BUSINESS LAW

Fourth Edition

Cavendish
Publishing
Limited

London • Sydney • Portland, Oregon

This book is supported by a Companion Website,
created to keep *Business Law* **up to date and to**
provide enhanced resources for both students and
lecturers.

Key features include:

- ◆ termly updates
- ◆ self-assessment tests
- ◆ links to useful websites
- ◆ links to 'ebooks' for introductory and further reading
- ◆ revision guidance
- ◆ guidelines on answering questions
- ◆ 'ask the author' – your questions answered

www.cavendishpublishing.com/businesslaw

BUSINESS LAW

Fourth Edition

David Kelly, PhD
Principal Lecturer in Law
Staffordshire University

Ann Holmes, M Phil, PGD
Associate Dean of the Law School
Staffordshire University

Ruth Hayward, LLB, LLM
Lecturer in Law
Staffordshire University

Cavendish
Publishing
Limited

London • Sydney • Portland, Oregon

Fourth edition first published in Great Britain 2002 by
Cavendish Publishing Limited, The Glass House,
Wharton Street, London WC1X 9PX, United Kingdom
Telephone: + 44 (0)20 7278 8000   Facsimile: + 44 (0)20 7278 8080
Email: info@cavendishpublishing.com
Website: www.cavendishpublishing.com

Published in the United States by Cavendish Publishing
c/o International Specialized Book Services,
5804 NE Hassalo Street, Portland,
Oregon 97213-3644, USA

Published in Australia by Cavendish Publishing (Australia) Pty Ltd
3/303 Barrenjoey Road, Newport, NSW 2106, Australia

© Kelly, D, Holmes, A
      and Hayward, R   2002
First edition   1995
Second edition   1997
Third edition   2000
Fourth edition   2002

British Library Cataloguing in Publication Data
Data available

Library of Congress Cataloguing in Publication Data
Data available

ISBN 1-85941-730-2

1 3 5 7 9 10 8 6 4 2

Printed and bound in Great Britain

PREFACE

Business and commercial enterprise takes place within a legal context and, in the final analysis, is governed and regulated by law. One of the problems facing the person studying business activity, and the one that is specifically addressed in this book, is the fact that business enterprise takes place within a general and wide ranging legal environment; but the student is required to have more than a passing knowledge of the legal rules and procedures which impact on business activity. The difficulty lies in acquiring an *adequate* knowledge of the many areas that govern such business activity. Law students legitimately may be expected to focus their attention on the minutiae of the law, but those studying law within, and as merely a component part of, a wider sphere of study cannot be expected to have the same detailed level of knowledge as law students. Nonetheless, they are expected to have a more than superficial knowledge of various legal topics.

For the author of a business law textbook, the difficulty lies in pitching the material considered at the appropriate level so that those studying the subject acquire a sufficient grasp to understand law as it relates *generally* to business enterprise, and of course to equip the student to pass the requisite exams. To achieve this goal, the text must not be too specialised and focus on too small a part of what is contained in most business law syllabuses. For example, although contract law is central to any business law course, to study it on its own, or with a few ancillary topics, is not sufficient. Nor, however, should the text be so wide ranging as to provide the student with no more than a superficial general knowledge of most of the possible interfaces between law and business enterprise. A selection has to be made and it is hoped that this text has made the correct one. No attempt has been made to cover all the areas within the potential scope of business law, but it is hoped that attention has been focused on the most important of these, without excluding any area of major importance. Additionally, it is hoped that the material provided deals with the topics selected in as thorough a way as is necessary.

In this fourth edition we have taken the opportunity to restructure the contract law section and to expand the treatment of other key areas, notably the company law and employment law sections. We have also been able to provide a more considered treatment of the Human Rights Act 1998 in the light of the most significant cases to have come before the courts since the previous edition. As usual, we have made every effort to ensure that the text is as up to date as we can make it.

David Kelly
Ann Holmes
Ruth Hayward
September 2000

CONTENTS

Contents

TABLE OF CASES

TABLE OF STATUTES

TABLE OF STATUTORY INSTRUMENTS

CONVENTIONS, TREATIES AND EC LEGISLATION

TREATIES AND CONVENTIONS

DIRECTIVES

TABLE OF ABBREVIATIONS

BNA	Business Names Act 1985
CA	Companies Act 1862/1985/1989
CAA	Criminal Appeal Act 1968/1995
CCA	Consumer Credit Act 1974
CDDA	Company Directors Disqualification Act 1986
CJA	Criminal Justice Act 1972/1988
CLSA	Courts and Legal Services Act 1990
CPA	Consumer Protection Act 1987
CPIA	Criminal Procedure and Investigations Act 1996
CPR	Civil Procedure Rules 1998
DCOA	Deregulation and Contracting Out Act 1994
DDA	Disability Discrimination Act 1995
EAT	Employment Appeal Tribunal
ECJ	European Court of Justice
ECHR	European Convention on Human Rights
EComHR	European Commission of Human Rights
ECtHR	European Court of Human Rights
EOC	Equal Opportunities Commission
EPA	Equal Pay Act 1970
ERA	Employment Rights Act 1996
GPSR	General Product Safety Regulations 1994
HRA	Human Rights Act 1998
IA	Insolvency Act 1986
IRA	Infants Relief Act 1874
LLPA	Limited Liability Partnership Act 2000
LLPR	Limited Liability Partnership Regulations 2001
MA	Misrepresentation Act 1967

NICA	Northern Ireland Court of Appeal
NMWA	National Minimum Wage Act 1998
PA	Partnership Act 1890
RRA	Race Relations Act 1976
SDA	Sex Discrimination Act 1975
SEA	Single European Act 1986
SGSA	Supply of Goods and Services Act 1982/1994
SoGA	Sale of Goods Act 1893/1979
SSGA	Sale and Supply of Goods Act 1994
TDA	Trade Descriptions Act 1968
TULR(C)A	Trade Union Labour Relations (Consolidation) Act 1992
TURERA	Trade Union Reform and Employment Rights Act 1993
UCTA	Unfair Contract Terms Act 1977
YJCEA	Youth Justice and Criminal Evidence Act 1999

CHAPTER 1

LAW AND LEGAL SOURCES

1.1 THE NATURE OF LAW

To a great extent, business activity across the world is carried on within a capitalist, market-based system. With regard to such a system, law provides and maintains an essential framework within which such business activity can take place, and without which it could not operate. In maintaining this framework, law establishes the rules and procedures for what is to be considered legitimate business activity and, as a corollary, what is not legitimate. It is essential, therefore, for the businessperson to be aware of the nature of the legal framework within which they have to operate. Even if they employ legal experts to deal with their legal problems, they will still need to be sufficiently knowledgeable to be able to recognise when to refer matters to those experts. It is the intention of this textbook to provide business students with an understanding of the most important aspects of law as they impinge on various aspects of business activity.

One of the most obvious and most central characteristics of all societies is that they must possess some degree of order, in order to permit their members to interact over a sustained period of time. Different societies, however, have different forms of order. Some societies are highly regimented with strictly enforced social rules, whereas others continue to function in what outsiders might consider a very unstructured manner, with apparently few strict rules being enforced.

Order is, therefore, necessary, but the form through which order is maintained is certainly not universal, as many anthropological studies have shown (see Mansell and Meteyard, *A Critical Introduction to Law*, 1999).

In our society, law plays an important part in the creation and maintenance of social order. We must be aware, however, that law, as we know it, is not the only means of creating order. Even in our society, order is not solely dependent on law, but also involves questions of a more general moral and political character. This book is not concerned with providing a general explanation of the form of order. It is concerned, more particularly, with describing and explaining the key institutional aspects of that particular form of order that is legal order.

The most obvious way in which law contributes to the maintenance of social order is the way in which it deals with disorder or conflict. This book, therefore, is particularly concerned with the institutions and procedures, both civil and criminal, through which law operates to ensure a particular form of social order by dealing with various conflicts when they arise.

Law is a formal mechanism of social control and, as such, it is essential that the student of law is fully aware of the nature of that formal structure. There are, however, other aspects to law that are less immediately apparent but of no less importance, such as the inescapably political nature of law. Some textbooks focus more on this particular aspect of law than others and these differences become evident in the particular approach adopted by the authors. The approach favoured by the authors of this book is to recognise that studying English law is not just about learning legal rules; it is also about considering a social institution of fundamental importance.

1.2 CATEGORIES OF LAW

There are various ways of categorising law, which initially tends to confuse the non-lawyer and the new student of law. What follows will set out these categorisations in their usual dual form, whilst, at the same time, trying to overcome the confusion inherent in such duality. It is impossible to avoid the confusing repetition of the same terms to mean different things and, indeed, the purpose of this section is to make sure that students are aware of the fact that the same words can have different meanings, depending upon the context in which they are used.

1.2.1   Common law and civil law

In this particular juxtaposition, these terms are used to distinguish two distinct legal systems and approaches to law. The use of the term 'common law' in this context refers to all those legal systems which have adopted the historic English legal system. Foremost amongst these is, of course, the US, but many other Commonwealth, and former Commonwealth, countries retain a common law system. The term 'civil law' refers to those other jurisdictions which have adopted the European continental system of law, which is derived essentially from ancient Roman law but owes much to the Germanic tradition.

The usual distinction to be made between the two systems is that the former, the common law system, tends to be case centred and, hence, judge centred, allowing scope for a discretionary, *ad hoc*, pragmatic approach to the particular problems that appear before the courts; whereas the latter, the civil law system, tends to be a codified body of general abstract principles which control the exercise of judicial discretion. In reality, both of these views are extremes, with the former overemphasising the extent to which the common law judge can impose his discretion and the latter underestimating the extent to which continental judges have the power to exercise judicial discretion. It is perhaps worth mentioning at this point that the European Court of Justice (ECJ), which was established, in theory, on civil law principles, is in practice increasingly recognising the benefits of establishing a body of case law.

It has to be recognised, and indeed the English courts do so, that although the ECJ is not bound by the operation of the doctrine of *stare decisis* (see below, 1.6), it still does not decide individual cases on an *ad hoc* basis and, therefore, in the light of a perfectly clear decision of the ECJ, national courts will be reluctant to refer similar cases to its jurisdiction. Thus, after the ECJ decided in *Grant v South West Trains Ltd* (1998) that Community law did not cover discrimination on grounds of sexual orientation, the High Court withdrew a similar reference in *R v Secretary of State for Defence ex p Perkins (No 2)* (1998) (see below, 1.4.3, for a detailed consideration of the ECJ).

1.2.2 Common law and equity

In this particular juxtaposition, these terms refer to a particular division within the English legal system.

The common law has been romantically and inaccurately described as 'the law of the common people of England'. In fact, the common law emerged as the product of a particular struggle for political power. Prior to the Norman Conquest of England in 1066, there was no unitary, national legal system. The emergence of the common law represented the imposition of such a unitary system under the auspices and control of a centralised power in the form of a sovereign king; and, in that respect, it represented the assertion and affirmation of that central sovereign power.

Traditionally, much play is made about the circuit of judges who travelled around the country, establishing the King's peace and, in so doing, selecting the best local customs and making them the basis of the law of England by means of a piecemeal but totally altruistic procedure. The reality of this process was that the judges were asserting the authority of the central State and its legal forms and institutions over the disparate and fragmented State and legal forms of the earlier feudal period. Hence, the common law was common *to* all in application, but certainly was not common *from* all. By the end of the 13th century, the central authority had established its precedence at least partly through the establishment of the common law. Originally, courts had been no more than an adjunct of the King's Council, the *Curia Regis*, but, gradually, the common law courts began to take on a distinct institutional existence in the form of the Courts of Exchequer, Common Pleas and King's Bench. With this institutional autonomy, however, there developed an institutional sclerosis, typified by a reluctance to deal with matters that were not, or could not be, processed in the proper form of action. Such a refusal to deal with substantive injustices, because they did not fall within the particular parameters of procedural and formal constraints, by necessity led to injustice and the need to remedy the perceived weaknesses in the common law system. The response was the development of equity.

Plaintiffs who were unable to gain access to the three common law courts might appeal directly to the Sovereign, and such pleas would be passed for consideration and decision to the Lord Chancellor, who acted as the 'King's conscience'. As the common law courts became more formalistic and more inaccessible, pleas to the Chancellor correspondingly increased and, eventually, this resulted in the emergence of a specific court which was constituted to deliver equitable or fair decisions in cases which the common law courts declined to deal with. As had happened with the common law, the decisions of the courts of equity established principles which were used to decide later cases, so it should not be thought that the use of equity meant that judges had discretion to decide cases on the basis of their personal ideas of what was just in each case.

The division between the common law courts and the courts of equity continued until they were eventually combined by the Judicature Acts 1873–75. Prior to this legislation, it was essential for a party to raise their action in the appropriate court; for example, the courts of law would not implement equitable principles. The Judicature Acts, however, provided that every court had the power and the duty to decide cases in line with common law and equity, with the latter being paramount in the final analysis.

Some would say that, as equity was never anything other than a gloss on common law, it is perhaps appropriate, if not ironic, that both systems have now effectively been subsumed under the one term: common law.

Common law remedies are available as of right. The classic common law remedy of damages can be subdivided into the following types:

- *Compensatory damages*: these are the standard awards, intended to achieve no more than to recompense the injured party to the extent of the injury suffered. Damages in contract can only be compensatory.

- *Aggravated damages*: these are compensatory in nature but are additional to ordinary compensatory awards and are awarded in relation to damage suffered to the injured party's dignity and pride. They are, therefore, akin to damages being paid in relation to mental distress. In *Khodaparast v Shad* (2000), the claimant was awarded aggravated damages after the defendant had been found liable for the malicious falsehood of distributing fake pictures of her in a state of undress, which resulted in her losing her job.

- *Exemplary damages*: these are awarded in tort in addition to compensatory damages. They may be awarded where the person who committed the tort intended to make a profit from their tortious action. The most obvious area in which such awards might be awarded is in libel cases where the publisher issues the libel to increase sales. Libel awards are considered in more detail in a later chapter, but an example of exemplary awards can be seen in the award of £50,000 (originally £275,000) awarded to Elton John as a result of his action against *The Mirror* newspaper (*John v MGN Ltd* (1996)).

- *Nominal damages*: these are awarded in the few cases which really do involve 'a matter of principle' but where no loss or injury to reputation is involved. There is no set figure in relation to nominal damages; it is merely a very small amount.

- *Contemptuous damages*: these are extremely small awards made where the claimant wins their case, but has suffered no loss and has failed to impress the court with the standard of their own behaviour or character. In *Reynolds v Times Newspaper Ltd* (1996), the former Prime Minster of Ireland was awarded one penny in his libel action against *The Times* newspaper; this award was actually made by the judge after the jury had awarded him no damages at all. Such an award can be considered nothing if not contemptuous.

The whole point of damages is compensatory, to recompense someone for the wrong they have suffered. There are, however, different ways in which someone can be compensated. For example, in contract law the object of awarding damages is to put the wronged person in the situation they would have been in had the contract been completed as agreed: that is, it places them in the position in which they would have been *after the event*. In tort, however, the object is to compensate the wronged person, to the extent that a monetary award can do so, for injury sustained: in other words to return them to the situation they were in *before the event*. The different treatment of damages in contract and tort will be considered in detail in Chapters 8 and 10.

Remedies in equity are discretionary; in other words, they are awarded at the will of the court and depend on the behaviour and situation of the party claiming such remedies. This means that, in effect, the court does not have to award an equitable remedy where it considers that the conduct of the party seeking such an award does not deserve such an award (*D & C Builders Ltd v Rees* (1965)). The usual equitable remedies are as follows:

- *injunction* – this is a court order requiring someone to do something or, alternatively, to stop doing something (*Warner Bros v Nelson* (1937));

- *specific performance* – this is a court order requiring one of the parties to a contractual agreement to complete their part of the contract. It is usually only awarded in respect of contracts relating to specific individual articles, such as land, and will not be awarded where the court cannot supervise the operation of its order (*Ryan v Mutual Tontine Westminster Chambers Association* (1893));

- *rectification* – this order relates to the alteration, under extremely limited circumstances, of contractual documents (*Joscelyne v Nissen* (1970));

- *rescission* – this order returns parties to a contractual agreement to the position they were in before the agreement was entered into. It is essential to distinguish this award from the common law award of damages, which is intended to place the parties in the position they would have been in had the contract been completed.

1.2.3 Common law and statute law

This particular conjunction follows on from the immediately preceding section, in that 'common law' here refers to the substantive law and procedural rules that have been created by the judiciary, through their decisions in the cases they have heard. Statute law, on the other hand, refers to law that has been created by Parliament in the form of legislation. Although there was a significant increase in statute law in the 20th century, the courts still have an important role to play in creating and operating law generally, and in determining the operation of legislation in particular. The relationship of this pair of concepts is of central importance and is considered in more detail below, 1.5 and 1.6.

1.2.4 Private law and public law

There are two different ways of understanding the division between private and public law.

At one level, the division relates specifically to actions of the State and its functionaries vis à vis the individual citizen, and the legal manner in which, and form of law through which, such relationships are regulated; that is, public law. In the 19th century, it was at least possible to claim, as Dicey did, that there was no such thing as public law in this distinct administrative sense, and that the powers of the State with regard to individuals was governed by the ordinary law of the land, operating through the normal courts. Whether such a claim was accurate when it was made, which is unlikely, there certainly can be no doubt now that public law constitutes a distinct and growing area of law in its own right. The growth of public law, in this sense, has mirrored the growth and increased activity of the contemporary State, and has seen its role as seeking to regulate such activity. The crucial role of judicial review in relation to public law will be considered in some detail below, 1.5.6.

There is, however, a second aspect to the division between private and public law. One corollary of the divide is that matters located within the private sphere are seen as purely a matter for individuals themselves to regulate, without the interference of the State, whose role is limited to the provision of the forum for deciding contentious issues and mechanisms for the enforcement of such decisions. Matters within the public sphere, however, are seen as issues relating to the interest of the State and general public and are, as such, to be protected and prosecuted by the State. It can be seen, therefore, that the category to which any dispute is allocated is of crucial importance to how it is dealt with. Contract may be thought of as the classic example of private law, but the extent to which this purely private legal area has been subjected to the regulation of public law in such areas as consumer protection should not be underestimated. Equally, the most obvious example of public law in this context would be criminal law. Feminists have argued, however, that the allocation of domestic matters to the sphere of private law has led to a denial of a general interest in the treatment and protection of women. By defining domestic matters as private, the State and its functionaries have denied women access to its power to protect themselves from abuse. In doing so, it is suggested that, in fact, such categorisation has reflected and maintained the social domination of men over women.

1.2.5 Civil law and criminal law

Civil law is a form of private law and involves the relationships between individual citizens. It is the legal mechanism through which individuals can assert claims against others and have those rights adjudicated and enforced. The purpose of civil law is to settle disputes between individuals and to provide remedies; it is not concerned with punishment as such. The role of the State in relation to civil law is to establish the general framework of legal rules and to provide the legal institutions for operating those rights, but the activation of the civil law is strictly a matter for the individuals concerned. Contract, tort and property law are generally aspects of civil law.

Criminal law, on the other hand, is an aspect of public law and relates to conduct which the State considers with disapproval and which it seeks to control and/or eradicate. Criminal law involves the enforcement of particular forms of behaviour, and the State, as the representative of society, acts positively to ensure compliance. Thus, criminal cases are brought by the State in the name of the Crown and cases are reported in the form of *Regina v* ... (*Regina* is simply Latin for 'Queen' and case references are usually abbreviated to *R v* ...), whereas civil cases are referred to by the names of the parties involved in the dispute, for example, *Smith v Jones*.

Decisions to prosecute in relation to criminal cases are taken by the Crown Prosecution Service, which is a legal agency operating independently of the police force.

In distinguishing between criminal and civil actions, it has to be remembered that the same event may give rise to both. For example, where the driver of a car injures someone through their reckless driving they will be liable to be prosecuted under the road traffic legislation, but at the same time, they will also be responsible to the injured party in the civil law relating to the tort of negligence.

A crucial distinction between criminal and civil law is the level of proof required in the different types of cases. In a criminal case, the prosecution is required to prove that the defendant is guilty beyond reasonable doubt, whereas, in a civil case, the degree of proof is much lower and has only to be on the balance of probabilities. This difference in the level of proof raises the possibility of someone being able to succeed in a civil case, although there may not be sufficient evidence for a criminal prosecution. Indeed, this strategy has been used successfully in a number of cases against the police where the

Crown Prosecution Service has considered there to be insufficient evidence to support a criminal conviction for assault.

Although prosecution of criminal offences is usually the prerogative of the Crown Prosecution Service as the agent of the State, it remains open to the private individual to initiate a private prosecution in relation to a criminal offence. It has to be remembered, however, that, even in the private prosecution, the test of the burden of proof remains the criminal one – requiring the facts to be proved beyond reasonable doubt. An example of the problems inherent in such private actions can be seen in the case of Stephen Lawrence, the young black man who was gratuitously stabbed to death by a gang of white racists whilst standing at a bus stop in London. Although there was strong suspicion, and indeed evidence, against particular individuals, the Crown Prosecution Service declined to press the charges against them on the basis of insufficiency of evidence. When the lawyers of the Lawrence family mounted a private prosecution against the suspects, the action failed for want of sufficient evidence to convict. As a consequence of the failure of the private prosecution, the current rule against double jeopardy meant that the accused could not be re-tried for the same offence at any time in the future, even if the police subsequently acquired sufficient new evidence to support a conviction. (The subsequent *Macpherson Inquiry* into the manner in which the police dealt with the Stephen Lawrence case recommended the removal of the double jeopardy rule.)

1.3 THE HUMAN RIGHTS ACT 1998

The UK was one of the initial signatories to the European Convention on Human Rights (ECHR) in 1950, which was set up in post-War Europe as a means of establishing and enforcing essential human rights. In 1966, it recognised the power of the European Commission on Human Rights to hear complaints from individual UK citizens and, at the same time, recognised the authority of the European Court of Human Rights (ECtHR) to adjudicate on such matters. It did not, however, at that time incorporate the European Convention into UK law.

The consequence of non-incorporation was that the Convention could not be directly enforced in English courts (*R v Secretary of State for the Home Department ex p Brind* (1991)). That situation has been remedied, however, by the passing of the Human Rights Act (HRA) 1998, which came into force in England and Wales in October 2000 and was by then already in effect in Scotland. The HRA 1998 incorporates the European Convention on Human Rights into UK law. The Articles incorporated into UK law and listed in Sched 1 to the Act cover the following matters:

- the right to life. Article 2 states that 'everyone's right to life shall be protected by law';

- prohibition of torture. Article 3 actually provides that 'no one shall be subjected to torture or inhuman or degrading treatment or punishment';
- prohibition of slavery and forced labour (Art 4);
- the right to liberty and security. After stating the general right, Art 5 is mainly concerned with the conditions under which individuals can lawfully be deprived of their liberty;
- the right to a fair trial. Article 6 provides that 'everyone is entitled to a fair and public hearing within a reasonable time by an independent and impartial tribunal established by law';
- the general prohibition of the enactment of retrospective criminal offences. Article 7 does, however, recognise the *post hoc* criminalisation of previous behaviour where it is 'criminal according to the general principles of law recognised by civilised nations';
- the right to respect for private and family life. Article 8 extends this right to cover a person's home and their correspondence;
- freedom of thought, conscience and religion (Art 9);
- freedom of expression. Article 10 extends the right to include 'freedom … to receive and impart information and ideas without interference by public authority and regardless of frontiers';
- freedom of assembly and association. Article 11 specifically includes the right to form and join trade unions;
- the right to marry (Art 12);
- prohibition of discrimination (Art 14);
- right to peaceful enjoyment of possessions and protection of property (Art 1 of Protocol 1);
- right to education (subject to a UK reservation) (Art 2 of Protocol 1);
- right to free elections (Art 3 of Protocol 1);
- right not to be subjected to the death penalty (Arts 1 and 2 of Protocol 6).

The rights listed can be relied on by any person, non-governmental organisation, or group of individuals. Importantly, it also applies, where appropriate, to companies, which are incorporated entities and hence legal persons. However, it cannot be relied on by governmental organisations, such as local authorities.

The above list of rights are not all seen in the same way. Some are absolute and inalienable and cannot be interfered with by the State. Others are merely contingent and are subject to derogation, that is, signatory States can opt out of them in particular circumstances. The absolute rights are those provided for in Arts 2, 3, 4, 7 and 14. All of the others are subject to potential limitations; and, in particular, the rights provided for under Arts 8, 9, 10 and 11 are subject to legal restrictions, such as are:

... necessary in a democratic society in the interests of national security or public safety, for the prevention of crime, for the protection of health or morals or the protection of the rights and freedoms of others (Art 11(2)).

In deciding the legality of any derogation, courts are required not just to be convinced that there is a need for the derogation, but they must also be sure that the State's action has been proportionate to that need. In other words, the State must not overreact to a perceived problem by removing more rights than is necessary to effect the solution. The UK entered such a derogation in relation to the extended detention of terrorist suspects without charge under the Prevention of Terrorism (Temporary Provisions) Act 1989, subsequently replaced and extended by the Terrorism Act 2000. Those powers had been held to be contrary to Art 5 of the Convention by the ECtHR in *Brogan v United Kingdom* (1989). The UK also entered a derogation with regards to the Anti-Terrorism, Crime and Security Act 2001, which was enacted in response to the attack on the World Trade Center in New York on 11 September that year. The Act allows for the detention without trial of foreign citizens suspected of being involved in terrorist activity.

With further regard to the possibility of derogation, s 19 of the Act requires a minister, responsible for the passage of any Bill through Parliament, either to make a written declaration that it is compatible the Convention or, alternatively, to declare that, although it may not be compatible, it is still the government's wish to proceed with it.

The HRA 1998 has profound implications for the operation of the English legal system. Section 2 of the Act requires future courts to take into account any previous decision of the ECtHR. This provision impacts on the operation of the doctrine of precedent within the English legal system, as it effectively sanctions the overruling of any previous English authority which is in conflict with a decision of the ECtHR. Also, s 3, which requires all legislation to be read so far as possible to give effect to the rights provided under the Convention, has the potential to invalidate previously accepted interpretations of statutes which were made, by necessity, without recourse to the Convention.

Section 6 of the HRA 1998 declares it unlawful for any public authority to act in a way which is incompatible with the Convention, and s 7 allows the victim of the unlawful act to bring proceedings against the public authority in breach. Section 8 empowers the court to grant such relief or remedy against the public authority in breach of the Act as it considers just and appropriate.

In order to understand the structure of the HRA 1998, it is essential to be aware of the nature of the changes introduced by the Act, especially in the apparent passing of such fundamental powers to the judiciary. Under the doctrine of parliamentary sovereignty, the legislature could pass such laws at it saw fit, even to the extent of removing the rights of its citizens. The new Act reflects a move towards the entrenchment of rights recognised under the Convention, but, given the sensitivity of the relationship between the elected Parliament and the unelected judiciary, it has been thought expedient to minimise the change in the constitutional relationship of Parliament and the judiciary. To that effect, the Act expressly states that the courts cannot invalidate any primary legislation (that is, essentially, Acts of Parliament) which is found to be incompatible with the Convention; they can only make a declaration of such incompatibility and leave it to the legislature to remedy the situation through new legislation (s 4).

To that effect, the Act provides for the provision of remedial legislation through a fast track procedure which gives a minister of the Crown the power to alter such primary legislation by way of statutory instrument.

Where a public authority is acting under the instructions of some primary legislation which is itself incompatible with the Convention, the public authority will not be liable under s 6 of the HRA 1998.

Reactions to the introduction of the Human Rights Act have been broadly welcoming, but some important criticisms have been raised. First, the Convention is a rather old document, and does not address some of the issues that contemporary citizens might consider as equally fundamental to those rights actually contained in the document. For example, it is silent on the rights to substantive equality relating to such issues as welfare and access to resources. Also, the actual provisions of the Convention are uncertain in the extent of their application. What exactly is covered by the 'right to a fair trial' or the right to 'respect for private and family life'? Such widely drawn rights are inherently uncertain and subject to argument for extension. It also has to be recognised that, at least to a degree, the rights provided under the Convention are contradictory. The most obvious difficulty arises from the need to reconcile Art 8's right to privacy with Art 10's freedom of expression. Newspapers have already expressed their concern in relation to this particular issue, and fear the development, at the hands of the court, of an overly limiting law of privacy that would prevent investigative journalism.

1.3.1 Cases decided under the Human Rights Act 1998

Proportionality

The way in which States can interfere with rights so long as they do so in a way that is proportionate to the attainment of a legitimate end can be seen in *Brown v Advocate General for Scotland* (2001). Brown had been arrested at a supermarket in relation to the theft of a bottle of gin. When the police officers noticed that she smelled of alcohol, they asked her how she had travelled to the superstore. Brown replied that she had driven and pointed out her car in the supermarket car park. Later, at the police station, the police used their powers under s 172(2)(a) of the Road Traffic Act 1988 to require her to say who had been driving her car at about 2.30 am; that is, at the time when she would have travelled in it to the supermarket. Brown admitted that she had been driving. After a positive breath test, Brown was charged with drunk driving, but appealed to the Scottish High Court of Justiciary for a declaration that the case could not go ahead on the grounds that her admission, as required under s 172, was contrary to the right to a fair trial under Art 6 of the Convention.

The High Court of Justiciary supported her claim on the basis that the right to silence and the right not to incriminate oneself at trial would be worthless if an accused person did not enjoy a right of silence in the course of the criminal investigation leading to the court proceedings. If this were not the case, then the police could require an accused person to provide an incriminating answer which subsequently could be used in evidence against them at their trial. Consequently, the use of evidence obtained under s 172 of the Road Traffic Act 1988 infringed Brown's rights under Art 6(1).

However, on 5 December 2000, the Privy Council reversed the judgment of the Scottish appeal court. The Privy Council reached its decision on the grounds that the rights contained in Art 6 of the Convention were not themselves absolute and could be restricted in certain limited conditions. Consequently, it was possible for individual States to introduce limited qualification of those rights so long as they were aimed at 'a clear public objective' and were 'proportionate to the situation' under consideration. The Convention had to be read as balancing community rights with individual rights. With specific regard to the Road Traffic Act, the objective to be attained was the prevention of injury and death from the misuse of cars, and s 172 was not a disproportionate response to that objective.

Section 3 duty to interpret legislation in line with the ECHR

It has long been a matter of concern that, in cases where rape has been alleged, the common defence strategy employed by lawyers has been to attempt to attack the credibility of the woman making the accusation. Judges had the discretion to allow questioning of the woman as to her sexual history where this was felt to be relevant, and in all too many cases this discretion was exercised in a way that allowed defence counsel to abuse and humiliate women accusers. Section 41 of the Youth Justice and Criminal Evidence Act 1999 (YJCEA) placed the court under a restriction that seriously limited evidence that could be raised in cross-examination of a sexual relationship between a complainant and an accused. Under s 41(3) of the 1999 Act, such evidence was limited to sexual behaviour 'at or about the same time' as the event giving rise to the charge that was 'so similar' in nature that it could not be explained as a coincidence.

In *R v A* (2000), the defendant in a case of alleged rape claimed that the provisions of the YJCEA 1999 were contrary to Art 6 of the European Convention to the extent that it prevented him from putting forward a full and complete defence. In reaching its decision, the House of Lords emphasised the need to protect women from humiliating cross-examination and prejudicial but valueless evidence in respect of their previous sex lives. It nonetheless held that the restrictions in s 41 of the 1999 Act were *prima facie* capable of preventing an accused from putting forward relevant evidence that could be crucial to his defence.

However, rather than make a declaration of incompatibility, the House of Lords preferred to make use of s 3 of the Human Rights Act 1998 to allow s 41 of the YJCEA 1999 to be read as permitting the admission of evidence or questioning relating to a relevant issue in the case where it was considered necessary by the trial judge to make the trial fair. The test of admissibility of evidence of previous sexual relations between an accused and a complainant under s 41(3) of the 1999 Act was whether the evidence was so relevant to the issue of consent that to exclude it would be to endanger the fairness of the trial under Art 6 of the Convention. Where the line is to be drawn is left to the judgment of trial judges. In reaching its decision, the House of Lords was well aware that its interpretation of s 41 did a violence to its actual meaning, but it nonetheless felt it within its power so to do.

Declarations of incompatibility

Where a court cannot interpret a piece of primary legislation in such a way as to make it compatible with the Convention, it cannot declare the legislation invalid, but it can make a declaration that the legislation in question is not compatible with the rights provided by the Convention. The first declaration of incompatibility was issued in *R v (1) Mental Health Review Tribunal, North & East London Region (2) Secretary Of State For Health ex p H* in March 2001. In that case, the Court of Appeal held that ss 72 and 73 of the Mental Health Act 1983 were incompatible with Arts 5(1) and 5(4) of the European Convention, inasmuch as they reversed the normal burden of proof by requiring the detained person to show that they should not be detained, rather than placing the burden on the authorities to show that they should be detained.

Wilson v First County Trust (2000) was, however, the first case in which a court indicated its likelihood of its making a declaration of incompatibility under s 4 of the Human Rights Act 1998. The legislation in question was the Consumer Credit Act 1974 and in particular s 127(3) of that Act, which proscribed the enforcement of any consumer credit agreement which did not comply with the requirements of the 1974 Act. Wilson had borrowed £5,000 from First County Trust (FCT) and had pledged her car as security for the loan. Wilson was to be charged a fee of £250 for drawing up the loan documentation but asked FCT to add it to the loan, which they agreed to do. The effect of this was that the loan document stated that the amount of the loan was £5,250. This, however, was inaccurate, as in reality the extra £250 was not part of the loan as such, rather it was part of the charge for the loan. The loan document had therefore been drawn up improperly and did not comply with the requirement of s 61 of the Consumer Credit Act 1974.

When Wilson subsequently failed to pay the loan at the end of the agreed period, FCT stated their intention of selling the car unless she paid £7,000. Wilson brought proceedings: (i) for a declaration that the agreement was unenforceable by reason of s 127(3) of the 1974 Act because of the misstatement of the amount of the loan; and (ii) for the agreement to be reopened on the basis that it was an extortionate credit bargain. The judge rejected Wilson's first claim but reopened the agreement and substituted a lower rate of interest, and Wilson subsequently redeemed her car on payment of £6,900. However, she then successfully appealed against the judge's decision as to the enforceability of the agreement, the Court of Appeal holding that s 127(3) clearly and undoubtedly had the effect of preventing the enforcement of the original agreement and Wilson was entitled to the repayment of the money she had paid to redeem her car. Consequently, Wilson not only got her car back but also retrieved the money she paid to FCT, who lost their money completely. In reaching its decision, however, the Court of Appeal expressed the opinion that it was at least arguable that s 127(3) was incompatible with Art 6(1) and/or Protocol 1 of Art 1 of the Convention. First, the absolute prohibition of enforcement of the agreement appeared to be a disproportionate restriction on the right of the lender to have the enforceability of its loan determined by the court contrary to Art 6(1); and secondly, to deprive FCT of its property – that is, the money which it had lent to Wilson – appeared to be contrary to Protocol 1 of Art 1.

Under those circumstances, the court considered it appropriate to give notice to the Crown under s 5 of the HRA 1998 that it was considering making a declaration of incompatibility, and such an order was made in due course.

1.4 SOURCES OF LAW

This section examines the various ways in which law comes into existence. Although it is possible to distinguish domestic and European sources of law, it is necessary to locate the former firmly within its wider European context; in line with that requirement, this section begins with an outline of that context.

1.4.1 European Community

Ever since the UK joined the European Economic Community (EEC), now the European Community (EC) (or European Union (EU) in some legal contexts), it has progressively, but effectively, passed the power to create laws which have effect in this country to the wider European institutions. In effect, the UK's legislative, executive and judicial powers are now controlled by, and can only be operated within, the framework of EC law. It is essential, therefore, that the contemporary law student is aware of the operation of the legislative and judicial powers of the EC.

The general aim of the EU is set out in Art 2 of the EC Treaty, as amended by the Treaty on European Union 1992 (the Maastricht Treaty), as follows:

The Community shall have as its task, by establishing a common market and an economic and monetary union and by implementing the common policies or activities referred to in Art 3, to promote throughout the Community a harmonious and balanced development of economic activities, sustainable and non-inflationary growth respecting the environment, a high degree of convergence of economic performance, a high level of employment and of social protection, the raising of the standard of living and quality of life, and economic and social cohesion and solidarity among Member States.

Amongst the policies originally detailed in Art 3 were:

- the elimination, between Member States, of custom duties and of quantitative restrictions on the import and export of goods;

- the establishment of a common customs tariff and a common commercial policy towards third countries;

- the abolition, between Member States, of obstacles to the freedom of movement for persons, services and capital;

- the adoption of a common agricultural policy;

- the adoption of a common transport policy;

- the harmonisation of laws of Member States to the extent required to facilitate the proper functioning of the single market;

- the creation of a European Social Fund, in order to improve the employment opportunities of workers in the EC and to improve their standard of living.

Article 3 has subsequently been extended to cover more social, as opposed to purely economic, matters and now incorporates policies relating to education, health, consumer protection, the environment, and culture generally. Before the UK joined the EU, its law was just as foreign as law made under any other jurisdiction. On joining the EU, however, the UK and its citizens accepted and became subject to EC law. This subjection to European law remains the case even where the parties to any transaction are themselves both UK subjects. In other words, in areas where it is applicable, EU law supersedes any existing UK law to the contrary.

An example of EC law invalidating the operation of UK legislation can be found in the first *Factortame* case (*Factortame Ltd v Secretary of State for Transport (No 1) (1989)*). The common fishing policy, established by the EEC, had placed limits on the amount of fish that any member country's fishing fleet was permitted to catch. In order to gain access to British fish stocks and quotas, Spanish fishing boat owners formed British companies and re-registered their boats as British. In order to prevent what it saw as an abuse and an encroachment on the rights of indigenous fishermen, the UK Government introduced the Merchant Shipping Act 1988, which provided that any fishing company seeking to register as British must have its principal place of business in the UK and at least 75% of its shareholders must be British nationals. This effectively debarred the Spanish boats from taking up any of the British fishing quota. Some 95 Spanish boat owners applied to the British courts for judicial review of the Merchant Shipping Act 1988 on the basis that it was contrary to EC law.

The High Court decided to refer the question of the legality of the legislation to the European Court of Justice (ECJ) under Art 234 (formerly 177), but in the meantime granted interim relief, in the form of an injunction disapplying the operation of the legislation, to the fishermen. On appeal, the Court of Appeal removed the injunction, a decision confirmed by the House of Lords. However, the House of Lords referred the question of the relationship of Community law and contrary domestic law to the ECJ. Effectively they were asking whether the domestic courts should follow the domestic law or Community law. The ECJ ruled that the Treaty of Rome requires domestic courts to give effect to the directly enforceable provisions of Community law and, in doing so, such courts are required to ignore any national law that runs counter to Community law. The House of Lords then renewed the interim injunction. The ECJ later ruled that, in relation to the original referral from the High Court, the Merchant Shipping Act 1988 was contrary to Community law and therefore the Spanish fishing companies should be able to sue for compensation in the UK courts. The subsequent claims also went all the way to the House of Lords before it was finally settled in October 2000 that the UK was liable to pay compensation, which has been estimated at between £50 million and £100 million.

1.4.2 Sources of EC law

Community law, depending on its nature and source, may have direct effect on the domestic laws of its various members; that is, it may be open to individuals to rely on it, without the need for their particular State to have enacted the law within its own legal system (see *Factortame (No 1)* (1989)).

There are two types of direct effect. Vertical direct effect means that the individual can rely on EC law in any action in relation to their government, but cannot use it against other individuals. Horizontal direct effect allows the individual to use an EC provision in an action against other individuals. Other EC provisions only take effect when they have been specifically enacted within the various legal systems within the EC.

The sources of EC law are fourfold:

(a) internal treaties and protocols;

(b) international agreements;

(c) secondary legislation;

(d) decisions of the ECJ.

Internal treaties

Internal treaties govern the Member States of the EU and anything contained therein supersedes domestic legal provisions. The primary treaty is the EC Treaty (formerly called the Treaty of Rome), as amended by such legislation as the Single European Act (SEA) 1986, the Maastricht Treaty 1992 and the Amsterdam Treaty 1997. Upon its joining the EC, the Treaty of Rome was incorporated into UK law by the European Communities Act 1972.

As long as Treaties are of a mandatory nature and are stated with sufficient clarity and precision, they have both vertical and horizontal effect (*Van Gend en Loos* (1963)).

International treaties

International treaties are negotiated with other nations by the European Commission on behalf of the EU as a whole and are binding on the individual Members of the EU.

Secondary legislation

Three types of legislation may be introduced by the European Council and Commission. These are as follows:

- *Regulations* apply to, and within, Member States generally, without the need for those States to pass their own legislation. They are binding and enforceable from the time of their creation, and individual States do not have to pass any legislation to give effect to regulations. Thus, in *Macarthys Ltd v Smith* (1979), on a referral from the Court of Appeal to the ECJ, it was held that Art 141 (formerly Art 119) entitled the claimant to assert rights that were not available to her under national legislation (the Equal Pay Act 1970) which had been enacted before the UK had joined the EEC. Whereas the national legislation clearly did not include a comparison between former and present employees, Art 141's reference to 'equal pay for equal work' did encompass such a situation. Smith was consequently entitled to receive a similar level of remuneration to that of the former male employee who had done her job previously.

  Regulations must be published in the Official Journal of the EU. The decision as to whether or not a law should be enacted in the form of a regulation is usually left to the Commission, but there are areas where the EC Treaty requires that the regulation form must be used. These areas relate to: the rights of workers to remain in Member States of which they are not nationals; the provision of State aid to particular indigenous undertakings or industries; the regulation of EU accounts; and budgetary procedures.

- *Directives*, on the other hand, state general goals and leave the precise implementation in the appropriate form to the individual Member States.

Directives, however, tend to state the means as well as the ends to which they are aimed and the ECJ will give direct effect to directives which are sufficiently clear and complete (see *Van Duyn v Home Office* (1974)). Directives usually provide Member States with a time limit within which they are required to implement the provision within their own national laws. If they fail to do so, or implement the directive incompletely, then individuals may be able to cite, and rely on, the directive in their dealings with the State in question. Further, *Francovich v Italy* (1991) established that individuals who have suffered as a consequence of a Member State's failure to implement EC law may seek damages against that State.

In contract law, the provisions in the Unfair Terms in Consumer Contracts Regulations 1994 (SI 1994/3159), repealed and replaced by the Unfair Terms in Consumer Contracts Regulations 1999 (SI 1999/2083), are an example of UK law being introduced in response to EU directives, and company law is continuously subject to the process of European harmonisation through directives.

- *Decisions* on the operation of European laws and policies are not intended to have general effect but are aimed at particular States or individuals. They have the force of law under Art 249 (formerly Art 189) of the EC Treaty.
- Additionally, Art 211 (formerly Art 155) provides for the Commission to issue recommendations and opinions in relation to the operation of Community law. These have no binding force, although they may be taken into account in trying to clarify any ambiguities in domestic law.

Judgments of the ECJ

The ECJ is the judicial arm of the EU and, in the field of Community law, its judgments overrule those of national courts. Under Art 234 (formerly Art 177) of the EC Treaty, national courts have the right to apply to the ECJ for a preliminary ruling on a point of Community law before deciding a case.

The mechanism through which Community law becomes immediately and directly effective in the UK is provided by s 2(1) of the European Communities Act 1972. Section 2(2) gives power to designated ministers or departments to introduce Orders in Council to give effect to other non-directly effective Community law.

1.4.3 The institutions of the EU

The major institutions of the EU are: the Council of Ministers; the European Parliament; the European Commission; and the ECJ.

The Council of Ministers

The Council is made up of ministerial representatives of each of the 15 Member States of the EU. The actual composition of the Council varies, depending on the nature of the matter to be considered: when considering economic matters, the various States will be represented by their finance ministers; if the matter before the Council relates to agriculture, the various agricultural ministers will attend. The Council of Ministers is the supreme decision making body of the EU and, as such, has the final say in deciding upon EU legislation. Although it acts on recommendations and proposals made to it by the Commission, it does have the power to instruct the Commission to undertake particular investigations and to submit detailed proposals for its consideration.

Council decisions are taken via a mixture of voting procedures. Some measures only require a simple majority; in others, a procedure of qualified majority voting is used; and, in yet others, unanimity is required. Qualified majority voting is the procedure by which the votes of the 15 Member States are weighted in proportion to their population, from 10 down to two votes each. There are a total of 87 votes to be cast and, in order to pass a vote on the basis of a qualified majority, a minimum of 62 votes in favour is required. The corollary of this is that a total of 26 votes are required to block any proposal that can be decided by qualified majority voting. It can be seen, therefore, that even qualified majority voting requires a substantial degree of agreement across the EU.

The European Parliament

The European Parliament is the directly elected European institution and, to that extent, it can be seen as the body which exercises democratic control over the operation of the EU. As in national Parliaments, members are elected to represent constituencies, the elections being held every five years. There are a total of 626 members, divided amongst the 15 members in approximate proportion to the size of their various populations. Members of the European Parliament do not sit in national groups but operate within political groupings.

The European Parliament's General Secretariat is based in Luxembourg and, although the Parliament sits in plenary session in Strasbourg for one week in each month, its detailed and preparatory work is carried out through 18 permanent committees, which usually meet in Brussels. These permanent committees consider proposals from the Commission and provide the full Parliament with reports of such proposals for discussion.

The Parliament is not a legislative institution and, in that respect, plays a subsidiary role to the Council of Ministers. Originally, its powers were merely advisory and supervisory and, since 1980, the Council has been required to wait for the Parliament's opinion before adopting any law. In its supervisory role, the Parliament scrutinises the activities of the Commission and has the power to remove the Commission by passing a motion of censure against it by a two-thirds majority.

The Parliament, together with the Council of Ministers, is the budgetary authority of the EU. The budget is drawn up by the Commission and is presented to both the Council and the Parliament. As regards what is known as obligatory expenditure, the Council has the final say, but, in relation to non-obligatory expenditure, the Parliament has the final decision as to whether to approve the budget or not.

The European Commission

The European Commission is the executive of the EU and, in that role, is responsible for the administration of EU policies. There are 20 Commissioners, chosen from the various Member States to serve for renewable terms of four years. Commissioners are appointed to head departments with specific responsibility for furthering particular areas of EU policy. Once appointed, Commissioners are expected to act in the general interest of the EU as a whole, rather than in the partial interest of their own home country.

In pursuit of EU policy, the Commission is responsible for ensuring that Treaty obligations between the Member States are met and that Community laws relating to individuals are enforced. In order to fulfil these functions, the Commission has been provided with extensive powers in relation to both the investigation of potential breaches of Community law and the subsequent punishment of offenders. The classic area in which these powers can be seen in operation is in the area of competition law. Under Arts 81 and 82 (formerly Arts 85 and 86) of the EC Treaty, the Commission has substantial powers to investigate and control potential monopolies and anti-competitive behaviour. It has used these powers to levy what, in the case of private individuals, would amount to huge fines where breaches of Community competition law have been discovered. In February 1993, the Commission imposed fines totalling more than £80 million on 17 steel producers for what was described as a very serious, illegal price fixing cartel. British Steel suffered the greatest individual imposition of £26.4 million.

In December 2000, the Staffordshire company JCB, the world's fifth largest producer of earthmoving equipment, was fined £22 million by the Commission. It had found that the company had engaged in what was described as 'a serious violation of EU competition law', in that JCB had created artificial barriers within the single market and had even at times fixed prices. It was stated that the company had entered into illegal agreements with its network of distributors that limited their ability to sell outside of their own territories, and prevented purchasers from enjoying any price differentials that existed within the EU.

In addition to these executive functions, the Commission also has a vital part to play in the EU's legislative process. The Council can only act on proposals put before it by the Commission. The Commission, therefore, has a duty to propose to the Council measures that will advance the achievement of the EU's general policies.

The ECJ

The ECJ is the judicial arm of the EU and, in the field of Community law, its judgments overrule those of national courts. It consists of 15 judges, assisted by nine Advocates General, and sits in Luxembourg. The role of the Advocate General is to investigate the matter submitted to the ECJ and to produce a report, together with a recommendation for the consideration of the Court. The ECJ is free to accept the report or not, as it sees fit.

The SEA 1986 provided for a new Court of First Instance to be attached to the existing ECJ. The jurisdiction of the Court of First Instance is limited mainly to internal claims by employees of the EC and to claims against fines made by the Commission under Community competition law. The aim is to reduce the burden of work on the ECJ, but there is a right of appeal, on points of law only, to the full Court of Justice. In July 2000, an appeal against a fine imposed by the Commission in 1998 against Europe's biggest car producer, Volkswagen (VW), was successful to the extent that the ECJ reduced the amount of the fine by £7.5 million. Unfortunately for VW, it upheld the essential finding of the Commission and imposed a fine of £57 million on it, a record for any individual company. VW was found guilty of 'an infringement which was particularly serious, the seriousness being magnified by the size of the Volkswagen group'. What the company had done was to prevent, essentially German and Austrian, customers from benefiting from the weakness of the Italian lire between 1993 and 1996 by instructing the Italian dealers not to sell to foreign customers on the false basis that different specifications and warranty terms prevented cross-border sales. Not only had VW instructed that this should happen, but it threatened that Italian dealers would lose their franchises if they failed to comply.

The ECJ performs two key functions:

- it decides whether any measures adopted, or rights denied, by the Commission, Council or any national government are compatible with Treaty obligations. In October 2000, the ECJ annulled EC Directive 98/43, which required Member States to impose a ban on advertising and sponsorship relating to tobacco products, because it had been adopted on the basis of the wrong provisions of the EC Treaty. The Directive had been adopted on the basis of the provisions relating to the elimination of obstacles to the completion of the internal market, but the Court decided that, under the circumstances, it was difficult to see how a ban on tobacco advertising or sponsorship could facilitate the trade in tobacco products.

  Although a partial prohibition on particular types of advertising or sponsorship might legitimately come within the internal market provisions of the Treaty, the Directive was clearly aimed at protecting public health and it was therefore improper to base its adoption on freedom to provide services (*Germany v European Parliament and EU Council* (Case C-376/98));

- it provides authoritative rulings at the request of national courts under Art 234 (formerly Art 177) of the EC Treaty on the interpretation of points of Community law. When an application is made under Art 234, the national proceedings are suspended until such time as the determination of the point in question is delivered by the ECJ. Whilst the case is being decided by the ECJ, the national court is expected to provide appropriate interim relief, even if this involves going against a domestic legal provision (as in the *Factortame* case).

1.5 LEGISLATION

If the institutions of the EC are sovereign within its boundaries, then, within the more limited boundaries of the UK, the sovereign power to make law lies with Parliament. Under UK constitutional law, it is recognised that Parliament has the power to enact, revoke or alter such, and any, law as it sees fit. Coupled to this wide power is the convention that no one Parliament can bind its successors in such a way as to limit their absolute legislative powers. Although we still refer to our legal system as a common law system, and although the courts still have an important role to play in the interpretation of statutes, it has to be recognised that legislation is the predominant method of law making in contemporary society. It is necessary, therefore, to have a knowledge of the workings of the legislative procedure through which law is made.

1.5.1 The legislative process

As an outcome of various historical political struggles, Parliament, and in particular the House of Commons, has asserted its authority as the ultimate source of law making in the UK. Parliament's prerogative to make law is encapsulated in the notion of the supremacy of Parliament.

Parliament consists of three distinct elements: the House of Commons, the House of Lords and the Monarch. Before any legislative proposal, known at that stage as a Bill, can become an Act of Parliament, it must proceed through and be approved by both Houses of Parliament and must receive the royal assent.

Before the formal law making procedure is started, the government of the day, which in practice decides and controls what actually becomes law, may enter into a process of consultation with concerned individuals or organisations.

Green Papers are consultation documents issued by the government which set out and invite comments from interested parties on particular proposals for legislation. After considering any response, the government may publish a second document in the form of a White Paper, in which it sets out its firm proposals for legislation.

A Bill must be given three readings in both the House of Commons and the House of Lords before it can be presented for the royal assent. It is possible to commence the procedure in either House, although money Bills must be placed before the Commons in the first instance.

Before it can become law, any Bill introduced in the Commons must go through five distinct procedures:

- First reading

  This is a purely formal procedure, in which the Bill's title is read and a date is set for its second reading.

- Second reading

  At this stage, the general principles of the Bill are subject to extensive debate. The second reading is the critical point in the process of a Bill. At the end, a vote may be taken on its merits and, if it is approved, it is likely that it will eventually find a place in the statute book.

- Committee stage

  After its second reading, the Bill is passed to a standing committee, whose job is to consider the provisions of the Bill in detail, clause by clause. The committee has the power to amend it in such a way as to ensure that it conforms with the general approval given by the House at its second reading.

- Report stage

  At this point, the standing committee reports the Bill back to the House for consideration of any amendments made during the committee stage.

- Third reading

  Further debate may take place during this stage, but it is restricted solely to matters relating to the content of the Bill; questions relating to the general principles of the Bill cannot be raised.

When a Bill has passed all of these stages, it is passed to the House of Lords for consideration. After this, the Bill is passed back to the Commons, which must then consider any amendments to the Bill that might have been introduced by the Lords. Where one House refuses to agree to the amendments made by the other, Bills can be repeatedly passed between them; but, since Bills must complete their process within the life of a particular parliamentary session, a failure to reach agreement within that period might lead to the total failure of the Bill.

Since the Parliament Acts of 1911 and 1949, the blocking power of the House of Lords has been restricted as follows:

- a 'Money Bill', that is, one containing only financial provisions, can be enacted without the approval of the House of Lords after a delay of one month;
- any other Bill can be delayed by one year by the House of Lords.

The royal assent is required before any Bill can become law. The procedural nature of the royal assent was highlighted by the Royal Assent Act 1967, which reduced the process of acquiring royal assent to a formal reading out of the short titles of any Act in both Houses of Parliament.

An Act of Parliament comes into effect on the date that royal assent is given, unless there is any provision to the contrary in the Act itself.

1.5.2 Types of legislation

Legislation can be categorised in a number of ways. For example, distinctions can be drawn between:

- *public Acts* – which relate to matters affecting the general public. These can be further sub-divided into either government Bills or Private Members' Bills;
- *private Acts* – which relate to the powers and interests of particular individuals or institutions, although the provision of statutory powers to particular institutions can have a major effect on the general public. For example, companies may be given the power to appropriate private property through compulsory purchase orders;
- *enabling legislation* – which gives power to a particular person or body to oversee the production of the specific details required for the implementation of the general purposes stated in the parent Act. These specifics are achieved through the enactment of statutory instruments. (See below, 1.5.3, for a consideration of delegated legislation.)

Acts of Parliament can also be distinguished on the basis of the function that they are designed to carry out. Some are unprecedented and cover new areas of activity previously not governed by legal rules, but other Acts are aimed at rationalising or amending existing legislative provisions:

- *consolidating legislation* is designed to bring together provisions previously contained in a number of different Acts, without actually altering them. The Companies Act 1985 is an example of a consolidation Act. It brought together provisions contained in numerous amending Acts which had been introduced since the previous Consolidation Act 1948;
- *codifying legislation* seeks not just to bring existing statutory provisions under one Act, but also looks to give statutory expression to common law rules. The classic examples of such legislation are the Partnership Act 1890 and the Sale of Goods Act 1893, now 1979;

- *amending legislation* is designed to alter some existing legal provision. Amendment of an existing legislative provision can take one of two forms:

  o a textual amendment, where the new provision substitutes new words for existing ones in a legislative text or introduces completely new words into that text. Altering legislation by means of textual amendment has one major drawback, in that the new provisions make very little sense on their own without the contextual reference of the original provision that it is designed to alter;

  o non-textual amendments do not alter the actual wording of the existing text, but alter the operation or effect of those words. Non-textual amendments may have more immediate meaning than textual alterations, but they, too, suffer from the problem that, because they do not alter the original provisions, the two provisions have to be read together to establish the legislative intention.

Neither method of amendment is completely satisfactory, but the Renton Committee on the Preparation of Legislation (1975, Cmnd 6053) favoured textual amendments over non-textual amendments.

1.5.3 Delegated legislation

In contemporary practice, the full scale procedure detailed above is usually only undergone in relation to enabling Acts. These Acts set out general principles and establish a framework within which certain individuals or organisations are given power to make particular rules designed to give practical effect to the enabling Act. The law produced through this procedure is referred to as 'delegated legislation'.

As has been stated, delegated legislation is law made by some person or body to whom Parliament has delegated its general law making power. A validly enacted piece of delegated legislation has the same legal force and effect as the Act of Parliament under which it is enacted; but, equally, it only has effect to the extent that its enabling Act authorises it. Any action taken in excess of the powers granted is said to be *ultra vires* and the legality of such legislation can be challenged in the courts, as considered below.

The Deregulation and Contracting Out Act (DCOA) 1994 is an example of the wide ranging power that enabling legislation can extend to ministers. The Act gives ministers the authority to amend legislation by means of statutory instruments, where they consider such legislation to impose unnecessary burdens on any trade, business, or profession. Although the DCOA 1994 imposes the requirement that ministers should consult with interested parties to any proposed alteration, it nonetheless gives them extremely wide powers to alter primary legislation without the necessity of following the same procedure as was required to enact that legislation in the first place. An example of the effect of the DCOA 1994 may be seen in the Deregulation

(Resolutions of Private Companies) Order 1996 (SI 1996/1471), which simplifies the procedures that private companies have to comply with in passing resolutions. The effect of this statutory instrument was to introduce new sections into the Companies Act 1985 which relax the previous provisions in the area in question. A second example is the Deregulation (Model Appeal Provisions) Order 1996 (SI 1996/1678), which set out a model structure for appeals against enforcement actions in business disputes.

The output of delegated legislation in any year greatly exceeds the output of Acts of Parliament. For example, in 2001, Parliament passed just 25 general public Acts, in comparison to more than 4,199 statutory instruments. In statistical terms, therefore, it is at least arguable that delegated legislation is actually more significant than primary Acts of Parliament.

There are various types of delegated legislation:

- *Orders in Council* permit the Government, through the Privy Council, to make law. The Privy Council is nominally a non-party political body of eminent parliamentarians, but, in effect, it is simply a means through which the government, in the form of a committee of ministers, can introduce legislation without the need to go through the full parliamentary process. Although it is usual to cite situations of State emergency as exemplifying occasions when the government will resort to the use of Orders in Council, in actual fact, a great number of Acts are brought into operation through Orders in Council. Perhaps the widest scope for Orders in Council is to be found in relation to EC law, for, under s 2(2) of the European Communities Act 1972, ministers can give effect to provisions of Community law which do not have direct effect;

- *statutory instruments* are the means through which government ministers introduce particular regulations under powers delegated to them by Parliament in enabling legislation. Examples have already been considered in relation to the DCOA 1994;

- *bylaws* are the means through which local authorities and other public bodies can make legally binding rules. Bylaws may be made by local authorities under such enabling legislation as the Local Government Act 1972, and public corporations are empowered to make regulations relating to their specific sphere of operation;

- *court rule committees* are empowered to make the rules which govern procedure in the particular courts over which they have delegated authority under such acts as the Supreme Court Act 1981, the County Courts Act 1984 and the Magistrates' Courts Act 1980;

- *professional regulations* governing particular occupations may be given the force of law under provisions delegating legislative authority to certain professional bodies which are empowered to regulate the conduct of their members. An example is the power given to The Law Society, under the Solicitors Act 1974, to control the conduct of practising solicitors.

1.5.4 Advantages of the use of delegated legislation

The advantages of using delegated legislation are as follows:

- Timesaving

  Delegated legislation can be introduced quickly where necessary in particular cases and permits rules to be changed in response to emergencies or unforeseen problems.

  The use of delegated legislation, however, also saves parliamentary time generally. Given the pressure on debating time in Parliament and the highly detailed nature of typical delegated legislation, not to mention its sheer volume, Parliament would not have time to consider each individual piece of law that is enacted in the form of delegated legislation.

- Access to particular expertise

  Related to the first advantage is the fact that the majority of Members of Parliament (MPs) simply do not have sufficient expertise to consider such provisions effectively. Given the highly specialised and extremely technical nature of many of the regulations that are introduced through delegated legislation, it is necessary that those who are authorised to introduce the legislation should have access to the external expertise required to formulate such regulations. With regard to bylaws, it practically goes without saying that local and specialist knowledge should give rise to more appropriate rules than reliance on the general enactments of Parliament.

- Flexibility

  The use of delegated legislation permits ministers to respond on an *ad hoc* basis to particular problems as and when they arise, and provides greater flexibility in the regulation of activity which is subject to the ministers' overview.

1.5.5 Disadvantages in the prevalence of delegated legislation

Disadvantages in the prevalence of delegated legislation are as follows:

- Accountability

  A key issue in the use of delegated legislation concerns the question of accountability and the erosion of the constitutional role of Parliament. Parliament is presumed to be the source of legislation, but, with respect to delegated legislation, individual MPs are not the source of the law. Certain people, notably government ministers and the civil servants who work under them to produce the detailed provisions of delegated legislation, are the real source of such regulations. Even allowing for the fact that they are in effect operating on powers delegated to them from Parliament, it is not beyond questioning whether this procedure does not give them more power than might be thought appropriate or, indeed, constitutionally correct.

- Scrutiny

    The question of general accountability raises the need for effective scrutiny, but the very form of delegated legislation makes it extremely difficult for ordinary MPs to fully understand what is being enacted and, therefore, to effectively monitor it. This difficulty arises in part from the tendency for such regulations to be highly specific, detailed and technical. This problem of comprehension and control is compounded by the fact that regulations appear outside the context of their enabling legislation but only have any real meaning in that context.

- Bulk

    The problems faced by ordinary MPs in effectively keeping abreast of delegated legislation are further increased by the sheer mass of such legislation; and, if parliamentarians cannot keep up with the flow of delegated legislation, the question has to be asked as to how the general public can be expected to do so.

1.5.6 Control over delegated legislation

The foregoing difficulties and potential shortcomings in the use of delegated legislation are, at least to a degree, mitigated by the fact that specific controls have been established to oversee the use of delegated legislation. These controls take two forms:

- Parliamentary control over delegated legislation

    Power to make delegated legislation is ultimately dependent upon the authority of Parliament, and Parliament retains general control over the procedure for enacting such law.

    New regulations, in the form of delegated legislation, are required to be laid before Parliament. This procedure takes one of two forms, depending on the provision of the enabling legislation. Some regulations require a positive resolution of one or both of the Houses of Parliament before they become law. Most Acts, however, simply require that regulations made under their auspices be placed before Parliament. They automatically become law after a period of 40 days, unless a resolution to annul them is passed.

    Since 1973, there has been a Joint Select Committee on Statutory Instruments, whose function it is to consider statutory instruments. This committee scrutinises statutory instruments from a technical point of view as regards drafting and has no power to question the substantive content or the policy implications of the regulation. Its effectiveness as a general control is, therefore, limited. EC legislation is overseen by a specific committee and local authority bylaws are usually subject to the approval of the Department for the Environment.

• Judicial control of delegated legislation

It is possible for delegated legislation to be challenged through the procedure of judicial review, on the basis that the person or body to whom Parliament has delegated its authority has acted in a way that exceeds the limited powers delegated to them. Any provision which does not have this authority is *ultra vires* and void. Additionally, there is a presumption that any power delegated by Parliament is to be used in a reasonable manner and the courts may, on occasion, hold particular delegated legislation to be void on the basis that it is unreasonable.

The power of the courts to scrutinise and control delegated legislation has been greatly increased by the introduction of the Human Rights Act 1998. As has been noted previously, that Act does not give courts the power to strike down primary legislation as being incompatible with the rights contained in the ECHR. However, as – by definition – delegated legislation is not primary legislation, it follows that the courts now do have the power to declare invalid any such legislation which conflicts with the ECHR.

1.6 CASE LAW

The foregoing has highlighted the increased importance of legislation in today's society, but, even allowing for this and the fact that case law can be overturned by legislation, the UK is still a common law system and the importance and effectiveness of judicial creativity and common law principles and practices cannot be discounted. 'Case law' is the name given to the creation and refinement of law in the course of judicial decisions.

1.6.1 The meaning of precedent

The doctrine of binding precedent, or *stare decisis*, lies at the heart of the English common law system. It refers to the fact that, within the hierarchical structure of the English courts, a decision of a higher court will be binding on any court which is lower than it in that hierarchy. In general terms, this means that, when judges try cases, they will check to see whether a similar situation has already come before a court. If the precedent was set by a court of equal or higher status to the court deciding the new case, then the judge in that case should follow the rule of law established in the earlier case. Where the precedent is set by a court lower in the hierarchy, the judge in the new case does not have to follow it, but he will certainly consider it and will not overrule it without due consideration.

The operation of the doctrine of binding precedent depends on the existence of an extensive reporting service to provide access to previous judicial decisions. The earliest summaries of cases appeared in the Year Books, but, since 1865, cases have been reported by the Council of Law Reporting, which produces the authoritative reports of cases. Modern technology has resulted in the establishment of Lexis, a computer based store of cases.

For reference purposes, the most commonly referenced law reports are cited as follows:

- *Law reports*
  Appeal Cases (AC)
  Chancery Division (Ch D)
  Family Division (Fam)
  King's/Queen's Bench (KB/QB)
- *Other general series of reports*
  All England Law Reports (All ER)
  Weekly Law Reports (WLR)
  Solicitors Journal (SJ)
  European Court Reports (ECR)
- *CD-ROMs and Internet facilities*

  As in most other fields, the growth of information technology has revolutionised law reporting and law finding. Many of the law reports mentioned above are both available on CD-ROM and on the Internet. See, for example, Justis, Lawtel, Lexis-Nexis and Westlaw UK, amongst others. Indeed, members of the public can now access law reports directly from their sources in the courts, both domestically and in Europe. The first major electronic cases database was the Lexis system, which gave immediate access to a huge range of case authorities, some unreported elsewhere. The problem for the courts was that lawyers with access to the system could simply cite lists of cases from the database without the courts having access to paper copies of the decisions. The courts soon expressed their displeasure at this indiscriminate citation of unreported cases trawled from the Lexis database (see *Stanley v International Harvester Co of Great Britain Ltd* (1983)).

1.6.2 The hierarchy of the courts and the setting of precedent

(See below, Figure 1 (p 50), for a diagram of the hierarchical structure of the courts.)

House of Lords

The House of Lords stands at the summit of the English court structure and its decisions are binding on all courts below it in the hierarchy. It must be recalled, however, that the ECJ is superior to the House of Lords in matters relating to EC law. As regards its own previous decisions, until 1966, the House of Lords regarded itself as bound by such decisions. In a *Practice Statement* (1966), Lord Gardiner indicated that the House of Lords would in future regard itself as being free to depart from its previous decisions where it appeared to be right to do so. Given the potentially destabilising effect on existing legal practice based on previous decisions of the House of Lords, this is not a discretion that the court exercises lightly. There have, however, been a number of cases in which the House of Lords has overruled or amended its own earlier decisions, for example: *Conway v Rimmer* (1968); *Herrington v BRB* (1972); *Miliangos v George Frank (Textiles) Ltd* (1976); and *R v Shivpuri* (1986). In *Herrington v BRB*, the House of Lords overturned the previous rule, established in *Addie v Dumbreck* (1929), that an occupier was only responsible for injury sustained to a trespassing child if the injury was caused either intentionally or recklessly by the occupier. In the modern context, the court preferred to establish responsibility on the basis of whether the occupier had done everything that a humane person should have done to protect the trespasser. And, in *Miliangos v George Frank (Textiles) Ltd*, the House of Lords decided that, in the light of changed foreign exchange conditions, the previous rule that damages in English courts could only be paid in sterling no longer applied. They allowed payment in the foreign currency as specified in the contract and, in so doing, overruled *Re United Rlys of the Havana & Regla Warehouses Ltd* (1961).

Court of Appeal

In civil cases, the Court of Appeal is generally bound by previous decisions of the House of Lords.

The Court of Appeal is also bound by its own previous decisions in civil cases. There are, however, a number of exceptions to this general rule. Lord Greene MR listed these exceptions in *Young v Bristol Aeroplane Co Ltd* (1944). They arise where:

- there is a conflict between two previous decisions of the Court of Appeal. In this situation, the later court must decide which decision to follow and, as a corollary, which decision to overrule (*Tiverton Estates Ltd v Wearwell Ltd* (1974));

- a previous decision of the Court of Appeal has been overruled, either expressly or impliedly, by the House of Lords. In this situation, the Court of Appeal is required to follow the decision of the House of Lords (*Family Housing Association v Jones* (1990));

- the previous decision was given *per incuriam*, in other words, that previous decision was taken in ignorance of some authority, either statutory or judge made, that would have led to a different conclusion. In this situation, the later court can ignore the previous decision in question (*Williams v Fawcett* (1985)).

There is also the possibility that, as a consequence of s 3 of the European Communities Act 1972, the Court of Appeal can ignore a previous decision of its own which is inconsistent with EC law or with a later decision of the ECJ.

Although, on the basis of *R v Spencer* (1985), it would appear that there is no difference, in principle, in the operation of the doctrine of *stare decisis* between the Criminal and Civil Divisions of the Court of Appeal, it is generally accepted that, in practice, precedent is not followed as strictly in the former as it is in the latter. Courts in the Criminal Division are not bound to follow their own previous decisions which they subsequently consider to have been based on either a misunderstanding or a misapplication of the law. The reason for this is that the criminal courts deal with matters which involve individual liberty and which, therefore, require greater discretion to prevent injustice.

High Court

The Divisional Courts, each located within the three divisions of the High Court, hear appeals from courts and tribunals below them in the hierarchy. They are bound by the doctrine of *stare decisis* in the normal way and must follow decisions of the House of Lords and the Court of Appeal. Each Divisional Court is usually also bound by its own previous decisions, although in civil cases it may make use of the exceptions open to the Court of Appeal in *Young v Bristol Aeroplane Co Ltd* (1944) and, in criminal appeal cases, the Queen's Bench Divisional Court may refuse to follow its own earlier decisions where it considers the earlier decision to have been made wrongly.

The High Court is also bound by the decisions of superior courts. Decisions by individual High Court judges are binding on courts which are inferior in the hierarchy, but such decisions are not binding on other High Court judges, although they are of strong persuasive authority and tend to be followed in practice.

Crown Courts cannot create precedent and their decisions can never amount to more than persuasive authority.

County courts and magistrates' courts do not create precedents.

1.6.3 The nature of precedent

Previous cases establish legal precedents which later courts must either follow or, if the decision was made by a court lower in the hierarchy, at least consider. It is essential to realise, however, that not every part of the case as reported in the law reports is part of the precedent. In theory, it is possible to divide cases into two parts: the *ratio decidendi* and *obiter dicta*.

- *Ratio decidendi*

  The *ratio decidendi* of a case may be understood as the statement of the law applied in deciding the legal problem raised by the concrete facts of the case. It is essential to establish that it is not the actual decision in a case that sets the precedent – it is the rule of law on which that decision is founded that does this. This rule, which is an abstraction from the facts of the case, is known as the *ratio decidendi* of the case.

- *Obiter dicta*

  Any statement of law that is not an essential part of the *ratio decidendi* is, strictly speaking, superfluous; and any such statement is referred to as *obiter dictum* (*obiter dicta* in the plural), that is, 'said by the way'. Although *obiter dicta* statements do not form part of the binding precedent, they are of persuasive authority and can be taken into consideration in later cases.

The division of cases into these two distinct parts is a theoretical procedure. It is the general misfortune of all those who study law that judges do not actually separate their judgments into the two clearly defined categories. It is the particular misfortune of a student of business law, however, that they tend to be led to believe that case reports are divided into two distinct parts: the *ratio*, in which the judge states what he takes to be the law; and *obiter* statements, in which the judge muses on alternative possibilities. Such is not the case: there is no such clear division and, in reality, it is actually later courts which effectively determine the *ratio* in any particular case. Indeed, later courts may declare *obiter* what was previously felt to be part of the *ratio*. One should never overestimate the objective, scientific nature of the legal process.

Students should always read cases fully; although it is tempting to rely on the headnote at the start of the case report, it should be remembered that this is a summary provided by the case reporter and merely reflects what he or she thinks the *ratio* is. It is not unknown for headnotes to miss an essential point in a case.

1.6.4 Evaluation

The foregoing has set out the doctrine of binding precedent as it operates, in theory, to control the ambit of judicial discretion. It has to be recognised, however, that the doctrine does not operate as stringently as it appears to at first sight, and there are particular shortcomings in the system that must be addressed in weighing up the undoubted advantages with the equally undoubted disadvantages.

1.6.5 Advantages of case law

There are numerous perceived advantages of the doctrine of *stare decisis*, amongst which are the following:

- Consistency

  This refers to the fact that like cases are decided on a like basis and are not apparently subject to the whim of the individual judge deciding the case in question. This aspect of formal justice is important in justifying the decisions taken in particular cases.

- Certainty

  This follows from, and indeed is presupposed by, the previous item. Lawyers and their clients are able to predict the likely outcome of a particular legal question in the light of previous judicial decisions. Also, once the legal rule has been established in one case, individuals can orient their behaviour with regard to that rule relatively secure in the knowledge that it will not be changed by some later court.

- Efficiency

  This particular advantage follows from the preceding one. As the judiciary are bound by precedent, lawyers and their clients can be reasonably certain as to the likely outcome of any particular case on the basis of established precedent. As a consequence, most disputes do not have to be re-argued before the courts. With regard to potential litigants, it saves them money in court expenses because they can apply to their solicitor/barrister for guidance as to how their particular case is likely to be decided in the light of previous cases on the same or similar points.

- Flexibility

  This refers to the fact that various mechanisms enable the judges to manipulate the common law in such a way as to provide them with an opportunity to develop law in particular areas without waiting for Parliament to enact legislation. It should be recognised that judges do have a considerable degree of discretion in electing whether or not to be bound by a particular authority.

  Flexibility is achieved through the possibility of previous decisions being either overruled or distinguished, or the possibility of a later court extending or modifying the effective ambit of a precedent. The main mechanisms through which judges alter or avoid precedents are overruling and distinguishing:

  - Overruling

    This is the procedure whereby a court which is higher in the hierarchy sets aside a legal ruling established in a previous case.

    It is somewhat anomalous that, within the system of *stare decisis*, precedents gain increased authority with the passage of time. As a consequence, courts tend to be reluctant to overrule long standing authorities, even though they may no longer accurately reflect contemporary practices. In addition to the wish to maintain a high degree of certainty in the law, the main reason for the judicial reluctance to overrule old decisions would appear to be the fact that overruling operates retrospectively and the principle of law being overruled is held never to have been law. Overruling a precedent, therefore, might have the consequence of disturbing important financial arrangements made in line with what were thought to be settled rules of law. It might even, in certain circumstances, lead to the imposition of criminal liability on previously lawful behaviour. It has to be emphasised, however, that the courts will not shrink from overruling authorities where they see them as no longer representing an appropriate statement of law. The legal recognition of the possibility of rape within marriage is one example of this process.

Overruling should not be confused with reversing, which is the procedure whereby a court higher in the hierarchy reverses the decision of a lower court in the same case.

o   Distinguishing

The main device for avoiding binding precedents is distinguishing. As has been previously stated, the *ratio decidendi* of any case is an abstraction from the material facts of the case. This opens up the possibility that a court may regard the facts of the case before it as significantly different from the facts of a cited precedent and, consequentially, it will not find itself bound to follow that precedent. Judges use the device of distinguishing where, for some reason, they are unwilling to follow a particular precedent, and the law reports provide many examples of strained distinctions where a court has quite evidently not wanted to follow an authority that it would otherwise have been bound by.

1.6.6   Disadvantages of case law

It should be noted that the advantage of flexibility at least potentially contradicts the alternative advantage of certainty, but there are other disadvantages in the doctrine which have to be considered. Amongst these are the following:

•   Uncertainty

This refers to the fact that the degree of certainty provided by the doctrine of *stare decisis* is undermined by the absolute number of cases that have been reported and can be cited as authorities. This uncertainty is compounded by the ability of the judiciary to select which authority to follow, through use of the mechanism of distinguishing cases on their facts.

•   Fixity

This refers to possibility that the law, in relation to any particular area, may become ossified on the basis of an unjust precedent, with the consequence that previous injustices are perpetuated. An example of this was the long delay in the recognition of the possibility of rape within marriage, which was only recognised a decade ago (*R v R* (1992)).

- Unconstitutionality

  This is a fundamental question that refers to the fact that the judiciary are in fact overstepping their theoretical constitutional role by actually making law, rather than restricting themselves to the role of simply applying it. It is now probably a commonplace of legal theory that judges do make law. Due to their position in the constitution, however, judges have to be circumspect in the way in which, and the extent to which, they use their powers to create law and impose values. To overtly assert or exercise the power would be to challenge the power of the legislature. For an unelected body to challenge a politically supreme Parliament would be unwise, to say the least.

Case study

Carlill v Carbolic Smoke Ball Co Ltd (1892) is one of the most famous examples of the case law in this area. A summary of the case is set out below.

Facts: Mrs Carlill made a retail purchase of one of the defendant's medicinal products: the Carbolic Smoke Ball. It was supposed to prevent people who used it in a specified way (three times a day for at least two weeks) from catching influenza. The company was very confident about its product and placed an advertisement in a newspaper, the *Pall Mall Gazette*, which praised the effectiveness of the smoke ball and promised to pay £100 (a huge sum of money at that time) to:

> ... any person who contracts the increasing epidemic influenza, colds, or any disease caused by taking cold, having used the ball three times daily for two weeks according to the printed directions supplied with each ball.

The advertisement went on to explain that the company had deposited £1,000 with the Alliance Bank (on Regent Street in London) as a sign of its sincerity in the matter. Any proper claimants could get their payment from that sum. On the faith of the advertisement, Mrs Carlill bought one of the balls at a chemist and used it as directed, but she caught influenza. She claimed £100 from the company but was refused it, so she sued for breach of contract. The company said that, for several reasons, there was no contract, the main reasons being that:

- the advert was too vague to amount to the basis of a contract;
- there was no time limit and no way of checking the way in which the customer used the ball;
- Mrs Carlill did not give any legally recognised value to the company;
- one cannot legally make an offer to the whole world, so the advert was not a proper offer;

- even if the advert could be seen as an offer, Mrs Carlill had not given a legal acceptance of that offer because she had not notified the company that she was accepting;
- the advert was a mere puff, that is, a piece of insincere rhetoric.

Decision: The Court of Appeal found that there was a legally enforceable agreement – a contract – between Mrs Carlill and the company. The company would have to pay damages to Mrs Carlill.

Ratio decidendi: The three Lords Justice of Appeal who gave judgments in this case all decided in favour of Mrs Carlill. Each, however, used slightly different reasoning, arguments and examples. The process, therefore, of distilling the reason for the decision of the court is quite a delicate art. The *ratio* of the case can be put as follows.

Offers must be sufficiently clear in order to allow the courts to enforce agreements that follow from them. The offer here was a distinct promise, expressed in language which was perfectly unmistakable. It could not be a mere puff in view of the £1,000 deposited specially to show good faith. An offer *may* be made to the world at large, and the advert was such an offer. It was accepted by any person, like Mrs Carlill, who bought the product and used it in the prescribed manner. Mrs Carlill had accepted the offer by her conduct when she did as she was invited to do and started to use the smoke ball. She had not been asked to let the company know that she was using it.

Obiter dicta: In the course of his reasoning, Bowen LJ gave the legal answer to a set of facts which were not in issue in this case. They are thus *obiter dicta*. He did this because it assisted him in clarifying the answer to Mrs Carlill's case. He said:

> If I advertise to the world that my dog is lost, and that anybody who brings the dog to a particular place will be paid some money, are all the police or other persons whose business it is to find lost dogs to be expected to sit down and write me a note saying that they have accepted my proposal? Why, of course, they at once look [for] the dog, and as soon as they find the dog they have performed the condition.

If such facts were ever subsequently in issue in a court case, the words of Bowen LJ could be used by counsel as persuasive precedent.

Carlill was applied in *Peck v Lateu* (1973) but was distinguished in *AM Satterthwaite & Co v New Zealand Shipping Co* (1972).

1.7 STATUTORY INTERPRETATION

The two previous sections have tended to present legislation and case law in terms of opposition: legislation being the product of Parliament and case law the product of the judiciary in the courts. Such stark opposition is, of course, misleading, for the two processes come together when consideration is given to the necessity for judges to interpret statute law in order to apply it.

1.7.1 Problems in interpreting legislation

In order to apply legislation, judges must ascertain its meaning and, in order to ascertain that meaning, they are faced with the difficulty of interpreting the legislation. Legislation, however, shares the general problem of uncertainty, which is inherent in any mode of verbal communication. Words can have more than one meaning and the meaning of a word can change, depending on its context.

One of the essential requirements of legislation is generality of application – the need for it to be written in such a way as to ensure that it can be effectively applied in various circumstances without the need to detail those situations individually. This requirement, however, can give rise to particular problems of interpretation; the need for generality can only really be achieved at the expense of clarity and precision of language.

Legislation, therefore, involves an inescapable measure of uncertainty, which can only be made certain through judicial interpretation. However, to the extent that the interpretation of legislative provisions is an active process, it is equally a creative process; and it inevitably involves the judiciary in creating law through determining the meaning and effect to being given to any particular piece of legislation.

1.7.2 Rules of interpretation

In attempting to decide upon the precise meaning of any statute, judges use well established rules of interpretation, of which there are three primary ones, together with a variety of other secondary aids to construction.

The rules of statutory interpretation are as follows:

- Literal rule

  Under this rule, the judge is required to consider what the legislation actually says, rather than considering what it might mean. In order to achieve this end, the judge should give words in legislation their literal meaning; that is, their plain, ordinary, everyday meaning, even if the effect of this is to produce what might be considered an otherwise unjust or undesirable outcome.

  A classic example of this approach from the area of contract law is *Fisher v Bell* (1961) (considered in detail below, 5.2.1), where, in line with general contract law principles, it was decided that the placing of an article in a window did not amount to offering but was merely an invitation to treat. Thus, the shopkeeper could not be charged with offering the goods for sale. In this case, the court chose to follow the 'contract law' literal interpretation of the meaning of 'offer' in the Act in question and declined to consider the usual, non-legal, literal interpretation of the word.

A problem in relation to the literal rule arises from the difficulty that judges face in determining the literal meaning of even the commonest of terms. In *R v Maginnis* (1987), the judges differed amongst themselves as to the literal meaning of the common word 'supply' in relation to a charge of supplying drugs.

- Golden rule

  This rule is generally considered to be an extension of the literal rule. It is applied in circumstances where the application of the literal rule is likely to result in an obviously absurd result.

  An example of the application of the golden rule is *Adler v George* (1964). In this case, the court held that the literal wording of the statute ('in the vicinity of') covered the action committed by the defendant who carried out her action within the area concerned.

  Another example of this approach is to be found in *Re Sigsworth* (1935), in which the court introduced common law rules into legislative provisions, which were silent on the matter, to prevent the estate of a murderer from benefiting from the property of the party he had murdered.

- Mischief rule

  This rule, sometimes known as the rule in *Heydon's Case* (1584), operates to enable judges to interpret a statute in such a way as to provide a remedy for the mischief that the statute was enacted to prevent. Contemporary practice is to go beyond the actual body of the legislation to determine what mischief a particular Act was aimed at redressing.

1.7.3 Aids to construction

In addition to the three main rules of interpretation, there are a number of secondary aids to construction. These can be categorised as either intrinsic or extrinsic in nature:

- Intrinsic assistance

  This is help which is actually derived from the statute which is the object of interpretation. The judge uses the full statute to understand the meaning of a particular part of it. Assistance may be found from various parts of the statute, such as: the title, long or short; any preamble, which is a statement preceding the actual provisions of the Act; and schedules, which appear as detailed additions at the end the Act. Section headings or marginal notes may also be considered, where they exist.

- Extrinsic assistance

  Sources outside of the Act itself may, on occasion, be resorted to in determining the meaning of legislation. For example, judges have always been entitled to refer to dictionaries in order to find the meaning of non-legal words. The Interpretation Act 1978 is also available for consultation with regard to the meaning of particular words generally used in statutes.

  Judges are also allowed to use extrinsic sources to determine the mischief at which particular legislation is aimed. For example, they are able to examine earlier statutes and they have been entitled for some time to look at Law Commission reports, Royal Commission reports and the reports of other official commissions.

  Until very recently, *Hansard,* the verbatim report of parliamentary debate, literally remained a closed book to the courts. In *Pepper v Hart* (1993), however, the House of Lords decided to overturn the previous rule. In a majority decision, it was held that, where the precise meaning of legislation was uncertain or ambiguous, or where the literal meaning of an Act would lead to a manifest absurdity, the courts could refer to *Hansard's Reports of Parliamentary Debates and Proceedings* as an aid to construing the meaning of the legislation.

1.7.4 Presumptions

In addition to the rules of interpretation, the courts may also make use of certain presumptions. As with all presumptions, they are rebuttable, which means that the presumption is subject to being overturned in argument in any particular case. The presumptions operate in the following ways:

- Against the alteration of the common law

  Parliament can alter the common law whenever it decides to do so. In order to do this, however, it must expressly enact legislation to that end. If there is no express intention to that effect, it is assumed that statute does not make any fundamental change to the common law. With regard to particular provisions, if there are alternative interpretations, one of which will maintain the existing common law situation, then that interpretation will be preferred.

- Against retrospective application

  As the War Crimes Act 1990 shows, Parliament can impose criminal responsibility retrospectively, where particular and extremely unusual circumstances dictate the need to do so; but such effect must be clearly expressed.

- Against the deprivation of an individual's liberty, property or rights

  Once again, the presumption can be rebutted by express provision and it is not uncommon for legislation to deprive people of their rights to enjoy particular benefits. Nor is it unusual for individuals to be deprived of their liberty under the Mental Health Act 1983.

- Against application to the Crown

Unless the legislation contains a clear statement to the contrary, it is presumed not to apply to the Crown.

- Against breaking international law

Where possible, legislation should be interpreted in such a way as to give effect to existing international legal obligations.

- In favour of the requirement that *mens rea* (a guilty mind) be a requirement in any criminal offence

The classic example of this presumption is *Sweet v Parsley* (1969), in which a landlord was eventually found not guilty of allowing her premises to be used for the purpose of taking drugs, as she had absolutely no knowledge of what was going on in her house. Offences which do not require the presence of *mens rea* are referred to as strict liability offences.

- In favour of words taking their meaning from the context in which they are used

This final presumption refers back to, and operates in conjunction with, the major rules for interpreting legislation considered previously. The general presumption appears as three distinct sub-rules, each of which carries a Latin tag:

o the *noscitur a sociis* rule is applied where statutory provisions include a list of examples of what is covered by the legislation. It is presumed that the words used have a related meaning and are to be interpreted in relation to each other (see *IRC v Frere* (1965));

o the *eiusdem generis* rule applies in situations where general words are appended to the end of a list of specific examples. The presumption is that the general words have to be interpreted in line with the prior restrictive examples. Thus, a provision which referred to a list that included, horses, cattle, sheep and other animals would be unlikely to apply to domestic animals such as cats and dogs (see *Powell v Kempton Park Racecourse* (1899));

o the *expressio unius exclusio alterius* rule simply means that, where a statute seeks to establish a list of what is covered by its provisions, then anything not expressly included in that list is specifically excluded (see *R v Inhabitants of Sedgley* (1831)).

1.8 CUSTOM

The traditional view of the development of the common law tends to adopt an overly romantic view as regards its emergence. This view suggests that the common law is no more than the crystallisation of ancient common customs; this distillation being accomplished by the judiciary in the course of their historic travels around the land in the Middle Ages. This view, however, tends to ignore the political process that gave rise to this procedure. The imposition of a common system of law represented the political victory of a State that had fought to establish and assert its central authority. Viewed in that light, the emergence of the common law can perhaps better be seen as the invention of the judges as representatives of the State and as representing what they wanted the law to be, rather than what people generally thought it was.

One source of customary practice that undoubtedly did find expression in the form of law was business and commercial practice. These customs and practices were originally constituted in the distinct form of the Law Merchant, but, gradually, this became subsumed under the control of the common law courts and ceased to exist apart from the common law.

Notwithstanding the foregoing, it is still possible for specific local customs to operate as a source of law. In certain circumstances, parties may assert the existence of customary practices in order to support their case. Such local custom may run counter to the strict application of the common law and, where they are found to be legitimate, they will effectively replace the common law. Even in this respect, however, reliance on customary law as opposed to common law, although not impossible, is made unlikely by the stringent tests that have to be satisfied (see *Egerton v Harding* (1974)). The requirements that a local custom must satisfy in order to be recognised are as follows:

- it must have existed from time immemorial, that is, 1189;
- it must have been exercised continuously within that period;
- it must have been exercised peacefully and without opposition;
- it must also have been felt to be obligatory;
- it must be capable of precise definition;
- it must have been consistent with other customs;
- it must be reasonable.

Given this list of requirements, it can be seen why local custom is not an important source of law.

1.8.1 Books of authority

In the very unusual situation of a court being unable to locate a precise or analogous precedent, it may refer to legal textbooks for guidance. Such books are subdivided, depending on when they were written. In strict terms, only certain works are actually treated as authoritative sources of law. Legal works produced after *Blackstone's Commentaries* of 1765 are considered to be of recent origin, and, although they cannot be treated as authoritative sources, the courts may consider what the most eminent works by accepted experts in particular fields have said in order to help determine what the law is or should be.

1.9 LAW REFORM

At one level, law reform is a product of either parliamentary or judicial activity, as has been considered previously. Parliament tends, however, to be concerned with particularities of law reform and the judiciary are constitutionally and practically disbarred from reforming the law on anything other than an opportunistic and piecemeal basis. Therefore, there remains a need for the question of law reform to be considered generally and a requirement that such consideration be conducted in an informed but disinterested manner.

Reference has already been made to the use of consultative Green Papers by the government as a mechanism for gauging the opinions of interested parties to particular reforms. More formal advice may be provided through various advisory standing committees. Amongst these is the Law Reform Committee. The function of this Committee is to consider the desirability of changes to the civil law which the Lord Chancellor may refer to it. The Criminal Law Revision Committee performs similar functions in relation to criminal law.

Royal Commissions may be constituted to consider the need for law reform in specific areas. For example, the Commission on Criminal Procedure (1980) led to the enactment of the Police and Criminal Evidence Act (PACE) 1984.

Committees may be set up in order to review the operation of particular areas of law, the most significant recent example being the Woolf review of the operation of the civil justice system. (Detailed analysis of the consequences flowing from the implementation of the recommendations of the Woolf Report will be considered subsequently.) Similarly, Sir Robin Auld conducted a review of the whole criminal justice system and Sir Andrew Leggatt carried out a similar task in relation to the tribunal system.

If a criticism is to be levelled at these committees and commissions, it is that they are all *ad hoc* bodies. Their remit is limited and they do not have the power either to widen the ambit of their investigation or initiate reform proposals.

The Law Commission fulfils the need for some institution to concern itself more generally with the question of law reform. Its general function is to keep the law as a whole under review and to make recommendations for its systematic reform.

The Commission is a purely advisory body and its scope is limited to those areas set out in its programme of law reform. Its seventh programme, set out in 2000, includes damages, limitation of actions, illegal transactions, property law, the law of trusts, the law of business associations, electronic commerce, third parties' rights against insurers, and criminal law. In addition, ministers may refer matters of particular importance to the Commission for its consideration. As was considered earlier at 1.2.5, it was just such a referral by the Home Secretary, after the Macpherson Inquiry into the Stephen Lawrence case, that gave rise to the Law Commission's recommendation that the rule against double jeopardy be removed in particular circumstances. The Law Commission only recommends reform after it has undertaken an extensive process of consultation with informed and/or interested parties. At the conclusion of a project, a report is submitted to the Lord Chancellor and Parliament for their consideration and action.

SUMMARY OF CHAPTER 1

LAW AND LEGAL SOURCES

The nature of law

Legal systems are particular ways of establishing and maintaining social order. Law is a formal mechanism of social control.

Categories of law

Law can be categorised in a number of ways, although the various categories are not mutually exclusive:

- Common law and civil law relate to distinct legal systems. The English legal system is a common law one.
- Common law and equity distinguish the two historical sources and systems of English law.
- Common law is judge made; statute law is produced by Parliament.
- Private law relates to individual citizens; public law relates to institutions of government.
- Civil law facilitates the interaction of individuals; criminal law enforces particular standards of behaviour.

The Human Rights Act 1998

The Human Rights Act 1998 incorporates the European Convention on Human Rights into UK law. The Articles of the Convention cover the following matters:

- the right to life (Art 2);
- the prohibition of torture (Art 3);
- the prohibition of slavery and forced labour (Art 4);
- the right to liberty and security (Art 5);
- the right to a fair trial (Art 6);
- the general prohibition of the enactment of retrospective criminal offences (Art 7);
- the right to respect for private and family life (Art 8);
- freedom of thought, conscience and religion (Art 9);

- freedom of expression (Art 10);
- freedom of assembly and association (Art 11);
- the right to marry (Art 12);
- the prohibition of discrimination (Art 14);
- the political activity of aliens may be restricted (Art 16).

The incorporation of the Convention into UK law means that UK courts can decide cases in line with the above Articles. This has the potential to create friction between the judiciary and the executive/legislature.

Domestic sources of law

- Legislation is the law produced through the parliamentary system. Then, it is given royal assent. The House of Lords has only limited scope to delay legislation.
- Delegated legislation is a sub-classification of legislation. It appears in the form of: Orders in Council; statutory instruments; bylaws; and professional regulations.

  Advantages of delegated legislation:
  - speed of implementation;
  - the saving of parliamentary time;
  - access to expertise; and
  - flexibility.

  The disadvantages relate to:
  - the lack of accountability;
  - the lack of scrutiny of proposals for such legislation; and
  - the sheer amount of delegated legislation.

  Controls over delegated legislation:
  - Joint Select Committee on Statutory Instruments; and
  - *ultra vires* provisions may be challenged in the courts.

Case law

- Created by judges in the course of deciding cases.
- The doctrine of *stare decisis*, or binding precedent, refers to the fact that courts are bound by previous decisions of courts which are equal or above them in the court hierarchy.
- The *ratio decidendi* is binding. Everything else is *obiter dicta*.
- Precedents may be avoided through either overruling or distinguishing.

The advantages of precedent are:

o   saving the time of all parties concerned;

o   certainty; and

o   flexibility.

The disadvantages are:

o   uncertainty;

o   fixity; and

o   unconstitutionality.

Statutory interpretation

The way in which judges give practical meaning to legislative provisions, using the following rules:

*   The *literal rule* gives words everyday meaning, even if this leads to an apparent injustice.

*   The *golden rule* is used in circumstances where the application of the literal rule is likely to result in an obviously absurd result.

*   The *mischief rule* permits the court to go beyond the words of the statute in question to consider the mischief at which it was aimed.

There are rebuttable presumptions against:

*   the alteration of the common law;

*   retrospective application;

*   the deprivation of an individual's liberty, property or rights; and

*   application to the Crown.
    And in favour of:

*   the requirement of *mens rea* in relation to criminal offences;

*   deriving the meaning of words from their contexts.
    Judges may seek assistance from:

*   intrinsic sources as the title of the Act, any preamble or any schedules to it;

*   extrinsic sources such as: dictionaries; textbooks; reports; other parliamentary papers; and, since *Pepper v Hart* (1993), *Hansard*.

Custom

Custom is of very limited importance as a contemporary source of law, although it was important in the establishment of business and commercial law in the form of the old Law Merchant.

Law reform

The need to reform the law may be assessed by a number of bodies:

- Royal Commissions;
- standing committees;
- *ad hoc* committees;
- the Law Commission.

CHAPTER 2

THE CRIMINAL AND CIVIL COURTS

2.1 INTRODUCTION

In the UK, the structure of the court system is divided into two distinct sectors, following the division between criminal and civil law. This chapter locates particular courts within the general hierarchical structure in ascending order of authority (see below, Figure 1). It is essential not just to be aware of the role and powers of the individual courts, but also to know the paths of appeal from one court to another within the hierarchy.

2.2 THE CRIMINAL COURT STRUCTURE

Crimes are offences against the law of the land and are usually prosecuted by the State. Criminal cases are normally cited in the form *R v Brown*. Cases are heard in different courts, depending on their seriousness. Offences can be divided into three categories:

- *summary offences* are the least serious and are tried by magistrates, without recourse to a jury;

- *indictable offences* are the most serious and are required to be tried before a judge and jury in the Crown Court;

- *either way offences*, as their title suggests, are open to trial in either of the preceding ways. At the moment, the decision as to whether the case is heard in the magistrates' court or the Crown Court is decided by the accused. The previous Labour Government twice attempted to introduce legislation to remove the defendant's right to elect for jury trial in relation to either way offences. On both occasions the proposed Bills were defeated in the House of Lords. In his review of the criminal justice system, published in 2001, Sir Robin Auld also recommended that defendants should lose the right to insist on jury trial. However, it now appears that the Government has decided that the best way of reducing jury trials is by increasing the sentencing powers of magistrates' courts from a maximum of six months to 12 months, with the introduction of a formal system of sentence discounts for those who plead guilty at an early stage.

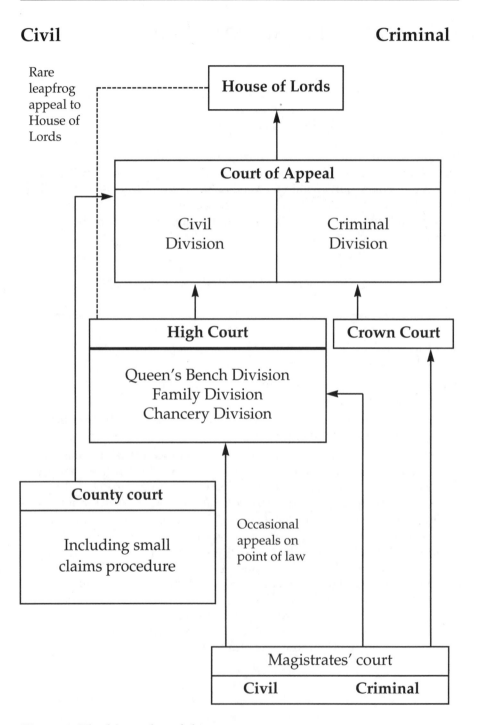

Figure 1: The hierarchy of the courts

2.3 MAGISTRATES' COURTS

The office of magistrate or justice of the peace (JP) dates from 1195, when Richard I appointed keepers of the peace to deal with those who were accused of breaking the King's peace. The JPs originally acted as local administrators for the King, in addition to carrying out their judicial responsibilities.

There are approximately 700 magistrates' courts in England and Wales, staffed by some 30,000 part time lay magistrates. In addition, there are 98 full time professional district judges (magistrates' courts) who sit in cities and large towns. The latter used to be known as stipendiary magistrates. Magistrates are empowered to hear and decide a wide variety of legal matters, and the amount and importance of the work they do should not be underestimated. It has been estimated that 97% of all criminal cases are dealt with by the magistrates' courts.

Lay magistrates are not usually legally qualified and sit as a bench of three. District judges are legally qualified and decide cases on their own.

A bench of lay magistrates is legally advised by a justices clerk, who is legally qualified and guides the justices on matters of law, sentencing and procedure, even when not specifically invited to do so. The clerk should not give any opinion on matters of fact. Magistrates are independent of the clerks and the latter should not instruct the magistrates as to what decision they should reach.

2.3.1 Powers of magistrates' courts

Magistrates' courts have considerable power. In relation to criminal law, they are empowered to try summary cases, that is, cases which are triable without a jury. Additionally, with the agreement of the accused, they may deal with triable either way cases, that is, cases which can either be tried summarily by the magistrates or on indictment before a jury in the Crown Court.

The maximum sentence that magistrates can normally impose is a £5,000 fine and/or a six month prison sentence. The maximum sentences for many summary offences, however, are much less than these limits. Where a defendant is convicted of two or more offences at the same hearing, consecutive sentences amounting to more than six months are not permitted, although this can rise to 12 months in cases involving offences triable either way. If the magistrates feel that their sentencing powers are insufficient to deal with the defendant, then the offender may be sent to the Crown Court for sentencing.

Magistrates can impose alternative sentences, such as community service orders or probation orders. They can also discharge offenders either conditionally or absolutely. In addition, they can issue compensation orders. Such orders are used not as a means of punishing the offender, but as a way of compensating the victims of the offender without them having to sue the offender in the civil courts. The maximum payment under any such order is £5,000.

Where magistrates decide that an offence triable either way should be tried in the Crown Court, they hold committal proceedings. These proceedings are also held where the defendant has been charged with an indictable offence. Acting in this way, the justices become examining magistrates. The object of these proceedings is to determine whether there is a *prima facie* case against the defendant. If the justices decide that there is a *prima facie* case, they must commit the defendant to a Crown Court for trial; if not, they must discharge him. Section 44 of the Criminal Procedure and Investigations Act (CPIA) 1996 repeals s 44 of the Criminal Justice and Public Order Act 1994 and, in effect, introduces a new, streamlined version of committal proceedings, in which no oral evidence can be given. The new system of committals is governed by s 47 and Sched 1 to the CPIA 1996. The effect of this law is to abolish the old style mini-trial committals and the right of the defendant to have witnesses called and cross-examined at the magistrates' court. Now, defendants may only use written evidence at committal stage.

Magistrates sit in youth courts to try children and young persons. A child is someone who has not reached his 14th birthday and young people are taken to be below the age of 18. These tribunals are not open to the public and sit separately from the ordinary magistrates' court in order to protect the young defendants from publicity.

2.4 THE CROWN COURT

The Crown Court, unlike the magistrates' court, is not a local court, but a single court which sits in over 90 centres. The Crown Court is part of the Supreme Court, which is defined as including the Court of Appeal, the High Court of Justice and the Crown Court. For the purposes of the operation of the Crown Court, England and Wales are divided into six circuits, each with its own headquarters and staff. The centres are divided into three tiers. In first tier centres, High Court judges hear civil and criminal cases, whereas circuit judges and recorders hear only criminal cases. Second tier centres are served by the same types of judge but hear criminal cases only. At third tier centres, recorders and circuit judges hear criminal cases only.

2.4.1 Jurisdiction

The Crown Court hears all cases involving trial on indictment. It also hears appeals from those convicted summarily in the magistrates' courts. At the conclusion of an appeal hearing, the Crown Court has the power to confirm, reverse or vary any part of the decision under appeal (s 48(2) of the Supreme Court Act 1981). If the appeal is decided against the accused, the Crown Court has the power to impose any sentence which the magistrates could have imposed, including one which is harsher than that originally imposed on the defendant.

2.5 CRIMINAL APPEALS

The process of appeal depends upon how a case was originally tried, that is, whether it was tried summarily or on indictment. The following sets out the various routes and procedures involved in appealing against the decisions of particular courts.

2.5.1   Appeals from magistrates' courts

Two routes of appeal are possible. The first route allows only a defendant to appeal. The appeal is to a judge and between two and four magistrates sitting in the Crown Court, and can be:

- against conviction (only if the defendant pleaded not guilty) on points of fact or law; or
- against sentence.

Such an appeal will take the form of a new trial (a trial *de novo*).

Alternatively, either the defendant or the prosecution can appeal by way of case stated to the High Court (the Divisional Court of the Queen's Bench Division). This court consists of two or more judges (but usually two), of whom one will be a Lord Justice of Appeal. This appeal is limited to matters relating to:

- points of law; or
- a claim that the magistrates acted beyond their jurisdiction.

Appeal from the Divisional Court is to the House of Lords. Either side may appeal, but only on a point of law and only if the Divisional Court certifies the point to be one of general public importance. Leave to appeal must also be granted either by the Court of Appeal or the House of Lords.

2.5.2   Appeals from the Crown Court

Appeals from this court lie to the Court of Appeal (Criminal Division), which hears appeals against conviction and sentence. The court hears around 6,000 criminal appeals and applications each year.

Appeals may be made by the defence against conviction, but the prosecution cannot appeal against an acquittal. Under s 36 of the Criminal

Justice Act (CJA) 1972, the Attorney General can refer a case which has resulted in an acquittal to the Court of Appeal where he believes the decision to have been questionable on a point of law. The Court of Appeal only considers the point of law and, even if its finding is contrary to the defendant's case, the acquittal is not affected. This procedure merely clarifies the law for future cases.

The Criminal Appeal Act (CAA) 1995 introduced significant changes to the criminal appeal system. Section 1 of this Act amended the CAA 1968 so as to bring appeals against conviction, appeals against a verdict of not guilty by reason of insanity and appeals against a finding of disability on a question of law alone into line with other appeals against conviction and sentence (that is, those involving questions of fact, or mixtures of law and fact). Now, all appeals against conviction and sentence must first have leave of the Court of Appeal or a certificate of fitness for appeal from the trial judge before the appeal can be taken. Before the new Act came into force, it was possible to appeal without the consent of the trial judge or Court of Appeal on a point of law alone.

Section 2 of the CAA 1995 changes the grounds for allowing an appeal under the CAA 1968. Under the old law, the Court of Appeal was required to allow an appeal where:

- the conviction, verdict or finding should have been set aside on the ground that, under all the circumstances, it was unsafe or unsatisfactory;

- the judgment of the court of trial or the order of the court giving effect to the verdict or finding should be set aside on the ground of a wrong decision of law; or

- there was a material irregularity in the course of the trial.

In all three situations, the Court of Appeal was allowed to dismiss the appeal if it considered that no miscarriage of justice had actually occurred. The new law requires the Court of Appeal to allow an appeal against conviction if it thinks that the conviction, verdict or finding is unsafe (as opposed to the old law, which used the unsafe or unsatisfactory formula).

Where there is an appeal against sentence, the court may confirm or alter the original sentence by way of changing the terms or substituting a new form of punishment. It cannot increase the sentence on appeal. However, under the CJA 1988, the Attorney General may refer indictable only cases to the Court of Appeal, where the sentence at trial is regarded as unduly lenient. In such circumstances, the court may impose a harsher sentence.

2.6 HOUSE OF LORDS

Following the determination of an appeal by the Court of Appeal or the Divisional Court, either the prosecution or the defence may appeal to the House of Lords. Leave from the court below or the House of Lords must be obtained and two other conditions must be fulfilled, according to s 33 of the CAA 1968:

- the court below must certify that a point of law of general public importance is involved; and
- either the court below or the House of Lords must be satisfied that the point of law is one which ought to be considered by the House of Lords.

2.7 JUDICIAL COMMITTEE OF THE PRIVY COUNCIL

The Privy Council is the final court of appeal for certain Commonwealth countries that have retained this option and for some independent members and associate members of the Commonwealth. The Committee comprises Privy Councillors who hold (or have held) high judicial office and five Lords of Appeal in Ordinary, sometimes assisted by a judge from the country concerned.

Most of the appeals heard by the Committee are civil cases. In the rare criminal cases, it is only on matters involving legal questions that appeals are heard; the Committee does not hear appeals against criminal sentence.

2.8 THE CIVIL COURT STRUCTURE

Civil actions are between individuals. The State merely provides the legal framework within which they determine and seek to enforce their mutual rights and obligations. Civil cases are cited in the form *Smith v Jones*.

2.9 MAGISTRATES' COURTS

Although they deal mainly with criminal matters, the magistrates' courts have a significant civil jurisdiction. They hear family proceedings under the Domestic Proceedings and Magistrates' Courts Act 1978 and the Children Act 1989. Under such circumstances, the court is termed a 'family proceedings court'. A family proceedings court must normally be composed of not more than three justices, including, as far as is practicable, both a man and a woman. Justices who sit on such benches must be members of the family panel, which comprises people specially appointed and trained to deal with family matters. Under the Children Act 1989, the court deals with adoption proceedings, applications for residence and contact orders, and maintenance relating to spouses and children. Under the Magistrates' Courts Act 1978, the court also has the power to make personal protection orders and exclusion orders in cases of matrimonial violence.

The magistrates' courts have powers of recovery in relation to the community charge and its replacement, council tax. They also have the power to enforce charges for water, gas and electricity. Magistrates' courts also function as licensing courts, under which guise they grant, renew or revoke licenses for selling liquor, betting or operating a taxi service.

2.10 THE WOOLF REFORMS TO THE CIVIL JUSTICE SYSTEM

Before considering the two most important civil courts, the county court and the High Court, it is necessary to have some understanding of the radical way in which civil law procedure has altered in the recent past. In 1994, Lord Woolf was invited to review the operation of the entire civil justice system and, in his *Interim Report* in 1995, he stated that:

> ... the key problems facing civil justice today are cost, delay and complexity. These three are interrelated and stem from the uncontrolled nature of the litigation process. In particular, there is no clear judicial responsibility for managing individual cases or for the overall administration of the civil courts [*Access to Justice – Interim Report*, 1995].

Lord Woolf's recommendations, which formed the basis of major changes to the system, were given effect by the Civil Procedure Act 1997 and Civil Procedure Rules (CPR) 1998, supplemented by a series of new practice directions and pre-action protocols. The new system came into effect in April 1999.

There are four main aspects to the reforms.

2.10.1 Judicial case management

The judge is a case manager under the new regime. The new system allocates cases to one of three tracks, depending upon the complexity and value of the dispute. Previously, lawyers from either side were permitted to wrangle almost endlessly with each other about who should disclose what information and documents to whom and at what stage. Now, the judge is under an obligation to actively manage cases. This includes:

* encouraging parties to co-operate with each other;
* identifying issues in the dispute at an early stage;
* disposing of summary issues which do not need full investigation;
* helping the parties to settle the whole or part of the case;

- fixing timetables for the case hearing and controlling the progress of the case; and
- considering whether the benefits of a particular method of hearing the dispute justify its costs.

If the parties refuse to comply with the new rules, practice directions or protocols, the judge will be able to exercise disciplinary powers. These include:

- using costs sanctions against parties (that is, refusing to allow the lawyers who have violated the rules to recover their costs from their client or the other side of the dispute);
- striking out;
- refusal to grant extensions of time; and
- refusal to allow documents not previously disclosed to the court and the other side to be relied upon.

2.10.2 Pre-action protocols

Part of the problem in the past arose from the fact that the courts could only start to exercise control over the progress of a case, and the way it was handled, once proceedings had been issued. Before that stage, lawyers were at liberty to take inordinate amounts of time to do things related to the case, to write to lawyers on the other side to the dispute, and so forth. Now, a mechanism allows new pre-action requirements to be enforced. The objects of the protocols are:

- to encourage greater contact between the parties at the earliest opportunity;
- to encourage a better exchange of information;
- to encourage better pre-action investigation;
- to put parties in a position where they can settle cases fairly and early; and
- to reduce the need for the case to go all the way to court.

2.10.3 Alternatives to going to court

Rule 4.1 of the CPR 1998 requires the court, as a part of its active case management, to encourage and facilitate the use of alternative dispute resolution (ADR) (see below, Chapter 3), and r 26.4 allows the court to stay proceedings (that is, halt them) in order to allow the parties to go to ADR either where the parties themselves request it or where the court of its own initiative considers it appropriate. The Commercial Court has already used this policy with notable success. It often acts to send cases to ADR where, for example, one side applies for a lengthy extension of time for the case to be heard.

2.10.4 Allocation to track (Pt 26 of the CPR 1998)

Allocation will be to one of three tracks: the small claims track; the fast track; or the multi-track. Each of the tracks offers a different degree of case management.

Small claims track

There is no longer any automatic reference to the small claims track. Claims are allocated to this track in exactly the same way as to the fast or multi-tracks. The concept of an arbitration, therefore, disappears and is replaced by a small claims hearing. The jurisdiction for small claims is increased to £5,000 (with the exception of claims for personal injury and actions for housing disrepair, where the limit is £1,000). Parties can consent to use the small claims track even if the value of their claim exceeds the normal value for that track, but this is subject to the court's approval.

Fast track

The fast track procedure handles cases with a value of more than £5,000 but less than £15,000. Amongst the features of the procedure which aim to achieve this are:

- standard directions for trial preparation which avoid complex procedures and multiple experts, with minimum case management intervention by the court;
- a maximum of one day (five hours) for trial;
- normally, no oral expert evidence is to be given at trial, and costs allowed for the trial are fixed and vary, depending on the level of advocate acting for the parties in the case.

Multi-track

The multi-track handles cases of higher value and more complexity, that is, those cases with a value of over £15,000.

This track does not provide any standard procedure, unlike those for small claims or claims in the fast track. Instead, it offers a range of case management tools, standard directions, case management conferences and pre-trial reviews, which can be used in a 'mix and match' way to suit the requirements of individual cases.

2.11 COUNTY COURTS

There are approximately 240 county courts, served by some 539 circuit judges and 337 district judges; and every county court has at least one specifically assigned circuit judge. District judges can try cases where the amount involved is £5,000 or less. A *Practice Direction* (1991) has stated that any case involving issues of particular importance or complexity should, as far as possible, be heard by a circuit judge. An appeal from the district judges' decision lies to the circuit judge.

Before the 1999 civil justice reforms, jurisdiction of the county courts was separated from that of the High Court on a strict financial limit basis; for example, a district judge heard cases where the amount was £5,000 or less. The CPR 1998 operate the same processes irrespective of whether the case forum is the High Court or the county court. Broadly, however, county courts will hear small claims and fast track cases, while the more challenging multi-track cases will be heard in the High Court. The changes brought about by the civil justice reforms are likely to put a considerable burden of work on the county courts.

A *Practice Direction* (1991) stated that certain types of actions set down for trial in the High Court are considered to be too important for transfer to a county court. These are cases involving:

- professional negligence;
- fatal accidents;
- allegations of fraud or undue influence;
- defamation;
- malicious prosecution or false imprisonment;
- claims against the police.

The county courts have an important role to play in the resolution of small claims, through their operation of an arbitration scheme. Consideration of the detailed operation of this scheme will be undertaken below, Chapter 3.

2.12 THE HIGH COURT OF JUSTICE

The High Court has three administrative Divisions: the Court of Chancery; the Queen's Bench Division; and the Family Division. In addition, each Division has a confusingly named Divisional Court, which hears appeals from other legal fora.

The majority of High Court judges sit in the Courts of Justice in the Strand, London, although it is possible for the High Court to sit anywhere in England and Wales.

2.12.1 The Queen's Bench Division

The main civil work of the Queen's Bench Division (QBD) is in contract and tort cases. The Commercial Court is part of this Division. It is staffed by judges with specialist experience in commercial law.

2.12.2 The Queen's Bench Divisional Court

The Queen's Bench Divisional Court, as distinct from the QBD, exercises appellate jurisdiction. Here, two, or sometimes three, judges sit to hear cases relating to the following circumstances:

- appeals on a point of law by way of case stated from magistrates' courts, tribunals and the Crown Court;
- applications for judicial review of the decisions made by governmental and public authorities, inferior courts and tribunals;
- applications for the writ of habeas corpus from persons who claim that they are being unlawfully detained.

2.12.3 The Chancery Division

The Chancery Division is the modern successor to the old Court of Chancery, that is, the Lord Chancellor's court from which equity was developed. Its jurisdiction includes matters relating to:

- the sale or partition of land and the raising of charges on land;
- the redemption or foreclosure of mortgages;
- the execution or declaration of trusts;
- the administration of the estates of the dead;
- bankruptcy;
- contentious probate business, for example, the validity and interpretation of wills;
- company law and partnerships;
- revenue law.

Like the QBD, Chancery contains specialist courts; these are the Patents Court and the Companies Court.

2.12.4 The Chancery Divisional Court

Comprising of one or two Chancery judges, the Chancery Divisional Court hears appeals from the Commissioners of Inland Revenue on income tax cases and from county courts on matters such as bankruptcy.

2.12.5 The Family Division

The Family Division of the High Court deals with all matrimonial matters, both at first instance and on appeal. It also considers proceedings relating to minors under the Children Act 1989.

2.12.6 The Family Divisional Court

The Family Divisional Court, which consists of two High Court judges, hears appeals from decisions of magistrates' courts and county courts in family matters. Commonly, these involve appeals against orders made about financial provision under the Domestic Proceedings and Magistrates' Courts Act 1978.

2.12.7 Specialist courts

In addition to the Divisions within the High Court, there also are two specialist courts which, although not actually part of the High Court, are equivalent in status. These are:

- the Restrictive Practices Court, established by statute in 1956, which hears cases relating to the area of commercial law concerned with whether an agreement is unlawful owing to the extent to which it restricts the trading capabilities of one of the parties. One QBD judge sits with specialist laypersons to hear these cases;
- the Employment Appeal Tribunal, which is presided over by similar panels, hearing appeals from employment tribunals.

2.13 THE COURT OF APPEAL (CIVIL DIVISION)

Appeals from decisions made by a judge in one of the three High Court Divisions will usually go to the Court of Appeal (Civil Division). An exception to this rule allows an appeal to miss out, or leapfrog, a visit to the Court of Appeal and go straight to the House of Lords. In order for this to happen, the trial judge must grant a certificate of satisfaction and the House of Lords must give permission to appeal. In order for the judge to grant a certificate, he must be satisfied that the case involves a point of law of general public importance which is concerned mainly with statutory interpretation. Alternatively, the court might find that it was bound by a previous Court of Appeal or House of Lords decision which appears to be in conflict with contemporary circumstances. Also, both parties must consent to the procedure.

The Court of Appeal hears appeals from the three Divisions of the High Court; the Divisional Courts; the county courts; and various tribunals (considered below). Usually, three judges will sit to hear an appeal, although five may sit for very important cases.

The appeal procedure takes the form of a rehearing of the case through the medium of the transcript of the case, together with the judge's notes. Witnesses are not re-examined and fresh evidence is not usually allowed.

2.13.1 The Civil Procedure Rules

From 2 May 2000, a new Pt 52 of the Civil Procedure Rules (CPR) 1998 combined with the Access to Justice Act 1999 to make new civil appeal rules covering the Court of Appeal, the High Court and the county court. The general rule is that permission to appeal in virtually all cases is mandatory. It should be obtained immediately following the judgment from the lower court or appellate court. Permission will only be given where the court considers that the appellant shows a real prospect of success or there is some other compelling reason.

All appeals will now be limited to a review rather than a complete rehearing, and the appeal will only be allowed if the decision of the lower court was wrong or unjust due to a serious procedural or other irregularity.

The rule now is that there should be only one appeal. An application for a second or subsequent appeal (from High Court or county court) must be made to the Court of Appeal, which will not allow it unless the appeal would raise an important point of principle or practice, or there is some other compelling reason.

The route of appeal has also been altered. The general rule is that the appeal lies to the next level of judge in the court hierarchy, that is, district judge to county court judge to High Court judge. The main exception relates to an appeal against a final decision in a multi-track claim, which will go straight to the Court of Appeal.

Great emphasis is placed on ensuring that cases are dealt with promptly and efficiently, and on weeding out and deterring unjustified appeals. The result is that the opportunity to appeal a decision at first instance in a lower court is much more restricted. It is vital, therefore, that practitioners be properly prepared at the initial hearing.

2.14 HOUSE OF LORDS

Acting in its judicial, as opposed to its legislative, capacity, the House of Lords is the final court of appeal in civil as well as criminal law. For most cases, five Lords will sit to hear the appeal, but seven are sometimes convened to hear very important cases.

2.15 JUDICIAL COMMITTEE OF THE PRIVY COUNCIL

As with criminal law, the Privy Council is the final court of appeal for certain Commonwealth countries which have retained this option and from some independent members and associate members of the Commonwealth. In practice, most of the appeals heard by the Committee are civil cases.

The decisions of the Privy Council are very influential in English courts, because they concern points of law that are applicable in this jurisdiction and are pronounced upon by Lords of Appeal in Ordinary in a way which is thus tantamount to a House of Lords ruling. Technically, however, these decisions are of persuasive authority only, although they are normally followed by English courts.

2.16 THE EUROPEAN COURT OF JUSTICE

The function of the European Court of Justice (ECJ), which sits in Luxembourg, is to ensure that 'in the interpretation and application of this Treaty the law is observed' (Art 220, formerly Art 164 of the EC Treaty). The ECJ is the ultimate authority on Community law. As the Treaty is often composed in general terms, the Court is often called upon to provide the necessary detail for EC law to operate. By virtue of the European Communities Act 1972, EC law has been enacted into English law, so the decisions of the court have direct authority in the English jurisdiction.

The court hears disputes between nations and between nations and the institutions of the European Union (EU), such as the European Commission. Individuals, however, can only bring an action if they are challenging a decision which affects them personally (see, further, above, Chapter 1).

2.17 THE EUROPEAN COURT OF HUMAN RIGHTS

This Court is the supreme court of the Council of Europe, that is, those States within Europe which have accepted to be bound by the European Convention on Human Rights. It has to be established, and emphasised, from the outset that the substance of this section has absolutely nothing to do with the EU as such; the Council of Europe is a completely distinct organisation and, although membership of the two organisations overlap, they are not the same. The Council of Europe is concerned not with economic matters but with the protection of civil rights and freedoms.

It is gratifying, at least to a degree, to recognise that the Convention and its Court (the ECtHR) are no longer a matter of mysterious external control, the Human Rights Act (HRA) 1998 having incorporated the Convention into UK law and having rendered the ECtHR the supreme court in matters related to its jurisdiction. Much attention was paid to the Convention and the HRA 1998 in Chapter 1 (see 1.3), so it only remains to consider the structure and operation of the ECtHR.

The Convention originally established two institutions:
* the European Commission of Human Rights. This body was charged with the task of examining and, if need be, investigating the circumstances of

petitions submitted to it. If the Commission was unable to reach a negotiated solution between the parties concerned, it referred the matter to the ECtHR;

- the ECtHR. The European Convention on Human Rights provides that the judgment of the Court shall be final and that parties to it will abide by the decisions of the Court. This body, sitting in Strasbourg, was, and remains, responsible for all matters relating to the interpretation and application of the current Convention.

However, in the 1980s, as the Convention and its Court became more popular and widely known as a forum for asserting human rights, so its workload increased. This pressure was exacerbated by the break up of the old Communist Eastern Bloc and the fact that the newly independent countries, in both senses of the words, became signatories to the Convention. The statistics support the view of the incipient sclerosis of the original structure:

Applications registered with the Commission

Year	Number of applications registered
1981	404
1993	2,037
1997	4,750

Cases referred to the ECtHR

Year	Number of cases referred
1981	7
1993	52
1997	119

As a consequence of such pressure, it became necessary to streamline the procedure by amalgamating the two previous institutions into one Court. In pursuit of this aim, Protocol 11 of the Convention was introduced in 1994. The new ECtHR came into operation on 1 November 1998, although the Commission continued to deal with cases which had already been declared admissible for a further year.

The ECtHR consists of 41 judges, representing the number of signatories to the Convention, although they do not have to be chosen from each State and, in any case, they sit as individuals rather than representatives of their State. Judges are generally elected, by the Parliamentary Assembly of the Council of Europe, for six years, but arrangements have been put in place so that one half of the membership of the judicial panel will be required to seek renewal every three years.

Structure of the Court

The Plenary Court elects its President, two Vice-Presidents and two Presidents of Section for a period of three years. The Court is divided into four Sections, whose composition, fixed for three years, is geographically and gender balanced, and takes account of the different legal systems of the Contracting States. Each Section is presided over by a President, two of the Section Presidents being at the same time Vice-Presidents of the Court. Committees of three judges within each Section deal with preliminary issues, and to that extent they do the filtering formerly done by the Commission. Cases are actually heard by Chambers of seven members, who are chosen on the basis of rotation. Additionally, there is a Grand Chamber of 17 judges – made up of the President, Vice-Presidents and Section Presidents and other judges by rotation. The Grand Chamber deals with the most important cases that require a reconsideration of the accepted interpretations of the Convention.

Judgments

Chambers decide by a majority vote and, usually, reports give a single decision. However, any judge in the case is entitled to append a separate opinion, either concurring or dissenting.

Within three months of delivery of the judgment of a Chamber, any party may request that a case be referred to the Grand Chamber if it raises a serious question of interpretation or application, or a serious issue of general importance. Consequently, the Chamber's judgment only becomes final at the expiry of a three month period, or earlier if the parties state that they do not intend to request a referral. If the case is referred to the Grand Chamber, its decision, taken on a majority vote, is final. All final judgments of the Court are binding on the respondent States concerned. Responsibility for supervising the execution of judgments lies with the Committee of Ministers of the Council of Europe, which is required to verify that States have taken adequate remedial measures in respect of any violation of the Convention.

Margin of appreciation and derogation

This refers to the fact that the court recognises that there may well be a range of responses to particular crises or social situations within individual States which might well involve some legitimate limitation on the rights established under the Convention. The Court recognises that in such areas, the response should be decided at the local level rather than being imposed centrally. The most obvious, but by no means the only, situations that involve the recognition of the margin of appreciation are the fields of morality and State security. Thus, *Wingrove v United Kingdom* (1996) concerned the refusal of the British Board of Film Classification to give a certificate of classification to the video-film *Visions of Ecstasy* on the ground that it was blasphemous, thus effectively banning it. The applicant, the director of the film, claimed that the refusal to grant a certificate of classification to the film amounted to a breach of his rights to free speech under Art 10 of the Convention. The Court rejected his claim, holding that the offence of blasphemy, by its very nature, did not lend itself to precise legal definition. Consequently, national authorities 'must be afforded a degree of flexibility in assessing whether the facts of a particular case fall within the accepted definition of the offence'.

In *Civil Service Union v United Kingdom* (1988), it was held that national security interests were of such paramount concern that they outweighed individual rights of freedom of association. Hence, the unions had no response under the Convention to the removal of their members' rights to join and be members of a trade union.

It should also be borne in mind that States can enter a derogation from particular provisions of the Convention, or the way in which they operate in particular areas or circumstances. The UK has entered such derogation in relation to the extended detention of terrorist suspects without charge under the Terrorism Act 2000 and the Anti-Terrorism, Crime and Security Act 2001.

Even where States avail themselves of the margin of appreciation, they are not at liberty to interfere with rights to any degree beyond what is required as a minimum to deal with the perceived problem within the context of a democratic society. In other words, the doctrine of proportionality requires that there must be a relationship of necessity between the end desired and the means used to achieve it.

An example of the way in which the system operates may be seen in the case of *R v Saunders* (1996). Earnest Saunders was one of the original defendants in the Guinness fraud trial of 1990. Prior to his trial, Saunders had been interviewed by Department of Trade and Industry inspectors and was required, under the provisions of the companies legislation, to answer questions without the right to silence. It was claimed that interviews under such conditions, and their subsequent use at the trial leading to his conviction, were in breach of the Convention on Human Rights. In October 1994, the Commission decided in Saunders' favour and the ECtHR confirmed that decision in 1996, although Saunders was not awarded damages. As a result, the Government has recognised that the powers given to DTI inspectors breach the Convention, and has declared an intention to alter them, but not in a retrospective way that would benefit Mr Saunders.

The ECtHR subsequently followed its *Saunders* ruling in the case of three others found guilty in the Guinness fraud trials: *IJL, GMR and AKP v United Kingdom* (2000).

SUMMARY OF CHAPTER 2

THE CRIMINAL AND CIVIL COURTS

Criminal courts

Trials take place in either the magistrates' courts or the Crown Court, depending on the nature of the offence:

- Summary offences cover less serious criminal activity and are decided by the magistrates.
- Indictable offences are the most serious and are tried before a jury in the Crown Court.
- Offences triable either way may be tried by magistrates with the agreement of the defendant; otherwise, they go to the Crown Court.

Appeals

- Appeals from magistrates' courts are to the Crown Court or the High Court (specifically, the Queen's Bench Divisional Court), by way of case stated.
- Appeals from the Crown Court are to the Court of Appeal, and may be as to sentence or conviction.
- Appeals from the Court of Appeal or the Queen's Bench Divisional Court are to the House of Lords, but only on a point of law of general public importance.

Civil courts

- *Magistrates' courts* have limited but important civil jurisdiction in licensing and, especially, as a family proceedings court under the Children Act 1989.
- *County courts* try personal injuries cases worth up to £50,000. Other actions up to £25,000 should normally be heard by them. Whether actions between £25,000 and £50,000 are heard in the county court or the High Court depends upon the substance, importance and complexity of the case.
- *The High Court* consists of three Divisions:
    - the Queen's Bench Division deals with contract and tort, amongst other things. Its Divisional Court hears applications for judicial review;

- o Chancery deals with matters relating to commercial matters, land, bankruptcy, probate, etc. Its Divisional Court hears taxation appeals;
- o the Family Division hears matrimonial and child related cases and its Divisional Court hears appeals from lower courts on these issues.

- *The Court of Appeal (Civil Division)* usually consisting of three judges, hears appeals from the High Court and county court and, in most cases, is the ultimate court of appeal.

- *The House of Lords* hears appeals on points of law of general importance. Appeals are heard from the Court of Appeal and may rarely, under the 'leapfrog' provision, hear appeals from the High Court.

- *The Judicial Committee of the Privy Council* is the final court of appeal for those Commonwealth countries which have retained it at the head of their national legal systems.

- *The European Court of Justice* interprets and determines the application of EC law throughout the Community. In such matters, its decisions bind all national courts.

- *The European Court of Human Rights* decides cases in the light of the European Convention on Human Rights. It has no mechanism for directly enforcing its decisions against Member States. However, the Human Rights Act 1998 has incorporated the Convention into UK law; consequently, UK courts are bound to decide cases in line with its provisions.

CHAPTER 3

ALTERNATIVE DISPUTE RESOLUTION

3.1 INTRODUCTION

Although attention tends to be focused on the courts as the forum for resolving conflicts when they arise, the court system is not necessarily the most effective way of deciding disputes, especially those which arise between people, or indeed businesses, which have enjoyed a close relationship. The problem with the court system is that it is essentially an antagonistic process, designed ultimately to determine a winner and a loser in any particular dispute. As a consequence, court procedure tends to emphasise and heighten the degree of conflict between the parties, rather than seek to produce a compromise solution. For various reasons, considered below, it is not always in the best long term interests of the parties to enter into such hostile relations as are involved in court procedure. In recognition of this fact, a number of alternative procedures to court action have been developed for dealing with such disputes.

The increased importance of alternative dispute resolution (ADR) mechanisms has been signalled in both legislation and court procedures. For example, the Commercial Court issued a *Practice Statement* in 1993, stating that it wished to encourage ADR, and followed this in 1996 with a further *Direction* that allows judges to consider whether a case is suitable for ADR at its outset, and to invite the parties to attempt a neutral, non-court settlement of their dispute. In cases in the Court of Appeal, the Master of the Rolls now writes to the parties, urging them to consider ADR and asking them for their reasons for declining to use it. Also, as part of the civil justice reforms, r 26.4 of the Civil Procedure Rules 1998 enables judges, either on their own account or at the agreement of both parties, to stop court proceedings where they consider the dispute to be better suited to solution by some alternative procedure, such as arbitration or mediation.

In particular, the Family Law Act 1996, which aimed to reform the operation of divorce law, emphasises the importance of mediation in this area and provides for the possibility of legal aid to finance it in appropriate instances. This will be considered further below, 3.5.

More generally, Lord Mackay, the former Lord Chancellor, considered various ADR mechanisms in the fourth of his Hamlyn Lectures, expressing the view that:

> ... the need seems to be not for further law based processes outside the courts ... but ... for processes which broaden the issues and available outcomes beyond those based in law.

The current Lord Chancellor has continued to look favourably on ADR, as is evident in his Inaugural Lecture to the Faculty of Mediation and ADR, in which he said:

> ADR has many supporters. But they, too, have a responsibility to proceed with care. ADR is not a panacea, nor is it cost free. But, I do believe that it can play a vital part in the opening of access to justice [www.open-gov.uk/lcd/speeches/1999/27-1-99.htm].

And in its 1999 Consultation Paper, *Alternative Dispute Resolution*, the Lord Chancellor's Department redefined Access to Justice as meaning:

> ... where people need help there are effective solutions that are proportionate to the issues at stake. In some circumstances, this will involve going to court, but in others, that will not be necessary. *For most people most of the time, litigation in the civil courts, and often in tribunals too, should be the method of dispute resolution of last resort.*

3.2 ARBITRATION

The first and oldest of these alternative procedures is arbitration. This is the procedure whereby parties in dispute refer the issue to a third party for resolution, rather than taking the case to the ordinary law courts. Studies have shown a reluctance on the part of commercial undertakings to have recourse to the law to resolve their disputes. At first sight, this appears to be paradoxical. The development of contract law can, to a great extent, be explained as the law's response to the need for regulation in relation to business activity, and yet, businesses decline to make use of its procedures. To some degree, questions of speed and cost explain this peculiar phenomenon, but it can be explained more fully by reference to the introduction to this chapter. It was stated there that informal procedures tend to be most effective where there is a high degree of mutuality and interdependency, and that is precisely the case in most business relationships. Businesses seek to establish and maintain long term relationships with other concerns. The problem with the law is that the court case tends to terminally rupture such relationships. It is not suggested that, in the final analysis, where the stakes are sufficiently high, recourse to the law will not be had; but such action does not represent the first, or indeed the preferred, option. In contemporary business practice, it is common, if not standard, practice for commercial contracts to contain express clauses referring any future disputes to arbitration. This practice is well established and its legal effectiveness has long been recognised by the law.

3.2.1 Arbitration procedure

The Arbitration Act 1996 repeals Pt 1 of the Arbitration Act 1950 and the whole of the Arbitration Acts of 1975 and 1979. As the Act is a relatively new piece of legislation, it is necessary to consider it in some detail.

Section 1 of the 1996 Act states that it is founded on the following principles:

(a) the object of arbitration is to obtain the fair resolution of disputes by an impartial tribunal without necessary delay or expense;

(b) the parties should be free to agree how their disputes are resolved, subject only to such safeguards as are necessary in the public interest;

(c) in matters governed by this part of the Act, the court should not intervene except as provided by this part.

This provision of general principles, which should inform the reading of the later detailed provisions of the Act, is unusual for UK legislation, but may be seen as reflecting the purposes behind the new Act, a major one of which was the wish to ensure that London did not lose its place as a leading centre for international arbitration. As a consequence of the demand-driven nature of the new legislation, it would seem that court interference in the arbitration process has had to be reduced to a minimum and replaced by party autonomy. Under the 1996 Act, the role of the arbitrator has been increased and that of the court has been reduced to the residual level of intervention where the arbitration process either requires legal assistance or is seen to be failing to provide a just settlement.

The Act follows the Model Arbitration Law, which was adopted in 1985 by the United Nations Commission on International Trade Law.

Whilst it is possible for there to be an oral arbitration agreement at common law, s 5 provides that Pt 1 of the Arbitration Act 1996 only applies to agreements in writing. What this means in practice, however, has been extended by s 5(3), which provides that, where the parties agree to an arbitration procedure which is in writing, that procedure will be operative, even though the agreement between the parties is not itself in writing. An example of such a situation would be where a salvage operation was negotiated between two vessels on the basis of Lloyds' standard salvage terms. It would be unlikely that the actual agreement would be reduced to written form, but, nonetheless, the arbitration element in those terms would be effective.

In analysing the Arbitration Act 1996, it is useful to consider it in three distinct parts: autonomy of the parties; powers of the court; and appellate rights.

Autonomy

It is significant that most of the provisions set out in the Arbitration Act 1996 are not compulsory. As is clearly stated in s 1, it is up to the parties to an arbitration agreement to agree on what procedures to adopt. The main purpose of the Act is to empower the parties to the dispute and to allow them to decide how it is to be decided. In pursuit of this aim, the mandatory parts of the Act only take effect where the parties involved do not agree otherwise. It is actually possible for the parties to agree that the dispute should not be decided in line with the strict legal rules; rather, they should be decided in line with commercial fairness, which might be a different thing altogether.

Powers of the arbitrator

Section 30 provides that, unless the parties agree otherwise, the arbitrator can rule on questions relating to jurisdiction, that is, in relation to:

- whether there actually is a valid arbitration agreement;
- whether the arbitration tribunal is properly constituted;
- what matters have been submitted to arbitration in accordance with the agreement.

Section 32 allows any of the parties to raise preliminary objections to the substantive jurisdiction of the arbitration tribunal in court, but provides that they may only do so on limited grounds, which require either: the agreement of the parties concerned; the permission of the arbitration tribunal; or the agreement of the court. Permission to appeal will only be granted where the court is satisfied that the question involves a point of law of general importance.

Section 28 expressly provides that the parties to the proceedings are jointly and severally liable to pay the arbitrators such reasonable fees and expenses as are appropriate. Previously, this was only an implied term.

Section 29 of the Arbitration Act 1996 provides that arbitrators are not liable for anything done or omitted in the discharge of their functions unless the act or omission was done in bad faith.

Section 33 provides that the tribunal has a general duty:

- to act fairly and impartially between the parties, giving each a reasonable opportunity to state their case; and
- to adopt procedures suitable for the circumstance of the case, avoiding unnecessary delay or expense.

Section 35 provides that, subject to the parties agreeing to the contrary, the tribunal shall have the following powers:

- to order parties to provide security for costs (previously a power reserved to the courts);
- to give directions in relation to property subject to the arbitration;

- to direct that a party or witness be examined on oath, and to administer the oath.

The parties may also empower the arbitrator to make provisional orders (s 39 of the Arbitration Act 1996).

Powers of the court

Where one party seeks to start a court action in the face of a valid arbitration agreement to the contrary, then the other party may request the court to stay the litigation in favour of the arbitration agreement under ss 9–11 of the Arbitration Act 1996. Where, however, both parties agree to ignore the arbitration agreement and seek recourse to litigation, then, following the party consensual nature of the Act, the agreement may be ignored.

The courts may order a party to comply with an order of the tribunal and may also order parties and witnesses to attend and to give oral evidence before tribunals (s 43).

The court has power to revoke the appointment of an arbitrator, on application of any of the parties, where there has been a failure in the appointment procedure under s 18, but it also has powers to revoke authority under s 24. This power comes into play on the application of one of the parties in circumstances where the arbitrator:

- has not acted impartially;
- does not possess the required qualifications;
- does not have either the physical or mental capacity to deal with the proceedings;
- has refused or failed to properly conduct the proceedings; or
- has been dilatory in dealing with the proceedings or in making an award, to the extent that it will cause substantial injustice to the party applying for their removal.

Under s 45, the court may, on application by one of the parties, decide any preliminary question of law arising in the course of the proceedings.

Arbitrators

The arbitration tribunal may consist of either a single arbitrator or a panel, as the parties decide (s 15). If one party fails to appoint an arbitrator, then the other party's nominee may act as sole arbitrator (s 17). Under s 20(4) of the Arbitration Act 1996, where there is a panel and it fails to reach a majority decision, the decision of the chair shall prevail.

The tribunal is required to fairly and impartially adopt procedures which are suitable to the circumstances of each case. It is also for the tribunal to decide all procedural and evidential matters. Parties may be represented by a lawyer or any other person, and the tribunal may appoint experts or legal advisers to report to it.

Arbitrators will be immune from action being taken against them, except in situations where they have acted in bad faith.

Appeal

Once the decision has been made, there are limited grounds for appeal. The first ground arises under s 67 of the Arbitration Act 1996, in relation to the substantive jurisdiction of the arbitral panel, although the right to appeal on this ground may be lost if the party attempting to make use of it took part in the arbitration proceedings without objecting to the alleged lack of jurisdiction. The second ground for appeal to the courts is on procedural grounds, under s 68, on the basis that some serious irregularity affected the operation of the tribunal. By serious irregularity is meant any of the following:

- failure to comply with the general duty set out in s 33;
- failure to conduct the tribunal as agreed by the parties;
- uncertainty or ambiguity as to the effect of the award;
- failure to comply with the requirement as to the form of the award.

Parties may also appeal on a point of law arising from the award under s 69 of the Arbitration Act 1996. However, the parties can agree beforehand to preclude such a possibility and, where they agree to the arbitral panel making a decision without providing a reasoned justification for it, they will also lose the right to appeal.

3.2.2 Relationship to ordinary courts

In general terms, the courts have no objection to individuals settling their disputes on a voluntary basis, but, at the same time, they are careful to maintain their supervisory role in such procedures. Arbitration agreements are no different from other terms of a contract and, in line with the normal rules of contract law, courts will strike out any attempt to oust their ultimate jurisdiction as being contrary to public policy. Thus, as has been stated above, arbitration proceedings are open to challenge, through judicial review, on the ground that they were not conducted in a judicial manner.

The Arbitration Act 1950 allowed for either party to the proceedings to have questions of law authoritatively determined by the High Court through the procedure of case stated. The High Court could also set aside the decision of the arbitrator on grounds of fact, law or procedure. Whereas the arbitration process was supposed to provide a quick and relatively cheap method of deciding disputes, the availability of the appeals procedures meant that parties could delay the final decision and, in so doing, increase the costs. In such circumstances, arbitration became the precursor to a court case, rather than a replacement of it. The Arbitration Act 1979 abolished the case stated procedure and curtailed the right to appeal, and, as has been seen, the Arbitration Act 1996 has reduced the grounds for appeal to the court system even further.

3.2.3 Advantages

There are numerous advantages to be gained from using arbitration rather than the court system:

- Privacy

  Arbitration tends to be a private procedure. This has the twofold advantage that outsiders do not get access to any potentially sensitive information and the parties to the arbitration do not run the risk of any damaging publicity arising out of reports of the proceedings.

- Informality

  The proceedings are less formal than a court case and they can be scheduled more flexibly than court proceedings.

- Speed

  Arbitration is generally much quicker than taking a case through the courts. Where, however, one of the parties makes use of the available grounds to challenge an arbitration award, the prior costs of the arbitration will have been largely wasted.

- Cost

  Arbitration is generally a much cheaper procedure than taking a case to the normal courts. Nonetheless, the costs of arbitration and the use of specialist arbitrators should not be underestimated.

- Expertise

  The use of a specialist arbitrator ensures that the person deciding the case has expert knowledge of the actual practice within the area under consideration and can form their conclusion in line with accepted practice.

It can be argued that arbitration represents a privatisation of the judicial process. It may be assumed, therefore, that, of all its virtues, perhaps the greatest (at least as far as the government is concerned) is the potential reduction in costs for the State in providing the legal framework within which disputes are resolved.

3.2.4 The small claims track (Pt 27 of the CPR)

After 1973, an arbitration service was available within the county court specifically for the settlement of relatively small claims. This small claims procedure, known as arbitration, was operated by county court district judges.

However, under the civil justice reforms, there is no longer any automatic reference to arbitration, which is replaced by reference to the small claims track (see 2.10.4 above). Claims are allocated to this track in exactly the same way as they are allocated to the fast or multi-tracks. The concept of an arbitration therefore disappears and is replaced by a small claims hearing. Aspects of the old small claims procedure that are retained include their informality, the interventionist approach adopted by the judiciary, the limited costs regime and the limited grounds for appeal (misconduct of the district judge or an error of law made by the court).

Changes to the handling of small claims are:

- *an increase in the jurisdiction from £3,000 to no more than £5,000* (with the exception of claims for personal injury where the damages claimed for pain and suffering and loss of amenity do not exceed £1,000 and the financial value of the whole claim does not exceed £5,000; and for housing disrepair where the claim for repairs and other work does not exceed £1,000 and the financial value of any other claim for damages is not more than £1,000);
- *hearings to be generally public hearings* – but subject to some exceptions (Pt 39 of the CPR);
- *paper adjudication, if parties consent* – where a judge thinks that paper adjudication may be appropriate, parties will be asked to say whether or not they have any objections within a given time period. If a party does object, the matter will be given a hearing in the normal way;
- *parties need not attend the hearing* – a party not wishing to attend a hearing will be able to give the court and the other party, or parties, written notice that they will not be attending. The notice must be filed with the court seven days before the start of the hearing. This will guarantee that the court will take into account any written evidence which that party has sent to the court. A consequence of this is that the judge must give reasons for the decision reached, which will be included in the judgment;
- *use of experts* – expert witnesses will only be allowed to give evidence with the permission of the court;
- *costs* – these are not generally awarded, but a small award may be made to cover costs in issuing the claim, court fees, and expenses incurred by the successful party, witnesses and experts. Under r 27.14 of the CPR, additional costs may be awarded against any party who has behaved unreasonably;
- *preliminary hearings* – these may be called:
  - where the judge considers that special instructions are needed to ensure a fair hearing;
  - to enable the judge to dispose of the claim where he is of the view that either of the parties has no real prospect of success at a full hearing;

○   to enable the judge to strike out either the whole or part of a statement of action on the basis that it provides no reasonable grounds for bringing such an action;

- *the introduction of tailored directions* – to be given for some of the most common small claims, for example, spoiled holidays or wedding videos, road traffic accidents, building disputes.

Parties can consent to use the small claims track even if the value of their claim exceeds the normal value for that track, although subject to the court's approval. The limited cost regime will not apply to these claims. But, costs will be limited to the costs that might have been awarded if the claim had been dealt with in the fast track. Parties will also be restricted to a maximum one day hearing.

The milestone events for the small claims track are the date for the return of the allocation questionnaire and the date of the hearing.

The right to appeal under the CPR is governed by new principles. An appeal can be made on the grounds that:

- there was a serious irregularity affecting the proceedings; or
- the court made a mistake of law.

An example would be where an arbitrator failed to allow submissions on any crucial point upon which he rested his judgment.

3.2.5   Small claims procedure

Arbitration proceedings begin with an individual filing a statement of case at the county court. This document details the grounds of their dispute and requests the other party to be summonsed to appear. There may be preliminary hearings, at which the issues involved are clarified, but it is possible for the dispute to be settled at such hearings. If no compromise can be reached at this stage, a date is set for the hearing of the small claims hearing.

Arbitration hearings are usually heard by the district judge, although the parties to the dispute may request that it be referred to the circuit judge or even an outside arbitrator. The judge hearing the case may, at any time before or after the hearing, with the agreement of the parties, consult an expert on the matter under consideration and, again with the approval of the parties, invite an expert to sit on the arbitration in the role of assessor.

If one of the parties fails to appear at the hearing, the dispute can be decided in their absence. Alternatively, the parties may agree to the case being decided by the arbitrator, solely on the basis of documents and written statements.

The arbitration procedure is intended to be a less formal forum than that provided by the ordinary courts and, to that end, the Civil Procedure Rules provide that the strict rules of evidence shall not be applied. Parties are encouraged to represent themselves, rather than make use of the services of professional lawyers, although they may be legally represented if they wish.

The Civil Procedure Rules give judges wide discretion to adopt any procedure they consider helpful to ensure that the parties have an equal opportunity to put their case. This discretion is not limitless, however, and it does not remove the normal principles of legal procedure, such as the right of direct cross-examination of one of the parties by the legal representative of the other party (see *Chilton v Saga Holidays plc* (1986), where the Court of Appeal held that a registrar was wrong to have refused to allow solicitors for the defendant in the case to cross-examine the plaintiff on the ground that that person was not also legally represented).

On the basis of the information provided, the judge decides the case and, if the claimant is successful, makes an award for appropriate compensation. A no-costs rule operates to ensure that the costs of legal representation cannot be recovered, although the losing party may be instructed to pay court fees and the expenses of witnesses. Judgments are legally enforceable.

3.2.6 Evaluation

Problems have become evident in the operation of the arbitration procedure, particularly in cases where one party has been represented whilst the other has not. In spite of the clear intention to facilitate the resolution of disputes cheaply and without the need for legal practitioners, some individuals, particularly large business enterprises, insisted on their right to legal representation. As legal aid is not available in respect of such actions, most individuals cannot afford to be legally represented and, therefore, find themselves at a distinct disadvantage when opposed by professional lawyers.

One solution to this difficulty would have been to make legal aid available in the case of arbitration. Such a proposal is very unlikely ever to come to fruition, mainly on economic grounds, but also on the ground that the use of professional lawyers in such cases would contradict the spirit and the whole purpose of the procedure.

Alternatively, it might have been provided that no party could be legally represented in arbitration procedures; but to introduce such a measure would have been a denial of an important civil right.

The actual method chosen to deal with the problem was to lift the restrictions on the rights of audience in small debt proceedings. Parties to the proceedings were entitled to be accompanied by a McKenzie friend to give them advice, but such people had no right of audience and, thus, had no right actually to represent their friend in any arbitration (see *McKenzie v McKenzie* (1970)). In October 1992, under the Courts and Legal Services Act 1990, the Lord Chancellor extended the right of audience to lay representatives in small claims courts. This decision has the effect of allowing individuals access to non-professional, but expert, advice and advocacy. Members of such organisations as citizens advice bureaux and legal advice centres will now be permitted to represent their clients, although they will still not be permitted to issue proceedings. In cases involving claims of more than £1,000, they may even charge a fee.

The increase in the maximum amount to be claimed to £5,000 introduces two particular difficulties with regard to representation. The first, and by far the more serious, is the fact that the raising of the ceiling to what is a not inconsiderable sum of money means that individuals will lose legal aid to fund their claims in such cases and, therefore, may not have access to the best possible legal advice with respect to their case. The second, and apparently contradictory, point is that the number of lawyers appearing in small claims proceedings may actually increase as a result of the rise in the limit. Whereas it might not be worth paying for legal representation in a £3,000 claim, it might make more economic sense to pay for professional help if the sum being claimed is much higher. Which alternative actually occurs remains to be seen.

Perhaps the major difficulty in regard to small claims procedures is the fact that the mere winning of a case and the awarding of compensation does not actually mean that the successful party will receive any recompense if the other party chooses simply to ignore the award. One study concluded that 36% of those who were successful in the small claims procedure actually received nothing by way of recompense awarded (*Handling Small Claims in the County Courts* (1996)). More stringent and efficient mechanisms for enforcing judgments, even in relation to the comparatively small awards as are made under the arbitration procedure, is a necessity.

The Lord Chancellor's Department's statistics revealed that in 1998, 694,000 warrants were issued to bailiffs instructing them to obtain payment or seize goods from debtors. However, only 240,000 of these resulted in payment. This situation is compounded by the fact that bailiffs' powers to seize property is likely to be in breach of the European Convention of Human Rights, and therefore directly challengeable under the Human Rights Act 1998. Consequently, in July 2000, the Lord Chancellor announced that bailiffs were to lose their rights to seize private property.

3.2.7 Arbitration under codes of conduct

When it was first established in 1973, the small claims procedure was seen as a mechanism through which consumers could enforce their rights against recalcitrant traders. In reality, the arbitration procedure has proved to be just as useful for, and used just as much by, traders and businesses as consumers. There remains one area of arbitration, however, that is specifically focused on the consumer: arbitration schemes that are run under the auspices of particular trade associations. As part of the regulation of trade practices and in the pursuit of effective measures of consumer protection, the Office of Fair Trading has encouraged the establishment of voluntary codes of practice within particular areas. It is usual to find that such codes of practice provide arbitration schemes to resolve particularly intractable problems between individual consumers and members of the association. Such schemes are never compulsory and do not seek to replace the consumers legal rights, but they do provide a relatively inexpensive mechanism for dealing with problems without the need even to bother the county court. Such schemes are numerous; the most famous one is probably the travel industry scheme operated under the auspices of the Association of British Travel Agents, but other associations run similar schemes in such areas as car sales, shoe retailing, dry cleaning, etc. Again, the point of such schemes is to provide a quick, cheap means of dealing with problems without running the risk of completely alienating the consumer from the trade in question.

Although many of the trade arbitration schemes offered consumers distinct advantages, some did not; and, in order to remedy any abuses, the Consumer Arbitration Act 1988 was introduced. This statute provides that, in the case of consumer contracts, no prior agreement between the parties that subsequent disputes will be referred to arbitration can be enforced. However, consumers will be bound by arbitration procedures where they have already entered into them as a consequence of a prior agreement, or have agreed to them subsequently.

3.3 ADMINISTRATIVE TRIBUNALS

Although attention tends to be focused on the operation of the courts as the forum within which legal decisions are taken, it is no longer the case that the bulk of legal and quasi-legal questions are determined within that court structure. There are, as alternatives to the court system, a large number of tribunals which have been set up under various Acts of Parliament to rule on the operation of the particular schemes established under those Acts. There are at least 70 different types of administrative tribunal and, within each type, there may well be hundreds of individual tribunals operating locally all over the country to hear particular cases. Almost one million cases are dealt with by tribunals each year, and, as the Royal Commission on Legal Services (Cmnd 7648) pointed out in 1979, the number of cases then being heard by tribunals was six times greater than the number of contested civil cases dealt with by the High Court and county court combined. It is evident, therefore, that tribunals are of major significance as alternatives to traditional courts in dealing with disputes.

The generally accepted explanation for the establishment and growth of tribunals in Britain since 1945 was the need to provide a specialist forum to deal with cases involving conflicts between an increasingly interventionist welfare State, its functionaries and the rights of private citizens. It is certainly true that, since 1945, the Welfare State has intervened more and more in every aspect of people's lives. The intention may have been to extend various social benefits to a wider constituency, but, in so doing, the machinery of the Welfare State, and in reality those who operate that machinery, have been granted powers to control access to its benefits. As a consequence, they have been given the power to interfere in, and control the lives of, individual subjects of the State. By their nature, welfare provision tends to be discretionary and dependent upon the particular circumstance of a given case. As a consequence, State functionaries were given extended discretionary power over the supply/withdrawal of welfare benefits. As the interventionist State replaced the completely free market as the source of welfare for many people, so access to the provisions made by the State became a matter of fundamental importance and a focus for potential contention, especially given the discretionary nature of its provision. At the same time as Welfare State provisions were being extended, the view was articulated that such provisions and projects should not be under the purview and control of the ordinary courts. It was felt that the judiciary reflected a culture which tended to favour a more market centred, individualistic approach to the provision of rights and welfare and that their essentially formalistic approach to the resolution of disputes would not fit with the operation of the new projects.

3.3.1 Tribunals and courts

There is some debate as to whether tribunals are merely part of the machinery of administration of particular projects or whether their function is the distinct one of adjudication. The Franks Committee (Cmnd 218, 1957) favoured the latter view, but others have disagreed and have emphasised the administrative role of such bodies. Parliament initiated various projects and schemes, and included within those projects specialist tribunals to deal with the problems that they inevitably generated. On that basis, it is suggested that tribunals are merely adjuncts to the parent project and that this, therefore, defines their role as more administrative than adjudicatory.

If the foregoing has suggested the theoretical possibility of distinguishing courts and tribunals in relation to their administrative or adjudicatory role, in practice it is difficult to implement such a distinction, for the reason that the members of tribunals may be, and usually are, acting in a judicial capacity. See *Pickering v Liverpool Daily Post and Echo Newspapers* (1991), in which it was held that a mental health review tribunal was a court whose proceedings were subject to the law of contempt. Although a newspaper was entitled to publish the fact that a named person had made an application to the tribunal, together with the date of the hearing and its decision, it was not allowed to publish the reasons for the decision or any conditions applied.

If the precise distinction between tribunals and courts is a matter of uncertainty, what is certain is that tribunals are inferior to the normal courts. One of the main purposes of the tribunal system is to prevent the ordinary courts of law from being overburdened by cases, but tribunals are still subject to judicial review on the basis of breach of natural justice; where it acts in an *ultra vires* manner; or, indeed, where it goes wrong in relation to the application of the law when deciding cases.

In addition to the control of the courts, tribunals are also subject to the supervision of the Council on Tribunals, which was originally established under the Tribunals and Inquiries Act 1958, as subsequently amended by the Tribunals and Inquiries Acts 1971 and 1992, the latter of which is the current legislation. Members of the Council are appointed by the Lord Chancellor and their role is to keep the general operation of the system under review.

In May 2000, Lord Irvine LC appointed High Court judge, Sir Andrew Leggatt to review the current operation of the Tribunal system as a whole. However, consideration of Sir Andrew's findings and recommendations will be postponed until later in this chapter.

3.3.2 Composition of tribunals

Tribunals are usually made up of three members, only one of whom, the chair, is expected to be legally qualified. The other two members are lay representatives. The lack of legal training is not considered to be a drawback, given the technical and administrative, as opposed to specifically legal, nature of the provisions they have to consider. Indeed, the fact of there being two lay representatives on tribunals provides them with one of their perceived advantages over courts. The non-legal members may provide specialist knowledge and, thus, may enable the tribunal to base its decision on actual practice, as opposed to abstract legal theory or mere legal formalism. An example of this can be seen with regard to the tribunals having responsibility or determining issues relating to employment, which usually have a trade union representative and an employers' representative sitting on the panel, and are, therefore, able to consider the immediate problem from both sides of the employment relationship.

The procedure for nominating tribunal members is set out in the parent statute, but, generally, it is the Minister of State with responsibility for the operation of the statute in question who ultimately decides the membership of the tribunal. As tribunals are established to deal largely with conflicts between the general public and government departments, this raises at least the possibility of suspicion that the members of tribunals are not truly neutral. In response to such doubts, the 1957 Franks Committee recommended that the appointment of the chairmen of tribunals should become the prerogative of the Lord Chancellor and that the appointment of the other members should become the responsibility of a Council on Tribunals. This recommendation was not implemented, and ministers, by and large, still retain the power to appoint tribunal members. As a compromise, however, the minister selects the chairperson from a panel appointed by the Lord Chancellor.

3.3.3 Statutory tribunals

There are a number of tribunals which have considerable power in their areas of operation, and it is necessary to have some detailed knowledge of a selection of the most important of these. Examples of such tribunals are:

- Employment tribunals

  These are governed by the Employment Tribunals Act 1996, which sets out their composition and major areas of competence and procedure. In practice, such tribunals are normally made up of a legally qualified chairperson, a representative chosen from a panel representing employers and another representative chosen from a panel representing the interests of employees.

  Employment tribunals have jurisdiction over a number of statutory provisions relating to employment issues. The majority of issues arise in relation to such matters as disputes over the meaning and operation of particular terms of employment, disputes in respect of redundancy payments, disputes involving issues of unfair dismissal and disputes as to the provision of maternity pay.

  They also have authority in other areas, under different legislation. Thus, they deal with complaints about racial discrimination in the employment field under the Race Relations Act 1976; complaints about sexual discrimination in employment under the Sex Discrimination Act 1975; complaints about equal pay under the Equal Pay Act 1970, as amended by the Sex Discrimination Act 1975; complaints under the Disability Discrimination Act 1995; complaints about unlawful deductions from wages under the Wages Act 1986; and appeals against the imposition of improvement notices under the Health and Safety at Work etc Act 1974. In addition, employment tribunals have to deal with various ancillary matters relating to trade union membership and activities.

  The tribunal hearing is relatively informal. As in arbitration hearings, the normal rules of evidence are not applied and parties can represent themselves, or be represented by solicitors or barristers. And, as appropriate, in an employment context they may also be represented by trade union officials or representatives, or indeed by any other person they wish to represent them. Appeal, on a point of law only, is to the Employment Appeal Tribunal, which also sits with lay representatives (see 2.12.7, above).

- Social security appeals tribunals

  Various Social Security Acts have provided for safety net provisions for the disadvantaged in society to ensure that they enjoy at least a basic standard of living. In the pursuit of this general goal, various State functionaries have been delegated the task of implementing the very complex provisions contained in the legislation and have been granted considerable discretionary power in the implementation of those provisions. The function of the social security tribunals is to ensure that such discretion is not abused and that the aims of the legislation are generally being met. The tribunals, of which there are some 200 in England and Wales, are charged with the duty of hearing and deciding upon the correctness of decisions made by adjudication officers, who are the people who actually determine the level of benefit that individuals are entitled to receive.

- Immigration Appeal Tribunal

  This body hears appeals from individuals who have been refused entry into the UK or who have been refused permission to extend their stay. Given the contemporary world situation, it can be appreciated that the work of this particular tribunal is not only politically sensitive but on the increase.

- Mental health review tribunals

  These operate under the Mental Health Act 1983. The tribunals have wide powers to decide whether individuals should be detained for the purposes of compulsory treatment. They can also dispose of the property of such individuals. Given the particular area within which the mental health review tribunals operate, it is essential that there are medical experts present to decide on medical issues. This latter requirement also applies in respect of social security issues relating to the state of the individual claimant's health.

- Lands Tribunal

  Established under the Lands Tribunal Act 1949, the Lands Tribunal's essential function is to determine the legality of, and the levels of compensation in relation to, compulsory purchase orders over land. It also considers matters relating to planning applications.

- Rent Assessment Committee

  This committee deals with matters specifically relating to the rent charged for property. It resolves disputes between landlords and tenants of private accommodation, hears appeals from decisions of rent officers and has the power to fix rent in relation to furnished and unfurnished residential tenancies.

3.3.4 Domestic tribunals

The foregoing has focused on public administrative tribunals set up under particular legislative provisions to deal with matters of public relevance. The term 'tribunal', however, is also used in relation to the internal disciplinary procedures of particular institutions. Whether these institutions are created under legislation or not is immaterial; the point is that domestic tribunals relate mainly to matters of private, rather than public, concern, although, at times, the two can overlap. Examples of domestic tribunals are the disciplinary committees of professional institutions such as the Bar, The Law Society or the British Medical Association; trade unions; and universities. The power that each of these tribunals has is very great and is controlled by means of the ordinary courts ensuring that the rules of natural justice are complied with and that the tribunal does not act *ultra vires*, that is, beyond its powers. Matters relating to trade union membership and discipline are additionally regulated by the Employment Rights Act 1996.

3.3.5 Advantages of tribunals

Advantages of tribunals over courts relate to such matters as:

* Speed

  The ordinary court system is notoriously dilatory in hearing and deciding cases. Tribunals are much quicker to hear cases. A related advantage of the tribunal system is the certainty that it will be heard on a specific date and will not be subject to the vagaries of the court system. That being said, there have been reports that the tribunal system is coming under increased pressure and is falling behind in relation to its caseload.

* Cost

  Tribunals are a much cheaper way of deciding cases than using the ordinary court system. One factor that leads to a reduction in cost is the fact that no specialised court building is required to hear the cases. Additionally, because those deciding the cases are less expensive to employ than judges and complainants do not have to rely on legal representation, the tribunal procedure is considerably less expensive than using the traditional court system. These reductions are further enhanced by the fact that there are no court fees involved in relation to tribunal proceedings and costs are not normally awarded against the loser.

* Informality

  Tribunals are supposed to be informal, in order to make them less intimidating than full court cases. The strict rules relating to evidence, pleading and procedure which apply in courts are not binding in tribunal proceedings. The lack of formality is strengthened by the fact that proceedings tend not to be inquisitorial or accusatorial, but are intended to encourage and help participants to express their views of the situation before the tribunal. Informality should not, however, be mistaken for a lack of order, and the Franks Committee Report itself emphasised the need for clear rules of procedure. The provision of this informal situation and procedure tends to suggest that complainants do not need to be represented by a lawyer in order to present their grievance. They may represent themselves or be represented by a more knowledgeable associate, such as a trade union representative or some other friend. This contentious point will be considered further below.

- Flexibility

  Tribunals are not bound by the strict rules of precedent, although some pay more regard to previous decisions than others. It should be remembered that, as tribunals are inferior and subject to the courts, they are governed by precedents made in the courts.

- Expertise

  Reference has already been made to the advantages to be gained from the particular expertise that is provided by the laymembers of tribunals, as against the more general legal expertise of the chairperson.

- Accessibility

  The aim of tribunals is to provide individuals with a readily accessible forum in which to air their grievances, and gaining access to tribunals is certainly not as difficult as getting a case into the ordinary courts.

- Privacy

  The final advantage is the fact that proceedings can be taken before a tribunal without triggering the publicity that might follow from a court case.

3.3.6 Disadvantages of tribunals

It is important that the supposed advantages of tribunals are not simply taken at face value. They represent significant improvements over the operation of the ordinary court system, but it is at least arguable that some of them are not as advantageous as they appear at first sight to be, and that others represent potential, if not actual, weaknesses in the tribunal system.

Tribunals are cheap, quick, flexible and informal; but their operation should not be viewed with complacency. These so called advantages could be seen as representing an attack on general legal standards, and the tribunal system could be portrayed as providing a second rate system of justice for those who cannot afford to pay to gain access to real law in the court system.

Vigilance is required on the part of the general community to ensure that this does not become an accurate representation of the tribunal system.

In addition to this general point, there are particular weaknesses in the system of tribunal adjudication. Some of these relate to the following:

- Appeals procedures

    There is ground for confusion due to the lack of uniformity in relation to appeals from tribunals. Rights of appeal from decisions of tribunals and the route of such appeals depend on the provision of the statute under which a particular tribunal operates. Where such rights exist, they may be exercised variously – to a further tribunal, to a minister or to a court of law. A measure of coherence would not come amiss in this procedure.

    Prior to the Report of the Franks Committee, tribunals were not required to provide reasons for their decisions and this prevented appeals in most cases. Subsequent to the Report, however, most tribunals, though still not all of them, are required to provide reasons for their decisions under s 10 of the Tribunals and Inquiries Act 1992. The importance of this provision is that, in cases where a tribunal has erred in its application of the law, the claimant can appeal to the High Court for an application for judicial review to have the decision of the tribunal set aside for error of law on the face of the record. All tribunals should be required to provide reasons for their decisions.

- Publicity

    It was stated above that lack of publicity in relation to tribunal proceedings was a potential advantage of the system. A lack of publicity, however, may be a distinct disadvantage, because it has the effect that cases involving issues of general public importance are not given the publicity and consideration that they might merit.

- The provision of legal aid

    It was claimed previously that one of the major advantages of the tribunal system is its lack of formality and non-legal atmosphere. Research has shown, however, that individual complainants fare better where they are represented by lawyers. Additionally, as a consequence of the Franks recommendations, the fact that chairpersons have to be legally qualified has led to an increase in the formality of tribunal proceedings. As a consequence, non-law experts find it increasingly difficult, in practice, to represent themselves effectively. This difficulty is compounded when the body which is the object of the complaint is itself legally represented; for, although the parties to hearings do not have to be legally represented, there is nothing to prevent them from being so represented.

This leads to a consideration of the major weakness in the operation of tribunals. Except for the Lands Tribunal, employment appeals tribunals, mental health tribunals and the Commons Commissioners, legal aid is not available to people pursuing cases at tribunals. They may be entitled to legal advice and assistance under the Green Form system, but such limited assistance is unlikely to provide potential complainants with sufficient help to permit them to pursue their case with any confidence of achieving a satisfactory conclusion.

Although Lord Mackay, the former Lord Chancellor, did not consider the operation of tribunals in his Hamlyn Lecture on ADR, he did make a comment that perhaps should be considered in this context. In justifying his refusal to provide legal aid for ADR generally, he stated that:

> Legal aid presupposes that there is a need, so undeniable that the taxpayer should support it, for legal advice or legal services relating to legal issues.

It is suggested that the operation of the tribunal system fits within these strictures and that, on the basis of the former Lord Chancellor's own reasoning, legal aid should be available to all those involved in and subject to the adjudication of tribunals. If tribunals are becoming increasingly important in determining individual rights and, at the same time, are becoming formalistic, then the refusal of legal aid to those seeking to use tribunals is tantamount to refusing them access to justice. The Council on Tribunals has consistently advocated the proposal that the provision of legal aid should be extended to all tribunals. Their case is unarguable on the grounds of justice; unfortunately, it appears to be defensible on the grounds of economics.

The effect of the replacement of legal aid by the Community Legal Service fund, under the Access to Justice Act 1999, remains to be seen. It is probably accurate to say, however, that in this particular area, it certainly cannot make matters worse and that the establishment of Community Legal Service Partnerships may well improve the availability of quality advice for those with problems to be decided by tribunals.

If, by and large, tribunals are quicker, cheaper and less formal than courts, then arbitration has similar advantages over tribunals. In the field of employment law, employers have accused employment tribunals of being over-formal, over-complicated, time consuming and expensive. Such complaints led to the setting up of an alternative arbitration procedure to replace the employment tribunal in relation to straightforward unfair dismissal cases. The new arbitration system operates under the auspices of the Advisory, Conciliation and Arbitration Service (ACAS) and came into force in May 2001.

The intention is that the resolution of disputes under the scheme will be confidential, relatively fast and cost-efficient. Procedures under the scheme are non-legalistic and far more informal and flexible than the employment tribunal. The process is inquisitorial rather than adversarial, with no formal pleadings or cross-examination by parties or representatives. Instead of applying strict law, the arbitrator will have regard to general principles of fairness and good conduct in employment relations. The latter will include, for example, principles referred to in the ACAS Code of Practice *Disciplinary and Grievance Procedures* and the ACAS Handbook *Discipline at Work*, which were current at the time of the dismissal. In addition, as it is only possible to appeal or otherwise challenge an arbitrator's award (decision) in very limited circumstances, the scheme should also provide quicker finality of outcome for the parties to an unfair dismissal dispute. Alternatively, this requirement to give up rights that could be insisted upon in the tribunal system might render the ACAS alternative inoperative from the outset.

3.3.7 The Leggatt Review of Tribunals

The obviously apparent proliferation of tribunals operating under a variety of powers gave rise to the perceived need to investigate the whole tribunal system. In May 2000, the Lord Chancellor announced a wide-ranging, independent review of tribunals in England and Wales, to be conducted by Sir Andrew Leggatt. In his report, Sir Andrew found that there were 70 different administrative tribunals in England and Wales, not counting regulatory bodies. Between them they deal with nearly one million cases a year, but only 20 each heard more than 500 cases a year and many were defunct. He concluded that it was necessary to rationalise and modernise the structure and operation of the tribunal system, and to that end his Review suggested the pursuit of the following main objects:

- To make the 70 tribunals into one tribunals system

  This would be achieved by combining the administration of different tribunals, which are concerned with disputes between citizen and State (in the guise of either central or local government) and those which are concerned with disputes between parties within one organisation. It was suggested that only on that basis would tribunals acquire a collective standing to match that of the court system and a collective power to fulfil the needs of users in the way that was originally intended. Within the overall system, the tribunals should be grouped by subject matter into divisions dealing with, for example, education, financial matters, health and social services, immigration, land and valuation, social security and pensions, transport, and employment.

- To render the tribunals independent of their sponsoring departments by having them administered by one Tribunals Service

  At present, departments of State may provide the administrative support for a tribunal, may pay the fees and expenses of tribunal members, may appoint some of them, may provide IT support (often in the form of access to departmental systems), and may promote legislation prescribing the procedure which it is to follow. On such a basis, the tribunal simply does not appear to be independent of the department it is regulating, nor is it independent in fact. The establishment of a distinct Tribunals Service with the duty to provide all of those services would stimulate both the appearance and reality of independence.

- To improve the training of chairmen and members

The review felt that there was a necessity to improve training in the interpersonal skills peculiar to tribunals, the aim being to encourage an atmosphere which would permit the people who use tribunals to represent themselves effectively. It also felt that every effort should be made to reduce the number of cases in which legal representation is needed. That could only be attained, however, by seeking to ensure:

- o that decision-makers give comprehensible decisions;
- o that the Tribunals Service provides users with all requisite information;
- o that voluntary and other advice groups are funded so that they can offer legal advice; and
- o that the tribunal chairmen are trained to afford such assistance as they legitimately can by ensuring that the proceedings are intelligible and by enabling users to present their cases.

Sir Andrew recognised that there will always be complex cases in which legal representation is a necessity. However, he suggested that voluntary and community bodies should be funded to provide it and that *only as a last resort should it be provided by legal aid*.

- There should be clear and effective rights of appeal, replacing the confused and confusing variety of appeal procedures that operate at present

He recommended that there should be a right of appeal on a point of law, by permission, on the generic ground that the decision of the tribunal was unlawful:

- o from the first-tier tribunals in each division to its corresponding appellate tribunal;
- o from appellate tribunals to the Court of Appeal; and
- o where there was no corresponding appellate tribunal, to any such court as may be prescribed by statute, or in default to such appellate tribunal as may be appointed by the Senior President.

- Lay members should not sit automatically in any particular case or category of cases

It was suggested that there was no justification for any members to sit, whether expert or lay, unless they have a particular function to fulfil, as they clearly do in the employment tribunal. In all other divisions, the President (or regional or district chairmen) should have a discretion to decide whether or not lay members should sit in particular classes of cases.

- There should be active case management of actions

It was found that, at present, too many cases took too long and were often ill prepared. It was suggested that their length should be measured from the date of the decision giving rise to the action, and that rigorous time constraints should be applied to them, supported by sanctions. In each division, one or more registrars should be responsible for determining what attention each case or type of case should receive.

3.4 OMBUDSMAN

As with tribunals, so the institution of the ombudsman reflects the increased activity of the contemporary State. As the State became more engaged in everyday social activity, it increasingly impinged on, and on occasion conflicted with, the individual citizen. Courts and tribunals were available to deal with substantive breaches of particular rules and procedures, but there remained some disquiet as to the possibility of the adverse effects of the implementation of general State policy on individuals. If tribunals may be categorised as an ADR procedure to the ordinary court system in relation to decisions taken in breach of rules, the institution of ombudsman represents a procedure for the redress of complaints about the way in which those decisions have been taken. It has to be admitted, however, that the two categories overlap to a considerable degree. The ombudsman procedure, however, is not just an alternative to the court and tribunal system; it is based upon a distinctly different approach to dealing with disputes. Indeed, the Parliamentary Commissioner Act 1967, which established the position of the first ombudsman, provides that complainants who have rights to pursue their complaints in either of those fora will be precluded from making use of the ombudsman procedure. (Such a prohibition is subject to the discretion of the ombudsman, who tends to interpret it in a generous manner in favour of the complainant.)

The concept of the ombudsman is Scandinavian in origin, and the function of the office holder is to investigate complaints of maladministration; that is, situations where the performance of a government department has fallen below acceptable standards of administration. The first ombudsman, appointed under the 1967 legislation, operated, as the present ombudsman still operates, under the title of the Parliamentary Commissioner for Administration (PCA) and was empowered to consider central government processes only. Since that date, a number of other ombudsmen have been appointed to oversee the administration of local government in England and Wales, under the Local Government Act 1974. Scotland and Northern Ireland have their own local government ombudsmen, who fulfil the same task. There are also Health Service Commissioners for England, Wales and Scotland, whose duty it is to investigate the administration and provision of services in the health service, and, in October 1994, Sir Peter Woodhead was appointed as the first Prisons Ombudsman. The ombudsman system has also spread beyond the realm of government administration and there are ombudsmen overseeing the operation of, amongst other things, legal services, banking and insurance. Some schemes, such as the legal services scheme, have been established by statute, but many others have been established by industry as a means of self-regulation; as regards this latter type, the Newspaper Ombudsman does not appear to have been a great success and it has been rumoured that the position might be disbanded.

The European Parliament appointed an ombudsman under the powers extended to it by Art 195 (formerly Art 138(e)) of the Treaty Establishing the European Community (now the EC Treaty). The European Ombudsman has the function of investigating maladministration in all Community institutions, including the non-judicial operation of the ECJ.

Before going on to consider the work of the Parliamentary Commissioner in some detail, mention should also be made of the various regulatory authorities which were established to control the operation of the privatised former State monopolies such as the water, gas and telephone and railway industries. Thus, OFWAT, OFGAS and OFTEL were set up, with part of their remit being to deal with particular consumer complaints as well as the general regulation of the various sectors.

3.4.1 Procedure

Although maladministration is not defined in the Parliamentary Commissioner Act 1967, it has been taken to refer to an error in the way that a decision was reached, rather than an error in the actual decision itself. Indeed, s 12(3) of the Parliamentary Commissioner Act 1967 expressly precludes the PCA from questioning the merits of particular decisions taken without maladministration. Maladministration, therefore, can be seen to refer to procedure used to reach a result, rather than the result itself. In an illuminating and much quoted speech introducing the Act, Richard Crossman, then leader of the House of Commons, gave an indicative, if non-definitive, list of what might be included within the term 'maladministration'. The list included the following: bias; neglect; inattention; delay; incompetence; ineptitude; perversity; turpitude; and arbitrariness.

Members of the public do not have the right to complain directly to the PCA; they must channel any such complaint through a Member of Parliament (MP). Complainants do not have to provide precise details of any maladministration; they simply have to indicate the difficulties they have experienced as a result of dealing with an agency of central government. It is the function of the PCA to discover whether the problem arose as a result of maladministration. There is a 12 month time limit for raising complaints, but the PCA has discretion to ignore this.

The powers of the PCA to investigate complaints are similar to those of a High Court judge; thus, they may require the attendance of witnesses and the production of documents and wilful obstruction of the investigation is treated as contempt of court.

On conclusion of an investigation, the PCA submits reports to the MP who raised the complaint and to the principal of the government office which was subject to the investigation. The ombudsman has no enforcement powers, but, if his recommendations are ignored and existing practices involving maladministration are not altered, he may submit a further report to both Houses of Parliament in order to highlight the continued bad practice. The assumption is that, on the submission of such a report, MPs will exert pressure on the appropriate minister of State to ensure that any necessary changes in procedure are made.

Annual reports are laid before Parliament and a Parliamentary Select Committee exists to oversee the operation of the PCA. The operation of the PCA is subject to judicial review (*R v PCA ex p Balchin* (1997)); however, the Parliamentary Commissioner for Public Standards, established after the Nolan Inquiry into 'cash for questions' in Parliament, is not subject to judicial review (*R v Parliamentary Comr for Standards ex p Al Fayed* (1997)).

The relationship between the PCA and government is highlighted by three case studies.

Barlow Clowes

The first of these concerned the Barlow Clowes group of companies. In 1988, Peter Clowes and three others were arrested and charged with offences in connection with the Prevention of Fraud (Investments) Act 1958 and theft. The prosecution alleged that there had been an investment fraud of over £115 million. The main allegation was that members of the public were induced to deposit their moneys in the belief that they would be invested in gilt-edged securities, but that only £1.9 million was in fact so invested. The rest was misappropriated by the defendants. Clowes alone faced charges of theft totalling some £62 million. The PCA received hundreds of complaints from investors who had lost their money in relation to the Barlow Clowes affair, all alleging maladministration on the part of the Department of Trade and Industry (DTI), which had responsibility for licensing such investment companies. The PCA made five findings of maladministration against the DTI and recommended that compensation should be paid to those who had suffered as a result of it. Surprisingly, the Government initially denied any responsibility for providing compensation. Subsequently, after the PCA had expressed his regret at the Government's initial stance, the latter agreed to pay the recommended compensation payments, amounting to £150 million, but with the rider that it still accepted no legal liability.

Child Support Agency

The much criticised Child Support Agency (CSA) had been established in an endeavour to ensure that absent parents, essentially fathers, would have to accept financial responsibility for the maintenance of their children as determined by the Agency. The PCA's report followed complaints referred to him by 95 MPs, covering the time that the Agency started its operations in April 1994 until the end of 1995. Although the PCA investigated 70 complaints, the report focused on seven of those as being representative of the whole. These complaints highlighted a number of failures on the part of the CSA: mistakes as to the identity of individuals subject to the determinations of the CSA; failure to answer correspondence; delay in assessing and reviewing maintenance assessments; delay in actually securing payments due; and the provision of incorrect or misleading advice. The conclusion of the PCA was that the CSA was liable for maladministration, inexcusable delays and slipshod service. In response to the report, the chief executive of the CSA wrote to the PCA, informing him that steps were being taken to deal with the problems highlighted in the report. Such changes in the way that the CSA operated has not staved off its proposed replacement by a more sympathetic and efficient organisation.

Channel Tunnel Rail Link

As a consequence of the four year delay on the part of the Department of Transport in deciding on a route for the Channel Tunnel Rail Link, the owners of properties along the various possible routes found the value of their properties blighted, if not unsaleable. The situation was not finalised until the Department announced its final selection in 1994.

According to the PCA:

> The effect of the Department of Transport's policy was to put the project in limbo, keeping it alive when it could not be funded.

As a consequence, he held that the Department:

> ... had a responsibility to consider the position of such persons suffering exceptional or extreme hardship and to provide redress where appropriate. They undertook no such considerations. That merits my criticism.

The unusual thing about this case, however, was the reaction of the Department of Transport, which rejected the findings of the PCA and refused to provide any compensation. The refusal of the Department of Transport led the PCA to lay a special report before Parliament, consequent upon a situation where an injustice has been found which has not, or will not be, remedied (s 10(3) of the Parliamentary Commissioner Act 1967). Even in the face of the implementation of this extremely rare form of censure, the Government maintained its original policy that it was not liable for the consequences of either general or particular blight. The matter was then taken up by the Select

Committee on the Parliamentary Commissioner for Administration, which supported the conclusions of the PCA and recommended that:

> ... the Department of Transport reconsider its response to the Ombudsman's findings, accept his conclusions that maladministration had occurred ... It would be most regrettable if the department were to remain obdurate. In such an event, we recommend that as a matter of urgency a debate on this matter be held on the floor of the House on a substantive motion in government time [Sixth Report of the PCA].

Such a demonstration of solidarity between the PCA and the Committee had the desired effect, leading to the Government's climb down and payments of £5,000 to those property owners who had suffered as a consequence of the housing blight.

3.4.2 Evaluation

All in all, the ombudsman system appears to function fairly well within its restricted sphere of operation, but there are major areas where it could be improved. The more important of the criticisms levelled at the PCA relate to the following:

- The retention of MPs as filters of complaints

  It is generally accepted that there is no need for such a filter mechanism. At one level, it represents a sop to the idea of parliamentary representation and control. Yet, at the practical level, PCAs have referred complaints made to them directly to the constituent's MP, in order to have them referred back to them in the appropriate form. It is suggested that there is no longer any need or justification for this farce.

- The restrictive nature of the definition of maladministration

  It is possible to argue that any procedure that leads to an unreasonable decision must involve an element of maladministration and that, therefore, the definition as currently stated is not overly restrictive. However, even if such reverse reasoning is valid, it would still be preferable for the definition of the scope of the PCA's investigations to be clearly stated, and be stated in wider terms than they are at present.

- The jurisdiction of the PCA

  This criticism tends to resolve itself into the view that many areas that *should* be covered by the PCA are not in fact covered by it. For example, as presently constituted, the ombudsman can only investigate the operation of general law. It could be claimed, not without some justification, that the process of making law in the form of delegated legislation could equally do with investigation.

- The lack of publicity given to complaints

  It is sometimes suggested that sufficient publicity is not given to either the existence of the various ombudsmen or the results of their investigations.

The argument is that, if more people were aware of the procedure and what it could achieve, then more people would make use of it, which would lead to an overall improvement in the administration of governmental policies.

• The reactive role of the ombudsman

This criticism refers to the fact that the ombudsmen are dependent upon receiving complaints before they can initiate investigations. It is suggested that a more pro-active role, in which the ombudsmen would be empowered to initiate investigation on their own authority, would lead to an improvement in general administration, as well as an increase the effectiveness of the activity of the ombudsman. This criticism is related to the way in which the role of ombudsmen is viewed. If they are simply a problem solving dispute resolution institution, then a reactive role is sufficient; if, however, they are seen as the means of improving general administrative performance, then a more proactive role is called for.

In his Hamlyn Lectures of 1994, the former Lord Chancellor, Lord Mackay, approvingly categorised the ombudsman as:

Popularly representing justice for the small against the great justice that is quick, inexpensive and unfettered by legalistic procedures, acceptance of the institution of ombudsman now extends well beyond central and local government administration. The concept is widely viewed as a desirable, and even necessary, avenue to fairness wherever the individual is perceived to be at the mercy of an impenetrable administrative system.

3.5 MEDIATION AND CONCILIATION

The final alternative dispute mechanisms to be considered – mediation and conciliation – are the most informal of all.

3.5.1 Mediation

Mediation is the process whereby a third party acts as the conduit through which two disputing parties communicate and negotiate, in an attempt to reach a common resolution of a problem. The mediator may move between the parties, communicating their opinions without their having to meet; or, alternatively, the mediator may operate in the presence of both parties. However, in either situation, the emphasis is upon the parties themselves working out a shared agreement as to how the dispute in question is to be settled.

In his Hamlyn Lecture, Lord Mackay considered three alternative systems of mediation and examined the possibility of annexing such schemes to the existing court system. One, involving lawyers advising parties as to the legal strengths of their relative positions, he rejected on the ground that it merely duplicated, without replacing or extending, what was already available in the courts. A second, based on judges adopting the role of mediators, he rejected on the ground that it might be seen as undermining the traditional impartiality of the judiciary. The third type, and the one that found most favour with him, broadened the issues beyond the legal, to explore solutions that were not available to the court. His approval, however, did not extend to financing such a system; the implication being that public money should, and does, finance the civil justice system and that any benefits that flow from a different system should be financed privately.

In March 1998, the Lord Chancellor's Department reported that take up of the voluntary mediation procedure offered in the pilot schemes had been fairly low. As regards the pilot scheme established in the Central London County Court, a monitoring report found that only 5% of cases referred to the ADR scheme actually took it up. However, in a more positive mode, the report did find that, in cases that did go to mediation, 62% settled during the process, without going on to court. The conclusion of the report was that mediation was capable of dealing with a wider range of cases than might have been expected, including personal injury cases. It also found that those who participated found the process satisfying and that it led to outcomes that the parties generally found acceptable.

In December 2001, a new mediation scheme was initiated at the Birmingham Civil Justice Centre. The Centre houses courts dealing with every form of civil action, from county court to High Court. Parties involved in any case, other than a small claims case of less than £5,000, will be able to request the mediation service. Mediation will only take place, however, if both parties agree to it. The procedure will involve a professionally trained mediator discussing the dispute with the parties on weekdays between 4.30 and 7.30 pm, when the courts have finished their business for the day. The hearings will be informal and held in private, and the parties may be accompanied by friends, advisors or legal representatives. The cost of the service will be between £75 and £250, depending on the amount in dispute. However, if the parties do not reach an agreed settlement, the action may proceed to court and the mediation fee will be lost.

3.5.2 Mediation in divorce

Mediation has an important part to play in family matters, where it is felt that the adversarial approach of the traditional legal system has tended to emphasise, if not increase, existing differences of view between individuals and has not been conducive to amicable settlements. Thus, in divorce cases, mediation has traditionally been used to enable the parties themselves to work out an agreed settlement, rather than having one imposed on them from outside by the courts.

This emphasis on mediation was strengthened in the Family Law Act 1996, but it is important to realise there are potential problems with mediation. The assumption that the parties freely negotiate the terms of their final agreement in a less than hostile manner may be deeply flawed, to the extent that it assumes equality of bargaining power and knowledge between the parties to the negotiation. Mediation may well ease pain, but, unless the mediation procedure is carefully and critically monitored, it may gloss over and perpetuate a previously exploitative relationship, allowing the more powerful participant to manipulate and dominate the more vulnerable and force an inequitable agreement. Establishing entitlements on the basis of clear legal advice may be preferable to apparently negotiating those entitlements away in the non-confrontational, therapeutic atmosphere of mediation.

Under the Divorce Reform Act 1969, the concept of no fault divorce was introduced for those couples who had been separated for two years, and it was assumed that this would provide the main grounds for divorce applications. This has not proved to be the case and it is commonly accepted that, because of the two year delay involved, 75% of those seeking divorces still apply on the basis of adultery or unreasonable behaviour, permitting them to complete the procedure in between three and six months.

The Family Law Act 1996 proposed to introduce real no fault divorce by abolishing the grounds of adultery and unreasonable behaviour, but couples would have to wait a minimum of 12 months before their divorce was confirmed. Instead of filing a divorce petition, the person seeking to be divorced would merely be required to submit a statement, certifying that their marriage has broken down. The process of divorce would require that the parties attend an informal meeting three months before they made their statement of marital breakdown. They would then have to wait a further nine months for their divorce, during which time they should reflect on whether the marriage could be saved, have an opportunity for reconciliation and consider arrangements relating to finance, property and children. The Act encourages the use of mediation in appropriate cases and allows the court, after it has received a statement of marital breakdown, to direct the parties to attend a meeting with a mediator for an explanation of the mediation process. The role of the mediator is restricted to sorting out the aspects of the divorce relating to finance and children, and should refer the case to an appropriate counsellor if it appears that the parties to the marriage might be open to reconciliation. During the cooling off period, State funding would be available for meetings with marriage guidance counsellors for those eligible for legal aid, and others would be encouraged to take advantage of such marriage support services.

Although the Family Law Act was passed in 1996, the proposed reforms were not implemented immediately and trials were conducted as to the appropriateness of the new procedures. Additionally, the fact that the Act was passed under the previous Conservative administration as a consequence of the strenuous endeavours of the then Lord Chancellor, Lord Mackay, did not prevent the incoming Labour administration's continued support for the proposed reforms. As Lord Irvine LC stated:

> ... in government, we have continued to encourage the use of mediation, most notably in the area of family law, where it is a central tenet of divorce law reform. The importance of mediation and ADR in family law cases can scarcely be understated, given the high incidence of family breakdown and the appaling social consequences which result [Lord Irvine LC, Speech to Faculty of Mediators, 1999].

However, in June 1999, Lord Irvine announced that the Government would not be implementing the new proposals in the Family Law Act in 2000, as had been previously intended. It has to be said that much academic and legal practitioner opinion was dubious, if not hostile, to the way in which the mediation procedure would operate. It was accepted generally that mediation might work in relation to children, but it was thought that it would be less likely to work where money was concerned and, in those circumstances, it was suggested that people would still be likely to look for their own personal legal representative rather than submit to mediation. It would appear that the results of the trials support such scepticism. Lord Irvine stated that the results of the mediation pilot schemes were disappointing, in that fewer than 10% of divorcing couples in the pilot areas were willing to make use of the preliminary information meetings, which would become compulsory under the Family Law Act's proposals. Of those attending the meetings, only 7% were successfully encouraged to opt for mediation and only 13% took up the offer to see a marriage counsellor. Almost 40% of those attending the meetings stated that they were more convinced of the need to see an independent lawyer to protect their legal rights.

Lord Irvine's announcement was merely as to the postponement of the implementation of the divorce law reforms. Many, however, believe that this postponement is merely a precursor to their future abandonment.

In a speech at the UK Family Law Conference in London on 25 June 1999, Lord Irvine recognised that his decision to postpone the implementation of Pt II of the Family Law Act 1996 raised a question mark over its future, but he went on to say that the final decision depended on the outcome of current and future research into the area.

Unfortunately, at least for proponents of no-fault divorce, the outcome of the research proved disagreeable to the Lord Chancellor's Department and, on 16 January 2001, Lord Irvine announced the Government's intention to repeal Pt II of the Family Law Act 1996. Six versions of the compulsory information meetings, intended to help couples either to save their marriages or to end them with minimum distress and acrimony, had been tested in pilot schemes over a period of two years. The research showed that, although those attending such meetings valued the information gained, it actually tended to incline those who were uncertain about their marriage towards divorce. The Lord Chancellor, however, stated that his concerns did not only relate to information meetings as the complex procedures in Pt II would be likely also to lead to significant delay and uncertainty in resolving arrangements for the future. The Government concluded that such delay would not be in the best interests of either couples or their children.

It is important to note that the repeal of Pt II of the Family Law Act does not mean the end of mediation. Both the Lord Chancellor and the Government remain strongly committed to advancing the role of mediation in family breakdown.

3.5.3 Conciliation

Conciliation takes mediation a step further and gives the mediator the power to suggest grounds for compromise and the possible basis for a conclusive agreement. Both mediation and conciliation have been available in relation to industrial disputes, under the auspices of the government funded Advisory Conciliation and Arbitration Service (ACAS). One of the statutory functions of ACAS is to try to resolve industrial disputes by means of discussion and negotiation; or, if the parties agree, it might take a more active role as arbitrator in relation to a particular dispute.

The essential weakness in the procedures of mediation and conciliation lies in the fact that, although they may lead to the resolution of a dispute, they do not necessarily achieve that end. Where they operate successfully, they are excellent methods of dealing with problems, as, essentially, the parties to the dispute determine their own solutions and, therefore, feel committed to the outcome. The problem is that they have no binding power and do not always lead to an outcome. As the Heilbron Report (*Civil Justice on Trial: The Case for Change*, 1993) emphasises, even if the civil law procedure is reformed to make it more litigant-friendly, ADR mechanisms will still have a very important part to play in dealing with problems in certain delicate areas that are not susceptible to resolution in the ordinary court system. Lord Mackay recognised this in his proposal for divorce reform, but he also resisted the call to fund a wider use of mediation, on the basis that for the State to fund it would lead to its use becoming compulsory. Yet it is the very lack of compulsion in the procedure that makes mediation work successfully.

SUMMARY OF CHAPTER 3

ALTERNATIVE DISPUTE RESOLUTION

Alternative dispute resolution has several features that make it preferable to the ordinary court system.

Its main advantages are that it is less antagonistic than the ordinary legal system and it is designed to achieve agreement between the parties involved:

- *Arbitration* is the procedure whereby parties in dispute refer the issue to a third party for resolution, rather than take the case to the ordinary law courts. Arbitration procedures can be contained in the original contract or agreed after a dispute arises. The procedure is governed by the Arbitration Act 1996.
- Advantages over the ordinary court system are:
  - privacy;
  - informality;
  - speed;
  - lower cost;
  - expertise;
  - less antagonistic.
- *Administrative tribunals* deal with cases involving conflicts between the State, its functionaries and private citizens. Tribunals are subject to the supervision of the Council on Tribunals but are subservient to, and under the control of, the ordinary courts.

Examples of tribunals are:

- employment tribunals;
- social security appeals tribunals;
- mental health review tribunal.

Advantages of tribunals over ordinary courts relate to:

- speed;
- cost;
- informality;
- flexibility;
- expertise;
- accessibility; and
- privacy.

Disadvantages relate to:

- appeals procedure;
- lack of publicity; and
- the lack of legal aid in most cases.

The Leggatt Review of Tribunals recommended:

- the creation of a single Tribunals System with different divisions;
- the creation of a single Tribunals Service;
- an improvement in training of tribunal chairs;
- active case management of claims;
- discretion to appoint lay members.

Ombudsmen investigate complaints of maladministration in various areas of State activity. Members of the public must channel complaints through an MP. On conclusion of an investigation, the Parliamentary Commissioner for Administration (PCA) submits reports to the MP who raised the complaint, and to the principal of the government office which was subject to the investigation. He can also report to Parliament.

Shortcomings in the procedure include:

- the MP filter;
- uncertain, if not narrow, jurisdiction;
- lack of publicity; and
- the reactive rather than proactive nature of the role.

Mediation is where a third party only acts as a go-between and cannot decide the matter at issue.

Conciliation is where the third party is more active in facilitating a reconciliation or agreement between the parties than is the case with mediation.

CHAPTER 4

THE NATURE AND FUNCTION
OF CONTRACT LAW

4.1 INTRODUCTION

Ours is a market system. This means that economic activity takes place through the exchange of commodities. Individual possessors of commodities meet in the market place and freely enter into negotiations to determine the terms on which they are willing to exchange those commodities. Contract law may be seen as the mechanism for facilitating, regulating and enforcing such market activities.

It is usual for textbooks to cite how all our daily transactions, from buying a newspaper or riding on a bus to our employment, are all examples of contracts, but the point is nonetheless valid and well made. We are all players in the contract game, even if we do not realise it. In fact, we probably will not have any need to recognise that particular contractual version of reality until we enter into some transaction that goes wrong, or at least does not go as we hoped it would. Then, we seek to assert rights and to look for remedies against the person with whom we have come into dispute. It is at this time that the analytical framework of contract law principles comes to bear on the situation, to determine what, if any, rights can be enforced and what, if any, remedies can be recovered. It is perhaps paradoxical that students of contract law have to approach their study of the subject from the opposite end from that at which the layperson begins. The layperson wants a remedy and focuses on that above all else; the student, or practitioner, realises that the availability of the remedy depends upon establishing contractual responsibility and, hence, their focus is on the establishment of the contractual relationship and the breach of that relationship, before any question of remedies can be considered. Such is the nature and relationship of law and ordinary, everyday reality.

Although people have always exchanged goods, market transactions only came to be the dominant form of economic activity during the 19th century, even in the UK. The general law of contract as it now operates is essentially the product of the common law and emerged in the course of the 19th century. It has been suggested that the general principles of contract law, or the 'classical model of contract', as they are known, are themselves based on an idealised model of how the market operates.

As the following chapters will evidence, there is much tension between the fit of the theoretical classical model and the practical demands of everyday business activity. Equally of note is the extent to which statutory inroads have been made into the common law, particularly in the area of consumer protection. For example, notable pieces of legislation that will require close attention are the Unfair Contract Terms Act 1977, which restricts the use of exclusion clauses in contracts, and the Contracts (Rights of Third Parties) Act 1999, which has made inroads into the common law doctrine of privity. The extent to which employment contracts are a matter of statutory regulation will be considered in detail in Chapter 14, below.

The purpose of this short chapter is to introduce contract law as the mechanism through which market activity is conducted and regulated.

4.2 DEFINITION

Given the examples of contracts cited above, it may be appreciated that the simplest possible description of a contract is a 'legally binding agreement'. It should be noted, however, that, although all contracts are the outcome of agreements, not all agreements are contracts; that is, not all agreements are legally enforceable. In order to be in a position to determine whether a particular agreement will be enforced by the courts, one must have an understanding of the rules and principles of contract law.

The emphasis placed on agreement highlights the consensual nature of contracts. It is sometimes said that contract is based on *consensus ad idem*, that is, a meeting of minds. This is slightly misleading, however, for the reason that English contract law applies an objective test in determining whether or not a contract exists. It is not so much a matter of what the parties actually had in mind as what their behaviour would lead others to conclude as to their state of mind. Consequently, contracts may be found and enforced, even though the parties themselves might not have thought that they had entered into such a relationship.

4.3 FORMALITIES

There is no general requirement that contracts be made in writing. They can be created by word of mouth or by action, as well as in writing. Contracts made in any of these ways are known as *parol* or *simple* contracts, whereas those made by deed are referred to as *speciality* contracts. It is generally left to the parties to decide on the actual form that a contract is to take, but, in certain circumstances, formalities are required:

• Contracts that must be made by deed

Essentially, this requirement applies to conveyances of land and leases of property extending over a period of more than three years. A conveyance is the legal process of the transfer of land. It is distinct from a contract to sell land, which is merely a legal agreement to transfer the land and not the actual process of transfer, which comes later. Agreements made by deed which would not otherwise be enforceable as contracts, because the required formation element of consideration is absent, will be implemented by the courts.

- Contracts that must be in writing (but not necessarily by deed)

  Among this group are: bills of exchange, cheques and promissory notes (by virtue of the Bills of Exchange Act 1882); consumer credit agreements, such as hire purchase agreements (by virtue of the Consumer Credit Act 1974); and contracts of marine insurance (by virtue of the Marine Insurance Act 1906). The Law of Property (Miscellaneous Provisions) Act 1989 requires all contracts for the sale or disposition of land to be made in writing. It should also be appreciated that some such agreements, for example hire purchase, must be signed by both parties. Increasingly, agreements are conducted by electronic means and, until recently, this created a problem where the law required a contract to be signed. Now the Electronic Communications Act 2000, which resulted from an EC Directive (1999/93/EC), deals with the issue; legal recognition is given to electronic signatures in that such signatures, accompanied by certification of authenticity, are now admissible as evidence in legal proceedings.

- Contracts that must be evidenced in writing

  This last category covers contracts of guarantee, derived from s 4 of the Statute of Frauds Act 1677.

4.4 THE LEGAL EFFECT OF AGREEMENT

It has already been pointed out that not all agreements are recognised as contracts in law; but it must also be borne in mind that, even where agreements do constitute contracts, they may not be given full effect by the courts. The legal effect of particular agreements may be distinguished as follows:

- Valid contracts

  These are agreements which the law recognises as being binding in full. By entering into to such contractual agreements, the parties establish rights and responsibilities and the court will enforce these by either insisting on performance of the promised action or awarding damages to the innocent party.

- Void contracts

  This is actually a contradiction in terms, for this type of agreement does not constitute a contract: it has no legal effect. Agreements may be void for a number of reasons, including mistake, illegality, public policy or the lack of a necessary requirement, such as consideration. The ownership of property exchanged does not pass under a void contract and remains with the original owner. The legal owner may recover it from the possession of the other party or, indeed, any third party, if it has been passed on to such a person. This is so even where the third party has acquired the property in good faith and has provided consideration for it.

- Voidable contracts

These are agreements which may be avoided, that is, set aside, by one of the parties. If, however, no steps are taken to avoid the agreement, then a valid contract ensues. Examples of contracts which may be voidable are those which have been entered into on the basis of fraud, misrepresentation or duress.

In relation to voidable contracts, the appropriate remedy is rescission of the original agreement. The effect of rescission is that both parties are returned to their original, pre-contractual position. Consequently, anyone who has transferred property to another on the basis of misrepresentation, for example, may recover that property. However, goods which have been exchanged under a voidable contract can be sold to an innocent third party. If such a transfer occurs before the first innocent party has rescinded the original contract, then the later innocent party receives good title to the property. This means that the property is now theirs and the innocent party to the first transaction can only seek a remedy such as damages against the other, non-innocent party to that contract.

- Unenforceable contracts

These are agreements which, although legal, cannot be sued upon for some reason. One example would be where the time limit for enforcing the contract has lapsed. The title to any goods exchanged under such a contract is treated as having been validly passed and cannot, therefore, be reclaimed.

The following four chapters will consider the major substantive rules relating to contracts, but, first, it is necessary to issue a warning in relation to examinations. Together with company law, contract forms the main component in most syllabuses. It is not possible to select particular areas as more important and, therefore, more likely to be examined than others. Unfortunately, any aspect of contract may be asked about, and so, candidates must be familiar with most, if not all, aspects of the subject. For example, it may be legitimate to expect a question on the vitiating factors in relation to contracts (see below, Chapter 7). It is not possible, however, to predict with any confidence which particular vitiating factor will be selected. To restrict one's study would be extremely hazardous. The candidate may have learnt mistake and misrepresentation very well, but that will be to no avail if the question asked actually relates to duress, as it might very well do. The warning, therefore, is to study contract thoroughly. Equally, students should be aware that a knowledge of remedies is of particular importance to all contractual topics; for example, an examination question on offer and acceptance or on misrepresentation may also require reference to appropriate remedies.

THE NATURE AND FUNCTION OF CONTRACT LAW

Definition

- A 'legally binding agreement' – enforceable in law.
- Enforceability is determined by legal rules.

Formalities

- Not normally required for *simple/parol* contracts.
- Some *simple* contracts need to be in writing/evidenced in writing.

The legal effect of agreements

- Valid contracts are enforceable.
- Void contracts have no legal effect.
- Voidable contracts can be set aside at one party's option; the contract is valid unless/until it is avoided.
- Unenforceable contracts are valid but no court action may be taken to enforce them.

CHAPTER 5

THE FORMATION OF A CONTRACT

5.1 INTRODUCTION

As has been seen, not every agreement, let alone every promise, will be enforced by the law. But what distinguishes the enforceable promise from the unenforceable one? The essential elements of a binding agreement, and the constituent elements of the classical model of contract, are as follows:

- offer;
- acceptance;
- consideration;
- capacity;
- intention to create legal relations;
- there must be no vitiating factors present.

The first five of these elements must be present, and the sixth one absent, for there to be a legally enforceable contractual relationship. This chapter will consider the first five elements in turn. Vitiating factors will be considered separately, in Chapter 7.

5.2 OFFER

An offer is a promise to be bound on particular terms, and it must be capable of acceptance. The person who makes the offer is the offeror; the person who receives the offer is the offeree. The offer sets out the terms upon which the offeror is willing to enter into contractual relations with the offeree. In order to be capable of acceptance, the offer must not be too vague; if the offeree accepts, each party should know what their rights and obligations are.

In *Scammel v Ouston* (1941), Ouston ordered a van from Scammel on the understanding that the balance of the purchase price could be paid on hire purchase terms over two years. Scammel used a number of different hire purchase terms and the specific terms of his agreement with Ouston were never actually fixed. When Scammel failed to deliver the van, Ouston sued for breach of contract. It was held that the action failed on the basis that no contract could be established, due to the uncertainty of the terms; no specific hire purchase terms had been identified.

5.2.1 Identifying an offer

An offer may, through acceptance by the offeree, result in a legally enforceable contract. It is important to be able to distinguish what the law will treat as an offer from other statements which will not form the basis of an enforceable contract. An offer must be distinguished from the following:

- A mere statement of intention

  Such a statement cannot form the basis of a contract, even though the party to whom it was made acts on it. See, for example, *Re Fickus* (1900), where a father informed his prospective son-in-law that his daughter would inherit under his will. It was held that the father's words were simply a statement of present intention, which he could alter as he wished in the future; they were not an offer. Therefore, the father could not be bound by them.

- A mere supply of information

  The case *Harvey v Facey* (1893) demonstrates this point. The plaintiff telegraphed the defendants as follows: 'Will you sell us Bumper Hall Pen? Telegraph lowest cash price.' The defendant answered, 'Lowest price for Bumper Hall Pen £900'. The plaintiff then telegraphed, 'We agree to buy Bumper Hall Pen for £900', and sued for specific performance when the defendants declined to transfer the property. It was held that the defendants' telegram was not an offer capable of being accepted by the plaintiff; it was simply a statement of information. This clearly has similarities with asking the price of goods in a retail outlet.

- An invitation to treat

  This is an invitation to others to make offers. The person extending the invitation is not bound to accept any offers made to him. The following are examples of common situations involving invitations to treat:

  o *The display of goods in a shop window.* The classic case in this area is *Fisher v Bell* (1961), in which a shopkeeper was prosecuted for offering offensive weapons for sale, by having flick-knives on display in his window. It was held that the shopkeeper was not guilty, as the display in the shop window was not an offer for sale; it was only an invitation to treat.

  o *The display of goods on the shelf of a self-service shop.* In this instance, the exemplary case is *Pharmaceutical Society of Great Britain v Boots Cash Chemists* (1953). The defendants were charged with breaking a law which provided that certain drugs could only be sold under the supervision of a qualified pharmacist. They had placed the drugs on open display in their self-service store and, although a qualified person was stationed at the cash desk, it was alleged that the contract of sale had been formed when the customer removed the goods from the shelf, the display being an offer to sell. It was held that Boots were not guilty. The display of goods on the shelf was only an invitation to treat. In law, the customer offered to buy the goods at the cash desk where the pharmacist was stationed. This decision is clearly practical, as the alternative would mean that, once customers had placed goods in their shopping baskets, they would be bound to accept them and could not change their minds and return the goods to the shelves.

○ *A public advertisement.* Once again, this does not amount to an offer. This can be seen from *Partridge v Crittenden* (1968), in which a person was charged with offering a wild bird for sale, contrary to the Protection of Birds Act 1954, after he had placed an advertisement relating to the sale of such birds in a magazine. It was held that he could not be guilty of offering the bird for sale, as the advertisement amounted to no more than an invitation to treat. Also, in *Harris v Nickerson* (1873), the plaintiff failed to recover damages for his costs in attending an advertised auction which was cancelled. In deciding against him, the court stated that he was attempting 'to make a mere declaration of intention a binding contract'. As a general rule, in auctions the bids are offers to buy.

However, there are exceptional circumstances where an advertisement may be treated as an offer; where the advertisement specifies performance of a task in return for a 'reward' and, on its terms, does not admit any room for negotiation, it may be treated as an offer. In *Carlill v Carbolic Smoke Ball Co* (1893), the facts of which are given in 5.2.2, the advertisement was held to be an offer, not an invitation to treat, because it specified performance of the task of using the smoke ball as directed and catching influenza in return for the reward of £100. Furthermore, there was no room to negotiate these terms, unlike the usual advertisement (such as the one in *Partridge v Crittenden,* above) where one would commonly expect to be able to negotiate on price.

Advertisements of goods on websites (internet shopping) are of particular interest. The legal issue is whether the advertisements are offers (in which case the customer ordering the goods accepts the offer and then a binding contract is made) or are invitations to treat, so that the customer's order is an offer to buy, which the advertiser can accept or reject. Many readers will be familiar with the widely reported dispute involving Argos in 1999. The Argos website advertised Sony televisions at £2.99 instead of £299 and customers placed orders at £2.99. Customers argued that they had accepted Argos' offer and that there was a binding contract to supply the goods for £2.99. A similar dispute arose recently where Kodak's website mistakenly advertised cameras for £100 instead of £329 (see www.bbc.co.uk/watchdog/reports/reports-wkodak.shtml). Such problems may be addressed on implementation of the E-Commerce Directive (2000/31/EC). Article 10 requires Member States to ensure that certain information is given by the 'service provider' to the recipient of the service. Unless otherwise agreed by parties who are not consumers, the relevant information is:

(1) the different technical steps to follow to conclude the contract;

(2) whether or not the concluded contract will be filed by the service provider;

(3) the technical means for identifying and correcting input errors before placing the order;

(4) the languages available for conclusion of the contract; and

(5) reference to any relevant codes of conduct and how they can be accessed.

These rules do not apply where the contract is conducted exclusively by email. The Directive also requires Member States to ensure that:

(1) the contract terms and general conditions provided to the recipient can be stored and reproduced by him/her;

(2) the service provider acknowledges receipt of the order, without delay and by electronic means.

○ A share prospectus. Contrary to common understanding, such a document is not an offer; it is merely an invitation to treat, inviting people to make offers to subscribe for shares in a company.

It can be seen that the decisions in both *Fisher v Bell* (1961) and *Partridge v Crittenden* (1968) run contrary to the common, non-legal understanding of the term 'offer'. It is interesting to note that later legislation, such as the Trade Descriptions Act 1968, has specifically been worded in such a way as to ensure that invitations to treat are subject to the same legal regulation as offers, where the protection of consumers from being misled is in issue.

5.2.2   Offers to particular people

An offer may be made to a particular person, or to a group of people, or to the world at large. If the offer is restricted, then only the people to whom it is addressed may accept it; but, if the offer is made to the public at large, it can be accepted by anyone.

In *Boulton v Jones* (1857), the defendant sent an order to a shop, not knowing that the shop had been sold to the plaintiff. The plaintiff supplied the goods, the defendant consumed them but did not pay, as he had a right to offset the debt against money the former owner owed him. The plaintiff sued for the price of the goods. The defendant argued that there was no contract obliging him to pay because his offer was an offer *only* to the former owner (because of the right of offset and lack of knowledge of the sale of the business), so only the former owner could accept, not the plaintiff. The court agreed with the defendant's argument; there was no contract, and so there was no contractual obligation to pay.

In *Carlill v Carbolic Smoke Ball Co* (1893), the company advertised that it would pay £100 to anyone who caught influenza after using their smoke ball as directed. Carlill used the smoke ball but still caught influenza and sued the company for the promised £100. Amongst the many defences argued for the company, it was suggested that the advertisement could not have been an offer, as it was not addressed to Carlill. It was held that the advertisement was an offer to the whole world, which Mrs Carlill had accepted by her conduct. There was, therefore, a valid contract between her and the company.

5.2.3   Knowledge of the offer

A person cannot accept an offer that he does not know about. Thus, if a person offers a reward for the return of a lost watch and someone returns it without knowing about the offer, he cannot claim the reward. Motive for accepting is not important, as long as the person accepting knows about the offer. In *Williams v Carwadine* (1883), a person was held to be entitled to receive a reward, although that was not the reason why he provided the information requested. (Acceptance is considered in detail below, 5.3.)

5.2.4   Rejection of offers

Express rejection of an offer has the effect of terminating the offer. The offeree cannot subsequently accept the original offer. A counter-offer, where the offeree tries to change the terms of the offer, has the same effect.

In *Hyde v Wrench* (1840), Wrench offered to sell his farm for £1,000. Hyde offered £950, which Wrench rejected. Hyde then informed Wrench that he accepted the original offer. It was held that there was no contract. Hyde's counter-offer had effectively ended the original offer and it was no longer open to him to accept it; Hyde was now making a new offer to buy for £1,000, which Wrench could accept or reject.

A counter-offer must not be confused with a request for information. Such a request does not end the offer, which can still be accepted after the new information has been elicited. See *Stevenson v McLean* (1880), where it was held that a request by the offeree as to the length of time that the offeror would give for payment did not terminate the original offer, which he was entitled to accept prior to revocation.

5.2.5 Revocation of offers

Revocation, the technical term for cancellation, occurs when the offeror withdraws the offer. There are a number of points that have to be borne in mind in relation to revocation:

- An offer may be revoked at any time before acceptance

    Once revoked, it is no longer open to the offeree to accept the original offer. In *Routledge v Grant* (1828), Grant offered to buy Routledge's house and gave him six weeks to accept the offer. Within that period, however, he withdrew the offer. It was held that Grant was entitled to withdraw the offer at any time before acceptance and, upon withdrawal, Routledge could no longer create a contract by purporting to accept it.

- Revocation is not effective until it is actually received by the offeree

    This means that the offeror must make sure that the offeree is made aware of the withdrawal of the offer, otherwise it might still be open to the offeree to accept the offer.

    In *Byrne v Van Tienhoven* (1880), the defendant offerors carried out their business in Cardiff and the plaintiff offerees were based in New York. On 1 October, an offer was made by post. On 8 October, a letter of revocation was posted, seeking to withdraw the offer. On 11 October, the plaintiffs telegraphed their acceptance of the offer. On 20 October, the letter of revocation was received by the plaintiffs.

    It was held that the revocation did not take effect until it arrived and the defendants were bound by the contract, which had been formed by the plaintiffs' earlier acceptance (which was effective on *sending* under the postal rule: see 5.3.2).

- Communication of revocation may be made through a reliable third party

    Where the offeree finds out about the withdrawal of the offer from a reliable third party, the revocation is effective and the offeree can no longer seek to accept the original offer.

    In *Dickinson v Dodds* (1876), Dodds offered to sell property to Dickinson and told him that the offer would be left open until Friday. On Thursday, the plaintiff was informed by a reliable third party, who was acting as an intermediary, that Dodds intended to sell the property to someone else. Dickinson still attempted to accept the offer on Friday, by which time the property had already been sold. It was held that the sale of the property amounted to revocation, which had been effectively communicated by the third party.

- A promise to keep an offer open is only binding where there is a separate contract to that effect

    This is known as an *option contract*, and the offeree/promisee must provide consideration for the promise to keep the offer open. If the offeree does not provide any consideration for the offer to be kept open, then the original offeror is at liberty to withdraw the offer at any time, as was seen in *Routledge v Grant*, above.

• In relation to unilateral contracts, revocation is not permissible once the offeree has started performing the task requested

A unilateral contract is one where one party promises something in return for some action on the part of another party. Rewards for finding lost property are examples of such unilateral promises, as was the advertisement in *Carlill v Carbolic Smoke Ball Co* (see 5.2.2). There is no compulsion placed on the party undertaking the action, but it would be unfair if the promisor were entitled to revoke their offer just before the offeree was about to complete their part of the contract.; for example, withdrawing a 'free gift for labels' offer before the expiry date, whilst customers were still collecting labels.

In *Errington v Errington and Woods* (1952), a father promised his son and daughter-in-law that he would convey a house to them when they had paid off the outstanding mortgage. After the father's death, his widow sought to revoke the promise. It was held that the promise could not be withdrawn as long as the mortgage payments continued to be met.

5.2.6 Lapse of offers

Offers lapse and are no longer capable of acceptance in the following circumstances:

• At the end of a stated period

It is possible for the parties to agree, or for the offeror to set, a time limit within which acceptance has to take place. If the offeree has not accepted the offer within that period, the offer lapses and can no longer be accepted.

• After a reasonable time

Where no time limit is set, then an offer will lapse after the passage of a reasonable time. What amounts to a reasonable time is, of course, dependent upon the particular circumstances of each case.

• Where the offeree dies

This automatically brings the offer to a close.

• Where the offeror dies and the contract was one of a personal nature

In such circumstances, the offer automatically comes to an end, but the outcome is less certain in relation to contracts that are not of a personal nature. See *Bradbury v Morgan* (1862) for an example of a case where it was held that the death of an offeror did not invalidate the offeree's acceptance.

It should be noted that the effect of death after acceptance also depends on whether or not the contract was one of a personal nature. In the case of a non-personal contract (for example, the sale of a car), the contract can be enforced by and against the representatives of the deceased. On the other hand, if performance of the contract depended upon the personal qualification or capacity of the deceased, then the contract will be frustrated (see below, 8.4).

5.3 ACCEPTANCE

Acceptance of the offer is necessary for the formation of a contract. Once the offeree has assented to the terms offered, a contract comes into effect. Both parties are bound: the offeror can no longer withdraw his offer and the offeree cannot withdraw his acceptance.

5.3.1 Form of acceptance

In order to form a binding agreement, the acceptance must correspond with the terms of the offer. Thus, the offeree must not seek to introduce new contractual terms into the acceptance.

In *Neale v Merrett* (1930), one party offered to sell some property for £280. The other party purported to accept the offer by sending £80 and promising to pay the remainder by monthly instalments. It was held that this purported acceptance was ineffective, as the offeree had not accepted the original offer as stated.

As was seen in *Hyde v Wrench* (1840), a counter-offer does not constitute acceptance. Analogously, it may also be stated that a conditional acceptance cannot create a contract relationship. Thus, any agreement subject to contract is not binding, but merely signifies the fact that the parties are in the process of finalising the terms on which they will be willing to be bound (*Winn v Bull* (1877)). However, the mere fact that a person adds a 'qualification' to their acceptance may not prevent acceptance from taking place. The dispute in *Society of Lloyd's v Twinn* (2000) arose from a settlement arrangement offered to Lloyd's 'names' in July 1996. Mr and Mrs Twinn indicated that they accepted the settlement agreement but added that they were unsure of their ability to actually carry out its terms; they queried whether any 'indulgence' would be granted them in such circumstances. Subsequently, the defendants argued that their acceptance had been conditional, so there was no contract enforceable against them. It was decided that it was a question of fact in each case whether there was an unconditional acceptance plus a collateral offer (which there was in the present case) or a counter-offer (that is, a conditional acceptance – 'I only accept the offer if …') which rejected the offer.

Acceptance may be in the form of express words, either oral or written; or it may be implied from conduct. Thus, in *Brogden v Metropolitan Rly Co* (1877), the plaintiff, having supplied the company with coal for a number of years, suggested that they should enter into a written contract. The company agreed and sent Brogden a draft contract. He altered some points and returned it, marked 'approved'. The company did nothing further about the document, but Brogden continued to deliver coal on the terms included in the draft contract. When a dispute arose, Brogden denied the existence of any contract. It was held that the draft became a full contract when both parties acted on it. More recently, acceptance by conduct was examined in *IRC v Fry* (2001). The defendant owed the Inland Revenue £100,000 and her husband sent a cheque for £10,000 to the Revenue, stating that cashing the cheque would be acceptance of his offer that it was 'full and final settlement' of the debt. As was normal practice, the Inland Revenue postroom sent the cheque for immediate banking and the accompanying letter to an inspector. The inspector informed the defendant that the cheque could not be full settlement; the defendant argued that cashing the cheque was acceptance of her husband's offer, so the debt was now fully settled. It should be noted here that part payment of a debt by a third party is an exception to the rule in *Pinnel's Case* (see 5.5.5), so the only issue was whether the husband's offer had been accepted. Jacobs J stated:

> Cashing a cheque is always strong evidence of acceptance, especially if it is not accompanied by an immediate rejection of the offer. Retention of the cheque without rejection is also strong evidence of acceptance, depending on the length of delay. But neither of these factors are conclusive and it would, I think, be artificial to draw a hard and fast line between cases where payment is accompanied by immediate rejection of the offer and cases where objection comes within a day or a few days.

It was decided that cashing the cheque raised a *rebuttable presumption* of acceptance of the offer but the fact that the Inland Revenue did not know of the offer at the time that the cheque was cashed, rebutted the presumption of acceptance (see 5.2.3).

5.3.2 Communication of acceptance

The general rule is that acceptance must be communicated to the offeror. As a consequence of this rule, silence cannot amount to acceptance. The classic case in this regard is *Felthouse v Bindley* (1863), where an uncle had been negotiating the purchase of his nephew's horse. He eventually wrote to the nephew, offering to buy it at a particular price, stating: 'If I hear no more about him I shall consider the horse mine'; the nephew made no reply. When the horse was mistakenly sold by an auctioneer, the uncle sued the auctioneer in conversion. It was held that the uncle had no cause of action, as the horse did not belong to him. Acceptance could not be imposed on the offeree on the basis of his silence.

There are, however, exceptions to the general rule that acceptance must be communicated, which arise in the following cases:

- Where the offeror has waived the right to receive communication

  In unilateral contracts, such as that in *Carlill v Carbolic Smoke Ball Co* (1893) or general reward cases, acceptance occurs when the offeree performs the required act. Thus, in the *Carlill* case, Mrs Carlill did not have to inform the Smoke Ball Co that she had used their treatment. Nor, in reward cases, do those seeking to benefit have to inform the person offering the reward that they have begun to perform the task that will lead to the reward.

- Where acceptance is through the postal service

  In such circumstances, acceptance is complete as soon as the letter, properly addressed and stamped, is posted. The contract is concluded, even if the letter subsequently fails to reach the offeror.

  In *Adams v Lindsell* (1818), the defendant made an offer to the plaintiff on 2 September. Due to misdirection, the letter was delayed. It arrived on 5 September and Adams immediately posted an acceptance. On 8 September, Lindsell sold the merchandise to a third party. On 9 September, the letter of acceptance from Adams arrived. It was held that a valid acceptance took place when Adams posted the letter. Lindsell was, therefore, liable for breach of contract.

As has already been seen in *Byrne v Van Tienhoven* (1880), the postal rule applies equally to telegrams. It does not apply, however, when means of instantaneous communication are used (see *Entores v Far East Corp* (1955) for a consideration of this point). It follows that, when acceptance is made by means of telephone, fax or telex, the offeror must actually receive the acceptance. This also raises issues concerning acceptance by email; it has been argued that this situation should be treated as a 'face to face' situation where receipt only occurs when the recipient reads the email. This argument would be in line with the decision in *Brinkibon Ltd v Stahag Stahl und Stahlwarenhandelsgesellshaft mbH* (1983). This, of course, begs the question of the effect of culpability in not reading emails quickly. It is suggested that, as a result of the decision in *The Brimnes* (1975), a court would take account of when the sender might reasonably expect the message to be received.

It should be noted that the postal rule will only apply where it is in the contemplation of the parties that the post will be used as the means of acceptance. If the parties have negotiated either face to face, for example in a shop, or over the telephone, then it might not be reasonable for the offeree to use the post as a means of communicating their acceptance and they would not gain the benefit of the postal rule (see *Henthorn v Fraser* (1892)).

In order to expressly exclude the operation of the postal rule, the offeror can insist that acceptance is only to be effective upon receipt (see *Holwell Securities v Hughes* (1974)). The offeror can also require that acceptance be communicated in a particular manner. Where the offeror does not actually insist that acceptance can only be made in the stated manner, then acceptance is effective if it is communicated in a way that is no less advantageous to the offeror (see *Yates Building Co v J Pulleyn & Sons* (1975)).

5.3.3 Tenders

These arise where one party wishes particular work to be done and issues a statement requesting interested parties to submit the terms on which they are willing to carry out the work. In the case of tenders, the person who invites the tender is simply making an invitation to treat. The person who submits a tender is the offeror and the other party is at liberty to accept or reject the offer as he pleases (see *Spencer v Harding* (1870)).

The effect of acceptance depends upon the wording of the invitation to tender. If the invitation states that the potential purchaser will require that a certain quantity of goods are supplied to him, then acceptance of a tender will form a contract and he will be in breach if he fails to order the stated quantity of goods from the tenderer.

If, on the other hand, the invitation states only that the potential purchaser may require goods, acceptance gives rise only to a standing offer. There is no compulsion on the purchaser to take any goods, but he must not deal with any other supplier. Each order given forms a separate contract and the supplier must deliver any goods required within the time stated in the tender. The supplier can revoke the standing offer, but he must supply any goods already ordered.

In *Great Northern Rly v Witham* (1873), the defendant successfully tendered to supply the company with 'such quantities as the company may order from time to time'. After fulfiling some orders, Witham refused to supply any more goods. It was held that he was in breach of contract in respect of the goods already ordered, but, once these were supplied, he was at liberty to revoke his standing offer.

5.4 OFFER, ACCEPTANCE AND THE CLASSICAL MODEL OF CONTRACT

The foregoing has presented the legal principles relating to offer and acceptance in line with the 'classical model' of contract. As has been stated, underlying that model is the operation of the market in which individuals freely negotiate the terms on which they are to be bound. The offeror sets out terms to which he is willing to be bound and, if the offeree accepts those terms, then a contract is formed. If, however, the offeree alters the terms, then the parties reverse their roles: the former offeree now becomes the offeror and the former offeror becomes the offeree, able to accept or reject the new terms as he chooses. This process of role reversal continues until an agreement is reached or the parties decide that there are no grounds on which they can form an agreement. Thus, the classical model of contract insists that there must be a correspondence of offer and acceptance, and that any failure to match acceptance to offer will not result in a binding contract.

Commercial reality, however, tends to differ from this theoretical model, and lack of genuine agreement as to terms in a commercial contract can leave the courts with a difficult task in determining whether there actually was a contract in the first place and, if there was, upon precisely which, or whose, terms was it entered into. This difficulty may be seen in relation to what is known as 'the battle of the forms', in which the parties do not actually enter into real negotiations but simply exchange standard form contracts, setting out their usual terms of trade. The point is that the contents of these standard form contracts might not agree and, indeed, might actually be contradictory. The question then arises as to whose terms are to be taken as forming the basis of the contract, if, indeed, a contract has actually been concluded.

Some judges, notably Lord Denning, have felt themselves to be too restricted by the constraints of the classical model of contract and have argued that, rather than being required to find, or construct, a correspondence of offer and acceptance, they should be able to examine the commercial reality of the situation in order to decide whether or not the parties had intended to enter into contractual relations. As Lord Denning would have had it, judges should not be restricted to looking for a precise matching of offer and acceptance, but should be at liberty to:

> ... look at the correspondence as a whole, and at the conduct of the parties, and see therefrom whether the parties have come to an agreement on everything that was material [*Gibson v Manchester CC* (1979)].

Gibson v Manchester CC (1979) concerned the sale of a council house to a tenant. The tenant had entered into negotiations with his local council about the purchase of his house. Before he had entered into a binding contract, the political make-up of the council changed and the policy of selling houses was reversed. It was clear that, under the classical model of contract, there was no correspondence of offer and acceptance, but the Court of Appeal nonetheless decided that the tenant could insist on the sale.

The status quo was restored by the House of Lords, which overturned the Court of Appeal's decision. In doing so, Lord Diplock expressed the view that:

> ... there may be certain types of contract, though they are exceptional, which do not easily fit in to the normal analysis of a contract as being constituted by offer and acceptance, but a contract alleged to have been made by an exchange of correspondence by the parties in which the successive communications other than the first are in reply to one another is not one of these.

Subsequent to this clear re-affirmation of the classical model, even Lord Denning was cowed in deciding *Butler Machine Tool Co Ltd v Ex-Cell-O Corp (England) Ltd* (1979). Although he did not hesitate to repeat his claim as to the unsuitability of the traditional offer/acceptance analysis in the particular case, which involved a clear battle of the forms, he did feel it necessary to frame his judgment in terms of the traditional analysis.

It is perhaps possible that Lord Denning's questioning of the classical model has been revitalised by the decision of the Court of Appeal in *Trentham Ltd v Archital Luxfer* (1993), another battle of the forms case, in which Steyn LJ stated that he was:

> ... satisfied that in this fully executed contract transaction a contract came into existence during performance, even if it cannot be precisely analysed in terms of offer and acceptance.

It must be pointed out, however, that the case involved a completed contract and the court was, therefore, faced with the problem of giving retrospective commercial effect to the parties' interactions and business relationship. It must also be emphasised that, in reaching its decision, the Court of Appeal relied on the authority of *Brogden v Metropolitan Rly Co* (1877). The case may not, therefore, be as significant in the attack on the classical model of contract as it appears at first sight; its full scope remains to be seen.

5.5 CONSIDERATION

English law does not enforce gratuitous promises unless they are made by deed. Consideration can be understood as the price paid for a promise. The element of bargain implicit in the idea of consideration is evident in the following definition by Sir Frederick Pollock, adopted by the House of Lords in *Dunlop v Selfridge* (1915):

> An act or forbearance of one party, or the promise thereof, is the price for which the promise of the other is bought, and the promise thus given for value is enforceable.

It is sometimes said that consideration consists of some benefit to the promisor or detriment to the promisee. It should be noted that both elements stated in that definition are not required to be present to support a legally enforceable agreement; though, in practice, they are usually present. If the promisee acts to their detriment, it is immaterial that the action does not directly benefit the promisor. However, that detriment must be suffered at the request of the promisor; for example, in *Carlill v Carbolic Smoke Ball Co* (see 5.2.2), Mrs Carlill gave consideration by way of detriment by undertaking the inconvenience of using the smoke ball as requested by the company in their advertisement.

5.5.1 Forbearance

Forbearance involves non-action or the relinquishing of some right. An example is forbearance to sue. If two parties, A and B, believe that A has a cause of legal action against B, then, if B promises to pay a sum of money to A if A will give up the right to pursue the action, there is a valid contract to that effect: A has provided consideration by giving up his right to have recourse to law. Such action would not amount to consideration if A knew that the claim was either hopeless or invalid, as was illustrated in *Wade v Simeon* (1846), where it transpired that the plaintiff had no legal claim for breach of the original contract.

5.5.2 Types of consideration

Consideration can be divided into the following categories:

* Executory consideration

  This is the promise to perform an action at some future time. A contract can be made on the basis of an exchange of promises as to future action. Such a contract is known as an executory contract.

* Executed consideration

  In the case of unilateral contracts, where the offeror promises something in return for the offeree's doing something, the promise only becomes enforceable when the offeree has actually performed the required act. If A offers a reward for the return of a lost watch, the reward only becomes enforceable once it has been found and returned.

* Past consideration

  This category does not actually count as valid consideration; that is, it is insufficient to make any agreement which is based on it a binding contract. Normally, consideration is provided either at the time of the creation of a contract or at a later date. In the case of past consideration, however, the action is performed before the promise that it is supposed to be the consideration for. Such action is not sufficient to support a promise, as consideration cannot consist of any action already wholly performed before the promise was made. The consideration must be given because of or in return for the other's promise.

  In *Re McArdle* (1951), a number of children were entitled to a house on the death of their mother. While the mother was still alive, her son and his wife had lived with her, and the wife had made various improvements to the house. The children later promised that they would pay the wife £488 for the work she had done. It was held that, as the work was completed when the promise was given, it was past consideration and the later promise could not be enforced; she had not carried out the work because of a promise of reimbursement.

  There are exceptions to the rule that past consideration will not support a valid contract:

- ○ under s 27 of the Bills of Exchange Act 1882, past consideration can create liability on a bill of exchange;

- ○ under s 29 of the Limitation Act 1980, a time barred debt becomes enforceable again if it is acknowledged in writing;

- ○ where the claimant performed the action at the request of the defendant and payment was expected, then any subsequent promise to pay will be enforceable, as can be seen in *Re Casey's Patents* (1892) where the joint owners of patent rights asked Casey to find licensees to work the patents. After he had done as requested, they promised to reward him. When one of the patent holders died, his executors denied the enforceability of the promise made to Casey on the basis of past consideration. It was held that the promise made to Casey was enforceable. There had been an implied promise to reward him before he had performed his action, and the later payment simply fixed the extent of that reward. In practical terms, it is usually implied that you are promising to pay where you ask a person to undertake work which is within the course of his/her trade or profession even though you do not actually promise to pay.

5.5.3 Rules relating to consideration

It has already been seen that consideration must not be past, but that is only one of the many rules that govern the legal definition and operation of consideration. Other rules are as follows:

- Performance must be legal

  The courts will not countenance a claim to enforce a promise to pay for any criminal act.

- Performance must be possible

  It is generally accepted that a promise to perform an impossible act cannot form the basis of a binding contractual agreement.

- Consideration must move from the promisee

  If A promises B £1,000 if B gives his car to C, then C cannot usually enforce B's promise, because C is not the party who has provided the consideration for the promise.

  In *Tweddle v Atkinson* (1861), on the occasion of the marriage of A and B, their respective fathers entered into a contract to pay money to A. When one of the parents died without having made the payment, A tried to enforce the contract against his estate. It was held that A could not enforce the contract, as he personally had provided no consideration for the promise. (This point should be considered in the context of the doctrine of privity of contract and its exceptions: see below, 5.6.)

- Consideration must be sufficient but need not be adequate

It is up to the parties themselves to decide the terms of their contract. The court will not intervene to require equality in the value exchanged; as long as the agreement has been freely entered into, the consideration exchanged need not be *adequate*.

In *Thomas v Thomas* (1842), the executors of a man's will promised to let his widow live in his house, in return for rent of £1 per year. It was held that £1 was sufficient consideration to validate the contract, although it did not represent an adequate rent in economic terms.

In *Chappell & Co v Nestlé Co* (1959), it was held that a used chocolate wrapper was consideration sufficient to form a contract, even though it had no economic value whatsoever to Nestlé and was in fact thrown away after it was returned to them.

However, the consideration must be *sufficient*; that is, something which the law recognises as amounting to consideration, as is examined in 5.5.4 below.

5.5.4 Performance of existing duties

It has generally been accepted that performance of an existing duty does not provide valid consideration. The rules relating to existing duty are as follows:

- The discharge of a public duty

As a matter of public policy, in order to forestall the possibility of corruption or extortion, it has long been held that those who are required to perform certain public duties cannot claim the performance of those duties as consideration for a promised reward.

In *Collins v Godefroy* (1831), the plaintiff was served with a subpoena, which meant that he was legally required to give evidence in the court case in question. Additionally, however, the defendant promised to pay him for giving his evidence. When the plaintiff tried to enforce the promised payment, it was held that there was no binding agreement, as he had provided no consideration by simply fulfiling his existing duty.

Where, however, a promisee does more than his duty, he is entitled to claim on the promise. See, for example, *Glasbrook v Glamorgan CC* (1925), where the police authority provided more protection than their public duty required; and the similar case of *Harris v Sheffield United FC* (1987), where the defendant football club was held liable to pay police costs for controlling crowds at their matches.

In cases where there is no possibility of corruption and no evidence of coercion, the courts have stretched the understanding of what is meant by 'consideration' in order to fit the facts of the case in question within the framework of the classical model of contract. See, for example, *Ward v*

Byham (1956), in which a mother was held to provide consideration by looking after her child well; and *Williams v Williams* (1957), in which the consideration for a husband's promise of maintenance to his estranged wife seemed to be the fact of her staying away from him. In both of these cases, Lord Denning introduced *obiter dicta* which directly questioned the reason why the performance of an existing duty should not amount to consideration, but the cases were ultimately decided on the basis that sufficient consideration was provided.

- The performance of a contractual duty

Lord Denning's challenge to the formalism of the classical model of contract is particularly pertinent when considered in the context of commercial contracts, where the mere performance of a contract may provide a benefit, or at least avoid a loss, for a promisor. The long established rule, however, was that the mere performance of a contractual duty already owed to the promisor could not be consideration for a new promise.

In *Stilk v Myrick* (1809), when two members of his crew deserted, a ship's captain promised the remaining members of the crew that they would share the deserters' wages if they completed the voyage. When the ship was returned to London, the owners refused to honour the promise and it was held that it could not be legally enforced, since the sailors had only done what they were already obliged to do by their contracts of employment.

Although *Stilk v Myrick* is cited as an authority in relation to consideration, it would appear that the public policy issue in the perceived need to preclude even the possibility of sailors in distant parts exerting coercive pressure to increase their rewards was just as important. Thus, although the reason for the decision was a matter of public policy, its legal justification was in terms of consideration.

As in the case of a public duty, so performance of more than the existing contractual duty will be valid consideration for a new promise. Thus, in *Hartley v Ponsonby* (1857), the facts of which were somewhat similar to those in *Stilk v Myrick*, it was decided that the crew had done more than they previously had agreed to do, because the number of deserters had been so great as to make the return of the ship unusually hazardous. On that basis, they were entitled to enforce the agreement to increase their wages. Once again, one finds in this case a reluctance to deny the theoretical application of the classical model of contract, whilst at the same time undermining its operation in practice.

The continued relevance and application of *Stilk v Myrick* in commercial cases has been placed in no little doubt in more recent years by a potentially extremely important decision of the Court of Appeal.

In *Williams v Roffey Bros* (1990), Roffey Bros had entered into a contract to refurbish a block of flats and sub-contracted with Williams to carry out carpentry work, for a fixed price of £20,000. It became apparent that Williams was in such financial difficulties that he might not be able to complete his work on time, with the consequence that Roffey Bros would be subject to a penalty clause in the main contract. As a result, Roffey Bros offered to pay Williams an additional £575 for each flat he completed. On that basis, Williams carried on working, but, when it seemed that Roffey Bros were not going to pay him, he stopped work and sued for the additional payment in relation to the eight flats he had completed after the promise of additional payment. The Court of Appeal held that Roffey Bros had enjoyed practical benefits as a consequence of their promise to increase Williams' payment: the work would be completed on time; they would not have to pay any penalty; and they would not suffer the bother and expense of getting someone else to complete the work. In the circumstances, these benefits were sufficient to provide consideration for the promise of extra money and Williams was held to be entitled to recover the extra money owed to him.

It should be emphasised that the Court of Appeal in *Williams v Roffey* made it clear that they were not to be understood as disapproving the *ratio* in *Stilk v Myrick* (1809). They distinguished the present case but, in so doing, effectively limited the application of the *ratio* in *Stilk v Myrick*. As the owners in *Stilk v Myrick* would appear to have enjoyed similar practical benefits to those enjoyed by Roffey Bros, it would seem that the reason for distinguishing the cases rests on the clear absence of any fraud, economic duress or other improper pressure. This was emphasised by the Court of Appeal in *Williams v Roffey Bros* (1990), where it was indicated that Williams did not put pressure on Roffey Bros for extra payment; it was Roffey Bros who approached Williams with the suggestion.

The legal situation would now seem to be that the performance of an existing contractual duty can amount to consideration for a new promise in circumstances where there is no question of fraud or duress, and where practical benefits accrue to the promisor. Such a conclusion not only concurs with the approach suggested earlier by Lord Denning in *Ward v Byham* (1956) and *Williams v Williams* (1957), but also reflects commercial practice, where contracts are frequently renegotiated in the course of their performance. However, it is important to note that in *Williams v Roffey Bros*, the court still felt constrained to find that consideration existed on the part of Williams, though some might consider such a finding artificial. It has been suggested that the court paid 'lip service' to the concept of consideration, not being prepared to depart entirely from its constraints in the interests of commercial reality.

The foregoing has considered the situation that operates between parties to an existing contract. It has long been recognised that the performance of a contractual duty owed to one person can amount to valid consideration for the promise made by another person.

In *Shadwell v Shadwell* (1860), the plaintiff had entered into a contract to marry. His uncle promised that, if he went ahead with the marriage, he would pay him £150 per year, until his earnings reached a certain sum. When the uncle died, owing several years' payment, the nephew successfully sued his estate for the outstanding money. It was held that going through with the marriage was sufficient consideration for the uncle's promise, even though the nephew was already contractually bound to his fiancée.

5.5.5 Consideration in relation to the waiver of existing rights

At common law, if A owes B £10 but B agrees to accept £5 in full settlement of the debt, B's promise to give up existing rights must be supported by consideration on the part of A. In *Pinnel's Case* (1602), it was stated that a payment of a lesser sum cannot be any satisfaction for the whole. This opinion was approved in *Foakes v Beer* (1884), where Mrs Beer had obtained a judgment in debt against Dr Foakes for £2,091. She had agreed in writing to accept payment of this amount in instalments. When payment was complete, she claimed a further £360 as interest due on the judgment debt. It was held that Mrs Beer was entitled to the interest, as her promise to accept the bare debt was not supported by any consideration from Foakes.

It can be appreciated that there are some similarities between the rules in *Foakes v Beer* and *Stilk v Myrick* in respect of the way in which promisors escape subsequent liability for their promises. In the former case, however, the promisor was being asked to give up what she was legally entitled to insist on; whereas, in the latter case, the promisors were being asked to provide more than they were legally required to provide.

As has been considered above, the rule in *Stilk v Myrick* (1809) has been subsequently modified and made less strict in its application by *Williams v Roffey Bros* (1990). However, no corresponding modification has taken place in relation to *Foakes v Beer* (1884); indeed, the Court of Appeal has rejected the argument that it should be so modified.

In *Re Selectmove Ltd* (1994), during negotiations relating to money owed to the Inland Revenue, the company had agreed with the collector of taxes that it would pay off the debt by instalments. The company began paying off the debt, only to be faced with a demand from the Revenue that the total be paid off immediately, on threat of liquidation. It was argued for the company, on the basis of *Williams v Roffey Bros*, that its payment of the debt was sufficient consideration for the promise of the Revenue to accept it in instalments. It was held that situations relating to the payment of debt were distinguishable from those relating to the supply of goods and services, and that, in the case of the former, the court was bound to follow the clear authority of the House of Lords in *Foakes v Beer* (1884).

The practical validity of the distinction drawn by the Court of Appeal is, to say the least, arguable. It ignores the fact that payment by instalments, and indeed part payment, is substantially better than no payment at all, which is a possible, if not likely, outcome of liquidating businesses in an attempt to recover the full amount of a debt. It is surely unnecessarily harsh to deny legal enforceability to renegotiated agreements in relation to debt where the terms have been renegotiated freely and without any suggestion of fraud or coercion. Nonetheless, the Court of Appeal clearly felt itself constrained by the doctrine of binding precedent and had less scope to distinguish *Foakes v Beer* than it had with regard to *Stilk v Myrick*. It remains to be seen whether the House of Lords will be asked to reconsider the operation of *Foakes v Beer* in the light of current commercial practice.

In any case, there are a number of situations in which the rule in *Foakes v Beer* does not apply. The following will operate to fully discharge an outstanding debt:

- Payment in kind

  Money's worth is just as capable of satisfying a debt as money. So, A may clear a debt if B agrees to accept something instead of money.

  As considered previously, consideration does not have to be adequate; thus, A can discharge a £10 debt by giving B £5 and a bar of chocolate. Payment by cheque is no longer treated as substitute payment in this respect (see *D & C Builders Ltd v Rees* (1966)).

- Payment of a lesser sum before the due date of payment

  The early payment has, of course, to be acceptable to the party to whom the debt is owed.

- Payment at a different place

  As in the previous case, this must be at the wish of the creditor.

- Payment of a lesser sum by a third party

  See *Welby v Drake* (1825).

- A composition arrangement

  This is an agreement between creditors to the effect that they will accept part payment of their debts. The individual creditors cannot subsequently seek to recover the unpaid element of the debt (see *Good v Cheesman* (1831)).

5.5.6 Promissory estoppel

It has been seen that English law will generally not enforce gratuitous promises, that is, promises which are not supported by consideration coming from the promisee. The equitable doctrine of promissory estoppel, however, can sometimes be relied upon to prevent promisors from going back on their promises to forgo their strict contractual rights. The doctrine first appeared in *Hughes v Metropolitan Rly Co* (1877) and was revived by Lord Denning in *Central London Pty Trust Ltd v High Trees House Ltd* (1947).

In the *High Trees* case, the plaintiffs let a block of flats to the defendants in 1937 at a fixed rent. Due to the Second World War, it became difficult to let the flats and the parties renegotiated the rent to half of the original amount. No consideration was provided for this agreement. By 1945, all the flats were let and the plaintiffs sought to return to the terms of the original agreement. They claimed that they were entitled to the full rent in the future and enquired as to whether they were owed additional rent for the previous period. It was held that the plaintiffs were entitled to the full rent in the future but were estopped from claiming the full rent for the period 1941–45.

The precise scope of the doctrine of promissory estoppel is far from certain. There are a number of conflicting judgments on the point, with some judges adopting a wide understanding of its operation, whilst others prefer to keep its effect narrowly constrained. However, the following points may be made:

- Promissory estoppel only arises where a party relies on the promise

  The promise must have been made with the intention that it be acted upon, and it must actually have been acted on. It was once thought that the promisee must have acted to their detriment, but such detriment is no longer considered necessary (see *WJ Alan & Co v El Nasr Export and Import Co* (1972)).

- Promissory estoppel only varies or discharges rights within an existing contract

  Promissory estoppel does not apply to the formation of contract and, therefore, does not avoid the need for consideration to establish a contract in the first instance. This point is sometimes made by stating that promissory estoppel is a shield and not a sword (see *Combe v Combe* (1951), where it was held that the doctrine could only be used as a defence, when sued on the terms of the original agreement, and not as a cause of action).

- Promissory estoppel normally only suspends rights

  It is usually open to the promisor, on the provision of reasonable notice, to retract the promise and revert to the original terms of the contract for the future (see *Tool Metal Manufacturing Co v Tungsten Electric Co* (1955)). Rights may be extinguished, however, in the case of a non-continuing obligation or where the parties cannot resume their original positions. (Consider *D &*

C Builders v Rees (1966), below. It is clear that, had the defendants been able to rely on promissory estoppel, the plaintiffs would have permanently lost their right to recover the full amount of the original debt.)

- The promise relied upon must be given voluntarily

As an equitable remedy, the benefit of promissory estoppel will not be extended to those who have behaved in an inequitable manner. Thus, if the promise has been extorted through fraud, duress, or any other inequitable act, it will not be relied on and the common law rules will apply.

In *D & C Builders Ltd v Rees* (1966), the defendants owed the plaintiffs £482 but would agree to pay only £300. As the plaintiffs were in financial difficulties, they accepted the £300 in full settlement of the account. The plaintiffs later successfully claimed the outstanding balance on the ground that they had been forced to accept the lesser sum. As the defendants themselves had not acted in an equitable manner, they were denied the protection of the equitable remedy and the case was decided on the basis of the rule in *Pinnel's Case* (1602).

- Promissory estoppel might only apply to future rights

It is not entirely clear whether the doctrine can apply to forgoing existing rights as well as future rights, but it should be noted that, in *Re Selectmove Ltd* (1994), it was stated that promissory estoppel could not be applied where the promise related to forgoing an existing debt; it only related to debts accruing in the future, such as rent due *after* the promise was made.

5.5.7 Promissory estoppel after *Williams v Roffey*

It is likely that the decision in *Williams v Roffey Bros* (1990) will reduce the need for reliance on promissory estoppel in cases involving the renegotiation of contracts for the supply of goods or services, since performance of existing duties may now provide consideration for new promises. As was stated previously with regard to *Re Selectmove* (1994), however, the same claim cannot be made in relation to partial payments of debts. Those situations are still subject to the rule in *Foakes v Beer* (1884), as modified, uncertainly, by the operation of promissory estoppel. As estoppel is generally only suspensory in effect, it is always open to the promisor, at least in the case of continuing debts, to reimpose the original terms by withdrawing their new promise.

5.6 PRIVITY OF CONTRACT

There is some debate as to whether privity is a principle in its own right, or whether it is simply a conclusion from the more general rules relating to consideration. In any case, it is a general rule that a contract can only impose rights or obligations on persons who are parties to it. This is the doctrine of privity and its operation may be seen in *Dunlop v Selfridge* (1915). In this case, Dunlop sold tyres to a distributor, Dew & Co, on terms that the distributor would not sell them at less than the manufacturer's list price and that they would extract a similar undertaking from anyone whom they supplied with tyres. Dew & Co resold the tyres to Selfridge, who agreed to abide by the restrictions and to pay Dunlop £5 for each tyre they sold in breach of them. When Selfridge sold tyres at below Dunlop's list price, Dunlop sought to recover the promised £5 per tyre. It was held that Dunlop could not recover damages on the basis of the contract between Dew and Selfridge, to which they were not a party.

There are, however, a number of ways in which consequences of the application of strict rule of privity may be avoided to allow a third party to enforce a contract. These occur in the following circumstances:

- The beneficiary sues in some other capacity

  Although an individual may not originally be party to a particular contract, they may, nonetheless, acquire the power to enforce the contract where they are legally appointed to administer the affairs of one of the original parties. An example of this can be seen in *Beswick v Beswick* (1967), where a coal merchant sold his business to his nephew in return for a consultancy fee of £6 10 s during his lifetime, and thereafter an annuity of £5 per week, payable to his widow. After the uncle died, the nephew stopped paying the widow. When she became administratrix of her husband's estate, she sued the nephew for specific performance of the agreement in that capacity, as well as in her personal capacity. It was held that, although she was not a party to the contract and, therefore, could not be granted specific performance in her personal capacity, such an order could be awarded to her as the administratrix of the deceased's estate. However, she *only* benefited personally because she was the beneficiary of the deceased's estate.

- The situation involves a collateral contract

  A collateral contract arises where one party promises something to another party if that other party enters into a contract with a third party; for example, A promises to give B something if B enters into a contract with C. In such a situation, the second party can enforce the original promise, that is, B can insist that A complies with the original promise. It may be seen from this that, although treated as an exception to the privity rule, a collateral contract conforms with the requirements relating to the establishment of any other contract, consideration for the original promise being the making of the second contract. An example of the operation of a collateral contract will demonstrate, however, the way in which the courts tend to construct collateral contracts in order to achieve what they see as fair dealing.

In *Shanklin Pier v Detel Products Ltd* (1951), the plaintiffs contracted to have their pier repainted. On the basis of promises as to its quality, the defendants persuaded the pier company to insist that a particular paint produced by Detel be used. The painters used the paint but it proved unsatisfactory. The plaintiffs sued for breach of the original promise as to the paint's suitability. The defendants countered that the only contract that they had entered into was with the painters to whom they had sold the paint, and that, as the pier company was not a party to that contract, they had no right of action against Detel. The pier company was successful. It was held that, in addition to the contract for the sale of paint, there was a second collateral contract between the plaintiffs and the defendants, by which the latter guaranteed the suitability of the paint in return for the pier company specifying that the painters used it.

- There is a valid assignment of the benefit of the contract

  A party to a contract can transfer the benefit of that contract to a third party through the formal process of assignment. The assignment must be in writing and the assignee receives no better rights under the contract than those which the assignor possessed. The burden of a contract cannot be assigned without the consent of the other party to the contract.

- Where it is foreseeable that damage caused by any breach of contract will cause a loss to a third party

  In *Linden Gardens Trust Ltd v Lenesta Sludge Disposals Ltd* (1994), the original parties had entered into a contract for work to be carried out on a property, with knowledge that the property was likely to subsequently be transferred to a third party. The defendants' poor work, amounting to a breach of contract, only became apparent after the property had been transferred. There had been no assignment of the original contract and, normally, under the doctrine of privity, the new owners would have no contractual rights against the defendants and the original owners of the property would have suffered only a nominal breach, as they had sold it at no loss to themselves. Nonetheless, the House of Lords held that, under such circumstances and within a commercial context, the original promisee should be able to claim full damages on behalf of the third party for the breach of contract.

- One of the parties has entered the contract as a trustee for a third party

  There exists the possibility that a party to a contract can create a contract specifically for the benefit of a third party. In such limited circumstances, the promisee is considered as a trustee of the contractual promise for the benefit of the third party. In order to enforce the contract, the third party must act through the promisee by making them a party to any action. For a consideration of this possibility, see *Les Affréteurs Réunis SA v Leopold Walford (London) Ltd* (1919).

The other main exception to the privity rule is agency, where the agent brings about contractual relations between two other parties, even where the existence of the agency has not been disclosed.

In the area of motoring insurance, statute law has intervened to permit third parties to claim directly against insurers. The Law Commission's draft Third Parties (Rights Against Insurers) Bill seeks to remedy some of the deficiencies of current legislation in this area.

5.6.1   Contracts (Rights of Third Parties) Act 1999

Significant inroads into the operation of the doctrine of privity have been made by the Contracts (Rights of Third Parties) Act 1999, which gives statutory effect to the recommendations of the 1996 Law Commission Report into this aspect of contract law (No 242, 1996). The Act establishes the circumstances in which third parties can enforce terms of contracts. Essentially, the requirement is that, in order for the third party to gain rights of enforcement, the contract in question must either expressly confer such a right on the third party or have been clearly made for their benefit (s 1). In order to benefit from the provisions of the Act, it is required that the third party be expressly identified in the contract by name, or as a member of a class of persons, or as answering a particular description. So, for example, *Tweddle v Atkinson* (1861) (see above, 5.5.3) would be differently decided today because the contract expressly named the son as beneficiary *and* stated that he could enforce the contract. Interestingly, however, the third person need not be in existence when the contract was made, so it is possible for parties to make contracts for the benefit of unborn children or a future marriage partner. This provision should also reduce the difficulties relating to pre-incorporation contracts in relation to registered companies. The third party may exercise the right to any remedy which would have been available had they been a party to the contract. Such rights are, however, subject to the terms and conditions contained in the contract; the third party can get no better rights than the original promisee; and the actual parties to the contract can place conditions on the rights of the third party.

Section 2 of the Act provides that where a third party has rights by virtue of the Act, the original parties to the contract cannot agree to rescind it or vary its terms without the consent of the third party, unless the original contract contained an express term to that effect.

Section 3 allows the promisor to make use of any defences or rights of set-off that they might have against the promisee in any action by the third party. Additionally, the promisor can also rely on any such rights against the third party. These rights are subject to any express provision in the contract to the contrary.

Section 5 removes the possibility of the promisor suffering from double liability in relation to the promisor and the third party. It provides, therefore, that any damages awarded to a third party for a breach of the contract be reduced by the amount recovered by the promisee in any previous action relating to the contract.

Section 6 of the Act specifically states that it does not alter the existing law relating to, and confers no new rights on third parties in relation to, negotiable instruments, s 14 of the Companies Act 1985, contracts of employment or contracts for the carriage of goods. However, a third party stated as benefiting from an exclusion clause in a contract for the carriage of goods by sea may rely on such a clause if sued. So, an independent firm of stevedores damaging a cargo during loading might claim the protection of a clause in the contract of carriage between the cargo owner and the shipowner.

Although the Contract (Rights of Third Parties) Act came into force on 11 November 1999, it does not apply in relation to contracts entered into before the end of the period of six months beginning with that date, unless the contract in question specifically provides for its application (s 10).

5.7 CAPACITY

Capacity refers to a person's ability to enter into a contract. In general, all adults of sound mind have full capacity. However, the capacity of certain individuals is limited.

5.7.1 Minors

A minor is a person under the age of 18 (the age of majority was reduced from 21 to 18 by the Family Reform Act 1969). The law tries to protect such persons by restricting their contractual capacity and, thus, preventing them from entering into disadvantageous agreements. The rules which apply are a mixture of common law and statute and depend on when the contract was made. Contracts entered into after 9 June 1987 are subject to the Minors' Contracts Act 1987, which replaced the Infants' Relief Act 1874. Agreements entered into by minors may be classified within three possible categories: valid, voidable and void.

Valid contracts

Contracts can be enforced against minors where they relate to the following:

• Contracts for necessaries

 A minor is bound to pay for necessaries, that is, things that are necessary to maintain the minor. Necessaries are defined in s 3 of the Sale of Goods Act 1979 as goods 'suitable to the condition in life of the minor and their actual requirements at the time of sale'. The operation of this section is demonstrated in *Nash v Inman* (1908), where a tailor sued a minor to whom he had supplied clothes, including 11 fancy waistcoats. The minor was an undergraduate at Cambridge University at the time. It was held that, although the clothes were suitable according to the minor's station in life, they were not necessary, as he already had sufficient clothing.

The minor is, in any case, only required to pay a reasonable price for any necessaries purchased.

- Beneficial contracts of service

  A minor is bound by a contract of apprenticeship or employment, as long as it is, on the whole, for their benefit.

  In *Doyle v White City Stadium* (1935), Doyle, a minor, obtained a professional boxer's licence, which was treated as a contract of apprenticeship. The licence provided that he would be bound by the rules of the Boxing Board of Control, which had the power to retain any prize money if he was ever disqualified in a fight. He claimed that the licence was void, as it was not for his benefit; but it was held that the conditions of the licence were enforceable. In spite of the penal clause, it was held that, taken as whole, it was beneficial to him.

There has to be an element of education or training in the contract; thus, ordinary trading contracts will not be enforced. See, for example, *Mercantile Union Guarantee Corp v Ball* (1937), where a minor who operated a haulage business was not held liable on a hire purchase contract that he had entered into in relation to that business.

Voidable contracts

Voidable contracts are binding on the minor, unless they are repudiated by the minor during the period of minority or within a reasonable time after reaching the age of majority. These are generally transactions in which the minor acquires an interest of a permanent nature with continuing obligations. Examples are contracts for shares, leases of property and partnership agreements.

If the minor has made payments prior to repudiation of the contract, such payment cannot be recovered unless there is a total failure of consideration and the minor has received no benefit whatsoever. An example is the case of *Steinberg v Scala (Leeds)* (1923). Miss Steinberg, while still a minor, applied for, and was allotted, shares in the defendant company. After paying some money on the shares, she defaulted on payment and repudiated the contract. The company agreed that her name be removed from its register of members but refused to return the money she had already paid. It was held that Miss Steinberg was not entitled to the return of the money paid. She had benefited from membership rights in the company; thus, there had not been a complete failure of consideration.

Void contracts

Under the Infants' Relief Act (IRA) 1874, the following contracts were stated to be absolutely void:

- contracts for the repayment of loans;
- contracts for goods other than necessaries;
- accounts stated, that is, admissions of money owed.

In addition, no action could be brought on the basis of the ratification, made after the attainment of full age, of an otherwise void contract.

The main effect of the Minors' Contracts Act 1987 was that the contracts set out in the IRA 1874 were no longer to be considered as absolutely void. As a consequence, unenforceable, as well as voidable, contracts may be ratified upon the minor attaining the age of majority.

Although the IRA 1874 stated that such contracts were absolutely void, this simply meant that, in effect, they could not be enforced against the minor. The other party could not normally recover goods or money transferred to the minor. Where, however, the goods had been obtained by fraud on the part of the minor and where they were still in the minor's possession, the other party could rely on the doctrine of restitution to reclaim them. The minor, on the other hand, could enforce the agreement against the other party. Specific performance would not be available, however, on the ground that it would be inequitable to grant such an order to minors while it could not be awarded against them.

The Minors' Contracts Act 1987 has given the courts wider powers to order the restoration of property acquired by a minor. They are no longer restricted to cases where the minor has acquired the property through fraud; they can now order restitution where they think it just and equitable to do so.

Minors' liability in tort

As there is no minimum age limit in relation to actions in tort, minors may be liable under a tortious action. The courts, however, will not permit a party to enforce a contract indirectly by substituting an action in tort or quasi-contract for an action in contract.

In *Leslie v Shiell* (1914), Shiell, a minor, obtained a loan from Leslie by lying about his age. Leslie sued to recover the money as damages in an action for the tort of deceit. It was held, however, that the action must fail, as it was simply an indirect means of enforcing the otherwise void contract.

5.7.2   Mental incapacity and intoxication

A contract made by a party who is of unsound mind or under the influence of drink or drugs is *prima facie* valid. In order to avoid a contract, such a person must show:

- that their mind was so affected at the time that they were incapable of understanding the nature of their actions; and

- that the other party either knew or ought to have known of their disability.

The person claiming such incapacity, nonetheless, must pay a reasonable price for necessaries sold and delivered to them. The Sale of Goods Act 1979 specifically applies the same rules to such people as those that are applicable to minors.

5.8 INTENTION TO CREATE LEGAL RELATIONS

All of the aspects considered previously may well be present in a particular agreement, and yet there still may not be a contract. In order to limit the number of cases that might otherwise be brought, the courts will only enforce those agreements which the parties' intended to have legal effect. Although expressed in terms of the parties intentions, the test for the presence of such intention is once again objective, rather than subjective. For the purposes of this topic, agreements can be divided into three categories, in which different presumptions apply.

5.8.1   Domestic and social agreements

In this type of agreement, there is a presumption that the parties do not intend to create legal relations.

In *Balfour v Balfour* (1919), a husband returned to Ceylon to take up employment and he promised his wife, who could not return with him due to health problems, that he would pay her £30 per month as maintenance. When the marriage later ended in divorce, the wife sued for the promised maintenance. It was held that the parties had not intended the original promise to be binding and, therefore, it was not legally enforceable.

It is essential to realise that the intention not to create legal relations in such relationships is only a presumption and that, as with all presumptions, it may be rebutted by the actual facts and circumstances of a particular case. A case in point is *Merritt v Merritt* (1970). After a husband had left the matrimonial home, he met his wife and promised to pay her £40 per month, from which she undertook to pay the outstanding mortgage on their house. The husband, at the wife's insistence, signed a note, agreeing to transfer the house into the wife's sole name when the mortgage was paid off. The wife paid off the mortgage but the husband refused to transfer the house. It was held that the agreement was enforceable, as, in the circumstances, the parties had clearly intended to enter into a legally enforceable agreement.

'Social' agreements, such as lottery syndicates, have also been the subject of legal dispute. In *Simpkins v Pays* (1955), a relatively vague agreement about contribution to postage and sharing of any winnings in competitions made between a lodger, a landlady and her granddaughter was alleged not to be a contract for lack of intention to create legal relations. However, the court decided that there was a binding contract to share winnings, despite the apparently social nature of the agreement. The agreement was commercial in nature and related to a matter unconnected with the running of a household; there was a degree of *mutuality* in the agreement which indicated an intention that it was binding. In *Albert v MIB* (1974), an agreement between colleagues in relation to lifts to work was held to be a contract because there was intention to create legal relations. It was said to be unnecessary to show whether the parties had thought about whether there was a contract, nor did it matter that, if asked, they would have said that they would not have sued if the arrangement failed. Clearly, therefore, the presumption does not purport to find the *actual* intention of the parties. Perhaps the best advice, particularly in relation to lottery syndicates, is to reduce the agreement to writing so that there is written evidence that the parties did intend the agreement to be a binding contract.

5.8.2 Commercial agreements

In commercial situations, the strong presumption is that the parties intend to enter into a legally binding relationship in consequence of their dealings.

In *Edwards v Skyways* (1964), employers undertook to make an *ex gratia* payment to an employee whom they had made redundant. It was held that, in such a situation, the use of the term *'ex gratia'* was not sufficient to rebut the presumption that the establishment of legal relations had been intended. The former employee was, therefore, entitled to the promised payment .

As with other presumptions, this, too, is open to rebuttal. In commercial situations, however, the presumption is so strong that it will usually take express wording to the contrary to avoid its operation. An example can be found in *Rose & Frank Co v Crompton Bros* (1925), in which it was held that an express clause which stated that no legal relations were to be created by a business transaction was effective. Another example is *Jones v Vernons Pools Ltd* (1938), where the plaintiff claimed to have submitted a correct pools forecast, but the defendants denied receiving it and relied on a clause in the coupon which stated that the transaction was binding in honour only. Under such circumstances, it was held that the plaintiff had no cause for an action in contract, as no legal relations had been created.

5.8.3 Collective agreements

Agreements between employers and trade unions may be considered as a distinct category of agreement, for, although they are commercial agreements, they are presumed not to give rise to legal relations and, therefore, are not normally enforceable in the courts. Such was the outcome of *Ford Motor Co v AUEFW* (1969), in which it was held that Ford could not take legal action against the defendant trade union, which had ignored previously negotiated terms of a collective agreement.

This presumption is now conclusive by virtue of s 179 of the Trade Union and Labour Relations (Consolidation) Act 1992, unless the agreement is in writing and expressly states that it is a binding agreement.

5.8.4 Letters of comfort

Letters of comfort are generally used by parent companies to encourage potential lenders to extend credit to their subsidiary companies by stating their intention to provide financial backing for those subsidiaries. It is generally the case that such letters merely amount to statements of present intention on the part of the parent company and, therefore, do not amount to offers that can be accepted by the creditors of any subsidiary companies. Given the operation of the doctrine of separate personality, this effectively leaves the creditors with no legal recourse against the parent company for any loans granted to the subsidiary.

In *Kleinwort Benson v Malaysian Mining Corp* (1989), the defendant company had issued a letter of comfort to the plaintiffs in respect of its subsidiary company, MMC Metals. However, when MMC Metals went into liquidation, the defendant failed to make good its debts to the plaintiffs.

At first instance, the judge decided in favour of the plaintiffs, holding that, in such commercial circumstances, the defendants had failed to rebut the presumption that there had been an intention to create legal relations. On appeal, it was held that, in the circumstances of the instant case, the letter of comfort did not amount to an offer; it was a statement of intention which could not bind the defendants contractually. Therefore, the Malaysian Mining Corporation was not legally responsible for the debt of its subsidiary.

It is important to note that the *Kleinwort Benson* case opens up the possibility that, under different circumstances, letters of comfort might be considered to constitute offers capable of being accepted and leading to contractual relations. Under such circumstances, the presumption as to the intention to create legal relations as they normally apply in commercial situations will operate, though it is almost inconceivable that a court would decide that a letter of comfort amounted to an offer without also finding an intention to create legal relations.

SUMMARY OF CHAPTER 5

THE FORMATION OF A CONTRACT

In order to create a contract, the following factors have to be present.

Offer

- An offer is a promise, which is capable of acceptance, to be bound on particular terms.
- An offer may be restricted to a particular person(s) or made to the public at large.
- A person can only accept an offer they are aware of.
- An offer may be revoked *before* acceptance or may come to an end in other ways.
- An offer must be distinguished from an invitation to treat, a statement of intention and a supply of information.

Acceptance

- Acceptance must correspond with the terms of the offer.
- Acceptance must be communicated to the offeror (subject to certain exceptions such as the *postal rule*).

Consideration

- Consists of some benefit to the promisor or detriment to the promisee.
- Consideration can be *executed* or *executory*, but not *past*.
- Consideration must be *sufficient*, but need not be *adequate*.

Promissory estoppel

- The doctrine may prevent a person from going back on a promise to forgo strict contractual rights.
- The doctrine operates as a defence, not a cause of action.

Privity

- Only a party to a contract can sue or be sued on it.
- There are common law and statutory exceptions to the doctrine of privity, notably the Contracts (Rights of Third Parties) Act 1999.

CAPACITY

- Minors, those of unsound mind or under the influence of drugs or alcohol have limited capacity to make binding contracts; nevertheless, contracts for necessaries bind them.
- Minors are also bound by beneficial contracts of service.
- Some contracts made by minors are voidable and only bind them if not repudiated by them before or within a reasonable time after reaching the age of majority.

INTENTION TO CREATE LEGAL RELATIONS

- In social/domestic agreements, there is a rebuttal presumption that legal relations were not intended.
- In commercial/business agreements, there is a rebuttal presumption that legal relations were intended.
- Collective agreements are usually presumed not to create legal relations.

CHAPTER 6

CONTENTS OF A CONTRACT

The previous chapter dealt with how a binding contractual agreement comes to be formed; this chapter will consider what the parties have actually agreed to do. What they have agreed to do are the *terms* of the contract.

6.1 CONTRACT TERMS AND MERE REPRESENTATIONS

As the parties will normally be bound to perform any promise that they have contracted to undertake, it is important to decide precisely what promises are included in the contract. Some statements do not form part of a contract, even though they might have induced the other party to enter into the contract. These pre-contractual statements are called *representations*. The consequences of such representations being false will be considered below (see below, 7.3), but for the moment, it is sufficient to distinguish them from contractual terms, which are statements which *do* form part of the contract. There are four tests for distinguishing a contractual term from a mere representation:

- Where the statement is of such major importance that the promisee would not have entered into the agreement without it, then it will be construed as a term. In *Bannerman v White* (1861), the defendant wanted to buy hops for brewing purposes and he asked the plaintiff if they had been treated with sulphur. On the basis of the plaintiff's false statement that they had not been so treated, he agreed to buy the hops. When he discovered later that they had been treated with sulphur, he refused to accept them. It was held that the plaintiff's statement about the sulphur was a fundamental term (the contract would not have been made *but for* the statement) of the contract and, since it was not true, the defendant was entitled to repudiate the contract.

- Where there is a time gap between the statement and the making of the contract, then the statement will most likely be treated as a representation.

  In *Routledge v McKay* (1954), on 23 October, the defendant told the plaintiff that a motorcycle was a 1942 model. On 30 October, a written contract for the sale of the bike was made, without reference to its age. The bike was actually a 1930 model. It was held that the statement about the date was a pre-contractual representation and the plaintiff could not sue for damages for breach of contract. However, this rule is not a hard and fast one. In *Schawell v Reade* (1913), the court held that a statement made three months before the final agreement was part of the contract.

- Where the statement is oral and the agreement is subsequently drawn up in written form, then its exclusion from the written document will suggest that the statement was not meant to be a contractual term. *Routledge v McKay* (1954) may also be cited as authority for this proposition.

- Where one of the parties to an agreement has special knowledge or skill, then statements made by them will be terms, but statements made *to* them will not.

  In *Dick Bentley Productions Ltd v Harold Smith (Motors) Ltd* (1965), the plaintiff bought a Bentley car from the defendant after being assured that it had only travelled 20,000 miles since its engine and gearbox were replaced. When this statement turned out to be untrue, the plaintiff sued for breach of contract. It was held that the statement was a term of the contract and the plaintiff was entitled to damages.

  In *Oscar Chess Ltd v Williams* (1957), Williams traded in one car when buying another from the plaintiffs. He told them that his trade-in was a 1948 model, whereas it was actually a 1939 model. The company unsuccessfully sued for breach of contract. The statement as to the age of the car was merely a representation, and the right to sue for misrepresentation had been lost, due to delay.

6.2 CONDITIONS, WARRANTIES AND INNOMINATE TERMS

Once it is decided that a statement is a term, rather than merely a pre-contractual representation, it is necessary to determine which type of term it is, in order to determine what remedies are available for its breach. Terms can be classified as one of three types.

6.2.1 Conditions

A condition is a fundamental part of the agreement and is something which goes to the root of the contract. Breach of a condition gives the innocent party the right either to terminate the contract and refuse to perform their part of it or to go through with the agreement and sue for damages.

6.2.2 Warranties

A warranty is a subsidiary obligation which is not vital to the overall agreement and does not totally destroy its efficacy. Breach of a warranty does not give the right to terminate the agreement. The innocent party has to complete their part of the agreement and can only sue for damages.

The difference between the two types of term can be seen in the following cases:

- In *Poussard v Spiers and Pond* (1876), the plaintiff had contracted with the defendants to sing in an opera that they were producing. Due to illness, she was unable to appear on the first night and for some nights thereafter. When Mme Poussard recovered, the defendants refused her services, as they had hired a replacement for the whole run of the opera. It was held that her failure to appear on the opening night had been a breach of a condition and the defendants were at liberty to treat the contract as discharged.

- In *Bettini v Gye* (1876), the plaintiff had contracted with the defendants to complete a number of engagements. He had also agreed to be in London for rehearsals six days before his opening performance. Due to illness, he only arrived three days before the opening night and the defendants refused his services. On this occasion, it was held that there was only a breach of warranty. The defendants were entitled to damages but could not treat the contract as discharged.

The distinction between the effects of a breach of condition as against the effects of a breach of warranty was enshrined in s 11 of the Sale of Goods Act (SoGA) 1893 (now the SoGA 1979). For some time, it was thought that these were the only two types of term possible, the nature of the remedy available being prescribed by the particular type of term concerned. This simple classification has subsequently been rejected by the courts as being too restrictive, and a third type of term has emerged: the innominate term.

6.2.3 Innominate terms

In this case, the remedy is not prescribed in advance simply by whether the term breached is a condition or a warranty, but depends on the consequence of the breach.

If the breach deprives the innocent party of substantially the whole benefit of the contract, then the right to repudiate will be permitted, even if the term might otherwise appear to be a mere warranty.

If, however, the innocent party does not lose the whole benefit of the contract, then they will not be permitted to repudiate but must settle for damages, even if the term might otherwise appear to be a condition.

In *Cehave v Bremer (The Hansa Nord)* (1976), a contract for the sale of a cargo of citrus pulp pellets, to be used as animal feed, provided that they were to be delivered in good condition. On delivery, the buyers rejected the cargo as not complying with this provision and claimed back the price paid from the sellers. The buyers eventually obtained the pellets when the cargo was sold off and used them for their original purpose. It was held that, since the breach had not been serious, the buyers had not been free to reject the cargo and the sellers had acted lawfully in retaining the money paid.

Not all judges are wholly in favour of this third category of term, feeling that, in the world of commerce, certainty as to the outcome of breach is necessary at the outset and should not be dependent on a court's findings after breach has occurred (see *Bunge Corp v Tradax Export SA* (1981)).

6.3 IMPLIED TERMS

So far, all of the cases considered have involved express terms: statements actually made by one of the parties, either by word of mouth or in writing. Implied terms, however, are not actually stated, but are introduced into the contract by implication. Implied terms can be divided into three types.

6.3.1 Terms implied by statute

For example, under the SoGA 1979, terms relating to description, quality and fitness for purpose are all implied into sale of goods contracts. (For consideration of these implied terms, see below, 9.2.4.)

6.3.2 Terms implied by custom

An agreement may be subject to customary terms not actually specified by the parties. For example, in *Hutton v Warren* (1836), it was held that customary usage permitted a farm tenant to claim an allowance for seed and labour on quitting his tenancy. It should be noted, however, that custom cannot override the express terms of an agreement (*Les Affréteurs Réunis v Walford* (1919)).

6.3.3 Terms implied by the courts

Generally, it is a matter for the parties concerned to decide the terms of a contract, but, on occasion, the court will presume that the parties intended to include a term which is not expressly stated. They will do so where it is necessary to give business efficacy to the contract.

Whether a term may be implied can be decided on the basis of the 'officious bystander' test. Imagine two parties, A and B, negotiating a contract. A third party, C, interrupts to suggest a particular provision. A and B reply that that particular term is understood. In such a way, the court will decide that a term should be implied into a contract.

In *The Moorcock* (1889), the appellants, the owners of a wharf, contracted with the respondents to permit them to discharge their ship at the wharf. It was apparent to both parties that, when the tide was out, the ship would rest on the river bed. When the tide was out, the ship sustained damage by settling on a ridge. It was held that there was an implied warranty in the contract that the place of anchorage should be safe for the ship. As a consequence, the shipowner was entitled to damages for breach of that term.

6.4 THE PAROL EVIDENCE RULE

If all the terms of a contract are in writing, then there is a strong presumption that no evidence supporting a different oral agreement will be permitted to vary those terms.

In *Hutton v Watling* (1948), on the sale of a business, together with its goodwill, a written agreement was drawn up and signed by the vendor. In an action to enforce one of the clauses in the agreement, the vendor claimed that it did not represent the whole contract. It was held that the vendor was not entitled to introduce evidence on this point, as the written document represented a true record of the contract.

The presumption against introducing contrary oral evidence can be rebutted, however, where it is shown that the document was not intended to set out all of the terms agreed by the parties.

In *Re SS Ardennes* (1951), a ship's bill of lading stated that it might proceed by any route directly or indirectly. The defendants promised that the ship would proceed directly to London from Spain with its cargo of tangerines. However, the ship called at Antwerp before heading for London and, as a result, the tangerines had to be sold at a reduced price. The shippers successfully sued for damages, as it was held that the bill of lading did not constitute the contract between the parties but merely evidenced their intentions. The verbal promise was part of the final contract.

The effect of the parol evidence rule has also been avoided by the willingness of the courts to find collateral contracts which import different, not to say contradictory, terms into the written contract. An example of this may be seen in *City and Westminster Properties (1934) Ltd v Mudd* (1959), where, although the written contract expressly provided that the defendant had no right to live on particular premises, the court recognised the contrary effect of a verbal collateral contract to allow him to do so. In return for agreeing to sign the new lease, the tenant (who had previously resided on the premises) was promised that he could continue to do so, despite the term of the new lease. Thus both parties provided consideration to support the collateral contract. (See, further, above, 5.6, for the use of collateral contracts to avoid the strict operation of the doctrine of privity.)

City and Westminster v Mudd at least suggests that the courts will find justification for avoiding the strict application of the parol evidence rule where they wish to do so. On that basis, it has been suggested that it should be removed from contract law entirely. Interestingly, however, a Law Commission Report (No 154) took the opposite view, stating that there was no need to provide legislation to remove the rule, as it was already a dead letter in practice.

6.5 EXEMPTION OR EXCLUSION CLAUSES

In a sense, an exemption clause is no different from any other clause, in that it seeks to define the rights and obligations of the parties to a contract. However, an exemption clause is a term in a contract which tries to exempt, or limit, the liability of a party in breach of the agreement. Exclusion clauses give rise to most concern when they are included in standard form contracts, in which one party, who is in a position of commercial dominance, imposes their terms on the other party, who has no choice (other than to take it or leave it) as far as the terms of the contract go. Such standard form contracts are contrary to the ideas of consensus and negotiation underpinning contract law; for this reason, they have received particular attention from both the judiciary and the legislature, in an endeavour to counteract their perceived unfairness. A typical example of a standard form agreement would be a holiday booking, made on the terms printed in a travel brochure.

The actual law relating to exclusion clauses is complicated by the interplay of the common law, the Unfair Contract Terms Act (UCTA) 1977 and the various Acts which imply certain terms into particular contracts. However, the following questions should always be asked with regard to exclusion clauses:

- has the exclusion clause been incorporated into the contract?;
- does the exclusion clause effectively cover the breach?;
- what effect do UCTA 1977 and the Unfair Terms in Consumer Contracts Regulations 1999 have on the exclusion clause?

6.5.1 Has the exclusion clause been incorporated into the contract?

An exclusion clause cannot be effective unless it is actually a term of a contract. There are three ways in which such a term may be inserted into a contractual agreement.

By signature

If a person signs a contractual document, then they are bound by its terms, even if they do not read it.

In *L'Estrange v Graucob* (1934), a café owner bought a vending machine, signing a contract without reading it, which took away all her rights under the SoGA 1893. When the machine proved faulty, she sought to take action against the vendors, but it was held that she had no cause of action, as she had signified her consent to the terms of the contract by signing it and the exclusion clause effectively exempted liability for breach.

The rule in *L'Estrange v Graucob* may be avoided where the party seeking to rely on the exclusion clause misled the other party into signing the contract (*Curtis v Chemical Cleaning and Dyeing Co* (1951)).

By notice

Apart from the above, an exclusion clause will not be incorporated into a contract unless the party affected actually knew of it or was given sufficient notice of it. In order for notice to be adequate, the document bearing the exclusion clause must be an integral part of the contract and must be given at the time that the contract is made.

In *Chapelton v Barry UDC* (1940), the plaintiff hired a deck chair and received a ticket, which stated on its back that the council would not be responsible for any injuries arising from the hire of the chairs. After he was injured when the chair collapsed, Chapelton successfully sued the council. It was held that the ticket was merely a receipt, the contract already having been made, and could not be used effectively to communicate the exclusion clause.

In *Olley v Marlborough Court Hotel Ltd* (1949), a couple arrived at a hotel and paid for a room in advance. On reaching their room, they found a notice purporting to exclude the hotel's liability in regard to thefts of goods not handed in to the manager. A thief later stole the wife's purse. It was held that the hotel could not escape liability, since the disclaimer had only been made after the contract had been formed.

The notice given must be sufficient for the average person to be aware of it; if it is sufficient, it matters not that this contracting party was not aware of it. In *Thompson v LM & S Rly* (1930), a woman who could not read was bound by a printed clause referred to on a railway timetable and ticket because the average person could have been aware of it.

Whether the degree of notice given has been sufficient is a matter of fact, but, in *Thornton v Shoe Lane Parking Ltd* (1971), it was stated that the greater the exemption, the greater the degree of notice required.

In *Interfoto Picture Library Ltd v Stiletto Programmes Ltd* (1988), the Court of Appeal decided that a particular clause was not to be considered as imported into a contract, even though it had been available for inspection before the contract was entered into. The clause in question sought to impose almost £4,000 liability for any delay in returning the photographic negatives which were the subject of the contract. It was held, following *Thornton v Shoe Lane Parking Ltd*, that this penalty was so severe that it could not have been fairly brought to the attention of the other party by indirect reference; it required notification in the most explicit way. This is sometimes referred to as the *red ink* or *red hand* principle and was recently re-examined in relation to scratch cards in *O'Brien v MGN Ltd* (2001).

By custom

Where the parties have had previous dealings on the basis of an exclusion clause, that clause may be included in later contracts (*Spurling v Bradshaw* (1956)), but it has to be shown that the party affected had actual knowledge of the exclusion clause.

In *Hollier v Rambler Motors* (1972), on each of the previous occasions that the plaintiff had had his car repaired at the defendants' garage, he had signed a form containing an exclusion clause. On the last occasion, he had not signed such a form. When the car was damaged by fire through negligence, the defendants sought to rely on the exclusion clause. It was held that there was no evidence that Hollier had been aware of the clause to which he had been agreeing and, therefore, it could not be considered to be a part of his last contract.

6.5.2 Does the exclusion clause effectively cover the breach?

As a consequence of the disfavour with which the judiciary have looked on exclusion clauses, a number of rules of construction have been developed which operate to restrict the effectiveness of exclusion clauses. These include the following:

* The *contra proferentem* rule

  This requires that any uncertainties or ambiguities in the exclusion clause be interpreted against the meaning claimed by the person seeking to rely on it.

  In *Andrews v Singer* (1934), the plaintiffs contracted to buy some new Singer cars from the defendant. A clause excluded all conditions, warranties and liabilities implied by statute, common law or otherwise. One car supplied was not new. It was held that the requirement that the cars be new was an express condition of the contract and, therefore, was not covered by the exclusion clause, which only referred to implied clauses.

  In *Hollier v Rambler* (1972), it was stated that, as the exclusion clause in question could be interpreted as applying only to non-negligent accidental damage or, alternatively, as including damage caused by negligence, it should be restricted to the former, narrower interpretation. As a consequence, the plaintiff could recover for damages caused to his car by the defendants' negligence.

  A more recent example of the operation of the *contra proferentem* rule may be seen in *Bovis Construction (Scotland) Ltd v Whatlings Construction Ltd* (1995). The details of the contract between the two parties were based on a standard form and a number of letters. One of the letters introduced a term which limited the defendants' liability in respect of time related costs to £100,000. The plaintiffs terminated the contract on the basis of the defendants' lack of diligence in carrying out the contracted work. When they subsequently sued for £2,741,000, the defendants relied on the limitation clause. The House of Lords decided that, as the defendants had introduced the limitation clause, it had to be interpreted strictly, although not as strictly as a full exclusion clause. It was held that the term 'time related costs' applied to losses arising as a consequence of delay in performance, and not non-performance. The defendants had been guilty of the latter and were, therefore, fully liable for the consequences of their reputiatory breach.

- The doctrine of fundamental breach

  In a series of complicated and conflicting cases, ending with the House of Lords' decision in *Photo Production v Securicor Transport* (1980), some courts attempted to develop a rule that it was impossible to exclude liability for breach of contract if a fundamental breach of the contract had occurred, that is, where the party in breach had failed altogether to perform the contract.

  In *Photo Production v Securicor Transport*, the defendants had entered into a contract with the plaintiffs to guard their factory. An exclusion clause exempted Securicor from liability, even if one of their employees caused damage to the factory. Later, one of the guards deliberately set fire to the factory. Securicor claimed the protection of the exclusion clause. It was ultimately decided by the House of Lords that whether an exclusion clause could operate after a fundamental breach was a matter of construction. There was no absolute rule that total failure of performance rendered such clauses inoperative. The exclusion clause in this particular case was wide enough to cover the events that took place, and so Photo Production's action failed.

6.5.3 What effect does UCTA 1977 have on the exclusion clause?

This Act represents the statutory attempt to control exclusion clauses. In spite of its title, it is really aimed at unfair exemption clauses, rather than contract terms generally. It also covers non-contractual notices which purport to exclude liability under the Occupiers' Liability Act 1957. The controls under UCTA 1977 relate to two areas:

- Negligence

  There is an absolute prohibition on exemption clauses in relation to liability in negligence resulting in death or injury (ss 2 and 5). Exemption clauses relating to liability for other damage caused by negligence will only be enforced to the extent that they satisfy the requirement of reasonableness (s 5).

In *Smith v Bush* (1989), the plaintiff bought a house on the basis of a valuation report carried out for her building society by the defendant. The surveyor had included a disclaimer of liability for negligence in his report to the building society and sought to rely on that fact when the plaintiff sued after the chimneys of the property collapsed. The House of Lords held that the disclaimer was an exemption clause and that it failed the requirement that such terms should be reasonable.

- Contract

The general rule of the Act (s 3) is that an exclusion clause imposed on a consumer (as defined in s 12(1)) or by standard terms of business is not binding unless it satisfies the Act's requirement of reasonableness. Effectively, therefore, the Act is dealing with clauses imposed by a person acting *in the course of business*. Section 12(1) states that a person deals as a consumer (so that he does *not act in the course of business*) if he neither makes the contract in the course of business nor holds himself out as so doing and the other party does make the contract in the course of business. Additionally, where goods are supplied under the contract, they must be of a type normally supplied for private consumption and they must be so used. The precise meaning of 'acting in the course of business' for the purposes of UCTA 1977 was considered in *R & B Customs Brokers Co Ltd v UDT* (1988). In deciding that the sellers of a car to a company could not rely on an exclusion clause contained in the contract, as the transaction had not been in the course of business, the Court of Appeal stated that the purchase had been:

> ... at highest, only incidental to the carrying on of the relevant business [and] ... a degree of regularity is required before it can be said that they are an integral part of the business carried on and so entered into in the course of business.

In reaching this decision, the Court of Appeal followed the House of Lords' decision in *Davies v Sumner* (1984), which dealt with a similar provision in the Trade Descriptions Act 1968. It would seem, however, that the meaning of selling 'in the course of business' for the purposes of s 14 of the SoGA 1979 is different. Section 14, which implies conditions of satisfactory quality and fitness for purpose into contracts for the sale of goods (see Chapter 9), applies where the seller 'sells in the course of business'. The meaning of selling 'in the course of business' under s 14 of the SoGA 1979 is wide enough to cover incidental sales by, for example, the professions, local and central government departments and public authorities. The meaning of selling 'in the course of business' in the context of s 14 was examined in *Stevenson v Rogers* (1999).

UCTA 1977 applies more specific rules to contracts for the sale of goods; which rules apply depends on whether the seller sells to a person 'dealing as a consumer' (as defined in s 12(1) of UCTA 1977; such sales are commonly referred to as 'consumer sales'). Under s 6(1) of UCTA 1977, the implied term of s 12(1) of the SoGA 1979 (transfer of title) cannot be excluded in consumer or non-consumer sales.

The other implied terms, namely, those as to description, fitness, satisfactory quality and sample, cannot be excluded in a consumer contract (s 6(2)); and, in a non-consumer transaction, any restriction is subject to the requirement of reasonableness (s 6(3)). Under s 7, similar rules apply to other contracts under which goods are supplied (for example hire contracts) by virtue of the Supply of Goods and Services Act 1982. Amendments to UCTA 1977, in so far as its provisions apply to contracts for the sale and supply of goods, are proposed by the Sale and Supply of Goods to Consumers Regulations 2002. These proposed amendments are dealt with in Chapter 9.

Indemnity clauses are covered by s 4 of UCTA 1977. These are provisions in contracts by means of which one party agrees to compensate the other for any liability incurred by them in the course of carrying out the contract. Although these may be legitimate ways of allocating risk and insurance responsibilities in a commercial context, they are of more dubious effect in consumer transactions and are, therefore, required to satisfy the requirement of reasonableness.

'The requirement of reasonableness means fair and reasonable ... having regard to the circumstances ... [s 11].' Schedule 2 to UCTA 1977 provides guidelines for the application of the reasonableness test in regard to non-consumer transactions, but it is likely that similar considerations will be taken into account by the courts in consumer transactions. Amongst these considerations are:

o the relative strength of the parties' bargaining power;

o whether any inducement was offered in return for the limitation on liability;

o whether the customer knew, or ought to have known, about the existence or extent of the exclusion;

o whether the goods were manufactured or adapted to the special order of the customer.

In *George Mitchell (Chesterhall) Ltd v Finney Lock Seeds Ltd* (1983), the respondents planted 63 acres with cabbage seed, which was supplied by the appellants. The crop failed, due partly to the fact that the wrong type of seed had been supplied and partly to the fact that the seed supplied was of inferior quality. When the respondents claimed damages, the sellers relied on a clause in their standard conditions of sale, which limited their liability to replacing the seeds supplied or refunding payment. It was held, however, that the respondents were entitled to compensation for the loss of the crop. The House of Lords decided that, although the exemption clause was sufficiently clear and unambiguous to be effective at common law, it failed the test of reasonableness under UCTA 1977.

In *Watford Electronics Ltd v Sanderson CFL Ltd* (2001), a contract between two businesses for the purchase of integrated software systems stated that:

o   the parties agreed no pre-contractual representations had been made;

o   liability for indirect/consequential loss was excluded;

o   liability for breach of contract was limited to the contract price of £104,596.

The system was unsatisfactory and the buyer claimed damages for breach of contract, misrepresentation and negligence, totalling (including loss of expected profits) £5.5 million. The seller sought to rely on the clauses to limit/escape liability; the buyer alleged that they were unreasonable under UCTA 1977. The Court of Appeal held that the clauses were reasonable because the contract was negotiated between two experienced businesses, both of which (on the facts) were of equal bargaining strength.

It is likely that many of the situations in the cases considered under the common law prior to UCTA 1977 would now be decided under that Act. It is still important, however, to understand the common law principles, for the very good reason that UCTA 1977 does not apply in many important situations. Amongst these are transactions relating to insurance; interests in land; patents and other intellectual property; the transfer of securities; and the formation of companies or partnerships.

6.5.4   The Unfair Terms in Consumer Contracts Regulations

The first Unfair Terms in Consumer Contracts Regulations were enacted in December 1994 (SI 1994/3159). They were introduced to implement the European Unfair Contract Terms Directive (93/13/EEC). Those original Regulations were repealed and replaced by the current Regulations (SI 1999/2083), which came into effect on 1 October 1999. The new Regulations are intended to reflect closely the wording of the original, but they also introduce significant alterations.

It has to be stated that there was some criticism that the previous Regulations merely introduced the Directive, without engaging in a comprehensive review of this area. Concern was expressed as to the precise way in which UCTA 1977 and the 1994 Regulations impacted on one another and how their interaction would affect consumer law generally. Unfortunately, the new Regulations have done nothing to improve this general problem and, in this particular respect, the criticisms of the 1994 Regulations are still relevant.

The 1999 Regulations apply to any term in a contract concluded between a seller or supplier and a consumer which has not been individually negotiated.

The Regulations are, therefore, wider in scope than UCTA 1977, in that they cover all terms, not just exclusion clauses. However, reg 6(2) states that, apart from the requirement in respect of plain language, neither the core provisions of a consumer contract, which set out its main subject matter, nor the adequacy of the price paid are open to assessment in terms of fairness. The Regulations would, therefore, still appear to focus on the formal procedure through which contracts are made, rather than the substantive content of the contract in question.

By virtue of reg 5, a term is unfair if, contrary to the requirements of good faith, it causes a significant imbalance in the parties' rights and obligations arising under the contract, to the detriment of the consumer. Schedule 2 sets out a long, indicative, but non-exhaustive, list of terms which may be regarded as unfair. Examples of terms included in this list are: a term which excludes or limits liability in the event of the supplier or seller causing the death or injury of the consumer; inappropriately excluding or limiting the legal rights of the consumer in the event of total or partial non-performance or inadequate performance; a term requiring any consumer who fails to fulfil his obligations to pay a disproportionately high sum in compensation; and a term enabling the seller or supplier to alter the terms of the contract unilaterally without a valid reason which is specified in the contract.

Any such term as outlined above will be assumed to be unfair and, under reg 8, if a term is found to be unfair, it will not be binding on the consumer, although the remainder of the contract will continue to operate if it can do so after the excision of the unfair term.

Two further provisions of the Regulations which are worthy of mention have been taken from the previous Regulations. First, there is the requirement that all contractual terms be in plain, intelligible language and that, when there is any doubt as to the meaning of any term, it will be construed in favour of the consumer (reg 7). This is somewhat similar to the *contra proferentem* rule in English common law.

Secondly, although the Regulations will be most used by consumers to defeat particular unfair terms, regs 10–12 give the Director General of Fair Trading the power to take action against the use of unfair terms by obtaining an injunction to prohibit the use of such terms. However, the power of the Director General to seek injunctions to control unfair contract terms has been extended to other qualifying bodies. These qualifying bodies are listed in Sched 1 to the Regulations and include the various regulatory bodies controlling the previous public utilities sector of the economy, the Data Protection Registrar and every weights and measures authority in Great Britain.

Various aspects of the original Regulations, which have implications for the current Regulations, have been examined by the House of Lords in *Director General of Fair Trading v First National Bank* (2001).

SUMMARY OF CHAPTER 6

CONTENTS OF A CONTRACT

Contract terms and mere representations

A pre-contract statement is likely to be a term if:
- the contract would not have been made but for the statement;
- the time gap between the statement and the contract is short;
- the statement is made by a person with special skill/knowledge.

A pre-contract statement is likely to be a representation only if:
- there is a long time gap between the statement and the contract;
- the statement is oral and the written contract does not refer to it;
- the person making the statement had no special skill/knowledge.

Terms

- A *condition* is a fundamental term, going to the root of the contract, breach of which gives a right to repudiate the contract.
- A *warranty* is a subsidiary term, breach of which gives a right to claim damages.
- If a term is *innominate*, the seriousness of the breach determines the remedies available.

Express and implied terms

- Express terms are those specifically agreed by the parties.
- Implied terms are not specifically agreed by the parties, but are implied into the contract by statute or custom or the courts.

The parol evidence rule

- Where there is a written contract, it is *presumed* that evidence cannot be adduced to show a differing oral agreement.

Exemption or exclusion clauses

The validity of such a clause depends on:

- whether it was incorporated into the contract;
- whether, on its wording, it covers the breach;
- whether a common law rule of construction, such as the *contra proferentem* rule, restricts its effect;
- the effect of statutory provisions.

Statutory regulation of exemption clauses

Under the Unfair Contract Terms Act 1977

- Liability for negligence causing death or injury cannot be excluded.
- Liability for breach of the implied terms of the SoGA 1979 cannot be excluded in consumer sales.
- Liability for breach of s 12(1) of the SoGA 1979 cannot be excluded in non-consumer sales but liability for breach of the other implied terms may be excluded, subject to the requirement of *reasonableness*.

Under the Unfair Terms in Consumer Contracts Regulations 1999

- Contract clauses not made *in good faith* are void.
- Authorised bodies may obtain injunctions to prevent the use of unfair terms.

CHAPTER 7

VITIATING FACTORS

7.1 INTRODUCTION

Vitiating factors are those elements which make an agreement either void or voidable, depending on which vitiating factor is present. The vitiating factors are:

- mistake;
- misrepresentation;
- duress;
- undue influence;
- public policy, rendering contracts void/illegal.

7.2 MISTAKE

Generally speaking, the parties to a contract will not be relieved from the burden of their agreement simply because they have made a mistake. If one party makes a bad bargain, that is no reason for setting the contract aside. Very few mistakes will affect the validity of a contract at common law, but, where a mistake is operative, it will render the contract void. This has the effect that property that is transferred under operative mistake can be recovered, even where it has been transferred to an innocent third party.

However, in cases where the mistake is not operative, an equitable remedy such as rescission may be available. The grant of such remedies is in the court's discretion and subject to the principles of equity. In *Leaf v International Galleries* (1950), there was a contract for the sale of a painting of Salisbury Cathedral, which both parties believed to be by Constable. Five years later, the buyer discovered that the painting was not by Constable but was refused rescission because of the lapse of time since purchase.

It is also important to appreciate that a mistake cannot affect a contract unless it exists at the time of contracting. In *Amalgamated Investment & Property Co Ltd v John Walker & Sons Ltd* (1976), a company purchased property for redevelopment. Just after the contract, the property was given listed building status, which would restrict the intended development. The purchaser could not rescind the contract on the basis of a mistake that the property could be redeveloped as intended, because at the time of sale it could have been so developed.

It is usual to divide mistakes into the following three categories:

- common mistake;
- mutual mistake;
- unilateral mistake.

7.2.1   Common mistake

This is where both parties to an agreement share the same mistake about the circumstances surrounding the transaction. In order for the mistake to be operative, it must be of a fundamental nature.

In *Bell v Lever Bros Ltd* (1932), Bell had been employed as chairman of the company by Lever Bros. When he became redundant, they paid off the remaining part of his service contract. Only then did they discover that Bell had been guilty of offences which would have permitted them to dismiss him without compensation. They claimed to have the payment set aside on the basis of the common mistake that neither party had considered the possibility of Bell's dismissal for breach of duty. It was held that the action must fail. The mistake was only as to quality and was not sufficiently fundamental to render the contract void. Similarly, in *Leaf v International Galleries* (above), the mistake was held to be one of quality; the court found that the contract was for the sale of a painting of Salisbury Cathedral (the value of which was mistaken), rather than a painting by Constable and as such could not render the contract void.

These cases suggest that a mistake as to quality can never render an agreement void for mistake, and that the doctrine of common mistake is restricted to the following two specific areas:

- *Res extincta*

    In this case, the mistake is as to the existence of the subject matter of the contract.

    In *Couturier v Hastie* (1856), a contract was made in London for the sale of some corn that was being shipped from Salonica. Unknown to the parties, however, the corn had already been sold. It was held that the London contract was void, since the subject matter of the contract was no longer in existence.

    It should be recognised, however, that in *Associated Japanese Bank v Credit du Nord* (1988), a contract was treated as void for common mistake on the basis of the non-existence of some gaming machines, although the agreement in point actually related to a contract of guarantee in relation to the non-existent machines. It might also be noted that there could be an argument, on the facts of *Leaf* (above), for saying that the mistake was not one of quality but as to the existence of the subject matter of the contract; that is, the contract was for the sale of a painting by Constable. Such a finding would mean that the common mistake rendered the contract void.

- *Res sua*

  In this case, the mistake is that one of the parties to the contract already owns what they are contracting to receive.

  In *Cooper v Phibbs* (1867), Cooper agreed to lease a fishery from Phibbs. It later transpired that he actually owned the fishery. The court decided that the lease had to be set aside at common law. In equity, however, Phibbs was given a *lien* over the fishery in respect of the money he had spent on improving it, permitting him to hold the property against payment.

  Though *Bell* and *Leaf* appear to restrict the circumstances in which a common mistake will render a contract void, it is interesting to note that not all judges are in agreement that mistakes as to quality cannot render a contract void. In *Bell*, Viscount Hailsham and Lord Warrington thought that a mistake as to quality could render the contract void; paying £50,000, when no payment need have been made to dismiss, rendered the contract fundamentally different from that intended. Similarly, in *Associated Japanese Bank v Credit du Nord* (above), Steyn J (*obiter*, at first instance) supported the view that a mistake as to quality might, in exceptional circumstances, render a contract void if it made the subject matter of the contract essentially and radically different from what the parties believed it to be.

  Cooper v Phibbs is an example of one possible way in which equity may intervene in regard to common mistake, namely, setting an agreement aside on particular terms. Alternatively, the agreement may even be set aside completely in equity.

  In *Magee v Pennine Insurance Co Ltd* (1969), a proposal form for car insurance had been improperly filled in by the plaintiff. When the car was subsequently written off, the insurance company offered Magee £375 as a compromise on his claim. After he had accepted this offer, the defendants discovered the error in the proposal form and sought to repudiate their agreement. It was held that, although it was not void at common law, the agreement could be set aside in equity.

7.2.2 Mutual mistake

This occurs where the parties are at cross-purposes. They have different views on the facts of the situation, but they do not realise it. However, an agreement will not necessarily be void simply because the parties to it are at cross-purposes. In order for mutual mistake to be operative, that is, to make the contract void, the terms of agreement must comply with an objective test. The court will try to decide which of the competing views of the situation a reasonable person would support, and the contract will be enforceable on such terms.

In *Smith v Hughes* (1871), the plaintiff offered to sell oats to the defendant, Hughes. Hughes wrongly believed that the oats were old, and, on discovering that they were new oats, he refused to complete the contract. It was held that the defendant's mistake as to the age of the oats did not make the contract void.

In *Scriven Bros v Hindley and Co* (1913), the defendants bid at an auction for two lots, believing both to be hemp. In fact, one of them was tow, an inferior and cheaper substance. Although the auctioneer had not induced the mistake, it was not normal practice to sell hemp and tow together. It was decided that, in such circumstances – where one party thought that he was buying hemp and the other thought that he was selling tow – the contract was not enforceable.

If the court is unable to decide the outcome on the basis of an objective 'reasonable person' test, then the contract will be void, as was illustrated in *Raffles v Wichelhaus* (1864), where the defendants agreed to buy cotton from the plaintiffs. The cotton was to arrive *ex Peerless* from Bombay. There were, however, two ships called *Peerless* sailing from Bombay; the first in October, the second in December. Wichelhaus thought that he was buying from the first, but Raffles thought that he was selling from the second. Under the exceptional circumstances, it was impossible for the court to decide which party's view was the correct one. It was decided, therefore, that the agreement was void for mutual mistake.

In respect of mutual mistake, equity follows the common law.

In *Tamplin v James* (1879), James purchased a public house at auction. He had wrongly believed that the property for sale included a field which the previous publican had used. The sale particulars stated the property for sale correctly, but James did not refer to them. When he discovered his mistake, James refused to complete the transaction. It was held that, in spite of his mistake, an order of specific performance would be granted against James. Objectively, the reasonable man would assume that the sale was made on the basis of the particulars (see also *Centrovincial Estates plc v Merchant Assurance Co Ltd* (1983) and *Great Peace Shipping Ltd v Tsavliros Salvage Ltd* (2001)).

The role of equity was considered in *Clarion Ltd v National Provident Institution* (2000), where one party's mistake as to the effect of the terms of a contract did not allow the contract to be rescinded. It was held that equity did not provide a remedy simply because of a bad bargain; mistake would only operate in equity where it related to the subject matter of the contract, the terms of the contract or the identity of the contracting party. The decision has been the subject of criticism as its effect is to narrow equitable relief to the same circumstances as common law.

7.2.3 Unilateral mistake

This occurs where only one of the parties to the agreement is mistaken as to the circumstances of the contract, and the other party is aware of that fact.

Most cases of unilateral mistake also involve misrepresentation (see 7.3), although this need not necessarily be so. It is important to distinguish between these two elements: whereas unilateral mistake makes a contract void and thus prevents the passing of title in any property acquired under it, misrepresentation merely makes a contract voidable and good title can be passed before the contract is avoided. This distinction will be seen in *Ingram v Little* (1960) and *Phillips v Brooks* (1919). A further important distinction relates to remedies available; damages are not available for mistake, but where there has been a misrepresentation, damages may be awarded.

The cases involving unilateral mistake relate mainly to mistakes as to identity. A contract will only be void for mistake where the seller intended to contract with a different person from the one with whom he did actually contract.

In *Cundy v Lindsay* (1878), a crook named Blenkarn ordered linen handkerchiefs from Lindsay & Co, a Belfast linen manufacturer. His order, from 37 Wood Street, was signed to look as if it were from Blenkiron & Co, a reputable firm which was known to Lindsay and which carried on business at 123 Wood Street. The goods were sent to Blenkarn, who sold them to Cundy. Lindsay successfully sued Cundy in the tort of conversion. It was held that Lindsay had intended only to deal with Blenkiron & Co, so the contract was void. Since there was no contract with Blenkarn, he received no title whatsoever to the goods and, therefore, could not pass title on to Cundy. The case is generally taken to indicate that, if you do not deal face to face, the identity of the other party is fundamental. This was recently confirmed in *Shogun Finance Ltd v Hudson* (2001), despite the fact that the decision defeated the objective of s 27 of the Hire Purchase Act 1964 to protect the innocent third party purchaser of a hire purchase motor vehicle. In that case, a con man obtained a car on hire purchase, using the identity of a Mr Patel, via a stolen driving licence. His contract was with the finance company, not the garage with whom he negotiated, so he did not deal face to face. The con man sold the car to Hudson and disappeared without paying the hire purchase instalments. The finance company sought damages in the tort of conversion from Hudson, on the basis that he had no title to the car. It should be noted that, where goods are acquired on hire purchase, ownership does not pass until all instalments are paid, so that the con man had no title to pass to Hudson. However, s 27 gives title to the innocent third party purchaser of a motor vehicle from a 'debtor' who acquired it on hire purchase. Nevertheless, the Court of Appeal held that, as the contract was not made face to face, the contracting party's identity was crucial, so the hire purchase contract was void for mistake. As it was void, there was no 'debtor' within the meaning of s 27; Hudson was not protected and was liable in conversion.

Although *Kings Norton Metal Co v Eldridge, Merrit and Co* (1897) appears to be similar to *Cundy*, it was decided differently, on the ground that the crook had made use of a completely fictitious company to carry out his fraud. The mistake, therefore, was with regard to the attributes of the company, rather than its identity.

Where the parties enter into a contract face to face, it is generally presumed that the seller intends to deal with the person before him; therefore, he cannot rely on unilateral mistake to avoid the contract; his concern is with the attributes (usually creditworthiness) of the other party rather than his identity. A shopkeeper will sell to you, no matter who you pretend to be, provided you pay.

In *Phillips v Brooks* (1919), a crook selected a number of items in the plaintiff's jewellery shop, and proposed to pay by cheque. On being informed that the goods would have to be retained until the cheque was cleared, he told the jeweller that he was Sir George Bullough of St James's Square. On checking in a directory that such a person did indeed live at that address, the jeweller permitted him to take away a valuable ring. The crook later pawned the ring to the defendant. Phillips then sued the defendant in conversion. It was decided that the contract between Phillips and the crook was not void for mistake. There had not been a mistake as to identity, but only as to the creditworthiness (that is, attributes) of the buyer. The contract had been voidable for misrepresentation, but the crook had passed title before Phillips took steps to avoid the contract.

A similar decision was reached by the Court of Appeal in *Lewis v Avery* (1971), in which a crook obtained possession of a car by misrepresenting his identity to the seller. The court declined to follow its earlier decision in *Ingram v Little* (1960), a very similar case. It is generally accepted that *Lewis v Avery* represents the more accurate statement of the law.

7.2.4 Mistake in respect of documents

There are two mechanisms for dealing with mistakes in written contracts:

* Rectification

  Where the written document fails to state the actual intentions of the parties, it may be altered under the equitable doctrine of rectification.

  In *Joscelyne v Nissen* (1970), the plaintiff agreed to transfer his car hire business to his daughter, in return for her agreeing to pay certain household expenses, although this was not stated in a later written contract. The father was entitled to have the agreement rectified to include the terms agreed.

- *Non est factum*

  Where a party signs a contract, they will usually be bound by its terms. It is assumed that the signatory has read, understood and agreed to the terms as stated, and the courts are generally reluctant to interfere in such circumstances.

  Where, however, someone signs a document under a misapprehension as to its true nature, the law may permit them to claim *non est factum*, that is, that the document is not their deed. Originally, the mistake relied on had to relate to the type of document signed, but it is now recognised that the defence is open to those who have made a fundamental mistake as to the content of the document they have signed. However, the person signing the document must not have been careless with regard to its content.

  In *Saunders v Anglia Building Society* (1970), Mrs Gallie, a 78 year old widow, signed a document without reading it, as her glasses were broken. She had been told, by a person named Lee, that it was a deed of gift to her nephew, but it was in fact a deed of gift to Lee. Lee later mortgaged the property to the respondent building society. Mrs Gallie sought to repudiate the deed of gift on the basis of *non est factum*. Her action failed; she was careless in not waiting until her glasses were mended. Furthermore, the document was not fundamentally different from the one she had expected to sign. She thought that she signed a document transferring ownership and that *was* the effect of the document. The conditions laid down in *Saunders* for *non est factum* to apply were confirmed in *Avon Finance Co Ltd v Bridger* (1985).

  This decision can be contrasted with a later successful reliance on the defence in *Lloyds Bank plc v Waterhouse* (1990), where the defendant, who was illiterate, intended to provide a guarantee in relation to his son's purchase of a farm. In actual fact, the document he signed was a guarantee in relation to all of his son's liabilities. In the Court of Appeal, it was decided that the father could rely on *non est factum*. He had not been careless – he had questioned the extent of his liability – and the document was fundamentally different from that which he had expected to sign.

7.3 MISREPRESENTATION

As was seen in Chapter 6, a statement which induces a person to enter into a contract, but which does not become a term of the contract, is a representation. A false statement of this kind is a misrepresentation and renders the contract voidable. The innocent party may rescind the contract or, in some circumstances, claim damages (see below, 7.3.4).

Misrepresentation can be defined as 'a false statement of fact, made by one party before or at the time of the contract, which induces the other party to enter into the contract'. The following points follow from this definition.

7.3.1 There must be a false statement of fact

- False

In most cases, it can be proved whether a statement is false, but the following situations need consideration:

- o Where the statement is a half-truth, it may be true, but misleading because of facts not given; it will be treated as false.

  In *Dimmock v Hallett* (1866), when selling property, it was truthfully stated that a farm was rented to a tenant for £290 per annum. The failure to indicate that the tenant was in arrears, had left the farm and a new tenant could not be found rendered the statement false.

- o Where the statement was true when made, but has subsequently become false before the contract is concluded, the change must be notified to avoid misrepresentation.

In *With v O'Flanagan* (1936), in January, the seller of a doctors' practice told the prospective buyer that it was worth an income of £2,000 per annum. By the time that the contract was concluded, its value had dropped substantially, to only £5 per week. The court held that the representation was of a continuing nature and, as it was false when it induced the contract, the buyer was entitled to rescind. The obligation to disclose changes relating to a representation of a continuing nature was affirmed by the Court of Appeal in *Spice Girls Ltd v Aprilia World Service BV* (2002).

- A statement

  There must be a written or oral statement. There is no general duty to disclose information, except in insurance contracts; silence does not generally amount to misrepresentation. In *Turner v Green* (1895), when negotiating a dispute settlement between T and G, T's solicitor failed to mention other legal proceedings he knew of which made the settlement G agreed to a 'bad deal' – one he would not have made had he known. G was bound by the settlement; he was not induced by a misrepresentation, as silence is not misrepresentation. However, it should be noted that there have been cases where courts have found that there is a misrepresentation by conduct; for example, *Gordon v Selico* (1986) and, at first instance, *Spice Girls Ltd v Aprilia World Service BV* (2002).

- A fact

  The following statements will not amount to representations because they are not facts:

○ Mere sales puffs – the statement must have some meaningful content. Thus, in *Dimmock v Hallett* (1866), it was held that a statement that land was fertile and improvable was not actionable as a misrepresentation.

○ Statements of law – everyone is presumed to know the law and, therefore, in theory, no one can be misled as to what the law is.

○ Statements of opinion – these are not actionable, because they are not statements of fact. In *Bisset v Wilkinson* (1927), the vendor of previously ungrazed land in New Zealand stated that it would be able to support 2,000 sheep. This turned out to be untrue, but it was held that the statement was only an expression of opinion and, as such, was not actionable; the purchaser knew that the vendor had no expertise. However, in *Smith v Land & House Property Corp* (1884), a statement that the tenant of a hotel was a 'desirable tenant' was a misrepresentation. Though descriptions like 'desirable' may seem to be subjective opinions, here there was expert knowledge that the tenant did not pay on time and was currently in arrears. That being so, the statement implied that there were facts on which it was based when there were not.

○ A statement of intention – this does not give rise to a misrepresentation even if the intention subsequently changes, unless it can be shown that there was no such intention at the time it was stated (see *Edgington v Fitzmaurice* (1884)).

7.3.2 The statement must actually induce the contract

That the statement must actually induce the contract means that:

• the statement must have been made by one party to the contract to the other, and not by a third party;

• the statement must have been addressed to the person claiming to have been misled;

• the person claiming to have been misled must have been aware of the statement;

• the person claiming to have been misled must have relied on the statement.

In *Horsfall v Thomas* (1962), Horsfall made and sold a gun to Thomas. He concealed a fault in it by means of a metal plug, and Thomas did not examine the gun. After short usage, the gun blew apart. Thomas claimed that he had been misled, by the presence of the plug, into buying the gun. It was held that the plug could not have misled him, as he had not examined the gun at the time of purchase. In *Attwood v Small* (1838), a false statement as to the profitability of a mine was not a misrepresentation as the purchaser did not rely on it; he commissioned an independent survey of the mine. On the other hand, in *Redgrave v Hurd* (1881), where the purchaser of a business declined to examine the accounts which would have revealed the falsity of a statement as to the business's profitability, there was no misrepresentation. Because he declined to examine the accounts, he clearly relied on what was said to him about profitability; he was not under a duty to check the truth of the statement.

Whether the reliance was reasonable or not is not material once the party claiming misrepresentation shows that they did, in fact, rely on the statement. See *Museprime Properties Ltd v Adhill Properties Ltd* (1990), in which an inaccurate statement contained in auction particulars, and repeated by the auctioneer, was held to constitute a misrepresentation, in spite of the claims that it should have been unreasonable for anyone to allow themselves to be influenced by the statement. However, it should be noted that, in *Barton v County Natwest Bank* (1999), the court indicated that an objective test would be applied to determine reliance. If, objectively, there was reliance, this was a presumption which was rebuttable.

7.3.3 Types of misrepresentation

Misrepresentation can be divided into three types, each of which involves distinct procedures and provides different remedies.

Fraudulent misrepresentation

In the case of fraudulent misrepresentation, the statement is made knowing it to be false, or believing it to be false, or recklessly careless as to whether it is true or false. The difficulty with this type of misrepresentation is proving the necessary mental element; it is notoriously difficult to show the required *mens rea*, or guilty mind, to demonstrate fraud.

In *Derry v Peek* (1889), the directors of a company issued a prospectus, inviting the public to subscribe for shares. The prospectus stated that the company had the power to run trams by steam power, but, in fact, it only had power to operate horsedrawn trams; it required the permission of the Board of Trade to run steam trams. The directors assumed that permission would be granted, but it was refused. When the company was wound up, the directors were sued for fraud. It was held that there was no fraud, since the directors had honestly believed the statement in the prospectus. They may have been negligent, but they were not fraudulent.

Negligent misrepresentation

With negligent misrepresentation, the false statement is made in the belief that it is true, but without reasonable grounds for that belief. (It follows that the directors in *Derry v Peek* (1889) would now be liable for negligent misrepresentation.) There are two categories of negligent misrepresentation:

- At common law

  Prior to 1963, the law did not recognise a concept of negligent misrepresentation. The possibility of liability in negligence for misstatements arose from *Hedley Byrne & Co v Heller and Partners* (1964). In that case, however, the parties were not in a contractual or a pre-contractual relationship, so there could not have been an action for misrepresentation. But, in *Esso Petroleum v Mardon* (1976), Mardon succeeded in an action for negligent misstatement, on the basis that he had been wrongly advised as to the amount of petrol he could expect to sell from a garage.

- Under the Misrepresentation Act (MA) 1967

  Although it might still be necessary, or beneficial, to sue at common law, it is more likely that such actions would now be taken under the statute. The reason for this is that s 2(1) of the MA 1967 reverses the normal burden of proof. In an action in negligence, the burden of proof is on the party raising the action to show that the other party acted in a negligent manner. However, where a misrepresentation has been made, then, under s 2(1) of the MA 1967, it is up to the party who made the statement to show that they had reasonable grounds for believing it to be true. In practice, a person making a statement in the course of his trade or profession might have difficulty providing such proof.

Innocent misrepresentation

Innocent misrepresentation occurs where the false statement is made by a person who not only believes it to be true, but also has reasonable grounds for that belief.

7.3.4 Remedies for misrepresentation

For fraudulent misrepresentation, the remedies are rescission and/or damages for any loss sustained. Rescission is an equitable remedy which is designed to return the parties to their original position. The action for damages is in the tort of deceit. In *Doyle v Olby (Ironmongers) Ltd* (1969), it was decided that, where a contract was induced by a fraudulent misrepresentation, the measure of damages was not merely what was foreseeable, but all damage which directly resulted as a consequence of the aggrieved party having entered into the contract. An example of this principle can be seen in *Smith and New Court Securities Ltd v Scrimgeour Vickers (Asset Management) Ltd* (1996), in which the plaintiffs were induced to buy 28 million shares in Ferranti plc on the basis of a fraudulently made claim about the shares. They had been told falsely that two other companies had already bid for the package of shares, and this led them to offer and pay 82.25 p per share, amounting to a total of £23,141,424. Without the false representation, they would not have offered more than 78 p per share and, as the defendants would not have sold at that price, Smith New Court would not have acquired any shares in Ferranti. When it transpired that Ferranti had been subject to a completely unrelated fraud, its share price fell considerably and, although the plaintiffs managed to sell their shareholding at prices ranging from 30 to 44 p, they suffered an overall loss of £11,353,220. The question to be decided was as to the amount that the defendants owed in damages. Was it the difference between the market value of the shares and the price actually paid at the time, a matter of 4.25 p per share, or was it the full loss, which was considerably larger? The House of Lords decided that the latter amount was due. The total loss was the direct result of the share purchase, which had been induced by the fraudulent statement; the defendants were, therefore, liable for that amount and the foreseeability test in relation to negligence, as stated in *The Wagon Mound (No 1)* (1961), did not apply (see below, Chapter 10, for a detailed consideration of this test).

For negligent misrepresentation, the remedies are rescission and/or damages. The action for damages may be in the tort of negligence at common law or under s 2(1) of the MA 1967. Under the statute, the measure of damages will still be determined as in a tort action (see *Royscot Trust Ltd v Rogerson* (1991), where the Court of Appeal confirmed this approach).

For innocent misrepresentation, the common law remedy is rescission. Under the MA 1967, however, the court may award damages instead of rescission, where it is considered equitable to do so (s 2(2)).

With regard to s 2(2) of the MA 1967, it was once thought that the court could only award damages, instead of rescission, where the remedy of rescission was itself available. The implication of that view was that, if the right to rescission was lost for some reason, such as the fact that the parties could not be restored to their original positions, then the right to damages under s 2(2) was also lost (*Atlantic Lines and Navigation Co Inc v Hallam* (1992)). However, in *Thomas Witter v TBP Industries* (1996) (see below), Jacob J examined and rejected that suggestion. In his opinion, the right to damages under s 2(2) depended not upon the right to rescission still being available, but upon the fact that the plaintiff had had such a right in the past. Thus, even if the right to rescission was ultimately lost, the plaintiff could still be awarded damages. This was confirmed in *Zanzibar v British Aerospace Ltd* (2000).

The right to rescind can be lost for any one of the following reasons:

- by affirmation, where the innocent party, with full knowledge of the misrepresentation, either expressly states that they intend to go on with the agreement or does some action from which it can be implied that they intend to go on with the agreement. Affirmation may be implied from lapse of time (see *Leaf v International Galleries* (1950));
- where the parties cannot be restored to their original positions;
- where third parties have acquired rights in the subject matter of the contract (see *Phillips v Brooks* (1919)).

Section 3 of the MA 1967 provides that any exclusion of liability for misrepresentation must comply with the requirement of reasonableness, a matter that was also considered in *Thomas Witter v TBP Industries* (1996). The facts of the *Witter* case involved the sale of a carpet manufacturing business. In the course of pre-contractual negotiation, the seller misrepresented the profitability of the business and, hence, the purchaser paid more than its real value for it. However, the eventual contract document contained the following purported exclusion clause:

> This Agreement sets forth the entire agreement and understanding between the parties or any of them in connection with the business and the sale and purchase described herein. In particular, but without prejudice to the generality of the foregoing, the purchaser acknowledges that it has not been induced to enter into this agreement by any representation warranty other than the statements contained in or referred to in schedule 6 [of the contract document].

In analysing the legal effect of the above clause, Jacob J held that, on its own wording, it could not provide any exemption in relation to any pre-contractual misrepresentations that had been included as express warranties within the document. Moreover, he held that the clause was ineffective, even as regards those pre-contractual misrepresentations which had not been included expressly in the contract. His first ground for striking down the clause, and in spite of its apparently perfectly clear wording, was that it was not sufficiently clear to remove the purchaser's right to rely on the misrepresentation. Secondly, and as an alternative, he held that the clause did not meet with the requirement of reasonableness under s 3 of the MA 1967. The scope of the clause was held to be far too wide, in that it purported to cover 'any liability' for 'any misrepresentation'. In Jacob J's view, it could never be possible to exclude liability for fraudulent misrepresentation and, although it might be possible to exclude liability for negligent and innocent misrepresentation, any such exclusion had to pass the reasonableness test, which the clause in question had failed to do.

Figure 2, below, shows both how statements may be classified and the consequence of such classification. It should be remembered that, in some instances, a pre-contract statement may be treated as a term of the contract, rather than a misrepresentation, so that remedies for breach of contract may be claimed (see 6.1).

Figure 2: Forms of misrepresentation

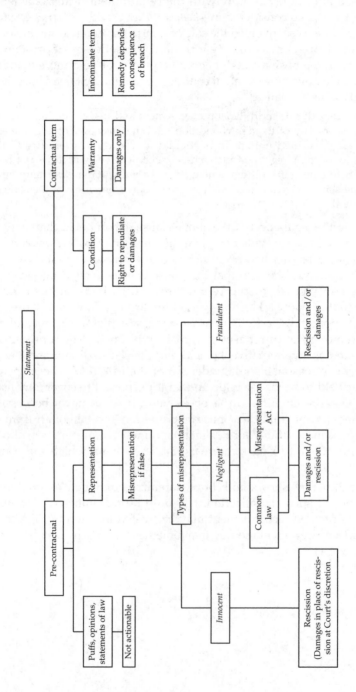

7.4 DURESS

Duress is some element of force, either physical or economic, which is used to override one party's freedom to choose whether or not to enter into a particular contract. Under such circumstances, the contract is voidable at the instance of the innocent party.

Its application used to be restricted to contracts entered into as a consequence of actual physical violence or the threat of such violence to a person.

In *Barton v Armstrong* (1975), the defendant threatened Barton with death if he did not arrange for his company to buy Armstrong's shares in it. Barton sought to have the agreement set aside. It was found that the threats had been made, but that, in addition, Barton thought that the transaction was a favourable one. Barton nonetheless succeeded. The court held that the proper inference was that duress was present, and the burden of proof was on Armstrong to show that the threats had played no part in Barton's decision. He had failed to discharge this burden.

Originally, it was held that threats to a person's goods could not amount to duress, but a doctrine of economic duress has now been developed by the courts. The germ of the doctrine, that an abuse of economic power can render a contract invalid, can be found in Lord Denning's decision in *D & C Builders Ltd v Rees* (1966) and was developed in later cases such as *The Siboen and The Sibotre* (1976) and *The Atlantic Baron* (1979).

In the latter case, fully cited as *North Ocean Shipping Company v Hyundai Construction* (1979), a contract had been entered into for the building of a ship. The builders then stated that they would not complete construction unless the purchasers paid an extra 10%. Without the ship, the buyers would have lost a lucrative contract with a third party, with whom they had already agreed to charter the ship. The buyers paid the extra money and then, at a later date, sued to recover it on the basis of, *inter alia*, economic duress. It was held that the threat to terminate the contract did constitute economic duress, which rendered the contract voidable. In the event, the buyers' delay in bringing the action acted as an affirmation of the agreement and they lost their right to rescission.

There is a difficulty in distinguishing ordinary commercial pressure from economic duress (see *Pao On v Lau Yiu Long* (1979)), but the existence of economic duress as a distinct principle of contract law finally received the approval of the House of Lords in *Universe Tankships Inc v ITWF* (1982), the *Universe Sentinel* case. The facts of the case concerned the blacking of the plaintiffs' ship by the defendant trade union, which meant that it could not leave the port. As part of negotiations to lift the blacking, the plaintiffs paid money into the union's benevolent fund. They subsequently and successfully reclaimed the money from the union, on the basis that it had been induced through economic duress.

In order to benefit from the doctrine of duress, plaintiffs must show the following two things:

- that pressure, which resulted in an absence of choice on their part, was brought to bear on them; and
- that that pressure was of a nature considered to be illegitimate by the courts.

Only under such circumstances will the court permit rescission of an agreement, as can be seen in *Atlas Express v Kafco* (1990). The defendant company had secured a highly profitable contract with Woolworths, the large retail outlet, and employed the plaintiffs as their carriers. After beginning to perform the contract, Atlas sought to increase their price. Although they protested, Kafco felt that they had no option but to agree to the demand, rather than break their contract with Woolworths, which would have proved economically disastrous for them. When Atlas sued to recover the increased charges, they failed, as it was held that the attempt to increase the charge was a clear case of economic duress. (This should be compared with the situation and outcome of *Williams v Roffey Bros* (1990); see above, 5.5.4.)

7.5 UNDUE INFLUENCE

Transactions, either under contract or as gifts, may be avoided where they have been entered into as a consequence of the undue influence of the person benefiting from them. The effect of undue influence is to make a contract voidable, but delay may bar the right to avoid the agreement. There are two possible situations relating to undue influence.

7.5.1 Special relationships

Where there is a special relationship between the parties, there is a presumption that the transaction is the consequence of undue influence. The burden of proof is on the person receiving the benefit to rebut the presumption.

In *Re Craig* (1971), after the death of his wife, Mr Craig, then aged 84, employed a Mrs Middleton as his secretary-companion. In the course of the six years for which she was employed, he gave her money to the extent of some £30,000. An action was taken to have the gifts set aside. The action succeeded, as it was held that the circumstances raised the presumption of undue influence, which Mrs Middleton had failed to rebut.

Examples of special relationships are:

- parent and child, while the latter is still a minor;
- guardian and ward;
- religious adviser and follower;

- doctor and patient;
- solicitor and client.

The list is not a closed one, however, and other relationships may be included within the scope of the special relationship (as in *Re Craig* (1971)).

Where a special relationship exists, then an important way in which the presumption of undue influence can be rebutted is to show that independent advice was taken by the other party, although all that is necessary is to show that the other party exercised their will freely.

Even where a special relationship exists, a transaction will not be set aside unless it is shown to be manifestly disadvantageous.

In *National Westminster Bank v Morgan* (1985), when a couple fell into financial difficulties, the plaintiff bank made financial arrangements which permitted them to remain in their house. The re-financing transaction secured against the house was arranged by a bank manager who had called at their home. Mrs Morgan had no independent legal advice. When the husband died, the bank obtained a possession order against the house in respect of outstanding debts. Mrs Morgan sought to have the refinancing arrangement set aside, on the ground of undue influence. The action failed, on the ground that the doctrine of undue influence had no place in agreements which did not involve any manifest disadvantage, and Mrs Morgan had actually benefited from the transaction by being able to remain in her home for a longer period. It might be noted, however, that recent cases are beginning to question whether this requirement of 'manifest disadvantage' is necessary before a contract can be avoided; for example, *Barclays Bank plc v Coleman* (2001).

The key element in deciding whether a relationship was a special one or not was whether one party was in a position of dominance over the other. *National Westminster Bank v Morgan* also decided that a normal relationship between a bank manager and his client is not a special relationship; but there may be circumstances where that relationship may be treated as 'special' (see *Lloyds Bank Ltd v Bundy* (1975)).

7.5.2 No special relationship

Where no special relationship exists between the parties, the burden of proof is on the party claiming the protection of the undue influence doctrine. It is of interest to note that relationships which are not included as special relationships include the relationships of husband and wife and bank and customer; yet these are precisely the relationships that are likely to generate the most problems.

The rule relating to manifest disadvantage, considered above in relation to special relationships, does not apply in the case where no such special relationship applies.

In *CIBC Mortgages plc v Pitt* (1993), Mrs Pitt sought to set aside a mortgage which she had signed against her home in favour of the plaintiffs, on the basis that her husband had exerted undue influence over her. Whereas the Court of Appeal had rejected her plea on the ground that the agreement was not to her manifest disadvantage, the House of Lords declared that such a principle did not apply in cases where undue influence was actual, rather than presumed. They did, however, recognise the validity of the mortgage, on the ground that the creditor had no knowledge, either actual or constructive, of the exercise of undue influence in relation to the transaction.

It is of interest to note in relation to this last case that the House of Lords in *Barclays Bank plc v O'Brien* (1993) referred to an implied duty on creditors in particular circumstances, which certainly included a marital relationship, to ensure that parties had not entered into agreements on the basis of misrepresentation or undue influence. In that particular case, the bank was held to have constructive notice of the undue influence wielded by the husband; that is, they *should* have known, whether they actually did or not. For that reason, the bank was not permitted to enforce the agreement entered into on the basis of that undue influence.

The situation relating to undue influence was most recently considered in *Dunbar Bank plc v Nadeem* (1998), in which it was clearly restated that, in order to rely on the presumption of undue influence, manifest disadvantage must be shown in addition to a relationship of trust and confidence. In the case in point, the wife's claim had to fail, as there was no such disadvantage and she had failed to show actual undue influence, which could be attached to the bank on the basis of the *O'Brien* case.

7.5.3 Inequality of bargaining power

It has been suggested that undue influence and duress are simply examples of a wider principle which is based on inequality of bargaining power. The existence of such a principle was suggested in a number of decisions involving Lord Denning. It was intended to provide protection for those who suffered as a consequence of being forced into particular agreements due to their lack of bargaining power. This doctrine, however, was considered and firmly rejected by the House of Lords in *National Westminster Bank v Morgan* (1985). It could be suggested that the very idea of inequality of bargaining power is incompatible with the reality of today's economic structure, which is dominated by large scale, if not monopolistic, organisations. It should be recognised, however, that, as considered in Chapter 6, the idea of inequality of bargaining power has found a place in determining how the Unfair Contract Terms Act 1977 is to operate.

7.6 CONTRACTS AND PUBLIC POLICY

It is evident that some agreements will tend to be contrary to public policy. The fact that some are considered to be more serious than others is reflected in the distinction drawn between those which are said to be illegal and those which are simply void.

7.6.1 Illegal contracts

A contract which breaks the law is illegal. The general rule is that no action can be brought by a party to an illegal contract, though in some circumstances, money or property transferred may be recovered. The contract may be either expressly prohibited by statute or implicitly prohibited by the common law. The following is a list of illegal contracts:

- contracts prohibited by statute;
- contracts to defraud the Inland Revenue;
- contracts involving the commission of a crime or a tort;
- contracts with a sexually immoral element, although contemporary attitudes may have changed in this respect (see *Armhouse Lee Ltd v Chappell* (1996));
- contracts against the interest of the UK or a friendly State;
- contracts leading to corruption in public life;
- contracts which interfere with the course of justice.

7.6.2 Void contracts

A void contract does not give rise to any rights or obligations. The contract is only void insofar as it is contrary to public policy; thus, the whole agreement may not be void. Severance is the procedure whereby the void part of a contract is excised, permitting the remainder to be enforced. Contracts may be void under statute or at common law.

Wagering contracts

A wagering contract is an agreement that, upon the happening of some uncertain event, one party shall give something of value to the other, the party who has to pay being dependent on the outcome of the event. Such contracts are governed by the Gaming Acts.

Anti-competitive practices

Certain agreements relating to matters such as price fixing and minimum resale prices may be void and unenforceable under the Competition Act 1998.

Contracts void at common law

- Contracts to oust the jurisdiction of the court

  Any contractual agreement which seeks to deny the parties the right to submit questions of law to the courts are void as being contrary to public policy. Agreements which provide for compulsory arbitration can be enforceable.

- Contracts prejudicial to the status of marriage

  It is considered a matter of public policy that the institution of marriage be maintained. Hence, any contract which seeks to restrain a person's freedom to marry, or undermines the institution of marriage in any way, will be considered void.

7.6.3   Contracts in restraint of trade

One area of particular importance which is subject to the control of the common law are contracts in restraint of trade. A contract in restraint of trade is an agreement whereby one party restricts their future freedom to engage in their trade, business or profession. The general rule is that such agreements are *prima facie* void, but they may be valid if it can be shown that they meet the following requirements:

- the person who imposes the restrictions has a legitimate interest to protect;
- the restriction is reasonable as between the parties;
- the restriction is not contrary to the public interest.

The doctrine of restraint of trade is flexible in its application and may be applied to new situations when they arise. Bearing this in mind, however, it is usual to classify the branches of the doctrine as follows.

Restraints on employees

Employers cannot protect themselves against competition from an ex-employee, except where they have a legitimate interest to protect. The only legitimate interests recognised by the law are trade secrets and trade connection.

Even in protecting those interests, the restraint must be of a reasonable nature. What constitutes reasonable in this context depends on the circumstances of the case.

In *Lamson Pneumatic Tube Co v Phillips* (1904), the plaintiffs manufactured specialised equipment for use in shops. The defendant's contract of employment stated that, on ceasing to work for the plaintiffs, he would not engage in a similar business for a period of five years, anywhere in the Eastern hemisphere. It was held that such a restriction was reasonable, bearing in mind the nature of the plaintiffs' business.

This has to be compared with *Empire Meat Co Ltd v Patrick* (1939), where Patrick had been employed as manager of the company's butchers business in Mill Road, Cambridge. The company sought to enforce the defendant's promise that he would not establish a rival business within five miles of their shop. In this situation, it was held that the restraint was too wide and could not be enforced.

The longer the period of time or the wider the geographical area covered by the restraint, the more likely it is to be struck down, but, in *Fitch v Dewes* (1921), it was held that a lifelong restriction placed on a solicitor was valid.

Restraints on vendors of business

The interest to be protected in this category is the goodwill of the business, that is, its profitability. Restrictions may legitimately be placed on previous owners to prevent them from competing in the future with new owners. Again, the restraint should not be greater than is necessary to protect that interest.

In *British Reinforced Concrete Engineering Co Ltd v Schleff* (1921), the plaintiffs sought to enforce a promise given by the defendant, on the sale of his business to them, that he would not compete with them in the manufacturing of road reinforcements. It was held that, given the small size and restricted nature of the business sold, the restraint was too wide to be enforceable.

However, in *Nordenfelt v Maxim Nordenfelt Guns and Ammunition Co* (1894), a worldwide restraint on competition was held to be enforceable, given the nature of the business sold.

Restraints on distributors/solus agreements

This category of restraint of trade is usually concerned with solus agreements between petrol companies and garage proprietors, by which a petrol company seeks to prevent the retailer from selling its competitors' petrol. It is recognised that petrol companies have a legitimate interest to protect, and the outcome depends on whether the restraint obtained in protection of that interest is reasonable.

In *Esso Petroleum v Harpers Garage* (1968), the parties had entered into an agreement whereby Harper undertook to buy all of the petrol to be sold from his two garages from Esso. In return, Esso lent him £7,000, secured by way of a mortgage over one of the garages. The monopoly right in respect of the garages was to last for four and a half years over one and 21 years over the other. When Harper broke his undertaking, Esso sued to enforce it. It was held that the agreements in respect of both garages were in restraint of trade. But, whereas the agreement which lasted for four and a half years was reasonable, the one which lasted for 21 years was unreasonable and void.

Until fairly recently, it was thought that *Esso v Harpers* had set down a rule that any solus agreement involving a restriction which was to last longer than five years would be void as being in restraint of trade. In *Alec Lobb (Garages) Ltd v Total Oil Ltd* (1985), however, the Court of Appeal made it clear that the outcome of each case depended on its own particular circumstances; and, in that case, it approved a solus agreement extending over a period of 21 years.

Exclusive service contracts

This category relates to contracts which are specifically structured to exploit one of the parties by controlling and limiting their output, rather than assisting them. The most famous cases involve musicians.

In *Schroeder Music Publishing Co v Macauley* (1974), an unknown songwriter, Macauley, entered into a five year agreement with Schroeder. Under it, he had to assign any music he wrote to them, but they were under no obligation to publish it. The agreement provided for automatic extension of the agreement if it yielded £5,000 in royalties, but the publishers could terminate it at any time with one month's notice. It was decided that the agreement was so one-sided as to amount to an unreasonable restraint of trade and, hence, was void.

Since the above case, numerous artists have made use of this ground for avoiding their contracts.

SUMMARY OF CHAPTER 7

VITIATING FACTORS

Mistake

- Operative (fundamental) mistake renders a contract void *ab initio*.
- Equitable remedies may be available where mistakes are not fundamental.
- Operative common mistake usually involves *res sua* or *res extincta*.
- An objective test is applied to determine whether a mutual mistake is operative.
- Generally, unilateral mistake is not operative where the parties deal face to face.
- Where the mistake relates to a written contract, rectification or *non est factum* may be claimed.

Misrepresentation

- Misrepresentation can be defined as 'a false statement of fact, made by one party before or at the time of the contract, which induces the other party to contract'.
- Some statements will not amount to representations, for example, statements of opinion and law.
- Some pre-contract statements may be treated as terms of the contract. This gives rise to an alternative cause of action for breach of contract, which should be noted for examination purposes.
- Rescission and damages in the tort of deceit are available for *fraudulent misrepresentation*.
- Rescission and/or damages under s 2(1) of the Misrepresentation Act (MA) 1967 are available for *negligent misrepresentation*.
- Rescission or damages under s 2(2) of the MA 1967 are available for *innocent misrepresentation*.

Duress

- A contract entered into in consequence of duress is voidable.
- Economic duress may render a contract voidable if there was illegitimate pressure, negating consent to the contract.

Undue influence

- Subject to delay, undue influence renders a contract voidable.
- Where there is a special relationship between the contracting parties, a rebuttal presumption of undue influence arises.
- Where there is no special relationship between the contracting parties, the party claiming undue influence has the burden of proof.

Contracts and public policy

- A contract rendered illegal by statute or common law cannot be the subject of legal action.
- Contracts rendered void as contrary to public policy (for example, contracts in restraint of trade) do not give rise to legal rights or obligations.

CHAPTER 8

DISCHARGE OF A CONTRACT

8.1 INTRODUCTION

When a contract is discharged, the parties to the agreement are freed from their contractual obligations. A contract is discharged in one of four ways:

- agreement;
- performance;
- frustration;
- breach.

8.2 DISCHARGE BY AGREEMENT

Emphasis has been placed on the consensual nature of contract law, and it follows that what has been made by agreement can be ended by agreement. The contract itself may contain provision for its discharge by either the passage of a fixed period of time or the occurrence of a particular event. Alternatively, it may provide, either expressly or by implication, that one or other of the parties can bring it to an end, as in a contract of employment.

Where there is no such provision in a contract, another contract will be required to cancel it before all of the obligations have been met. There are two possible situations:

- where the contract is executory, the mutual exchange of promises to release one another from future performance will be sufficient consideration;
- where the contract is executed, that is, one party has performed, or partly performed, their obligations, the other party must provide consideration (that is, make a new contract) in order to be released from performing their part of the contract (unless the release is made under seal). The provision of this consideration discharges the original contract and there is said to be accord and satisfaction. This was found to have occurred in *Williams v Roffey Bros* (1990) (see 5.5.4).

8.3 DISCHARGE BY PERFORMANCE

This occurs where the parties to a contract perform their obligations under it. Performance is the normal way in which contracts are discharged. As a general rule, discharge requires complete and exact performance of the obligations in the contract.

In *Cutter v Powell* (1795), Cutter was employed as second mate on a ship that was sailing from Jamaica to Liverpool. The agreement was that he was to receive 30 guineas when the journey was completed. Before the ship reached Liverpool, Cutter died and his widow sued Powell, the ship's master, to recover a proportion of the wages due to her husband. It was held that the widow was entitled to nothing, as the contract required complete performance.

There are four exceptions to the general rule requiring complete performance:

- Where the contract is divisible

  In an ordinary contract of employment, where it is usual for payment to be made periodically, the harshness of the outcome of *Cutter v Powell* is avoided.

  In *Bolton v Mahadeva* (1972), the plaintiff had contracted to install central heating for the defendant for £560. It turned out to be defective and required a further £179 to put the defect right. It was held that Bolton could not claim any of the money, as he had failed to perform the contract. An agreement to supply a bathroom suite was divisible from the overall agreement, however, and had to be paid for.

- Where the contract is capable of being fulfilled by substantial performance

  This occurs where the essential element of an agreement has been performed but some minor part or fault remains to be done or remedied. The party who performed the act can claim the contract price, although they remain liable for any deduction for the work outstanding.

  In *Hoenig v Isaacs* (1952), Hoenig was employed by Isaacs to decorate his flat. The contract price was £750, to be paid as the work progressed. Isaacs paid a total of £400, but refused to pay the remainder, as he objected to the quality of the work carried out. Hoenig sued for the outstanding £350. It was held that Isaacs had to pay the outstanding money less the cost of putting right the defects in performance. These latter costs amounted to just under £56. A similar issue arose in *Williams v Roffey* (1990).

  This should be compared with *Bolton v Mahadeva* (1972), in which no payment was allowed for work done in a totally unsatisfactory manner.

- Where performance has been prevented by the other party

  Under such circumstances, as occurred in *Planche v Colburn* (1831), the party prevented from performance can sue either for breach of contract or on a *quantum meruit* basis (see below, 8.7.4).

- Where partial performance has been accepted by the other party

  This occurs in the following circumstances: A orders a case of 12 bottles of wine from B. B only has 10, and delivers those to A. A is at liberty to reject the 10 bottles if he or she wants to, but, once the goods are accepted, he or she must pay a proportionate price for them.

8.3.1 Tender of performance

'Tender of performance' simply means an offer to perform the contractual obligations. For example, if a buyer refuses to accept the goods offered (where there are no legal grounds to do so, for example where the goods are defective), but later sues for breach of contract, the seller can rely on the fact that they tendered performance as discharging their liability under the contract. The seller would also be entitled to claim for breach of contract.

In *Macdonald v Startup* (1843), Macdonald promised to deliver 10 tons of oil to the defendant within the last 14 days of March. He tried to deliver on Saturday 31 March at 8.30 pm, and Startup refused to accept the oil. It was held that the tender of performance was equivalent to actual performance, and Macdonald was entitled to claim damages for breach of contract.

Section 29(5) of the Sale of Goods Act 1979 now provides that tender is ineffectual unless made at a reasonable hour. It is unlikely that 8.30 pm on a Saturday evening would be considered reasonable.

8.4 DISCHARGE BY FRUSTRATION

Where it is impossible to perform an obligation from the outset, no contract can come into existence. Early cases held that subsequent impossibility was no excuse for non-performance. In the 19th century, however, the doctrine of frustration was developed to permit a party to a contract, in some circumstances, to be excused performance on the grounds of impossibility arising after formation of the contract.

A contract will be discharged by reason of frustration in the following circumstances:

- Where destruction of the subject matter of the contract has occurred

  In *Taylor v Caldwell* (1863), Caldwell had agreed to let a hall to the plaintiff for a number of concerts. Before the day of the first concert, the hall was destroyed by fire. Taylor sued for breach of contract. It was held that the destruction of the hall had made performance impossible and, therefore, the defendant was not liable under the contract.

- Where government interference, or supervening illegality, prevents performance

  The performance of the contract may be made illegal by a change in the law. The outbreak of war, making the other party an enemy alien, will have a similar effect.

In *Re Shipton, Anderson & Co* (1915), a contract was made for the sale of some wheat, which was stored in a warehouse in Liverpool. Before the seller could deliver, it was requisitioned by the Government under wartime emergency powers. It was held that the seller was excused from performance. Due to the requisition, it was no longer possible to lawfully deliver the wheat.

- Where a particular event, which is the sole reason for the contract, fails to take place

In *Krell v Henry* (1903), Krell let a room to the defendant for the purpose of viewing the Coronation procession of Edward VII. When the procession was cancelled, due to the King's ill health, Krell sued Henry for the due rent. It was held that the contract was discharged by frustration, since its purpose could no longer be achieved. This only applies where the cancelled event was the sole purpose of the contract.

In *Herne Bay Steamboat Co v Hutton* (1903), a naval review, which had been arranged as part of Edward VII's coronation celebrations, also had to be cancelled due to illness. Hutton had contracted to hire a boat from the plaintiffs for the purpose of seeing the review. It was held that Hutton was liable for breach of contract. The sole foundation of the contract was not lost, as the ship could still have been used to view the assembled fleet.

- Where the commercial purpose of the contract is defeated

This applies where the circumstances have so changed that to hold a party to their promise would require them to do something which, although not impossible, would be radically different from the original agreement.

In *Jackson v Union Marine Insurance Co* (1874), the plaintiff's ship was chartered to proceed to Newport to load a cargo bound for San Francisco. On the way, it ran aground. It could not be refloated for over a month, and needed repairs. The charterers hired another ship and the plaintiff claimed under an insurance policy which he had taken out to cover the eventuality of his failure to carry out the contract. The insurance company denied responsibility, on the basis that the plaintiff could claim against the charterer for breach of contract. The court decided, however, that the delay had put an end to the commercial sense of the contract. As a consequence, the charterers had been released from their obligations under the contract and were entitled to hire another ship.

- Where, in the case of a contract of personal service, the party dies or becomes otherwise incapacitated

In *Condor v Barron Knights* (1966), Condor contracted to be the drummer in a pop group. After he became ill, he was medically advised that he could only play on four nights per week, not every night as required. It was decided that the contract was discharged by reason of the failure in the plaintiff's health preventing him from performing his duties under it; thus, any contractual obligations were unenforceable. In *Hare v Murphy Bros*

(1974), a foreman's employment contract was frustrated when he was jailed for unlawful wounding. This was not self-induced frustration (see 8.4.1), though there was fault on the part of the foreman; he did not have a choice as to his availability for work.

8.4.1 Situations in which the doctrine of frustration does not apply

In *Tsakiroglou & Co v Noblee and Thorl* (1962), it was stated that frustration is a doctrine which is only too often invoked by a party to a contract who finds performance difficult or unprofitable, but it is very rarely relied on with success. It is, in fact, a kind of last resort and is a conclusion which should be reached rarely and with reluctance. A contract will not be discharged by reason of frustration in the following circumstances:

- Where the parties have made express provision in the contract for the event which has occurred

  In this case, the provision in the contract will be applied.

- Where the frustrating event is self-induced

  An example of such a situation is the case of *Maritime National Fish Ltd v Ocean Trawlers Ltd* (1935). Maritime were charterers of a ship, equipped for otter trawling, which was owned by Ocean Trawlers. Permits were required for otter trawling, and Maritime, which owned four ships of its own, applied for five permits. They were only granted three permits, however, and they assigned those permits to their own ships. They claimed that their contract with Ocean Trawlers was frustrated, on the basis that they could not lawfully use the ship. It was held, however, that the frustrating event was a result of their action in assigning the permits to their own ships and, therefore, they could not rely on it as discharging their contractual obligations. Effectively, self-induced frustration amounts to breach of contract (see 8.5.1).

- Where an alternative method of performance is still possible

  In such a situation, the person performing the contract will be expected to use the available alternative method.

  In *Tsakiroglou & Co v Noblee and Thorl* (1962), a 'cif' contract was entered into to supply 300 tons of Sudanese groundnuts to Hamburg. It had been intended that the cargo should go via the Suez Canal, and the appellants refused to deliver the nuts when the canal was closed. It was argued that the contract was frustrated, as to use the Cape of Good Hope route would make the contract commercially and fundamentally different from that which was agreed. The court decided that the contract was not fundamentally altered by the closure of the canal and, therefore, was not discharged by frustration. Thus, the appellants were liable for breach of contract. Obviously, if the cargo had been perishable, performance may not have been possible.

- Where the contract simply becomes more expensive to perform

In such circumstances, the court will not allow frustration to be used as a means of escaping from a bad bargain.

In *Davis Contractors v Fareham UDC* (1956), the plaintiffs contracted to build 78 houses in eight months, at a total cost of £94,000. Due to a shortage of labour, it actually took 22 months to build the houses, at a cost of £115,000. The plaintiffs sought to have the contract set aside as having been frustrated, and to claim on a *quantum meruit* basis. The court determined that the contract had not been frustrated by the shortage of labour and the plaintiffs were, thus, bound by their contractual undertaking with regard to the price.

8.4.2 The effect of frustration

At common law, the effect of frustration was to make the contract void as from the time of the frustrating event. It did not make the contract void *ab initio*, that is, from the beginning. The effect of this was that each party had to perform any obligation which had become due before the frustrating event, and was only excused from obligations which would arise after that event. On occasion, this could lead to injustice. For example, in *Krell v Henry* (1903), the plaintiff could not claim the rent, as it was not due to be paid until after the coronation event had been cancelled. However, in *Chandler v Webster* (1904), the plaintiff had already paid £100 of the total rent of £141 15 s for a room from which to watch the coronation procession, before it was cancelled. He sued to recover his money. It was decided that not only could he not recover the £100, but he also had to pay the outstanding £41 15 s, as the rent had fallen due for payment before the frustrating event had taken place.

8.4.3 Law Reform (Frustrated Contracts) Act 1943

Statute intervened to remedy the potential injustice of the common law with the introduction of Law Reform (Frustrated Contracts) Act 1943. The position is now as follows:

- any money paid is recoverable;
- any money due to be paid ceases to be payable;
- the parties may be permitted, at the discretion of the court, to retain expenses incurred from any money received; or to recover those expenses from money due to be paid before the frustrating event. If no money was paid, or was due to be paid, before the event, then nothing can be retained or recovered;
- a party who has received valuable benefit from the other's performance before the frustrating event may have to pay for that benefit.

The Act does not apply to contracts of insurance, contracts for the carriage of goods by sea and contracts covered by s 7 of the SoGA 1979 (see 9.2.12).

8.5 DISCHARGE BY BREACH

Breach of a contract occurs where one of the parties to the agreement fails to comply, either completely or satisfactorily, with their obligations under it. A breach of contract may occur in three ways:

- where a party, prior to the time of performance, states that they will not fulfil their contractual obligation;
- where a party fails to perform their contractual obligation;
- where a party performs their obligation in a defective manner.

8.5.1 Effect of breach

Any breach will result in the innocent party being able to sue for damages. In addition, however, some breaches will permit the innocent party to treat the contract as having been discharged. In this situation, they can refuse either to perform their part of the contract or to accept further performance from the party in breach. The right to treat a contract as discharged arises in the following instances:

- where the other party has repudiated the contract before performance is due, or before they have completed performance;
- where the other party has committed a fundamental breach of contract. As has already been pointed out in Chapter 7, above, there are two methods of determining whether a breach is fundamental or not: the first is by relying on the distinction between conditions and warranties; and the other is by relying on the seriousness of the consequences that flow from the breach.

8.5.2 Anticipatory breach

Anticipatory breach arises where one party, prior to the actual due date of performance, demonstrates an intention not to perform their contractual obligations. The intention not to fulfil the contract can be either express or implied:

- Express

  This occurs where a party actually states that they will not perform their contractual obligations.

  In *Hochster v De La Tour* (1853), in April, De La Tour engaged Hochster to act as courier on his European tour, starting on 1 June. On 11 May, De La

Tour wrote to Hochster, stating that he would no longer be needing his services. The plaintiff started proceedings for breach of contract on 22 May and the defendant claimed that there could be no cause of action until 1 June. It was held, however, that the plaintiff was entitled to start his action as soon as the anticipatory breach occurred (that is, when De La Tour stated that he would not need Hochster's services).

- Implied

  This occurs where a party carries out some act which makes performance impossible.

  In *Omnium D'Enterprises v Sutherland* (1919), the defendant had agreed to let a ship to the plaintiff. Prior to the actual time for performance, he sold the ship to another party. It was held that the sale of the ship amounted to repudiation of the contract and the plaintiff could sue from that date.

With regard to anticipatory breach, the innocent party can sue for damages immediately, as in *Hochster v De La Tour*. Alternatively, they can wait until the actual time for performance before taking action, thus giving the other party a chance to perform. In the latter instance, they are entitled to make preparations for performance and claim for actual breach if the other party fails to perform on the due date, even though this apparently conflicts with the duty to mitigate losses (see below, 8.7.2).

In *White and Carter (Councils) v McGregor* (1961), McGregor contracted with the plaintiffs to have advertisements placed on litter bins which were supplied to local authorities. The defendant wrote to the plaintiffs, asking them to cancel the contract. The plaintiffs refused to cancel, and produced and displayed the adverts as required under the contract. They then claimed payment. It was held that the plaintiffs were not obliged to accept the defendant's repudiation. They were entitled to perform the contract and claim the agreed price. Thus the duty to mitigate loss did not place the plaintiffs under an obligation to accept anticipatory breach and stop their own performance; as they were allowing the defendants a 'second chance', the plaintiffs had to commence their performance in case the defendants did perform on the due date.

Where the innocent party elects to wait for the time of performance, they take the risk of the contract being discharged for some other reason, such as frustration, and, thus, of losing their right to sue.

In *Avery v Bowden* (1856), Bowden chartered the plaintiff's ship in order to load grain at Odessa within a period of 45 days. Although Bowden later told the ship's captain that he no longer intended to load the grain, the ship stayed in Odessa in the hope that he would change his mind. Before the end of the 45 days, the Crimean War started and, thus, the contract was discharged by frustration. Avery then sued for breach of contract. It was held that the action failed. Bowden had committed anticipatory breach, but the captain had waived the right to discharge the contract on that basis. The contract continued and was brought to an end by frustration, not by breach.

A more recent case sheds some light on the operation and effect of anticipatory breach. In *Vitol SA v Norelf Ltd* (1996), the parties entered into a contract for the purchase of a cargo of propane gas by the plaintiff. The contract was made on 11 February, but, on 8 March, Vitol sent a telex to Norelf which purported to repudiate the agreement on the basis of an alleged breach by the latter party. As the allegation of breach on the part of Norelf subsequently turned out to be unfounded, the telex of 8 March was itself an anticipatory breach of the contract on the part of Vitol. Norelf did not communicate with Vitol and sold the cargo to another party on 15 March. In arbitration, it was decided that this subsequent sale effectively represented Norelf's acceptance of the anticipatory breach and left Vitol with no action in relation to the cargo. In the Court of Appeal, however, it was held that Norelf should have indicated their acceptance of the anticipatory breach in a clear and unequivocal manner, and that silence could not amount to such acceptance. In restoring the decision of the arbitrator, the House of Lords decided that the fact that Norelf had not taken the next step in the contract by delivering a bill of lading was sufficient notification that they had accepted Vitol's repudiatory breach. In so doing, they set out three principles that govern the acceptance of repudiatory breach:

- in the event of repudiatory breach, the other party has the right either to accept the repudiation or to affirm the contract;
- the aggrieved party does not specifically have to inform the other party of their acceptance of the anticipatory breach, and conduct which clearly indicates that the injured party is treating the contract as at an end is sufficient (though, of course, each case must be considered on its specific facts);
- the aggrieved party need not personally notify the other of the decision to accept the repudiation; it is sufficient that they learn from some other party.

8.6 REMEDIES FOR BREACH OF CONTRACT

The principal remedies for breach of contract are:
- damages;
- *quantum meruit*;
- specific performance;
- injunction;
- action for the agreed contract price;
- repudiation.

Which of these remedies is available for a particular breach depends on issues such as whether the breach is of condition or warranty (see Chapter 6).

8.7 DAMAGES

According to Lord Diplock in *Photo Productions Ltd v Securicor Transport Ltd* (1980):

> Every failure to perform a primary obligation is a breach of contract. The secondary obligation on the part of the contract breaker to which it gives rise by implication of the common law is to pay monetary compensation to the other party for the loss sustained by him in consequence of the breach.

Such monetary compensation for breach of contract is referred to as 'damages'. The estimation of what damages are to be paid by a party in breach of contract can be divided into two parts: remoteness and measure.

8.7.1 Remoteness of damage

What kind of damage can the innocent party claim? This involves a consideration of causation and the remoteness of cause from effect, in order to determine how far down a chain of events a defendant is liable. The rule in *Hadley v Baxendale* (1854) states that damages will only be awarded in respect of losses which arise naturally, that is, in the natural course of things; or which both parties may reasonably be supposed to have contemplated, when the contract was made, as a probable result of its breach.

In *Hadley v Baxendale*, Hadley, a miller in Gloucester, had engaged the defendant to take a broken mill-shaft to Greenwich so that it could be used as a pattern for a new one. The defendant delayed in delivering the shaft, thus causing the mill to be out of action for longer than it would otherwise have been. Hadley sued for loss of profit during that period of additional delay. It was held that it was not a natural consequence of the delay in delivering the shaft that the mill should be out of action. The mill might, for example, have had a spare shaft. So, the first part of the rule stated above did not apply. In addition, Baxendale was unaware that the mill would be out of action during the period of delay, so the second part of the rule did not apply, either. Baxendale, therefore, although liable for breach of contract, was not liable for the loss of profit caused by the delay.

The effect of the first part of the rule in *Hadley v Baxendale* is that the party in breach is deemed to expect the normal consequences of the breach, whether they actually expected them or not.

Under the second part of the rule, however, the party in breach can only be held liable for abnormal consequences where they have actual knowledge that the abnormal consequences might follow.

In *Victoria Laundry Ltd v Newham Industries Ltd* (1949), the defendants contracted to deliver a new boiler to the plaintiffs, but delayed in delivery. The plaintiffs claimed for normal loss of profit during the period of delay, and also for the loss of abnormal profits from a highly lucrative contract which they could have undertaken, had the boiler been delivered on time. In this case, it was decided that damages could be recovered in regard to the normal profits, as that loss was a natural consequence of the delay. The second claim failed, however, on the ground that the loss was not a normal one; it was a consequence of an especially lucrative contract, about which the defendant knew nothing.

The decision in the *Victoria Laundry* case was confirmed by the House of Lords in *Czarnikow v Koufos* (*The Heron II*) (1967), although the actual test for remoteness was reformulated in terms of whether the consequence should have been within the reasonable contemplation of the parties at the time of the contract.

In *The Heron II*, the defendants contracted to carry sugar from Constanza to Basra. They knew that the plaintiffs were sugar merchants, but did not know that they intended to sell the sugar as soon as it reached Basra. During a period that the ship was delayed, the market price of sugar fell. The plaintiffs claimed damages for the loss from the defendants. It was held that the plaintiffs could recover. It was common knowledge that the market value of such commodities could fluctuate; therefore, the loss was within the reasonable contemplation of the parties (see also *Bailey* v *HSS Alarms* (2000)).

As a consequence of the test for remoteness, a party may be liable for consequences which, although within the reasonable contemplation of the parties, are much more serious in effect than would be expected of them.

In *H Parsons (Livestock) Ltd v Uttley Ingham & Co* (1978), the plaintiffs, who were pig farmers, bought a large food hopper from the defendants. While erecting it, the plaintiffs failed to unseal a ventilator on the top of the hopper. Because of a lack of ventilation, the pig food stored in the hopper became mouldy. The pigs that ate the mouldy food contracted a rare intestinal disease and died. It was held that the defendants were liable for the loss of the pigs. The food that was affected by bad storage caused the illness as a natural consequence of the breach, and the death from such illness was not too remote.

8.7.2 Measure of damages

Damages in contract are intended to compensate an injured party for any financial loss sustained as a consequence of another party's breach. The object is not to punish the party in breach, so the amount of damages awarded can never be greater than the actual loss suffered. The aim is to put the injured party in the same position they would have been in, had the contract been properly performed. There are a number of procedures which seek to achieve this end:

- The market rule

  Where the breach relates to a contract for the sale of goods, damages are usually assessed in line with the market rule. This means that, if goods are not delivered under a contract, the buyer is entitled to go into the market and buy similar goods, paying the market price prevailing at the time. They can then claim the difference in price between what they paid and the original contract price as damages. Conversely, if a buyer refuses to accept goods under a contract, the seller can sell the goods in the market and accept the prevailing market price. Any difference between the price they receive and the contract price can be claimed in damages (see ss 50 and 51 of the SoGA 1979, and below, 9.2.6 and 9.2.8).

- The duty to mitigate losses

  The injured party is under a duty to take all reasonable steps to minimise their loss. So, in the above examples, the buyer of goods which are not delivered has to buy the replacements as cheaply as possible; and the seller of goods which are not accepted has to try to get as good a price as they can when they sell them.

  In *Payzu v Saunders* (1919), the parties entered into a contract for the sale of fabric, which was to be delivered and paid for in instalments. When the purchaser, Payzu, failed to pay the first instalment on time, Saunders refused to make any further deliveries unless Payzu agreed to pay cash on delivery. The plaintiff refused to accept this and sued for breach of contract. The court decided that the delay in payment had not given the defendant the right to repudiate the contract. As a consequence, he had breached the contract by refusing further delivery. The buyer, however, should have mitigated his loss by accepting the offer of cash on delivery terms. His damages were restricted, therefore, to what he would have lost under those terms, namely, interest over the repayment period.

  A more recent case highlights the problems that can arise in relation to both the market rule and the duty to mitigate losses.

  In *Western Web Offset Printers Ltd v Independent Media Ltd* (1995), the parties had entered into a contract, under which the plaintiff was to publish 48 issues of a weekly newspaper for the defendant. In the action which followed the defendant's repudiation of the contract, the only issue in question was the extent of damages to be awarded. The plaintiff argued that damages should be decided on the basis of gross profits, merely subtracting direct expenses such as paper and ink, but not labour costs and other overheads; this would result in a total claim of some £177,000. The defendant argued that damages should be on the basis of net profits, with labour and other overheads being taken into account; this would result in a claim of some £38,000. Although the trial judge awarded the lesser sum, the Court of Appeal decided that he had drawn an incorrect analogy from cases involving sale of goods. In this situation, it was not simply a matter of working out the difference in cost price from selling price in order to reach a nominal profit. The plaintiff had been unable to replace the work, due to the recession in the economy, and, therefore, had not been able to mitigate the loss. In the circumstances, the plaintiff was entitled to receive the full amount that would have been due in order to allow it to defray the expenses that it would have had to pay during the period that the contract should have lasted.

- Non-pecuniary loss

At one time, damages could not be recovered where the loss sustained through breach of contract was of a non-financial nature. The modern position is that such non-pecuniary damages can be recovered.

In *Jarvis v Swan Tours Ltd* (1973), the defendant's brochure stated that various facilities were available at a particular ski resort. The facilities available were, in fact, much inferior to those advertised. The plaintiff sued for breach of contract. The court decided that Jarvis was entitled to recover not just the financial loss he suffered, which was not substantial, but also damages for loss of entertainment and enjoyment. The Court of Appeal stated that damages could be recovered for mental distress in appropriate cases, and this was one of them. The scope of recovery of damages for 'distress and disappointment' was recently examined by the House of Lords in *Farley v Skinner* (2001).

Particular problems arise in relation to estimating the damages liable in relation to construction contracts. Where a builder has either not carried out work required or has carried it out inadequately, they will be in breach of contract and the aggrieved party will be entitled to claim damages. The usual measure of such damages is the cost of carrying out the work or repairing the faulty work. However, this may not be the case where the costs of remedying the defects are disproportionate to the difference in value between what was supplied and what was ordered.

In *Ruxley Electronics and Construction Ltd v Forsyth* (1995), the parties had entered into a contract for the construction of a swimming pool and surrounding building. Although the contract stated that the pool was to be 7 ft 6 in deep at one end, the actual depth of the pool was only 6 ft 9 in. The total contract price was £70,000. Fixing the error would have required a full reconstruction at a cost of £20,000. The trial judge decided that the measure of damages for the plaintiff's breach was the difference between the value of the pool actually provided and the value of the pool contracted for. He decided that the difference was nil, but awarded the defendant £2,500 for loss of amenity. On appeal, the Court of Appeal overturned that award, holding that Forsyth was entitled to the full cost of reconstruction. On further appeal, the House of Lords reinstated the decision of the trial judge. They considered that, in building contracts, there were two possible ways of determining damages: either the difference in value, as used by the trial judge; or the cost of reinstatement, as preferred by the Court of Appeal. As the costs of reinstatement would have been out of all proportion to the benefit gained, the House of Lords awarded the difference in value. According to Lord Jauncey, 'damages are designed to compensate for an established loss and not to provide a gratuity to the aggrieved party'. Lord Lloyd said that the plaintiff could not, in all cases, 'obtain the monetary equivalent of specific performance'.

It should be noted that such construction contracts are evidently to be treated differently from contracts for the sale of goods, for purchasers of goods can reject them under s 13 of the SoGA 1979 where they do not match their description, even if they are otherwise fit for the purpose for which they were bought (see below, 9.2.4).

8.7.3 Liquidated damages and penalties

It is possible, and common in business contracts, for the parties to an agreement to make provisions for possible breach by stating in advance the amount of damages that will have to be paid in the event of any breach occurring. Damages under such a provision are known as liquidated damages. They will only be recognised by the court if they represent a genuine pre-estimate of loss, and are not intended to operate as a penalty against the party in breach. If the court considers the provision to be a penalty, it will not give it effect, but will award damages in the normal way, that is, unliquidated damages assessed by the court.

In *Dunlop v New Garage & Motor Co* (1915), the plaintiffs supplied the defendants with tyres, under a contract designed to achieve resale price maintenance. The contract provided that the defendants had to pay Dunlop £5 for every tyre they sold in breach of the resale price agreement. When the garage sold tyres at less than the agreed minimum price, they resisted Dunlop's claim for £5 per tyre, on the grounds that it represented a penalty clause. On the facts of the situation, the court decided that the provision was a genuine attempt to fix damages and was not a penalty. It was, therefore, enforceable.

In deciding the legality of such clauses, the courts will consider the effect, rather than the form, of the clause, as can be seen in *Cellulose Acetate Silk Co Ltd v Widnes Foundry (1925) Ltd* (1933). In that case, the contract expressly stated that damages for late payment would be paid by way of penalty at the rate of £20 per week. In fact, the sum of £20 was in no way excessive and represented a reasonable estimate of the likely loss. On that basis, the House of Lords enforced the clause, in spite of its actual wording.

In *Duffen v FRA Bo SpA* (1998), it was held that a term in an agency contract which established so called 'liquidated damages' for the dismissal of the agent at £100,000 was, in fact, a penalty clause and could not be enforced. This was in spite of the fact that the agreement specifically stated that the £100,000 was 'a reasonable pre-estimate of the loss and damage which the agent will suffer on the termination of the agreement'. In reaching its conclusion, the court held that, although the wording of the agreement was persuasive, it was outweighed by the fact that the level of damages did not alter in proportion to the time remaining to be served in the agreement. The claimant was consequently only allowed to claim for normal damages, although these could be augmented under the Commercial Agents (Council Directive) Regulations 1993 (SI 1993/3053) (see below, 11.5.3).

The whole question of penalty clauses is fraught. It is obviously advantageous, in a business context, for the parties to a contract to know with certainty what the financial consequences of any breach of the contract will be, so as to allow them to manage their risk properly. However, the possibility of the courts subsequently holding a damages clause to be punitive introduces the very uncertainty that the clause was designed to avoid.

In any case, why should businesses not be bound by clauses, as long as they have been freely negotiated? This point leads to a comparison of liquidated damages clauses and limitation and exclusion clauses. Usually, penalty clauses are thought of as overestimating the damages, but it should be considered that such a pre-estimation may be much lower than the damages suffered, in which case the clause will effectively operate as a limitation clause. It would surely be better all round if the liquidated damages/penalties clause question was subject to a similar regime as regulates exclusion/limitation clauses under the Unfair Contract Terms Act 1977. The courts would then be required to examine whether the clause was the product of truly free negotiation and not the outcome of an abuse of power, in which case it would be effective; or, alternatively, whether it was imposed on one of the parties against their wishes, in which case it would be inoperative.

8.7.4 *Quantum meruit*

The term *quantum meruit* means that a party should be awarded as much as he had earned, and such an award can be either contractual or quasi-contractual (see below, 8.12) in nature. If the parties enter into a contractual agreement without determining the reward that is to be provided for performance, then, in the event of any dispute, the court will award a reasonable sum.

Payment may also be claimed on the basis of *quantum meruit* where a party has carried out work in respect of a void contract and the other party has accepted that work.

In *Craven-Ellis v Canons Ltd* (1936), the plaintiff had acted as the managing director of a company under a deed of contract. However, since he had not acquired any shares in the company, as required by its articles, his appointment was void. He sued to recover remuneration for the service he had provided prior to his removal. The court decided that, although he could not claim under contract, he was entitled to recover a reasonable sum on the basis of *quantum meruit*.

Furthermore, where the defendant has prevented the claimant from completing performance, the claimant may be entitled to payment for work done so far. In *Planche v Colburn* (1831), the plaintiff was under contract to write a book for the defendants, payment to be made on completion of the manuscript. The defendants abandoned publication plans before the manuscript was completed; the plaintiff, having done some of the research for and writing of the manuscript, could claim for that work done.

8.8 SPECIFIC PERFORMANCE

It will sometimes suit a party to break their contractual obligations and pay damages; but, through an order for specific performance, the party in breach may be instructed to complete their part of the contract. The following rules govern the award of such a remedy:

- An order of specific performance will only be granted in cases where the common law remedy of damages is inadequate. It is not usually applied to contracts concerning the sale of goods where replacements are readily available. It is most commonly granted in cases involving the sale of land and where the subject matter of the contract is unique (for example, a painting by Picasso).

- Specific performance will not be granted where the court cannot supervise its enforcement. For this reason, it will not be available in respect of contracts of employment or personal service.

In *Ryan v Mutual Tontine Westminster Chambers Association* (1893), the landlords of a flat undertook to provide a porter, who was to be constantly in attendance to provide services such as cleaning the common passages and stairs and delivering letters. The person appointed spent much of his time working as a chef at a nearby club. During his absence, his duties were performed by a cleaner or by various boys. The plaintiff sought to enforce the contractual undertaking. It was held that, although the landlords were in breach of their contract, the court would not award an order of specific performance. The only remedy available was an action for damages.

Similarly, in *Co-operative Insurance Society Ltd v Argyll Stores (Holdings) Ltd* (1997), the House of Lords held that it would be inappropriate to enforce a covenant to trade entered into by the defendant company. The case concerned a shopping centre owned by the claimants, in which the defendant's Safeway supermarket was the largest attraction. Although it had contracted in its lease to keep its supermarket open during usual trading hours, the defendant company decided to close the shop, causing significant threat to the continued operation of the shopping centre. The claimant's action for specific performance to force Argyll to keep the store open was unsuccessful at first instance, although it was supported in the Court of Appeal. The House of Lords, however, restored the traditional approach by refusing to issue an order for specific performance in such circumstances where it would require constant supervision by the court. Damages were held to be the appropriate remedy.

- Specific performance is an equitable remedy which the court grants at its discretion. It will not be granted where the claimant has not acted properly on their part; neither will it be granted where mutuality is lacking. Thus, a minor will not be granted specific performance, because no such order could be awarded against them.

8.9 INJUNCTION

This is also an equitable order of the court, which directs a person not to break their contract. It can have the effect of indirectly enforcing contracts for personal service.

In *Warner Bros v Nelson* (1937), the defendant, the actress Bette Davis, had entered a contract which stipulated that she was to work exclusively for the plaintiffs for a period of one year. When she came to England, the plaintiffs applied for an injunction to prevent her from working for someone else. The court granted the order to Warner Bros. In doing so, it rejected Nelson's argument that granting it would force her either to work for the claimants or not to work at all.

An injunction will only be granted to enforce negative covenants within the agreement and cannot be used to enforce positive obligations.

In *Whitwood Chemical Co v Hardman* (1891), the defendant had contracted to give the whole of his time to the plaintiffs, his employers, but he occasionally worked for others. The plaintiffs applied for an injunction to prevent him working for anyone else. No injunction was granted. Hardman had said what he would do, not what he would not do; therefore, there was no negative promise to enforce.

8.10 ACTION FOR THE AGREED CONTRACT PRICE

In some circumstances, a party may sue for non-payment of the price rather than seeking damages for breach. For example, s 49 of the SoGA 1979 gives this right to the seller where either the buyer fails to pay on the agreed date or ownership in the goods has been transferred to the buyer.

8.11 REPUDIATION

As already discussed in Chapter 6, where there is a breach of condition, the party not in breach has the option of treating the contract as repudiated, so that he need not perform his contractual obligations (see 8.5).

8.12 QUASI-CONTRACTUAL REMEDIES

Quasi-contractual remedies are based on the assumption that a person should not receive any undue advantage from the fact that there is no contractual remedy to force them to account for it. An important quasi-contractual remedy is an action for money paid and received.

If no contract comes into existence by reason of a total failure of consideration, then, under this action, any goods or money received will have to be returned to the party who supplied them.

A recent case of particular interest is *HM Attorney General v Blake* (2000). Blake, jailed for treason for spying for the Soviet Union, escaped and subsequently wrote his autobiography. This was alleged to be a breach of his contract of employment with the British Intelligence Service and the AG sought an injunction to prevent the publishers from paying Blake £90,000 royalties on the book. The Court of Appeal granted the injunction on the ground that it was against public policy for a criminal to profit from his crime.

The House of Lords did not uphold grant of the injunction as they could find no statutory or common law authority for such grant; accordingly, the money could be paid to Blake. However, Blake's treachery made the case exceptional, allowing application of the principle of restitution to Blake's breach of contract. Accordingly, the AG was allowed an account of all profits resulting from the breach. Effectively, therefore, the AG recovered the royalties from Blake.

SUMMARY OF CHAPTER 8

DISCHARGE OF A CONTRACT

Discharge by agreement

- Executory contracts may be discharged by mutual exchange of promises to discharge.
- Where one party has executed the contract, the other is only released from the obligation to perform by providing new consideration.

Discharge by performance

- As a general rule, discharge by performance requires complete and exact performance of the obligations in the contract, except where the contract is divisible, is capable of being fulfilled by substantial performance, performance has been prevented by the other party or partial performance has been accepted by the other party.

Tender of performance

- Tender of performance (an offer to perform the contractual obligations) discharges liability under a contract.

Discharge by frustration

- Frustrating events, such as destruction of the subject matter of the contract, discharge the contract.
- A contract will not be frustrated where the contract expressly provides for the frustrating event, nor where the frustration is self-induced nor where an alternative method of performance is available.
- Contracts frustrated at common law are void from the time of frustration.
- Under the Law Reform (Frustrated Contracts) Act 1943, money paid before frustration is recoverable and money due is recoverable/not payable. In the court's discretion, claims may be made for expenses incurred prior to frustration.

Discharge by breach

- Breach may be anticipatory or by failure to perform/defective performance of the contract.
- Breach of a contract entitles the innocent party to damages. Additionally, a breach of condition entitles the innocent party to treat the contract as being discharged.

Damages

- Damages may be *liquidated* or *unliquidated*.
- Assessment of unliquidated damages is determined by the rules of *remoteness* (reasonable forseeability) and *mitigation of loss*.

Quantum meruit

- Where the contract does not fix the price, a reasonable sum is payable.
- Where a person is prevented from completing performance by the other party, payment can be claimed for work done so far.
- Payment may be claimed for work done under a void contract which is accepted by the other party.

Specific performance

A party in breach may be instructed to complete their part of the contract:

- An order of specific performance will only be granted in cases where the common law remedy of damages is inadequate and supervision of enforcement is not required.
- Specific performance is an equitable remedy which the court grants at its discretion.

Injunction

- This is also an equitable order of the court, which directs a person not to break their contract.

Quasi-contractual remedies

- These are based on the assumption that a person should not receive any undue advantage from the fact that there is no contractual remedy to force them to account for it.

CHAPTER 9

SALE AND SUPPLY OF GOODS

9.1 INTRODUCTION

One of the most common transactions entered into by businesses is the contract for the sale of goods to other businesses or consumers. However, goods may be supplied under contracts other than sale; for example:

*   Contracts of hire

    Here, the owner of goods transfers possession for a fixed period but retains ownership; common examples are television rental and car hire.

*   Contracts of hire purchase

    The owner of goods transfers possession of the goods, but does not transfer ownership of them unless and until the hirer has paid all of the agreed instalments and has exercised his or her option to purchase.

Furthermore, a person may be supplied with goods other than under a contract; for example:

*   By gift

    Gifts are voluntary transfers of ownership to a person who does not give any consideration in return for the ownership.

It should also be appreciated that the sale and supply of goods can give rise to both civil and criminal liability, the latter being of particular importance in relation to the protection of consumers.

A detailed examination of the laws relating to all transactions for the sale or supply of goods is outside the remit of this book; civil and criminal laws relating to the commonest of such transactions will be considered, namely:

*   Civil liability:
    o   Sale of Goods Act 1979;
    o   Supply of Goods and Services Act 1982;
    o   Consumer Protection (Distance Selling) Regulations 2000;
    o   Pt I of the Consumer Protection Act 1987.
*   Criminal liability:
    o   Pt II of the Consumer Protection Act 1987;
    o   General Product Safety Regulations 1994;
    o   Trade Descriptions Act 1968.

9.2 THE SALE OF GOODS ACT 1979

This Act has been amended by the Sale and Supply of Goods Act (SSGA) 1994, the Sale of Goods (Amendment) Act 1994 and the Sale of Goods (Amendment) Act 1995. All references to the Sale of Goods Act (SoGA) 1979 are to the provisions as amended.

Note should also be taken of the Department of Trade and Industry's draft regulations, the Sale and Supply of Goods to Consumers Regulations 2002 (2002 Regulations); these result from an EC Directive (1999/44/EC). Certain issues have yet to be incorporated into the draft regulations, but the regulations are expected to be implemented late in 2002. When implemented, the 2002 Regulations will make amendments to the SoGA 1979, mainly where the buyer of goods is a consumer; the regulations define a 'consumer' as a natural person who is acting for purposes which are outside his business. The SoGA 1979, in its current form, will apply to contracts made before the commencement date of the 2002 Regulations.

The SoGA 1979 will be examined in its current form, with reference to the proposed amendments of the 2002 Regulations.

9.2.1 Definition

Under s 2(1), a contract for the sale of goods is 'a contract by which the seller transfers or agrees to transfer the property in the goods to the buyer for a money consideration, called the price'.

In this context, 'property' means 'ownership', so the object of such a contract is to transfer ownership in the goods to the buyer; however, the contract is only covered by the SoGA 1979 if the buyer's consideration is money. Accordingly, an exchange of goods is not within the Act, but, following the decision in *Connell Estate Agents v Begej* (1993), it can be argued that part exchange contracts are within the Act, particularly where the value of the goods given in part exchange is apparent. Section 2(1) also requires that 'goods', as defined in s 61(1) of the SoGA 1979, are the subject matter of the contract. In general, the word 'goods' includes personal property of a moveable type (that is, anything which can be physically possessed in some way and is not attached to the land). For example, crops become goods on harvesting and money becomes goods when antique or collectable. However, there are specific exclusions from the definition of 'goods', for example:

- real property (for example, land and buildings);
- choses in action (for example, debts, cheques and currency in circulation).

9.2.2 Form of the agreement

The basic essentials for forming any contract (see Chapter 5), such as capacity to contract, must be met, but there are no formal requirements – the contract can be oral, written or even inferred from conduct, as might be the case in a supermarket sale, where the parties are unlikely to actually state that they wish to buy and sell the goods!

9.2.3 The price of the goods

Being an essential part of the contract by virtue of s 2(1), the price of the goods is usually expressly agreed; for example, when buying goods in a shop, the buyer agrees to pay the marked price. Section 8(1) of the SoGA 1979 confirms that the price may be fixed by the contract and also indicates that the price can be determined by a course of dealing between the parties or in a manner agreed by the contract. Thus, when re-ordering goods without reference to the price, the parties could be taken to agree that the price paid in a previous transaction was applicable to this contract. Equally, the parties might validly agree that an independent third party should determine the price payable. Of course, the question arises of what happens if that third party does not make, or is prevented from making, that determination of the price payable. Section 9 of the SoGA 1979 solves these issues:

(1) Where there is an agreement to sell goods on the terms that the price is to be fixed by the valuation of a third party, and he cannot or does not make the valuation, the agreement is avoided; but if the goods or any part of them have been delivered to and appropriated by the buyer, he must pay a reasonable price for them.

(2) Where the third party is prevented from making the valuation by the fault of the seller or buyer, the party not at fault may maintain an action for damages against the party at fault.

Some problems arising from determination of the price, however, are not specifically addressed by the SoGA 1979. Though the Act indicates in s 8(2) that 'a reasonable price' is payable where the price has not been determined under s 8(1), it has been suggested that failure to agree a price or a manner of fixing it means that there is no contract concluded and s 8(2) cannot operate to make such an arrangement a contract.

In *May and Butcher v The King* (1934), an agreement for the purchase of government tentage provided that the price was to be agreed from time to time; effectively, they agreed to make later agreements as to the price. Had there been no mention of the price at all, then failure to actually agree a price would not mean that there was no contract – a 'reasonable price' would have been payable, under the SoGA 1893. However, as the parties had expressly stated that the price was to be agreed later, it was held that they were simply agreeing to agree and had not intended to make a binding contract.

In *Foley v Classique Coaches Ltd* (1934), the defendants agreed to purchase supplies of petrol from the plaintiffs, at a price 'to be agreed by the parties from time to time'. Failing agreement, the price was to be settled by arbitration. The agreement was held to be a binding contract by the Court of Appeal.

The distinction between the two cases would appear to be based on the fact that, by providing a method (arbitration) by which the price could be fixed, the parties had shown an intention to make a legally binding agreement. Accordingly, it would seem that intention to be bound can be regarded as the key issue and agreement as to price is merely a factor in determination of such intention.

9.2.4 Seller's implied obligations

As well as performing any express undertakings in the contract, the seller must also comply with certain terms implied into the contract by the SoGA 1979, regardless of whether he or she sells to a consumer or a business. These implied terms are of particular interest to the consumer, who rarely negotiates and agrees express terms. In supermarket sales, for example, it is unlikely that there will be any discussion, let alone specific undertakings given, as to the quality and functions of the goods sold. Nevertheless, the implied terms will place a seller under an obligation as to matters such as quality and functions of the goods that he or she sells. It is also important to note that the seller's obligations under the implied terms apply even though the seller is not actually at fault; he or she undertakes liability by the act of selling the goods. Thus, if a new stereo system does not function properly because of a manufacturing defect, the buyer may still sue the seller for breach of contract. Furthermore, in some cases, the Contracts (Rights of Third Parties) Act 1999 (considered above, Chapter 5) might give a non-buyer the same rights against the seller.

Finally, it should be realised that the implied terms of the SoGA 1979 are classified as conditions or warranties (see above, Chapter 6), which give rise to different remedies for breach (see below, 9.2.8):

- Title (s 12 of the SoGA 1979)

  We have already seen that the objective of a contract for the sale of goods is to buy ownership in the goods; accordingly, s 12(1) implies a condition into the contract that the seller has the 'right to sell' the goods. If the seller cannot transfer ownership, he or she does not have the 'right to sell'. In *Rowland v Divall* (1923), the buyer of a car did not receive ownership, as the garage which sold him the car did not own it. There was a breach of s 12(1) and he was able to recover the full purchase price paid, even though he had used the car for four months. Where ownership is not transferred, there is a total failure of consideration, as the buyer does not receive what he contracted to buy. Clearly, legal ownership is of paramount importance and transferring use and possession of goods is not sufficient for performance of a sale of goods contract.

Section 12(2) also implies into the contract warranties of quiet possession and freedom from encumbrances (s 12(2) of the SoGA 1979). Effectively, the seller undertakes that the buyer's title will not be interfered with or be subject to anyone else's rights, except insofar as such are known by or disclosed to the buyer before the contract is made.

In *Microbeads AC v Vinhurst Road Markings* (1975), the seller sold some road marking machines to the buyers. Unbeknown to the seller at the time of the sale, another firm was in the process of patenting this type of equipment, although rights to enforce the patent did not commence until after the contract between the seller and buyer was made. A patent action was subsequently brought against the buyer, who then claimed that the seller was in breach of the implied condition, as he had no right to sell and was in breach of the warranty of quiet possession. It was held that, at the time of sale, the seller had every right to sell the goods, but was in breach of the warranty for quiet possession, because that amounted to an undertaking as to the future.

- Description (s 13 of the SoGA 1979)

Where the sale of goods is by description, the goods must correspond with that description. Goods are sold 'by description' either where the buyer does not see the goods but relies on a description of them or where the buyer sees the goods but relies on terms describing features of the goods or a description on the goods themselves. So, descriptive words printed on packaging could form part of the description; one would buy a packet labelled 'Cornflakes' because one would rely on that word as indicating that the contents were cornflakes.

Not all words used by the seller will be part of the contract description (it might be a 'moot' point whether the ingredients list on the 'Cornflakes' packet also forms part of the contract description under s 13). *Reliance* on the words as *identifying* the goods being bought is the important issue (see *Harlingdon and Leinster Enterprises Ltd v Christopher Hull Fine Art Ltd* (1990)), as was illustrated in *Beale v Taylor* (1967), where the buyer answered an advertisement for the sale of a 'Herald Convertible 1961'. On the back of the car was a disc which stated '1200'. He bought the car. Later, he found that the car consisted of the back half of a 1961 model welded to the front half of an earlier model. It was held that the description in the advertisement was clearly relied on in buying the car and was, therefore, part of the contract description under s 13, which had not been complied with.

The description may be very simple; in *Grant v Australian Knitting Mills* (1936), the buyer asked for 'underpants', which was held to be the contract description, as that was the way in which the buyer identified what he was purchasing. It is interesting to note that the court also indicated that retail sales, where goods were asked for over the counter or chosen from a display, were still sales by description. In other contracts, the description may be a very detailed one, such as a formula (see, for example, *Ashington Piggeries v Christopher Hill Ltd* (1972)) or design specifications. It is not always easy to determine which words used are part of the contract description. In *Re Moore and Co and Landauer and Co* (1921), the contract required tins of fruit to be packed in cases of 30. The correct quantity of tins was delivered, but some were in cases of 24 tins; there was held to be a breach of the contract description. The court decided that a stipulated method of packaging was part of the contract description.

Where goods are 'sold as seen', this is an indication that the goods are not sold under any description within the meaning of s 13.

Once the contractual description of the goods has been established, the question arises of whether or not it has been complied with. This may be easy to determine in some cases, but is often less obvious. In *Arcos Ltd v Ronaasen & Son* (1933), a delivery of staves which were 9-16ths of an inch thick instead of half an inch thick, as required by the contract, was a breach of description. In *Ashington Piggeries v Christopher Hill* (1972), in a written contract, the seller agreed to make up a formula specified by the buyer to produce a 'vitamin fortified' mink food to be called 'King Size'. One of the ingredients in the formula was herring meal, and the herring meal used by the seller was contaminated and harmful to mink. If 'mink food' was part of the contract description under s 13, there would have been a breach of condition, as a product which harmed mink could hardly be correctly described as 'mink food'. However, the House of Lords decided that the statement that the end product was to be a 'mink food' was not part of the contract description; the contract description was the specified formula which indicated what the end product was. Therefore, it was the words 'herring meal' which were in issue as regards compliance with the contract description. Despite the fact the contaminated herring meal was harmful to mink, and even potentially harmful to other animals, it was decided that the contract description was complied with, as the meal was still identifiable as 'herring meal'. This finding has been criticised on the basis that 'herring meal' should be regarded as meaning 'a food which can be safely fed to animals'; if it cannot fulfil that function, it is not 'herring meal'.

Though strict compliance with the description was required in cases such as *Arcos Ltd v Ronaasen and Son* (above), where there was a breach of s 13 even though the staves could still have been used as the buyer intended, namely, to make barrels, the *'de minimis'* rule may allow minor deviations in certain situations. Where a description has acquired a meaning in the trade, goods which comply with that trade meaning will comply with s 13 even if they do not comply with the strict wording of the contract description. In *Peter Darlington Partners Ltd v Gosho Co Ltd* (1964), there was a contract for the purchase of canary seed on a 'pure basis'. The buyers refused to accept 98% pure seed, but, because 98% pure was the highest standard in the trade, there was no breach of description and the buyers were in breach themselves for wrongfully refusing the seed.

Section 13 also indicates that, where goods are sold by sample and description, there must be compliance with both sample and description. It is not sufficient that the goods comply with either description or sample. Sale by sample is the subject of s 15 of the SoGA 1979 (see below).

Finally, it should be noted that s 13 does not require that the seller is undertaking a business transaction, so the private seller, such as a person selling goods through a classified advertisement column, has the obligation to supply goods complying with the contract description.

- Satisfactory quality (s 14(2) of the SoGA 1979)

The SSGA 1994 repealed the implied condition of 'merchantable quality' and replaced it with the current s 14(2).

There is an implied term that the goods shall be of satisfactory quality, according to s 14(2) of the SoGA 1979. While the new s 14(2) uses the word 'term', it is clear from the new s 14(6) that the term is a condition. Unlike s 13, s 14 does not apply to private sales; that is, the goods must be sold in the course of a business. The term 'sale in the course of a business' is not defined in the SoGA 1979, but, in *Stevenson v Rogers* (1999), it was held that a fisherman 'acted in the course of business' when he sold his trawler. Even though he did not deal in vessels, it was a sale connected with his business. (Note, however, *R & B Customs Brokers Ltd v United Dominions Trust* (1988), which discusses the meaning of 'in the course of business' in the context of s 12(1) of the Unfair Contract Terms Act (UCTA) 1977 (see 6.5.3).) Thus, goods which come within s 14(2) include not only goods sold in the normal course of business, but also goods used in or connected with the business, for example, the sale of a van which has been used in a grocery business.

The meaning of the requirement of 'satisfactory quality' must also be considered. Section 14(2A) states that 'goods are of satisfactory quality if they meet the standard that a reasonable person would regard as satisfactory, taking account of any description of the goods, the price (if relevant) and all other relevant circumstances'. This provision must then be read subject to s 14(2B), which states:

> ... the quality of the goods includes their state and condition and the following factors (among others) are in appropriate cases aspects of the quality of goods:
>
> (i) fitness for all the purposes for which goods of the kind in question are commonly supplied; [the 2002 Regulations will add the words 'or normally used']

(ii) appearance and finish;

(iii) freedom from minor defects;

(iv) safety; and

(v) durability.

The SSGA 1994, in replacing s 14(6) of the SoGA 1979, attempts to clarify the meaning of 'satisfactory quality'. An objective test based on the reasonable man is introduced, as well as statutory recognition that second hand goods may have some acceptable minor defects. The factors are to be regarded as a non-exhaustive list and failure to comply with one of the factors will not necessarily result in goods being classified as being of unsatisfactory quality. Existing case law may still be relevant in interpreting both s 14(2A) and s 14(2B). For example, the price of the goods may be extremely relevant in the case of second hand goods, but may not be of significance in relation to new goods sold at a reduced price in a sale (see *Business Appliances Specialists Ltd v Nationwide Credit Corp Ltd* (1988)).

In *Rogers v Parish (Scarborough) Ltd* (1987), the buyer bought a Range Rover for £16,000. It transpired that it had a defective engine, gear box and bodywork, all of which were below the standard normally expected of a vehicle costing that much. It was held that the vehicle was not of merchantable quality. The fact that it was driveable and repairable did not satisfy s 14 of the SoGA 1979, as this could only be judged by considering whether it was of a reasonable standard for a vehicle of its type. As a result, the buyer's rejection was valid and he was entitled to recover the purchase price and damages.

With regard to new cars, in *Bernstein v Pamsons Motors (Golders Green) Ltd* (1987), the buyer purchased a new Nissan car for £8,000. He drove it for three weeks, covering some 140 miles. The engine then seized and had to undergo extensive repairs. The buyer rejected the car and refused to take it back after it had been repaired. The court felt that the buyer of a new car was entitled to expect more than the buyer of a second hand car, although how much more was dependent upon the nature of the defect, the length of time that it took to repair it and the price of the vehicle. The court distinguished between 'the merest cosmetic blemish on a new Rolls Royce which might render it unmerchantable, whereas on a humbler car it might not'. However, whilst the car was unmerchantable at the time of delivery, it was further held that a period of three weeks and 140 miles was a reasonable time to examine and try out the goods. The buyer was, therefore, deemed to have accepted the goods within the meaning of s 35 (see below, 9.2.9) and could, therefore, only claim for breach of warranty.

It is unlikely that the decisions in *Rogers* and *Bernstein* in relation to breach of s 14(2) would have been different in the light of the new definition. However, the goods have to be suitable for all their common purposes under s 14(2B), which is an extension of the s 14(6) definition. As a result, *Aswan Engineering Establishment v Lupdine* (1987) (where containers which could fulfil some, though not all, of their normal uses, as now required by s 14(2B), were of merchantable quality) may need to be reconsidered. However, the decision would probably stand in *Kendall (Henry) and Sons v William Lillico and Sons Ltd* (1968) (where groundnut extraction which harmed pheasants was still of merchantable quality, as it could be safely fed to other poultry, which was one of its normal uses) and *Brown and Sons Ltd v Craiks Ltd* (1970) (where cloth which was suitable for its normal industrial use was of merchantable quality, though it was not fit for the buyer's intended purpose of dressmaking).

The factors now specifically include appearance and finish, as well as freedom from minor defects. The former clearly refer to cosmetic defects which may or may not affect the quality of the goods by reference to the type of goods, price, etc. The same is true of minor defects. For example, a scratch on a Rolls Royce may affect quality, whereas a scratch on a second hand Ford Fiesta may not.

Safety is now a specific factor in assessing satisfactory quality, and it would appear that any matter which results in the goods being unsafe will fall within the new s 14(2).

Finally, durability of the goods also falls to be considered. This raises the contentious issue of the length of time for which a buyer can expect goods to remain of satisfactory quality. However, the test to be applied is that of the reasonable man, that is, an objective test. Again, an assessment of durability can only be made by reference to description, purpose, price, etc. Indeed, it would appear that it will only be in rare situations that these factors are considered in isolation from each other.

From the foregoing analysis of s 14(2), it seems clear that the new legislation was designed to address the shortcomings of the old law which the courts had striven to overcome. A clear illustration of this can be found in the fact that the condition of satisfactory quality applies not simply to the goods sold, but to the 'goods supplied under the contract', which could clearly include 'free gifts' supplied with goods and is a confirmation of the Court of Appeal's decision in *Wilson v Rickett Cockerell* (1954). There, an argument that explosives supplied in a bag of Coalite did not amount to a breach of s 14(2), as the section only applied to the goods purchased – the Coalite – was rejected.

Finally, note should be taken of s 14(2C), which provides for exceptions to the 'satisfactory quality' requirement. Section 14(2C) states that the term does not extend to any 'matter' making the quality of goods unsatisfactory:

o which is specifically drawn to the buyer's attention before the contract is made;

   o   which examination ought to reveal, where the buyer examines the goods before the contract is made; or

   o   which, in the case of a contract for sale by sample, would have been apparent on reasonable examination of the sample.

These exceptions are essentially the same as those found previously in the SoGA 1979; so, for example, if somebody buys a sweater labelled 'shop soiled', he or she cannot later argue that marks on the goods rendered them of unsatisfactory quality. Of course, if the sweater also had a hole in the sleeve which had not been drawn to the buyer's attention, this defect could mean that the sweater was not of satisfactory quality.

Nevertheless, it could be argued that the seller may now be able to invoke this exception, not by actually specifying the defect (as was previously necessary), but by simply mentioning a 'matter' which could affect quality. Case law on this point is awaited with interest.

It should be remembered that the buyer is under no obligation to actually examine the goods before sale. If, however, the buyer chooses to undertake such an examination, then defects which that examination actually reveal, or ought to have revealed, will be excluded from s 14(2).

The 2002 Regulations add four new sub-sections to s 14(2). The effect of these additions is that, in determining whether goods are of 'satisfactory quality', the s 14(2B) factors that the court should consider will also include any 'public statements on the specific characteristics of the goods made about them by the seller, the producer or his representative, particularly in advertising or on labelling'. A 'producer' is not only the manufacturer but also a person who imports the goods into the EC or puts his name, sign or trademark on the goods. The English courts have already taken account of this factor but, as far as the retailer is concerned, having the obligation specifically stated in the 2002 Regulations may mean that more care is taken to check advertisements and labelling of goods. Of course, many such statements will be taken to be 'sales puff', which will not affect the legal position; this was one of the arguments put forward by the company in *Carlill v Carbolic Smoke Ball Co* (1893) as to why their advertisement was not an offer.

It should be noted that this additional factor will not apply:

- to second hand goods;

- to sales at public auctions which consumers can attend in person (therefore, online auctions would be excluded);

- if the seller shows that he was not/could not have been aware of the statement or it had been corrected at the time of contracting or the buyer could not have been influenced to buy by the statement.

Though the additional factor, relating to advertising and labelling statements, only has to be considered by the courts where the buyer is a consumer, nevertheless, where the buyer is a business, the factor may be considered as a 'relevant circumstance' determining 'satisfactory quality' for the purposes of s 14(2A). Thus, those who sell to businesses (for example, manufacturers) may consider their advertising and labelling more carefully.

- Reasonable fitness for purpose (s 14(3) of the SoGA 1979)

There is an implied condition in a contract for the sale of goods that the goods supplied are reasonably fit for any purpose expressly or impliedly made known to the seller or credit-broker under s 14(3) of the SoGA 1979. A breach of this section is to be treated as a breach of a condition. A credit-broker is an intermediary; for instance, a furniture shop might allow a buyer to have goods under a credit sale (see Chapter 18). To achieve this, the goods are sold, 'on paper', to a finance company with whom the buyer then contracts to buy the goods and pay by instalments. Where goods have a normal purpose, the law implies that one buys those goods for that purpose, unless stated otherwise. For example, in the case of *Grant v Australian Knitting Mills* (1936), the purpose of 'underpants' was that they could be worn; and, in *Godley v Perry* (1960), in purchasing a toy catapult, the buyer did not have to state specifically the purpose for which the object was being bought. Note, also, *Kendall and Sons v Lillico and Sons Ltd* (1969), where resale was held to be a normal purpose of goods. If the purpose is unusual or the goods have several normal but distinct uses, for example, timber for paper or for furniture, then the purpose must be made known expressly – that is, it must be spelt out clearly, either verbally or in writing – to the seller before the buyer can rely on this section. An example of this is the case of *Ashington Piggeries v Christopher Hill Ltd* (1972), where the buyers made it clear to the seller that the end product would be fed to mink, even though they supplied the formula.

Whether goods are reasonably fit for the purpose is a question of fact. In *Crowther v Shannon Motor Co* (1975), in determining whether a second hand car which needed a new engine after 2,300 miles was 'reasonably fit', the court said that the age, condition and make of the car should be considered in order to determine what could reasonably be expected of it.

It should also be noted that poor instructions for use or a failure to give warning of dangers related to the use of the goods which are not generally known can render the goods unfit for the buyer's purpose (see *Vacwell Engineering Co Ltd v BDH Chemicals Ltd* (1969) and *Wormell v RHM Agriculture (East) Ltd* (1986)). This may explain rather bizarre warnings in instruction booklets, such as advice not to dry underwear or newspapers in microwave ovens!

Section 14(3) indicates that this condition does not apply where the buyer does not rely on the skill and judgment of the seller or credit-broker, for example, where a brand other than that recommended by the seller is chosen or where it is unreasonable for the buyer to have relied on that skill and judgment if he or she had greater expertise (see *Teheran-Europe Corp v ST Belton Ltd* (1968)). However, even if the buyer selects the product him or herself (for example, from a supermarket shelf), he or she still relies on the seller that the product will fulfil its normal functions.

In *Slater v Finning Ltd* (1996), the seller installed a camshaft in the buyer's vessel. Following a number of repairs and replacements, a new engine had to be installed. The old engine was installed in another vessel with no problems. On the facts, it was concluded that excessive torsional resonance in the vessel caused damage to the camshaft. The buyer argued that, as the seller knew that the camshaft was to be installed in a particular ship, there was reliance on the seller to supply a suitable camshaft for that ship. It was held that there was no breach of condition where the failure of the goods to meet a particular purpose arose from an abnormal feature or idiosyncrasy in the buyer or, as in this case, in the circumstances in which the buyer used the goods, and such was not made known to the seller. In the present case, the camshaft was suitable for use on this type of vessel, which was the extent of the buyer's reliance on the seller. It was only a particular idiosyncrasy of this vessel which made the usual type of camshaft unsuitable. (Compare this case with *Manchester Liners Ltd v Rea* (1922) and see also *Griffiths v Peter Conway Ltd* (1939).)

A final point to note is that reliance on the seller's skill and judgment may be partial, as was shown in *Ashington Piggeries v Christopher Hill Ltd* (1972) (above), where it was held that the buyer, in supplying the formula, did not rely on the seller's skill and judgment that the end product would be suitable for mink (in the sense that he did not rely on the seller that the specified combination of ingredients was suitable for mink), but he did rely on the seller to use ingredients which were not defective. Accordingly, there was a breach of s 14(3).

Whereas s 14(3) currently indicates that the goods must be fit for the purpose made known, 'whether or not that is a purpose for which such goods are commonly supplied', the 2002 Regulations will add the words 'or normally used'. The 2002 Regulations add further sub-sections to s 14(3), which have the effect that:

o Where the buyer is a consumer, the implied term of s 14(3) will not apply 'unless the seller or credit-broker has accepted that the goods are fit for the purpose in question'. It is suggested that the effect of this amendment is to cover situations where the seller or credit-broker indicates that he does not undertake that the goods are fit for the purpose. Presumably, this would not negate the restrictions on exclusion of liability under s 6 of UCTA 1977 (see 6.5.3) but might apply, for example, where a buyer asks whether goods can be used in a particular way but the seller says he has no idea.

o Where the buyer does not deal as a consumer, the implied term of s 14(3) does not apply if the circumstances show that the buyer did not rely on the seller's or credit-broker's skill and judgment or it was unreasonable for him or her to so rely. This provision already applies on the current wording of s 14(3).

- Sale by sample (s 15 of the SoGA 1979)

Section 15 of the SoGA 1979 imposes an implied condition that, where goods are sold by sample, they will comply with that sample. Furthermore, such goods will be free from any defect making their quality unsatisfactory which would not be apparent on reasonable examination of the sample.

This section applies only if there is a term of the contract which states that it is a contract of sale by sample. This could be an oral term, but, if it is in writing, then the term about sale by sample must be written into the contract. The mere act of showing a sample of the goods during negotiations does not make the sale one of sale by sample unless the parties agree to this. In *Drummond v Van Ingen* (1887), Lord MacNaughten examined the function of a sample, stating that:

> ... the office of a sample is to present to the real meaning and intention of the parties with regard to the subject matter of the contract, which, owing to the imperfection of language, it may be difficult or impossible to express in words. The sample speaks for itself.

Everyday examples could be the purchase of carpets or wallpaper by reference to a sample book.

It is no defence under s 15(2) to say that the bulk can easily be made to correspond with the sample. In *E & S Ruben Ltd v Faire Bros & Co Ltd* (1949), a material known as Linatex was sold which was crinkled, whereas the sample had been soft and smooth. The seller argued that, by a simple process of warming, the bulk could have been made as soft as the sample. It was held that there had been a breach of s 15(2) and the sellers were, therefore, liable to pay damages to the buyer.

A buyer may not be able to claim damages under s 15(2) of the SoGA 1979 for defects which he or she could reasonably have discovered upon examination of the goods. He or she may still have an action under s 14(2) and (3). It is important to remember that the implied conditions under s 15 are:

o that the bulk shall correspond with the sample;

o that the buyer shall have a reasonable opportunity to compare the goods with the sample;

o that the goods will be free from any defect rendering them unsatisfactory which would not be apparent on reasonable examination of the sample.

9.2.5 Delivery and payment obligations

By virtue of s 27 of the SoGA 1979, the seller has an obligation to deliver the goods to the buyer and the buyer has a duty to accept the goods and pay for them:

- Seller's delivery obligation

  The seller's obligation is to deliver the goods at the right time and place and by the correct method.

  A stipulated time for delivery will be considered to be 'of the essence' (that is, a condition of the contract), as will a specified date of shipment of goods. Where the time of delivery is not complied with or, in the absence of an agreed time, a reasonable time has elapsed, the buyer may treat the contract as repudiated for breach of condition. Alternatively, he or she can accept late delivery and sue for damages only.

  In *Rickards v Oppenheim* (1950), the seller contracted to build a car for the buyer by 20 March. It was not ready by that date. The buyer did not repudiate the contract, but pressed for early delivery. When it was still not finished by the end of June, the buyer informed the seller that, if it was not ready in another four weeks, he would regard the contract as repudiated. At the end of four weeks, the car was still not ready. It was held that the buyer had acted within his rights. He lost the right to regard the contract as repudiated on 20 March by his waiver, but it was a condition of that waiver, under those circumstances, that delivery should take place as soon as possible. The buyer could, therefore, revive his right to repudiate the contract by giving reasonable notice. The buyer was under no obligation, after four weeks, to buy the car.

- Buyer's obligation to accept and pay for the goods

  Unless the buyer has a right to repudiate the contract for the seller's breach (for example, due to delivery of defective goods), he or she must take and pay for the goods. Failure to do so means that the buyer is in breach of contract and the seller will be able to maintain an action against him or her for the contract price or for damages for non-acceptance (see below, 9.2.6). It should be noted, however, that the *time* of payment is not normally perceived as a condition of the contract unless the parties have expressly agreed otherwise.

9.2.6 Seller's personal remedies

Where the buyer is in breach of contract, the seller may seek a remedy against the buyer personally:

- Action for the price of the goods

  The seller can sue for the contract price, under s 49 of the SoGA 1979, where the buyer has failed to pay on the date fixed in the contract or he or she wrongfully fails to pay, the property in the goods having passed to the buyer (see below, 9.2.12).

If neither of these conditions applies and the buyer wrongfully refuses to take and pay for the goods, he or she cannot be sued for the contract price. If this were allowed, the seller would have both the money and the goods. Instead, the seller may sue for damages for non-acceptance.

The Late Payment of Commercial Debts (Interest) Act 1998 provides for statutory interest to accrue on debts paid late in certain circumstances.

- Damages for non-acceptance of the goods

This right is given by s 50(1) and, according to sub-s (2), the measure of damages, as in *Hadley v Baxendale* (1854), is the loss arising naturally from the breach. However, in this context, note should be taken of sub-s (3), which imposes an obligation on the seller to mitigate his or her loss by reselling the goods that the buyer has refused to accept. Where there is an available market for the goods in question, the measure of damages is *prima facie* to be ascertained by the difference between the contract price and the market or current price at the time or times when the goods ought to have been accepted or, if no time was fixed for acceptance, at the time of refusal to accept (see *WL Thompson Ltd v Robinson Gunmakers Ltd* (1955) and *Charter v Sullivan* (1957)). Currently, problems might arise in applying sub-s (3) because of constant 'price wars', which may make it difficult to determine the 'market' or 'current' price.

9.2.7 Seller's real remedies

A seller may not be able to pursue personal remedies against the buyer because, for example, the buyer has gone into liquidation. However, in such circumstances, he or she may be able to use his or her 'real' remedies by taking action against the goods:

- Lien (ss 41–43 of the SoGA 1979)

The seller has the right to retain possession of the goods, even though the property has passed to the buyer. The SoGA 1979 assumes that delivery and payment are normally concurrent events, except where sales are on credit. The lien, or right to keep the goods, is based on possession of the goods and is only available for the price of the goods, and not for other debts such as storage charges. It may be a useful remedy in times of economic stress where there are rumours of bankruptcies and liquidations. The unpaid seller may well be better off financially with the goods in his or her possession than if he or she had simply become a creditor in the bankruptcy.

Delivery of part of the goods will not destroy the unpaid seller's lien unless the circumstances show an intention to waive the lien. The unpaid seller will lose his or her lien if the goods are delivered for carriage to the buyer and he or she does not reserve the right of disposal over them or if the buyer lawfully obtains possession of the goods.

- Stoppage in transit (ss 44–46 of the SoGA 1979)

If the buyer becomes insolvent and the goods are still in transit between the seller and the buyer, the unpaid seller is given the right of stoppage in transit and can recover the goods from the carrier. The cost of re-delivery must be borne by the seller in this case.

- Right of resale

An unpaid seller can pass a good title to the goods to a second buyer after exercising a right of lien or stoppage in transit. In these cases, the contract with the first buyer is automatically rescinded, so that the property in the goods reverts to the seller, who can keep any further profit made from the resale and any deposit put down by the buyer. If a loss is made on the resale, then he or she can claim damages from the original buyer. There is no requirement that the second purchaser takes delivery or buys in good faith (that is, without knowledge of the first sale).

In *Ward (RV) Ltd v Bignall* (1967), two cars were being sold for £850. After paying a deposit of £25, the buyer refused to pay the remainder. The seller informed the buyer in writing that, if he did not pay the balance by a given date, he would resell the cars. The buyer did not pay. The seller sold one car at £350 but failed to find a purchaser for the other. He brought a claim against the purchaser for the balance of the price and advertising expenses. It was held that the seller could not recover any of the price, since the ownership had reverted back to him, but he could recover damages. The remaining car was worth £450, so that his total loss on resale would be £50, minus the £25 deposit originally paid. He was entitled to this £25 plus advertising expenses.

- Reservation of title (s 19 of the SoGA 1979)

Section 19(1) of the SoGA 1979 indicates that, in contracts for the sale of specific goods, or where goods have been appropriated to the contract (see below, 9.2.12), the seller can reserve the right to dispose of the goods. Effectively, he or she can insert a clause in the contract under which the property in the goods does not pass to the buyer (even if he or she is in possession of the goods) until payment is made. This could protect an unpaid seller where the buyer is in liquidation. If the buyer owns the goods, the liquidator can sell them and the money raised goes towards paying all creditors. The seller would merely be a creditor for the purchase price and might only receive a small part of the price if there is insufficient to pay all creditors in full. Clearly, it is better for the seller to retain ownership, so that he or she can resell the goods.

- The *Romalpa* clause

This arose from the case of *Aluminium Industrie Vassen BV v Romalpa Aluminium Ltd* (1976), which established that the manufacturer or supplier of goods had rights to retain some proprietary interest over the goods until paid for, even when the goods supplied had been processed or sold. Furthermore, proprietary rights could be maintained even after a sub-sale of the goods (sale by the buyer to another party), so that debts owed to the buyer could be transferred to the manufacturer or supplier if an appropriate *Romalpa* clause had been inserted.

9.2.8 Buyer's remedies

- Action for specific performance (s 52(1) of the SoGA 1979)

  The court can make an order of specific performance against the seller in the case of a contract to deliver specific or ascertained goods; the order cannot be made for unascertained or future goods (see below, 9.2.12). The seller is required to deliver the goods and is not given the option of paying damages instead. The courts will not make the order for such a remedy unless damages for non-delivery would not be adequate. Damages will generally be adequate, except where the goods are in some way unique or rare.

- Remedies for breach of condition

  Where the seller is in *breach of condition*, the buyer can treat the contract as repudiated. Accordingly, he or she can *reject* the goods, claim a *refund* of the price paid or refuse payment and claim *damages* for further loss suffered; but, where the seller is in *breach of warranty*, the buyer may only sue for damages for breach of contract.

  It is useful to note that, from a practical point of view, the buyer who sues for breach of implied terms of the SoGA 1979 would be well advised to sue for breach of more than one implied term, in order to increase his or her chances of success. In *Godley v Perry* (1960) (see above), the child successfully pleaded breaches of s 14(2) and (3). There may appear to be an overlap of the provisions of the implied terms on the facts of some cases, but all the implied terms are needed to protect a buyer. For example, if one purchased a brand new washing machine and it was delivered badly dented but in full working order, one could claim that it was not of satisfactory quality under s 14(2). However, as it worked properly, there would be no breach of ss 13 or 14(3).

  Rejection of goods means refusing to take delivery or informing the seller that they are rejected and returning the goods. A buyer in possession of rejected goods will often take them back to the seller, but is under no obligation to do so; the seller has the obligation to collect rejected goods from the buyer (s 36 of the SoGA 1979). The buyer does not have a lien over rejected goods and must hand them back, even if the purchase price paid has not been refunded.

  The new s 15A of the SoGA 1979 may now limit the right to reject goods for 'technical' breaches of condition, as occurred in cases such as *Re Moore*

& *Co v Landauer* & *Co* (1921). The courts are now given the right to refuse to allow rejection of goods by a business buyer for breach of s 13, 14 or 15 where 'the breach is so slight that it would be unreasonable for him to reject them'. In such circumstances, the buyer may instead sue for damages for breach of warranty, though it should be noted that the effect of s 15A can be circumvented by a 'contrary intention' in or be 'implied from' the contract. Whether the breach is 'slight' is a question of fact in each case. Section 15A does not apply where the buyer is a consumer. Guidance on whether or not a person 'deals as consumer' can be found in UCTA 1977, which provides that a person deals as consumer if the contract is not made in the course of a business, if the other party does not make the contract in the course of a business and if the goods are of a type ordinarily supplied for private use of consumption. This has a wide remit and, since the burden is on the seller to prove that the buyer does not deal as consumer, the average sale of goods contract is unlikely to be affected.

The new s 35A of the SoGA 1979 deserves consideration, as it gives the buyer a wider right of *partial* rejection than did s 30(4), which has been repealed. In line with what many businesspersons would do in practice, the buyer has now been given the right to choose to accept those goods which do conform with the contract and to reject those which do not.

Where the buyer claims a *refund* of the price paid, he or she can recover all payments made if the consideration has failed. This may apply to cases of non-delivery, but may also apply where there has been a breach of condition of the sale. If the contract is severable (for example, where there are separate delivery times and instalments for different parts of the goods), the buyer can accept part and reject part of the goods and recover the price paid on the rejected goods.

The buyer's *claim for damages* may be for non-delivery or for breach of condition or warranty. Where the claim is for damages for non-delivery, damages may be recovered for losses arising naturally from the breach (s 51(2) of the SoGA 1979), but this may not allow a buyer to claim the whole of the profit he or she expected to gain by resale of the goods which the seller has failed to deliver. He or she is required to mitigate his or her loss by purchasing replacement goods for resale, and the measure of damages which he or she is entitled to is the difference between the contract price and the current or market price which he or she would have to pay for replacements, assuming that it is higher (s 51(3) of the SoGA 1979).

Damages for breach of condition are assessed according to the usual contractual rules, but it should be noted that, if the buyer has 'accepted' a breach of condition, he or she can only treat it as a breach of warranty (s 11(4) of the SoGA; but note also that s 11(4) must be read subject to s 35, which is discussed below, 9.2.9).

- Damages for breach of warranty

These are assessed according to the provisions of s 53 of the SoGA 1979, which, in particular, indicate the measure as *prima facie* the difference between the value of the goods at the time of delivery to the buyer and the value they would have had if they had fulfilled the warranty.

The buyer's right to claim any of the remedies described above may be affected by:

  o   acceptance of a breach of condition;

  o   an exclusion or limitation clause.

The 2002 Regulations will give additional remedies to the buyer of goods which do not conform with the contract of sale, who deals as a 'consumer'; these remedies are not available in relation to second hand goods or where the goods are sold at a public auction which consumers can attend in person. The additional remedies are replacement, repair, reduction in price and rescission. Whilst such remedies may currently be given voluntarily by sellers, there is no legal obligation to do so. The 2002 Regulations also indicate that if the buyer chooses replacement or repair, he cannot reject for breach of condition *until* he has given the seller a reasonable time to carry out the chosen remedial action.

The 2002 Regulations also indicate that, if the goods do not conform with the contract of sale at any time within six months of the transfer of ownership to the buyer, it will be presumed that they did not conform at the time property was transferred. The effect of this provision is that the buyer would not bear the burden of proving that non-conformity existed at the time the goods were supplied to him. However, it should be appreciated that:

(a)   as a presumption, it is rebuttable by evidence to the contrary;

(b)   under the 2002 Regulations, currently the 'six month' rule only applies in relation to a claim for the additional remedies given by the Regulations.

Furthermore, note should be taken of the fact that the 2002 Regulations have not yet addressed the issue of the two year limitation period for action of the EC Directive. The current six year limitation period on breach of contract actions may continue to apply; alternatively, the two year limitation period may be applied only to the 'additional remedies'. It seems unlikely that the two year period would be applied across the board, even to existing remedies. The EC Directive also proposed that a consumer should be required to make complaint within two months of discovering non-conformity of the goods. It has been decided not to include such a requirement in the 2002 Regulations; in any case, the SoGA 1979 rules relating to 'acceptance' (see 9.2.9) probably ensure that complaints are made quickly.

9.2.9 Acceptance

As already stated above, acceptance of a breach of condition deprives the buyer of the right to reject the goods and claim a refund or refuse payment. It does not deprive him or her of all remedies; he or she is still entitled to claim damages for breach of warranty. The rules relating to what amounts to 'acceptance' are contained in s 35 of the SoGA 1979 (these rules were amended by the SSGA 1994), which indicates that acceptance occurs when either:

- the buyer states to the seller that the goods are acceptable, for example, where an acceptance note is signed; or

- the goods have been delivered to the buyer and he or she does an act in relation to them which is inconsistent with the ownership of the seller, for example, selling the goods or processing them.

The rules on when acceptance takes place are subject to s 35(2), which provides the buyer with an opportunity to examine the goods in the following circumstances:

Where goods are delivered to the buyer, and he has not previously examined them, he is not deemed to have accepted them until he has had a reasonable opportunity of examining them for the purpose –

(a) of ascertaining whether they are in conformity with the contract; and

(b) in the case of a contract for sale by sample, of comparing the bulk with the sample.

This right cannot be removed or excluded in consumer sales.

Although s 34(1) of the SoGA 1979 has been repealed, s 34 continues to provide that, subject to agreement, the seller is bound on request to afford the buyer a reasonable opportunity of examining the goods for the purpose of ascertaining whether they conform with the contract. Following s 35(2), acceptance cannot take place until this examination has been carried out.

Section 35(4) continues to provide that acceptance is also deemed to have taken place when the buyer retains the goods after a reasonable length of time without intimating to the seller that they will be rejected. What amounts to a reasonable length of time has to be considered in conjunction with the reasonable opportunity to examine the goods. It will be a question of fact in each case, as illustrated in *Bernstein v Pamsons Motors* (1987) (see 9.2.4), where the car was held to be neither of merchantable quality nor fit for the purpose, but the plaintiff was deemed to have accepted the car under s 35 and, therefore, could only treat the breach of condition as a warranty and claim damages. The court felt that 'reasonable time' meant a reasonable time to try out the goods, not a reasonable time to discover the defect.

As a result of the new provisions, it is likely that the decision in *Bernstein* would be different today.

A further clarification of the rules on acceptance has been provided by s 35(6). A buyer is not deemed to have accepted the goods merely because he or she has requested or agreed to their repair. As it had been thought that agreeing to repair may amount to acceptance, this section provides a useful addition to consumer protection.

9.2.10 Exclusion and limitation of liability

The rules of UCTA 1977 relating to the ability to exclude or limit liability for breach of contract are discussed above (see Chapter 6) but, insofar as they apply to contracts for the sale of goods, they can be summarised as follows:

- Section 12 of the SoGA 1979 cannot be excluded in consumer or non-consumer sales (the distinction between consumer and non-consumer sales is covered by s 12(1) of UCTA 1977).

- In consumer sales (for example, where an individual buys goods from a shop), liability for breach of ss 13–15 of the SoGA 1979 cannot be excluded. Businesses should be aware that it is a criminal offence to include a term in a contract, or to display a notice, which purports to exclude the statutory implied terms or restrict liability for their breach as against a person who deals as a consumer (by virtue of the Consumer Transactions (Restrictions on Statements) Order 1976 (SI 1976/1813), as amended by SI 1998/127). Accordingly, a notice in a shop which states 'No refunds' is a criminal offence, but one which states 'No refunds, except on faulty goods' does not contravene the Order, as there is no obligation to give refunds, except where they are legally faulty under ss 13–15 of the SoGA 1979.

  The 2002 Regulations indicate that, for the purposes of ss 13–15 of the SoGA 1979, the definition of a consumer sale in s 12(1) of UCTA 1977 will not apply. Instead, there is a new definition:

  > ... a party deals as a consumer where –
  >
  > (a) he is a natural person who makes the contract otherwise than in the course of a business; and
  >
  > (b) the other party does make the contract in the course of a business.

  Thus, the s 12(1) of UCTA 1977 requirement that the goods be of a type ordinarily supplied for private use and consumption is omitted. Equally, there will not be a consumer sale for the purposes of exclusion of liability for breaches of ss 13–15 of the SoGA 1979 if the goods are second hand or sold at public auction where consumers may attend in person.

- In non-consumer sales, it is possible to exclude liability for breach of ss 13–15 of the SoGA 1979, provided that the exclusion clause satisfies the test of 'reasonableness'. The requirement of reasonableness means that the exclusion clause 'shall be a fair and reasonable one to be included, having regard to the circumstances which were or ought to have been known to or in the contemplation of the parties when the contract was made'.

UCTA 1977 provides that, in determining 'reasonableness', regard shall be had in particular to guidelines stated in Sched 2 (as listed above, Chapter 6), such as 'whether the customer received an inducement to agree to the term'. A clause in a contract which states that 'The seller undertakes no liability for defects in the goods sold in return for granting the purchaser a 20% price discount' could be considered under this guideline.

- Any other liability for breach of contract can be excluded or restricted only to the extent that it is reasonable.
- Exclusion of liability for death and personal injury is prohibited.
- It is possible to exclude liability for other loss or damage arising from negligence or misrepresentation only to the extent that the clause is deemed to be reasonable.

In addition, the Unfair Terms in Consumer Contracts Regulations 1994 (SI 1994/3159), which implement EC Directive 93/13, provide further protection with respect to exclusion or other unfair terms in consumer contracts where the term has not been individually negotiated, such as may be found in a standard form contract. 'Consumer' in this context is confined to natural persons and is, therefore, currently narrower than UCTA 1977 (see 6.5.4).

An unfair term is defined in reg 4(1) as 'any term which, contrary to the requirement of good faith, causes a significant imbalance in the parties' rights and obligations under the contract to the detriment of the consumer'. Such terms are not unlawful *per se*, but can be challenged on the basis that they are contrary to good faith. The criteria for assessing good faith are laid down in Sched 2 to the Regulations, in which it is stated that regard shall be had in particular to:

(a) the strength of the bargaining positions of the parties;

(b) whether the consumer had an inducement to agree to the term;

(c) whether the goods or services were sold or supplied to the special order of the consumer; and

(d) the extent to which the seller or supplier has dealt fairly and suitably with the consumer.

These criteria are very similar to the 'reasonableness' criteria in UCTA 1977, but Sched 3 to the Regulations also gives an illustrative list of terms which may be considered unfair. A consumer wishing to challenge a term under the Regulations can ask the court to find that the unfair term should not be binding. This allows the remaining terms of the contract to stand. In addition, the Director General of Fair Trading, on receipt of a complaint, has the power to obtain an injunction against unfair terms which would allow a challenge to be made against particular terms in standard form contracts.

The 1994 Regulations apply to contracts made between 1 July 1995 and 1 October 1999. Contracts made after that date will be governed by the Unfair Contract Terms Regulations 1999, which do not change the 1994 Regulations extensively, though there are some differences. For example, the right of the Director General of Fair Trading to obtain an injunction against a person using an unfair term has been extended to other bodies, such as Weights and Measures Authorities and the Data Protection Registrar.

9.2.11 Guarantees

Many consumer goods, such as electrical appliances, are sold with a voluntary guarantee given by the seller or manufacturer. These often give the right to replacement or repair. It should be noted that these rights are not given *instead* of statutory rights under ss 13–15 of the SoGA 1979; they are simply rights which the consumer may choose to exercise against the person giving the guarantee. The person giving the guarantee is obliged by law to insert a statement to the effect that 'Statutory rights are not affected' (Consumer Transactions (Restrictions on Statements) Order 1976 (SI 1976/1813), as amended). Furthermore, it should be noted that exercising the right to repair under a guarantee does not necessarily amount to 'acceptance' of the goods depriving the buyer of the right to reject them for breach of condition (see above, 9.2.9).

Under the 2002 Regulations, these voluntary (or 'commercial') guarantees will be further controlled. The new controls will operate where a natural person who acts outside the course of a business is supplied with goods under a contract and is also given a guarantee. The main provisions of the 2002 Regulations are as follows:

- the guarantee creates a contract between the consumer and the guarantor, subject to any conditions stated in the guarantee or associated advertising;

- the guarantee must be in plain, intelligible language, written in English where the goods are supplied within the UK, and must indicate how to claim under the guarantee, its duration and the name and address of the guarantor. Furthermore, the consumer may require that a copy of the guarantee, in writing or other durable medium, be made available to him or her within a reasonable time.

Failure to comply with these provisions allows enforcement of an injunction against the guarantor.

9.2.12 Transfer of property and risk

The main essential of the s 2 of the SoGA 1979 definition is the transfer of property (ownership) to the buyer. It is important to know when property is transferred because:

- if the property has passed, the unpaid seller can sue the buyer for the agreed contract price (s 49(1) of the SoGA 1979; see above, 9.2.6); and

- as a general rule, risk passes with property (s 20(1) of the SoGA 1979), although this rule may be varied by agreement or custom. In such circumstances, it will become necessary to ascertain who bears the financial risk of loss of the goods – the seller or the buyer. ('Risk' determines who bears the cost of accidental loss or damage; that is, loss or damage caused by reasons beyond the control of the seller, buyer or their employees.) Various possibilities can complicate the situation. It is possible that the title to the goods has passed to the buyer and yet he or she still does not have possession. Similarly, it is possible that the buyer has the goods in his or her possession but the title to the goods and, therefore, the risk has not yet passed.

The Act gives detailed rules for determining when property is transferred and divides goods into four categories:

- Specific goods

    These are goods which are identified and agreed upon at the time of contracting (for example, a contract to buy a particular second hand car). The term also includes a share in a specific bulk which has not been divided up at the time of contracting, expressed as a percentage or fraction (s 61 of the SoGA 1979). For example, a contract for the sale of '50% of the seller's 100 tons of grain in the warehouse' would be a sale of specific goods, but the sale of '50 tons of the 100 tons of grain in the seller's warehouse' would not be a sale of specific goods, as the goods are not expressed as a percentage or fraction of the 100 tons.

- Unascertained goods

    This means that the seller possesses goods of the type that the buyer (B) agrees to buy, but, at the time of contracting, B does not know exactly which goods he or she will get. For example, B agrees to buy a sofa like the one on show, but, at the time of contracting, B does not know which of six such sofas in stock he or she will actually get. In this context, note s 16, which states: '... where there is a contract for the sale of unascertained goods, no property in the goods is transferred to the buyer unless and until the goods are ascertained.' However, s 16 must now be read subject to s 20A (see below).

- Ascertained goods

  These are goods identified after the making of the contract. Thus, when B agrees to buy one of the six sofas that the shop has in stock, the goods will not be ascertained until one of the sofas is labelled/set aside for B.

- Future goods

  These are goods to be manufactured or acquired by the seller after the making of the contract of sale. As a general rule, future goods will be unascertained.

  Subject, of course, to the provisions of s 16, s 17 of the SoGA 1979 provides that the property passes when the parties intend it to pass and, in determining this, regard should be had to the terms of the contract, the conduct of the parties and all other circumstances. A reservation of title clause (see above, 9.2.7) is a common example of an expression of the parties' intention. Where the parties have not agreed on a time at which property is to pass (as would be common in consumer transactions), s 18 determines the time of transfer, as described below.

The passing of property in specific goods

The general rule for the passing of property in specific goods is that, if a contract of sale is unconditional, property passes to the buyer when the contract is made (s 18 r 1). This is subject to the intention of the parties. In *Re Anchor Line (Henderson Bros Ltd)* (1937), a crane was sold to buyers, who agreed to pay annual sums for depreciation. It was held that the buyers would not have paid depreciation on their own goods; so, the intention must be inferred that the property in the goods remained with the sellers until the price was fully paid.

In *Dennant v Skinner and Collam* (1948), a gentleman bought a car at an auction and, later, signed a form to the effect that the ownership of the vehicle would not pass to him until his cheque had been cleared. He sold the car to a third party and there followed a dispute about the ownership of the car. It was held that the contract was complete and ownership passed as the auctioneer's hammer fell. The third party therefore acquired a good title to the car. If s 18 r 1 is satisfied, property passes immediately.

If the contract is for the sale of specific goods but the seller is bound to do something to them to put them in a deliverable state, then ownership does not pass until that thing is done and the buyer has notice that it is done (s 18 r 2).

In *Underwood v Burgh Castle Brick and Cement Syndicate* (1922), the parties entered a contract for the sale of an engine weighing 30 tons. At the time that the contract was made, the engine was embedded in a concrete floor. Whilst it was being removed and loaded onto a truck, it was damaged. The seller still sued for the price. It was held that the engine was not in a deliverable state when the contract was made and, applying r 2, property would not pass until the engine was safely loaded on the truck; the seller must, therefore, bear the risk.

If the goods are to be weighed, tested or measured by the seller, or are to be subjected to some other act or thing for the purpose of ascertaining the price, the property will not pass until the process is complete and the buyer is informed, unless there is a specific agreement to the contrary (s 18 r 3).

Where goods are supplied on sale or return or on approval, property passes to the buyer when:

- the buyer signifies approval or acceptance to the seller (see *Kirkham v Attenborough* (1897)); or

- the buyer does any other act adopting the transaction; or

- the buyer, whilst not giving approval or acceptance, retains the goods beyond the agreed time or, if no time is agreed, beyond a reasonable time (s 18 r 4). In *Poole v Smith's Car Sales (Balham) Ltd* (1962), following several requests by the seller for the return of his car, which had been left at a garage on a sale or return basis, the car was returned damaged. It was held that, as the car had not been returned within a reasonable time, property had passed to the defendant, who would then be liable for the price.

Section 18 rr 1–4 clearly apply where the specific goods are those identified and agreed upon at the time of sale, but the s 61 of the SoGA 1979 definition of specific goods also includes a share in a specific bulk which has not been divided up at the time of contracting and which is expressed as a percentage or fraction. Though such goods would be unascertained at the time of contracting, they are defined as 'specific goods'. Unfortunately, there is no statutory provision stating when the property is to pass.

The passing of property in unascertained goods

No property passes in unascertained or future goods, unless and until the goods become ascertained (s 16). Section 18 r 5 provides that:

> ... where there is a contract for the sale of unascertained or future goods by description, and goods of that description and in a deliverable state are unconditionally appropriated to the contract, either by the seller with the assent of the buyer or by the buyer with the assent of the seller, the property in the goods then passes to the buyer and the assent may be express or implied, and may be given either before or after the appropriation is made.

In *Carlos Federspiel and Co v Charles Twigg and Co Ltd* (1957), it was held that goods are unconditionally appropriated to the contract if they have been 'irrevocably earmarked' for use in that contract.

Where the seller places the goods in the hands of a carrier for transmission to the buyer, this is deemed to be 'unconditional appropriation', unless he or she reserves the right to dispose of the goods (s 18 r 5(2)).

This is further illustrated by the case of *McDougall v Aeromarine of Emsworth Ltd* (1958), in which the seller agreed to build a yacht for the buyer. As part of the agreement, after the first instalment was paid, the yacht and all the materials were intended to become the 'absolute property' of the buyer. It was held that no property could pass to the buyer, since the goods were not physically in existence at that time.

In *Healy v Howlett* (1917), 190 boxes of fish were carried by rail. The buyer was to purchase 20 boxes and the seller directed the railway company to set aside 20 boxes. However, before this could be done, the fish went rotten. The seller had sent the buyer an invoice, stating that the fish were carried at the buyer's sole risk. It was held that, since the fish had gone rotten before the goods were ascertained, property could not pass to the buyer, who was, therefore, entitled to reject the goods. Obviously, the critical factor in this case was the failure on the part of the railway company to identify the 20 boxes by setting them aside for the buyer. It would have been untenable for future buyers if the courts had made the buyer 'bear the loss' in these circumstances.

Section 18 r 5(3) provides for ascertainment by exhaustion. This occurs where the goods are part of a designated bulk and the bulk is reduced to a quantity which is equal or less than the contract quantity. In these circumstances, the goods will be deemed to be appropriated. For example, a buyer agrees to buy 200 cases of wine from 500 cases stored in the seller's warehouse. The seller then sells and delivers 300 cases to another buyer. The remaining 200 cases are then deemed to be appropriated to the contract and property passes to the buyer when the 300 cases are removed from the warehouse.

Section 16 must be considered in the light of the new s 20A, which provides that, where the buyer purchases a specified quantity (for example, 100 tons, but not a quantity expressed as a percentage or fraction of the whole) from an identified bulk source, and has paid for some or all of the goods forming part of the bulk, the buyer becomes co-owner of the bulk. No specific provision is made for the passing of risk in such situations, but it has been suggested that, if the bulk is partially destroyed before the shares of several buyers are divided, they bear the risk, and so suffer loss proportionate to the size of their undivided shares. (See Dobson, P, 'Sale of goods forming part of a bulk' (1995) 16 SLR 11.)

Exceptions to s 20(1) of the SoGA 1979

Though the general rule is that property and risk pass together, there are exceptions to this rule:

- Under s 20(2), 'where delivery has been delayed through the fault of either buyer or seller, the goods are at the risk of the party at fault as regards any loss which might not have occurred but for such fault'.

- The contract or trade custom may indicate that the passing of property and risk is separated. For example, in a 'cif' (cost, insurance and freight) contract, goods are sold abroad and carriage by sea is part of the contract. In such contracts, property passes to the buyer on loading for sea transit; risk does not pass until later, when the seller sends the shipping documents to the buyer against payment.

Consequences of bearing the 'risk'

- If the buyer bears the risk at the time of loss or damage, he or she must pay for the goods and cannot claim for breach of condition when he or she receives no goods or damaged goods.
- If the seller bears the risk at the time of loss or damage and the contract was for future or unascertained goods, he or she must, at his or her own expense, get a replacement to deliver; otherwise, he or she will be in breach of condition by failure to deliver or by delivering damaged goods.
- Under s 7 of the SoGA 1979, where there is a contract for the sale of specific goods and they perish whilst at the seller's risk, the contract is frustrated (see above, 8.4). Note that the rules of the Law Reform (Frustrated Contracts) Act 1943 do not apply to s 7 situations.

9.2.13 Sale by a person who is not the owner

There is an implied condition in s 12 of the SoGA 1979 that the seller has a right to sell the goods, that is, pass on a good title to them. The rule *nemo dat quod non habet* means that a person cannot give what he or she has not got, so that, in general, ownership is protected. The general rule is that, where goods are sold by a person who is not the owner, the buyer acquires no better title than the seller (s 21 of the SoGA 1979). However, there are exceptions and the law may often have to choose between the rights of two innocent parties – the innocent purchaser and the real owner of the goods. Generally, the buyer will have to return the goods to the true owner, usually without any recompense, although where the goods have been 'improved', the buyer may be entitled to some reimbursement.

If the innocent purchaser does not get good title, he or she may sue the seller for breach of s 12(1) of the SoGA 1979. See *Rowland v Divall* (1923) (above, 9.2.4). The exceptions to the *nemo dat* rule are as follows:

- Estoppel

  If the seller or buyer, by his or her conduct, makes the other party believe that a certain fact is true, and the other party alters his or her position, then that same party will later be estopped (or prevented) from saying that the fact is untrue. This has arisen where a party has, for complicated reasons, signed a statement that their own property belongs to someone else and then ends up 'buying back' their own property. They may be estopped from denying the statement that they made falsely about the ownership of the property (*Eastern Distributors Ltd v Goldring* (1957)).

In order to make a successful claim, estoppel can only be raised against a person who had actual knowledge of the facts and actually agreed to them knowing that a third party might rely on the 'apparent' authority.

- Agency

  If a principal appoints an agent to sell his or her goods to a third party, then any sale by the agent, in accordance with the instructions given, will pass on a good title to the third party. If, however, the agent has exceeded the instructions in some way, then no title will pass to the third party unless the agent had apparent authority (*Central Newbury Car Auctions v Unity Finance* (1957)).

- Mercantile agency

  A third party has an even stronger claim to the title of the goods where the agent is a mercantile agent. A mercantile agent is one 'having in the customary course of business as such agent, authority either to sell goods or to consign goods for the purposes of sale or to buy goods, or to raise money on the security of goods' (s 1(1) of the Factors Act 1889). So, for example, where the third party, as a consumer, buys a car from an agent who is in the car trade, this provision may apply.

  The Factors Act 1889 states that the owner is bound by the actions of a mercantile agent in the following circumstances:

  o If the agent has possession of the goods or the documents of title, with the owner's consent, and makes any sale, pledge or other disposition of them in the ordinary course of business, whether or not the owner authorised it (s 2(1); *Folkes v King* (1923)). Any third party claiming against the owner in this situation must prove, *inter alia*, that, at the time of the sale, he or she had no notice of the lack of authority on the part of the agent.

    In *Pearson v Rose and Young* (1951), the owner of a car took it to a dealer and asked him to obtain offers. The owner did not intend to hand over the registration book, but left it with the dealer by mistake. The dealer sold the car with the book to an innocent buyer. The question of true ownership of the car was raised. It was held that the dealer had obtained the car 'with the consent of the owner' but this consent did not extend to the registration book; hence, the sale must be treated as a sale without registration book which was not in the ordinary course of business, and the buyer could not get a good title to the car.

  o If the mercantile agent pledges goods as security for a prior debt, the pledgee acquires no better right to the goods than the factor has against his or her principal at the time of the pledge (s 4).

- o If the mercantile agent pledges goods in consideration of either the delivery of the goods or a document of title to goods or a negotiable security, the pledgee acquires no right in the goods pledged beyond the value of the goods, documents or security when so delivered in exchange (s 5).

- o If the mercantile agent has received possession of goods from their owner for the purpose of consignment or sale and the consignee has no notice that the agent is not the owner, the consignee has a lien on the goods for any advances he or she has made to the agent (s 7).

- • Sales authorised by law

  There are cases in which the title does not pass directly from the owner, because the sale is authorised by the court, for example, the sale of goods which are the subject matter of legal proceedings. Similarly, in common law or by statute, it is sometimes declared that a non-owner is entitled to sell goods, for example, an unpaid seller (see above, 9.2.7).

- • Sale in market overt (s 22 of the SoGA 1979)

  This was a rule relating to well established open public markets in England and shops within the City of London. These rules did not apply in Scotland and Wales. When goods were sold in such 'markets', at business premises, in the normal hours of business between sunrise and sunset, the buyer would obtain a good title as long as he bought the goods in good faith and without notice of the defect in title on the part of the seller (*Reid v Metropolitan Police Comr* (1974)). The Sale of Goods (Amendment) Act 1994, which came into force in January 1995, has abolished this exception to the *nemo dat* rule, although it should be noted that its effect is not retrospective.

- • Sale under a voidable title (s 23 of the SoGA 1979)

  Where a buyer obtains goods by fraud, he or she acquires a voidable title in them and has title unless and until the seller avoids the contract, so that the title in the goods reverts to him or her. The seller may avoid the contract by telling the buyer that he or she avoids or by, for example, informing the police. If the person who obtained the goods by fraud resells them before the original seller avoids the contract, the buyer in good faith who did not know that the person who sold the goods to him or her had a defective title acquires good title and keeps the goods. In *Car & Universal Finance Co v Caldwell* (1965), the buyer obtained a car by fraud, paying by a cheque, which was dishonoured. The seller told the police and then the buyer resold the car to a purchaser, who was later found by the court not to have acted in good faith. The original owner had good title and could recover the car, because he had avoided the buyer's title *before* he resold the car *and* the person who subsequently purchased the car was not an innocent purchaser.

- Disposition by a seller in possession (s 24 of the SoGA 1979)

  A contract of sale can be complete and valid even where the goods are still in the possession of the seller, for example, when they are awaiting delivery. If, in this scenario, the seller sells the goods a second buyer, the second buyer will obtain a good title to those goods if delivery of them is taken. However, the goods must be taken in good faith and without notice of the original sale. This leaves the first buyer in the position of having to sue the seller for breach of contract.

  In *Pacific Motor Auctions Ltd v Motor Credits (Hire Finance) Ltd* (1965), a car dealer sold a number of vehicles to the plaintiffs under a 'display agreement'. This allowed the seller to retain possession of the cars for display in their showroom. He was paid 90% of the purchase price and was authorised to sell the cars as agent for the plaintiff. The seller got into financial difficulties and the plaintiffs revoked their authority to sell the cars. However, the dealer sold a number of them to the defendants, who took them in good faith and without notice of the previous sale. Whilst the defendants knew about the 'display agreement', it was presumed that the dealer had the authority to sell the cars; as a result, it was held that s 24 applied and that, as the defendant had obtained a good title to the car, the plaintiff would fail in their claim for the return of the vehicles.

- Disposition by a buyer in possession (s 25 of the SoGA 1979)

  Disposition by a buyer in possession is a corresponding situation, where the buyer possesses the goods but the seller has retained property in them. Then, if the buyer has the goods and any necessary documents of title with the consent of the seller and transfers these to an innocent transferee (second buyer), that transferee will obtain a good title to the goods; again, this is subject to the proviso that the second buyer takes the goods in good faith and without notice of any lien or other claim on the goods by the original seller. In *Cahn v Pockett's Bristol Channel Co* (1899), it was held that possession of a bill of lading (a document of title) with the owner's consent was sufficient to pass a good title to a third party under s 25(1); in *Re Highway Foods International Ltd* (1995), it was held that, where there is a reservation of title clause, the sub-purchaser may not be able to rely on s 25.

  In *Newtons of Wembley Ltd v Williams* (1965), a car was sold with an agreement that the property would not pass until the price was paid. The cheque for payment was dishonoured, which meant that no title had passed because of the provisions of the contract; the buyer was, therefore, a buyer in possession without any title when he sold the car in a London street market. The car was then sold to the defendant. It was held that, as the buyer took the car in good faith when it was resold in the market, he obtained a good title under s 25, which he then transferred by sale to the defendant. It should be stressed, however, that s 25 only applies where the buyer in possession resells as if he were 'a mercantile agent'; in the *Newtons of Wembley* case, this aspect was satisfied by sale in the street market.

It is worth comparing *Newtons of Wembley* with *Caldwell* (1965); once the buyer's title was avoided in *Caldwell*, he became a buyer in possession within the meaning of s 25. However, s 25 could not have operated because the subsequent purchaser did *not* act in good faith.

- Sale of motor vehicles which are subject to hire purchase agreements

  The law changed in 1964 (by Pt III of Hire Purchase Act 1964 (re-enacted in the Consumer Credit Act 1974)) to protect 'private purchasers' of motor vehicles which were subject to a hire purchase agreement. The original hirer will still have the same obligation to the finance company. The purchaser who takes the car in good faith, without notice of the hire purchase agreement, gets a good title thereto. However, it appears that the original hire purchase contract must be valid for the third party to be protected (see *Shogun Finance Ltd v Hudson* (2001); see 7.2.3).

In conclusion, it should be noted that, if none of the exceptions to the *nemo dat* rule apply, the original owner retains title and may sue in the tort of conversion anyone who does possess or has possessed the goods since they were obtained from the original owner.

9.3 THE SUPPLY OF GOODS AND SERVICES ACT 1982

9.3.1 Implied terms

The Supply of Goods and Services Act (SGSA) 1982 provides protection in respect of agreements which do not fulfil the definition of the SoGA 1979 but under which goods are supplied, usually along with a service. For example, an exchange contract and a car service which included purchase of new parts would come within the Act. The SGSA 1982 itself mirrors the SoGA 1979, in that it implies conditions with respect to goods supplied. These implied conditions are contained in ss 2–5 and are very similar to ss 12–15 of the SoGA 1979; that is, there are implied conditions regarding title, description, quality and fitness for purpose, as well as sample. The SGSA 1982 also applies to contracts of hire, in that ss 6–10 imply in hire contracts terms similar to those implied by ss 12–15 of the SoGA 1979 in sale of goods contracts. The SGSA 1982 is also subject to similar amendments, introduced by the SSGA 1994. These amendments can be found in Sched 2. The 2002 Regulations will amend the rules relating to implied terms and remedies in the same way as for contracts for the sale of goods (see 9.2.8).

Furthermore, the SGSA 1982 provides protection for the victims of poor quality workmanship, including the time it takes to provide services and the price for such services. It applies to all contracts where a 'person agrees to carry out a service in the course of a business'. Dry cleaning and window cleaning contracts would come within this definition. The implied terms as to services can be found in ss 13–15.

Section 13 of the SGSA 1982 states that there is an implied term that, where the supplier is acting in the course of a business, the supplier will carry out the service with reasonable skill and care.

Section 14 states that, where the supplier is acting within the course of a business and the time for the service to be carried out is not fixed by the contract or determined by a course of dealings between the parties, the supplier will carry out the service within a reasonable time.

Section 15 states that, where the consideration is not determined by the contract or in a manner agreed in the contract or by the course of dealing between the parties, the party contracting with the supplier will pay a reasonable price.

Obviously, some contracts coming within the SGSA 1982 are 'hybrids'; a decorating contract would involve supply of goods (paint, wallpaper, etc) and supply of a service (the labour involved in carrying out the decorating). In such a case, the provisions of ss 2–5, relating to the supply of goods, apply to the paint and wallpaper and the provisions of ss 13–15, relating to the supply of a service, apply to the carrying out of the work.

9.3.2 Exclusion clauses

UCTA 1977 governs exclusion and limitation of liability under the SGSA 1982. Title cannot be excluded and any attempt to exclude renders the clause void. In consumer sales, any attempt to exclude the terms contained in ss 2–5 will render the clause void. If the buyer does not deal as a consumer, any attempt to exclude these terms will be subject to the test of reasonableness. The 2002 Regulations will make similar amendments to such rules as for sale of goods (see 9.2.10).

However, where there is a contract of hire, the terms as to title and quiet possession can be excluded or restricted by an exemption clause, subject to the test of reasonableness.

Where an exclusion clause relates to s 13, it must satisfy the test of reasonableness. Liability for death or personal injury cannot be excluded.

9.4 THE CONSUMER PROTECTION (DISTANCE SELLING) REGULATIONS 2000

9.4.1 Application

The Regulations apply to contracts for the supply of goods or services which are concluded solely by distance communication (no face to face meeting) where the supplier normally contracts in this way (not a one-off transaction). For example, they apply to press advertisements with order forms, catalogues, telephone sales, internet shopping, email, fax and letter. However, some contracts are specifically excluded; for example, financial services, vending machine sales, contracts concluded via pay phone operator and internet auctions.

9.4.2 Main provisions

- The consumer must receive clear information about the goods/services *before* he or she decides whether to contract. For example, he or she must be told the name of the supplier, the price, delivery arrangements and costs, the cost of using distance communication (for example, premium telephone rate) and (where it applies) of his or her right to cancel the contract.

  So, for example, internet shopping channels should allow access to this information at the time people might order; catalogues should contain such information.

- The consumer must also receive confirmation of this information in a 'durable medium' (for example, email, fax, letter) and the confirmation must also contain certain other information, such as details of any guarantee and how to exercise the right to cancel. The confirmation must be received by the consumer, at the latest, on delivery of the goods or commencement of the supply of services.

- The consumer can withdraw from the contract without liability on it (that is, exercise the right of cancellation) up to seven working days (excluding weekends and bank holidays) from receipt of the confirmation of information (see above). However, the right of cancellation is not available in some circumstances, for example perishable goods (such as supermarket 'home shopping' via the internet); sale of videos and software which the customer has 'unsealed'; supply of newspapers and magazines; goods made to order. If the consumer is not given prior notice of the right to cancel, the cancellation period is extended by three months. The consumer has to give written notice of cancellation (by, for example, email, letter, fax), but cannot cancel where he or she has used or damaged the goods. If the consumer who cancels already has possession of the goods, then (unless the details sent of the right to cancel state otherwise) the supplier must collect them within 21 days of cancellation, after giving the consumer notice of when they will be collected. Whilst awaiting collection, the consumer must take reasonable care of the goods for 21 days. On cancellation, the consumer is entitled to a refund of money paid.

9.5 THE CONSUMER PROTECTION ACT 1987

9.5.1 Introduction

The Consumer Protection Act (CPA) 1987 was passed to implement the EC Directive on Product Liability (85/374/EEC). The CPA 1987 provides a means of redress for a consumer against the 'producer' of a product for injury or property damage caused by that product. This means of redress is of particular importance to the non-buyer (for example, the recipient of a gift), but a buyer might pursue an action under the CPA 1987 where, for example, it is not worth suing an insolvent seller. Although a consumer would have had an action against the manufacturer in negligence (*Donoghue v Stevenson* (1932); see below, Chapter 10), this would involve establishing fault; the CPA 1987 does not require such evidence in order to establish liability.

A consumer might also encounter problems in suing a manufacturer abroad; apart from the expense involved, English law may not be applied by a foreign court to determine the issue. The CPA 1987 solves this problem by providing for the possibility of an action against a person or body in this country. Accordingly, a business which does not manufacture the defective goods or sell them to the consumer may nevertheless find itself liable to compensate a consumer who suffers loss because of the defects in the goods, because it is a 'producer'.

In order to succeed in a claim, the claimant must show that:

- the product contained a defect; and
- the claimant suffered damage; and
- the damage was caused by the defect; and
- the defendant was a producer, own brander or importer of the product into the EU.

9.5.2 Meaning of 'producer'

A 'producer' of a product is defined as including the manufacturer of a finished product or of a component; any person who won or abstracted the product; or, where goods are not manufactured or abstracted, any person responsible for an industrial or other process to which any essential characteristic of the product is attributable, for example, a person who processes agricultural produce (s 2(2) of the CPA 1987).

Although a supplier of a defective product (for example a retail outlet) does not have primary liability, the supplier will be liable if he or she fails to identify the producer or importer when requested to do so (s 2(2)).

A person may be deemed to be a 'producer' of a defective product if that person claims to be a producer by putting his or her name or trademark on the product.

9.5.3 'Defective' product

A product will be 'defective' within the meaning of s 3 of the CPA 1987 if the safety of the product is not such as persons generally are entitled to expect, taking all circumstances into account, including the marketing of the product; the presentation of the product, including instructions and warnings; the use to which it might reasonably be expected to be put; and the time when it was supplied, that is, the state of the product at the time of supply.

A 'product' is 'any goods or electricity and ... includes a product which is comprised in another product, whether by virtue of being a component part or raw materials or otherwise' (s 1 of the CPA 1987). 'Goods' includes substances (which can be natural or artificial, solid, liquid, gaseous or in the form of a vapour), things comprised in land by virtue of being attached to it (but not land itself), ships, aircraft and vehicles (s 45).

Thus, for example, all processed and manufactured goods supplied by a business are covered by the CPA 1987, as are raw materials and components incorporated into them. However, services such as advice are not included and agricultural produce and game which have not undergone an industrial process were specifically exempted from the provisions of the CPA. So, for example, a farmer who supplied eggs infected with salmonella would not be liable under the CPA 1987, though, of course, the seller of such could be liable to a buyer under the SoGA 1979. However, probably because of the BSE crisis, EC Directive 99/34 required a change in the law by 4 December 2000 to include primary agricultural products within the scope of the CPA 1987, which has now been implemented.

9.5.4 Extent of liability

A person suffering loss because of a defective product can claim, but, under s 5, damages can only be awarded for property damage over £275 and for death or injury. No claim can be made for 'pure' economic loss or for damage to the defective product itself.

9.5.5 Exclusion of liability

Under s 7, liability cannot be excluded, though an action for damages is subject to the defences of the CPA 1987 and the time limitations of the Limitation Act 1980.

9.5.6 Defences

Although the CPA 1987 imposes strict liability, there are a number of defences provided by s 4.

Any person has a defence if it can be shown that:

- the defect is attributable to compliance with a domestic or EC enactment;
- the person was not at any time the supplier of the product;
- the supply was not in the course of business;
- the defect did not exist in the product at the time it was supplied;
- the state of scientific and technical knowledge at the relevant time was not such that the producer might be expected to have discovered the defect;
- the defect was in a product in which the product in question had been comprised and was wholly attributable to the design of the subsequent product;
- more than 10 years has elapsed since the product was first supplied.

The 'development risks' defence allows the producer to show that the defect was not discoverable at the time of supplying the product. What is required of a producer for this defence to operate is an area of contention, awaiting clarification by the courts. Should the producer make sure that he or she is aware of all available knowledge related to the product and then ensure that it is applied; or will it suffice to do limited research, bearing in mind the cost of development and the potentially small risk to the consumer?

Section 6(4) indicates that the defence of contributory negligence is available.

9.5.7 Limitations on action

There is a three year limitation period for claims, the start date being the date of the injury or damage. Where the injury or damage is not apparent, the date runs from the time that the claimant knew or could reasonably have known of the claim.

It should also be made clear that products supplied before 1 March 1988 cannot be the subject of claims under the CPA 1987, as the Act is not retrospective.

9.6 CRIMINAL LIABILITY

9.6.1 Introduction

The businessman must be aware that, as well as seeking to protect buyers and consumers generally by providing remedies, the law also strives to prevent consumers being misled and defective products being supplied by imposing criminal liability. The conviction of a business could cause harm to its commercial reputation, apart from any other consequences, such as payment of a fine and seizure of dangerous goods.

9.6.2 Part II of the CPA 1987

This part of the Act provides protection for the public from unsafe consumer goods by imposing criminal liability. It enables the Secretary of State to make safety regulations in respect of specific products. Safety regulations already exist in respect of a wide range of products, including children's nightdresses and the coverings and fillings of upholstered furniture.

The CPA 1987 creates a criminal offence of 'supplying consumer goods which are not reasonably safe' (s 10). It allows the Secretary of State to serve either a 'prohibition notice' on a supplier, prohibiting him or her from supplying goods which are unsafe, or a 'notice to warn', which requires the supplier to publish warnings about the unsafe goods (s 13).

A consumer may have a civil action for breach of statutory duty against the supplier of unsafe goods under this part of the CPA 1987.

9.6.3 The General Product Safety Regulations 1994

Even if there are no specific safety regulations relating to a particular product, the General Product Safety Regulations (GPSR) 1994 (SI 1994/2328) can impose criminal liability for supplying *unsafe products* onto the market.

The GPSR 1994 arose out of EC Directive 92/59, which requires Member States to introduce general product safety requirements and develop and implement procedures for the notification and exchange of information relating to dangerous products. The Regulations apply to all manufacturers and producers within the EC. If the manufacturer/producer does not have a base within the EC, the onus will fall on the distributor/importer (reg 2). The main requirement states that no producer shall place a product on the market unless the product is safe (reg 7).

The GPSR 1994 apply to any product intended for or likely to be used by consumers. They also cover second hand and reconditioned goods, subject to reg 3 (reg 2). 'Product' has a wider meaning than that found in the CPA 1987; for example, tobacco was specifically excluded from the CPA 1987 but is covered by the GPSR 1994.

A 'safe product' is further defined by reg 2 of the GPSR 1994 as:

... any product which, under normal or reasonably foreseeable conditions of use, including duration, does not present any risk or only the minimum risks compatible with the product's use, considered as acceptable and consistent with a high level of protection for the safety and health of persons, taking into account in particular:

- the characteristics of the product, including its composition, packaging, instructions for assembly and maintenance;

- the effect on other products, where it is reasonably foreseeable that it will be used with other products;

- the presentation of the product, the labelling, any instructions for its use and disposal and any other indication or information provided by the producer; and

- the categories of consumers at risk when using the product, in particular children.

Clearly, the packaging itself, or misleading or inadequate instructions on it, can render a product unsafe and result in a breach of the Regulations.

Where the producer or distributor is accused of an offence under the GPSR 1994, the due diligence defence may be raised (reg 14), that is, it can be shown that all reasonable steps were taken and all due diligence was exercised to avoid committing the offence.

On conviction of an offence under the GPSR 1994, the penalty may either be imprisonment for up to three months and/or a fine (reg 17).

The GPSR 1994 specifically preserve application of s 13 of the CPA 1987 in relation to products coming under the GPSR 1994 (provisions regarding prohibition notices and notices to warn – see above, 9.6.2).

9.6.4   Misleading price indications

It has been common practice for businesses to mislead or give inadequate information to consumers in relation to prices. For example, a notice stating '10% off' with no reference to the original price means that the consumer is unable to determine whether the price now charged is a 'bargain'.

Section 20 of the CPA 1987 provides that a person is guilty of an offence if, in the course of a business, consumers are given a misleading indication as to the price at which any goods, services, accommodation or facilities are available (see *Toyota (GB) Ltd v North Yorkshire CC* (1998)). Evidence of an offence is provided by compliance or non-compliance with the Code of Practice for Traders on Price Indications, published by the Office of Fair Trading. Under the guidelines of the Code, where goods are 'reduced' in price, the last previous price during the preceding six months must also be shown and the product must have been available at that price for at least 28 consecutive days in those six months at the same outlet where the reduced price is now offered. Also, a retailer should not compare his prices with an amount described only as 'worth' or 'value', for example, 'worth £20, our price £15'. Under s 20(2) of the CPA 1987, a criminal offence is also committed where the price indication, though not misleading when given, has become misleading before the consumer enters a contract (see *Link Stores Ltd v Harrow LBC* (2001)).

A number of defences are provided in s 24 of the CPA 1987. The defendant may prove that all reasonable precautions were taken and that he or she exercised all due diligence to avoid the commission of an offence; or that he or she was an innocent publisher/advertiser who was unaware of the fact that, and had no grounds to suspect that, the advertisement contained a misleading price indication.

The provisions of the CPA 1987 and the Code of Practice can be supplemented by regulations made by the Secretary of State under s 26 of that Act. Under the Price Indications (Method of Payment) Regulations 1991, where a trader charges different prices according to the method of payment, the differences must be made clear to consumers. It is common practice for garages to charge more for payment by credit card than for cash.

9.6.5 The Trade Descriptions Act 1968

The Trade Descriptions Act (TDA) 1968 provides criminal sanctions for offences relating to the sale of goods involving the use of false or misleading descriptions, as well as misleading statements about services. It also provides facilities for the court to make a compensation order for the consumer who has suffered loss.

Under the TDA 1968, it is a criminal offence to apply, in the course of a trade or business, a false description to goods or to sell goods where such a description is applied (ss 1 and 3 of the TDA 1968; see *Formula One Autocentres Ltd v Birmingham CC* (1998)). Private sales are outside the remit of the TDA 1968.

The professions fall within the scope of the TDA 1968. For example, in *Roberts v Leonard* (1995), a veterinary surgeon was held to be carrying on a trade or business. 'False' means 'false to a material degree'; therefore, in effect, any deviation from the description must be significant. The meaning of 'trade description' is indicated in s 2(1) as including statements about quantity, size and method of manufacture; fitness for purpose; other physical characteristics; testing and the results of such tests; approvals by any person; place, date and name of manufacturer, producer or processor; and any history, including ownership and use.

In *Sherratt v Geralds The American Jewellers Ltd* (1970), a watch, described by the maker as a 'diver's watch' and inscribed 'waterproof', filled with water and stopped on its first immersion. The defendant was found guilty of a breach of s 1 of the TDA 1968 in supplying goods to which a false description had been applied by another person.

The TDA 1968 not only makes it unlawful for the trader to apply a false trade description to goods, but extends to supplying goods, exposing goods for supply or having goods in his or her possession for the purposes of supply and to services, accommodation or facilities (ss 6 and 14 of the TDA 1968). In *Yugo Tours Ltd v Wadsley* (1988), a tour operator advertised a holiday on board a three-masted schooner under full sail and included a photograph. It was held that the tour operator was in breach of the TDA 1968, as customers, having relied on the brochure to book their holiday, then found themselves on a two-masted schooner without sails.

A person may be guilty of an offence, even where the description is technically correct, where it is likely to mislead a customer without specialist knowledge, although this is subject to the general provision that the description must be false or misleading to a material degree. For example, to describe a car as 'beautiful' when it is in a poor mechanical state could be a false description to a material degree (*Robertson v Dicocco* (1972)).

The TDA 1968 provides two defences (s 24):

- that the misdescription was due to a mistake; or to reliance on information supplied by a third party; or to the act or default of a third party or some other cause beyond the control of the defendant;

- that all reasonable precautions were taken and due diligence was exercised to avoid the commission of an offence. The defence of due diligence was recently examined in *DSG Retail Ltd v Oxfordshire CC* (2001).

In *Lewin v Rothersthorpe Road Garage* (1984), a defendant raised the s 24 defence by establishing that he was a member of the Motor Agents Association and had adopted the code of practice drawn up by the Association, as approved by the Office of Fair Trading. This was sufficient for the court to accept that the defendant had taken reasonable precautions to avoid commission of an offence by his employee.

It is also open to a 'trader' who is supplying goods to issue a disclaimer. This will provide a defence as long as it is sufficiently bold to equal that of the description supplied In *Norman v Bennett* (1974), though the mileage recorded on a car's odometer was incorrect, there was no contravention of s 1(1)(b) of the TDA 1968 because the buyer signed a sales agreement which he knew contained the words 'odometer reading not guaranteed'. (Compare this with *Holloway v Cross* (1981).) Such a disclaimer is not available where the trader is actually applying the trade description him or herself, as occurred in *Newham LBC v Singh* (1988). It seems fair that a dealer should be able to say that he is not liable for odometer readings which he cannot check, but, clearly, he should not be allowed to exclude liability where he knows, or ought to know, that a description is false.

SUMMARY OF CHAPTER 9

SALE AND SUPPLY OF GOODS

Goods may be supplied onto the market by several means, such as sale and hire. As a result of supply, there may be civil liability to a person suffering loss and a criminal offence may be committed in respect of supplying defective goods.

Sale of Goods Act 1979

- The price may be expressly agreed by the parties, but otherwise a reasonable price is payable.

- The Act implies conditions into contracts for the sale of goods: the goods must correspond with the contract description, must be of satisfactory quality, must be reasonably fit for the purpose made known by the buyer and must correspond with any sample by reference to which the goods are sold. The draft Sale and Supply of Goods to Consumers Regulations 2002 propose amendments to the implied conditions.

- It is the duty of the seller to deliver the goods and of the buyer to accept and pay for them.

- Acceptance of a breach of condition deprives the buyer of the right to reject the goods and claim a refund; however, damages may be claimed.

- The seller's remedies for breach of contract are an action for the price, damages for non-acceptance, lien, stoppage in transit and the right of resale.

- The buyer's remedies for breach of contract are specific performance, rejection of the goods, damages and recovery of the price paid. Additional remedies are proposed by the draft Sale and Supply of Goods to Consumers Regulations 2002.

- Liability for loss caused by breach of the contract cannot be excluded in consumer sales. In non-consumer sales, liability for failure to transfer title cannot be excluded but exclusion of liability for other implied conditions of the Act may be valid, subject to the requirement of reasonableness.

- Guarantees must state that 'Statutory rights are not affected'. New controls on voluntary guarantees are proposed by the draft Sale and Supply of Goods to Consumers Regulations 2002.

- The purpose of sale of goods contracts is the transfer of property (ownership). The time of such transfer is important because, once property has passed to the buyer, the risk of accidental loss is usually transferred and an unpaid seller can sue for the contract price. The time of transfer of property depends on whether the contract is for the sale of specific, ascertained or unascertained goods.

Sale of goods by non-owners

- Generally, a person who does not own goods cannot transfer title in them by sale. There are several statutory exceptions to this rule, contained mainly in the SoGA 1979.

The Supply of Goods and Services Act 1982

- Where goods are supplied, terms similar to those of ss 13–15 of the SoGA 1979 are implied.

  The ability to exclude these terms is governed by UCTA 1977. Amendments are proposed by the draft Sale and Supply of Goods to Consumers Regulations 2002.

- In relation to any service aspect of the contract, there are implied terms that the work will be carried out with reasonable skill and care, that the work will be carried out within a reasonable time (if no time is agreed) and that a reasonable price is payable where none was agreed.

The Consumer Protection (Distance Selling) Regulations 2000

- The Regulations control contracts for the supply of goods and services which are not made face to face, such as online shopping. Some such contracts are not covered, such as internet auctions.

- The Regulations cover information to be given to the consumer before contracting, require confirmation of orders by the supplier and give consumers the right to cancel the contract.

Part I of the Consumer Protection Act 1987

- The Act imposes strict liability on the 'producer' of 'defective' products in relation to a person suffering property loss over £275, death or injury.

- Liability cannot be excluded (s 7) but defences are available under the Act (s 4 and s 6(4)).

- To succeed in an action under the Act, the claimant must show that he or she suffered loss, that the product was defective and that it was the defective product which caused the loss.

Part II of the Consumer Protection Act 1987

- Breach of safety regulations made under the Act is a criminal offence.
- The Secretary of State may make safety regulations and issue prohibition notices and notices to warn.

General Product Safety Regulations 1994

- It is a criminal offence to supply unsafe goods on to the market.
- The regulations can apply to new, second hand and reconditioned goods.

Misleading price indications

- It is a criminal offence to give a misleading indication to consumers as to the price of goods, services, accommodation or facilities available.
- Evidence of an offence is provided by non-compliance with the Office of Fair Trading's Code of Practice.

Trade Descriptions Act 1968

- It is a criminal offence for a trader to apply a false description to goods or to sell goods to which such a description applied.
- The trader may plead as a defence that he or she exercised all due diligence and took all reasonable precautions to avoid committing the offence.

CHAPTER 10

NEGLIGENCE

10.1 INTRODUCTION

Negligence is a tort. It is, however, necessary to define what is meant by 'a tort' before considering the essentials of negligence. A tort is a wrongful act against an individual or body corporate and his, her or its property, which gives rise to a civil action (usually for damages, although other remedies are available). Principally, liability is based on fault, although there are exceptions to this, for example, breach of statutory duty, vicarious liability and the tort established in *Rylands v Fletcher* (1865). The motive of the defendant in committing the tort is generally irrelevant.

Negligence is the most important of all the torts, not only because an understanding of it is vital to the comprehension of other torts, such as employers' and occupiers' liability, but also because it is the one tort which is constantly developing in the light of social and economic change. This can be seen by reference to product liability, professional negligence and economic loss, all of which were originally only compensated if there was in existence a valid contract; in other words, 'no contract, no claim'. After a period of continual development in the scope and application of this tort, there are signs that the courts are beginning to be more cautious. They are aware of the economic implications on the public and private sector if they continue to extend the scope of actions in negligence. Whether this should be an issue for the courts is always open to debate, but, if the courts are to be pragmatic, then they may have no choice but to be restrained in the current economic climate.

A professional person, such as an auditor, accountant, lawyer or doctor, may find themselves in a non-contractual relationship with another who will have little choice but to pursue an action in negligence if they are injured as a result of professional malpractice. Indeed, in order to cover potential actions in negligence and contract, many professional bodies require, as part of membership approval and the issue of practising certificates, that their members take out insurance cover to meet the cost of potential claims (usually, a minimum amount of cover is stipulated for an individual claim). This is known as professional indemnity insurance.

The prime object of the tort of negligence is to provide compensation for the injured person. It has also been suggested that liability in tort provides a deterrent and that negligence is no exception; that is, it helps to define what is or is not acceptable conduct and, therefore, sets the boundaries of such behaviour. Unfortunately, people rarely act by reference to the civil law and the only real deterrent is through market forces – the economic impact being passed on to those who have a higher risk of causing injury. Alternative compensation systems have been considered, as these would largely eradicate the need of the injured party to pursue legal action. The alternatives on offer are no fault compensation schemes – see the Pearson Commission's *Report on Civil Liability and Compensation for Personal Injury* (Cmnd 7054, 1978) – and extending public and private insurance schemes.

The possible impact of the Human Rights Act (HRA) 1998 in opening up the boundaries of the duty of care also needs to be considered. This may be particularly relevant where, for example, the duty of care is restricted on policy grounds. As a result of the decision in *Osman v UK* (1999), an individual may be able to pursue an action using the HRA 1998 as the basis of the claim. In the *Osman* case, an action against the police failed in the Court of Appeal on the basis of public service immunity. However, the claimant succeeded before the European Court of Human Rights on the basis of a breach of Art 6 of the European Convention on Human Rights (ECHR), which guarantees access to justice.

Now that the HRA 1998 is in force, the courts have to implement the ECHR and interpret existing law so as to avoid conflict with the ECHR's underlying principles.

10.2 ELEMENTS OF THE TORT

There are specific elements of the tort of negligence, which have to be established in the correct order if a claim by an injured party is to succeed. The burden of proof is on the claimant to show, on a balance of probabilities, that certain elements exist.

10.3 DUTY OF CARE

A person is not automatically liable for every negligent act that he or she commits. The need to establish the essentials, particularly a duty of care, sets a legal limit on who can bring an action, as a duty is not owed to the world at large. The onus is on the claimant to establish that the defendant owes him or her a duty of care. Unless this first hurdle is crossed, no liability can arise. The test for establishing whether a duty of care exists arises out of the case of *Donoghue v Stevenson* (1932). Prior to this case, the duty of care was only owed in limited circumstances. Now, it is said that the categories of negligence are never closed, in that the law can change to take into account new circumstances and social or technical change. Where, therefore, there is unintentional damage, there is, potentially, an action in negligence.

In *Donoghue v Stevenson* (1932), a lady went into a café with her friend, who bought her a bottle of ginger beer. After she had drunk half from the bottle, she poured the remainder of the ginger beer into a glass. She then saw the remains of a decomposed snail at the bottom. She suffered nervous shock and sued the manufacturer, as the snail must have got into the bottle at the manufacturer's premises, since the bottle top was securely sealed when her friend bought it. It was held that a manufacturer owes a duty of care to the ultimate consumer of his or her goods. He or she must therefore exercise reasonable care to prevent injury to the consumer. The fact that there is no contractual relationship between the manufacturer and the consumer is irrelevant to this action.

The most important aspect of this case is the test laid down by Lord Atkin. He stated that:

> You must take reasonable care to avoid acts and omissions which you could reasonably foresee would be likely to injure your neighbour. Who, then, in law is my neighbour? ... any person so closely and directly affected by my act that I ought reasonably to have them in contemplation as being so affected when I am directing my mind to the acts and omissions which are called in question.

This test forms the basis for deciding the existence of a duty. It follows that, if a duty of care is to exist, the question for the court is somewhat hypothetical, in that the court does not look at the reality (that is, 'did you contemplate the effect of your actions on the injured party?') but asks, 'should you have done so?'; that is, the question is objective, rather than subjective. This does not require specific identity of the injured person; it merely requires ascertainment of the identity of the class of person, for example, pedestrians, children, etc.

The test in *Donoghue v Stevenson* was qualified in *Anns v Merton LBC* (1978). Lord Wilberforce in this case introduced the two stage test for establishing the existence of a duty:

- is there a sufficient relationship of proximity or neighbourhood between the alleged wrongdoer and the person who has suffered damage such that, in the reasonable contemplation of the former, carelessness on his part may be likely to cause damage to the latter?;

- if the first question is answered in the affirmative, are there then any considerations which ought to negate, reduce or limit the scope of the duty or the class of persons to whom it is owed or the damages to which a breach of duty may give rise?

The first question clearly corresponds with the 'neighbour test' in *Donoghue v Stevenson* (1932), although it is referred to as the 'proximity test'. The second question introduces the consideration of public policy issues, which may be grounds for limiting the situations where a duty of care is found to exist. As far as new situations are concerned, the following are some of the policy reasons which, if justified, may prevent a duty of care from being actionable:

- the 'floodgates' argument, that is, will an extension of duty to cover this situation lead to a flood of litigation?;

- will it lead to an increase in the number of fraudulent claims either against insurance companies or in the courts?;

- what are the financial or commercial consequences of extending the duty?

The impact of *Anns* (1978) led to the expansion of negligence, as the policy reasons acted only to limit liability once a duty had been found to exist, as opposed to limiting the existence of the duty itself. This was illustrated in the case of *Junior Books Ltd v Veitchi Co Ltd* (1983), in which the House of Lords extended the duty of care because of the close proximity between the parties, in that their relationship was quasi-contractual. As a result, the defendants were found to be liable for pure economic loss resulting from their negligent actions. It should be noted that the decision in *Junior Books* has come to be regarded as a special case, providing a narrow exception to the rule that, in general, there can be no liability in negligence for pure economic loss. However, there was gradual criticism of and retraction from the approach taken by Lord Wilberforce, as can be seen in two cases: *Peabody Donation Fund v Sir Lindsay Parkinson and Co Ltd* (1984), in which the court stressed that the proximity test had to be satisfied before a duty of care could be found to exist; and *Leigh and Sillivan Ltd v Aliakmon Shipping Co Ltd* (1986) (known as *The Aliakmon*), in which Lord Brandon stated that, when Lord Wilberforce laid down the two phase test in *Anns*, he was:

> ... dealing with the approach to the questions of existence and scope of duty of care in a novel type of factual situation, which was not analogous to any factual situation in which the existence of such a duty had already been held to exist. He was not suggesting that the same approach should be adopted to the existence of a duty of care in a factual situation in which the existence of such a duty had repeatedly been held not to exist.

This further limitation was developed in *Yuen Kun Yeu v AG of Hong Kong* (1987), in which Lord Keith stated that Lord Wilberforce's approach 'had been elevated to a degree of importance greater than it merits and greater, perhaps, than its author intended'. Finally, the decision in *Anns* was overruled by *Murphy v Brentwood DC* (1990), where it was held that local authorities owed a duty of care to a building owner to avoid damage to the building which would create a danger to the health and safety of the occupants. The duty arose out of the local authority's powers to require compliance with building regulations. However, as the damage was held to be pure economic loss, it was irrecoverable.

The present position, following this rapid retraction from *Anns*, appears to be that, in establishing the existence of a duty of care in negligence, an incremental approach must be taken.

The claimant must show that the defendant foresaw that damage would occur to the claimant, that is, that there was sufficient proximity in time, space and relationship between the claimant and the defendant (see *Bourhill v Young* (1943)). In practical terms, foreseeability of damage will determine proximity in the majority of personal injury cases. The courts will then, where appropriate, consider whether it is just and reasonable to impose a duty and whether there are any policy reasons for denying or limiting the existence of a duty, for example, under the floodgates argument. The courts will not necessarily consider these in all cases.

The final retraction from *Anns* (1978) and support for the incremental approach was seen in *Caparo Industries plc v Dickman* (1990), where the application of a three stage test for establishing a duty of care was recommended. This requires consideration of the following questions:

* was the harm caused reasonably foreseeable?;

* was there a relationship of proximity between the defendant and the claimant?;

* in all the circumstances, is it just, fair and reasonable to impose a duty of care?

This decision has since been followed in *Marc Rich Co AG v Bishop Rock Marine Co Ltd (The Nicholas H)* (1994). The Court of Appeal held in this case that a duty of care would only be imposed if the three aims of the test expounded in *Caparo* could be satisfied. These would have to be applied irrespective of the type of loss suffered. If anything, this takes the retraction from *Anns* one step further, as, in the past, it could always be argued that *Anns* applied to new duty situations, as opposed to all situations.

A clear application of policy reasons limiting the existence of a duty of care can be seen in *Hill v CC of West Yorkshire* (1989). Mrs Hill's daughter was the last victim of the Yorkshire Ripper. She alleged that the police had failed to take reasonable care in apprehending the murderer, as they had interviewed him but had not arrested him prior to her daughter's unlawful killing. The House of Lords had to determine whether the police owed her a duty of care. After confirming the need to establish foresight and proximity, the court went on to state that there were policy reasons for not allowing the existence of a duty in this case, namely, that any other result may lead to police discretion being limited and exercised in a defensive frame of mind. This may, in turn, distract the police from their most important function – 'the suppression of crime'.

A further illustration of public policy influences on whether there is a duty of care owed by the police can be seen in *Alexandrou v Oxford* (1993), in which it was held that there was no duty owed by the police to the owners of premises that had a burglar alarm system connected to a police station.

It is apparent that the courts' current position is to continue to retreat from *Anns* (1978) to a more 'category based' approach, as referred to in the *ratio* of *Donoghue v Stevenson* (1932). This was clearly summed up by Lord Hoffman in *Stovin v Wise* (1996), as follows:

The trend of authorities has been to discourage the assumption that anyone who suffers loss is *prima facie* entitled to compensation from a person ... whose act or omission can be said to have caused it. The default position is that he is not.

Public policy or not, it is still the case that, unless harm to the claimant can be foreseen, a duty of care cannot be established. In *Goodwin v British Pregnancy Advisory Service* (1996), the defendants performed a vasectomy on a man who was subsequently to become Goodwin's lover. It transpired that the vasectomy had not been a success, and the plaintiff became pregnant. The plaintiff claimed that the defendants owed her a duty of care and were negligent in not warning her lover that a small number of vasectomies spontaneously reverse, leading to the possibility of fertility being restored. Her claim was struck out. The only possible duty of care would have been to the wife of the patient, had he been married at the time of the vasectomy. The plaintiff, however, could not be foreseen by the defendants, as she fell within an indeterminate class of women with whom the patient could have a sexual relationship.

Even where harm to the claimant is foreseen, an omission to act will not result in liability unless there is an existing relationship between the parties, for example, between a member of the public and the fire service or a doctor and patient. Liability may also arise through custom and practice resulting in wilful neglect (see *X v Bedfordshire CC* (1995)). This can be seen in *Vellino v Chief Constable of Greater Manchester* (2001), in which the claimant sustained serious injuries whilst trying to escape from police custody. The claimant had a history of being arrested at his flat, and of trying to evade arrest by jumping out of his flat windows. He argued that two police officers had sought to arrest him, but made no attempt to prevent him from jumping out of the window. The Court of Appeal held that a police officer carrying out an arrest did not owe the person being arrested a duty of care to prevent him from injuring himself in a foreseeable attempt to escape. The act of escaping from custody constituted a common law crime and therefore could not attract tortious liability (*ex turpi causa*).

10.4 NERVOUS SHOCK

Nervous shock (or post-traumatic stress disorder, to give it its medical name) is a form of personal injury and, thus, may give rise to an action for damages. The Law Commission Report, *Liability for Psychiatric Illness* (No 249, 1998), highlights the continuing problem for the courts in determining the extent of liability for post-traumatic stress disorder. If damages are to be recoverable, nervous shock must take the form of a recognised mental illness; mental suffering, such as grief, is generally not recoverable (see *Vernon v Bosley (No 1)* (1997)). No physical injury need be suffered. The basis of liability for nervous shock depends on whether this type of injury was reasonably foreseeable and whether there was sufficient proximity between the claimant and the defendant.

In *Bourhill v Young* (1943), the plaintiff, a pregnant woman, heard a motor accident as she alighted from a tram. A little while later, she saw some blood on the road. She alleged that, as a result of seeing the aftermath of the accident, she suffered nervous shock, which led to a miscarriage. It was held that the plaintiff did not fall within the class of persons to whom it could be reasonably foreseen that harm might occur.

Indeed, it was made clear in this case that one could expect passers-by to have the necessary 'phlegm and fortitude' not to suffer nervous shock as a result of seeing the aftermath of an accident. As a result, the abnormally sensitive claimant will not recover for nervous shock unless the person with normal phlegm and fortitude would have sustained shock in those circumstances (see *Jaensch v Coffey* (1984)).

At present, the courts appear to be treating the professional rescuer as a bystander for the purposes of nervous shock claims and expect them to have the requisite phlegm and fortitude, as described in *Bourhill v Young* (1943).

As far as the courts are concerned, persons claiming for nervous shock fall into distinct categories:

- The claimant experiences shock and illness after fearing for his or her own safety

  In this situation, the claimant is a primary victim. In claiming nervous shock, there is a clear distinction between how the courts view primary and secondary victims (the latter being those who are not in danger themselves but who witness the aftermath). In *Dulieu v White* (1901), a pregnant woman was serving in a public house when the defendant's employee negligently drove a van into the front of the building. The plaintiff was not physically injured, but suffered severe shock, which led to illness. It was held that she was allowed to recover damages, as the shock and illness arose out of a fear of immediate personal injury to herself.

  Further application of the decision in *Dulieu* can be seen in *Page v Smith* (1995), where the House of Lords held that foreseeability of physical injury was sufficient to enable the plaintiff, who was directly involved in an accident, to recover damages for nervous shock, even though he had not actually been physically hurt. Interestingly, Lord Keith, in a dissenting judgment, felt that the plaintiff's claim for nervous shock should be defeated on the basis of remoteness of damage; that is, the class of injury was unforeseen.

- Where the claimant fears for the personal safety of a close relative

  In *Hambrook v Stokes Bros* (1925), an unattended lorry began to roll down a hill. A mother had just left her children when she saw the lorry go out of control. She could not see her children, but heard the crash. She was told that a child wearing glasses had been hurt. One of her children wore glasses. She suffered shock, which was so severe that it eventually led to her death. It was held that her estate could recover damages, even though her illness was caused by fear for her children, not for herself. The defendant, the lorry driver, should have foreseen that his negligence might put someone in such fear of bodily injury, that is, that they would suffer nervous shock, and that this could be extended to cover fear for one's children.

In *McLoughlin v O'Brian* (1982), a mother was informed at home that her family had been injured in a road accident two miles away. As a result, she suffered psychiatric illness, caused by the shock of hearing this news and seeing her family in hospital, who were still in a particular bloody state because they had not yet received any treatment; also, one child had been killed. It was held that she should recover damages, as the shock was a foreseeable consequence of the defendant's negligence. The courts felt that the proximity of the plaintiff to the accident was relevant. However 'proximity' here meant closeness in time and space. Furthermore, the shock must be caused by the sight or hearing of the event or its immediate aftermath.

The essential elements for establishing a duty in similar cases arose out of Lord Wilberforce's *dictum* in *McLoughlin*, which was that, in addition to foresight, the claimant must show that there was a close relationship between him or her and the person suffering injury; secondly, that there was sufficient proximity between the claimant and the accident in terms of time and space; and, finally, it was concluded that being told about the accident by a third party was outside the scope of the duty. The application of Lord Wilberforce's *dictum* was seen in *Alcock and Others v Chief Constable of South Yorkshire* (1991). This case arose out of the accident at Hillsborough stadium in Sheffield, involving Liverpool supporters who were crushed as a result of a surge of supporters being allowed into the ground by the police. The nervous shock claim was made by those friends and relatives who witnessed the scenes either first hand at the ground or saw or heard them on television or radio. The House of Lords repeated the requirements for establishing duty of care in cases of nervous shock. There should be:

o a close and loving relationship with the victim if reasonable foresight is to be established;

o proximity in time and space to the accident or its aftermath;

o nervous shock resulting from seeing or hearing the accident or its immediate aftermath.

It is still open to debate whether viewing live television is equivalent to seeing the accident. It is generally considered not to be, because broadcasting guidelines prevent the showing of suffering by recognisable individuals. Furthermore, any such transmission may be regarded as a *novus actus interveniens*.

- Where the claimant suffers nervous shock through seeing injury to others, even though he or she is in no danger him or herself

In *Dooley v Cammell Laird and Co* (1951), a faulty rope was being used on a crane to secure a load as it was hoisted into the hold of a ship. The rope broke, causing the load to fall into the hold, where people were working. The crane driver suffered shock arising out of a fear for the safety of his fellow employees. It was held that the crane driver could recover damages, as it was foreseeable that he was likely to be affected if the rope broke.

It would appear that the decision in *Dooley* is confined to situations where the employee making the claim was directly involved in the incident, rather than a mere 'bystander'. In *Robertson and Rough v Forth Road Bridge Joint Board* (1995), two employees claimed damages for nervous shock after witnessing another colleague, who was working alongside them on the Forth Road Bridge, fall to his death. It was held that their claim would fail, as they were in effect mere bystanders and their illness was not, therefore, reasonably foreseeable.

This was confirmed in *Hegarty v EE Caledonia Ltd* (1996), in which the plaintiff, who was on one of the support vessels, witnessed at close range the Piper Alpha oil rig disaster, in which over 150 men died. He claimed nervous shock but was found to be a person of normal fortitude who, as a 'mere bystander', was close to the danger but not actually in danger himself. However, it could now be argued that damages for psychiatric harm suffered by an employee who witnesses the event and is in danger himself may be recoverable, following the decision in *Young v Charles Church (Southern) Ltd* (1996), in which an employee working alongside a man who was electrocuted and killed was also held to be a 'primary victim'.

In *Chadwick v British Rlys Board* (1967), Chadwick took part in the rescue operation after a train crash. He suffered a severe mental condition as a result of the horrific scenes. He had a previous history of mental illness. It was held that the British Railways Board was liable. It was reasonably foreseeable that, in the event of an accident, someone other than the defendant's employees would intervene and suffer injury. Injury to a rescuer in the form of shock was reasonably foreseeable, even if he suffered no physical injury.

One of the more controversial decisions arose in *White (formerly Frost) v CC of South Yorkshire* (1997), in which a number of policemen involved in the Hillsborough stadium disaster (in which 95 football supporters were crushed to death) brought claims for psychiatric damage attributable to witnessing the events. It was held by the Court of Appeal that the police who attended the scene in the immediate aftermath of the incident were rescuers and were entitled to recover on that basis. It was further held that a rescuer, whether a policeman or layperson, may recover against a tortfeasor for physical or psychiatric injury sustained during a rescue. Among the factors to be considered in determining whether a particular person is a rescuer are the character and extent of the initial incident caused by the tortfeasor; whether that incident has finished or is continuing; whether there is any danger, continuing or otherwise, to the victim or to the claimant; the character of the claimant's conduct, both in itself and in relation to the victim; and how proximate, in time and place, the claimant's conduct is to the incident.

However, the findings of the Court of Appeal were reversed by the House of Lords (*White v Chief Constable of South Yorkshire Police* (1999)). The House of Lords concluded that the police officers who were present should not be treated as primary victims. They were secondary victims, like any person who witnesses injury to others but is not in danger him or herself. As such a victim, the conditions laid down in *Alcock* (1991) must, therefore, be met. Furthermore, they were not to be treated as a special category of rescuer. To claim as 'rescuers', the police officers would still have show that they met the criteria under which rescuers could recover as secondary victims. (For further discussion of the law in this area, see Mullany and Handford, 'Hillsborough replayed' (1997) 113 LQR 410; and Teff, 'Liability for negligently inflicted psychiatric harm: justifications and boundaries' [1998] CLJ 91.)

It is certainly possible for the law to be extended in this area. For example, in *Attia v British Gas* (1987), the plaintiff was able to recover damages for nervous shock resulting from the sight of her house being burned down as a result of the defendant's negligence.

Finally, returning to the principle that grief alone will not normally sustain a claim for nervous shock, the case of *Vernon v Bosley (No 1)* (1997) shows that it may be possible to recover for a condition which falls short of post-traumatic stress disorder, but which amounts to pathological grief disorder. In *Vernon*, the plaintiff's children were killed when their car, which was being driven by their nanny, left the road and crashed into a river. The plaintiff was called to the scene of the accident and witnessed the attempts of the emergency services to rescue the children. He subsequently became mentally ill and his business and marriage failed. The plaintiff accepted that his illness was due to the deaths of his children, but argued that it was not caused by shock, but by pathological grief. The Court of Appeal held that, as a secondary victim who met the general preconditions for such a claim, he could recover, even though his illness was linked to pathological grief rather than post-traumatic stress disorder. It could, however, be argued that, given the facts of this case, there is a very fine dividing line between the two notional heads of claim.

10.5 ECONOMIC LOSS

There are two categories of economic loss which may form the basis of a claim in negligence. First, there is economic loss arising out of physical injury or damage to property; and, secondly, there is what is known as 'pure' economic loss, which is the sole loss sustained, unconnected with physical damage. Following more recent developments, only the former is now recoverable, unless the claimant can show that there was a 'special relationship' between him or her and the defendant, in which the defendant assumed responsibility for the claimant's economic welfare (see *Williams v Natural Life Health Foods Ltd* (1998)). In effect, the law has reverted to the decision in the following case for defining the extent of liability for economic loss.

In *Spartan Steel and Alloys Ltd v Martin and Co* (1973), the plaintiffs manufactured steel alloys 24 hours a day. This required continuous power. The defendant's employees damaged a power cable, which resulted in a lack of power for 14 hours. There was a danger of damage to the furnace, so this had to be shut down and the products in the process of manufacture removed, thereby reducing their value. The plaintiffs also suffered loss of profits. It was held that the defendants were liable for physical damage to the products and the loss of profit arising out of this. There was, however, no liability for economic loss which was unconnected with the physical damage.

The rule that economic loss was only recoverable where it was directly the consequence of physical damage was challenged in *Junior Books Ltd v Veitchi Ltd* (1983), in which a claim for pure economic loss was allowed on the basis of there being sufficiently close proximity between the plaintiffs and the sub-contractor who had carried out the work for the main contractor. However, following this case, there was a gradual retraction from recovery for pure economic loss – see *Muirhead v Industrial Tank Specialties Ltd* (1986), where it was held that there was insufficient proximity between the purchaser of goods and the manufacturer of the goods with respect to a claim for economic loss. This was reinforced in the cases of *Simaan General Contracting Co v Pilkington Glass Ltd (No 2)* (1988) and *Greater Nottingham Co-Operative Society Ltd v Cementation Piling and Foundations Ltd* (1988), where the courts refused to find sufficient proximity in tripartite business relationships, although the decision in *Junior Books* appears to stand, at least for the moment.

The expansion of the law in this area was seen to result from Lord Wilberforce's two stage test in *Anns v Merton LBC* (1978). As the gradual withdrawal from that decision grew apace, it was inevitable that a final blow would be dealt to this test. First, in *D and F Estates Ltd v Church Comrs for England* (1988), it was held that a builder was not liable in negligence to the owner for defects in quality, only for personal injury or damage to other property, thereby bringing back the distinction between actions in tort and contract. Additionally, it was held that pure economic loss could only be recovered in an action for negligent misstatement or where the circumstances fell within *Junior Books*. Secondly, in *Murphy v Brentwood DC* (1990), the decision in *Anns* was overruled; it was made clear that liability for pure economic loss could only be sustained in an action for negligent misstatement based on *Hedley Byrne & Co v Heller and Partners* (1964).

For further discussion of this area, see Cane, *Tort Law and Economic Interests*, 2nd edn, 1996.

10.6 NEGLIGENT MISSTATEMENTS

The importance of the neighbour, or proximity, test can be seen in the extension of the duty of care to cover negligent misstatements which result in economic loss. Indeed, as we have seen, this is the only heading under which pure economic loss can be claimed. This expansion of the duty arose out of the case of *Hedley Byrne* (1964). Prior to this case, there was only liability for negligent misstatements causing physical damage, intentionally dishonest or fraudulent statements, or where there was a fiduciary or contractual relationship between the parties (*Derry v Peek* (1889)).

In *Hedley Byrne* (1964), Hedley Byrne asked their bank to make inquiries into the financial position of Heller, one of their clients. The bank made enquiries of Heller's bank, which gave a favourable reply about the client's financial position, adding the words 'without responsibility'. Hedley Byrne relied on this advice and lost a lot of money when their clients went into liquidation. However, they lost their action against the bank because of the exclusion clause, which at that time was held to be valid. The importance of the case is the *dictum* on negligent misstatements. It was held that a duty of care exists where:

> ... one party seeking information and advice was trusting the other to exercise such a degree of care as the circumstances required, where it was reasonable for him to do that, and where the other party gave the information or advice when he knew or ought to have known the enquirer was relying on him.

Liability for negligent misstatements is based on the existence of a special relationship; that is, the defendant must hold himself out in some way as having specialised knowledge, knowing that any information that he or she gives will be relied upon by the claimant. Interestingly, it has recently been decided that there may be concurrent liability in tort and contract, so that the claimant may choose which cause of action provides him or her with the best remedy. This is illustrated in *Henderson v Merrett Syndicates Ltd* (1994), in which it was held that an assumption of responsibility by a person providing professional or quasi-professional services, coupled with reliance by the person for whom the services were provided, could give rise to tortious liability, irrespective of whether there was a contractual relationship between the parties. (This decision finally lays to rest the decision in *Tai Hing Cotton*

Mill Ltd v Liu Chong Hing Bank Ltd (1986), which excluded concurrent liability in contract and tort.) Obviously, lawyers, accountants, bankers, surveyors, etc, come within this 'special relationship'. (See Hepple, R, 'The search for coherence' (1997) 50 CLP 69.)

However, as the law has developed, some attempts to limit liability can be found in the case law. For example, in *Mutual Life and Citizens Assurance Co v Evatt* (1971), it was held that the defendant should be in the business of giving such advice, although the minority in this case required the plaintiff to make it clear to the defendant that he was seeking advice which he may then have relied on. There is, in general, no liability for information given on a purely social occasion, but advice from friends on other occasions may result in liability, as can be seen in *Chaudry v Prabhakar* (1988). Silence or inaction can rarely amount to misstatement, unless there was a duty on the defendant to disclose or take action. In *Legal and General Assurance Ltd v Kirk* (2002), the Court of Appeal held that, for a claim based on negligent misstatement in respect of an employment reference, a statement must actually have been made to a third party. The fact that Mr Kirk had not applied for a reference in the knowledge that the contents of the reference would inevitably have led to his being rejected by a prospective employer was insufficient to establish liability on the part of the employer. The courts have recognised that it is possible for there to be a voluntary assumption of responsibility by the defendant and reliance by the claimant on that assumption (*La Banque Financière de la Cité v Westgate Insurance Co Ltd* (1990)). Any attempt at excluding liability may be subject to the Unfair Contract Terms Act (UCTA) 1977 and would then have to satisfy the test of reasonableness laid down in s 2(2). It should also be noted that any attempt to exclude liability for death or personal injury is not permitted by virtue of s 2 of UCTA 1977.

10.7 PROFESSIONAL NEGLIGENCE

In considering whether a duty of care is owed by the defendant to the claimant, it is necessary to consider the particular position of the professional person who, through the nature of his or her job, will be giving advice or carrying out acts which may leave him or her open to an action in negligence.

10.7.1 Accountants and auditors

While there may be a contractual relationship between an accountant and his client, on which the client can sue, the contentious legal area arises in respect of other people who may rely on reports made or advice given in a non-contractual capacity. Indeed, in many situations, the potential claimant may be unknown to the accountant. Whether there is liability appears to depend upon the purpose for which reports are made or accounts prepared.

In *JEB Fasteners v Marks Bloom and Co* (1983), the defendant accountants negligently overstated the value of stock in preparing accounts for their client. At the time of preparation, the accountants were aware that their client was in financial difficulties and was actively seeking financial assistance. After seeing the accounts, the plaintiff decided to take over the company. They then discovered the true financial position and sued the accountants for negligent misstatement. It was held that a duty of care was owed by the accountants, as it was foreseeable that someone contemplating a takeover might rely on the accuracy of the accounts; but they were not liable, as their negligence had not caused the loss to the plaintiff. The evidence revealed that, when they took over the company, they were interested not in the value of the stock, but in acquiring the expertise of the directors. Thus, although they relied on the accounts, the accounts were not the cause of the loss, as they would have taken over the company in any event.

The case of *Caparo Industries plc v Dickman* (1990) served to limit the potential liability of auditors in auditing company accounts. Accounts were audited in accordance with the Companies Act 1985. The respondents, who already owned shares in the company, decided to purchase more shares and take over the company after seeing the accounts. The accounts were inaccurate. The respondents then incurred a loss, which they blamed on the negligently audited accounts. It was held that, when the accounts were prepared, a duty of care was owed to members of the company (that is, the shareholders), but only so far as to allow them to exercise proper control over the company. This duty did not extend to members as individuals and potential purchasers of shares. The onus was clearly on the appellants in these circumstances to make their own independent inquiries, as it was unreasonable to rely on the auditors.

However, where express representations are made about the accounts and the financial state of a company by its directors or financial advisers, with the intention that the person interested in the takeover will rely on them, a duty of care is owed (*Morgan Crucible Co plc v Hill Samuel Bank Ltd* (1991)).

The case of *James McNaughten Paper Group Ltd v Hicks Anderson & Co* (1991) reaffirmed the key elements in determining liability for negligent misstatements. In this case, the accountants were asked, at short notice, to draw up draft accounts for a company chairman. The plaintiffs, who were planning a takeover bid, inspected the accounts, and on that basis took over the company. They subsequently claimed that the draft accounts were inaccurate and that they had suffered a loss. The Court of Appeal held that in determining liability, the following needed to be considered:

- the purpose for which the statement is made;
- the purpose for which the statement is communicated;
- the relationship between the adviser, the one advised and any relevant third party;

- the size of any class to which the person advised belonged;
- the state of knowledge of the adviser.

10.7.2 Lawyers

Solicitors are usually in a contractual relationship with their client; however, there may be circumstances outside this relationship where they are liable in tort for negligent misstatements. The definitive position was stated in *Ross v Caunters* (1980), where the defendant solicitors prepared a will, under which the plaintiff was a beneficiary. The solicitors sent the will to the person instructing them, but failed to warn him that it should not be witnessed by the spouse of a beneficiary. When the will was returned to them, they failed to notice that one of the witnesses was the plaintiff's spouse. As a result, the plaintiff lost her benefit under the will. It was held that a solicitor may be liable in negligence to persons who are not his clients, either on the basis of the principle in *Hedley Byrne* (1964) or under *Donoghue v Stevenson* (1932). The latter was specifically applied in this case, the plaintiff being someone so closely and directly affected by the solicitors' acts that it was reasonably foreseeable that they were likely to be injured by any act or omission.

The decision in *Ross v Caunters* was further supported by the decision of the House of Lords in *White v Jones* (1995), in which the plaintiff was cut out of his father's will. The father then instructed his solicitors to reinstate him. Unfortunately, the solicitors delayed some six weeks in carrying out the change and, in the meantime, the father died. It was held that the solicitors owed a duty of care to the son as a potential beneficiary. The loss to the plaintiff was reasonably foreseeable and the duty of care was broken by their omission to act promptly.

Barristers are in the position of not being in a contractual relationship with their 'client', that is, the person they are representing; neither are they liable in tort for the way in which they conduct a case in court. There are policy reasons for this, as the duty to the court is higher than the duty to the client and must be put first, as can be seen *Rondel v Worsley* (1969). In *Saif Ali v Sidney Mitchell* (1980), it was confirmed that a barrister was neither liable for conduct of the case in court, nor was he liable for pre-trial work connected with the conduct of the case in court. However, he would be liable in tort for negligent opinions, that is, written advice where there was no error on the part of the solicitor briefing him.

Further limits on immunity for solicitors can be seen in *Arthur JS Hall & Co v Simons* (2000), in which solicitors who were being sued for negligence in civil proceedings attempted to rely on *Rondel v Worsley*. The House of Lords held that public policy arguments in favour of exemption were no longer appropriate and that *Rondel v Worsley* was disapproved. It was felt that the courts would be able to judge between errors of judgment which were an inevitable part of advocacy and true negligence and, as a result, the floodgates would not be opened. This has resulted in immunity being removed in both criminal and civil proceedings.

10.7.3 Surveyors

A duty of care is owed by surveyors, builders and architects, etc, to the client, with whom they are usually in a contractual relationship. However, there may also be liability in tort as a result of *Hedley Byrne*, although this hinges on the questions of reasonable reliance by the third party and whether the defendant ought to have foreseen such reliance.

In *Yianni v Edwin Evans and Sons* (1982), surveyors who were acting for the defendant building society valued a house at £15,000 and, as a result, the plaintiffs were able to secure a mortgage of £12,000. The house was, in fact, suffering from severe structural damage and repairs were estimated at £18,000. The basis of the plaintiffs' claim was not only the surveyor's negligence, but also the fact that he ought reasonably to have contemplated that the statement would be passed on by the building society to the plaintiffs and that they would rely on it, which they did. It was held that a duty of care was owed by the defendants. An important factor was that the price of the house indicated that the plaintiff was of modest means, would not be expected to obtain an independent valuation and would, in all probability, rely on the defendant's survey, which was communicated to them by the building society. The court was also confident that the defendants knew that the building society would pass the survey to the purchasers and that they would rely on it.

The decision in *Yianni* was approved in *Smith v Eric Bush* (1989) and *Harris v Wyre Forest DC* (1989). The facts of the former case are very similar to *Yianni*, in that the plaintiff was sent a copy of the surveyor's report by the defendant building society. This report stated that no essential repairs were necessary and, although it contained a recommendation on obtaining independent advice, the plaintiff chose to rely on the report. In fact, the property had defective chimneys. In *Harris*, the plaintiffs did not see the surveyor's report, as it was stated on the mortgage application that the valuation was confidential and that no responsibility would be accepted for the valuation. However, the plaintiff paid the valuation fee and accepted the 95% mortgage on offer. When they attempted to sell the house three years later, structural defects were revealed and the property was deemed to be uninhabitable and unsaleable. It was held, in both cases, that there was sufficient proximity between the surveyor and the purchaser and that it was foreseeable that the plaintiff was likely to suffer damage as a result of the negligent advice. It was felt that, in general, surveyors knew that 90% of purchasers relied on their valuation for the building society; it was, therefore, just and reasonable for a duty to be imposed. The limitation on this decision is that it does not extend protection to subsequent purchasers or where the property is of a high value (although this will need to be determined on the facts of each case). The attempt to exclude liability in this case was seen as an attempt to exclude the existence of a duty of care, which, it was felt, was not within the spirit of UCTA 1977 and could not be permitted. In *Merrett v Babb* (2001), the defendant was held to have assumed personal responsibility to the buyers of a house he surveyed. This was despite the fact that he had not met the client, nor was the fee paid to him individually. However, he signed the valuation report personally and this report proved to be defective.

The decision in *Murphy v Brentwood DC* (1990) has seriously limited the potential liability of builders, architects and quantity surveyors in respect of claims arising out of defective buildings. Where the defect is discovered prior to any injury to person or health or damage to property other than the defective premises itself, this is to be regarded as pure economic loss, not physical damage to property, and is not, therefore, recoverable in negligence.

10.8 BREACH OF THE DUTY OF CARE

Once the claimant has established that the defendant owes him or her a duty of care, he or she must then establish that the defendant is in breach of this duty. The test for establishing breach of duty was laid down in *Blyth v Birmingham Waterworks Co* (1856). A breach of duty occurs if the defendant:

> ... fails to do something which a reasonable man, guided upon those considerations which ordinarily regulate the conduct of human affairs, would do; or does something which a prudent and reasonable man would not do [*per* Alderson B].

The test is an objective test, judged through the eyes of the reasonable man. The fact that the defendant has acted less skilfully than the reasonable man would expect will usually result in breach being established. This is the case even where the defendant is inexperienced in his particular trade or activity. One cannot condone the incompetence of such defendants. For example, a learner driver must drive in the manner of a driver of skill, experience and care (*Nettleship v Weston* (1971)). It is, however, clear from the case law that, depending on the age of the child, the standard of care expected from a child may be lower than that of an adult. Children should be judged on whether they have the 'foresight and prudence of a normal child of that age' (see *Mullin v Richards* (1998)). The degree or standard of care to be exercised by such a person will vary, as there are factors, such as the age of the claimant, which can increase the standard of care to be exercised by the defendant. The test is, therefore, flexible. The following factors are relevant:

- The likelihood of injury

  In deciding whether the defendant has failed to act as the reasonable man would act, the degree of care must be balanced against the degree of risk involved if the defendant fails in his duty. It follows, therefore, that the greater the risk of injury or the more likely it is to occur, the more the defendant will have to do to fulfil his duty.

In *Bolton v Stone* (1951), a cricket ground was surrounded by a 17 ft high wall and the pitch was situated some way from the road. A batsman hit a ball exceptionally hard, driving it over the wall, where it struck the plaintiff, who was standing on the highway. It was held that the plaintiff could not succeed in his action, as the likelihood of such injury occurring was small, as was the risk involved. The slight risk was outweighed by the height of the wall and the fact that a ball had been hit out of the ground only six times in 30 years.

- The seriousness of the risk

The degree of care to be exercised by the defendant may be increased if the claimant is very young, old or less able bodied in some way. The rule is that 'you must take your victim as you find him'. This is illustrated in *Haley v London Electricity Board* (1965), in which the defendants, in order to carry out repairs, had made a hole in the pavement. Haley, who was blind, often walked along this stretch of pavement. He was usually able to avoid obstacles by using his white stick. The precautions taken by the Electricity Board would have prevented a sighted person from injuring himself, but not a blind person. Haley fell into the hole, striking his head on the pavement, and became deaf as a consequence. It was held that the Electricity Board was in breach of its duty of care to pedestrians. It had failed to ensure that the excavation was safe for all pedestrians, not just sighted persons. It was clearly not reasonably safe for blind persons, yet it was foreseeable that they may use this pavement.

There are other cases in this field which should be referred to, for example, *Gough v Thorne* (1966), concerning young children; *Daly v Liverpool Corp* (1939), concerning old people; and *Paris v Stepney BC* (1951), concerning disability.

- Cost and practicability

Another factor in deciding whether the defendant is in breach of his duty to the claimant is the cost and practicability of overcoming the risk. The foreseeable risk has to be balanced against the measures necessary to eliminate it. If the cost of these measures far outweighs the risk, the defendant will probably not be in breach of duty for failing to carry out these measures. This is illustrated by the case of *Latimer v AEC Ltd* (1952). A factory belonging to AEC became flooded after an abnormally heavy rainstorm. The rain mixed with oily deposits on the floor, making the floor very slippery. Sawdust was spread on the floor, but it was insufficient to cover the whole area. Latimer, an employee, slipped on a part of the floor to which sawdust had not been applied. It was held that AEC Ltd was not in breach of its duty to the plaintiff. It had taken all reasonable precautions and had eliminated the risk as far as it practicably could without going so far as to close the factory. There was no evidence to suggest that the reasonably prudent employer would have closed down the factory and, as far as the court was concerned, the cost of doing that far outweighed the risk to the employees.

Compare this case with *Haley*, where the provision of 2 ft barriers around excavations in the pavement would have been practicable and would have eliminated the risk to blind people.

- Social utility

The degree of risk has to be balanced against the social utility and importance of the defendant's activity. If the activity is of particular importance to the community, then the taking of greater risks may be justified in the circumstances.

In *Watt v Hertfordshire CC* (1954), the plaintiff, a fireman, was called out to rescue a woman trapped beneath a lorry. The lifting jack had to be carried on an ordinary lorry, as a suitable vehicle was unavailable. The jack slipped, injuring the plaintiff. It was held that the employer was not in breach of duty. The importance of the activity and the fact that it was an emergency was found to justify the risk involved.

- Common practice

If the defendant can show that what he or she has done is common practice, then this is evidence that a proper standard of care has been exercised. However, if the common practice is in itself negligent, then his or her actions in conforming to such a practice will be actionable, as can be seen in *Paris v Stepney BC* (1951). There, the common practice of not wearing safety glasses could not be condoned, as it was in itself inherently negligent.

- Skilled persons

The standard of care to be exercised by people professing to have a particular skill is not be judged on the basis of the reasonable man. The actions of a skilled person must be judged by what the ordinary skilled man in that job or profession would have done, for example, the reasonable doctor, plumber, engineer, etc. Such a person is judged on the standard of knowledge possessed by the profession at the time that the accident occurred. Obviously, there is an onus on the skilled person to keep himself abreast of changes and improvements in technology.

In *Roe v Minister of Health* (1954), a patient was paralysed after being given a spinal injection. This occurred because the fluid being injected had become contaminated with the storage liquid, which had seeped through minute cracks in the phials. It was held that there was no breach of duty, since the doctor who administered the injection had no way of detecting the contamination at that time.

Furthermore, the common practice of the profession may, if this is followed, prevent liability. This can be seen in *Bolam v Friern Hospital Management Committee* (1957). Bolam broke his pelvis whilst undergoing electro-convulsive therapy treatment at the defendant's hospital. He alleged that the doctor had not warned him of the risks; he had not been given relaxant drugs prior to treatment; and no one had held him down during treatment. It was held that the doctor was not in breach of duty (and there was, therefore, no vicarious liability), because this form of treatment was accepted at that time by a certain body of the medical profession. This has been qualified by the decision in *Bolitho v City and Hackney HA* (1998): in order to be accepted, expert opinion must be shown to be reasonable and responsible and to have a logical basis (*per* Lord Browne-Wilkinson).

10.9 *RES IPSA LOQUITUR*

The burden of proof in establishing breach of duty normally rests on the claimant. In certain circumstances, the inference of negligence may be drawn from the facts. If this can be done, the claimant is relieved of the burden, which moves to the defendant to rebut the presumption of negligence. This is known as *res ipsa loquitur*, that is, the thing speaks for itself. It can only be used where the only explanation for what happened is the negligence of the defendant, yet the claimant has insufficient evidence to establish the defendant's negligence in the normal way. There are three criteria for the maxim to apply:

- Sole management or control

  It must be shown that the damage was caused by something under the sole management or control of the defendant, or by someone for whom he or she is responsible or whom he or she has a right to control (*Gee v Metropolitan Rly* (1873)).

- The occurrence cannot have happened without negligence

  This depends on the facts of each case. If there are other possible explanations as to how the incident occurred, *res ipsa loquitur* will fail. In *Mahon v Osborne* (1939), a patient died after a swab was left in her body after an operation. No one could explain how this had happened; therefore, *res ipsa loquitur* applied.

- The cause of the occurrence is unknown

  If the defendant can put forward a satisfactory explanation as to how the accident occurred which shows no negligence on his part, then the maxim is inapplicable. In *Pearson v NW Gas Board* (1968), the plaintiff's husband was killed and her house destroyed when a gas main fractured. She pleaded *res ipsa loquitur*. However, the Gas Board put forward the explanation that the gas main could have fractured due to earth movement after a heavy frost. This explanation was plausible and, as it showed no negligence on the board's part, it was not liable.

If the defendant can rebut the presumption of negligence by giving a satisfactory explanation, it is open to the claimant to establish negligence in the normal way. In practice, he or she is unlikely to succeed because, if sufficient evidence were available in the first place, *res ipsa loquitur* would not have been pleaded.

10.10 CAUSATION

The claimant must show that he or she has suffered some injury, but it does not necessarily have to be physical injury. Furthermore, he or she must show that this injury was caused by the defendant's negligence. This is known as causation in fact. The 'but for' test is used to establish whether the defendant's negligence was the cause of the injury to the claimant.

10.10.1 The 'but for' test

In order to satisfy the test, the claimant must show that, 'but for' the defendant's actions, the damage would not have occurred. If the damage would have occurred irrespective of a breach of duty on the part of the defendant, then the breach is not the cause.

In *Cutler v Vauxhall Motors Ltd* (1971), the plaintiff suffered a grazed ankle whilst at work, due to the defendant's negligence. The graze became ulcerated because of existing varicose veins and the plaintiff had to undergo an immediate operation to remove the veins. It was held that the plaintiff could not recover damages for the operation, because the evidence was that he would have to undergo the operation within five years anyway, irrespective of the accident at work.

If the same result would have occurred regardless of the breach, then the courts are unlikely to find that the breach caused the injury. This is illustrated in *Barnett v Chelsea and Kensington HMC* (1969), in which a doctor in a casualty department sent home a patient without treating him, telling him to go and see his own doctor. The patient died from arsenic poisoning. While it was held that the doctor was negligent, the evidence indicated that the patient would have died anyway. The doctor's conduct did not, therefore, cause his death. This is further supported by the case of *Robinson v Post Office* (1974), where a doctor failed to test for an allergic reaction before giving an anti-tetanus injection. However, it was held that the doctor would not be liable for the reaction of the patient, because the test would not have revealed the allergy in time.

Recent case law has not been sympathetic to the claimant where there has been a number of potential causes of the injury. The onus is on the claimant to show that the defendant's breach was a material contributory cause of his or her injury.

Where there are a number of possible causes, establishing causation may prove difficult, particularly in medical negligence cases. In *Wilsher v Essex AHA* (1988), the plaintiff was born three months premature. He suffered almost total blindness as a result of a condition known as retrolental fibroplasia. It was claimed on behalf of the plaintiff that this was caused by the negligence of the doctor, who had failed to notice that the device for adding oxygen to the blood had been wrongly attached, resulting in an excessive dose of oxygen. However, medical evidence showed at least six potential causes of the plaintiff's blindness, the majority of which were inherent in premature babies. The House of Lords held that there was insufficient evidence to show which of the six caused the injury to the plaintiff.

The court in *Hotson v East Berkshire AHA* (1987) considered whether the defendant could be liable for loss of a chance. Here, a boy fell from a tree and injured his hip. At the hospital, his injury was misdiagnosed and, by the time the mistake was discovered, he was left with a permanent disability. It was held that, as 75% of such cases were inoperable, there was no lost chance and, therefore, the plaintiff could not recover. Where there are two or more independent tortfeasors, there can also be problems in establishing how far each one is responsible for the damage caused.

In *Baker v Willoughby* (1970), the plaintiff injured his leg through the defendant's negligence, and he was left partially disabled. Subsequently, the plaintiff was shot in the same leg by another person and, as a result of the shooting, the leg had to be amputated. It was held that the first defendant was only liable for the first injury (and not the amputation). Irrespective of the amputation, it would have been a continuing disability, and this was reflected in the responsibility imposed on the defendant. The liability for the existing disability did not cease when the second incident took place.

The 'but for' test cannot solve all questions of factual causation. Indeed, where there has been an omission to act or an act which does not in itself have physical consequences, it may not be an appropriate test. In *Joyce v Merton, Sutton and Wandsworth HA* (1996), the plaintiff underwent an operation which resulted in a partially blocked artery. This, in turn, resulted in total paralysis. The procedure itself was not necessarily negligent; however, it was concluded that the immediate aftercare *was* negligent, in that the plaintiff was discharged from hospital without proper instruction and advice. A vascular surgeon should have seen the plaintiff within the first 48 hours and he should have operated to deal with the blockage. In order to succeed on the point of causation, it was held that the plaintiff would have to prove either that, had the vascular surgeon been summoned, he would have operated, or that it would have been negligent for him not to do so. The correct test in these circumstances was to satisfy one of two questions. First, what steps would have been taken if proper care had been taken? Or, secondly, what would have been the outcome of any further steps that ought to have been taken? In this case, the plaintiff was able to satisfy the first question by establishing that his injuries would have been avoided if proper care had been taken.

Recovery for a lost opportunity or chance may at times be problematic, in *Spring v Guardian Assurance plc* (1995), an employee who was provided with a poor reference by his employer recovered for his lost chance of employment, even though he could not prove that he would have got the job.

The 'but for' test can be used to establish causation on the facts. However, once this has been established, it does not mean that the defendant will be liable for all of the damage to the claimant. There must be causation in law. This can be seen through the maxim, *novus actus interveniens*, or 'a new intervening act'.

10.10.2 *Novus actus interveniens*

Where there is a break in the chain of causation, the defendant will not be liable for damage caused after the break. The issues are whether the whole sequence of events is the probable consequence of the defendant's actions and whether it is reasonably foreseeable that these events may happen. This break in the chain is caused by an intervening act and the law recognises that such acts fall into three categories.

- A natural event

  A natural event does not automatically break the chain of causation. If the defendant's breach has placed the claimant in a position where the natural event can add to that damage, the chain will not be broken unless the natural event was totally unforeseen.

  In *Carslogie Steamship Co Ltd v Royal Norwegian Government* (1952), a ship which was owned by Carslogie had been damaged in a collision caused by the defendant's negligence. The ship was sent for repair and, on this voyage, suffered extra damage, caused by the severe weather conditions. This resulted in the repairs taking 40 days longer than anticipated. It was held that the bad weather acted as a new intervening act, for which the defendant was not liable. The effect of the new act in this case prevented the plaintiff from recovering compensation for the time that it would have taken to repair the vessel in respect of the collision damage, as the ship would have been out of use in any case, due to the damage caused by the weather.

- Act of a third party

  Where the act of a third party following the breach of the defendant causes further damage to the claimant, such act may be deemed to be a *novus actus*; the defendant will not then be liable for damage occurring after the third party's act.

In *Lamb v Camden LBC* (1981), due to the defendant's negligence, a water main was damaged, causing the plaintiff's house to be damaged and the house to be vacated until it had been repaired. While the house was empty, squatters moved in and caused further damage to the property. It was held that the defendant was not liable for the squatters' damage. Although it was a reasonably foreseeable risk, it was not a likely event. Furthermore, it was not the duty of the council to keep the squatters out.

The third party's act need not be negligent in itself in order to break the chain of causation, although the courts take the view that a negligent act is more likely to break the chain than one that is not negligent, as can be seen in *Knightley v Johns* (1982).

- Act of the claimant him or herself

In *McKew v Holland, Hannen and Cubbitts (Scotland) Ltd* (1969), the plaintiff was injured at work. As a result, his leg sometimes gave way without warning. He was coming downstairs when his leg gave way, so he jumped in order to avoid falling head first and badly injured his ankle. It was held that the defendants were not liable for this additional injury. The plaintiff had not acted reasonably in attempting to negotiate the stairs without assistance and his actions amounted to a *novus actus interveniens*.

The case of *Reeves v Commissioner of Police* (2000) questions whether an act of suicide amounts to a *novus actus*. In this case, D, apparently of sound mind, committed suicide in police custody. At first instance, the police were held to be in breach of their duty of care, but the court treated the deceased's behaviour as a totally voluntary act, which broke the chain of causation. The Court of Appeal initially allowed the Commissioner's appeal. However, the House of Lords found the police liable on the basis that they were under a specific duty to protect D from the risk of suicide and had failed to do so. The defence of voluntary assumption of risk was not compatible with this duty.

The House of Lords allowed the appeal and the amount of damages was reduced. A deliberate act of suicide was not a *novus actus interveniens* negating the casual connection between breach of duty and death. To hold as such would lead to the absurd result that the very act which the duty sought to prevent would be fatal to establishing a causative link. On the issue of causation, both the police, who had been negligent in leaving the door hatch open, and the deceased, who had responsibility for his own life, were the causes of his death. The deceased was held to be contributorily negligent and damages were reduced by 50%.

Where it is the act of the claimant which breaks the chain, it is not a question of foresight but of unreasonable conduct.

10.11 REMOTENESS OF DAMAGE

It must be understood that, even where causation is established, the defendant will not necessarily be liable for all of the damage resulting from the breach. This was not always the case and the way in which the law has developed must be considered.

In *Re Polemis and Furness, Withy and Co* (1921), the plaintiff's ship was destroyed by fire when one of the employees of the company to whom the ship had been chartered negligently knocked a plank into the hold. The hold was full of petrol vapour. The plank caused a spark as it struck the side and this ignited the vapour. It was held that the defendants were liable for the loss of the ship, even though the presence of petrol vapour and the causing of the spark were unforeseen. The fire was the direct result of the breach of duty and the defendant was liable for the full extent of the damage, even where the manner in which it took place was unforeseen.

The case of *Re Polemis* is no longer regarded as the current test for remoteness of damage. The test currently used arose out of *The Wagon Mound (No 1)* (1961). The defendants negligently allowed furnace oil to spill from a ship into Sydney harbour. The oil spread and came to lie beneath a wharf, which was owned by the plaintiffs. The plaintiffs had been carrying out welding operations and, on seeing the oil, they stopped welding in order to ascertain whether it was safe. They were assured that the oil would not catch fire, and so resumed welding. Cotton waste, which had fallen into the oil, caught fire. This in turn ignited the oil and a fire spread to the plaintiff's wharf. It was held that the defendants were in breach of duty. However, they were only liable for the damage caused to the wharf and slipway through the fouling of the oil. They were not liable for the damage caused by fire because damage by fire was at that time unforeseeable. This particular oil had a high ignition point and it could not be foreseen that it would ignite on water. The court refused to apply the rule in *Re Polemis*.

The test of reasonable foresight arising out of *The Wagon Mound* clearly takes into account such things as scientific knowledge at the time of the negligent act. The question to be asked in determining the extent of liability is, 'is the damage of such a kind as the reasonable man should have foreseen?'. This does not mean that the defendant should have foreseen precisely the sequence or nature of the events. Lord Denning in *Stewart v West African Air Terminals* (1964) said:

> It is not necessary that the precise concatenation of circumstances should be envisaged. If the consequence was one which was within the general range which any reasonable person might foresee (and was not of an entirely different kind which no one would anticipate), then it is within the rule that a person who has been guilty of negligence is liable for the consequences.

This is illustrated in the case of *Hughes v Lord Advocate* (1963), where employees of the Post Office, who were working down a manhole, left it without a cover but with a tent over it and lamps around it. A child picked up a lamp and went into the tent. He tripped over the lamp, knocking it into the hole. An explosion occurred and the child was burned. The risk of the child being burned by the lamp was foreseeable. However, the vapourisation of the paraffin in the lamp and its ignition were not foreseeable. It was held that the defendants were liable for the injury to the plaintiff. It was foreseeable that the child might be burned and it was immaterial that neither the extent of his injury nor the precise chain of events leading to it was foreseeable.

The test of remoteness is not easy to apply. The cases themselves highlight the uncertainty of the courts. For example, in *Doughty v Turner Manufacturing Co Ltd* (1964), an asbestos cover was knocked into a bath of molten metal. This led to a chemical reaction, which was at that time unforeseeable. The molten metal erupted and burned the plaintiff, who was standing nearby. It was held that only burning by splashing was foreseeable and that burning by an unforeseen chemical reaction was not a variant on this. It could be argued that the proper question in this case should have been, 'was burning foreseeable?', as this was the question asked in *Hughes*.

A similar issue surrounding the questions asked to establish whether the harm is foreseeable can be seen in *Tremain v Pike* (1969), in which a farmhand contracted a rare disease transmitted by rat's urine. It was foreseeable that the plaintiff may sustain injury from rat bites or from contaminated food, but not from the contraction of this disease. Once again, this case raises the issue of whether the correct question was asked (see *Robinson v Post Office* (1974), which was considered above).

10.12 DEFENCES

The extent of the liability of the defendant may be reduced or limited by one of the defences commonly pleaded in negligence actions.

10.12.1 Contributory negligence

Where the claimant is found in some way to have contributed through his or her own fault to his or her injury, the amount awarded as damages will be reduced accordingly (under the Law Reform (Contributory Negligence) Act 1945). The onus is on the defendant to show that the claimant was at fault and that this contributed to his or her injury.

The court, if satisfied that the claimant is at fault, will reduce the amount of damages by an amount which is just and reasonable, depending on the claimant's share of the blame. For example, damages may be reduced by anything from 10% to 75%. However, a 100% reduction has been made, as can be seen in *Jayes v IMI (Kynoch) Ltd* (1985).

10.12.2 *Volenti non fit injuria*

Volenti, or consent, as it applies to negligent acts, is a defence to future conduct of the defendant which involves the risk of a tort being committed. *Volenti* may arise from the express agreement of the claimant and defendant or it may be implied from the claimant's conduct.

In *ICI v Shatwell* (1965), the plaintiff and his brother ignored the safety precautions issued by their employer and breached the regulations in testing detonators. As a result, the plaintiff was injured in an explosion. The action against the employer was based on vicarious liability and breach of statutory duty on the part of the plaintiff's brother. It was held that the defence of *volenti* would succeed. The plaintiff not only consented to each act of negligence and breach of statute on the part of his brother, but also participated in it quite willingly.

It must be stressed that this particular case highlights extreme circumstances where *volenti* is likely to succeed. However, if the defence is to succeed, it must be shown that the claimant was fully informed of the risks when he or she gave his or her consent.

In *Dann v Hamilton* (1939), a girl accepted a lift in the car of a driver whom she knew to be drunk. She could have used alternative transport. She was injured as a result of his negligent driving. It was held that, although she knew of the risk, this was insufficient to support the defence of *volenti*. It was necessary to show that she had consented to the risk, which could not be established. She therefore succeeded in her action against the driver.

Following this case, it is unlikely that this defence will succeed where the implied consent is given before the negligent act occurs. In practice, the courts do not look favourably on this defence in respect of negligent actions and, therefore, it is not usually pleaded.

Finally, there is a limitation period for commencing an action in tort. The Limitation Act 1980 states that, generally, an action must be brought within six years from the date on which it occurred. If the action is for personal injury, the period is three years from the date on which it occurred or the date of knowledge, that is, the date that the injury becomes attributable to another person's negligent actions, whichever is the later.

NEGLIGENCE

The tort of negligence imposes a duty to take reasonable care to prevent harm or loss occurring from one's actions.

The elements of the tort, which must be established by the claimant, are:

- duty of care;
- breach of duty;
- resultant damage.

Duty of care

- Established by the 'neighbour' test:
  - *Donoghue v Stevenson* (1932);
  - *Peabody Donation Fund v Sir Lindsay Parkinson and Co Ltd* (1984); *Leigh and Sullivan Ltd v Aliakmon Shipping Co Ltd* (1986); *Anns v Merton LBC* (1978);
  - *Caparo Industries plc v Dickman* (1990), which introduced a three stage test for establishing the existence of a duty of care. This test appears to apply to all situations.
- The test is incremental, requiring consideration of the following:
  - foresight;
  - proximity;
  - 'just and reasonable'.

It was approved in *Marc Rich and Co AG v Bishop Rock Marine Co Ltd (The Nicholas H)* (1994).

Nervous shock

The tort of negligence also recognises liability for nervous shock, sometimes known as post-traumatic stress disorder. The claimant must establish:

- a recognised medical condition which goes beyond grief and distress;
- foresight;
- proximity.

The courts clearly distinguish between:

- fearing for one's own safety (*Dulieu v White* (1901));
- merely being a passing witness to an accident (*Bourhill v Young* (1943); *Hegarty v EE Caledonia Ltd* (1996)).

A further contentious issue arises where the claimant who witnesses the accident or its immediate aftermath has a close relationship with the victim. In these circumstances, the claimant must establish:

- a close loving relationship;
- proximity to the accident in terms of time and space;
- *Hambrook v Stokes Bros* (1925);
- *McLoughlin v O'Brian* (1982);
- *Alcock and Others v Chief Constable of South Yorkshire* (1991).

Rescuers are usually treated as a special case, particularly where they are not professional rescuers:

- *Chadwick v BRB* (1967);
- *White v Chief Constable of South Yorkshire* (1999).

Economic loss

Liability for economic loss arising out of physical injury or damage to property may be compensated in negligence. Liability for pure economic loss cannot, in general, be compensated:

- *Spartan Steel & Alloys Ltd v Martin and Co* (1973);
- *Junior Books Ltd v Veitchi Ltd* (1983);
- liability for pure economic loss will generally only be upheld where negligent misstatement is proven (*Murphy v Brentwood DC* (1990);
- where a special relationship is found to exist between the parties which falls short of contract, the defendant may be liable for giving negligent advice (*Hedley Byrne & Co v Heller and Partners* (1964); see, also, *Mutual Life and Citizens Assurance Co v Evatt* (1971); *Chaudry v Prabhakar* (1988)).

However, the claimant will have to show that he or she actually relied on the advice:

- *JEB Fasteners v Marks Bloom and Co* (1983);
- *Caparo Industries plc v Dickman* (1990);
- *White v Jones* (1995);
- *Merrett v Babb* (2001).

Breach of duty

Once the claimant has established a duty of care, breach of duty must be proven. The test for establishing breach of duty is whether the defendant has acted as a reasonable person in all the circumstances of the case. The courts will take the following into account:

- likelihood of harm occurring (*Bolton v Stone* (1951));
- egg-shell skull rule (*Haley v London Electricity Board* (1965); *Paris v Stepney BC* (1951));
- cost and practicability of taking precautions (*Latimer v AEC* (1952));
- social utility of the act (*Watt v Hertfordshire CC* (1954));
- common practice (*Roe v Minister of Health* (1954)).

In certain circumstances, the claimant may rely on the maxim *res ipsa loquitur* in order to establish breach. However, the following must be shown:

- sole management or control on the part of the defendant;
- the occurrence could not have happened without negligence;
- the cause of the occurrence is unknown.

Resultant damage

Finally, the claimant must show that the breach of duty on the part of the defendant was the cause of his or her loss. The test for establishing causation in fact is the 'but for' test:

- If there is another acceptable explanation for the injury, causation may not be proven (see *Cutler v Vauxhall Motors Ltd* (1971)).
- The onus rests on the claimant to show that the defendant's breach was a material contributory cause, as in *Wilsher v Essex AHA* (1988); *Hotson v East Berkshire AHA* (1987).
- The extent of the defendant's liability may be further limited by the rules for determining remoteness of damage (for example, *novus actus interveniens*).
- Where the cause and extent of the harm is unforeseen, the loss will not be recoverable. The test for establishing remoteness is that of reasonable foresight, as expounded in *Wagon Mound (No 1)* (1961).
- As a general rule, it is not necessary to foresee the exact cause of the harm, as long as it is within the general range which any reasonable person might foresee:
  - *Stewart v West African Air Terminals* (1964);
  - *Hughes v Lord Advocate* (1963);

- *Doughty v Turner Manufacturing Co Ltd* (1964);
- *Tremain v Pike* (1969).

Defences

Damages may be reduced by the claimant's contributory negligence (Law Reform (Contributory Negligence) Act 1945).

The defence of *volenti* or consent may operate as a complete defence (*ICI v Shatwell* (1965); *Dann v Hamilton* (1939)).

CHAPTER 11

AGENCY

11.1 INTRODUCTION

The principles of agency law provide the basis for an understanding of many issues relating to partnerships and some of those relating to registered companies. The general assumption is that individuals engaging in business activity carry on that business by themselves, and on their own behalf, either individually or collectively. It is not uncommon, however, for such individuals to engage others to represent them and negotiate business deals on their behalf. Indeed, the role of the 'middleman' is a commonplace one in business and commerce. The legal relationship between such a representative, or middleman, and the business person making use of them is governed by the law of agency. Agency principles also apply in relation to companies registered under the companies legislation and the directors and other officers of such companies.

11.2 DEFINITION OF 'AGENCY'

An agent is a person who is empowered to represent another legal party, called the principal, and brings the principal into a legal relationship with a third party. It should be emphasised that the contract entered into is between the principal and the third party. In the normal course of events, the agent has no personal rights or liabilities in relation to the contract. This outcome represents an accepted exception to the usual operation of the doctrine of privity in contract law (see above, 5.6).

Since the agent is not actually entering into contractual relations with the third party, there is no requirement that the agent has contractual capacity, although, based on the same reasoning, it is essential that the principal has full contractual capacity. Thus, it is possible for a principal to use a minor as an agent, even though the minor might not have contractual capacity to enter into the contract on their own behalf.

There are numerous examples of agency relationships. For example, as their names imply, estate agents and travel agents are expressly appointed to facilitate particular transactions. Additionally, employees may act as agents of their employers in certain circumstances; or friends may act as agents for one another.

Some forms of agency merit particular consideration:

- A general agent, as the title indicates, has the power to act for a principal generally in relation to a particular area of business, whereas a special agent only has the authority to act in one particular transaction.

- A *del credere* agent is one who, in return for an additional commission by way of payment, guarantees to the principal that, in the event of a third party's failure to pay for goods received, the agent will make good the loss.

- A commission agent is a hybrid form which lies midway between a full principal/agent relationship and the relationship of an independent trader and client. In essence, the agent stands between the principal and the third party and establishes no contract between those two parties. The effect is that, although the commission agent owes the duties of an agent to his or her principal, he or she contracts with the third party as a principal in his or her own right. The effectiveness of this procedure is undermined by the normal operation of the agency law relating to an undisclosed principal (see below, 11.6.2).

- The position of a mercantile agent/factor is defined in the Factors Act 1889 as an agent:

  ... having in the customary course of his business as such agent authority either to sell goods, or to consign goods for the purpose of sale, or to buy goods, or to raise money on the security of goods.

However, of perhaps more contemporary importance are marketing agents, distribution agents and the question of franchising.

- Marketing agents have only limited authority. They can only introduce potential customers to their principals and do not have the authority either to negotiate or to enter into contracts on behalf of their principals.

- Distribution agents are appointed by suppliers to arrange the distribution of their products within a particular area. The distributors ordinarily cannot bind the supplier, except where they have expressly been given the authority to do so.

- Franchising arrangements arise where the original developer of a business decides, for whatever reason, to allow others to use their goodwill to conduct an independent business, using the original name of the business. Two prominent examples of franchises are McDonalds and The Body Shop, although there are many others. It is essential to emphasise that any such relationship does not arise from, or give rise to, a relationship of principal and agent. Indeed, it is commonplace, if not universal, that franchise agreements include an express clause to the effect that no such relationship is to be established.

- Commercial agents are specifically covered by the Commercial Agents (Council Directive) Regulations 1993, which were enacted in order to comply with EC Directive 86/653. The Regulations define a commercial agent as a self-employed intermediary who has continuing authority to negotiate the sale or purchase of goods on behalf of another person, or to negotiate and conclude such transactions on behalf of that person. Although intended to harmonise the operation and effect of agency law within the European Union, the regulations do not introduce any major substantive change into UK agency law. The effect of the Regulations will be considered in more detail below at 11.5.3.

- A power of attorney arises where an agency is specifically created by way of a deed.

11.3 CREATION OF AGENCY

No one can act as an agent without the consent of the principal, although consent need not be expressly stated.

In *White v Lucas* (1887), a firm of estate agents claimed to act on behalf of the owner of a particular property, though that person had denied them permission to act on his behalf. When the owner sold the property to a third party, who was introduced through the estate agents, they claimed their commission. It was held that the estate agents had no entitlement to commission, as the property owner had not agreed to their acting as his agent.

The principal/agent relationship can be created in a number of ways. It may arise as the outcome of a distinct contract, which may be made either orally or in writing, or it may be established purely gratuitously, where some person simply agrees to act for another. The relationship may also arise from the actions of the parties.

It is usual to consider the creation of the principal/agency relationship under five distinct categories.

11.3.1 Express appointment

This is the most common manner in which a principal/agent relationship comes into existence. In this situation, the agent is specifically appointed by the principal to carry out a particular task or to undertake some general function. In most situations, the appointment of the agent will itself involve the establishment of a contractual relationship between the principal and the agent, but need not necessarily depend upon a contract between those parties.

For the most part, there are no formal requirements for the appointment of an agent, although, where the agent is to be given the power to execute deeds in the principal's name, they must themselves be appointed by way of a deed (that is, they are given power of attorney).

11.3.2 Ratification

An agency is created by ratification when a person who has no authority purports to contract with a third party on behalf of a principal. Ratification is the express acceptance of the contract by the principal. Where the principal elects to ratify the contract, it gives retrospective validity to the action of the purported agent. There are, however, certain conditions which have to be fully complied with before the principal can effectively adopt the contract:

- The principal must have been in existence at the time that the agent entered into the contract

  Thus, for example, in *Kelner v Baxter* (1866), where promoters attempted to enter into a contract on behalf of the, as yet unformed, company, it was held that the company could not ratify the contract after it was created and that the promoters, as agents, were personally liable on the contract. (This is now given statutory effect under s 36C of the Companies Act 1985.)

- The principal must have had legal capacity to enter into the contract when it was made

  When the capacity of companies to enter into a business transaction was limited by the operation of the doctrine of *ultra vires*, it was clearly established that they could not ratify any such *ultra vires* contracts. Similarly, it is not possible for minors to ratify a contract, even though it was made in their name.

- An undisclosed principal cannot ratify a contract

  The agent must have declared that he or she was acting for the principal. If the agent appeared to be acting on his or her own account, then the principal cannot later adopt the contact (see *Keighley, Maxted and Co v Durant* (1901)).

- The principal must adopt the whole of the contract

  It is not open to the principal to pick and choose which parts of the contract to adopt; they must accept all of its terms.

- Ratification must take place within a reasonable time

  It is not possible to state with certainty what will be considered as a reasonable time in any particular case. Where, however, the third party with whom the agent contracted becomes aware that the agent has acted without authority, a time limit can be set, within which the principal must indicate their adoption of the contract for it to be effective.

11.3.3 Implication

This form of agency arises from the relationship that exists between the principal and the agent and from which it is assumed that the principal has given authority to the other person to act as his or her agent. Thus, it is implied from the particular position held by individuals that they have the authority to enter into contractual relations on behalf of their principal. So, whether an employee has the actual authority to contract on behalf of his or her employer depends on the position held by the employee; and, for example, it was decided in *Panorama Developments v Fidelis Furnishing Fabrics Ltd* (1971) that a company secretary had the implied authority to make contracts in the company's name relating to the day to day running of the company.

Problems most often occur in relation to the implied extent of a person's authority, rather than their actual appointment (but see *Hely-Hutchinson v Brayhead Ltd* (1967) as an example of the latter).

11.3.4 Necessity

Agency by necessity occurs under circumstances where, although there is no agreement between the parties, an emergency requires that an agent take particular action in order to protect the interests of the principal. The usual situation which gives rise to agency by necessity occurs where the agent is in possession of the principal's property and, due to some unforeseen emergency, the agent has to take action to safeguard that property:

- In order for agency by necessity to arise, there needs to be a genuine emergency.

  In *Great Northern Rly Co v Swaffield* (1874), the railway company transported the defendant's horse and, when no one arrived to collect it at its destination, it was placed in a livery stable. It was held that the company was entitled to recover the cost of stabling, as necessity had forced them to act as they had done as the defendant's agents.

- There must also be no practical way of obtaining further instructions from the principal.

  In *Springer v Great Western Rly Co* (1921), a consignment of tomatoes arrived at port, after a delayed journey due to storms. A railway strike would have caused further delay in getting the tomatoes to their destination, so the railway company decided to sell the tomatoes locally. It was held that the railway company was responsible to the plaintiff for the difference between the price achieved and the market price in London. The defence of agency of necessity was not available, as the railway company could have contacted the plaintiff to seek his further instructions.

- The person seeking to establish the agency by necessity must have acted *bona fide* in the interests of the principal (see *Sachs v Miklos* (1948)).

11.3.5 Estoppel

This form of agency is also known as 'agency by holding out' and arises where the principal has led other parties to believe that a person has the authority to represent him or her. (The authority possessed by the agent is referred to as 'apparent authority' – see below, 11.4.2.) In such circumstances, even though no principal/agency relationship actually exists in fact, the principal is prevented (estopped) from denying the existence of the agency relationship and is bound by the action of his or her purported agent as regards any third party who acted in the belief of its existence:

- To rely on agency by estoppel, the principal must have made a representation as to the authority of the agent

  In *Freeman and Lockyer v Buckhurst Park Properties Ltd* (1964), a property company had four directors, but one director effectively controlled the company and made contracts as if he were the managing director, even though he had never actually been appointed to that position and, therefore, as an individual, had no authority to bind the company. The other directors, however, were aware of this activity and acquiesced in it. When the company was sued in relation to one of the contracts entered into by the unauthorised director, it was held that it was liable, as the board which had the actual authority to bind the company had held out the individual director as having the necessary authority to enter such contracts. It was, therefore, a case of agency by estoppel.

- As with estoppel generally, the party seeking to use it must have relied on the representation

  In *Overbrooke Estates Ltd v Glencombe Properties Ltd* (1974), a notice which expressly denied the authority of an auctioneer to make such statements as actually turned out to be false was successfully relied on as a defence by the auctioneer's employers.

11.4 THE AUTHORITY OF AN AGENT

In order to bind a principal, any contract entered into must be within the limits of the authority extended to the agent. The authority of an agent can be either actual or apparent.

11.4.1 Actual authority

Actual authority can arise in two ways:

- Express actual authority

  This is explicitly granted by the principal to the agent. The agent is instructed as to what particular tasks are required to perform and is informed of the precise powers given in order to fulfil those tasks.

- Implied actual authority

  This refers to the way in which the scope of express authority may be increased. Third parties are entitled to assume that agents holding a particular position have all the powers that are usually provided to such an agent. Without actual knowledge to the contrary, they may safely assume that the agent has the usual authority that goes with their position. (This has been referred to above in relation to implied agency.)

  In *Watteau v Fenwick* (1893), the new owners of a hotel continued to employ the previous owner as its manager. They expressly forbade him to buy certain articles, including cigars. The manager, however, bought cigars from a third party, who later sued the owners for payment as the manager's principal. It was held that the purchase of cigars was within the usual authority of a manager of such an establishment and that, for a limitation on such usual authority to be effective, it must be communicated to any third party.

11.4.2 Apparent authority

Apparent authority is an aspect of agency by estoppel considered above. It can arise in two distinct ways:

- Where a person makes a representation to third parties that a particular person has the authority to act as their agent without actually appointing the agent

  In such a case, the person making the representation is bound by the actions of the apparent agent (see *Freeman and Lockyer v Buckhurst Park Properties Ltd* (1964)). The principal is also liable for the actions of the agent where it is known that the agent claims to be his or her agent and yet does nothing to correct that impression.

- Where a principal has previously represented to a third party that an agent has the authority to act on their behalf

  Even if the principal has subsequently revoked the agent's authority, he or she may still be liable for the actions of the former agent, unless he or she has informed third parties who had previously dealt with the agent about the new situation (see *Willis Faber and Co Ltd v Joyce* (1911)).

11.4.3 Warrant of authority

If a person claims to act as agent, but without the authority to do so, the supposed principal will not be bound by any agreement entered into. Neither is there a contract between the supposed agent and the third party, for the reason that the third party intended to deal not with the purported agent but with the supposed principal. However, the supposed agent may lay themselves open to an action for breach of warrant of authority.

If an agent contracts with a third party on behalf of a principal, the agent impliedly guarantees that the principal exists and has contractual capacity. The agent also implies that he or she has the authority to make contracts on behalf of that principal. If any of these implied warranties prove to be untrue, then the third party may sue the agent in quasi-contract for breach of warrant of authority. Such an action may arise even though the agent was genuinely unaware of any lack of authority.

In *Yonge v Toynbee* (1910), a firm of solicitors was instructed to institute proceedings against a third party. Without their knowledge, their client was certified insane and, although this automatically ended the agency relationship, they continued with the proceedings. The third party successfully recovered damages for breach of warrant of authority, since the solicitors were no longer acting for their former client.

11.5 THE RELATIONSHIP OF PRINCIPAL AND AGENT

The following considers the reciprocal rights and duties which principal and agent owe to each other.

11.5.1 The duties of agent to principal

The agent owes a number of duties, both express and implied, to the principal. These duties are as follows:

* To perform the agreed undertaking according to the instructions of the principal

    A failure to carry out instructions will leave the agent open to an action for breach of contract. This, of course, does not apply in the case of gratuitous agencies, where there is no obligation whatsoever on the agent to perform the agreed task. See *Turpin v Bilton* (1843), where an agent was held liable for the loss sustained by his failure to insure his principal's ship prior to its sinking.

* To exercise due care and skill

    An agent will owe a duty to act with reasonable care and skill, regardless of whether the agency relationship is contractual or gratuitous. The level of skill to be exercised, however, should be that appropriate to the agent's professional capacity and this may introduce a distinction in the levels expected of different agents. For example, a solicitor would be expected to show the level of care and skill that would be expected of a competent member of that profession; whereas a layperson acting in a gratuitous capacity would only be expected to perform with such degree of care and skill as a reasonable person would exercise in the conduct of their own affairs. See *Keppel v Wheeler* (1927), where the defendant estate agents were held liable for failing to secure the maximum possible price for a property.

- To carry out instructions personally

  Unless expressly or impliedly authorised to delegate the work, an agent owes a duty to the principal to act personally in the completion of the task. The right to delegate may be agreed expressly by the principal, or it may be implied from customary practice or arise as a matter of necessity. In any such case, the agent remains liable to the principal for the proper performance of the agreed contract.

- To account

  There is an implied duty that the agent keep proper accounts of all transactions entered into on behalf of the principal. The agent is required to account for all money and other property received on the principal's behalf and should keep his or her own property separate from that of the principal.

In addition to these contractual duties, there are general equitable duties which flow from the fact that the agency relationship is a fiduciary one, that is, one based on trust. These general fiduciary duties are:

- Not to permit a conflict of interest to arise

  An agent must not allow the possibility of personal interest to conflict with the interests of his or her principal without disclosing that possibility to the principal. Upon full disclosure, it is up to the principal to decide whether or not to proceed with the particular transaction. If there is a breach of this duty, the principal may set aside the contract so affected and claim any profit which might have been made by the agent.

  In *McPherson v Watt* (1877), a solicitor used his brother as a nominee to purchase property which he was engaged to sell. It was held that, since the solicitor had allowed a conflict of interest to arise, the sale could be set aside. It was immaterial that a fair price was offered for the property.

  The corollary to the above case is that the agent must not sell his or her own property to the principal without fully disclosing the fact (see *Harrods v Lemon* (1931)). This leads into the next duty.

- Not to make a secret profit or misuse confidential information

  An agent who uses his or her position as an agent to secure financial advantage for him or herself, without full disclosure to his principal, is in breach of fiduciary duty. Upon disclosure, the principal may authorise the agent's profit, but full disclosure is a necessary precondition (see *Hippisley v Knee Bros* (1905) for a clear-cut case). An example of the strictness with which this principle is enforced may be seen in the case of *Boardman v Phipps* (1967), in which agents were held to account for profits made from information which they had gained from their position as agents, even though their action also benefited the company they were acting for.

- Not to take a bribe

  This duty may be seen as merely a particular aspect of the general duty not to make a secret profit, but it goes so much to the root of the agency relationship that it is usually treated as a distinct heading in its own right. Again, for a clear-cut case, see *Mahesan v Malaysian Government Officers Co-operative Housing Society* (1978), where the plaintiff received a bribe to permit a third party to profit at his principal's expense.

Where it is found that an agent has taken a bribe, the following civil remedies are open to the principal:

- to repudiate the contract with the third party;
- to dismiss the agent without notice;
- to refuse to pay any money owed to the agent or to recover such money already paid;
- to claim the amount of the bribe;
- to claim damages in the tort of deceit for any loss sustained as a result of the payment of the bribe.

The payment of the bribe may also have constituted a breach of criminal law.

11.5.2 The rights of an agent

It is a simple matter of fact that the common law does not generally provide agents with as many rights in relation to the number of duties that it imposes on them. The agent, however, does benefit from the clear establishment of three general rights. These rights are:

- To claim remuneration for services performed

  It is usual in agency agreements for the amount of payment to be stated, either in the form of wages or commission, or, indeed, both. Where a commercial agreement is silent on the matter of payment, the court will imply a term into the agreement, requiring the payment of a reasonable remuneration. Such a term will not be implied in contradiction of the express terms of the agreement. See *Re Richmond Gate Property Co Ltd* (1965), where it was held that no remuneration could be claimed where an agreement stated that payment would be determined by the directors of the company, but they had not actually decided on any payment.

- To claim indemnity against the principal for all expenses legitimately incurred in the performance of services

  Both contractual and non-contractual agents are entitled to recover money spent in the course of performing their agreed task. In the case of the former, the remedy is based on an implied contractual term; and, in the case of a gratuitous agent, it is based on the remedy of restitution. Money can, of course, only be claimed where the agent has been acting within his or her actual authority.

- To exercise a lien over property owned by the principal

  This is a right to retain the principal's goods, where they have lawfully come into the agent's possession, and hold them against any debts outstanding to him or her as a result of the agency agreement. The nature of the lien is usually a particular one relating to specific goods which are subject to the agreement, not a general one which entitles the agent to retain any of the principal's goods, even where no money is owed in relation to those specific goods. The general lien is only recognised on the basis of an express term in the contract or as a result of judicially recognised custom, as in the area of banking.

11.5.3 Commercial Agents (Council Directive) Regulations 1993

These Regulations implement Council Directive 86/653/EEC on the Co-ordination of the Laws of Member States relating to Self-employed Commercial Agents, and came into force at the beginning of 1994. Regulations 3–5 set out the rights and obligations as between commercial agents and their principals; regs 6–12 deal with remuneration; and regs 13–16 deal with the conclusion and termination of the agency contract. Regulations 17–19 contain provisions relating to the indemnity or compensation payable to a commercial agent on termination of his agency contract, and reg 20 relates to the validity of restraint of trade clauses.

Considering the provisions in more detail:

- Regulation 3 provides that agents must act dutifully and in good faith in the interests of their principal. The agents must negotiate in a proper manner, execute the contracts they are contracted to undertake, communicate all necessary information to, and comply with all reasonable instructions from, their principal.

- Regulation 4 relates to principals' duties and requires that they provide their agent with the necessary documentation relating to the goods concerned, obtain information necessary for the performance of the agency contract, and, in particular, notify the commercial agent within a reasonable period once they anticipate that the volume of commercial transactions will be significantly lower than that which the commercial agent could normally have expected. Additionally, a principal shall, in addition, inform the commercial agent, within a reasonable period, of his acceptance or refusal of a commercial transaction which the commercial agent has procured for him.

- Regulation 14 provides that agents are entitled to notice of termination of their situation.

- Regulation 17 states that commercial agents are entitled to indemnity or compensation on termination of the agency agreement.

- Regulation 20 states that any agreements in restraint of trade in agency contracts are only effective if they are in writing. Such restraints must relate solely to the type of goods dealt with under the agency agreement and must be limited to the geographical area, or the particular customer group, allocated to the agent. In any case, such restraints may only be valid for a maximum period of two years (cf general contracts in restraint of trade at 7.6.3).

The relationship of the Commercial Agents (Council Directive) Regulations 1993 (SI 1993/3053) and the common law was considered in *Duffen v FRA Bo SpA* (1998), in which it was held that, although a dismissed agent could not enforce a 'liquidated damages' clause in his contract because it was really a penalty clause, he might not be restricted to merely claiming common law damages, as the Regulations allowed him to claim 'compensation' which might well involve a premium over the level of ordinary damages (see further, above at 8.7.3).

Recently, however, controversy, not to say confusion, has arisen over the way in which the level of compensation provided for in reg 17 should be calculated. As has been stated, the regulation itself simply provides that, in the event of a principal terminating a relationship with a commercial agent, the latter is entitled to compensation. The regulations do not, however, state precisely how such compensation should be calculated and it this lack of detail that has led to the confusion:

- In *Douglas King v T Tunnock Ltd* (2000), the Inner House of the Scottish Court of Session determined that, as the EC Directive was based on French law, it would be appropriate to operate the system for the calculation of compensation on the same basis as was adopted by the French courts. On that basis, the Inner House held that the agent should receive compensation equal to the gross commission paid during the previous two years of the agency. Alternatively, the court held that a multiple of twice the average commission earned during the last three years could be used.

- In *Barrett McKenzie & Co Ltd v Escada (UK) Ltd* (2001), the High Court reached a different conclusion as to the way in which compensation should be calculated. It did so on the basis that the aim of the original Directive was simply to establish a general right to an entitlement and that the particular method of assessing the value of that entitlement was to be left to the individual Member States to decide upon. The Court, therefore, thought it inappropriate simply to follow the method of calculation operated by the French courts. Following *Duffen v FRA Bo SpA*, the High Court, contrary to general common law principles, held that, under the Regulations, an independent agency had a value, which was akin to the value of the goodwill in a business. Any assessment of that value, at or just before termination, required consideration of various factors, including the agent's expenditure incurred in earning the commission, the duration and history of the agreement, provision for notice, etc, and was not susceptible to the application of a simple formula.

- In *Ingmar GB Ltd v Eaton Leonard Inc (formerly Eaton Leonard Technologies Inc)* (2001), whilst Morland J felt himself bound to recognise the hierarchical superiority of the Scottish Court of Session decision as stated in *Douglas King v T Tunnock Ltd* in relation to a piece of British legislation, he nonetheless felt more in sympathy with the approach adopted by the High Court in *Barrett McKenzie & Co Ltd v Escada (UK) Ltd*. His mechanism for achieving both ends was to decide that the Scottish court had laid down 'not a principle of law but a guideline that in many cases ... may be appropriate'. However, in the present case, he found it not appropriate and thus he could effectively avoid following the Court of Session's decision.

The situation as to the precise way in which s 17 compensation payments are to be calculated remains uncertain. Although much academic work supports the approach of the English High Court, it remains for the final resolution to be determined by the House of Lords, either in that form or as the Privy Council in relation to Scottish cases.

11.6 RELATIONS WITH THIRD PARTIES

In the words of Wright J in *Montgomerie v UK Mutual Steamship Association* (1891), once an agent creates a contract between the principal and a third party, *prima facie* at common law, 'the only person who can sue is the principal and the only person who can be sued is the principal'. In other words, the agent has no further responsibility. This general rule is, however, subject to the following particular exceptions, which in turn tend to depend upon whether or not the agent has actually disclosed the existence of the principal.

11.6.1 Where the principal's existence is disclosed

Although the actual identity of the principal need not be mentioned, where the agent indicates that he is acting as an agent, the general rule is as stated above; only the principal and the third party have rights and obligations under the contract.

Exceptionally, however, the agent may be held liable as a party to the contract. This can occur:

- At third party insistence

  Where the agent has expressly accepted liability with the principal in order to induce the third party to enter the contract, he or she will attract liability.

- By implication

    Where the agent has signed the contractual agreement in his or her own name, without clearly stating that he or she is merely acting as a representative of the principal, he or she will most likely be liable on it.

- In relation to bills of exchange

    As in the previous situation, where an agent signs a bill of exchange without sufficiently indicating that he or she is merely acting as the agent of a named principal, he or she will become personally liable on it.

- In relation to the execution of a deed

    Where the agent signs the deed other than under a power of attorney, he or she will be personally liable on it.

- Where the agent acts for a non-existent principal

    In such circumstances, the other party to the agreement can take action against the purported agent.

11.6.2 Where the principal's existence is not disclosed

Even in the case of an undisclosed principal, where the agent has authority but has failed to disclose that he or she is acting for a principal, the general rule is still that a contract exists between the principal and the third party, which can be enforced by either of them. The following, however, are some modifications to this general rule:

- the third party is entitled to enforce the contract against the agent and, in turn, the agent can enforce the contract against the third party. In both cases, the principal can intervene to enforce or defend the action on his or her own behalf;

- as stated previously, an undisclosed principal cannot ratify any contract made outside of the agent's actual authority;

- where the third party had a special reason to contract with the agent, the principal may be excluded from the contract. This will certainly apply in relation to personal contracts, such as contracts of employment and, possibly, on the authority of *Greer v Downs Supply Co* (1927), where the third party has a right to set off debts against the agent;

- authority exists in *Said v Butt* (1920), where a theatre critic employed someone to get him a ticket for a performance he would not have been allowed into, for claiming that an undisclosed principal will not be permitted to enforce a contract where particular reasons exist as to why the third party would not wish to deal with him or her. This decision appears to run contrary to normal commercial practice and is of doubtful merit.

It is certain, however, that, where the agent actually misrepresents the identity of the principal, knowing that the third party would not otherwise enter into the contract, the principal will not be permitted to enforce the contract (see *Archer v Stone* (1898)).

11.6.3 Payment by means of an agent

Payment by means of an agent can take two forms:

- Payment by the third party to the agent to pass on to the principal

  In this situation, if the principal is undisclosed, then the third party has discharged liability on the contract and is not responsible if the agent absconds with the money. However, if the principal is disclosed, then any payment to the agent only discharges the third party's responsibility if it can be shown that the agent had authority, either express or implied, to receive money.

- Payment by the principal to the agent to pass on to the third party

  In this situation, the general rule is that, if the agent does not pay the third party, the principal remains liable. This remains the case with an undisclosed principal (see *Irvine and Co v Watson and Sons* (1880)).

11.6.4 Breach of warrant of authority

As has been stated above (11.4.3), where an agent purports to act for a principal without actually having the necessary authority, the agent is said to have breached his or her warrant of authority. In such circumstances, the third party may take action against the purported agent.

11.6.5 Liability in tort

An agent is liable to be sued in tort for any damages thus caused. However, the agent's right to indemnity extends to tortious acts done in the performance of his or her actual authority. In addition, the principal may have action taken against him or her directly, on the basis of vicarious liability.

11.7 TERMINATION OF AGENCY

The principal/agent relationship can come to end in two distinct ways: either by the acts of the parties themselves, either jointly or unilaterally; or as an effect of the operation of law.

11.7.1 Termination by the parties

There are a number of ways in which the parties can bring an agency agreement to an end:

- By mutual agreement

  Where the agency agreement is a continuing one, the parties may simply agree to bring the agency relationship to an end on such terms as they wish. Where the agency was established for a particular purpose, then it will automatically come to an end when that purpose has been achieved. Equally, where the agency was only intended to last for a definite period of time, then the end of that period will bring the agency to an end.

- By the unilateral action of one of the parties

  Because of the essentially consensual nature of the principal/agency relationship, it is possible for either of the parties to bring it to an end simply by giving notice of termination of the agreement. Although the agency relationship will be ended by such unilateral action, in situations where the principal has formed a contractual relationship with the agent, such unilateral termination may leave the principal open to an action for damages in breach of contract.

- Irrevocable agreements

  In some circumstances, it is not possible to revoke an agency agreement. This situation arises where the agent has authority coupled with an interest. Such an irrevocable agency might arise where a principal owes money to the agent and the payment of the debt was the reason for the formation of the agency relationship. For example, where, in order to raise the money to pay off his debt, the principal appoints his creditor as his agent to sell some particular piece of property, the principal may not be at liberty to bring the agency to an end until the sale has taken place and the debt has been paid off.

11.7.2 Termination by operation of law

This refers to the fact that an agency relationship will be brought to an end by any of the following:

- Frustration

  Contracts of agency are subject to discharge by frustration in the same way that ordinary contracts are (see above, 8.4, for the general operation of the doctrine of frustration).

- The death of either party

  Death of the agent clearly brings the agreement to an end, as does the death of the principal. The latter situation may, however, give rise to problems where the agent is unaware of the death and continues to act in the capacity of agent. In such circumstances, the agent will be in breach of his or her warrant of authority and will be personally liable to third parties.

- Insanity of either party

  As in the previous situation, the insanity of either party will bring the agency to an end; similarly, agents will have to be careful not to breach their warrant of authority by continuing to act after the principal has become insane (see *Yonge v Toynbee* (1910), above, 11.4.3).

- Bankruptcy

  Generally, the bankruptcy of the principal will end the agency agreement, but the bankruptcy of the agent will only bring it to an end where it renders him or her unfit to continue to act as an agent.

AGENCY

Definition

An agent is a person who is empowered to represent another legal party, called the principal, and brings the principal into a legal relationship with a third party.

Agency agreements may be either contractual or gratuitous.

Commercial agents are specifically covered by the Commercial Agents (Council Directive) Regulations 1993.

Creation of agency

Agency may arise:

- expressly;
- by ratification;
- by implication;
- by necessity;
- by estoppel.

Nature of agent's authority

Actual authority may be divided into:

- express actual authority; and
- implied actual authority.

Apparent authority is based on estoppel and operates in such a way as to make the principal responsible for their action or inaction as regards someone who claims to be their agent.

Warrant of authority

If an agent contracts with a third party on behalf of a principal, the agent impliedly guarantees that the principal exists and has contractual capacity and that he or she has that person's authority to act as his or her agent. If this is not the case, the agent is personally liable to third parties for breach of warrant of authority.

The duties of agent to principal

The duties of the agent to the principal are:
- to perform the undertaking according to instructions;
- to exercise due care and skill;
- to carry out instructions personally;
- to account;
- not to permit a conflict of interest to arise;
- not to make a secret profit or misuse confidential information;
- not to take a bribe.

The rights of an agent

The rights of an agent are:
- to claim remuneration for services performed;
- to claim indemnity for all expenses legitimately incurred in the performance of services;
- to exercise a lien over property owned by the principal.

Commercial Agents (Council Directive) Regulations 1993

- Regulations 3–5 set out the rights and obligations as between commercial agents and their principals.
- Regulations 6–12 deal with remuneration.
- Regulations 13–16 deal with the conclusion and termination of the agency contract.
- Regulations 17–19 contain provisions relating to the indemnity or compensation payable to a commercial agent on termination of his agency contract.
- Regulation 20 relates to the validity of restraint of trade clauses.

Relations with third parties

Where the agent indicates that he or she is acting as an agent, the general rule is that only the principal and the third party have rights and obligations under the contract.

There are exceptions to this:
- at the insistence of the third party;
- by implication;
- in relation to bills of exchange;
- in relation to deeds.

Where the principal's existence is not disclosed:
- the agent can enforce the contract against the third party;
- the principal can enforce the contract against the third party;
- the third party can choose to enforce the contract against the agent or the principal;
- an undisclosed principal cannot ratify any contract made outside of the agent's actual authority.

Where the third party had a special reason to contract with the agent, the principal may be excluded from the contract.

Where the agent misrepresents the identity of the principal, the third party may not be bound by the contract.

Payment by means of an agent

- If the agent does not pay the third party, the principal remains liable.
- If the agent absconds with money paid by the third party, then, if the principal is undisclosed, he or she sustains the loss. If, however, the principal is disclosed, the agent must have had authority to accept money, or else the third party is liable.

Termination of agency

Agreements may end:
- by mutual agreement;
- by the unilateral action of one of the parties;
- through frustration;
- due to the death, insanity or bankruptcy of either party.

CHAPTER 12

PARTNERSHIP LAW

12.1 INTRODUCTION

The partnership is a fundamental form of business/commercial organisation. Historically, the partnership predated the registered limited company as a means for uniting the capital of separate individuals and it was of the utmost importance in financing the Industrial Revolution in the UK in the 18th and 19th centuries.

As an economic form, the partnership is still important. However, since the last quarter of the 19th century, as unlimited partnerships have transformed themselves into private limited companies, partnership law has given way to the control of company law as a form of legal regulation. It could be argued that, nowadays, the important partnership cases take place in the Companies Court. The continued relevance of partnership law should not be underestimated, however, since it remains the essential form of organisation within the sphere of such professional activities as the law, accountancy and medicine, where there is no wish, or need, for limited liability.

The situation has been further complicated by the availability of the new legal form of the incorporated and limited partnership under the Limited Liability Partnership Act 2000.

12.2 THE PARTNERSHIP ACTS

12.2.5 Standard partnerships

The legal regulation of standard partnerships is mainly to be found in the Partnership Act (PA) 1890. The PA 1890 recognised the existing business and commercial practice and at least some of the previous decisions of common law and equity as they affected partnerships.

In line with the consensual nature of partnership undertakings, the PA 1890 did not seek to set out to achieve a complete codification of the law; it merely sought to establish a basic framework, whilst leaving open the possibility of partners establishing their own terms. The limited nature of the PA 1890 means that reference has to be made to cases decided by the courts both before and after the PA 1890 in order to understand the full scope of partnership law (s 46 expressly maintains all the rules of the common law and equity, except where they are inconsistent with the provisions of the PA 1890).

12.2.2 Limited partnerships

A key attribute of the standard partnership is the fact that its members are liable to the full extent of their personal wealth for the debts of the business. The Limited Partnership Act 1907, however, allows for the formation of limited partnerships. In order for members of a partnership to gain the benefit of limited liability under this legislation, the following rules apply:

- limited partners are not liable for partnership debts beyond the extent of their capital contribution, but, in the ordinary course of events, they are not permitted to remove their capital;

- one or more of the partners must retain full, that is, unlimited, liability for the debts of the partnership;

- a partner with limited liability is not permitted to take part in the management of the business enterprise and cannot usually bind the partnership in any transaction (contravention of this rule will result in the loss of limited liability);

- the partnership must be registered with the Companies Registry.

In practice, the Limited Partnership Act 1907 has had little effect and has been seldom used. The simple reason for such a situation is the emergence, legal recognition and development of the private limited company as an alternative form of organisation. At least to the extent that it affords the protection of limited liability, limited small businesses have seen the private company as the better and preferred form. The famous company law case of *Salomon v Salomon and Co* (1897) recognised the legal validity of the private limited company and predestined the failure of the Limited Partnership Act (see, further below, 13.2.2).

12.2.3 Limited liability partnerships

The Limited Liability Partnership Act (LLPA) 2000 provides for a new form of business entity, the limited liability partnership. Although stated to be a partnership, the new form is a corporation, with a distinct legal existence apart from its members. It will have perpetual succession and consequently, alterations in its membership will not have any effect on its existence. Most importantly, however, the new legal entity will allow all of its members to benefit from limited liability, in that they will not be liable for more than the amount they have agreed to contribute to its capital.

This last advantage is significantly different from the previous limitation on liability available under the Limited Partnership Act 1907, which, as has been seen, required at least one general partner to remain fully liable for partnership debts. The provisions of the LLPA 2000 and its likely effect will be considered in detail below at 12.9, and what follows before then will relate to the ordinary standard partnership.

12.3 DEFINITION OF 'PARTNERSHIP'

Section 1 of the PA 1890 states that partnership is the relation which subsists between persons carrying on a business in common with a view to profit.

In relation to this definition, it should be noted that:

- The section expressly excludes companies registered under the companies legislation.

- The nature of the relationship is a contractual one

  Partners enter into the agreement on the terms that they themselves have negotiated and acceded to. As a consequence, they are contractually bound by those terms, as long as they do not conflict with the express provisions of the PA 1890, and they may be enforced by the law in the same way as other contractual terms.

- It is a requirement that a business be carried on

  The term 'business' includes any trade, occupation or profession. The mere fact that individuals jointly own property does not necessarily mean that they are partners if the property is not being used by them to pursue some collective business activity. See also *Britton v Comrs of Customs and Excise* (1986), where it was held that the fact that a wife received a share of the profits of her husband's business did not make her a partner in the business, since this was a purely domestic arrangement.

- Any business must be carried out in common

  Partnerships are by definition collective organisations. Under English law, however, they are no more than a collection of individuals and do not enjoy the benefits of separate personality (see below, 12.4).

- Partnerships may be created for the purposes of a single venture

  It is usually the case that partnerships continue over an extended period of time, but this is not necessarily the case.

- The business must be carried on with a view to profit

  An immediate result of this provision is that neither charitable nor mutual benefit schemes are to be considered as partnerships.

  It used to be the case that the mere receipt of a share of profit was enough to make a person a partner and responsible for partnership debts (see *Waugh v Carver* (1793)). Nowadays, although the receipt of a share of profits may be *prima facie* evidence of a partnership relationship, it is not conclusive.

  Section 2(2) of the PA 1890 expressly states that the sharing of gross returns does not in itself indicate the existence of a partnership agreement, since such an arrangement may simply represent a form of payment for the individual concerned. Thus, by way of example, the authors of this book will receive a percentage of the total sales value of the book. That, however, does not make them partners of the publishers, so, if publication of the book results in massive losses for the publishers, third parties cannot look to the authors for any money owed.

Even receiving a share of net profits does not necessarily indicate a partnership. For example, a person would not be treated as a partner where they received payment of a debt by instalments made from business profits; or where they received wages in the form of a share of profit; or where they received interest on a loan to a business, the rate of which varied in relation to the level of the business profits. Thus, in *Strathearn Gordon Associates Ltd v Comrs of Customs and Excise* (1985), the company acted as management consultant to seven separate enterprises, receiving a share of their individual profits as part of its payment. The company argued that the consultancy was part of seven separate partnership agreements and, therefore, did not accrue value added tax (VAT), as would be the case if it were merely supplying its services to the various enterprises. The VAT tribunal found against the company, on the basis that merely receiving a share of profit was not sufficient to establish a partnership relationship. (See, also, *Britton v Comrs of Customs and Excise* (1986).)

12.3.1 Types of partners

It is sometimes thought to be necessary to distinguish between different types of partners, but, in reality, such a division is of most use in pointing out particular dangers inherent in a failure to adopt an active, if only supervisory, role in a partnership enterprise. Thus, a general partner is the typical member of a partnership. The term is actually used in the Limited Partnership Act 1907 to distinguish that usual type from the unusual limited partner. The general partner is one who is actively engaged in the day to day running of the business enterprise, whereas the limited partner is actually precluded from participating in the management of the enterprise.

Section 24(5) of the PA 1890 provides that every partner is entitled to take part in the management of the partnership business. The partnership agreement may place limitations on the actual authority of any such person, but, unless an outsider is aware of the limitation, the partnership is responsible for any business transaction entered into by a partner within his or her usual authority. (For further consideration of these types of authority, see below, 12.7.1.)

A dormant or 'sleeping' partner is a person who merely invests money in a partnership enterprise but, apart from receiving a return on capital invested, takes no active part in the day to day running of the business. The limited partner in a limited partnership may be seen as a dormant partner. The term is used more generally, however, to refer to people who simply put money into partnership enterprises without taking an active part in the business and yet do not comply with the formalities required for establishing a limited partnership. The essential point that has to be emphasised in this regard is that, in so doing, such people place themselves at great risk. The law will consider them as general partners in the enterprise and will hold them personally and fully liable for the debts of the partnership to the extent of their ability to pay. By remaining outside the day to day operation of the business, such people merely surrender their personal unlimited liability into the control of the active parties in the partnership.

12.4 THE LEGAL STATUS OF A PARTNERSHIP

The standard partnership is an organisation established by individuals to pursue some business activity. Although the law is permissive in relation to the establishment of such enterprises, there are particular ways in which the law impinges on and controls, not just the operation of partnerships, but their very formation and existence.

12.4.1 Legal personality

The definition of a partnership expressly states that it is a relationship between persons. The corollary of this is that the partnership has no existence outside of, or apart from, that relationship. In other words, the partnership has no separate legal personality apart from its members, unlike a joint stock company.

Although Scottish law does grant corporate personality to the partnership without the benefit of limited liability, in English law a partnership is no more than a group of individuals collectively involved in a business activity. Section 4 of the PA 1890, however, does recognise an element of unity within the partnership organisation, to the extent that it permits the partnership to be known collectively as a firm and permits the business to be carried out under the firm's name. In addition, the procedural Rules of the Supreme Court, Ord 81 provide that legal action may be taken by, and against, the partners in the firm's name, although any award against the partnership may be executed against any of the individual partners.

Limited liability partnerships formed under the LLPA 2000 are incorporated and, as such, have a distinct legal personality apart from their members. (See 12.9 for limited liability partnerships and 13.2 for an analysis of corporations.)

It follows from the lack of separate personality in the standard partnership that the partners are self-employed. The partnership can, of course, employ others. However, an interesting juxtaposition of the requirement to carry out a business collectively in the pursuit of profit and the requirements of employment law may be found in *Rennison and Sons v Minister of Social Security* (1970). It is essential for the purposes of employment law to distinguish between those who are self-employed (or in contracts for services) and those who are employees (in contracts of service), as different rights appertain to the different categories. In deciding any question, the courts will look at the reality of the situation, rather than the mere title that someone bares.

In the *Rennison* case, a firm of solicitors had purported to enter into contracts of service with their clerical staff and, subsequently, all of the staff had entered into a partnership agreement, under which the profits and losses were to be divided on terms to be agreed. In fact, the clerical staff continued to work as they had done before and continued to be paid at exactly the same hourly rate that they had previously been paid. The only difference was that the wages were paid in a lump sum to one of them who was responsible for dividing it out amongst the rest. When the issue of responsibility for payment of national insurance was raised, as was required in relation to employees but not the self-employed, the court held that neither of the devices successfully removed the reality that the staff concerned were employees. Simply calling them 'self-employed' did not alter their status as employees, nor did calling them 'partners'. In reality, the agreement simply affected the way in which they were paid, rather than their employment status. (See below, Chapter 15, for more detailed treatment of the employment law issues.)

12.4.2 Illegal partnerships

A partnership is illegal if it is formed to carry out an illegal purpose or to carry out a legal purpose in an illegal manner. In such circumstances, the courts will not recognise any partnership rights between the persons involved, but will permit innocent third parties who have no knowledge of any illegality to recover against them.

Partnerships are generally not lawful if they consist of more than 20 persons, as provided by s 716 of the Companies Act (CA) 1985. However, certain professional partnerships, such as solicitors, accountants and surveyors, etc, are exempt from this maximum limit.

12.4.3 Capacity

There are two distinct aspects relating to capacity:

• Capacity of individuals to join a partnership

The general common law rules relating to capacity to enter into contracts apply in the particular case of the membership of a partnership. Thus, any partnership agreement entered into by a minor is voidable during that person's minority and for a reasonable time after they have reached the age of majority. If the former minor does not repudiate the partnership agreement within a reasonable time of reaching the age of majority, then they will be liable for any debts as a *de facto* partner. Third parties cannot recover against partners who are minors, but they can recover against any other adult partners.

Mental incapacity does not necessarily prevent someone from entering into a partnership, but subsequent mental incapacity of a partner may be grounds for the dissolution of a partnership.

- Capacity of the partnership

  A particular consequence of the fact that the partnership is, at least in the perception of the law, no more than a relationship between individuals is that there are no specific rules controlling the contractual capacity of partnerships, other than those general rules which constrain individuals' capacity to enter into contracts. This point was of more significance when companies were more strictly constrained by the operation of the *ultra vires* doctrine, but, as will be seen below, 13.5.1, company law doctrine has been much relaxed.

  Section 5 of the PA 1890 provides that each partner is the agent of the firm and the other partners for the purpose of the business of the partnership, but, as that purpose is determined by the members, and as it is not fixed by law, it can be changed by the unanimous agreement of those members. (See below, 12.5.2, on the alteration of the partnership agreement.)

12.5 FORMATION OF A PARTNERSHIP

There are no specific legal requirements governing the formation of a partnership. Partnerships arise from the agreement of the parties involved and are governed by the general principles of contract law. An agreement to enter into a partnership, therefore, may be made by deed, in writing or by word of mouth. Such agreement may even be implied from the conduct of the parties.

12.5.1 The partnership agreement

It is usual for the terms of the partnership to be set out in written form. The document produced is known as the 'articles of partnership'. The parties involved, no doubt after some negotiation, decide what they wish to be specifically included in the articles. Any gaps in the articles will be filled in by reference to the PA 1890 or the existing common law and equitable rules relating to partnerships, but it is necessary for the future partners to provide for any unusual or specialised terms to be included in the articles.

The detailed provisions in articles of partnership usually refer to such matters as the nature of the business to be transacted, the name of the firm, the capital contributions to be made by the individual partners, the drawing up of the business accounts, the method of determining and sharing profits and the dissolution of the partnership. It is also usual for there to be a provision for disputes between partners to be referred to arbitration for solution.

The partnership agreement is an internal document and, although it has effect between the partners, it does not necessarily affect the rights of third parties. Thus, where the agreement seeks to place limitations on the usual authority of a partner, it is effective with regard to the internal relations of the partners but does not have any effect as regards an outsider who deals with the partner without knowledge of the limitation.

In *Mercantile Credit v Garrod* (1962), Parkin and Garrod were partners in a garage business, which was mainly concerned with letting garages and repairing cars. The partnership agreement expressly excluded the sale of cars. After Parkin had sold a car, to which he had no title, to the plaintiffs, they claimed back the money they had paid from Garrod.

It was held that, since selling cars was within the usual scope of a garage business, it was within the usual authority of a partner in such a business. Parkin, therefore, had acted within his implied authority and the partnership was responsible for his actions. The plaintiffs had no knowledge of the limitation contained within the articles and could not be subject to it.

12.5.2 Alteration of the partnership agreement

Just as the consensual nature of the partnership relationship allows the parties to make the agreement in such terms as they wish, so are they equally free to alter those terms at a later date. Section 19 of the PA 1890, however, enacts the common law rule that any decision to alter the terms of partnership articles must be made unanimously. Consent does not have to be expressed but may be inferred from the conduct of the partners.

In *Pilling v Pilling* (1887), the articles of partnership entered into between a father and his two sons stated that the business was to be financed by the father's capital and that such capital was to remain his personal property and was not to be treated as the partnership property. The articles also stated that the father should receive interest on his capital. In practice, however, the sons, as well as the father, received interest on the partnership capital. It was held that the capital originally provided by the father was partnership property and that the conduct of the parties in treating it as such had amounted to a valid alteration of the written agreement.

12.5.3 The firm's name

Partnerships may use the words 'and Company' or its alternative form, 'and Co', in their name; for example, a firm of solicitors may call itself 'Brown, Smith and Co'. This merely indicates that the names of all the partners are not included in the firm's name. As has been seen above, it in no way indicates that the partnership has any existence apart from its constituent members or that those members have the benefit of limited liability. Even in the case of limited partnerships, someone must accept full liability for partnership debts. Section 34 of the CA 1985 consequently makes it a criminal offence for a partnership to use the word 'Limited' (or the abbreviation 'Ltd') in its name.

A partnership may trade under the names of the individual partners or it may trade under a collective name. Any name must comply with both the Business Names Act (BNA) 1985 and the common law provisions relating to the tort of passing off.

12.5.4 The Business Names Act 1985

Section 4 of the BNA 1985 requires that, where a partnership does not trade under the names of all of its members, the names of individuals must be displayed on the business premises and on the firm's business documents. Where the partnership is a large one with more than 20 members, the individual names do not have to be listed on business documents, but a list of all partners must be available for inspection at the firm's principal place of business. Any failure to comply with this requirement may result in the person in breach not being able to enforce a claim against another party who was disadvantaged by the breach.

There is no longer any requirement that business names be registered as such, but the BNA 1985 requires the approval of the Secretary of State for Trade and Industry before certain names can be used. Such names may imply that the business is related in some way to the Crown, the government, local authorities or other official bodies.

12.5.5 Passing off

The BNA 1985 does not prevent one business from using the same, or a very similar, name as another business. However, the tort of passing off prevents one person from using any name which is likely to divert business their way by suggesting that the business is actually that of some other person or is connected in any way with that other business. It thus enables people to protect the goodwill they have built up in relation to their business activity. See *Ewing v Buttercup Margarine Co Ltd* (1917), where the plaintiff successfully prevented the defendants from using a name that suggested a link with his existing dairy company. For a more up to date and less serious case, see *Stringfellow v McCain Foods GB Ltd* (1984), in which the owner of the famous *Stringfellow's* night club failed to prevent a manufacturer of long, thin, oven chips from calling their product by the same name.

12.5.6 Arbitration clauses

The consensual nature of the relationship on which any partnership is based has been repeatedly emphasised. It should always be remembered, however, that even the best of friends can fall out; when they are engaged in a joint business venture, any such conflict may be disastrous for the business. In an attempt to forestall such an eventuality, and to avoid the cost, delay and publicity involved in court procedure, it is standard practice for partnership articles to contain a clause referring disputes to arbitration for solution.

The actual procedure of arbitration has been considered in Chapter 3, above, but it should be recognised that arbitration, although relatively cheaper than the court system, is not cheap in absolute terms. Nor can it deal with situations where the partners have reached the stage where their continued conflict prevents the effective operation of the business. In such circumstances, it is probably wiser if the partnership is wound up on just and equitable grounds under s 35 of the PA 1890. (See below and see also *Re Yenidje Tobacco Co Ltd* (1916) as an example of the partnership principle being extended to a quasi-partnership company.)

12.6 THE RELATIONSHIP BETWEEN PARTNERS

The partnership agreement is contractual in nature. The partnership also involves a principal/agency relationship, but is complicated by the fact that partners are, at one and the same time, both agents of the firm and their fellow partners, and principals as regards those other partners. Partners are equally subject to the equitable rights and duties that derive from their being in a fiduciary position in relation to another. Thus, the legal nature of the partnership involves a complicated mixture of elements of contract, agency and equity.

Section 24(8) of the PA 1890 provides that, subject of course to any agreement to the contrary, any differences arising as to the ordinary matters connected with the partnership business are to be decided by a majority of the partners, although they must not impose their views without actually consulting the minority (see *Const v Harris* (1824)). Thus, the day to day business is conducted in line with the wishes of the majority. However, s 24(8) also states that the nature of that business cannot be changed without the unanimous agreement of the partners.

12.6.1 Duties of partners

The fiduciary nature of the partnership relationship imports the usual duties that derive from such a relationship, which can be summed up under the general heading of a duty to act in good faith. In addition to these general fiduciary duties, ss 28–30 of the PA 1890 lay down specific duties as follows:

* The duty of disclosure

  Section 28 provides that partners must render true accounts and full information in relation to all things affecting the partnership to the other partners or their legal representatives.

  In *Law v Law* (1905), one partner accepted an offer from the other to buy his share of the firm. He later discovered that certain partnership assets had not been disclosed to him and sought to have the contract set aside. The court decided that, as the purchasing partner had breached the duty of disclosure, the agreement could have been set aside. In actual fact, the parties had come to an arrangement, so it was not necessary for such an order to be granted.

* The duty to account

  Section 29 of the PA 1980 provides that partners must account to the firm for any benefit obtained, without consent, from any transaction concerning the partnership; its property, including information derived from membership of the partnership; its name; or its business connection. As with fiduciary duties generally, such profit is only open to challenge where it is undisclosed. Full disclosure is necessary and sufficient to justify the making of an individual profit from a partnership position.

  In *Bentley v Craven* (1853), Craven was in partnership with the plaintiff in a sugar refinery business. He bought sugar on his own account and later sold it to the partnership at a profit, without declaring his interest to the other partners. It was held that the partnership was entitled to recover the profit from the defendant.

* The duty not to compete

  Section 30 provides that, where a partner competes with the partnership business, without the consent of the other partners, then that person shall be liable to account to the partnership for any profits made in the course of that business. In *Glassington v Thwaites* (1823), a member of a partnership, which produced a morning paper, was held to account for the profit he made from publishing an evening paper. Once again, it is essential to note that full disclosure is necessary to validate any such profits made in competition with the partnership. (See *Trimble v Goldberg* (1906), where the court declined to recognise competition in relation to a partnership; but the likely severity of the courts' approach can be surmised from the company law case of *Industrial Development Consultants v Cooley* (1972).)

12.6.2 Rights of partners

Subject to express provision to the contrary in the partnership agreement, and it should be remembered that the consensual nature of the partnership allows the parties to avoid the provisions of the Act, s 24 of the PA 1890 sets out the rights of partners. Amongst the most important of these are the following rights:

• To share equally in the capital and profits of the business

Even where the partnership agreement is silent on the matter, s 24 does not mean that someone who has contributed all, or the greater part, of the capital of a firm must share it equally with the other partners. In such circumstances, it would most likely be decided that the facts of the case provided evidence of such contrary intention as to rebut the statement in the PA 1890. What the section does mean is that, even in the same circumstances, the partners will share profits equally, although it is not unusual to find clauses in agreements which recognise differences in capital input by providing for profits to be shared on an unequal basis. The same effect can be achieved by permitting interest to be paid on capital before profits are determined. Where partners advance additional capital to the firm by way of a loan, they are entitled to interest at 5% unless there is an agreement to the contrary.

The corollary of this right is the duty to contribute equally to any losses of capital, even where no capital was originally brought into the business. For example, if A and B enter into a partnership, with A providing all of the capital of £10,000 but A and B sharing the profits equally, and, upon winding up, the business has accrued a loss of £2,000, then both parties are required to contribute to the loss. In effect, B will have to contribute £1,000 and A will only receive a return of £9,000.

• To be indemnified by the firm for any liabilities incurred or payments made in the course of the firm's business

This may be seen as merely an express declaration of the usual right of an agent to indemnity. The right of an agent to act outside their authority in the case of necessity is also expressly set out in s 24.

• To take part in the management of the business

The unlimited nature of the ordinary partnership means that involvement in such a business brings with it the risk to one's personal wealth. It is essential under such circumstances, therefore, that partners are able to protect their interests by taking an active part in the operation of the business in order to assess and control the level of their risk. It is for this reason that the right to take part in the management of the business is stated expressly. In the case of quasi-partnership companies, the courts will imply such a right.

A partner is generally not entitled to receive any salary for acting in the partnership business, but it is not unusual for the agreement effectively to provide for the payment of a salary to particular partners before the determination of net profit.

- To have access to the firm's books

  This right follows from, and is based on, the same reasoning as the previous provision. The books are normally kept at the firm's principal place of business.

- To prevent the admission of a new partner or prevent any change in the nature of the partnership business

  As has been seen, any differences relating to the partnership business can be decided by the majority, but unanimity is required to change the nature of the business. Again, this reflects the need for individual partners to accept risk voluntarily. They have only accepted existing business risks and cannot be forced to alter or increase that risk.

  Similarly, as principals, they have agreed to give their authority to bind them and make them liable for partnership debts to particular individuals. They cannot be forced to extend that authority against their wishes.

In addition to the above rights, s 25 of the PA 1980 provides that no majority can expel another partner, unless such power is contained in the partnership agreement. Even where such a power is included, it must be exercised in good faith. See *Blisset v Daniel* (1853), where the majority attempted to expel a partner in order to acquire his share of the business cheaply; and *Green v Howell* (1910), where a partner was properly expelled for a flagrant breach of his duties. For more recent cases, see *Kerr v Morris* (1987) and *Walters v Bingham* (1988).

12.6.3 Partnership property

Property may be owned collectively by all of the partners and may thus amount to partnership property. Alternatively, it is possible for property to be used by the partnership as a whole and yet remain the personal property of only one of the partners.

Section 20 of the PA 1890 states that partnership property consists of all property brought into the partnership stock or acquired on account for the purposes of the firm. Section 21 further states that any property bought with money belonging to the firm is deemed to have been bought on account of the firm.

Whether or not any particular item of property belongs to the firm is always a matter of fact, to be determined in relation to the particular circumstances of any case. If there is no express agreement that property is to be brought into the firm as partnership property, the court will only imply such a term to the extent required to make the partnership agreement effective.

In *Miles v Clarke* (1953), Clarke had carried on a photography business for some time before taking Miles into partnership. The partnership agreement merely provided that the profits should be divided equally. When the partners fell out, a dispute arose as to who owned the assets used by the partnership. It was held that only the consumable stock-in-trade could be considered as partnership property. The leases of the business premises and other plant and equipment remained the personal property of the partner who introduced them into the business.

It is important to distinguish between partnership property and personal property for the following reasons:

• Partnership property must be used exclusively for partnership purposes (s 20 of the PA 1980)

This may been seen as a statement of the general duty not to make a personal profit from a fiduciary position without full disclosure. Thus, partners are not supposed to use partnership property for their own personal benefit or gain, and, if they were to do so, they would be liable to account to the partnership for any profit made.

It is also made clear that partners do not own the firm's assets directly. All they have, under s 30, is the partnership lien over those assets, which entitles them, on dissolution, to participate in any surplus after their realised value has been used to pay off partnership debts.

• Any increase in the value of partnership property belongs to the partnership

As a consequence, the increased value when realised will be divided amongst all the partners.

• Any increase in the value of personal property belongs to the person who owns the property

Consequently, the increased value will not have to be shared with the other partners.

• On the dissolution of the firm, partnership property is used to pay debts before personal property

This is clearly stated in s 39, which has been considered above in relation to the nature of the partnership lien.

• Partnership and personal property are treated differently in the satisfaction of claims made by partnership creditors, as opposed to personal creditors

Under s 23, a writ of execution can only be issued against partnership property in respect of a judgment against the partnership. A personal creditor of a partner may not, therefore, take action against partnership property. They can, however, apply for a charging order against that partner's share in the partnership, which would entitle them to receive the partner's share of profits, or assets on dissolution, to the extent of the debt and interest. The other partners may redeem the charge at any time by paying off the debt, in which case the charge becomes vested in them.

- On the death of a partner, any interest in partnership land will pass as personalty, whereas land owned personally will pass as realty

In effect, this means that the interest may pass to different people, depending on whether or not the party has made an appropriate will.

Specifically in relation to land, s 22 enacts the equitable doctrine of conversion by providing that any such partnership property is to be treated as personal property.

12.6.4 Assignment of a share in a partnership

Unless the partnership agreement states otherwise, partners are at liberty to mortgage or assign absolutely their shares in partnerships to outsiders. The assignee is, however, only entitled to the share of profits due to the partner assigning the shares, or on dissolution, to the appropriate share of partnership assets. Section 31 makes it clear that any such assignee does not become a partner and has no right whatsoever to become involved in the management of the business. In *Garwood v Paynter* (1903), Garwood charged his shares to a trust, of which his wife was one of the beneficiaries. When the other partners began to pay themselves salaries, Mrs Garwood objected on the ground that such payment reduced the net profit of the firm and, hence, indirectly, the income to the trust. It was held that the payment of salaries was an internal management matter and, therefore, the trustees, who were assignees, by virtue of s 31 could not interfere in the absence of fraud.

The assignee does not take over responsibility for partnership debts. These remain the liability of the assignor. Where, however, the assignment is absolute, the assignee must indemnify the assignor in respect of future liabilities arising from the business.

12.7 THE RELATIONSHIP BETWEEN PARTNERS AND OUTSIDERS

Of equal importance to the internal relationships of the partnership is the relationship of the members of the partnership to outsiders who deal with the partnership and, in particular, the extent to which the partnership and, hence, the partners are liable for the actions of the individual partners.

12.7.1 The authority of partners to bind the firm

As stated in s 5 of the PA 1890, every partner is an agent of the firm and of the other partners. Each partner, therefore, has the power to bind co-partners and make them liable on business transactions. The partnership agreement may, however, expressly seek to limit the powers of particular members. The effect of such limitations depends on the circumstances of each case. They do not apply where the other partners have effectively countermanded the restriction. This can occur in two ways:

- if the other partners give their prior approval for a partner to exceed his actual authority, then the partner in question has express actual authority and the firm is bound by his action;
- if the other partners give their approval after the event, then they have ratified the transaction and the partnership is again liable.

The firm may be liable even where the other partners have not expressly approved the action in excess of authority, as long as the partner has acted within his or her implied powers, that is, within the usual scope of a partner's powers in the particular business concerned (see *Mercantile Credit v Garrod* (1962), above). If, however, the outsider had actual knowledge of the partner's lack of authority, then the partnership is not bound by the transaction.

Every partner, other than a limited partner, is presumed to have the implied authority to enter into the following transactions:

- to sell the firm's goods;
- to buy goods of a kind normally required by the firm;
- to engage employees;
- to receive payment of debts due to the partnership;
- to pay debts owed by the partnership and to draw cheques for that purpose;
- to employ a solicitor to act for the firm in defence of an action or in pursuit of a debt.

The above implied powers apply equally to trading and non-trading partnerships. Partners in trading firms, that is, those which essentially buy and sell goods, have the following additional implied powers:

- to accept, draw, issue or endorse bills of exchange or other negotiable instruments on behalf of the firm;
- to borrow money on the credit of the firm;
- to pledge the firm's goods as security for borrowed money.

12.7.2 The nature of partners' liability

Every partner is responsible for the full amount of the firm's liability. Outsiders have the choice of taking action either against the firm collectively or against the individual partners. Where damages are recovered from one partner only, the other partners are under a duty to contribute equally to the amount paid:

- Liability on debts and contracts

  Under s 9 of the PA 1890, the liability of partners as regards debts or contracts is joint. The effect of joint liability used to be that, although the partners were collectively responsible, a person who took action against one of the partners could take no further action against the other partners, even if they had not recovered all that was owing to them.

  That situation was remedied by the Civil Liability (Contributions) Act 1978, which effectively provided that a judgment against one partner *does* bar a subsequent action against the other partners.

- Liability for torts

  Under s 10 of the PA 1890, the liability of partners with regard to torts or other wrongs committed in the ordinary course of the partnership business is joint and several. In such a situation, there is no bar on taking successive actions against partners in order to recover all that is due.

  It should be emphasised that, in order for the partnership to be responsible, the wrong sued on must have been committed in the ordinary course of partnership business or with the express approval of all the partners. If a tort is committed outside this scope, then the partner responsible is personally liable.

  In *Hamlyn v Houston and Co* (1905), one of the partners in the defendant company bribed a clerk employed by the plaintiff, in order to get information about their rival's business. Hamlyn sued the defendant partnership to recover the loss he claimed to have suffered as a consequence. It was held that the defendant firm was liable for the wrongful act of the individual partner, as he had acted within the usual scope of his authority, although he had used illegal methods in doing so.

  However, see *Arbuckle v Taylor* (1815), where the partnership was not liable because the individual partner had gone beyond the general scope of the partnership business.

  As was stated in 12.4.1, partners may be sued in the firm's name, although they remain individually liable for any awards made as a consequence of any such action.

12.7.3 The liability of incoming and outgoing partners

A person who is admitted into an existing firm is not liable to creditors of the firm for anything done before they became a partner (see s 17 of the PA 1890). The new partner can, however, assume such responsibility by way of a device known as novation. This is the process whereby a retiring partner is discharged from existing liability and the newly constituted partnership takes the liability on themselves. Novation is essentially a tripartite contract involving the retiring partner, the new firm and the existing creditors. As creditors effectively give up rights against the retiring partner, their approval is required. Such approval may be express, or it may be implied from the course of dealing between the creditor and the firm.

In *Thompson v Percival* (1834), Charles Thompson and James Percival had been in partnership until Thompson retired. The plaintiff creditors, on applying for payment, were informed that Percival alone would be responsible for payment, as Thompson had retired. As a consequence, they drew a bill for payment against Percival alone. Subsequently, it was held that they no longer had a right of action against Thompson, since their action showed that they had accepted his discharge from liability.

Creditors do not have to accept a novation. A creditor may still hold the retired partner responsible for any debts due at the time of retirement. The newly constituted firm may, however, agree to indemnify the retiring partner against any such claims.

Apart from novation, a retired partner remains liable for any debts or obligations incurred by the partnership prior to retirement. The date of any contract determines responsibility: if the person was a partner when the contract was entered into, then they are responsible, even if the goods under the contract are delivered after they have left the firm. The estate of a deceased person is only liable for those debts or obligations arising before death.

Where someone deals with a partnership after a change in membership, they are entitled to treat all of the apparent members of the old firm as still being members, until they receive notice of any change in membership. In order to avoid liability for future contracts, a retiring partner must take the following action:

- ensure that individual notice is given to existing customers of the partnership; and

- advertise the retirement in the *London Gazette*. This serves as general notice to people who were not customers of the firm prior to the partner's retirement but who knew that that person had been a partner in the business. Such an advert is effective whether or not it comes to the attention of third parties.

A retired partner owes no responsibility to someone who had neither dealings with the partnership nor previous knowledge of his or her membership.

In *Tower Cabinet Co Ltd v Ingram* (1949), Ingram and Christmas had been partners in a firm known as Merry's. After it was dissolved by mutual agreement, Christmas carried on trading under the firm's name. Notice was given to those dealing with the firm that Ingram was no longer connected with the business, but no notice was placed in the *London Gazette*. New note paper was printed without Ingram's name. However, the plaintiffs, who had had no previous dealings with the partnership, received an order on old note paper, on which Ingram's name was included. When Tower Cabinet sought to enforce a judgment against Ingram, it was held that he was not liable, since he had not represented himself as being a partner, nor had the plaintiffs been aware of his membership prior to dissolution.

12.7.4 Partnership by estoppel

Failure to give notice of retirement is one way in which liability arises on the basis of estoppel or holding out. Alternatively, anyone who represents themselves, or knowingly permits themselves to be represented, as a partner is liable to any person who gives the partnership credit on the basis of that representation. Although they may become liable for partnership debts, they are not, however, partners in any other sense. (In *Tower Cabinet Co Ltd v Ingram*, the defendant was not affected by partnership by estoppel, since he was never actually aware that he had been represented as being a partner.)

12.8 DISSOLUTION AND WINDING UP OF THE PARTNERSHIP

There are a number of possible reasons for bringing a partnership to an end. It may have been established for a particular purpose and that purpose has been achieved, or one of the partners might wish to retire from the business, or the good relationship between the members, which is essential to the operation of a partnership, may have broken down. In all such cases, the existing partnership is dissolved, although, in the second case, a new partnership may be established to take over the old business.

12.8.1 Grounds for dissolution

As has been repeatedly emphasised, the partnership is based on agreement. It is created by agreement and it may be brought to an end in the same way. However, subject to any provision to the contrary in the partnership agreement, the PA 1890 provides for the automatic dissolution of a partnership on the following grounds:

- The expiry of a fixed term or the completion of a specified enterprise (s 32(a) and (b))

If the partnership continues after the pre-set limit, it is known as a 'partnership at will' and it can be ended at any time thereafter at the wish of any of the partners.

- The giving of notice (s 32(c))

  If the partnership is of indefinite duration, it can be brought to an end by any one of the partners giving notice of an intention to dissolve the partnership.

- The death or bankruptcy of any partner (s 33(1))

  Although the occurrence of either of these events will bring the partnership to an end, it is usual for partnership agreements to provide for the continuation of the business under the control of the remaining/solvent partners. The dead partner's interest will be valued and paid to his or her personal representative, and the bankrupt's interest will be paid to his or her trustee in bankruptcy.

- Where a partner's share becomes subject to a charge under s 23 (s 33(2))

  Under such circumstances, dissolution is not automatic; it is open to the other partners to dissolve the partnership.

- Illegality (s 34)

  The occurrence of events making the continuation of the partnership illegal will bring it to an end. An obvious case would be where the continuation of the partnership would result in trading with the enemy (see *R v Kupfer* (1915)). The principle applied equally, however, in the more recent and perhaps more relevant case of *Hudgell, Yeates and Co v Watson* (1978). Practising solicitors are legally required to have a practice certificate. However, one of the members of a three-person partnership forgot to renew his practice certificate and, thus, was not legally entitled to act as a solicitor. It was held that the failure to renew the practice certificate brought the partnership to an end, although a new partnership continued between the other two members of the old partnership.

In addition to the provisions listed above, the court may, mainly by virtue of s 35 of the PA 1890, order the dissolution of the partnership in the following circumstances:

- Where a partner becomes a patient under the Mental Health Act 1983

  The procedure is no longer taken under s 35 of the PA 1890, but, where the person is no longer able to manage their affairs because of mental incapacity, the Court of Protection may dissolve a partnership at the request of the person's receiver or the other partners.

- Where a partner suffers some other permanent incapacity

  This provision is analogous to the previous one. It should be noted that it is for the other partners to apply for dissolution and that the incapacity alleged as the basis of dissolution must be permanent. It is not unusual for partnerships to include specific clauses in their agreement in order to permit dissolution on the basis of extended absence from the business (see *Peyton v Mindham* (1971), where a clause in a partnership covering medical practice provided for termination after nine months' continuous absence or a total of 300 days in any period of 24 months).

- Where a partner engages in an activity prejudicial to the business

  Such activity may be directly related to the business, such as the misappropriation of funds. Alternatively, it may take place outside the business but operate to its detriment – an example of this might be a criminal conviction for fraud.

- Where a partner persistently breaches the partnership agreement

  This provision also relates to conduct which makes it unreasonable for the other partners to carry on in business with the party at fault.

- Where the business can only be carried on at a loss

  This provision is a corollary of the very first section of the PA 1890, in which the pursuit of profit is part of the definition of the partnership form. If such profit cannot be achieved, then the partners are entitled to avoid loss by bringing the partnership to an end.

- Where it is just and equitable to do so

  The courts have wide discretion in relation to the implementation of this power. A similar provision operates within company legislation and the two provisions come together in the cases involving quasi-partnerships. On occasion, courts have wound up companies on the ground that they would have been wound up had the business assumed the legal form of a partnership. For examples of this approach, see *Re Yenidje Tobacco Co Ltd* (1916) and *Ebrahimi v Westbourne Galleries Ltd* (1973).

After dissolution, the authority of each partner to bind the firm continues so far as is necessary to wind up the firm's affairs and complete transactions that have begun but are unfinished at the time of dissolution (s 38 of the PA 1980). Partners cannot, however, enter into new contracts.

12.8.2 Winding up

Since the introduction of the Insolvency Act 1986, partnerships as such are not subject to bankruptcy, although the individual partners may be open to such procedure. Partnerships may be wound up as unregistered companies under Pt V of the Insolvency Act 1986 where they are unable to pay their debts.

12.8.3 Treatment of assets on dissolution

Upon dissolution, the value of the partnership property is realised and the proceeds are applied in the following order:

- in paying debts to outsiders;
- in paying to the partners any advance made to the firm beyond their capital contribution;
- in paying the capital contribution of the individual partners.

Any residue is divided between the partners in the same proportion as they shared in profits (s 44 of the PA 1890).

If the assets are insufficient to meet debts, partners advances and capital repayments, then the deficiency has to be made good out of any profits held back from previous years, or out of partners' capital, or by the partners individually in the proportion to which they were entitled to share in profits.

An example will clarify this procedure. Partners A, B and C contribute £5,000, £3,000 and £1,000 respectively. In addition, A makes an advance to the firm of £1,000. Upon dissolution, the assets realise £8,000, and the firm has outstanding debts amounting to £2,500. The procedure is as follows:

First, the creditors are paid what is due to them from the realised value of the assets. Thus, £8,000 – £2,500 = £5,500.

Secondly, an advance of £1,000 is paid back, leaving £4,500.

Assuming that there was no agreement to the contrary, profits and losses will be shared equally. The actual loss is determined as follows:

Original capital:	£9,000
Minus money left:	£4,500
	£4,500

This loss of £4,500 has to be shared equally in this case. Each partner has to provide £1,500 in order to make good the shortfall in capital. In the case of A and B, this is a paper transaction, as the payment due is simply subtracted from their original capital contribution. C, however, actually has to make a contribution of £500 from his personal wealth, as his due payment exceeds his original capital. The outcome is as follows:

A's share of net assets:	£5,000 – £1,500	=	£3,500
B's share of net assets:	£3,000 – £1,500	=	£1,500
C's share of net assets:	£1,000 – £1,500	=	– £500

A provision in the partnership agreement for profits to be shared in proportion to capital contribution, that is, in the ratio 5:3:1, would have the following effect:

A would contribute five-ninths of the £4,500 loss, that is, £2,500

B would contribute three-ninths of the £4,500 loss, that is, £1,500

C would contribute one-ninth of the £4,500 loss, that is, £500

Their shares in net assets would, therefore, be as follows:

A: (£5,000 – £2,500) = £2,500

B: (£3,000 – £1,500) = £1,500

C: (£1,000 – £500) = £500

12.8.4 Bankruptcy of partners

Where a partner is bankrupt on the dissolution of a firm, the partnership assets are still used to pay partnership debts. It is only after the payment of partnership debts that any surplus due to that partner is made available for the payment of the partner's personal debts.

Where one partner is insolvent and there is a deficiency of partnership assets to repay the firm's creditors and any advances, the burden of making good the shortfall has to be borne by the solvent partners in proportion to their share in profits. If, however, the shortfall only relates to capital, then the situation is governed by the rule in *Garner v Murray* (1904). This rule means that, in any such situation, the solvent partners are not required to make good the capital deficiency due to the insolvency of their co-partner. But, as a consequence, there will be a shortfall in the capital fund, which has to be borne by the solvent partners in proportion to their capitals.

To return to the original example, the net assets were £4,500 and the capital deficiency was £4,500. All three partners were to contribute £1,500. In effect, C was the only one who actually had to pay out any money, since A and B merely suffered an abatement in the capital returned to them. However, if it is now assumed that C is insolvent and can make no contribution, the situation is as follows:

C loses his right of repayment, so this reduces the capital fund required to pay back partners' contributions to £8,000.

As previously, A and B contribute their portion of the total loss, taking the available capital fund up to £7,500 (that is, £4,500 + (2 x £1,500)).

There still remains a shortfall of £500. This is borne by A and B in proportion to their capital contribution. Thus, A suffers a loss of five-eighths of £500; and B suffers a loss of three-eighths of £500.

So, from the capital fund of £7,500 they receive the following:

A: £5,000 – (5/8 x £500) = £4,687.50 (in reality, he or she simply receives £3,187.50)

B: £3,000 – (3/8 x £500) = £2,812.50 (in reality, he or she simply receives £1,312.50)

12.9 LIMITED LIABILITY PARTNERSHIPS

As has already been seen, the main shortcoming with regard to the standard partnership is the lack of limited liability for its members: members have joint and several liability for the debts of their partnership to the full extent of their personal wealth. The risk of such unlimited liability is increased by the fact that due to the nature of the partnership, all members can enter into contracts on behalf of the partnership, and is further compounded when the membership of the partnership is extensive, as it is in the case of many professional partnerships. The dangers inherent in such partnerships were revealed in America in the early 1990s, with the collapse of the savings and loans system. Many firms of accountants and lawyers who had advised on such schemes found themselves being sued for negligence and the partners in those firms found themselves personally liable for extremely large amounts of debt, even though they had had absolutely nothing to do with the transaction in question. Whilst such firms of professionals were reluctant to incorporate and turn themselves into limited liability companies, they clearly saw the benefit of limiting the liability of the individual partners in relation to the misbehaviour of one of their fellow members. The limited liability partnership was the device for achieving the desired end of limiting claims for such vicarious liability (for a consideration of vicarious liability, see 17.6). It should be noted, however, that although the limited liability partnership (LLP) was introduced to offer protection to the large scale professional firms, it is not in any way limited to them and it is open to any type of partnership, no matter how small, no matter what their business, to register as an LLP.

The possibility of registering as an LLP was introduced into the UK in 2000 with the passage of the Limited Liability Partnership Act (LLPA) of that year, although the Act did not come into effect until April 2001. The Act itself was a remarkable example of enabling legislation, merely providing a general framework and leaving the details to be supplied by the Limited Liability Partnership Regulations (LLPR) 2001. Section 1 of the LLPA 2000 states quite clearly that the LLP is a new form of legal entity, but before going on to consider the LLP in detail, it has to be stated at the outset that the LLP is something of a hybrid legal form, seeking, as will be seen, to amalgamate the advantages of the company's corporate form with the flexibility of the partnership form. However, s 1(5) states categorically that:

> ... except as far as otherwise provided by this Act ... the law relating to partnerships does not apply to a limited liability partnership.

12.9.1 Legal personality and limited liability

Although called a partnership, the LLP is a corporation, with a distinct legal existence apart from its members. As such, it will have the ability to:

- hold property in its own right;
- create floating charges over its property;
- enter into contracts in its own name;
- sue and be sued in its own name.

It will also have perpetual succession and consequently, alterations in its membership will not have any effect on its existence. Similarly, the death or personal insolvency of a member will not affect the existence of the LLP. Most importantly, however, the new legal entity will allow its members to benefit from limited liability, in that they will not be liable for more than the amount they have agreed to contribute to its capital. There is no minimum amount for such agreed capital contribution. (For a further consideration of these attributes of incorporation, see 13.2.)

12.9.2 Creation

In order to form an LLP, the appropriate form must be registered with the Registrar of Companies. The form must contain:

- the signatures of at least two persons who are associated for the purposes of carrying on a lawful business with a view to profit;
- the name of the LLP, which must end with the words 'Limited Liability Partnership' or the abbreviation 'LLP';
- the location of the LLP's registered office, in England and Wales, in Wales or in Scotland;
- the address of the registered office of the LLP;
- the names and addresses of those persons who will be members on the incorporation of the LLP and a statement whether some or all of them are to be designated members (see below);
- a statement of compliance.

On registration of the company, the Registrar will issue a certificate of incorporation.

12.9.3 Membership

There must be a minimum of two members of the LLP. If the membership should fall below two for a period of six months, then the remaining member will lose their limited liability and will assume personal liability for any liabilities incurred during that period that the LLP cannot meet.

There is no maximum limit on membership. This is clearly indicative of the fact that LLPs were initially designed to offer limited liability to large-scale professional firms, which were not limited to 20 members as were ordinary trading partnerships. However, as has been seen, the LLP form is in fact open to any partnership. Membership is not limited to individuals and other incorporated bodies can be members of an LLP, as can other LLPs.

Within the LLP, there is a special type of membership, known as *designated membership*. As will be seen, such members are responsible for ensuring that the LLP conforms with its duty to file its accounts with the Registrar of Companies.

Becoming a member

Section 4(1) states that the original subscribers to the incorporation document are automatically members of the LLP. Other members may join with the agreement of the existing members (s 4(2)).

Ceasing to be a member

Under s 4(3), membership ceases on the occurrence of any of the following eventualities:

- death;
- dissolution (if the member is a corporation);
- on gaining the agreement of the other members;
- after the giving of reasonable notice.

12.9.4 Disclosure requirements

Just as with limited companies, members of LLPs get the benefit of limited liability, but equally, as with limited companies, such a benefit has to be paid for in the form of publicity and disclosure. People dealing with limited business are put on notice of that fact by the need to indicate their limited status in the names of the LLPs; this applies to both companies and LLPs. In addition, both are required to submit their accounts and some of their affairs to public scrutiny by filing them with the Registrar of Companies. In respect of LLPs, the essential filing requirements relate to:

- accounts;
- annual returns;
- changes in membership generally;
- changes in designated membership;
- change to the registered office.

Accounts

The provisions that apply to limited companies with regard to auditing apply equally to LLPs, and therefore they will be required to submit properly audited accounts which give a true and fair view of the affairs of the LLP.

However, the exemptions open to small and medium sized companies also apply to LLPs.

12.9.5 Relationship between members and the LLP

Section 6(1) provides that every member of the LLP is an agent of the LLP and, consequently, they will bind the LLP to any agreement entered into within the scope of their actual or apparent authority. However, the LLP will not be liable where the third party is aware of the lack of authority or does not know, or believe, that the other party is a member of the LLP. The LLP is also liable to the same extent as the member for any wrongful acts or omissions of individual members.

12.9.6 Relationship between members

Section 5 makes clear the intention to retain the flexible and consensual nature of the internal regulation of standard partnerships by providing that the mutual rights and duties of the members shall be governed 'by agreement between the members'. It is expected that LLPs will draw up specific agreements, but in the absence of any agreement, the default provisions of the LLPR 2001 will apply, which in turn are generally based on the previous rules set out in the Partnership Act 1890.

12.9.7 Relationship between members and third parties

As the LLP is a distinct legal person in its own right with full contractual capacity, it follows that there is usually no relationship between a member as agent and third parties who contract with the LLP as principal. However, it is possible that, as stated previously, the member may be personally liable for any wrongful act or omission, in which case he or she will consequently make the LLP equally liable.

12.9.8 Creditor protection

Members' liability is limited to the amount of capital introduced into the partnership. However, unlike limited companies, there are no controls on the withdrawal of capital by members, so creditors are not protected by the doctrine of capital maintenance. Creditors, however, are protected by the following general mechanisms:

- the requirement for LLPs to file audited accounts;
- the rules relating to fraud or misconduct under the Insolvency Act 1986;

- actions to recover money from members in relation to misfeasance, fraudulent and wrongful trading and other potential compensatory provisions under the Insolvency Act (see further below, 12.9.10);
- the power to disqualify members.

12.9.9 Taxation

Although the LLP enjoys corporate status, it is not taxed as a separate entity from its members. Section 10 of the LLPA 2000 expressly provides that where a LLP carries on business with a view to profit, the members will be treated for the purposes of income tax, corporation tax and capital gains tax as if they were partners in a standard partnership. Thus, members of LLPs gain the benefits of limited liability whilst retaining the tax advantages of a partnership.

12.9.10 Insolvency and winding up

The LLPR 2001 extend the provisions relating to the insolvency and winding up of registered companies to LLPs. Thus, the relevant sections of the Companies Act 1985, the Insolvency Act 1986, the Company Directors Disqualification Act 1986 and the Financial Services and Markets Act 2000 have been appropriately modified to apply to LLPs.

Of particular interest are two alterations to the Insolvency Act 1986. Section 1(4) of the LLPA 2000 merely stated that members of LLPs should have liability to contribute to its assets in the event of its winding up as 'is provided for by virtue of this Act'. The actual extent of that liability is established by a new s 74 introduced into the Insolvency Act 1986 under the LLPR 2001.

The new section provides that:

> ... when a limited liability partnership is wound up every present and past member of the limited liability partnership who has agreed with the other members or with the limited liability partnership that he will, in circumstances which have arisen, be liable to contribute to the assets of the limited liability partnership in the event that the limited liability partnership goes into liquidation is liable, to the extent that he has so agreed, to contribute to its assets to any amount sufficient for payment of its debts and liabilities, and the expenses of the winding up, and for the adjustment of the rights of the contributories among themselves.

Thus, it is a matter for the members to agree the level of their potential liability, which may be set at a nominal level, as there is no minimum level established in the section. Indeed, there is no compulsion for the members to agree to pay any debts of the LLP.

As has been stated previously, members of LLPs are subject to the usual controls exerted over company members in relation to their conduct in relation to their insolvent companies, such as actions for misfeasance, fraudulent trading and wrongful trading (see further 13.7 below). In addition to these, however, the LLPR 2001 introduce a new s 214A into the Insolvency Act 1986, which allows a liquidator to recover assets from members who have previously withdrawn property from their LLP. This measure strengthens the degree of creditor protection and is necessary in the light of the lack of the capital maintenance provisions which apply to companies. Section 214A applies in the following circumstances:

- A member withdrew property from the LLP in the two years prior to the start of its winding up. The property may be in the form of a share of profits, salary, repayment or payment of interest on a loan to the limited liability partnership, or any other withdrawal of property.
- It can be shown that, at the time of the withdrawal, the member knew or had reasonable grounds to believe that the LLP:
  o was unable to pay its debts; or
  o became unable to pay its debts as a result of the withdrawal.

In deciding whether a person had reasonable grounds to believe in the continued solvency of the LLP, the court will apply a minimum objective test, based on what they ought to have known in their position, as well as a potentially more onerous subjective test – what they ought to have known, given their personal attributes.

Under s 214A, the court may declare that the person who made the withdrawal is liable to make such contribution (if any) to the LLP's assets as it thinks proper. However, the court cannot make a declaration which exceeds the aggregate of the amounts of all the withdrawals made by that person within the period of two years previously referred to.

12.9.11 The future of the LLP

As yet, the availability of the LLP form of business organisation is too new to accurately assess its impact on traditional partnerships. However, by January 2002, Companies House reported that 1,161 firms had registered as LLPs. It is generally thought that the relatively slow take-up of the new form is due to a reluctance on the parts of professional partnerships to comply with the publicity requirements required under the LLP regime. It would appear that they would rather not have limited liability than have to reveal their finances to the public. Whether this remains the case is a matter for speculation for the moment, but there are indications that interest in the new form is increasing as awareness of it spreads. It is certainly an area of business law to be watched in the future.

PARTNERSHIP LAW

Definition of 'partnership'

- Section 1 of the Partnership Act 1890 states that partnership is the relation which subsists between persons carrying on a business in common with a view to profit.

The legal status of a partnership

- A partnership, unlike a joint stock company, has no separate legal personality apart from its members, although the limited liability partnership formed under the Limited Liability Partnership Act (LLPA) 2000 does have separate legal personality.
- Partnerships are generally limited to 20 members; however, certain professional partnerships are exempt from this maximum limit.

Formation of a partnership

- There are no specific legal requirements governing the formation of a partnership. Partnerships arise from the agreement of the parties involved and are governed by the general principles of contract law.

Duties of partners

- General fiduciary duties.
- Sections 28–30 of the Partnership Act 1890 lay down the specific duties:
  - of disclosure;
  - to account;
  - not to compete.

Rights of partners

Subject to express provision to the contrary in the partnership agreement, s 24 of the Partnership Act 1890 sets out the rights of partners. Among the most important of these are the rights:

- to share equally in the capital and profits of the business;
- to be indemnified by the firm for any liabilities incurred or payments made in the course of the firm's business;
  - o to take part in the management of the business;
  - o to have access to the firm's books;
  - o to prevent the admission of a new partner;
  - o to prevent any change in the nature of the partnership business.

Partnership property

It is important to distinguish between partnership property and personal property for the following reasons:

- partnership property must be used exclusively for partnership purposes;
- any increase in the value of partnership property belongs to the partnership;
- any increase in the value of personal property belongs to the person who owns the property;
- on the dissolution of the firm, partnership property is used to pay debts before personal property;
- partnership and personal property are treated differently in the satisfaction of claims made by partnership creditors, as opposed to personal creditors;
- on the death of a partner, any interest in partnership land will pass as personalty, whereas land owned personally will pass as realty.

The authority of partners to bind the firm

Authority can be actual or implied on the basis of the usual authority possessed by a partner in the particular line of business carried out by the firm.

Partners' liability on debts

Every partner is responsible for the full amount of the firm's liability.

Outsiders have the choice of taking action against:

- the firm collectively; or
- against the individual partners;
- where damages are recovered from one partner only, the other partners are under a duty to contribute equally to the amount paid.

Partnership by estoppel

Failure to give notice of retirement is one way in which liability arises on the basis of estoppel or holding out. Alternatively, anyone who represents themselves, or knowingly permits themselves to be represented, as a partner is liable to any person who gives the partnership credit on the basis of that representation.

Dissolution

Grounds for dissolution are:
- the expiry of a fixed term or the completion of a specified enterprise;
- the giving of notice;
- the death or bankruptcy of any partner;
- where a partner's share becomes subject to a charge;
- illegality;
- where a partner becomes a patient under the Mental Health Act 1893;
- where a partner suffers some other permanent incapacity;
- where a partner engages in activity prejudicial to the business;
- where a partner persistently breaches the partnership agreement;
- where the business can only be carried on at a loss;
- where it is just and equitable to do so.

Winding up

Since the introduction of the Insolvency Act 1986, partnerships as such are not subject to bankruptcy. Partnerships may be wound up as unregistered companies under Pt V of the Insolvency Act 1986.

Treatment of assets on dissolution

On dissolution, the value of the partnership property is applied in the following order:
- in paying debts to outsiders;
- in paying to the partners any advance made to the firm beyond their capital contribution;
- in paying the capital contribution of the individual partners;
- any residue is divided between the partners in the same proportion as they shared in profits.

Limited liability partnerships

The LLPA 2000, together with the Limited Liability Partnership Regulations (LLPR) 2001, provides for a new form of business entity, the limited liability partnership. Although stated to be a partnership, the new form is a corporation, with a distinct legal existence apart from its members. As such, it will have the ability:

- to hold property in its own right;
- to sue and be sued in its own name.

It will have perpetual succession and consequently alterations in its membership will not have any effect on its existence.

Most importantly, however, the new legal entity will allow its members to benefit from limited liability, in that they will not be liable for more than the amount they have agreed to contribute to its capital.

Formation

To form a limited liability partnership:

- two or more persons must subscribe to an incorporation document;
- the incorporation document must be delivered to the companies' registry;
- a statement of compliance must be completed by a solicitor or subscriber to the incorporation document.

The incorporation document must include:

- the name of the LLP (subject to restrictions);
- the address of the registered office;
- the names and addresses of those who will be members on incorporation of the LLP;
- the names of at least two designated members, whose duty it is to ensure that the administrative and filing duties of the LLP are complied with. If no such members are designated, then all members will be assumed to be designated members.

Regulation between members

The rights and duties of members will be governed by any agreement entered into. In the absence of any agreement, the default provisions of the LLPR 2001 will apply. These default rules are based on the previous rules set out in the Partnership Act 1890.

Section 6 of the LLPA 2000 provides that every member of the LLP is an agent of the LLP rather than a principal, and agent of the other members, as in an ordinary partnership. The extent of such authority is subject to the usual agency rules.

Liability and creditor protection

Members' liability is limited to the amount of capital introduced into the partnership. However, unlike limited companies, there are no controls on the withdrawal of capital by members, so creditors are not protected by the doctrine of capital maintenance. Creditors are protected by the following general mechanisms:

* the requirement for LLPs to file audited accounts;
* the rules relating to fraud or misconduct under the Insolvency Act 1986.

Insolvency and winding up

The LLPR 2001 extend the provisions relating to the insolvency and winding up of registered companies to LLPs. Thus, the relevant sections of the Companies Act 1985, the Insolvency Act 1986, the Company Directors Disqualification Act 1986 and the Financial Services and Markets Act 2000 have been appropriately modified to apply to LLPs.

CHAPTER 13

COMPANY LAW

13.1 INTRODUCTION

This chapter deals with the formation and regulation of a common alternative form of business association to the partnership, namely, the registered company. The flexibility of the company form of organisation is shown by the fact that it is used by businesses of widely different sizes and needs; from the one-man business to the transnational corporation. In fact, the register of all companies shows that the overwhelming number (almost 99%) are, in fact, private companies, which may be seen as sole traders or partnerships which have assumed the legal form of the registered company (see below, 13.3.2).

As yet, it is too early to estimate the likely impact of the availability of the limited liability partnership (LLP) form (see 12.9), but it may be reasonably expected that it will provide a useful alternative to the private company form.

The major general legislation governing company law is the Companies Act (CA) 1985, as amended by the Companies Act 1989. There are, however, other Acts that govern specific aspects of company law, such as the Insolvency Act (IA) 1986, the Company Directors Disqualification Act (CDDA) 1986 and the Criminal Justice Act (CJA) 1993, which covers insider dealing. In this chapter, if no reference is made to any specific Act, then it can be assumed that reference is to the CA 1985. All other Acts will be specifically named.

13.2 CORPORATIONS AND THEIR LEGAL CHARACTERISTICS

Partnerships may trade as, for example, 'J Smith and Co'. But the use of the term 'company' in this instance does not mean that such a business is to be understood, or treated in the same way, as a company registered under the companies legislation. In terms of legal form, companies differ from partnerships, in that they are bodies corporate or corporations. In other words, they have a legal existence in their own right, apart from and independent of their members. Such is not the case with respect to partnerships.

13.2.1 Types of corporation

Corporations can be created in one of four ways:

*   By grant of royal charter

    Such corporations are governed mainly by the common law. The very earliest trading companies were created by royal charter, but this was essentially in order to secure monopoly privileges from the Crown, which could not be given to individuals. Nowadays, this method of incorporation tends to be restricted to professional, educational and charitable institutions and is not used in relation to business enterprises.

- By special Act of Parliament

  Such bodies are known as statutory corporations, although this method of incorporation was the only alternative to charters before the introduction of registration and was common during the 19th century. This was particularly true in relation to railway and public utility companies, which usually required powers of compulsory purchase of land. It is not greatly used nowadays, and certainly not by ordinary trading companies.

- By registration under the Companies Acts

  Since 1844, companies have been permitted to acquire the status of a corporation simply by complying with the requirements for registration set out in general Acts of Parliament. This is the method by which the great majority of trading enterprises are incorporated. The current legislation is the CA 1985, as subsequently amended by various other Acts of Parliament.

- By registration under the Limited Liability Partnership Act 2000

  As has already been seen, at 12.9, LLPs are granted the privilege of incorporation on registration with the companies' registry.

13.2.2 The doctrine of separate personality

English law, unlike continental or Scottish law, treats a partnership simply as a group of individuals trading collectively. The effect of incorporation, however, is that a company, once formed, has its own distinct legal personality, separate from its members.

The doctrine of separate, or corporate, personality is an ancient one and may be found in Roman law. An early example of its application in relation to English business law can be seen in *Salomon v The Hamborough Co* (1671). That being said, the usual case cited in relation to separate personality is *Salomon v Salomon and Co* (1897). Salomon had been in the boot and leather trade for some time. Together with other members of his family, he formed a limited company and sold his previous business to it. Payment was in the form of cash, shares and debentures (the latter is loan stock which gives the holder priority over unsecured creditors if the company is wound up; see below, 13.6.6). When the company was eventually wound up, it was argued that Salomon and the company were the same and, as he could not be his own creditor, Salomon's debentures should have no effect. Although previous courts had decided against Salomon, the House of Lords held that, under the circumstances, in the absence of fraud, his debentures were valid. The company had been properly constituted and, consequently, it was, in law, a distinct legal person, completely separate from Salomon.

It is important to note that, contrary to what some, if not most, textbooks state, the *Salomon* case did not establish the doctrine of separate personality. It merely permitted its application to one-man and private companies (see below, 13.3.2).

Following the European Community's 12th Directive on Company Law (89/667), which was enacted in the UK in the form of the Companies (Single Member Private Limited Companies) Regulations 1992, provision has been made for the establishment of true one-man companies. These Regulations permit the incorporation of private limited companies by one person and with only one member. Thus, there is no longer any need for any pretence in the registration of sole traders as companies. As a matter of interest, it should be noted that the Limited Liability Partnership Act 2000 does not permit individuals to register as an LLP as, by definition, a partnership involves more than one person.

It should be noted, as a matter of related interest, that the Law Commission is currently engaged in examining the whole question of limited liability as it applies, or as it should be applied, to economic partnerships.

13.2.3 The effects of incorporation

A number of consequences flow from the fact that corporations are treated as having legal personality in their own right:

- Limited liability

  No one is responsible for anyone else's debts unless they agree to accept such responsibility. Similarly, at common law, members of a corporation are not responsible for its debts without agreement. However, registered companies, that is, those formed under the CA 1985 and CA 1989, are not permitted unless the shareholders agree to accept liability for their company's debts. In return for this agreement, the extent of their liability is set at a fixed amount. In the case of a company limited by shares, the level of liability is the amount remaining unpaid on the nominal value of the shares held. In the case of a company limited by guarantee, it is the amount that shareholders have agreed to pay in the event of the company being wound up.

- Perpetual succession

  As the corporation exists in its own right, changes in its membership have no effect on its status or existence. In contrast to the partnership, members of companies may die or be declared bankrupt or insane without any effect on the company. More importantly, however, members may transfer their shares to a third party without having any effect on the continuation of the business. In public limited companies, and certainly those listed on the stock exchange, freedom to transfer shares is unrestricted, although it is common for some restrictions to be placed on the transferability of shares in private companies (this is merely one of the many legal differences between the two forms of company, which reflects their essential difference as economic forms; see below, 13.3.2).

As an abstract legal person, the company cannot die, although its existence can be brought to an end through the winding up procedure (see below, 13.11).

- Business property is owned by the company

Any business assets are owned by the company itself, not the shareholders. This is normally a major advantage, in that the company's assets are not subject to claims based on the ownership rights of its members. It can, however, cause unforeseen problems.

In *Macaura v Northern Assurance* (1925), the plaintiff owned a timber estate. He later formed a one-man company and transferred the estate to it. He continued to insure the estate in his own name. When the timber was lost in a fire, it was held that Macaura could not claim on the insurance, since he had no personal interest in the timber, which belonged to the company.

What the member owns is a number of shares in the company. The precise nature of the share will be considered below (see 13.6.1).

- The company has contractual capacity in its own right and can sue and be sued in its own name

The nature and extent of a company's contractual capacity will be considered in detail later (see 13.5.1). For the moment, it should be noted that contracts are entered into in the company's name and it is liable on any such contracts. The extent of the company's liability, as opposed to the members' liability, is unlimited, and all of its assets may be used to pay off debts.

As a corollary of this, the members of the board of directors are the agents of the company. Members as such are not agents of the company; they have no right to be involved in the day to day operation of the business and they cannot bind the company in any way. This lack of power on the part of the members is one of the key differences between the registered company and the partnership, as partners have the express power to bind the partnership (s 5 of the Partnership Act 1890). However, members of private, quasi-partnership companies may have a legitimate expectation to be involved in the management of their company and may take action under s 459 of the CA 1985 to remedy any exclusion from the management.

- The rule in *Foss v Harbottle* (1843)

This states that, where a company suffers an injury, it is for the company, acting through the majority of the members, to take the appropriate remedial action. Perhaps of more importance is the corollary of the rule, which is that an individual cannot raise an action in response to a wrong suffered by the company (exceptions to the rule in *Foss v Harbottle*, both at common law and under statute, will be considered in detail below, 13.11).

Contemporary company lawyers explain the foregoing attributes as being the consequence of, and see them as following from, the doctrine of separate personality. It is possible, however, to reverse the causality contained in such conventional approaches. Consequently, it may be suggested that the doctrine of separate personality, as we now know it, is itself the product, rather than the cause, of these various attributes, which were recognised and developed independently by the courts.

13.2.4 Lifting the veil of incorporation

There are a number of occasions, both statutory and at common law, when the doctrine of separate personality will not be followed. On these occasions, it is said that the veil of incorporation, which separates the company from its members, is pierced, lifted or drawn aside and the members are revealed and made responsible for the actions of the company. Such situations arise in the following circumstances:

- Under the companies legislation

    Section 24 of the CA 1985 provides for personal liability of the member where a company carries on trading with fewer than two members; and s 229 requires consolidated accounts to be prepared by a group of related companies.

    Section 213 of the IA 1986 provides for personal liability in relation to fraudulent trading; s 214 does the same in relation to wrongful trading (see below, 13.7.6). And, as has already been seen, the new s 214A, introduced into the IA 1986 by the Limited Liability Partnership Regulations 2001, operates in a similar way with regard to LLPs.

- At common law

    As in most areas of law that are based on the application of policy decisions, it is difficult to predict with any certainty when the courts will ignore separate personality. What is certain is that the courts will not permit the corporate form to be used for a clearly fraudulent purpose or to evade a legal duty. In such instances, the courts tend to refer to the company using terms such as sham, cloak and mask, and ignore it in order to fix ultimate responsibility on the person who tries to hide behind it. For example, in *Gilford Motor Co Ltd v Horne* (1933), an employee had entered into a contractual agreement not to solicit his former employers' customers. After he left their employment, he formed a company to solicit those customers. It was held that the company was a sham and the court would not permit it to be used to avoid the prior contract.

As would be expected, the courts are prepared to ignore separate personality in times of war to defeat the activity of shareholders who might be enemy aliens. See *Daimler Co Ltd v Continental Tyre and Rubber Co (GB) Ltd* (1917).

Where groups of companies have been set up for particular business ends, the courts will not usually ignore the separate existence of the various companies, unless they are being used for fraud. *Adams v Cape Industries plc* (1990) is a particularly strong example of this approach. In that case, it was held that an award made in relation to asbestos-related injuries against a company in the US could not be enforced against the UK parent company. The basis for the decision was the doctrine of separate personality, even though it might have appeared that the company structure had been deliberately set up to avoid such a claim. Such ingenuity was not fraud.

There is authority for treating separate companies as a single group, as in *DHN Food Distributors Ltd v Borough of Tower Hamlets* (1976); but later authorities have cast extreme doubt on this decision and, although it has never been overruled, it is probably true to say that it is no longer an accurate statement of the law (see *Woolfson v Strathclyde Regional Council* (1978); *National Dock Labour Board v Pinn and Wheeler Ltd* (1989); and *Adams v Cape Industries plc* (1990)).

At one time, it appeared that the courts were increasingly willing to use and extend their essential discretionary power in such a way as to achieve results they considered right. However, in *Ord v Bellhaven Pubs Ltd* (1998), Hobhouse LJ expressed what appears to be the contemporary reluctance of the courts to ignore separate personality simply to achieve what might be considered a subjectively fair decision. In overturning the decision at first instance, and at the same time overruling *Creasey v Breachwood Motors* (1993), he stated that:

> The approach of the judge in the present case was simply to look at the economic unit, to disregard the distinction between the legal entities that were involved and then to say: since the company cannot pay, the shareholders who are the people financially interested should be made to pay instead. That, of course, is radically at odds with the whole concept of corporate personality and limited liability and [from] the decision of the House of Lords in *Salomon v Salomon and Co Ltd* it is clear that ... there must be some impropriety before the corporate veil can be pierced.

13.3 TYPES OF COMPANIES

Although the distinction between public and private companies is probably the most important, there are a number of ways in which companies can be classified.

13.3.1 Limited and unlimited companies

One of the major advantages of forming a company is limited liability, but companies can be formed without limited liability. Such companies receive all the benefits that flow from incorporation, except limited liability, but, in return, they do not have to submit their accounts or make them available for public inspection.

The great majority of companies, however, are limited liability companies. This means, as explained above, that the maximum liability of shareholders is fixed and cannot be increased without their agreement. There are two ways of establishing limited liability:

* By shares

  This is the most common procedure. It limits liability to the amount remaining unpaid on shares held. If the shareholder has paid the full nominal value of the shares, plus any premium that might be due to the company, then that is the end of their responsibility with regard to company debts. So, even if the company goes into insolvent liquidation with insufficient assets to pay its creditors, the individual shareholder cannot be required to make any further contribution to its funds.

* By guarantee

  This type of limited liability is usually restricted to non-trading enterprises such as charities and professional and educational bodies. It limits liability to an agreed amount, which is only called on if the company cannot pay its debts on being wound up. In reality, the sum guaranteed is usually a nominal sum, so no real risk is involved on the part of the guarantor.

13.3.2 Public and private companies

Rather oddly, previous legislation defined the public company in relation to the private company. The current legislation, however, makes the public company the essential form, with the private company as the exceptional form. Thus, the Companies Act 1985 defines a public company as essentially a company:

(a) the memorandum of which states that it is a public company;

(b) in relation to which the appropriate registration requirements have been complied with.

The Act then defines a private company as any company which is not a public company.

The essential difference between these two forms is an economic one, although different legal rules have been developed to apply to each of them:

- Private companies

  Private companies tend to be small scale enterprises, owned and operated by a small number of individuals who are actively involved in the day to day running of the enterprise. Outsiders do not invest in such companies and, indeed, private companies are precluded from offering their shares to the public at large. Their shares are not quoted on any share market, and in practice tend not to be freely transferable, with restrictions being placed on them in the company's articles of association. Many such companies, and they make up the vast majority of registered companies, are sole traders or partnerships which have registered as companies in order to take advantage of limited liability. When limited liability was made available to registered companies in 1855 and under the later CA 1862, it was clearly not intended that it should be open to partnerships or individuals. Nonetheless, it became apparent that such businesses could acquire the benefit of limited liability by simply complying with the formal procedures of the CA 1862, and a great many businesses converted to limited companies. The legal validity of such private companies was clearly established only in the House of Lords' decision in the *Salomon* case, but since then the courts and the legislature have developed specific rules governing their operation.

- Public limited companies

  Public companies, on the other hand, tend to be large and are controlled by directors and managers rather than the shareholders. This division is sometimes referred to as the separation of ownership and control. These public companies are essentially a source of investment for their shareholders and have freely transferable shares which may be quoted on the stock exchange.

As a consequence of the difference with regard to ownership and control, many of the provisions of the companies legislation, which is designed to protect the interests of shareholders in public companies, are not applicable to private companies. In his leading text on company law, Professor John Farrar lists some 18 differences in the way in which the legislation operates as between public and private companies (Farrar, JH, *Company Law*, 4th edn, 1998). The most important of these are as follows:

- public companies must have at least two directors, whereas private companies need only have one. This recognises the reality of the true one-man business. It is important to note that the Companies (Single Member Private Companies) Regulations 1992 (SI 1992/1699) provide for the formation of a limited company with only one member. These Regulations are in line with the 12th European Company Law Directive;

- public companies must have a minimum issued capital of £50,000, which must be paid up to the extent of 25%. There is no such requirement in relation to private companies (see further at 13.6);

- the requirement to keep accounting records is shorter for private companies – three years, as opposed to six years for public companies;

- the controls over distribution of dividend payments is relaxed in relation to private companies;

- private companies may purchase their own shares out of capital, whereas public companies are strictly forbidden from doing so;

- private companies can provide financial assistance for the purchase of their own shares where public companies cannot;

- there are fewer and looser controls over directors in private companies with regard to their financial dealings with their companies than there are in public companies;

- in a private company, anything that might be done by way of a resolution of a general meeting or a meeting of a class of members may instead be achieved by a resolution in writing, signed by all the members of the company, without the need to convene any such meeting;

- private companies may pass an elective resolution dispensing with the need to appoint auditors annually, to lay accounts before an annual general meeting or, indeed, to hold annual general meetings at all. An elective resolution also permits private companies to reduce the majority needed to call meetings at short notice from 95% to 90%.

It may also be suggested that, in cases involving private limited companies, which the courts view as quasi-partnerships, other general company law principles are applied less rigorously or not at all. See, for example, *Ebrahimi v Westbourne Galleries Ltd* (1973) (otherwise known as *Re Westbourne Galleries*), where the court seemed to play down the effect of separate personality in such instances. Consider also *Clemens v Clemens Bros Ltd* (1976), over which much ink has been spilled in trying to establish a general rule concerning the duties owed by majority to minority shareholders. The reality is that there was no general principle that could be applied: the case merely reflects the courts' willingness to treat what they see as quasi-partnerships in an equitable manner. What is certain about the *Clemens* case is that it would find no application in public limited companies.

Many of the above issues will be dealt with in more detail below, but, for the moment, it might be pointed out that there is much to be said for the suggestion that private limited companies should be removed from the ambit of the general companies legislation and be given their own particular legislation. It is apparent that they are not the same as public companies and cannot be expected to submit to the same regulatory regime as applies to the latter. In practice, the law recognises this, but only in a roundabout way, by treating them as exceptions to the general law relating to public companies. The argument, however, is that they are not exceptions; they are completely different, and this difference should be clearly recognised by treating them as a legal form *sui generis*. The introduction of the possibility of limited liability partnerships may be seen as a measure to address and rationalise this particular matter, although as yet, it is too early to assess its impact.

13.3.3 Parent and subsidiary companies

This description of companies relates to the way in which large business enterprises tend to operate through a linked structure of distinct companies. Each of these companies exists as a separate corporate entity in its own right but, nonetheless, the group is required to be treated as a single entity in relation to the group accounting provisions under s 229 of the CA 1985.

Section 736 of the CA 1985 states that one company, S, is a subsidiary of another company, H, its holding company, in any of the following circumstances:

- where H holds a majority of voting rights in S;
- where H is a member of S and has a right to appoint or remove a majority of its board of directors;
- where H is a member of S and controls a majority of the voting rights in it;
- where S is a subsidiary of a company which is in turn a subsidiary of H.

Section 258, which relates to accounting requirements, defines the relationship of parent and subsidiary companies in a similar way but introduces the additional idea of the parent exercising a dominant influence over the subsidiary company.

13.3.4 Small, medium and large companies

Companies can be categorised in relation to their size. Small and medium sized companies are subjected to relaxation in relation to the submission of accounts under s 246 of the CA 1985. Which category a company fits into depends on its turnover, balance sheet valuation and number of employees.

A small company must satisfy two of the following requirements:

Turnover	not more than £2.8 million
Balance sheet	not more than £1.4 million
Employees	not more than 50

A medium sized company must satisfy two of the following requirements:

Turnover	not more than £11.2 million
Balance sheet	not more than £5.6 million
Employees	not more than 250

It should be remembered that, as discussed above at 13.2.2, it is now open to individuals to form companies and the companies legislation will apply subject to appropriate alterations.

13.4 FORMATION OF COMPANIES

The CA 1985 establishes a strict procedure with which companies have to comply before they can operate legally. The procedure, which in the case of public companies involves two stages, is described below.

13.4.1 Registration

There are two companies registries in the UK, one in Cardiff, which deals with companies registered within England and Wales, and one in Edinburgh, which deals with Scottish companies. A registered company is incorporated when particular documents are delivered to the registrar of companies (s 10 of the CA 1985). On registration of these documents, the registrar issues a certificate on incorporation (s 13 of the CA 1985). The documents required under s 10 are:

- a memorandum of association;
- articles of association (unless Table A articles are to apply – see below);
- a statement detailing the first directors and secretary of the company with their written consent and the address of the company's registered office;
- a statutory declaration that the necessary requirements of the CA 1985 have been complied with must be submitted under s 12. This declaration can be made by a solicitor engaged in the formation of the company, or a director, or the company secretary.

The duty of the registrar of companies is to ensure that:

- the requirements of the Companies Act have been complied with;
- the memorandum and articles of association do not infringe the Companies Act;
- the objects of the company are lawful;
- the name of the company is lawful;
- in the case of a public company, that its share capital is not less than the authorised minimum.

If the registrar is satisfied that the above requirements have been complied with, a certificate of incorporation will be issued. Such a certificate is conclusive evidence that the company has been properly incorporated (see *Jubilee Cotton Mills v Lewis* (1924)).

The registrar can refuse to register a company if he or she considers it to have been formed for some unlawful purpose. Such a refusal can be challenged under judicial review (*R v Registrar of Joint Stock Companies ex p Moore* (1931)), as can the improper registration of a company formed for unlawful purposes (*R v Registrar of Companies ex p AG* (1991), where the company had been formed for the purposes of conducting prostitution).

13.4.2 Commencement of business

A company exists from the date of its registration, and a private company may start its business and use its borrowing powers as soon as the certificate of registration is issued. A public company, however, cannot start a business or borrow money until it has obtained an additional certificate from the registrar under s 117 of the CA 1985. In relation to public companies, there is a requirement that they have a minimum allotted share capital, at present £50,000 (ss 11, 118 of the CA 1985), and, under s 101, they must not allot shares unless they have been as paid up at least as to one-quarter of their nominal value (it follows that the statutory minimum issued and paid up capital for a public company is £12,5000). The s 117 certificate confirms that the company has met these requirements.

13.5 THE CONSTITUTION OF THE COMPANY

The constitution of a company is established by two documents: the memorandum of association and the articles of association. If there is any conflict between the two documents, the contents of the memorandum prevail over anything to the contrary contained in the articles; although provisions in the articles may be used to clarify particular uncertainties in the memorandum.

As will be seen, there is a large measure of freedom as to what is actually included in such documents, but this latitude is extended within a clearly established framework of statutory and common law rules. Model memorandums and articles of association are set out in the Companies (Tables A to F) Regulations 1985 (SI 1985/805), although companies may alter the models to suit their particular circumstances and requirements.

13.5.1 The memorandum of association

The memorandum of association is a compulsory document which mainly governs the company's external affairs. It represents the company to the outside world, stating its capital structure, its powers and its objects. The document submitted to the registrar of companies must be signed by at least two subscribers from amongst the company's first shareholders. Every memorandum must contain the following clauses:

- The name clause

  Except in relation to specifically exempted companies such as those involved in charitable work, companies are required to indicate that they are operating on the basis of limited liability. Thus, private companies are required to end their names either with the word 'Limited' or the abbreviation 'Ltd'; and public companies must end their names with the words 'public limited company' or the abbreviation 'plc'. Welsh companies may use the Welsh language equivalents (ss 25 and 27). Equally, it amounts to a criminal offence to use the words 'public limited company' or 'Limited' in an improper manner (ss 33 and 34).

  A further aspect of this requirement for publicity is that companies display their names outside their business premises, on business documents and on their seal. In addition to committing a criminal offence, any person who fails to use a company's full name on any document will be personally liable for any default. See *Penrose v Martyr* (1858), where a company secretary was held personally liable when he failed to indicate that the company against which he had drawn a bill of exchange was in fact a limited company.

  A company's name must not be the same as any already registered, nor should it constitute a criminal offence or be offensive (s 26(1)). Any suggestion of connection with the government or any local authority in a company's name requires the approval of the Secretary of State (s 26(2)), as does the use of any of the many words listed in the Company and Business Names Regulations 1981 (SI 1981/1699) (s 29). Among the words in the Regulations are such as imply connection with royalty, such as 'king', 'queen', 'prince', 'princess', 'royal', etc. Amongst other controlled words in titles are: abortion, benevolent, co-operative; through to stock exchange, trade union and university.

  A passing-off action may be taken against a company, as previously considered in relation to partnership law (see above, 12.5.5).

  The name of a company can be changed by a special resolution of the company (s 28).

- The registered office clause

  This is the company's legal address. It is the place where legal documents such as writs or summonses can be served on the company. It is also the place where particular documents and statutory registers such as the register of members (s 353), the register of directors interests in shares (s 325), the register of debenture holders (s 190) and the register of charges held against the company's property (s 407) are required to be kept available for inspection. The memorandum does not state the actual address of the registered office, but only the country within which the company is registered, be it Scotland or England and Wales. The precise location of the registered office, however, has to be stated on all business correspondence (s 351). It is not necessary that the registered office be the company's main place of business and, indeed, it is not unusual for a company's registered office to be the address of its accountant or lawyer.

- The objects clause

Companies registered under the various Companies Acts are not corporations in the same way as common law corporations are. It was established in *Ashbury Rly Carriage and Iron Co Ltd v Riche* (1875) that such companies were established only to pursue particular purposes. Those purposes were stated in the objects clause of the company's memorandum of association and any attempt to contract outside of that limited authority was said to be *ultra vires* and, as a consequence, was void.

It was felt for a long time that the operation of the *ultra vires* doctrine operated unfairly on outsiders and various attempts were made to reduce the scope of its application. Since the introduction of the CA 1989, it is fortunately no longer necessary to enter into a detailed consideration of the history and operation of the doctrine of *ultra vires*. After the CA 1989, *ultra vires* has been effectively reduced to an internal matter and does not affect outsiders; even as a means of limiting the actions of directors it has been considerably weakened (see ss 35, 35A and 35B of the CA 1989).

Whereas in the past, companies used to register extended objects clauses to provide for unforeseen eventualities, they can now simply register as a general commercial company, which will empower them to carry on any trade or business whatsoever and to do all such things as are incidental or conducive to the carrying on of any trade or business (s 3A).

Companies can alter their objects clause by passing a special resolution, by virtue of s 4, although such procedure is subject to a right of appeal to the courts within 21 days, by the holders, of 15% of the issued capital of the company. However, given the effect of the CA 1989, this element of control will only have indirect effect on the external relations of the company to the extent that members may bring proceedings to prevent directors from acting beyond the stated objects of the company (s 35(2) of the CA 1989).

- The limited liability clause

This clause simply states that the liability of the members is limited. It must be included even where the company has permission not to use the word 'Limited' in its name.

- The authorised share capital clause

This states the maximum amount of share capital that a company is authorised to issue. The capital has to be divided into shares of a fixed monetary amount, as no-fixed-value shares are not permissible in UK law.

- The association clause

  This states that the subscribers to the memorandum wish to form a company and agree to take the number of shares placed opposite their names.

It should also be recalled that the memorandum of public companies must contain a clause stating that they are public companies.

13.5.2 The articles of association

The articles primarily regulate the internal working of the company. They govern the rights and relations of the members to the company and vice versa, and the relations of the members between themselves. As provided in s 14 of the CA 1989, the articles are to be treated as an enforceable contract; although it has to be stated that it is a peculiar contract, in that its terms can be altered by the majority of the members without the consent of each member.

The articles deal with such matters as the allotment and transfer of shares, the rights attaching to particular shares, the rules relating to the holding of meetings and the powers of directors.

A company is at liberty to draw up its own articles, but regulations made under the CA 1989 provide a set of model articles known as Table A. Companies do not have to submit their own articles and, if they do not, then Table A applies automatically. The provisions contained in Table A also apply to the extent that they have not been expressly excluded by the company's particular articles. Usually, companies adopt Table A and modify it to suit their own situation.

Alteration of articles

Articles can be altered by the passing of a special resolution (s 9 of the CA 1985). Any such alteration has to be made *bona fide* in the interest of the company as a whole, but the exact meaning of this phrase is not altogether clear. It is evident that it involves a subjective element in that those deciding the alteration must actually believe they are acting in the interest of the company. There is additionally, however, an objective element. In *Greenhalgh v Arderne Cinemas Ltd* (1951), it was stated that any alteration had to be in the interests of the individual hypothetical member; thus, the alteration that took a pre-emptive right from a particular member was held to be to the advantage of such a hypothetical member, although it severely reduced the rights of a real member. Such differentiation between concrete and hypothetical benefits is a matter of fine distinction, although it can be justified. In any case, persons suffering from substantive injustice are now at liberty to make an application under s 459 for an order to remedy any unfairly prejudicial conduct (see below, 13.11.2).

The following two cases may demonstrate the difference between the legitimate use and the abuse of the provision for altering articles; each of them relates to circumstances where existing shareholders' rights were removed.

In *Brown v British Abrasive Wheel Co* (1919), an alteration to the articles of the company was proposed, to give the majority shareholders the right to buy shares of the minority. It was held, under the circumstances of the case, that the alteration was invalid, since it would benefit the majority shareholders rather than the company as a whole.

In *Sidebottom v Kershaw Leese and Co* (1920), the alteration to the articles gave the directors the power to require any shareholder who entered into competition with the company to transfer their shares to nominees of the directors at a fair price. It was held that, under these circumstances, the alteration permitting the expropriation of members interests was valid, since it would benefit the company as a whole.

As the power to alter their articles is a statutory provision, companies cannot be prevented from using that power, even if the consequence of so doing results in a breach of contract. Thus, in *Southern Foundries Ltd v Shirlaw* (1940), it was held that the company could not be prevented from altering its articles in such a way that eventually would lead to the breach of the managing director's contract of employment. Shirlaw was, of course, entitled to damages for the breach.

13.5.3 Effect of memorandum and articles

Section 14 of the CA 1985 provides that:

> ... the memorandum and articles, when registered, bind the company and its members to the same extent as if they had respectively had been signed and sealed by each member and contained covenants on the part of each member to observe all the provision of the memorandum and articles.

Thus, the memorandum and articles constitute a statutory contract. The effect of this is that:

- the constitutional documents establish a contract between each member and the company and binds each member to the terms of that contract. Thus, in *Hickman v Kent or Romney Marsh Sheep Breeders Association* (1915), the company was able to insist that a member complied with an article which provided that disputes between the company and any member should go to arbitration;

- the company is contractually bound to each member to abide by the terms of the documents. Thus, in *Pender v Lushington* (1877), a member was able to enforce his constitutional right in the face of the company's refusal to permit him to vote at a company meeting;

- the members are bound *inter se*, that is, to each other. Authority for this was provided by *Rayfield v Hands* (1960), in which the directors of a company were required to abide by the articles of association, which required them to buy the shares of any members who wished to transfer their shares.

It is essential to note, however, that the memorandum and articles only create a contractual relationship in respect of membership rights. Consequently, although members can enforce such rights, non-members, or any member suing in some other capacity than that of a member, cannot enforce the provisions contained in those documents. In *Eley v Positive Government Life Assurance* (1876), the company's articles stated that the plaintiff was to be appointed as its solicitor. It was held, however, that Eley could not use the article to establish a contract between himself and the company. The articles only created a contract between the company and its members, and, although Eley was a member of the company, he was not suing in that capacity but in a different capacity, namely, as the company's solicitor.

13.5.4 Class rights

A company might only issue one class of shares giving the holders the same rights. However, it is possible, and quite common, for companies to issue shares with different rights. Thus, preference shares may have priority rights over ordinary shares with respect to dividends or the repayment of capital. Nor is it uncommon for shares to carry different voting rights. Each of these instances is an example of class rights and the holders of shares which provide such rights constitute distinct classes within the generality of shareholders. It is usual for class rights to attach to particular shares and to be provided in the memorandum of association, although it is more usual for such rights to be provided for in the articles of association. It is now recognised, however, that such class rights may be created by external agreements and may be conferred upon a person in the capacity of shareholder of a company, although not attached to any particular shares. Thus, in *Cumbrian Newspapers Group Ltd v Cumberland and Westmorland Herald Newspaper and Printing Co Ltd* (1986), following a merger between the plaintiff and defendant companies, the defendant's articles were altered so as to give the plaintiff certain rights of pre-emption and also the right to appoint a director, so long as it held at least 10% of the defendant's ordinary shares. Scott J held that these rights were in the nature of class rights and could not be altered without going through the procedure for altering such rights.

As the *Cumbrian Newspapers* case demonstrates, class rights become an issue when the company looks to alter them. When it is realised that class rights usually provide their holders with some distinct advantage or benefit not enjoyed by the holders of ordinary shares, and that the class members are usually in a minority within the company, it can be appreciated that the procedure for varying such rights requires some sensitivity towards the class members.

Alteration of class rights

The procedure for altering class rights are set out in ss 125–27 of the CA 1985. The precise procedure depends upon two matters: first, where the rights are set out; and, secondly, whether there is a pre-established procedure for altering the rights:

- where the original articles set out a procedure for varying class rights, then that procedure should be followed, even if the rights are provided by the memorandum (s 125(4));

- where the rights are attached to a class of shares otherwise than by the memorandum, that is, by the articles or an external contract, and there is no pre-established procedure for altering them, then the consent of a three-quarters majority of nominal value of the shares in that class is necessary. The majority may be acquired in writing or by passing a special resolution at a separate meeting of the holders of the shares in question. This is the most common way of attaching and varying class rights (s 125(2));

- where the articles are attached by the memorandum and there is no pre-established procedure for alteration, then the consent of all members of the company is required to alter the rights (s 125(5)).

Any alteration of class rights under s 125 is subject to challenge in the courts. To raise such a challenge, any objectors must:

- hold no less than 15% of the issued shares in the class in question (s 127(2));

- not have voted in favour of the alteration (s 127(2)); and

- apply to the court within 21 of the consent being given to the alteration (s 127(3)).

The court has the power to either confirm the alteration or cancel it as unfairly prejudicial.

In *Greenhalgh v Arderne Cinemas* (1946), it was held that the sub-division of 50 p shares, which had previously carried one vote each, into five 10 p shares, which each carried one vote, did not vary the rights of another class of shares. Note that although, strictly speaking, such an alteration did not effect the rights held by the other shares, it did alter their real voting power. Also, in *House of Fraser plc v ACGE Investments Ltd* (1987), it was held that the return of all the capital held in the form of preference shares amounted to a total extinction of right. It could not, therefore, be seen as a variation of those rights and the s 125 procedure did not have to be followed. However, in *Re Northern Engineering Industries plc* (1994), it was held that a specific provision in the articles, designed to prevent the reduction of preference share capital with the approval of its holders, was equally effective to prevent to the complete extinction of the preference share capital.

13.6 CAPITAL

There are many different definitions of 'capital'. For the purposes of this chapter, attention will be focused on the way in which companies raise such money as they need to finance their operation. The essential distinction in company law is between share capital and loan capital.

13.6.1 Share capital

Company law and company lawyers have been extremely hesitant in offering any precise definition of the share, being content to deal with shares in a pragmatic rather than a theoretical manner. The most generally accepted definition of the share states that it is:

> ... the interest of the shareholder in the company measured by a sum of money, for the purposes of liability in the first place and of interest in the second, but also consisting of a series of mutual covenants entered into by all the shareholders [*Borlands Trustees v Steel* (1901)].

This definition can be divided into three elements:

- Liability

  The nominal value of the share normally fixes the amount which the shareholder is required to contribute to the assets of the company. Shareholders must pay at least the full nominal value of any shares issued to them (that is, shares must not be issued at a discount (s 100)), but where, as is quite common, the company issues shares at a premium, that is, at more than the nominal value of the shares, then the holders of those shares will be liable to pay the amount owed over and above the nominal value. The excess will form part of the company's capital and be included in the share premium account (s 130).

- Interest

  Legal definitions usually state that the share is a form of property, representing a proportionate interest in the business of the company, but tend to be much less certain as to the precise nature of such an interest. What is clear is that, as a consequence of separate personality, the share does not represent, in any other than a very contingent way, a claim against the assets owned by the company. What shareholders possess is not a right to own and control the capital assets operated by their company, but, rather, a right to receive a part of the profit generated by the use of those assets. As McPherson put it:

  > The market value of a modern corporation consists not of its plant and stocks of material but its presumed ability to produce a revenue for itself and its shareholders by its organisation of skills and its manipulation of the markets. Its value as a property is its ability to produce a revenue. The

property of its shareholders have is the right to a revenue from that ability ['Capitalism and the changing concept of property', in Kamenka, E and Neale, RS (eds), *Feudalism, Capitalism and Beyond*, 1975].

It also has to be recognised that even this right is contingent upon the company making a profit and the directors of the company recommending the declaration of a dividend.

- Mutual covenants

  The effect of s 14 of the CA 1985 has already been considered above, 13.5.3.

Section 182 of the CA 1985 provides that shares are personal property and are transferable in the manner provided for in the company's articles of association. Although the articles of private limited companies tend to restrict the transfer of shares within a close group of people, it is an essential aspect of shares in public limited companies that the investment they represent is open to immediate realisation; to that end, they are made freely transferable, subject to the appropriate procedure being followed.

13.6.2 Types of share capital

The word 'capital' is used in a number of different ways in relation to shares:

- Nominal or authorised capital

  This is the figure stated in the company's memorandum of association. It sets the maximum number of shares that the company can issue, together with the value of each share. There is no requirement that companies issue shares to the full extent of their authorised capital.

- Issued or allotted capital

  This represents the nominal value of the shares actually issued by the company. It is more important than authorised capital as a true measure of the substance of the company. If a company is willing to pay the registration fee, it can register with an authorised capital of £1 million yet only actually issue two £1 shares. Public companies must have a minimum issued capital of £50,000 (s 11 of the CA 1985).

- Paid up capital

  This is the proportion of the nominal value of the issued capital actually paid by the shareholder. It may be the full nominal value, in which case it fulfils the shareholders responsibility to outsiders; or it can be a mere part payment, in which case the company has an outstanding claim against the shareholder. Shares in public companies must be paid up to the extent of at least one-quarter of their nominal value (s 101 of the CA 1985).

- Called and uncalled capital

  Where a company has issued shares as not fully paid up, it can at a later time make a call on those shares. This means that the shareholders are required to provide more capital, up to the amount remaining unpaid on the nominal value of their shares. Called capital should equal paid up capital; uncalled capital is the amount remaining unpaid on issued capital.

- Reserve capital

    This arises where a company passes a resolution that it will not make a call on any unpaid capital. The unpaid capital then becomes a reserve, only to be called upon if the company cannot pay its debts from existing assets in the event of its liquidation.

The following could be a theoretical capital structure for a public limited company:

Authorised capital	£100,000
Issued capital	£50,000
Paid up capital	£12,500

13.6.3 Types of shares

Companies can issue shares of different value, and with different rights attached to them. Such classes of shares can be distinguished and categorised as follows:

- Ordinary shares

    These shares are sometimes referred to as 'equity in the company'. Of all the various types of shares, they carry the greatest risk, but in recompense receive the greatest return. The nominal value of shares is fixed but the exchange value of the shares in the stock market fluctuates in relation to the performance of the company and the perception of those dealing in the stock exchange. It is perhaps a matter of regret that the typical shareholder, and that includes the institutional investor, relates more to the performance of their shares in the market than to the actual performance of their company in productive terms. Ownership of ordinary shares entitles the holder to attend and vote at general meetings, although, once again, it is a matter of regret that very few shareholders do actually exercise these rights.

- Preference shares

    These shares involve less of a risk than ordinary shares. They may have priority over ordinary shares in two respects: dividends and repayment. They carry a fixed rate of dividend which has to be paid before any payment can be made to ordinary shareholders. Such rights are cumulative unless otherwise provided. This means that a failure to pay a dividend in any one year has to be made good in subsequent years.

    As regards repayment of capital, preference shares do not have priority unless, as is usually the case, this is specifically provided for. Also, without specific provision, preference shares have the same rights as ordinary shares; but it is usual for their voting rights to be restricted. Preference shareholders are entitled to vote at class meetings convened to consider any alteration to their particular rights, but, apart from that, they are usually restricted to voting in general meetings when their dividends are in arrears.

- Deferred shares

  This type of share postpones the rights of its holder to dividends until after the ordinary shareholders have received a fixed return. In effect, the ordinary shares are treated as preference shares and the deferred shares as ordinary shares. It is no longer a common form of organisation.

- Redeemable shares

  These are shares issued on the understanding that they may be bought back by the company (s 159). Redemption may be at the option of either the company or the shareholder, depending on the terms of issue. Companies, in any case, now have the right, subject to conditions, to purchase their own shares, and, therefore, are no longer restricted to buying redeemable shares (s 162).

13.6.4 Issue of shares

Directors generally are not allowed to issue shares without the authority of the members. In practice, however, it is usual for them to be granted general authority to issue the company's shares as they see fit, as long as that authority does not extend beyond a period of five years (s 80). The directors must not use their power to issue shares for an improper purpose. Thus, it was held in *Hogg v Cramphorn* (1967) that the issue of shares as a way of defeating a takeover bid was an improper use of the directors' power. Conversely, in *Howard Smith v Ampol Petroleum* (1974), issuing shares in order to facilitate a takeover bid was also unlawful.

It should be noted that any such breach of directors' powers can be ratified by a subsequent vote of the members in a general meeting (*Bamford v Bamford* (1970)).

13.6.5 Payment for shares

Under s 99 of the CA 1985, shares are only treated as paid up to the extent that the company has received money or money's worth. Any shortfall in payment will have to be made up in the future and this is especially true if the company goes into insolvent liquidation.

Issuing shares at a discount

This responsibility to make good any difference between consideration provided and the nominal value of the shares received is re-emphasised in s 100, which expressly prohibits the issuing of shares at a discount. The strictness of the rule may be seen in *Ooregeum Gold Mining Co of India Ltd v Roper* (1892). The £1 shares of the company were trading at only 12.5 p and, in an attempt to refinance it, new £1 preference shares were issued and credited with 75 p already paid. When the company subsequently went into liquidation, the holders of the preference shares were required to pay their full value and, therefore, had to subscribe a further 75 p. The court does have the power to grant relief from such payment in appropriate circumstances (s 113). Section 314 extends criminal liability to both the company and any officer of the company who has breached the rules relating to issuing shares at a discount.

Issuing shares at a premium

It is possible, and indeed quite common, for companies to issue their shares at a premium, that is, to charge those who take the shares more than their nominal value. In such circumstances, any additional payment received must be transferred into a share premium account, which may only be used for specific limited purposes such as paying any premium due on the redemption of preference shares or paying for previously unissued shares to be issued to the existing members.

It was held in *Henry Head v Ropner Holdings* (1952), and subsequently confirmed in *Shearer v Bercain* (1980), that the requirement to create a share premium account applied to situations where non-cash assets were transferred to pay for shares. The perceived inequity of this decision led to the provision of specific relief relating to mergers where assets are transferred in consideration of shares between formerly distinct companies (ss 131 and 132 of the Companies Act 1985).

Where public companies accept non-cash consideration for the issue of shares, they are required to have the value of the consideration provided independently reported on by some person who is qualified to act as a company auditor (ss 103 and 108). Such reports must be filed with the companies registry (s 111). Private companies, as usual, are less restricted in what they can do and they may accept non-cash consideration without the need to have it independently valued, as long as a copy of the contract is delivered to the registry (s 88).

13.6.6 Capital maintenance

The immediately preceding section focused on the way in which the law insists on companies receiving the full capital value for the shares they issue.

Once the capital has been received by the company, there are equally as important rules controlling what can be done with it, or, more accurately, controlling what cannot be done with it.

Thus, in *Flitcroft's Case* (1882), Jessel MR stated:

> The creditor has no debtor but the impalpable thing the corporation, which has no property except the assets of the business. The creditor, therefore, I may say, gives credit to that capital, gives credit to the company on the faith of the implied representation that the capital shall be applied only for the purposes of the business, and he has therefore a right to say that the corporation shall keep its capital and not return it to the shareholders ...

This quotation highlights two aspects of the doctrine of capital maintenance: first, that creditors have a right to see that the capital is not dissipated unlawfully; and, secondly, that members must not have the capital returned to them surreptitiously. These two aspects of the single doctrine of capital maintenance are governed by the rules relating to capital reduction and company distributions.

Capital reduction

The procedures under which companies can reduce the amount of their issued share capital are set out in ss 135–41 of the CA 1985. Section 135 states that a company may reduce its capital in any way, if so authorised in its articles, by passing a special resolution to that end. The section sets out three particular ways in which such capital can be reduced by:

- removing or reducing liability for any capital remaining as yet unpaid, that is, deciding that the company will not need to make any call on that unpaid capital in the future;

- cancelling any paid up share capital which has been lost through trading and is unrepresented in the current assets of the company, that is, bringing the balance sheet into balance at a lower level by reducing the capital liabilities in acknowledgement of the loss of assets;

- paying off any already paid up share capital that is in excess of the company's requirement, either now or in the future, that is, giving the shareholders back some of the capital that they have invested in the company.

Any proposal to reduce a company's capital is subject to confirmation by the court (s 136), on such terms as it thinks fit (s 137). For example, it is possible that the court will require the company to add the words 'and reduced' after its name, in order to warn the general public that the company has undergone such an alteration to its capital structure. In considering any capital reduction scheme, the court will take into account the interests not just of the members and creditors of the company, but of the general public as well. It should be noted that the process of capital reduction is distinct from, and treated more restrictively than, the process of capital alteration, which is governed by s 121 and is an essentially internal affair which does not affect the interests of creditors. Amongst the alterations governed by s 121 is the procedure for increasing a company's capital. As long as its articles allow for such a process, this may be achieved by the passing of an ordinary resolution to that effect. Clearly, outside creditors have no say in relation to any such decision to increases the company's capital, as it would actually increase their security. Of equal importance is the fact that existing members cannot be required to subscribe for any of the increased capital.

Distribution/dividend law

As has been seen, it is a fundamental rule of company law that capital must be maintained and that any reduction in capital is strictly controlled by the courts. This doctrine of capital maintenance led to two statements of a general rule with respect to the payment of dividends:

- dividends may only be paid out of profits;
- dividends may not be paid out of capital.

However, just as with capital, there are a number of different, not to say contradictory, ways to determine profit. The lack of certainty in this regard led to an extremely lax regulation of the manner in which dividends could be paid out to shareholders, which was only remedied by the introduction of clear and stricter rules under the CA 1980. The current rules about what may be distributed to shareholders are to be found in Pt VIII of the CA 1985 and, once again, the rules relating to public limited companies are more restrictive than those governing private companies. Section 263 of the CA 1985 imposes restrictions on companies generally and sets out the basic requirement that any distribution of a company's assets to its members must come from 'profits available for that purpose'. This latter phrase is then defined as 'accumulated realised profits (which have not been distributed or capitalised) less accumulated realised losses (which have not been written off in a reduction of capital)'. Any such profits may be either revenue or capital in origin, the key requirement being that they are realised, that is, that they are not merely paper profits.

Public companies are subject to the additional controls of s 264, which imposes a balance sheet approach to the determination of profits by requiring that:

- net assets at the time of distribution must exceed the total of called up capital plus undistributable reserves;
- the distribution must not reduce the value of the net assets below the aggregate of the total called up capital plus undistributable reserves.

The undistributable reserves include: the share premium account; capital redemption reserve fund; and the excess of accumulated unrealised profits. There are special and distinct rules relating to investment companies.

At common law, directors who knowingly paid dividends out of capital were liable to the company to replace any money so paid out, although they could seek to be indemnified by shareholders who knowingly received the payments. Section 277 of the CA 1985 additionally provides that shareholders who receive payments, with reasonable grounds to know that they are made in breach of the rules, shall be liable to repay the amount received to the company.

Purchase of own shares

It was once an extremely strict rule of company law that companies were not allowed to buy their own shares. Any such purchase was treated as a major contravention of the capital maintenance rules (*Trevor v Whitworth* (1887)). Subsequently, companies were granted the power to issue specifically redeemable shares and such a power still finds expression in s 159 of the Companies Act 1985, although there are strict controls over how any such redemption has to be financed (s 160). However, in a Green Paper in 1980, the leading academic company lawyer, Professor Gower, recommended that the right to buy back should be extended to cover all, rather than just redeemable, shares. Professor Gower's recommendations were accepted and are currently enacted in ss 162–81 of the Companies Act 1985.

The Act provides for three distinct ways in which companies can buy their own shares:

- through a market purchase, conducted under the rules of recognised investment exchange (s 166);
- through an off-market purchase, which effectively relates to any other method of purchase (s 164);
- through a contingent purchase contract, which essentially relates to options to buy shares (s 165).

The rules for financing the purchase by a company of its own shares are the same as those that apply to the redemption of redeemable shares, and are to be found in s 160 of the Companies Act 1985. The most essential rule is that no purchase or redemption is to be financed from the company's capital, and can only be paid from profits properly available for distribution to the company's members (see immediately above).

However, as in most areas of company law, there are relaxations of the strict rules in relation to private limited companies. Thus, in ss 171–75, private companies are permitted to use the company's capital to finance the purchase of their own shares, although even here the controls established are extremely rigorous.

Financial assistance for the purchase of the company's own shares

Section 151 of the CA 1985 makes it illegal for a company to provide financial assistance to any person to enable them to buy shares in the company. The company, and any officer, in breach of the section is liable to criminal sanctions. The section applies to both direct and indirect assistance, no matter whether it is given before or after the share purchase. Thus, it covers gifts, loans and any other transactions that allow the purchaser of the shares to use the company's assets to pay for those shares.

Section 153, however, provides for general exceptions to the application of s 151. Thus, lending in the ordinary course of business is not covered, nor is assistance provided for employees' share schemes. The most significant exception, however, is that provided under s 153(1), which allows the company to finance share purchases as long as it is done in good faith and in the pursuit of some larger purpose. The precise extent of this relaxation is uncertain and was not helped by the refusal to consider it in the Guinness trials or the House of Lords' confused, and confusing, decision in *Brady v Brady* (1989).

As usual, exceptions to the general rule are to be found in relation to private companies (ss 155–58), which are allowed to provide financial assistance, as long as it does not come out of the company's capital, but only from profits available for distribution.

13.6.7 Loan capital

Companies usually acquire the capital they need to engage in their particular business through the issue of shares. It is, however, also common practice for companies to borrow additional money to finance their operation. It is usual for the memorandum of association of companies to contain an express power allowing the company to borrow money, but, in any event, such power is implied as incidental to the conduct of the business of any trading company. Nonetheless, it should be remembered that public limited companies are prohibited from using their borrowing powers until they have been issued with a trading certificate under s 117 of the CA 1985. It is also possible for the articles of association to attempt to limit the borrowing powers of the directors, to whom the general power to borrow is delegated. Again, it should be remembered that, as a consequence of s 35, any such purported limitation remains an internal issue and is not effective as against an outsider.

Loans may be provided simply by a company's bank extending to it an overdraft facility. Alternatively, however, the company may use special facilities to borrow from individuals, either individually or as a group. In either case, the lender is likely to require that security is given for the loan, in order to allow them to recover the value of the loan from the company if it defaults on its interest payments or its final repayment. Even where the lender is given such security, it is essential to realise that borrowing, even when it is secured, does not give the lender any interest in the company but represents a claim against the company. The relationship between company and the provider of loan capital is the ordinary relationship of debtor/creditor, even where specific mechanisms exist to facilitate the borrowing of companies and to secure the interests of their creditors.

Debentures

In strict legal terms, a debenture is a document which acknowledges the fact that a company has borrowed money and does not refer to any security that may have been given in relation to the loan. In business practice, however, the use of the term 'debenture' is extended to cover the loan itself and usually designates a secured loan, as opposed to an unsecured one. Debentures may be issued in a variety of ways:

- Single debentures

  A debenture may be issued to a single creditor, for example a bank or other financial institution or, indeed, an individual. The debenture document will set out the terms of the loan: interest, repayment and security.

- Debentures issued in series

  Alternatively, the company may raise the specific capital that it requires from a number of different lenders. In this case, the global sum of the loan is made up from all of the individual loans. In such a situation, the intention is that each of the participant lenders should rank equally (*pari passu*) in terms of rights and security. Thus, although each lender receives a debenture, they are all identified as being part of a series and consequently have equality of rights.

- Debenture stock

  This third method is the way in which companies raise loans from the public at large. The global sum of the loan is once again raised from a large number of people, each of whom holds a proportional part of the total loan stock. The individual lender receives a debenture stock certificate, which in some ways is similar to a share certificate, at least to the extent that such debenture stock is freely transferable and may be dealt with on the stock exchange.

  The loan and the rights appertaining to it are set out in a deed of trust and a trustee for the debenture stock holders is appointed to represent and pursue the interests of the individual stockholders. In law, it is the trustee, rather than the individual lender, who is the creditor of the company, and the individual debenture stockholders have no direct relationship with the company. In this way, the individuals are relieved of the need to pursue their own causes and the company is relieved of the need to deal with a multiplicity of lenders. Of course, if the trustee fails to pursue the interests of the beneficiaries, they can have recourse to the courts to instruct him to pursue his duties. The content of the trust deed sets out the terms relating to the loan, and in particular it will detail any security and the powers of the trustee to act on behalf of the lenders to enforce that security.

Debentures may be issued as redeemable or irredeemable under s 193 of the CA 1985. In addition, they may carry the right to convert into ordinary shares at some later time. Just as with shares, debentures may be transferred from the current holder to another party, subject to the proper procedure under s 183 of the CA 1985.

However, debentures differ from shares in the following respects:

- debenture holders are creditors of the company – they are not members, as shareholders are;

- as creditors, they receive interest on their loans – they do not receive dividends, as shareholders do;

- they are entitled to receive interest, whether the company is profitable or not, even if the payment is made out of the company's capital – shareholders' dividends must not be paid out of capital;

- debentures may be issued at a discount, that is, at less than their nominal value – shares must not be issued at a discount and the company must receive the equivalent to the shares nominal value.

Company charges

As has been stated previously, it is usual for debentures to provide security for the amount loaned. 'Security' means that, in the event of the company being wound up, the creditor with a secured debt will have priority as regards repayment over any unsecured creditor. There are two types of security for company loans: fixed charge and floating charge:

- Fixed charge

  In this case, a specific asset of the company is made subject to a charge in order to secure a debt. The company cannot thereafter dispose of the property without the consent of the debenture holders. If the company fails to honour its commitments, then the debenture holders can sell the asset to recover the money owed. The asset most commonly subject to fixed charges is land, although any other long term capital asset may also be charged, as may such intangible assets as book debts. It would not be appropriate, however, to place a fixed charge against stock in trade, as the company would be prevented from freely dealing with it without the prior approval of the debenture holders. This would obviously frustrate the business purpose of the enterprise.

- Floating charge

  This category of charge does not attach to any specific property of the company until it crystallises through the company committing some act or default in relation to the loan. On the occurrence of such a crystallising event, the floating charge becomes a fixed equitable charge over the assets detailed, the value of which may be realised in order to pay the debt owed to the floating charge holder. It is usual for the document creating the floating charge to include a list of events which will effect crystallisation of the floating charge. Examples of such occurrences are typically that the company is in a position where it is unable to pay its debts; or some other holder of a charge appoints a receiver; or it ceases business or goes into liquidation.

The floating charge is most commonly made in relation to the undertaking and assets of a company. In such a situation the security is provided by all the property owned by the company, some of which may be continuously changing, such as stock in trade. The use of the floating charge permits the company to deal with its property without the need to seek the approval of the debenture holders.

Registration of charges

All charges, including both fixed and floating charges, have to be registered with the Companies Registry within 21 days of their creation (ss 395 and 396 of the CA 1985). If they are not registered, then the charge is void, that is, ineffective, against any other creditor or the liquidator of the company; but it is still valid against the company. This means that the charge holder loses priority as against other creditors.

Under s 404 of the CA 1985, the court has the power to permit late registration, that is, at some time after the initial 21 day period. In allowing any late registration, the court can impose such terms and conditions 'as seem to the court to be just and expedient'. Where the court accedes to a request for late registration, as a matter of custom, it does so with the proviso that any rights acquired as a consequence of the late registration are deemed to be without prejudice to the rights of any parties acquired before the time of actual registration. Thus, parties who lent money to the company and received security for their loans will be protected and will not lose out to the rights given under the late registration.

In addition to registration at the Companies Registry, companies are required to maintain a register of all charges on their property (s 407 of the CA 1985). Such a register has to be available for inspection by members and creditors of the company. Failure to comply with this requirement constitutes an offence but it does not invalidate the charge.

Priority of charges

In relation to properly registered charges of the same type, charges take priority according to their date of creation. Thus, although it is perfectly open for a company to create a second fixed or floating charge over assets that are already subject to such pre-existing charges, it is not possible for the company to give the later charge equality with, let alone priority over, the charge already in existence.

However, with regard to charges of different types, a fixed charge takes priority over a floating charge even though it was created after it. Generally, there is nothing to prevent the creation of a fixed charge after the issuing of a floating charge, and, as a legal charge against specific property, that fixed charge will still take priority over the earlier floating charge. The reason for this apparent anomoly lies in the whole purpose of the floating charge.

As has been seen, the floating charge was designed specifically to allow companies to continue to deal with their assets in the ordinary course of their business, without being subject to the interference of the holder of the floating charge. Consequently, the courts have held that this freedom extended to the ability to create fixed charges over the assets in order to secure later borrowings in the course of the business (*Wheatley v Silkstone and Haigh Moor Coal Co* (1885)). It is possible, however, for the debenture creating the original floating charge to include a provision preventing the creation of a later fixed charge taking priority over that floating charge. The question then is whether the registration of that restriction has any effect on subsequent debenture holders. The current position is that, for such a restrictive provision to be effective, it is necessary that the holder of the subsequent charge should have knowledge of the specific restriction in the original debenture. As registration has been held only to give constructive notice of the existence of a debenture, and not its contents, it is likely that the courts will maintain the position that subsequent charge holders are not subject to limitations contained in previous debentures, unless they actually have knowledge of the existence of such restrictions. Sections 92–107 of the CA 1989 set out procedures to deal with this particular problem, amongst others, in relation to the operation of the registration process for debentures; but unfortunately, due to several inadequacies of the proposed alterations, it was decided that the new procedures would not be introduced.

13.7 DIRECTORS

Shareholders in public limited companies typically remain external to the actual operation of the enterprise in which they have invested. They also tend to assess the performance of their investment in relation to the level of dividend payment and the related short term movement of share prices on the stock exchange rather than in relation to any long term business strategy. These factors have led to the emergence of what is known as the separation of ownership and control. As it suggests, this idea refers to the fact that those who provide a company's capital are not actually concerned in determining how that capital is used within the specific business enterprise. In effect, the day to day operation of the business enterprise is left in the hands of a small number of company directors, whilst the large majority of shareholders remain powerless to participate in the actual business from which they derive their dividend payments.

In theory, the shareholders exercise ultimate control over the directors through the mechanism of the general meeting. The separation of ownership and control, however, has resulted in the concentration of power in the hands of the directors and has given rise to the possibility that directors might operate as a self-perpetuating oligarchy which seeks to run the company in its own interests, rather than in the interests of the majority of shareholders. In light of the lack of fit between theory and practice, statute law has intervened to place a number of specific controls on the way in which directors act.

13.7.1 The position of directors

It is a feature of the companies legislation that it tends to define terms in a tautological way, using the term to be defined as part of the definition. Thus, s 741 of the CA 1989 defines the term 'director' to include any person occupying the position of director, by whatever name that person is called. The point of this definition is that it emphasises the fact that it is the function that the person performs, rather than the title given to them, that determines whether they are directors or not. Section 741 also introduces the concept of the shadow director. This is a person who, although not actually appointed to the board, instructs the directors of a company as to how to act. The point is that such a person is subject to all the controls and liabilities that the ordinary directors are subject to.

The actual position of a director may be described in a number of ways.

- they are officers of the company (s 744 of the CA 1985);
- the board of directors is the agent of the company and, under Art 84 of Table A, the board may appoint one or more managing directors. They are, therefore, able to bind the company without incurring personal liability. It should be noted that directors are not the agents of the shareholders (see below in relation to the powers of directors);
- directors are in a fiduciary relationship with their company. This means that they are in a similar position to trustees. The importance of this lies in the nature of the duties that it imposes on directors (see below);
- directors are not employees of their companies *per se*. They may, however, be employed by the company, in which case they will usually have a distinct service contract detailing their duties and remuneration. Apart from service contracts, the articles usually provide for the remuneration of directors in the exercise of their general duties.

13.7.2 Appointment of directors

The first directors are usually named in the articles or memorandum. Subsequent directors are appointed under the procedure stated in the articles. The usual procedure is for the company in general meeting to elect the directors by an ordinary resolution.

Casual vacancies are usually filled by the board of directors co-opting someone to act as director. That person then serves until the next Annual General Meeting (AGM), when they must stand for election in the usual manner.

13.7.3 Removal of directors

There are a number of ways in which a person may be obliged to give up their position as a director:

* Rotation

  Table A provides that one-third of the directors shall retire at each AGM, being those with longest service. They are, however, open to re-election and in practice are usually re-elected.

* Retirement

  Directors of public companies are required to retire at the first AGM after they have reached the age of 70. They may retire at any time before then.

* Removal

  A director can be removed at any time by the passing of an ordinary resolution of the company (s 303). The company must be given special notice (28 days) of the intention to propose such a resolution.

  The power to remove a director under s 303 cannot be taken away or restricted by any provision in the company's documents or any external contract. It is possible, however, for the effect of the section to be avoided in private companies by the use of weighted voting rights.

  In *Bushell v Faith* (1969), the articles of association of a company which had three equal shareholders, each of whom was a director, provided that, on a vote to remove a director, that person's shares would carry three votes as against its usual one. The effect of this was that a s 303 resolution could never be passed. The House of Lords held that such a procedure was legitimate, although it has to be recognised that it is unlikely that such a decision would be extended to public limited companies.

  As regards private/quasi-partnership companies, it has been held, in *Re Bird Precision Bellows Ltd* (1984), that exclusion from the right to participate in management provides a ground for an action for a court order to remedy unfairly prejudicial conduct under s 459 of the CA 1985 (see below, 13.11.2).

- Disqualification

  The articles of association usually provide for the disqualification of directors on the occurrence of certain circumstances: bankruptcy; mental illness; or prolonged absence from board meetings. In addition, there are statutory controls over directors, other officers and promoters of companies.

13.7.4 Company Directors Disqualification Act 1986

Individuals can be disqualified from acting as directors up to a maximum period of 15 years under the CDDA 1986. The Act was introduced in an attempt to prevent the misuse of the company form. One of its specific aims was the control of what are described as 'phoenix companies'. These are companies which trade until they get into financial trouble and accrue extensive debts. Upon this eventuality, the company ceases trading, only for the person behind the company to set up another company to carry on essentially the same business, but with no liability to the creditors of the former company. Such behaviour is reprehensible and is clearly an abuse of limited liability. The CDDA 1986 seeks to remedy this practice by preventing certain individuals from acting as company director, but the ambit of the Act's control is much wider than this one instance.

The CDDA 1986 identifies three distinct categories of conduct which may, and in some circumstances must, lead the court to disqualify certain persons from being involved in the management of companies:

- General misconduct in connection with companies

  This first category involves the following:

  o A conviction for an indictable offence in connection with the promotion, formation, management or liquidation of a company or with the receivership or management of a company's property (s 2 of the CDDA 1986). The maximum period for disqualification under s 2 is five years where the order is made by a court of summary jurisdiction, and 15 years in any other case.

  o Persistent breaches of companies legislation in relation to provisions which require any return, account or other document to be filed with, or notice of any matter to be given to, the registrar (s 3 of the CDDA 1986). Section 3 provides that a person is conclusively proved to be persistently in default where it is shown that, in the five years ending with the date of the application, he has been adjudged guilty of three or more defaults (s 3(2) of the CDDA 1986). This is without prejudice to proof of persistent default in any other manner. The maximum period of disqualification under this section is five years.

○ Fraud in connection with winding up (s 4 of the CDDA 1986). A court may make a disqualification order if, in the course of the winding up of a company, it appears that a person:

(1) has been guilty of an offence for which he is liable under s 458 of the CA 1985, that is, that he has knowingly been a party to the carrying on of the business of the company either with the intention of defrauding the company's creditors or any other person or for any other fraudulent purpose; or

(2) has otherwise been guilty, while an officer or liquidator of the company or receiver or manager of the property of the company, of any fraud in relation to the company or of any breach of his duty as such officer, liquidator, receiver or manager (s 4(1)(b) of the CDDA 1986).

The maximum period of disqualification under this category is 15 years.

- Disqualification for unfitness

The second category covers:

○ disqualification of directors of companies which have become insolvent, who are found by the court to be unfit to be directors (s 6 of the CDDA 1986). Under s 6, the minimum period of disqualification is two years, up to a maximum of 15 years;

○ disqualification after investigation of a company under Pt XIV of the CA 1985 (s 8 of the CDDA 1986).

A disqualification order may be made as the result of an investigation of a company under the companies legislation. Under s 8 of the CDDA 1986, the Secretary of State may apply to the court for a disqualification order to be made against a person who has been a director or shadow director of any company, if it appears from a report made by an inspector under s 437 of the CA or s 94 or 177 of the Financial Services Act 1986 that 'it is expedient in the public interest' that such a disqualification order should be made. Once again, the maximum period of disqualification is 15 years.

The CDDA 1986 sets out certain particulars to which the court is to have regard where it has to determine whether a person's conduct as a director makes them unfit to be concerned in the management of a company (s 9). The detailed list is of matters to be considered is set out in Sched 1 to the Act.

In addition, the courts have given indications as to what sort of behaviour will render a person liable to be considered unfit to act as a company director. Thus, in *Re Lo-Line Electric Motors Ltd* (1988), it was stated that:

> Ordinary commercial misjudgment is in itself not sufficient to justify disqualification. In the normal case, the conduct complained of must display a lack of commercial probity, although ... in an extreme case of gross negligence or total incompetence, disqualification could be appropriate.

A 'lack of commercial probity', therefore, will certainly render a director unfit, but, as Vinelott J stated in *Re Stanford Services Ltd* (1987):

> ... the public is entitled to be protected, not only against the activities of those guilty of the more obvious breaches of commercial morality, but also against someone who has shown in his conduct of a company a failure to appreciate or observe the duties attendant on the privilege of conducting business with the protection of limited liability.

Consequently, even where there is no dishonesty, incompetence may render a director unfit. Thus, in *Re Sevenoaks Stationers Ltd* (1990), the Court of Appeal held that the a director was unfit to be concerned in the management of a company on the basis that:

> His trouble is not dishonesty, but incompetence or negligence in a very marked degree, and that is enough to render him unfit; I do not think it is necessary for incompetence to be 'total' to render a director unfit to take part in the management of a company.

- Other cases for disqualification

This third category relates to:

- o participation in fraudulent or wrongful trading under s 213 of the IA 1986 (s 10 of the CDDA 1986);
- o undischarged bankrupts acting as directors (s 11 of the CDDA 1986); and
- o failure to pay under a county court administration order (s 12 of the CDDA 1986).

Disqualification orders

For the purposes of most of the CDDA 1986, the court has a discretion to make a disqualification order. Where, however, a person has been found to be an unfit director of an insolvent company, the court has a duty to make a disqualification order (s 6 of the CDDA 1986).

The precise nature of any such order is set out in s 1, under which the court may make an order preventing any person (without leave of the court) from being:

- a director of a company;
- a liquidator or administrator of a company;
- a receiver or manager of a company's property; or
- in any way, whether directly or indirectly, concerned with or taking part in the promotion, formation or management of a company.

However, a disqualification order may be made:

- with leave to continue to act as a director for a short period of time, in order to enable the disqualified director to arrange his business affairs (*Re Ipcon Fashions Ltd* (1989));

- with leave to continue as a director of a named company, subject to conditions (*Re Lo-Line Electric Motors Ltd* (1988));
- with leave to act in some other managerial capacity but not as director (*Re Cargo Agency Ltd* (1992)).

Period of disqualification

With regard to the period of disqualification, in *Re Sevenoaks Stationers (Retail) Ltd* (1990), Dillon LJ in the Court of Appeal divided the potential maximum 15 year period of disqualification into three distinct brackets:

- over 10 years for particularly serious cases (for example, where a director has been disqualified previously);
- two to five years for 'relatively not very serious' cases;
- a middle bracket of between six and 10 years for serious cases not meriting the top bracket.

Penalty for breach of a disqualification order

Anyone who acts in contravention of a disqualification order is liable:

- to imprisonment for up to two years and/or a fine, on conviction on indictment; or
- to imprisonment for up to six months and/or a fine not exceeding the statutory maximum, on conviction summarily (s 13 of the CDDA 1986).

13.7.5 Directors' powers

In considering the topic of directors' powers, it necessary to distinguish between the power of the directors as a board and the powers of individual directors.

The power of directors as a board

Article 70 of Table A provides that the directors of a company may exercise all the powers of the company. It is important to note that this power is given to the board as a whole and not to individual directors, although Art 72 does allow for the delegation of the board's powers to one or more directors.

Article 70 gives the board of directors general power, but the Articles may seek to restrict the authority of the board within limits expressly stated in the company's constitutional documents. The effectiveness of such restrictions has been greatly reduced by the operation of s 35 of the CA 1985, as amended by the CA 1989. As a consequence of s 35, as it now is, not only can the power of a company not be challenged on the grounds of lack of capacity: neither can the actions of its directors be challenged on the basis of any limitation contained in the company's documents. This provision is subject to the requirement that any third party must act in good faith, although such good faith is presumed, subject to proof to the contrary.

The power of individual directors

There are three ways in which the power of the board of directors may be extended to individual directors. These ways are, however, simply particular applications of the general law of agency, considered above (see 11.3).

- Express actual authority

  This category is unproblematic, in that it arises from the express conferral by the board of a particular authority onto an individual director. For example, it is possible for the board to specifically authorise an individual director to negotiate and bind the company to a particular transaction.

- Implied actual authority

  In this situation, the person's authority flows from their position. Article 84 of Table A's model articles (see above, 13.5.2) provides for the board of directors to appoint a managing director. The board of directors may confer any of their powers on the managing director as they see fit. The mere fact of appointment, however, will mean that the person so appointed will have the implied authority to bind the company in the same way as the board, whose delegate they are. Outsiders, therefore, can safely assume that a person appointed as managing director has all the powers usually exercised by a person acting as a managing director.

  Implied actual authority to bind a company may also arise as a consequence of the appointment of an individual to a position other than that of managing director.

  In *Hely-Hutchinson v Brayhead Ltd* (1968), although the chairman and chief executive of a company acted as its *de facto* managing director, he had never been formally appointed to that position. Nevertheless, he purported to bind the company to a particular transaction. When the other party to the agreement sought to enforce it, the company claimed that the chairman had no authority to bind it. It was held that, although the director derived no authority from his position as chairman of the board, he did acquire such authority from his position as chief executive; thus, the company was bound by the contract he had entered into on its behalf.

- Apparent or ostensible authority/agency by estoppel

  This arises where an individual director has neither express or implied authority. Nonetheless, the director is held out by the other members of the board of directors as having the authority to bind the company. If a third party acts on such a representation, then the company will be estopped from denying its truth.

  Problems tend to arise where someone acts as a managing director without having been properly appointed to that position. In such a situation, although the individual concerned may not have the actual authority to bind the company, they may still have apparent authority and the company may be estopped from denying their power to bind it to particular transactions.

In *Freeman and Lockyer v Buckhurst Park Properties (Mangal) Ltd* (1964), although a particular director had never been appointed as managing director, he acted as such with the clear knowledge of the other directors and entered into a contract with the plaintiffs on behalf of the company. When the plaintiffs sought to recover fees due to them under that contract, it was held that the company was liable: a properly appointed managing director would have been able to enter into such a contract and the third party was entitled to rely on the representation of the other directors that the person in question had been properly appointed to that position.

13.7.6 Directors' duties

At common law, the duties owed by directors to their company and the shareholders, employees and creditors of that company were at worst non-existent or at best notoriously lax. Statute has, by necessity, been forced to intervene to increase such duties in order to provide a measure of protection for those concerned.

Fiduciary duties

As fiduciaries, directors owe the following duties to their company (it is imperative to note that the duty is owed to the company as a distinct legal person and not the shareholders of the company, so the rule in *Foss v Harbottle* applies – see above, 13.2.3):

- The duty to act *bona fide* in the interests of the company

  In effect, this means that directors are under an obligation to act in what they genuinely believe to be the interests of the company.

- The duty not to act for any collateral purpose

  This may be seen as a corollary of the preceding duty, in that directors cannot be said to be acting *bona fide* if they use their powers for some ulterior or collateral purpose. For example, directors should not issue shares to particular individuals in order merely to facilitate, or indeed prevent, a prospective takeover bid (see *Howard Smith v Ampol Petroleum* (1974) and *Hogg v Cramphorn* (1967)). The breach of such a fiduciary duty is, however, subject to *post hoc* ratification (see *Bamford v Bamford* (1970)).

- The duty not to permit a conflict of interest and duty to arise

  This equitable rule is strictly applied by the courts and the effect of its operations may be seen in *Regal (Hastings) v Gulliver* (1942), where the directors of a company which owned one cinema provided money for the creation of a subsidiary company to purchase two other cinemas. After the parent and subsidiary companies had been sold at a later date, the directors were required to repay the profit they had made on the sale of their shares in the subsidiary company on the ground that they had only been in the situation to make that profit because of their positions as directors of the parent company. (The profits made went back to the parent company, which was by then in the hands of the person who had paid the money to the directors in the first place.)

Duty of care and skill

Common law did not place any great burden on directors in this regard. Damages could be recovered against directors for losses caused by their negligence but the level of such negligence was high. As was stated in *Lagunas Nitrate Co v Lagunas Syndicate* (1989), it must, in a business sense, be culpable or gross. The classic statement is to be found in *Re City Equitable Fire Assurance Co* (1925), which established three points:

* First, in determining the degree of skill to be expected, the common law applied a subjective test and established no minimum standard. A director was expected to show the degree of skill which might reasonably be expected of a person of their knowledge and experience. As a result, if they were particularly experienced and skilled in the affairs of their business, then they would be expected to exercise such skill in the performance of their functions. On the other hand, however, if the director was a complete incompetent, he would only be expected to perform to the level of a complete incompetent. The reasoning behind this seemed to be that the courts left it to the shareholders to elect and control the directors as their representatives. If the shareholders elected incompetents, then that was a matter for them and the courts would not interfere.

* Secondly, the duties of directors were held to be of an intermittent nature and, consequently, directors were not required to give continuous attention to the affairs of their company. In *Re Cardiff Savings Bank* (the *Marquis of Bute's* case) (1892), it emerged that the Marquis had inherited his position as president of the bank at the age of six months and, in the course of 38 years, he had only ever attended one board meeting.

* Thirdly, in the absence of any grounds for suspicion, directors were entitled to leave the day to day operation of the company's business in the hands of managers and to trust them to perform their tasks honestly.

Fraudulent and wrongful trading

The laxity of the situation at common law has been much tightened by statute, particularly by the development of the possibility of wrongful trading, which was introduced by s 214 of the IA 1986.

It should be noted that there has long been civil liability for any activity amounting to fraudulent trading. Thus, s 213 of the IA 1986 governs situations where, in the course of a winding up, it appears that the business of a company has been carried on with intent to defraud creditors, or for any fraudulent purpose. In such cases, the court, on the application of the liquidator, may declare that any persons who were knowingly parties to such carrying on of the business are liable to make such contributions (if any) to the company's assets as the court thinks proper. There is a major problem in making use of s 213, however, and that lies in meeting the very high burden of proof involved in proving dishonesty on the part of the person against whom it is alleged. It should be noted that there is also a criminal offence of fraudulent trading under s 458 of the Companies Act 1985, which applies to anyone who has been party to the carrying on of the business of a company with intent to defraud creditors or any other person, or for any other fraudulent purpose. Wrongful trading does not involve dishonesty but, nonetheless, it still makes particular individuals potentially liable for the debts of their companies. Section 214 applies where a company is being wound up and it appears that, at some time before the start of the winding up, a director knew, or ought to have known, that there was no reasonable chance of the company avoiding insolvent liquidation. In such circumstances, then, unless the directors took every reasonable step to minimise the potential loss to the company's creditors, they may be liable to contribute such money to the assets of the company as the court thinks proper. In deciding what directors ought to have known, the court will apply an objective test, as well as a subjective one. As in common law, if the director is particularly well qualified, they will be expected to perform in line with those standards. Additionally, however, s 214 of the IA 1986 establishes a minimum standard by applying an objective test which requires directors to have the general knowledge, skill and experience which may reasonably be expected of a person carrying out the same functions as are carried out by that director in relation to the company.

The manner in which incompetent directors will become liable to contribute the assets of their companies was shown in *Re Produce Marketing Consortium Ltd* (1989), in which two directors were held liable to pay compensation from the time that they ought to have known that their company could not avoid insolvent liquidation, rather than the later time when they actually realised that fact. In that case, the two directors were ordered to contribute £75,000 to the company's assets. In reaching that decision, Knox J stated that:

> In my judgement, the jurisdiction under s 214 is primarily compensatory rather than penal. *Prima facie*, the appropriate amount that a director is declared to be liable to contribute is the amount by which the company's assets can be discerned to have been depleted by the director's conduct which caused the discretion under s 214(1) to arise ... The fact that there was no fraudulent intent is not of itself a reason for fixing the amount at a nominal or low figure, for that

would amount to frustrating what I discern as Parliament's intention in adding s 214 to s 213 in the Insolvency Act 1986 ...

It should also be recalled, as considered previously, that directors may be disqualified from holding office for a period of up to 15 years under the provisions of the CDDA 1986 if they are found liable for either fraudulent or wrongful trading.

Interestingly, the common law approach to directors' duty of care has recently been extended to accommodate the requirements of s 214. Thus, in *Re D'Jan of London Ltd* (1993), Hoffman LJ, as he then was, held that the common law duty of care owed by a director to his company was as was stated in s 214 of the IA 1986, and contained both objective and subjective tests. In that particular case, the managing director of a small company had signed a proposal for fire insurance which had been filled in by his insurance broker and which contained inaccurate answers to some questions. When the insurers subsequently declined liability for a fire which destroyed the company's premises and stock, Hoffman LJ held that the director was liable to the company for breaching his duty of care.

13.8 COMPANY SECRETARY

Section 744 of the CA 1989 includes the company secretary among the officers of a company. Every company must have a company secretary and, although there are no specific qualifications required to perform such a role in a private company, s 286 of the CA 1985 requires that the directors of public company must ensure that the company secretary has the requisite knowledge and experience to discharge their functions. Section 286(2) sets out a list of professional bodies, including the ICA, ACCA, ICMA and ICSA, membership of which enables a person to act as a company secretary.

13.8.1 Duties of company secretaries

The duties of company secretaries are set by the board of directors, and therefore vary from company to company, but as an officer of the company, the secretary will be responsible for ensuring that the company complies with its statutory obligations. The following are some of the most important duties undertaken by company secretaries:

- to ensure that the necessary registers required to be kept by the Companies Acts are established and properly maintained;
- to ensure that all returns required to be lodged with the companies registry are prepared and filed within the appropriate time limits;
- to organise and attend meetings of the shareholders and directors;

- to ensure that the company's books of accounts are kept in accordance with the Companies Acts and that the annual accounts and reports are prepared in the form and at the time required by the Acts;

- to be aware of all the statutory requirements placed on the company's activities and to ensure that the company complies with them;

- to sign such documents as require their signature under the Companies Acts.

13.8.2 Powers of company secretaries

Although old authorities, such as *Houghton and Co v Northard Lowe and Wills* (1928), suggest that company secretaries have extremely limited authority to bind their company, later cases have recognised the reality of the contemporary situation and have extended to company secretaries potentially significant powers to bind their companies. As an example, consider *Panorama Developments Ltd v Fidelis Furnishing Fabrics Ltd* (1971), in which a company secretary hired cars for his own use, although he signed the documents as 'company secretary'. His company was held liable to pay for the hire of the cars. In the Court of Appeal, Lord Denning stated that a company secretary was entitled:

> ... to sign contracts connected with the administrative side of a company's affairs, such as employing staff and ordering cars and so forth. All such matters now come within the ostensible authority of a company's secretary.

Although Lord Denning dealt with the secretary's authority on the basis of ostensible authority, it would be more accurate to define it as an example of implied actual authority (see above, 11.4.1).

13.9 COMPANY AUDITOR

Section 384 of the CA 1985 requires all companies to appoint an auditor, whose duty it is under s 235 of the CA 1985 to report to the company's members as to whether or not the company's accounts have been properly prepared and to consider whether the directors' report is consistent with those accounts.

In the case of a newly registered company, the first auditors are appointed by the directors until the first general meeting, at which they may be reappointed by the members of the company. Thereafter, auditors are appointed annually at general meetings at which accounts are laid (s 385 of the CA 1985). It should be recalled that private companies may, by means of an elective resolution, dispense with the requirement to appoint auditors annually. In such circumstances, the existing auditor is deemed to be reappointed for each succeeding year (s 386 of the CA 1985). The Secretary of

State has the power to appoint an auditor where the company has not appointed one (s 387 of the CA 1985).

Section 389 provides that a person can only be appointed as an auditor where he is a member of a recognised supervisory body such as the Institute of Certified Accountants or the Chartered Association of Certified Accountants. A person cannot be appointed where he is an officer or employee of the company in question.

Auditors are appointed to ensure that the company is being run on a proper basis. They represent the interests of the shareholders and report to them. They are, however, employed by the company and owe their contractual duty to the company rather than the shareholders. As partnerships may now be appointed as auditors (s 26 of the CA 1989), some concern has been expressed that the large accountancy firms might offer auditor services as a loss leader, in order to acquire more lucrative accountancy deals with the company. The concern is that this might lead to a conflict of interest between the accountancy firm's role as auditor and its other roles in relation to the company.

Auditors are required to make a report on all annual accounts laid before the company in general meeting during their tenure of office (s 235(1)). The report must state the names of the auditors and must be signed by them (s 236(1) and (3)).

The auditors are required to report (s 235(2)): whether the accounts have been properly prepared in accordance with the CA 1989; and whether the individual and group accounts show a true and fair view of the profit or loss and state of affairs of the company and of the group, so far as concerns the members of the company.

Auditors are required to make the necessary investigations and consider the following, which need only be reported on if there are deficiencies: whether the company has kept proper accounting records and obtained proper accounting returns from branches (s 237(1) and (2)); whether the accounts are in agreement with the records (s 237(1) and (2)); whether they have obtained all the information and explanations that they considered necessary (s 237(3)); whether the requirements of Sched 6, concerning disclosure of information about directors and officers remuneration, loans and other transactions, have been met; and whether the information in the directors' report is consistent with the accounts (s 235(3)).

Where the company circulates a summary financial statement, the auditors are required to give a report on whether the summary statement is consistent with the company's annual accounts and directors' report, and whether it complies with the requirements of the CA 1985 and regulations in relation to this statement (s 251(4)(b)).

If the auditors' report does not state that, in their unqualified opinion, the accounts have been properly prepared in accordance with the relevant legislation governing the relevant undertakings accounts (s 262(1)), then the accounts are said to be qualified.

Auditors have the right of access at all times to the company's books and accounts, and officers of the company are required to provide such information and explanations as the auditors consider necessary (s 389A of the CA 1985). It is a criminal offence to make false or reckless statements to auditors (s 389A). Auditors are entitled to receive notices and other documents in connection with all general meetings, to attend such meetings and to speak when the business affects their role as auditors (s 390). Where a company operates on the basis of written resolutions rather than meetings, then the auditor is entitled to receive copies of all such proposed resolutions as are to be sent to members (s 381B).

An auditor may be removed at any time by ordinary resolution of the company (s 391(1) of the CA 1985). This does, however, require special notice. Any auditor who is to be removed or not reappointed is entitled to make written representations and require these to be circulated or have them read out at the meeting (s 391A).

An auditor may resign at any time (s 392 of the CA 1985). Notice of resignation must be accompanied by a statement of any circumstances that the auditor believes ought to be brought to the attention of members and creditors, or, alternatively, a statement that there are no such circumstances (s 394). The company is required to file a copy of the notice with the registrar of companies within 14 days (s 392). Where the auditor's resignation statement states that there are circumstances that should be brought to the attention of members, then he may require the company to call a meeting to allow an explanation of those circumstance to the members of the company (s 392A(1)).

The tortious liability of auditors is considered above, 10.7.1.

13.10 COMPANY MEETINGS

In theory, the ultimate control over a company's business lies with the members in general meeting. In practice, however, the residual powers of the membership are restricted to their ultimate control over the company's memorandum and articles of association, although this control has been reduced by the introduction of the new s 35 of the CA 1985, as effected by the CA 1989, together with their control over the composition of the board of directors. The reality of such limited theoretical powers are further constrained by the practicalities involved with the operation of company meetings.

In line with this approach, some powers are specifically reserved to the members by statute, such as the right to petition for voluntary winding up;

and Art 70 of Table A provides that the shareholders, by passing a special resolution, can instruct the directors to act in a particular way. In reality, the ideal typical shareholder tends either not to be bothered to take an active part in the conduct of company meetings or to use their votes in a way directed by the board of directors.

One would obviously conclude that a meeting involved more than one person and, indeed, there is authority to that effect in *Sharp v Dawes* (1876). In that case, a meeting between a lone member and the company secretary was held not to be validly constituted. It is possible, however, for a meeting of only one person to take place in the following circumstances:

- in the case of a meeting of a particular class of shareholders and all the shares of that class are owned by the one member;

- by virtue of s 371 of the CA 1985, the court may order the holding of a general meeting, at which the quorum is to be one member. This eventuality might arise in a quasi-partnership where a recalcitrant member of a two-person company refused to attend any meetings, thus preventing the continuation of the enterprise.

13.10.1 Types of meetings

There are three types of meeting:

- Annual general meeting

  By virtue of s 366 of the CA 1985, every company is required to hold an AGM every calendar year, subject to a maximum period of 15 months between meetings. This means that, if a company holds its AGM on 1 January 2001, then it must hold its next AGM by 31 March 2002 at the latest.

  In line with the recognised distinction between public and private companies, the CA 1989 introduced a provision in the form of a new s 366A, which permitted private companies, subject to approval by a unanimous vote, to dispense with the holding of an AGM.

  If a company fails to hold an AGM, then any member may apply to the Secretary of State, under s 367 of the CA 1989, to call a meeting in default.

- Extraordinary general meeting

  An extraordinary general meeting (EGM) is any meeting other than an AGM. EGMs are usually called by the directors, although members holding 10% of the voting shares may requisition such a meeting.

- Class meeting

  This refers to the meeting of a particular class of shareholder, that is, those who hold a type of share providing particular rights, such as preference shares (considered above, 13.6.3).

Under s 381A of the CA 1985, it is no longer necessary for a private company to convene a general meeting where the members have unanimously signed a written resolution setting out a particular course of action.

13.10.2 Calling meetings

Meetings may be convened in a number of ways by various people:

- by the *directors* of the company under Art 37 of Table A. Apart from this usual power, directors of public limited companies are required, under s 142 of the CA 1985, to call meetings where there has been a serious loss of capital, defined as the assets falling to half or less than the nominal value of the called up share capital;

- by the *members* using the power to requisition a meeting under s 368 of the CA 1985. To require the convening of a company meeting, any shareholders must hold at least one-10th of the share capital carrying voting rights. If the directors fail to convene a meeting as required within 21 days of the deposit of the requisition, although the actual date of the meeting may be within eight weeks of the date of requisition, then the requisitionists may themselves convene a meeting and recover any expenses from the company;

- by the *auditor* of a company under s 392A of the CA 1985, which provides for a resigning auditor to require the directors to convene a meeting in order to explain the reason for the auditor's resignation;

- the *Secretary of State* may, under s 367 of the CA 1985, on the application of any member, call a meeting of a company where it has failed to hold an AGM as required under s 366;

- the *court* may order a meeting under s 371 of the CA 1985 where it is otherwise impracticable to call a meeting.

13.10.3 Notice of meetings

Proper and adequate notice must be sent to all those who are entitled to attend any meeting, although the precise nature of the notice is governed by the articles of association.

Details of the following must be given:

- Time

  This is set out in s 369 of the CA 1985. The minimum period of notice is 21 clear days for an AGM and 14 clear days for all other meetings, except those called to consider a special resolution, which also require 21 clear days' notice. Shorter notice is permissible in the case of an AGM where all the members entitled to attend agree; and in the case of any other meeting where holders of 95% of the nominal value of the voting shares agree.

Private companies, by means of an elective resolution, may reduce this latter requirement to 90%.

• Content

Adequate notice of the content of any resolution must be sent to members, so that they can decide whether to attend the meeting or to appoint a proxy to vote in line with their instructions. In respect of anything other than standard business, it is desirable that the full text of any resolution to be put to the meeting be circulated to all of the members entitled to vote on it.

13.10.4 Agenda

It is usually the prerogative of the directors to decide which motions will be put to the company in the general meeting. Members, however, may set the agenda where they have requisitioned an EGM under the procedure established in s 368 (see above, 13.10.2). In relation to an AGM, s 376 provides a procedure whereby a minority of members, amounting to one-20th of the total voting rights or 100 members holding an average of £100 worth of shares, may have a motion considered. This mechanism is complicated and expensive, and the difficulties involved in putting it into practice, especially in large public companies, means that it is not often used.

The difficulties involved in ordinary members getting issues onto the agenda also extend to resolutions to remove directors. Although s 303 provides for the removal of directors on the passing of an ordinary resolution, it was held in *Pedley v Inland Waterways Association Ltd* (1977) that a disgruntled member could only get such a resolution onto the agenda if he satisfied the requirements of s 376.

13.10.5 Types of resolutions

There are essentially three types of resolution:

• Ordinary resolution

This requires a simple majority of those voting. Members who do not attend or appoint a proxy, or who attend but do not vote, are disregarded.

Notice in relation to an ordinary resolution depends on the type of meeting at which it is proposed: the required period is 21 days for an AGM and 14 days for an EGM, although, in relation to an ordinary resolution to remove a director under s 303, the company must be given special notice of 28 days. It should be noted that, in this latter case, the notice is given to the company, whereas it is usually the company that is required to give notice to the members.

- Extraordinary resolution

  Section 378(1) of the CA 1985 provides that an extraordinary resolution is one passed by a three-quarters majority of votes cast at a meeting convened by a notice specifying the intention to propose such a resolution. As no period of notice is stated in s 378, it would appear that, unless the articles provide for a longer period, the minimum period of notice will be the 14 days ordinarily laid down for EGMs, or 21 days for AGMs, under s 369 of the CA 1985. The effect of linking the notice of the resolution to the notice for the meeting is that the minimum 14 day period of notice can be reduced with the approval of the appropriate majority, that is, those representing at least 95% of the authorised capital of the company (s 369(4) of the CA 1985). This latter majority may be reduced by the passing of an elective resolution to that effect in a private company (see below).

  The requirement for meetings to pass extraordinary resolutions is not a common one. However, s 125 of the CA 1985 provides for the variation of class rights, other than those contained in the memorandum, by an extraordinary resolution of the class concerned, where the articles of association do not provide for variation. Also, although it is normally necessary for the company to pass a special resolution in order to be wound up voluntarily, an extraordinary resolution can be used on the grounds of insolvency (s 84 of the IA 1986).

- Special resolution

  A special resolution is one that has been passed by a majority of not less than three-quarters at a general meeting, of which not less than 21 days' notice has been given, such notice having specified the intention to propose the resolution as a special resolution (s 378(2) of the CA 1985). The 21 day notice period may be shortened, as with extraordinary resolutions, under s 368 of the CA 1985. The companies legislation requires special resolutions to be passed in so many situations that they cannot all be listed here. Amongst those in the CA 1985 are the following examples:

  - alteration to objects clause (s 4);
  - alteration of articles (s 9);
  - change of company name (s 28);
  - re-registration of a private company as a public company (s 430) and vice versa (s 53);
  - reduction of capital (s 135).

Written resolutions

By virtue of s 381A of the CA 1985, anything which in the case of a private company might be done by resolution in a general or class meeting may be done by resolution in writing, signed by, or on behalf of, all members who would be entitled to attend and vote at such meeting. However, resolutions for the removal of directors or auditors before expiry of their term of office cannot be the subject of written resolutions. The effect of s 381A is that private companies no longer have to call meetings or give notice for resolutions.

The written resolution requires unanimity. The members can, however, sign different pieces of paper, so long as each accurately states the terms of the resolution (s 381A(2) of the CA 1985).

Directors or the secretary must ensure that the company's auditor receives a copy of the resolution before the members receive it, but, although failure to comply with this provision may render the person liable to a fine, it does not affect the validity of the resolution. The date of a written resolution is the date when the last member signs it (s 381B(3) of the CA 1985) and the company is required keep a record of any written resolutions.

Elective resolutions

Under s 379A of the CA 1985, a private company may dispense with certain procedural requirements of the Act by passing an elective resolution to that effect. Five possibilities are set out in s 379A, but the Secretary of State can alter the list by statutory instrument (s 117 of the CA 1989).

Elective resolutions may be passed:

- to provide directors with permanent authority to allot shares (s 80A);
- to dispense with laying accounts and reports before the general meeting (s 252);
- to dispense with the holding of AGMs (s 366A);
- to reduce the majority required to consent to short notice of a meeting (s 369);
- to dispense with the appointment of auditors annually (s 386).

An elective resolution requires 21 days' notice to be given of the meeting at which it is to be proposed. It also and requires unanimity of all members entitled to attend and vote. The members may agree unanimously to dispense with the notice requirement. An elective resolution may be revoked by an ordinary resolution. Finally, it should be noted that an elective resolution may be passed by written resolution.

It *was* the case that elective resolutions required 21 days' notice; however, under the Deregulation (Resolutions of Private Companies) Order 1996, itself made under the Deregulation and Contracting Out Act 1994, that requirement has been removed and such a resolution is effective notwithstanding that less than 21 days' notice was given. It is still the case that unanimity is required both to pass the resolution and to accept the shorter notice. So, all those entitled to attend and vote at a meeting must approve of the resolution, but it should also be noted that elective resolutions can themselves be passed, using the procedure for passing written resolutions.

13.10.6 Quorum

This is the minimum number of persons whose presence is required for the transaction of business at any meeting. The precise details are set out in the articles of association, although s 370 and Art 41 of Table A set the minimum at two, who must be continuously present at the meeting.

13.10.7 Votes

A resolution is decided upon initially by a show of hands, unless a poll is demanded. On a show of hands, every member has one vote. In a poll, it is usual for each share to carry a vote and, thus, for the outcome of the poll to reflect concentration of interest in the company (for exceptions to this, see *Bushell v Faith* (1969), above, 13.7.3).

Article 41 of Table A enables any two members or the chairman to call for a poll.

13.10.8 Proxies

Section 372 of the CA 1985 provides that any member of a company who is entitled to attend and vote at a meeting may appoint another person as their proxy, that is, to act as their agent in exercising the member's voting right. Every notice of a meeting must state the member's right to appoint a proxy and, although the articles may require notice of the appointment of a proxy to be given to the company, they may not require more than 48 hours' notice. Proxies need not be members of the company. They have no right to speak at meetings of public companies but may speak in private companies. They are not allowed to vote on a show of hands, but only in regard to a poll vote.

13.10.9 Chairman

Although s 370 provides that any member may act as chair, Art 43 of Table A (see above, 13.5.2) states that the chairman of the board of directors shall preside. The chairman conducts the meeting and must preserve order and ensure that it complies with the provisions of the companies legislation and the company's articles. He or she may adjourn it with the consent of, or where instructed to do so by, the meeting. The chairman has a casting vote in the case of equality. He or she is under a general duty at all times to act *bona fide* in the interests of the company as a whole, and thus must use his or her vote appropriately.

13.10.10 Minutes

Section 382 requires that minutes of all general meetings and directors' meetings must be kept and are regarded as evidence of the proceedings when signed by the chairman.

13.11 MAJORITY RULE AND MINORITY PROTECTION

It has been seen how the day to day operation of a company's business is left in the hands of its directors and managers, with shareholders having no direct input into business decisions. Even when the members convene in general meetings, the individual shareholder is subject to the wishes of the majority, as expressed in the passing of appropriate resolutions. In normal circumstances, the minority has no grounds to complain, even though the effect of majority rule may place them in a situation they do not agree with. Even where the minority shareholders suspect that some wrong has been done to the company, it is not normally open to them to take action. This situation is encapsulated in what is known as the rule in *Foss v Harbottle* (1843) (see above, 13.2.3), where individual members were not permitted to institute proceedings against the directors of their company. It was held that, if any wrong had been committed, it had been committed against the company, and it was for the company acting through the majority to decide to institute proceedings. A more recent example of the operation of this rule may be seen in *Stein v Blake* (1998), in which the court refused to allow an individual shareholder to pursue an action against a sole director for his alleged misappropriation of the company's property. Although the shareholder did suffer a loss as a consequence of the fall of value in his shares, that loss was a reflection of the loss sustained by the company; consequently, it was for the company, and not the shareholder, to take any action against the director.

It is important to distinguish the various ways in which one or more minority shareholders may take action against the company, the directors or the majority shareholders.

In a personal action, shareholders sue in their own name to enforce personal rights. An example might be where the individuals' voting rights are denied, as in *Pender v Lushington* (1877).

A representative action is a collective action taken where the rights of other shareholders have been affected by the alleged wrongdoing. Once again, if the rights in question are membership rights, the rule in *Foss v Harbottle* does not apply.

A derivative action is the usual form of action, where minority shareholders sue under the fraud on the minority exception to the rule in *Foss v Harbottle* (see below, 13.11.1). The claimants sue in their own name, usually in representative form on behalf of themselves and all the other shareholders, except those who are named as defendants. The defendants in the action are, first, the alleged wrongdoers and, secondly, the company itself. As the claimant shareholders are seeking to redress a corporate wrong, they are actually seeking a remedy on the company's behalf. As a result, if the action is successful, the judgment takes the form of an order against the first defendants and in favour of the company as second defendant. With regard to the costs of such an action, it was held in *Wallersteiner v Moir (No 2)* (1975) that, where the minority shareholder has reasonable grounds for bringing the action, the company itself should be liable, on the basis that the individual was acting not for himself but for the company.

Particular problems may arise where those in effective control of a company use their power in such a way as either to benefit themselves or cause a detriment to the minority shareholders. In the light of such a possibility, the law has intervened to offer protection to minority shareholders. The source of the protection may be considered in three areas.

13.11.1 Common law – fraud on the minority

At common law, it has long been established that those controlling the majority of shares are not to be allowed to use their position of control to perpetrate what is known as a fraud on the minority. In such circumstances, the individual shareholder will be able to take legal action in order to remedy their situation. Thus, in *Menier v Hooper's Telegraph Works* (1874), the plaintiff, who was the majority shareholder in the company, had entered into a contract with it to lay a submarine telegraph cable. However, he was approached by another party with a more lucrative offer to lay a cable for them. As a result, he used his majority power to cause his company to abandon its contract, allowing him to pursue the other one. It was held that, in the face of such an abuse of power amounting to fraud, a minority shareholder could pursue a derivative action, the result of which required the majority shareholder to account to the company for any profits made on the second contract. Similarly, in *Cook v Deeks* (1916), directors, who were also the majority shareholders of a company, negotiated a contract on its behalf. They then took the contract for themselves and used their majority voting power to pass a resolution declaring that the company had no interest in the contract. On an action by the minority shareholder in the company, it was held that the majority could not use their votes to ratify what was a fraud on the minority. The contract belonged to the company in equity and the directors had to account to the company for the profits they made on it. Thus, the minority shareholder was not excluded from benefiting from the contract.

Fraud

The foregoing cases provide clear cut examples of fraudulent activity, but there are less clear cut situations relating to the issue of fraud. What is certain is that mere negligence, in the absence of any more serious allegation of fraud, will not permit a derivative action. Thus, in *Pavlides v Jensen* (1956), a company sold an asbestos mine for £182,000, although a minority shareholder claimed that it was worth £1 million. An action by the minority shareholder failed, on the basis that the directors had done nothing unlawful, and, in the absence of any assertion of fraud on their part, any negligence they had shown could have been ratified by the majority of shareholders. The case, therefore, clearly fell within the scope of the rule in *Foss v Harbottle*. However, the meaning of fraud, with specific reference to fraud on the minority, was extended in *Daniels v Daniels* (1977). In this case, a married couple were the directors and majority shareholders in the company. The company bought land for £4,250 and later sold it, at the same price, to the female director. She subsequently sold it for £120,000. A minority shareholder's action was successful, in spite of *Pavlides v Jensen*, and the fact that no allegation of fraud was raised against the majority shareholders. In the view of Templeman J:

> If a minority shareholder can sue if there is fraud, I see no reason why they cannot sue where the action of the majority, and the directors, though without fraud, confers some benefit on those directors or majority shareholders.

Thus, it can be seen that the meaning of 'fraud' in this regard has been extended to cover negligence on the part of the majority where the majority themselves benefit from that negligence.

Minority

In normal circumstances, control is the correlation of holding the majority of the voting shares in a company. However, the meaning of 'control' has also been extended by the courts in relation to fraud on the minority. In *Prudential Assurance Co Ltd v Newman Industries Ltd (No 2)* (1980), the chair and vice chair of a public company controlled a substantial, but nonetheless minority, shareholding in that company through another company. They proposed that the public company should buy the share capital of the second company, on the basis of the latter's supposed asset value. It was subsequently alleged that the information provided by the chair and vice chair to the general meeting which approved the purchase was incomplete and misleading. Prudential, which was a minority shareholder in the company, sought to pursue a derivative action on the basis of the common law exceptions to the rule in *Foss v Harbottle*. At first instance, it was held that the action could proceed, as, although the chair and vice chair did not constitute majority shareholders, they did control the flow of information to the company's board, its advisers and the general meeting. On that basis, they could be said to control the company. Although the directors' appeal on the substance of the allegation was upheld in the Court of Appeal, the above point was not overruled, and so remains effective.

In relation to voting rights, it was stated in *Greenhalgh v Arderne Cinemas Ltd* (1950) that shareholders were entitled to pursue their own interests when voting. However, there is judicial authority for the suggestion that special restrictions apply to the way in which majority shareholders are permitted to use their voting powers. Thus, in *Clemens v Clemens Bros Ltd* (1976), a majority shareholder was prevented from using her voting power in such a way as would affect the rights of a minority shareholder. Much time has been spent trying to explain, and justify, the decision in *Clemens*, but it should be recognised that the case involved a private, family-run company and its application should be restricted to such a case. It certainly will not be applied in regard to public companies (*Re Astec (BSR) plc* (1998)).

The Law Commission Report, *Shareholder Remedies* (No 246, Cm 3769), which was issued in October 1997, recommended the partial abolition of the rule in *Foss v Harbottle* and its exceptions and the replacement of the existing procedure by a new statutory action.

13.11.2 Statutory protection

In circumstances where the minority shareholders disagree with the actions of the majority, but without that action amounting to fraud on the minority, one remedy is simply to leave the company. In a listed public limited company, this procedure is easily achieved by selling the shares held, but things are more difficult in the case of small, private companies. In these quasi-partnership cases, an alternative to bringing a derivative action in the name of the company is to petition to have the company wound up or to apply to the court for an order to remedy any unfairly prejudicial conduct.

Just and equitable winding up

Section 122(g) of the IA 1986 gives the court the power to wind up a company if it considers it just and equitable to do so. Such an order may be applied for where there is evidence of a lack of probity on the part of some of the members. It may also be used in small private companies to provide a remedy where either there is deadlock on the board or a member is removed from the board altogether or refused a part in the management of the business.

In *Re Yenidje Tobacco Co Ltd* (1916), the company only had two shareholders, who also acted as its directors. After quarrelling, the two directors refused to communicate with one another, except through the company secretary. It was held that the company was essentially a partnership and that, as a partnership would have been wound up in this eventuality, the company should be wound up as well.

In *Re Westbourne Galleries* (1973), a business which two parties had previously carried on as a partnership was transformed into a private limited company. After a time, one of the two original partners was removed from the board of directors of the company. It was held that the removal from the board and the consequential loss of the right to participate in the management of the business were grounds for winding up the company. In reaching his decision in the House of Lords, Lord Wilberforce made the following observations, which go a long way to explain *Clemens v Clemens Ltd* (1976) and have important implications for the operation of actions for unfairly prejudicial conduct under s 459 of the CA 1985 (see below):

> The words ['just and equitable'] are a recognition of the fact that a limited company is more than a mere judicial entity, with a personality in law of its own; that there is room in company law for recognition of the fact that behind it, or amongst it; there are individuals, with rights, expectations and obligations *inter se* which are not necessarily submerged in the company structure ... The 'just and equitable' provision does not, as the respondents suggest, entitle one party to disregard the obligation he assumed by entering a company, nor the court to dispense him from it. It does, as equity always does, enable the court to subject the exercise of legal rights to equitable considerations; considerations, that is, of a personal character arising between one individual and another, which may make it unjust, or inequitable, to insist on legal rights or to exercise them in a particular way.

> It would be impossible, and wholly undesirable, to define the circumstances in which these considerations may arise. Certainly, the fact that a company is a small one, or a private company, is not enough. There are very many of these where the association is a purely commercial one, of which it can safely be said that the basis of association is adequately and exhaustively laid down in the articles. The superimposition of equitable considerations requires something more, which typically may include one, or probably more, of the following elements: (a) an association formed or continued on the basis of a personal relationship, involving mutual confidence – this element will often be found where a pre-existing partnership has been converted into a limited company; (b) an agreement, or understanding, that all, or some (for there may be 'sleeping' members), of the shareholders shall participate in the conduct of the business; (c) restriction on the transfer of the members' interest in the company so that, if confidence is lost, or one member is removed from management, he cannot take out his stake and go elsewhere.

Unfairly prejudicial conduct

Use of the procedure under s 122 of the IA 1986 is likely to have extremely serious consequences for a business. Indeed, the fact that the company has to be wound up will probably result in losses for all the parties concerned. It is much better if some less mutually destructive process can be used to resolve disputes between members of private companies.

Under s 459 of the CA 1985, any member may petition the court for an order on the ground that the affairs of the company are being conducted in a way that is unfairly prejudicial to the interests of some of the members or the members generally. Section 461 gives the court general discretion as to the precise nature and content of any order it makes to remedy the situation. The following case demonstrates the operation and scope of the procedure.

In *Re London School of Electronics* (1986), the petitioner held 25% of the shares in the company LSE. The remaining 75% were held by another company, CTC. Two directors of LSE, who were also directors and the principal shareholders in CTC, diverted students from LSE to CTC. The petitioner claimed that such action deprived him of his share in the potential profit to be derived from those students. It was held that the action was unfairly prejudicial and the court instructed CTC to purchase the petitioners shares in LSE at a value which was to be calculated as if the students had never been transferred.

In *Re Ringtower Holdings plc* (1989), Gibson J made the following four points in relation to the operation of s 459:

(1) the relevant conduct (of commission or omission) must relate to the affairs of the company of which the petitioners are members;

(2) the conduct must be both prejudicial (in the sense of causing prejudice or harm) to the relevant interests and also unfairly so: conduct may be unfair without being prejudicial or prejudicial without being unfair and in neither case would the section be satisfied;

(3) the test is of unfair prejudice, not of unlawfulness, and conduct may be lawful but unfairly prejudicial;

(4) the relevant interests are the interests of members (including the petitioners) as members, but such interests are not necessarily limited to strict legal rights under the company's constitution, and the court may take into account wider equitable considerations such as any legitimate expectation which a member has which go beyond his legal rights.

The s 459 procedure has also been used in cases where a member has been excluded from exercising a 'legitimate expectation' of participating in the management of a company business (see *Re Bird Precision Bellows Ltd* (1984)). And, in *Re Sam Weller and Sons Ltd* (1990), the court decided that a failure to pay dividends may amount to unfairly prejudicial conduct.

In *Re Elgindata Ltd* (1991), it was held that, depending on the circumstances of the case, serious mismanagement could constitute unfairly prejudicial conduct, although the court would normally be reluctant to make such a finding. On the facts of that case, evidence of mismanagement was found, together with a lack of managerial purposefulness, but it was not sufficient to amount to unfairly prejudicial conduct. However, in *Re Macro (Ipswich) Ltd* (1994), the court found that mismanagement in relation to two companies had been so bad as to warrant the requirement that the majority shareholder and sole director in both companies should buy out the minority. The order was made to the effect that the price to be paid should ignore the current value of the shares and value them as if the mismanagement had not taken place.

Although s 459 is referred to, and tends to be thought of, as a minority shareholders' remedy, it has been held that it is equally open to the majority shareholders to use it under appropriate circumstances (*Re Legal Costs Negotiators Ltd* (1998)).

As stated previously, the powers of the court under s 461 are extremely wide and extent to making 'such orders as it thinks fit for giving relief in respect of the matters complained of'. Section 461(2) provides examples of such orders but expressly states that any such are 'without prejudice to the generality of sub-s (1)'. The examples cited in the section are powers to:

- regulate the conduct of the company's affairs in the future;
- require the company to refrain from doing or continuing an act complained of by the petitioner or to do an act which the petitioner has complained that it omitted to do;
- authorise civil proceedings to be brought in the name and on behalf of the company, by such person or persons and on such terms as the court may direct;
- provide for the purchase of the shares of any members of the company by other members or by the company itself, and, in the case of a purchase by the company itself, the reduction of the company's capital accordingly.

The ambit of judicial discretion extends to not providing a remedy, even where there has been unfairly prejudicial conduct (*Re Full Cup International Trading Ltd* (1998)).

It should be noted, however, that when the House of Lords came to consider the ambit of s 459 in *O'Neill v Phillips* (1999), it adopted a restraining role in the extent to which the term 'legitimate expectation' should be interpreted in order to permit access to the remedies available under s 459. As Lord Hoffman put it, the term should not be allowed to 'lead a life of its own' as a way of justifying judicial intervention in business relationships. On the facts of the case, the House of Lords declined to award a remedy under s 459 simply on the basis of a breakdown of a previous relationship of trust and confidence. Rather, it required that prejudicial conduct should be clearly demonstrated, which was not the situation in the immediate case.

Section 459 is an extremely active area of company law and has replaced s 122 of the IA 1986 as the most appropriate mechanism for alleviating the distress suffered by minority shareholders. It is essential, however, to note that the cases considered above all involved economic partnerships which had merely assumed the company legal form as a matter of internal and external convenience. The same outcomes would not be forthcoming in relation to public limited companies. The statutory protections still apply in the case of public companies but it is extremely unlikely that they would be used as freely or as widely as they are in quasi-partnership cases. As evidence of this claim, see *Re A Company 003843* (1986), in which the exclusion of a party from management was held not to be unfairly prejudicial, as the business had not been established on a quasi-partnership basis (see, also, *Re Astec (BSR) plc* (1999)).

The Law Commission Report, *Shareholder Remedies* (see above, 13.11.1), made a number of proposals designed to reduce the number of, and speed up the trials of, such actions. Amongst the recommendations were:

- that there should be greater use of case management powers by the courts;

- that there should be a statutory presumption that, in quasi-partnerships instances, the exclusion of a member from management is unfairly prejudicial conduct justifying the award of a buyout order on a *pro rata* basis;

- that actions under s 459 of the CA 1985 should be subject to a limitation period;

- that a petitioner should, with the leave of the court, be able to seek the winding up of the company as a form of s 459 of the CA 1985.

In addition, the Report recommended that there should be a new, but non-compulsory, provision in Table A, providing 'exit rights' for shareholders. This would give shareholders the right to require their fellow shareholders to buy out their shareholding.

13.11.3 Investigations

In order for minority shareholders to complain, they must know what is going on in their company. It is part of their situation as minority shareholders, however, that they do not have access to all the information that is available to the directors of the company. As a possible means of remedying this lack of information and, thus, as a means of supporting minority protection, the Department of Trade and Industry has been given extremely wide powers to conduct investigations into the general affairs of companies, their membership and their dealings in their securities. Such powers are framed extremely widely and the courts have accepted the need for such wide powers. As Lord Denning stated in *Norwest Holst Ltd v Secretary of State for Trade* (1978):

> It is because companies are beyond the reach of ordinary individuals that this legislation has been passed so as to enable the Department of Trade to appoint inspectors to investigate the affairs of a company.

Such theoretical power as is possessed by the Secretary of State for Trade and Industry is much diluted in practice by a reluctance on the part of government to finance their use.

Bearing in mind the foregoing caveat, the Secretary of State has the power under s 431 of the CA 1985 to appoint inspectors to investigate the affairs of a company on application by the following:

- the company itself, after passing an ordinary resolution;
- members holding 10% of the company's issued share capital;
- 200 or more members.

However, s 431(3) requires that any such application must be supported by such evidence as the Secretary of State may require for the purpose of showing that the applicant has good reason for requiring the investigation. This at least somewhat undermines the whole purpose of the exercise. Shareholders may want an investigation because, although they might suspect that something untoward is going on, they do not know exactly what is happening in their company. Yet, before they can get such an investigation, they have to supply evidence that something is going on, which is exactly the reason why they want the investigation in the first place.

The Secretary of State may also require the applicant to give security of up to £5,000 before appointing inspectors (s 431(4)).

Under s 432 of the CA 1985, the Secretary of State may order such an investigation where:

- the company's affairs have been conducted with intent to defraud creditors, or for an unlawful or fraudulent purpose;
- the company's affairs have been conducted in a manner which is unfairly prejudicial to some of the members;
- the promoters or managers have been found guilty of fraud;
- the shareholders have not been supplied with proper information.

Once appointed, the investigators have very wide powers. Thus, inspectors appointed under ss 431 or 432 of the CA 1985 may also investigate the affairs of any other body corporate which is or has been in the same group, if they consider it necessary (s 433).

The inspectors also have extensive powers to require production of company documents, that is, any information recorded in any form. Information which is not in legible form can be required to be produced in legible form. All officers and agents of the company being investigated and of any related company that is being investigated are required:

- to produce for the inspectors all documents concerning the company or related company which are in their custody or power;
- to attend before the inspectors when required to do so; and
- otherwise to give the inspectors all assistance in connection with the investigation which they are reasonably able to give (s 434(1) of the CA 1985).

The inspectors' powers extend to any person who is or may be in possession of information relating to a matter which the inspectors believe may be relevant to the investigation (s 434(2) of the CA 1985); so, for example, banks may be required to provide information about any clients who are under investigation.

Failure to comply with these requirements renders an individual liable for contempt of the court (s 436 of the CA 1985).

Both during and at the end of an investigation, inspectors are required to report to the Secretary of State (s 437 of the CA 1985). Inspectors may or, if the Secretary of State so directs, must inform the Secretary of State of any matters coming to their knowledge as a result of their investigations (s 437).

The Secretary of State may, if he thinks fit, cause the report to be printed and published (s 437(3)(c)). The Secretary of State has a discretion as to whether to publish the report (*R v Secretary of State for Trade and Industry ex p Lonrho plc* (1989)).

Where the investigation has been carried out on the order of the court under s 432 of the CA 1985, the Secretary of State must provide a copy of any report to the court.

Under s 439 of the CA 1985, the expenses of an investigation are met in the first instance by the Secretary of State. The following persons, however, may be liable to reimburse the Secretary:

- any person who is convicted on a prosecution as a result of the investigation or who is ordered to pay damages or restore property may, in the same proceedings, be ordered to pay the expenses or part of them;

- any company in whose name proceedings are brought is liable to the amount or value or any sums or property recovered as a result of the proceedings;

- any company dealt with by the report where the inspector was not appointed at the Secretary of State's initiative, unless the company was the applicant for the investigation and the Secretary of State directs otherwise; and

- the applicants for the investigation, where the inspector was appointed under s 431 or 442, to the extent that the Secretary of State directs.

In an investigation, individuals cannot only be required to attend; they must answer any questions that are put to them. There is no privilege against self-incrimination and all the evidence given may be used in subsequent proceedings. Section 441 renders the report admissible evidence of the inspectors' opinion in any legal proceedings. In contrast, where a disqualification order is sought under s 8 of the CDDA 1986, it may be treated as 'evidence of any fact stated therein'.

In *R v Seelig* (1991), the Court of Appeal rejected an argument that answers given under s 434 should be inadmissible in criminal proceedings as being oppressive under s 76(2) of the Police and Criminal Evidence Act 1984 (see, also, *Re London United Investments plc* (1992)).

However, the European Court of Human Rights (ECtHR) has decided that the use, in criminal proceedings, of evidence obtained by inspectors under their compulsory powers is an infringement of Art 6(1) of the European Convention on Human Rights (*Saunders v UK* (1996)). Even before the Human Rights Act 1998 was introduced, the Secretary of State had made in clear that, in light of the *Saunders* decision in the ECtHR, the prosecution would no longer rely on evidence compelled from the accused under the mandatory powers conferred on company inspectors. However, it has been decided subsequently that evidence acquired through the use of such powers of compulsion can still be used in actions taken in relation to the CDDA 1986. The reason for such a conclusion, and the means of distinguishing *Saunders*, was that such actions are not criminal in nature (*R v Secretary of State for Trade and Industry ex p McCormick* (1998)). It remains to be seen whether such a fine distinction can survive the increased emphasis on human rights ushered in by the Human Rights Act 1998.

On receipt of the final report of the investigation, the Secretary of State may take any of the following actions:

- institute criminal proceedings against any person believed to be guilty of offences;
- petition to have the company wound up under s 124 of the IA 1986;
- petition for an order under s 459;
- bring a civil action in the name of the company against any party;
- apply to the courts to have any director disqualified from acting as a director in future, under s 8 of the CDDA 1986.

In addition to the above investigation into the affairs of a company, the Secretary of State has the power, under s 442, to appoint inspectors to investigate the ownership and control of companies. In this regard, the general powers of the inspector are the same as those relating to an investigation into the affairs of the company (s 443). Additionally, however, an inspector may require documents and evidence from all persons who are or have been, or whom the inspector has reasonable cause to believe to be or to have been financially interested in, the success or failure of the company or related company. This provision also applies to those able to control or materially to influence the policy of the company or related company (s 444).

Where there is difficulty in finding out the relevant facts about the ownership of particular shares, the court may impose restrictions on those shares (s 454). These restrictions, commonly known as 'freezing orders', provide that:

- any transfer of the securities or, in the case of unissued securities, any transfer of the right to be issued with securities, and any issue of them, will be void;
- voting rights may not be exercised in respect of those securities;
- no further securities shall be issued in right of those securities or in pursuance of any offer made to the holder of them;
- except in a liquidation, no payment shall be made of any sums due from the company on the securities.

Investigations may also be instigated into directors' share dealings under s 446 of the CA 1985, and into insider dealing under s 177 of the Financial Services Act 1986.

The foregoing has focused on full scale investigation, but it has to be recognised that such investigations can be not only extremely time consuming, but also extremely expensive, not to mention potentially very damaging to the company that is the object of the investigation. In the light of these patent disadvantages of a full investigation, a possible alternative, and perhaps a precursor to a full investigation, exists in the investigation of a company's documents, supported by the power to require an explanation of such documents, where necessary. These investigations are carried out by officials of the Department of Trade and Industry.

Thus, under s 447 of the CA 1985, the Secretary of State may require a company, or any person who is in possession of them, to produce specified documents. Section 447 also empowers the Secretary of State to take copies of the documents and to require the person who produces them, or any other person who is a present or past officer or employee of the company, to provide an explanation of them.

The Secretary of State may obtain a search warrant, enabling the police to enter and search premises and take possession of documents (s 448 of the CA 1985). Any information obtained under s 447 of the CA 1985 may not be published or disclosed, except for specified purposes set out in s 449 of that Act, including criminal proceedings and proceedings for a disqualification order under the CDDA 1986. Any company officer who destroys, mutilates or falsifies a document relating to the company's property or affairs is guilty of an offence (s 450 of the CA 1985), and any person who makes a materially false statement in relation to a requirement under s 447, whether recklessly or deliberately, is also liable to a criminal charge.

Given the extent of the powers possessed by the Secretary of State and the investigators appointed by him, it is a little ironic, if not symptomatic of the failures in the system of company investigations, that some of the most famous cases of the early 1970s, that is, *Re Pergamon Press Ltd* (1971) and *Maxwell v Department of Trade and Industry* (1974), involved the late, and generally unlamented, publishing mogul, Robert Maxwell. Maxwell's death in

1991 revealed the corruption and criminal illegality on which his business empire was based and had been sustained. The blameworthy part of the Maxwell saga was, however, that his corrupt behaviour was an open secret that should have been investigated before it reached its inevitably disastrous conclusion. The manner in which Maxwell used the threat of libel actions to ensure his immunity from criticism is also to be regretted, but is a matter beyond the scope of this book.

13.12 WINDING UP AND ADMINISTRATION ORDERS

Winding up and administrative orders are alternative mechanisms for dealing with companies whose business activity is in a state of potentially terminal decline.

13.12.1 Winding up

Winding up, or liquidation, is the process whereby the life of the company is terminated. It is the formal and strictly regulated procedure whereby the business is brought to an end and the company's assets are realised and distributed to its creditors and members. The procedure is governed by the IA 1986 and may be divided into three distinct categories:

- Member's voluntary winding up

  This takes place when the directors of a company are of the opinion that the company is solvent, that is, capable of paying off its creditors. The directors are required to make a statutory declaration to that effect and the actual liquidation process is initiated by a special resolution of the company.

  Section 89 of the Insolvency Act 1986 requires that the directors of the company which wishes to go into voluntary winding up must make a declaration that the company will be able to pay its debts within 12 months from the date of the commencement of the winding up. If the directors make a false declaration, they may be criminally liable under s 89(4).

  A company may be wound up voluntarily in the following ways:

  o where an event takes place, which the articles provide should bring about the liquidation of the company, then the members need only pass an ordinary resolution;

  o where the company is to be wound up for any other reason, a special resolution is required; except

  o where the company's liabilities make it advisable to wind up, in which case, an extraordinary resolution has to be passed.

On the appointment of a liquidator, all directors' powers cease, although the liquidator may continue to employ them. On appointment, the liquidator proceeds to wind up the affairs of the company. When this is achieved, the liquidator calls a final meeting of the members and presents a report to members of how the procedure has been carried out. The liquidator must also send a copy of the report and a notice that the final meeting has been held to the registrar of companies. Three months after registration, the company is deemed to be dissolved and no longer exists.

If at any time during the winding up process, the liquidator forms the opinion that the company will not be able to pay its debts in full, then a meeting of the company's creditors must be called and the winding up will proceed as a creditors' winding up.

- Creditor's voluntary winding up

This occurs when the directors of the company do not believe that it will be able to pay off its debts and thus do not make the necessary declaration required for a members voluntary winding up. The liquidation is initiated by an extraordinary resolution of the company. Within 14 days of the passing of the resolution to wind up the company, a meeting of its creditors has to be called, at which the directors are required to present a full statement of the company's affairs together with a list of its creditors and an estimation of how much is owed to them. The creditors' meeting may require the formation of a committee of inspection, consisting of representatives of the creditors and the members. The purpose of the committee is to assist the liquidator and does away with the need to call full creditors' meetings to get approval for particular actions. In the event of any disagreement as to who should act as liquidator, the nomination of the creditors prevails over that of the members.

As in a members' voluntary winding up, once appointed, the liquidator proceeds to wind the company up and on completion of that task calls meetings of both the members and creditors to account for his actions in so doing. Once again, a copy of the account has to be sent to the registrar of companies, and three months after registration, the company is deemed to be dissolved.

- Compulsory winding up

This is a winding up ordered by the court under s 122 of the IA 1986. Although there are seven distinct grounds for such a winding up, one of which, depending upon just and equitable grounds, has already been considered (see above, 13.11.2), the most common reason for the winding up of a company is its inability to pay its debts. Section 123 provides that, if a company with a debt exceeding £750 fails to pay it within three weeks of receiving a written demand, then it is deemed unable to pay its debts.

On the presentation of a petition to wind a company up compulsorily, the court will normally appoint the Official Receiver to be the company's provisional liquidator. The Official Receiver will require the present or past officers, or indeed employees of the company to prepare a statement of the company's affairs. This statement must reveal:

o   particulars of the company's assets and liabilities;

o   names and addresses of its creditors;

o   any securities held by the creditors (fixed or floating charges) and the dates on which they were granted;

o   any other information which the Official Receiver may require.

After his appointment, the Official Receiver calls meetings of the company's members and creditors in order to select a liquidator to replace him and to select a liquidation committee if required. Once again, in the event of disagreement, the choice of the creditors prevails.

Section 142 of the IA 1986 states that the functions of the liquidator are 'to secure that the assets of the company are got in, realised and distributed to the company's creditors and, if there is a surplus, to the persons entitled to it'. Once the liquidator has performed these functions, he must call a final meeting of the creditors, at which he gives an account of the liquidation and secures his release from the creditors. Notice of the final meeting has to be submitted to the registrar of companies and, three months after that date, the company is deemed to be dissolved.

13.12.2 Order of payment of company debts

The assets of a company being wound up are to be applied in the following order:

*   *Secured creditors holding fixed charges*

    This category of creditor is entitled to have their debt met from the assets before any other payment is made. If, however, the security is insufficient to meet the full amount owed, then the creditor ranks merely as an unsecured creditor for the balance.

*   *Expenses incurred in the winding up*

    Thus, liquidators are entitled to recover their remuneration plus the costs of the winding up.

*   *Preferential creditors who all rank equally*

    Section 175 and Sched 6 to the IA 1986 set out what are to be treated as preferred payments and include the following:

    o   any income tax which became payable within 12 months of the appropriate date, also VAT due within a six month period;

    o   wages of employees together with all accrued holiday pay (£800 maximum);

    o   national insurance contributions outstanding.

- *Creditors secured by a floating charge*

  See above, 13.6.7.

- *Ordinary unsecured creditors*

  This category is the one that stands to lose most. It comprises the customers and trade creditors of the company. As creditors, they rank equally, but, as is likely, if the company cannot fully pay its debts, they will receive an equal proportion of what is available.

- *The deferred debts of the company*

  These are debts owed to the members as members, for example, dividends declared but not paid.

- *Members' capital*

  After the debts of the company are paid, the members are entitled to the return of their capital, depending on, and in proportion to, the provisions of the articles of association.

- Any remaining surplus is distributed amongst the members, subject to the rights given in the articles of association or other documents.

13.12.3 Administration orders

Administration is a relatively new procedure, having been introduced in line with the recommendations of the Cork Report of 1982. The aim of the administration order is to save the business as a going concern by taking control of the company out of the hands of its directors and placing it in the hands of an administrator. Alternatively, the procedure is aimed at maximising the realised value of the business assets.

The rules are set out in the IA 1986. Section 8 of that Act provides that, where the court is satisfied that the company is, or is likely to become, unable to pay its debts, it may issue an administrative order to achieve one or more of the following purposes:

- the survival of the whole or part of the business as a going concern;

- the approval of a voluntary arrangement under Pt 1 of the IA 1986, by which the creditors reach an agreement between themselves and the company as to the satisfaction of their debts;

- the sanctioning of a compromise or arrangement under s 425 of the CA 1985;

- a more advantageous realisation of the assets of the company than would be effected on the winding up of the company.

Once an administration order has been issued, it is no longer possible to commence winding up proceedings against the company or enforce charges, retention of title clauses or even hire-purchase agreements against the company. This major advantage is in no small way undermined by the fact that an administration order cannot be made after a company has begun the liquidation process. Since companies are required to inform any person who is entitled to appoint a receiver of the fact that the company is applying for an administration order, it is open to any secured creditor to enforce their rights and to forestall the administration procedure. This would cause the secured creditor no harm, since their debt would more than likely be covered by the security, but it could well lead to the end of the company as a going concern.

13.13 INSIDER DEALING

It is essential to distinguish between the nominal value of a share and its market value, that is, what it is actually worth. Whilst the former is fixed, the latter is free to fluctuate with demand. The fluctuation in the exchange value of shares in listed public limited companies is readily apparent in the constantly changing value of shares on the stock exchange. It is, of course, the fact that share prices do fluctuate in this way that provides the possibility of individuals making large profits, or losses, in speculating in shares. Speculation, which is not unlike gambling, refers to the purchase of shares in the hope of a quick capital gain and should be distinguished from investment, which refers to the purchase of shares as a longer term basis for income as well as capital gain. The stock exchange is insistent on its role as a mechanism for facilitating investment rather than speculation, but, nonetheless, that does not prevent it from being a mechanism for a huge amount of such short term speculation. The question remains to be asked, however, as to what actually causes the fluctuation in share prices. The obvious answer, that it is the result of the working out of the law of supply and demand, merely begs the question and prompts the further question as to why particular shares should be in more demand than others. A more fundamental answer to the original question may be located in the nature of the share itself.

It will be recalled that one of the essential attributes of the share is the right it provides to participate in the profits generated by the company. At least at a very basic level, the value of shares may be seen as a reflection of the underlying profitability of the company: the more profitable the company, the greater its potential to pay dividends and the higher the value of its shares. In such a simplified model, the function of the market is to act in a rational way to ascribe a fitting capital value to the business undertaking of the company. However, it will be appreciated that the accuracy of any such valuation relies on the information provided intermittently in the company's published accounts. Once the actual performance of a company is revealed in its accounts and statements, the market value of its share capital will be adjusted in the market to reflect its true worth: either upwards, if it has done better than expected; or downwards, if it has done worse than was expected. It will be seen, therefore, that the accuracy of any current valuation is always uncertain in the face of a shortage of accurate information relating to the company's current performance, which itself may fluctuate considerably over time.

The market's valuation of the company's performance and, consequently, the market value of the individual share in that company can never be completely accurate. Speculators, in particular, look to make large capital gains by capitalising on large disparities between performance and share value through buying shares that are currently undervalued and selling them at a profit when the market adjusts the share value in line with performance. It has actually been claimed that the distorting effect of speculation is so strong that it undermines the rational operation of the market. Consequently, share prices are described as assuming a 'random walk' pattern; that is, there is no way of accurately predicting which direction they will go in, rather like a drunk man staggering back from the pub. It might be thought that the current success of the internet '.com' companies undermine the foregoing analysis, in that very few of them have generated any profit to sustain the value of the many millions of pounds they have been valued at. The answer to this apparent anomaly is that, in these cases, individuals are investing in the prospects of future large scale profits, not to mention the immediate short term capital gains to be made as interest in such shares intensifies.

Current valuation of the worth of these '.com' companies may be seen, therefore, as the product of multiple speculation as to future income and immediate capital gain. Substantial capital gains can also be made as a result of a takeover bid, for it is usual for the predator company to pay a premium, over and above the market value of the shares in the company it has targeted for takeover. Once again, speculators may buy shares in companies which they think will be likely targets of a takeover bid, in the hope of receiving such premium payoffs.

To reiterate, it can be seen that share valuation depends upon accurate information as to a company's performance or its prospects. To that extent, knowledge is money, but such price sensitive/affected information is usually only available to the individual share purchaser on a *post hoc* basis, that is, after the company has issued its information to the public. If, however, the share buyer could gain prior access to such information, then they would be in the position to predict the way in which share prices would be likely to move and, consequently, to make substantial profits. Such dealing in shares, on the basis of access to unpublished price sensitive information, provides the basis for what is referred to as 'insider dealing' and is governed by Pt V of the CJA 1993.

13.13.1 The CJA 1993

Section 52 of the CJA 1993 sets out the three distinct offences of insider dealing:

- an individual is guilty of insider dealing if they have information as an insider and deal in price-affected securities on the basis of that information;

- an individual who has information as an insider will also be guilty of insider dealing if they encourage another person to deal in price-affected securities in relation to that information;

- an individual who has information as an insider will also be guilty of insider dealing if they disclose it to anyone other than in the proper performance of their employment, office or profession.

It should be noted that s 52(3) of the CJA 1993 makes it clear that any dealing must be carried out on a regulated market or through a professional intermediary.

The CJA 1993 goes on to explain the meaning of some of the above terms. Thus, s 54 defines which securities are covered by the legislation. These are set out in the second Schedule to the Act and specifically include: shares; debt securities, for example, debentures; warrants; options; futures; and contracts for differences (the latter do not involve the exchange of the security but merely require one party to pay or receive any change in value of the security in question).

'Dealing' is defined in s 55 as, amongst other things, acquiring or disposing of securities, whether as an principal or agent, or agreeing to acquire securities.

Who are insiders and what amounts to insider information are clearly crucial questions and s 56 defines 'inside information' as:

- relating to particular securities;

- being specific or precise;

- not having been made public; and

- being likely to have a significant effect on the price of the securities (this latter definition applies the meaning of 'price sensitive' and 'price affected').

Section 57 of the CJA 1993 goes on to provide that a person has information as an insider only if they know that it is inside information and they have it from an inside source. The section then considers what might be described as primary and secondary insiders. The first category of primary insiders covers those who get the inside information directly, through either:

- being a director, employee or shareholder of an issuer of securities; or

- having access to the information by virtue of their employment, office or profession.

Significantly, the term 'insider' is extended to the secondary category of anyone who receives, either directly or indirectly, any inside information from anyone who is a primary insider. Thus, anyone receiving information from an insider, even second or third hand, is to be treated as an insider. It is important to note that, if the primary insider merely recommends that the second party should buy shares, without passing on information, then, although the tipper has committed an offence under s 52(2) in recommending the shares, the tipee does not commit any offence under the CJA 1993 because they have not received any specific information, as required by s 56.

The requirement that information must not have been made public is dealt with in s 58 of the CJA 1993, although not exhaustively. Of interest is the fact that information is treated as public even if it can only be acquired through the exercise of skill or expertise.

Schedule 1 to the CJA 1993 sets out special defences for those who act in good faith in the course of their jobs as market makers, but perhaps of more importance are the general defences set out in s 53 of the Act. These require the individual concerned to show one of three things:

- that they did not expect the dealing to result in a profit attributable to the price sensitive information; or

- that they reasonably believed that the information had been previously disclosed widely enough to ensure that those taking part in the dealing would be prejudiced by not having the information; or

- that they would have done what they did, even if they did not have the information.

Remembering that the legislation applies to individuals who are seeking to avoid losses, as well as to those seeking to make gains, an example of the last defence listed above would be where an individual who had access to inside information nonetheless had to sell shares in order to realise money to pay a pressing debt because they had no other funds to pay it.

The seriousness of the offence is highlighted by penalties available to the courts in the event of a conviction for insider dealing. Thus, on summary conviction, an individual who is found guilty of insider dealing is liable to a fine not exceeding the current statutory maximum and/or maximum of six months' imprisonment. On indictment, the penalty is an unlimited fine and/or a maximum of seven years' imprisonment.

13.13.2 The reality of insider dealing

From the foregoing exposition of the CJA 1993, it can be seen that insider dealing is viewed as a very serious offence, with severe penalties for those found guilty of engaging in it. However, doubts have to be expressed about how the law actually operates in practice in order to control the activities of insiders. The fact that insider dealing continues to be carried out is reflected in the 'spike' that quite often appears in the graph of share prices just before a takeover bid is announced. This spike reflects a sudden, and otherwise inexplicable, rise in market value of the shares in question and suggests, if it cannot categorically prove, that some people have been trading on the basis of inside information about the takeover. The stock exchange employs a small body of people to monitor and investigate such abnormal share price rises, and they pass any doubtful cases to the Department of Trade and Industry for further investigation (see below).

When legislation against insider dealing was first introduced in the CA 1980, there was no provision for any independent investigation of suspected dealing. This shortcoming was remedied, at least to a degree, by the provision of s 177 of the Financial Services Act 1986, which gives the Secretary of State for Trade and Industry power to appoint inspectors to carry out investigations into suspected insider dealing. The powers of any such inspectors appointed are considerable (see above, 13.11.3).

It has been claimed that insider dealing is a 'victimless crime', to the extent that no one is forced to sell or buy shares that they would not have bought or sold in any case. Take, for example, a company that is the target of a takeover bid. The insider knows about the bid and, equally, knows that, if they buy shares before the bid becomes public knowledge, they will stand to make a considerable profit on any shares bought. It is quite clear that the possessor of inside information will benefit from that knowledge, but the question is as to who actually loses in the share dealing. One argument is that the sellers of the shares are in no way coerced into selling at the prevailing price, so they get what they want and, therefore, have no grounds for complaint. From this perspective, the only shareholder who could complain about losing would be the one who was mistakenly persuaded to sell by the market activity generated by the insider dealing. Some have even gone as far as to suggest that the profits derived from insider dealing are a legitimate perk of those in the know, and that they cut down the need to pay such people even higher salaries than those that they already enjoy.

There is, however, an overpowering argument against the practice of insider dealing, and not just in the fact that it unjustly rewards particular individuals. Perhaps more importantly, in so doing, it undermines the faith in, and the integrity of, the whole investment mechanism. In a system designed to encourage the concept of shareholder democracy, how can ordinary individuals be persuaded to invest in shares if they are faced with the reality of insider dealing?

13.14 ELECTRONIC COMMUNICATIONS

No treatment of company law can be considered complete without reference to the Companies Act 1985 (Electronic Communications) Order 2000, but, as its consequences are so disparate, it is better to postpone any mention of it until a general understanding of at least some of the areas which it impacts on have been considered. As its title suggests, the Electronic Communications Order recognises the impact of the computer revolution and the Internet on communication by allowing electronic communication to replace what were formerly requirements for paper-based systems. The Order applies to communication between the company and the Registrar of Companies, the company and its member and the members and the company. Although there are many consequential amendments to the Companies Act, the most significant alterations recognise electronic statements of compliance as equivalent to statutory declarations. Thus, for example, it applies in relation to statements regarding:

- company registration;
- company re-registration;
- public companies' share capital requirements;
- the provision of financial assistance for the purchase of shares in private companies.

The Order also allows companies to issue their annual reports electronically. This can be done by either emailing individual members or, if the members agree, placing them on a web page for members to access on notification by email. Similar arrangements can be made with regard to the notification of company meetings and the appointment of proxies.

Not only does the Order alter Table A as regards future companies, but it also provides that existing companies can take advantage of its provisions, even if there is anything contrary in their existing articles.

SUMMARY OF CHAPTER 13

COMPANY LAW

The effects of incorporation

- *Separate personality* is where the company exists as a legal person in its own right, completely distinct from the members who own shares in it.
- *Limited liability* refers to the fact that the potential liability of shareholders is fixed at a maximum level, equal to the nominal value of the shares held.
- *Perpetual succession* refers to the fact that the company continues to exist, irrespective of any change in its membership. The company only ceases to exist when it is formally wound up.
- The company owns the business property in its own right. Shareholders own shares; they do not own the assets of the business they have invested in.
- The company has contractual capacity in its own right and can sue and be sued in its own name. Members, as such, are not able to bind the company.

Lifting the veil of incorporation

The courts will, on occasion, ignore separate personality. Examples:
- statutory provisions;
- the use of the company form as a mechanism for perpetrating fraud;
- it is difficult, however, to provide a general rule to predict when the courts will lift the veil of incorporation.

Public and private companies

This is an essential distinction which causes/explains the need for different legal provisions to be applied to the two forms. The essential difference is to be found in the fact that the private company is really an economic partnership seeking the protection of limited liability.

The company's documents

- The memorandum of association governs the company's external affairs. It represents the company to the outside world, stating its capital structure, its powers and its objects.
- The articles of association regulate the internal working of the company.
- If there is any conflict between the two documents, the contents of the memorandum prevail.

Share capital

A 'share' has been defined as 'the interest of the shareholder in the company measured by a sum of money, for the purposes of liability in the first place and of interest in the second, but also consisting of a series of mutual covenants entered into by all the shareholders' (*Borlands Trustees v Steel* (1901)).

The main ways of categorising shares are in terms of:

- nominal or authorised capital;
- issued or allotted capital;
- paid up and unpaid capital;
- called and uncalled capital.

Types of shares

Shares can be divided into:

- ordinary;
- preference;
- deferred; and
- redeemable shares.

Loan capital

The term 'debenture' refers to the document which acknowledges the fact that a company has borrowed money, and also refers to the actual debt:

- a fixed charge is a claim against a specific asset of the company;
- a floating charge does not attach to any specific property of the company until it crystallises through the company committing some act or default;
- all charges, both fixed and floating, have to be registered with the Companies Registry within 21 days of their creation;
- a fixed charge takes priority over a floating charge, even though it was created after the floating charge;
- similar charges take priority according to their date of creation.

Directors

- The board of directors is the agent of the company and may exercise all the powers of the company.
- Individual directors may be described as being in a fiduciary relationship with their companies.

A director can be removed at any time by the passing of an ordinary resolution of the company (s 303 of the Companies Act 1985).

Individuals can be disqualified from acting as directors up to a maximum period of 15 years under the Company Directors Disqualification Act 1986.

As fiduciaries, directors owe the following duties to their company:

- to act *bona fide* in the interests of the company;
- not to act for a collateral purpose; and
- not to permit a conflict of interest to arise.

They also owe the company a duty of care and skill. This has been enhanced by s 214 of the Insolvency Act 1986.

Meetings

In theory, the ultimate control over a company's business lies with the members in general meeting. In practice, however, the residual powers of the membership are extremely limited.

There are three types of meeting:

- annual general meeting;
- extraordinary general meeting; and
- class meeting.

Proper and adequate notice must be sent to all those who are entitled to attend any meeting, although the precise nature of the notice is governed by the articles of association.

There are three types of resolutions:

- ordinary resolution;
- extraordinary resolution; and
- special resolution.

Voting is by a show of hands or according to the shareholding on a poll. Proxies may exercise voting rights if properly appointed.

Majority rule and minority protection

The majority usually dictate the action of a company and the minority is usually bound by the decisions of the majority. Problems may arise where those in effective control of a company use their power in such a way as to benefit themselves or to cause a detriment to the minority shareholders.

Three remedies are available to minority shareholders:

- the minority may seek court action to prevent the majority from committing a fraud on the minority;

- an order to have the company wound up on just and equitable grounds may be applied for where there is evidence of a lack of probity on the part of some of the members. It may also be used in small private companies to provide a remedy where there is either deadlock on the board or a member is removed from the board altogether or refused a part in the management of the business;

- under s 459 of the Companies Act 1985, any member may petition the court for an order, on the ground that the affairs of the company are being conducted in a way that is unfairly prejudicial to the interests of some of the members.

In addition to the above remedies, the Secretary of State has the power under s 431 of the Companies Act 1985 to appoint inspectors to investigate the affairs of a company.

Winding up

Liquidation is the process whereby the life of the company is brought to an end.

There are three possible procedures:

- compulsory winding up;
- a member's voluntary winding up; and
- a creditor's voluntary winding up.

Administration

This is a relatively new procedure, aimed at saving the business as a going concern by taking control of the company out of the hands of its directors and placing it in the hands of an administrator. Alternatively, the procedure is aimed at maximising the realised value of the business assets.

Insider dealing is governed by Pt V of the Criminal Justice Act (CJA) 1993:

- Section 52 of the CJA states that an individual who has information as an insider is guilty of insider dealing if they deal in securities that are price affected securities in relation to the information.

- They are also guilty of an offence if they encourage others to deal in securities that are linked with this information, or if they disclose the information otherwise than in the proper performance of their employment, office or profession.

- Section 56 makes it clear that securities are price affected in relation to inside information if the information, made public, would be likely to have a significant effect on the price of those securities.

- Section 57 defines an insider as a person who knows that they have inside information and knows that they have the information from an inside source. 'Inside source' refers to information acquired through:
  o being a director, employee or shareholder of an issuer of securities; or
  o having access to information by virtue of their employment;
  o it also applies to those who acquire their information from primary insiders previously mentioned.
- Section 53 makes it clear that no person can be so charged if they did not expect the dealing to result in any profit or the avoidance of any loss.
- On summary conviction, an individual found guilty of insider dealing is liable to a fine not exceeding the statutory maximum and/or a maximum of six months' imprisonment.
- On indictment, the penalty is an unlimited fine and/or a maximum of seven years' imprisonment.

Companies Act 1985 (Electronic Communications) Order 2000

This allows electronic communication to replace what were formerly requirements for paper-based systems. It also alters Table A articles of association.

CHAPTER 14

INDIVIDUAL EMPLOYMENT RIGHTS (1): THE CONTRACT OF EMPLOYMENT

14.1 INTRODUCTION

Prior to the 1970s, the traditional approach in the UK to industrial relations and employment law was non-interventionist. A change to this legal abstentionism came about during the office of the Labour Government 1974–79, which resulted in the enactment of a statutory floor of employment rights as part of the ' Social Contract', for example, the Employment Protection (Consolidation) Act 1978, the Sex Discrimination Act 1975, the Race Relations Act 1976 and the Health and Safety at Work etc Act 1974.

The law relating to individual employment rights has undergone numerous changes over the past two decades, either in the form of statutory regulation or through the interpretation of the law by the employment tribunals (formerly industrial tribunals) or courts. In recent times, the policy has been one of deregulation, which has led to some abuse of individual employment rights by employers, clearly illustrated by the reduction in State support for collective bargaining and trade union rights. However, the impact of EC law has halted the deregulation progress, particularly in the fields of discrimination and maternity rights and transfer of undertakings. A further halt has been called for in the Labour Government's White Paper on *Fairness at Work* (Cm No 3968, 1998), in which the Prime Minister stated that the White Paper:

> ... steers a way between the absence of minimum standards of protection at the workplace and a return to the laws of the past. It is based on the rights of the individual, whether exercised on their own or with others, as a matter of their choice. It matches rights and responsibilities. It seeks to draw a line under the issue of industrial relations law.

The Prime Minister went on to make it clear that there would be no return to the days of strikes without ballots, mass picketing or closed shops. The three main elements of the *Fairness at Work* framework are:

- provisions for the basic fair treatment of employees;
- new procedures for collective representation at work;
- policies that enhance family life, while making it easier for people – both men and women – to go to work.

A notable feature of the *Fairness at Work* legislation was that it left a substantial amount of the detail to regulations. In practical terms, this means that consultation is made in the lead-up to specific regulations being passed. It also allows for such regulations to be further developed and amended swiftly.

There has been some criticism of the *Fairness at Work* White Paper as being too cautious and extremely qualified – see Simpson, 'Review of the Department of Trade and Industry: fairness at work' (1998) 27 ILJ 245 – although many of the proposals have been implemented by the Employment Relations Act 1999.

When considering individual employment rights, it must be borne in mind that the legislation was originally drafted to protect full time, rather than part time, employees. As a result, thousands of workers did not qualify for employment protection on the basis that they are either self-employed or work part time, even though the trend in working patterns shows that there has been an increase in these groups of workers. For example, a recent Labour Force survey shows that around 5 million people now work less than 30 hours per week, with married women accounting for 75% of all part time workers. These changes have come about because of changes in the labour market, with a reduction in full time employment in the manufacturing industries and a growth in employment in the service sector, which has traditionally employed a greater proportion of part time workers.

However, the Part-Time Workers Directive (97/81 EC) provides for 'the removal of discrimination against part time workers and to improve the quality of part time work and to facilitate the development of part time work'. Section 19 of the Employment Relations Act 1999 gave the Secretary of State the power to make regulations to implement the Directive, which resulted in the Part-Time Workers (Prevention of Less Favourable Treatment) Regulations 2000 (SI 2000/1551).

14.2 CONTRACT OF EMPLOYMENT

The relationship between employee and employer is governed by the contract of employment, which forms the basis of the employee's employment rights. The distinction between contracts of employment and those of self-employment is of fundamental importance, because only 'employees' qualify for employment rights such as unfair dismissal, redundancy payments, minimum notice on termination, etc. Wider protection is provided under the discrimination and equal pay legislation, which applies to both a contract of service and a contract 'personally to execute any work or labour', which in effect includes some self-employed relationships. The Health and Safety at Work etc Act 1974 is also broader in scope, as it protects employees, the self-employed and, indeed, the general public. It is, therefore, important to understand the meaning of this term. Employees are employed under a contract of employment or contract of service, whereas self-employed persons, that is, independent contractors, are employed under a contract for services. The following example assists in distinguishing between employees and independent contractors.

If A employs a plumber to install his washing machine, A does not become an employer, as the plumber is an independent contractor, although a firm of plumbers may employ him or her. If A was to employ a nanny, then, as a general rule, he or she would become A's employee and would, therefore, be responsible for such things as deductions from his or her salary (for example, tax, National Insurance, etc); as well as this, the nanny would benefit from employment protection rights.

There is very limited guidance in the legislation as to what is meant by the term 'employee'. However, s 230 of the Employment Rights Act (ERA) 1996 offers the following definition:

(1) In this Act, 'employee' means an individual who has entered into or works under (or, where the employment has ceased, worked under) a contract of employment.

(2) In this Act, 'contract of employment' means a contract of service or apprenticeship, whether express or implied, and (if it is express) whether oral or in writing.

Tests have been developed through the case law for determining whether a person is an employee and, therefore, employed under a contract of service or employment, or whether he or she is self-employed and engaged under a contract for services. (See *Chung and Shun Sing Lee v Construction and Engineering Co Ltd* (1990), in which Lord Griffith argued that the question of employee status was largely one of fact.) These enable the courts to distinguish between the two types of contract and, clearly, s 230 should be read in the light of those tests. Although, for the majority of people at work, there is no problem in deciding whether they are employees or independent contractors, there may be occasions on which the distinction is not clear-cut. These tests will be considered in chronological order, since, although the early tests are still of relevance, the multiple test and the mutuality of obligations test are now at the forefront, should the question of employment status arise.

14.2.1 Control test

In applying the control test, the question to be asked is, does the person who is to be regarded as the employer control the employee or servant? Control extends to not just what the employee does, but how it is done. If the answer is in the affirmative, there is an employer/employee relationship. The reasoning behind this question was that an independent contractor might be told what to do, but probably had discretion as to how to do the work. However, in the modern workplace, this question has become a little unreal and, therefore, has fallen into decline as the sole test applied by the courts, although it is still a vital element in the multiple test.

In *Walker v Crystal Palace Football Club* (1910), Walker was employed as a professional footballer with the defendant club. It became necessary to decide whether he was employed under a contract of service or a contract for services. It was held that he was employed under a contract of service (or employment) because he was subject to the control of his master in the form of training, discipline and method of play.

One problem in applying the control test was that, if interpreted strictly, it resulted in skilled and professional people being categorised as independent contractors, which, at a time when there were limited employment rights, was not a problem for them, but proved to be a problem for persons injured as a result of their negligence at work, as such a person would be unable to rely on the principle of vicarious liability to claim against the employer. As a result, the courts saw fit to develop another test, which would reflect this development in the workplace by recognising that skilled and professional people could also be employees.

14.2.2 Integration test

This test was developed to counter the deficiencies of the control test. In applying the integration test, the question to be asked is, how far is the servant/employee integrated into the employer's business? If it can be shown that the employee is fully integrated into the employer's business, then there is in existence a contract of employment. It is clear that an independent contractor does not become part of the employer's business. The use of this test was confirmed in *Stevenson Jordan and Harrison Ltd v MacDonald and Evans* (1952), in which Lord Denning expressed the following view:

> One feature which seems to run through the instances is that, under a contract of service, a man is employed as part of the business and his work is done as an integral part of the business; whereas, under a contract for services, his work, although done for the business, is not integrated into it but is only accessory to it.

In *Whittaker v Minister of Pensions and National Insurance* (1967), Whittaker was employed as a trapeze artist in a circus. She claimed industrial injury benefit as a result of an accident sustained at work. Initially, this was refused, on the basis that she was not an employee of the circus. She was, however, able to show that, for at least half of her working day, she was expected to undertake general duties other than trapeze work, such as acting as usherette and working in the ticket office. It was held that her general duties showed that she was an integral part of the business of running a circus and was, therefore, employed under a contract of employment.

Although this test developed due to the impracticalities of the control test, it never gained popularity with the courts. It was successfully used in cases such as *Cassidy v Ministry of Health* (1951) to establish that highly skilled workers, such as doctors and engineers, can be employed under a contract of employment, and may even have a type of duel employment, where in some circumstances they are to be regarded as employees and in others they are seen as self-employed. The control test was clearly inapplicable to these situations. The need to develop a test which would suit all circumstances became of paramount importance. Employers were able to avoid various aspects of the statutory provisions by categorising employees as self-employed when, in reality, this was not necessarily the case, but at that time there was no test to cover these situations. For example, an employer could avoid tax and national insurance provisions, as well as liability for accidents caused by these persons whilst going about their jobs. As a result, the following test was developed.

14.2.3 Multiple test

The multiple test is, by definition, much wider than either the control test or integration test. It requires numerous factors to be taken into account in deciding whether a person is employed under a contract of service or a contract for services. It arose out of the case of *Ready Mixed Concrete (South East) Ltd v Minister of Pensions and National Insurance* (1968). RMC previously employed a number of lorry drivers under a contract of employment. The company then decided to dismiss the drivers as employees. However, it allowed them to purchase their vehicles, which had to be painted in RMC's colours. The contract between the drivers and the company stated that the drivers were independent contractors. The Minister of Pensions, who believed that the drivers were employees and, therefore, that RMC was liable for National Insurance contributions, disputed this. There were a number of stipulations under the contract. The drivers had to wear the company's uniform and the company could require repairs to be carried out to the vehicles at the drivers' expense. The vehicle could only be used for carrying RMC's products for a fixed period and the drivers were told where and when to deliver their loads, although, if a driver was ill, a substitute driver could be used. It was held by MacKenna J that a contract of service exists if three conditions are fulfilled:

- the servant agrees that, in consideration of a wage or other remuneration, he or she will provide his or her own work and skill in the performance of some service for his or her master;

- he or she agrees, expressly or impliedly, that, in the performance of that service, he or she will be subject to the other's control in a sufficient degree to make that other master;

- the other provisions of the contract are consistent with its being a contract of service.

In this case, it was decided that the drivers were independent contractors, as there were factors which were inconsistent with the existence of a contract of employment, for example, the ability to provide a replacement driver if the need arose.

This test has proved to be most adaptable, in that it only requires evaluation of the factors which are inconsistent with the existence of a contract of employment. It is important to appreciate that there is no exhaustive list of inconsistent factors. The courts will ask questions such as: who pays the wages? Who pays income tax and national insurance? Is the person employed entitled to holiday pay?

They will treat as irrelevant the fact that there is a contract in which someone is termed 'independent contractor' when the other factors point to him or her being an employee. This is illustrated in *Market Investigations Ltd v Minister of Social Security* (1969), in which Market Investigations employed Mrs Irving as an interviewer on an occasional basis. If she was selected from the pool of interviewers maintained by the firm, she was not obliged to accept the work. However, if she accepted, she would be given precise instructions of the methods to be used in carrying out the market research and the time in which the work had to be completed. However, she could choose the hours she wanted to work and do other work at the same time, as long as she met Market Investigations' deadlines. It was held that she was an employee of the company every time she decided to undertake work for them. It was felt that the question to be asked is, 'is the person who has engaged himself to perform these services performing them as a person in business on his own account?'. If the answer is yes, then there is a contract for services; if the answer is no, there is a contract of service. Cooke J in that case stated that no exhaustive list could be compiled of the considerations which are relevant to this question, nor could strict rules be laid down as to the relevant weight which the various considerations should carry in particular cases. The most that could be said is that control will always have to be considered, although it will not be the sole determining factor. Whilst this multifactorial test found approval in *Lee v Chung and Shun Sing Construction and Engineering Co Ltd* (1990), the Court of Appeal in *Hall (HM Inspector of Taxes) v Lorimer* (1994) warned against adopting a mechanistic application of Cooke J's checklist.

A further illustration of the problem of defining status and the implications for the individual can be seen in *Lane v Shire Roofing Co (Oxford) Ltd* (1995). The plaintiff was a roofer who traded as a one-man firm and was categorised as self-employed for tax purposes. In 1986, he was hired by the defendants, a newly established roofing business, which had not wanted to take on direct labour and so had taken on the plaintiff on a 'payment by job' basis. While re-roofing a porch of a house, he fell off a ladder, sustaining serious injuries. It was held initially that the defendants did not owe the plaintiff a duty of care, as he was not an employee. However, on appeal, the Court of Appeal found for the plaintiff. They concluded, in recognition of greater flexibility in employment patterns, that many factors had to be taken into account in determining status. First, control and provision of materials were relevant but were not decisive factors; secondly, the question may have to be broadened to 'whose business was it?'; finally, these questions must be asked in the context of who is responsible for the overall safety of the men doing the work in question. There were clear policy grounds for adopting this interpretation, the safety of the individual being of paramount importance. Whether such an interpretation would have been adopted in an unfair dismissal case is open to debate.

Obviously, as was seen in the *Ready Mixed Concrete* case (1968), there are other factors which may have to be taken into account, even though there may be some reluctance on the part of the courts to articulate what these other factors might be, with the exception of control. It is important that the multiple test continues to be flexible, so that it can adapt with changes in the labour environment. Unfortunately, these tests have tended to result in the atypical worker, that is, those with irregular working patterns, being categorised as self-employed. This is particularly true of casual or seasonal workers, even though, in practical terms, they may see themselves tied to a particular firm and, therefore, have an obligation to that business. There have, however, been some developments in this area which provide possible redress for such workers.

The test which has developed is known as the 'mutuality of obligation' test. This arose out of the case of *O'Kelly v Trusthouse Forte plc* (1983). O'Kelly and his fellow appellants worked on a casual basis as wine waiters at the Grosvenor House Hotel. They were regarded as regular casuals, in that they were given preference in the work rota over other casual staff. They had no other employment. They sought to be classified as employees, so that they could pursue an action for unfair dismissal. They argued that, if they were to be classified as employees, then each independent period of work for the defendant could be added together and the qualifying period of employment under the Employment Protection (Consolidation) Act 1978 would be met. It was held that the regular casuals in this case were self-employed, as there was no mutuality of obligation on the part of either party, in that Trusthouse Forte was not obliged to offer work, nor were O'Kelly and his colleagues obliged to accept it when it was offered. The preferential rota system was not a contractual promise.

The court made it clear that an important factor in determining whether there is a contract of service in this type of situation is the custom and practise of the particular industry. The case of *Wickens v Champion Employment* (1984) supports the decision in *O'Kelly*. In *Wickens*, 'temps' engaged by a private employment agency were not accorded employment status because of the lack of binding obligation on the part of the agency to make bookings for work and the absence of any obligation on the worker to accept them. Such an approach by the courts is obviously disadvantageous to atypical workers. However, a more liberal approach was taken in *Nethermore (St Neots) v Gardiner and Taverna* (1984), in which home workers who were making clothes on a piecework basis were accorded employee status, on the basis that a mutuality of obligation arose out of an irreducible minimum obligation to work for that company 'by the regular giving and taking of work over periods of a year or more'.

However, it was held by the Court of Appeal in *McMeecham v Secretary of State for Employment* (1997) that a temporary worker can have the status of employee of an employment agency in respect of each assignment actually worked, notwithstanding that the same worker may not be entitled to employee status under his or her general terms of engagement.

While the decision in *McMeecham* goes some way to supporting the position of the temporary worker, the same cannot be said of the decision in *Express and Echo Publications Ltd v Tanton* (1999). There, Mr Tanton worked for the claimants as an employee until he was made redundant. He was then re-engaged as a driver, ostensibly on a self-employed basis. One clause in his contract stated that, if he was unable or unwilling to perform the services personally, he should, at his own expense, find another suitable person. Mr Tanton found the agreement unacceptable and refused to sign it. He did, however, continue to work in accordance with its terms and, on occasions, utilised a substitute driver. He then brought a claim to an employment tribunal that he had not been provided with written particulars – thereby confirming his employee status. The employment tribunal found in Mr Tanton's favour on the basis of what had actually occurred, particularly the element of control exercised by the company. It was also concluded by the employment tribunal, and then on appeal by the Employment Appeal Tribunal (EAT), that the substitution clause was not fatal to the existence of a contract of employment. However, the Court of Appeal ruled that the right to provide a substitute driver was 'inherently inconsistent' with employment status, as a contract of employment must necessarily contain an obligation on the part of the employee to provide services personally.

There has been some criticism of this judgment (see Rubenstein, M, 'Highlights' [1999] IRLR 337), as it may allow unscrupulous employers to:

... draft contracts which will negate employment status for certain workers by including a substitution clause in their contracts. Clearly, the whole issue of employment status needs clarification. The position of atypical workers or those on zero hours contracts is particularly vulnerable until this issue is resolved.

A return to the *Wickens* approach is again in evidence in *Montgomery v Johnson Underwood Ltd* (2001). Mrs Montgomery was registered with an agency and was sent to work as a receptionist for the same client company for more than two years. Following her dismissal, she named both the agency and the client as respondents. The employment tribunal and the Employment Appeal Tribunal both held that she was an employee of the agency, but this view was rejected by the Court of Appeal. Buckley J stated that 'mutuality of obligation' and 'control' are the 'irreducible minimum legal requirement for a contract of employment to exist'. According to Buckley J, 'a contractual relationship concerning work to be carried out in which one party has no control over the other could not possibly be called a contract of employment'. In Mrs Montgomery's case, there may have been sufficient mutuality, but a finding of fact that there was no control by the agency was fatal to the argument that she was an employee of the agency.

Yet more confusion relating to the status of agency work was introduced by the decision of the Scottish EAT in *Motorola v Davidson and Melville Craig* (2001). Davidson worked for Motorola as a mobile telephone repairer. His contract was with Melville Craig, who assigned him to work for Motorola. Motorola paid Melville Craig for his services, and Melville Craig paid Davidson. Davidson was largely subject to Motorola's control. They gave him instructions, provided tools, and he arranged holidays with them. He wore their uniform and badges, and obeyed their rules. If Davidson chose not to work for Motorola, that might have breached his contract with Melville Craig, but not a contract with Motorola. The agreement between Motorola and Melville Craig gave Motorola the right to return Davidson to them if they found him 'unacceptable'. His assignment was terminated by Motorola following a disciplinary hearing held by one of their managers. Mr Davidson claimed unfair dismissal against Motorola, who maintained that he was an employee of Melville Craig. However, the employment tribunal concluded that there was sufficient control to make Motorola the employer and the EAT agreed. In the view of the EAT, in determining whether there is a sufficient degree of control to establish a relationship of employer and employee, there is no good reason to ignore practical aspects of control that fall short of legal rights. Nor is it a necessary component of the type of control exercised by an employer over an employee that it should be exercised only directly between them and not by way of a third party acting upon the directions, or at the request of the third party.

In the case of *Carmichael v National Power plc* (1998), where a tourist guide employed on a casual basis was found to be an employee, the Court of Appeal held that there was the requisite mutuality of obligations between the parties, because there was an implied term in the contract that the applicants would take on a reasonable amount of work and that the employers would take on a reasonable share of such guiding work as it became available. *Carmichael* went on appeal to the House of Lords (*Carmichael v National Power plc* (2000)). It was held that the relationship, on its facts, did not have the mutuality of obligations necessary to create an employment relationship. However, in determining the terms of the contract of employment, the House of Lords concluded that, where the parties intended all of the terms of the contract to be contained in documents, the terms should be determined solely by reference to these documents. In other situations, the court can look beyond the written documentation to the evidence of the parties in relation to what they understand their respective obligations to be, and to their subsequent conduct as evidence of the terms of the contract. It is argued that this approach, while it did not assist Carmichael, would assist many other marginal workers.

A number of wider implications flow from *Carmichael*. The decision has erected significant obstacles in the way of any attempts to extend employment status to casual workers. Furthermore, it could be used by employers to try to question the employment status of other workers on the margins of employment protection, for example, agency workers and homeworkers. Finally, 'highly evolved' human resource practitioners have always faced an uphill struggle in trying to convince line managers that it was not sufficient to label a worker as 'casual' and then assume that they possessed no employment rights. The *Carmichael* decision does not aid the HR manager's cause (see Leighton, P and Painter, RW, 'Casual workers: still marginal after all these years' (2001) 23(1), (2) Employee Relations 75).

Finally, in *Stevedoring & Haulage Services Ltd v Fuller and Others* (2001), workers who voluntarily accepted redundancy were then re-employed as casual workers. A letter from the company offering employment made it clear that they were not employees and that there was no obligation on either the part of the company to provide work or on the applicants to accept it. However, they worked for the company on more days than not and did not work for any other employer. After three years, they applied to an employment tribunal for written particulars of their employment under s 1 of the ERA 1996. The employment tribunal and EAT concluded that the applicants were employed because there was an 'overarching contract of employment', evidenced by the implied mutuality of obligation which reflected the reality of the agreement. However, the company successfully appealed to the Court of Appeal on the basis that the implied term and express terms contained in the documents could not be reconciled.

This case therefore opens up the possibility that employers will be able to avoid legal responsibilities by including express terms denying 'employee' status to their workers. In effect, an express term will be able to override statutory employment rights.

It is still open to the Government to ensure that legislation is extended to provide cover to such workers. Section 23 of the Employment Relations Act 1999 provides the Secretary of State with such a power and the broadening of the scope of legislative provisions can be seen in the Working Time Regulations 1998 and the National Minimum Wage Act 1998, both of which extend protection to 'workers' (see Painter, RW, Puttick, K and Holmes, AEM, *The Gateway to Employment Rights, Employment Rights*, 2nd edn, 1998, Chapter 1). Part time workers as well as casuals have also found themselves to be in a vulnerable position in the labour market (see Dickens, L, *Whose Flexibility? Discrimination and Equality Issues in Atypical Work*, 1992). The Part-Time Workers Directive (EC 97/81), which the UK Government had originally opposed on the ground that it would have a negative employment effect, has finally been adopted in the Part-Time Workers (Prevention of Less Favourable Treatment) Regulations 2000. The main thrust of the Regulations is to ensure that part time employees will be treated no less favourably than comparable full time employees in relation to a variety of matters, including pay, leave, training and pensions. A part time employee is defined under the Regulations as 'one who is not identifiable as a full time employee'. Comparison will be made with a full time employee 'who is engaged in the same or broadly similar work as a part time employee ... [and] works at the same establishment or, where no full time employee working at the establishment meets the preceding criteria, works at a different establishment and satisfies those requirements'. A defence of objective justification is provided in the Regulations. In theory, it provides all atypical and part time workers with an action for direct discrimination, distinct from that provided under the Equal Pay Act 1970 and the Sex Discrimination Act 1975. (See Jeffery, M, 'Not really going to work? Of the Directive on part time work, atypical work and attempts to regulate it' (1998) 27 ILJ 193.)

In the past, the threshold qualifying hours have also imposed a barrier for part time and casual workers qualifying for employment protection rights, for example, the requirement that a worker has worked 16 hours per week for a minimum of two years in order to qualify for unfair dismissal or redundancy payments. However, this has been changed by the decision in *R v Secretary for Employment ex p Equal Opportunities Commission* (1995). As a result of this, the Employment Protection (Part-Time Employees) Regulations 1995 were introduced, which removed the 16 hours per week qualification. Despite the broadening of the coverage of the Regulations to 'workers' as opposed to 'employees', the Regulations retain the potential to disenfranchise many economically dependent workers from the scope of their protection. This is because comparisons under the Regulations can only be employed under the Regulations between an actual comparator (cf the Sex Discrimination Act 1975 and the Race Relations Act 1976) employed under the same contract. Thus, for example, a part time worker employed as a fixed term contract worker cannot compare his or her treatment with that of a full time worker employed on a permanent contract. Similarly, workers employed under contracts of employment ('workers') cannot compare their treatment with full time workers employed under contracts of employment ('employees') – see reg 2(3). In other words, the *Carmichael* problem is not resolved. The only cases in which a claim may be made without reference to an actual full time comparator are set out in Regulations. Broadly, these exceptions cover (a) a full time worker who becomes part time (reg 3), and (b) full time workers returning to work part time for the same employer within a period of 12 months (reg 4). The decision of the European Court of Justice in *R v Secretary of State for Employment ex p Seymour-Smith* (1999) goes one step further, in concluding that the two year qualifying period discriminated against part time employees, who are predominantly female. Such a qualifying period may, therefore, contravene Art 141 of the EC Treaty. However, in *R v Secretary of State for Employment ex p Seymour-Smith and Perez* (2000), the House of Lords concluded that, although the qualifying period was discriminatory, it was justified on the basis that, when it was introduced, there was evidence that a shorter qualifying period might inhibit employers recruiting employees. To some extent, the Employment Relations Act 1999, in which the qualifying period for unfair dismissal was reduced to one year, has overtaken the final outcome of the *Seymour-Smith* case.

14.3 LOANING OR HIRING OUT EMPLOYEES

One area of contention involves the loaning or hiring out of an employee; the issue is, whose is the employee? This is particularly important in respect of who should be vicariously liable for the employee's torts. As can be seen in *Mersey Docks and Harbour Board v Coggins and Griffiths (Liverpool) Ltd* (1947), there is a rebuttable presumption that, when an employee is loaned out, he or she remains the employee of the first/original employer. In *Mersey Docks*, a crane and its driver were hired out to C and G to assist in the loading of a ship. C and G paid the driver's wages. While the crane driver was doing this work, he negligently injured an employee of the stevedores, C and G. The issue to be decided by the courts was whether the harbour board or C and G were vicariously liable for the crane driver's negligence. It was held that the harbour board remained the employer of the crane driver. He was under their ultimate control in respect of the work he should do, even though he was under the temporary direction of the stevedores; that is, the original employer retained the right to hire, dismiss and decide on his work, even though day to day control passed to the stevedores.

The courts are reluctant to find that there has been a transfer of employment where employees are loaned or hired out, unless there is consent on the part of the employee or there is an agreement which clearly states the position in the event of liability accruing. There may, however, be exceptional circumstances where the courts may declare that, *pro hac vice* (for that one occasion), a loaned or hired employee has become the employee of the 'second' employer, as in *Sime v Sutcliffe Catering* (1990).

14.4 CONTINUITY: PERIODS AWAY FROM WORK

In order to acquire employment protection rights, there should normally be continuity of employment. It is, therefore, necessary to consider the impact of weeks away from work. Section 212 of the ERA 1996 is the main legislative provision. The key point is that any week or part of a week in which the employee's relations with his employer are governed by a contract of employment must count in computing the employee's period of employment. The section also reinforces the point that absence through pregnancy or childbirth, sickness or injury, temporary cessation of work or custom or practise will generally count in computing the period of employment. Any such custom or practise must be established before or at the time that the absence commences. Even where employers engage employees on a series of short term contracts, they may find that these will be added together for the purpose of computing the period of employment – *Ford v Warwickshire CC* (1983). This mathematical approach may be used where the gaps in employment are regular, whereas where the pattern is irregular, the courts should be flexible and adopt a 'broad brush' approach – *Flack v Kodak Ltd* (1986). This approach is of benefit to many workers, such as part time or temporary teachers, and makes it more difficult for employers to avoid the employment protection laws by offering a succession of fixed term contracts. However, where patterns of employment are more irregular, it may not be appropriate to consider continuity in this way. Indeed, in *Flack v Kodak Ltd* (1986), where the periods of employment were particularly irregular, a broad brush approach was adopted, whereby the whole of the employment period was deemed to be relevant; to do otherwise would have led to a most misleading comparison being drawn.

Booth v United States of America (1999) is a prime example of the vulnerability of workers on fixed term contracts. The case concerned a US airbase in the UK, where maintenance workers were employed under a series of fixed term contracts for a total period in excess of two years but with a gap of about two weeks between each contract. Despite the fact that the aim of this arrangement was to evade the employment protection legislation, the Employment Appeal Tribunal declined to adopt a purposive approach and to find continuity. As Morrison J put it:

> Whilst it is generally desirable that employees should enjoy statutory protection during their employment, Parliament has laid down the conditions under which that protection is afforded. If, by so arranging their affairs, an employer is lawfully able to employ people in such a manner that the employees cannot complain of unfair dismissal or seek a redundancy payment, that is a matter for him. The courts simply try and apply the law as it stands. It is for the legislators to close any loopholes that might be perceived to exist.

The position of such workers will be improved once the EC Directive on Fixed-Term Work has been implemented in the UK. It was due to be implemented by the Fixed-Term Employees (Prevention of Less Favourable Treatment) Regulations, on 10 July 2001, but this was delayed in order to meet employers' concerns that they had had insufficient time to prepare for it. The key aim of the Directive is to ensure that fixed term employees are not, without justification, treated less favourably than comparable permanent staff. The Directive does not cover pay or pensions and so, without further legislation, or evidence of sex/race/disability discrimination, it would be lawful to continue to pay a fixed term worker less than a member of the permanent staff.

The use of a succession of fixed term engagements – the issue in *Booth* – will also be addressed by the Regulations, which may set a maximum number of successive renewals of a fixed term contract; a maximum total duration of a series of fixed term contract; or a combination of more than one of these options.

The Government announced on 8 November 2001 that it would be using the Employment Bill 2002 to prevent pay and pensions discrimination against fixed term workers and to transpose the Fixed-Term Work Directive.

14.5 INDUSTRIAL DISPUTES

Any week in which an employee takes part in a strike does not count towards continuity (s 212 of the ERA 1996) but, at the same time, continuity is not broken. The same is true of absences due to lock-outs by the employer.

14.6 FORMATION OF THE CONTRACT OF EMPLOYMENT

In general terms, there are no formalities involved in the formation of a contract of employment. The contract itself may be oral or in writing, with the exception of apprenticeship deeds and articles for merchant seamen, which obviously, by their nature, have to be in writing. Therefore, it follows that, within reason, the parties to the contract, that is, the employer and employee, can decide on whatever terms they wish. This, however, raises the issue of the respective bargaining position of the parties, as the employer will always be in the strongest position. In industries which have traditionally had strong trade union representation, a collective agreement may form the basis of the employment terms, where it is expressly agreed that such agreements should be incorporated into the contract. The contract may also be subject to implied terms, which will be considered subsequently.

14.6.1 Written statement of terms

Although the contract of employment itself need not be in writing, the employee must be given written particulars of the main terms. This is required by Pt 1 of the ERA 1996. These written particulars must be supplied within two months of the date on which employment commenced. The particulars must contain the following:

- the names of the parties and the date on which the employment commenced; if there is a change of employer, resulting in continuity of employment, the date on which continuity commences must be specified;

- the rate of pay or the method of calculating it;
- the intervals at which wages are to be paid, for example, weekly or monthly;
- terms and conditions relating to hours of work;
- terms and conditions relating to holidays and holiday pay;
- the length of notice which the employee must give and the amount that he or she is entitled to receive on termination of his or her employment;
- job title and description.

The Trade Union Reform and Employment Rights Act (TURERA) 1993 made further changes, so that the statement must also include the following:

- where the employment is non-permanent, the period for which it is expected to continue;
- either the place of work or, where the employee is required or permitted to work at various places, an indication of that fact, plus the address of the employer;
- any collective agreement which directly affects the terms and conditions of employment, including, where the employer is not a party, the persons by whom they were made;
- where an employee is required to work outside the UK for more than a month, the period of such work, the currency of remuneration, any additional remuneration or benefit by reason of the requirement to work outside the UK and any terms and conditions relating to his or her return to the UK.

These form the basis of the written particulars and the employer must provide this information in one document (s 2 of the ERA 1996; see below, fig 3). In addition, the employer must specify the following:

- any disciplinary rules which apply to the employee or reference to the document containing them;
- the person to whom he or she can apply if he or she is dissatisfied with any disciplinary decision relating to him or her;
- the grievance procedure, including the person to whom he or she can apply if he or she has a grievance relating to his or her employment;
- the document containing rights to sick pay and pension schemes.

Figure 3: Specimen statement of terms of employment

The following statement of written particulars is provided in accordance with the ERA 1996. It is not intended to be a comprehensive statement of the terms and conditions of your employment.

The parties:

Employer: (name and address)

Employee: (name and address)

Job title and description: (as flexible as possible)

Place of work:

Date of commencement:

Remuneration: (for example, rate x hours) payable weekly/monthly

Hours of work: (for example, 8.45 am to 5.15 pm Mondays to Fridays inclusive, plus one Saturday in four)

Holiday entitlement: (for example, whether paid leave and when it can be taken; statutory holidays)

Notice: (period to be given by the employer and employee in order to terminate the contract of employment subject to the statutory periods)

The terms and conditions relating to pensions, sick leave and pay; the grievance and disciplinary procedures; the works rules; and the safety policy are set out in reference documents. Copies can be seen on the main notice board and are contained in the staff handbook or are available from the Personnel Office.

You will be notified in writing of any changes to your terms and conditions within one month of the date of such change.

Acknowledgment

I have received and read a copy of the terms and conditions of employment, which are correct and which I accept.

At the very least, the employee must have reasonable access to this information. Any agreed changes must be communicated to the employee in writing within one month of the change. It is permissible for the employer to refer the employee to additional terms contained in a document, such as a collective agreement, as long as it is reasonably accessible. The written statement, whilst not being a contract, is *prima facie* evidence of what is agreed between the employee and the employer. (See *Gascol Conversions Ltd v Mercer* (1974) and *Systems Floors (UK) Ltd v Daniel* (1982) for consideration of the distinction between signing an acknowledgment and signing a statement described as a 'contract'.) If the employer fails to provide a statement, or if there is a disagreement with respect to its contents, or if a change has not been properly notified, the employee may apply to an employment tribunal in order to determine which particulars ought to be included in the statement (s 11 of the ERA 1996) (see *Mears v Safecar Security Ltd* (1982)). In such cases, applications must be brought within three months of termination of the contract of employment.

Following amendments implemented by TURERA 1993 and the Employment Protection (Part-Time Employees) Regulations 1995, the eight hour threshold has been removed and the right to receive a written statement has been extended to all part time employees, as well as full time employees whose contract subsists for one month. However, certain categories of employee are still excluded, including Crown employees, registered dock workers and those employees who work wholly or mainly outside Great Britain.

If there is a change to any of the terms about which particulars must be provided or referred to in the document, the employer must notify employees individually in writing.

Sections 35–38 of the Employment Act 2002 make a number of positive changes in relation to the supply of written statements and conditions. These are as follows:

- Section 35 provides for part of the written statement dealing with disciplinary and grievance matters to cover the procedure which applies when the employee is dismissed or disciplined, whereas at present, it must only describe what he must do if dissatisfied with disciplinary action taken against him. This ensures that all stages of the new minimum statutory disciplinary and dismissal procedures must be set out in a written statement.

- Section 36 removes the current exemption, relating to the need for details of disciplinary rules and procedures, for employers with less than 20 employees. This means that all employers, of whatever size, will have to mention their disciplinary rules and the new minimum procedures in the written statement. This is a long overdue reform.

- Section 37 provides flexibility for employers by allowing particulars included in a copy of the contract of employment or letter of engagement given to the employee to form, or to form part of, the written statement. This reduces the need to duplicate existing documents. It also enables such documents to be given to the employee before his or her employment begins.

- Section 38 provides for employment tribunals to award compensation to an employee where the lack, incompleteness or inaccuracy of the written statement becomes evident upon a claim being made under specified tribunal jurisdictions (which cover the main areas such as unfair dismissal, and all types of discrimination – Sched 4). This is done by requiring the tribunal to increase any award made against the employer in respect of the complaint under the other jurisdiction by between the greater of 5%, or one or two weeks' pay, and 25%, according to whether the statement is merely incomplete or inaccurate or has never been issued at all. One or two weeks' pay is also the award where compensation is not a remedy available for the particular complaint or where it is not the remedy that the tribunal chooses.

14.6.2 Terms

Terms may be incorporated into the contract of employment from a variety of sources. Such terms may be express or implied. Section 179 of the Trade Union and Labour Relations (Consolidation) Act (TULR(C)A) 1992 provides that a written collective agreement which states that the parties intend all or part of it to be legally enforceable is then expressly incorporated into the contract.

The express terms are those agreed upon by the employer and employee on entering into the contract of employment. They may be oral or in writing and will cover such things as the point on the salary scale at which the employee will commence employment. However, oral terms may be open to dispute and it is in the interests of both parties to have such terms in writing; for example, a restraint of trade clause is unlikely to be enforceable unless it is in writing. Disputes about oral terms may result in the employee pursuing an action for clarification before an employment tribunal. A breach of an express term of the contract may result in the dismissal of the employee and, if it is a breach by the employer, may enable the employee to resign and bring an action for constructive dismissal. As we have seen, a collective agreement made between the employer or his association and a trade union may be expressly incorporated into the contract of employment (s 179 of TULR(C)A 1992). Such agreements usually provide a comprehensive set of terms and conditions for particular types of employees. In such cases, the trade union usually has equal bargaining power to the employer. Where they are expressly incorporated under s 1 of the ERA 1996, they will bind both employer and employee. However, as Kerr LJ stated in *Robertson v British Gas Corp* (1983):

> ... it is only if and when those terms are varied collectively by agreement that the individual contracts of employment will also be varied. If the collective scheme is not varied by agreement, but by some unilateral abrogation or withdrawal or variation to which the other side does not agree, then it seems to me that the individual contracts of employment remain unaffected.

There may be a subtle distinction between a 'collective agreement', which is legally binding, and a 'local arrangement', which is not (*Cadoux v Central Regional Council* (1986); see, also, Napier, B, 'Incorporation of collective agreements' (1986) 15 ILJ 52). It is possible, in the absence of express agreement, for terms to be incorporated by conduct, for example, where collectively bargained terms and conditions are uniformly observed for a group of workers of which the employer is a member. Another issue which may arise relates to the validity of all the terms of the agreement. Some terms may be deemed to be inappropriate for incorporation, as they relate to the individual, as opposed to collective, relationship. In *Alexander v Standard Telephone and Cables Ltd (No 2)* (1991), a redundancy agreement written into a collective agreement was held to be unenforceable as being inappropriate for incorporation. Part of the reasoning in this case was that the redundancy provisions were to be found in a part of the agreement containing other provisions incapable of incorporation, that is, statements of policy. (See Rubenstein, M, 'Highlights' [1991] IRLR 282 for a critique of this decision.)

14.6.3 National minimum wage

Before considering the terms which may be implied into a contract of employment, it is pertinent, in the light of the more interventionist approach taken by the Government, to consider the national minimum wage. It is anticipated that the statutory requirement to pay a minimum wage will impact not only on the nature of the labour market, but also on equality, as it relates to pay.

The statutory provisions are to be found in the National Minimum Wage Act (NMWA) 1998. With effect from 1 April 1999, all relevant workers are entitled to the national minimum wage, which is currently set at £4.10 per hour for those aged 22 years and over and £3.50 per hour for those aged 18–21. This is expected to increase to £4.20 per hour and £3.60 per hour from October 2002. People under the age of 18 are currently excluded from the Act. The national minimum wage applies to all workers, whether they are paid hourly, monthly, etc. The Low Pay Commission has been set up to advise the Secretary of State for Employment in respect of the key issues relating to the minimum wage. The Low Pay Commission monitors the level at which the rate is set and makes recommendations for change on an annual basis. The Commission also reviews the working of the NMWA with a view to correcting anomalies, closing loopholes, etc – see Low Pay Commission, *Second Report*, 2000, Stationery Office. For example, the number of exempted categories of worker has been increased – National Minimum Wage (Amendment) Regulations 2000.

The First Annual Report on the national minimum wage showed that over £2 million had been won back by enforcement officers – *National Minimum Wage Annual Report, 1999–2000* – available from the DTI.

The enforcement officers are appointed by the Inland Revenue.

As part of the requirements under the NMWA 1998, employers are required to keep adequate records to show that the wage has been paid and must produce such records on request (by workers, the enforcement agency, tribunals and courts). In proceedings, the onus is generally on the employer to show that the wage has been paid correctly. It is a criminal offence to refuse to pay the minimum wage or to fail to keep proper records. There is no provision for employers or workers to 'opt out' of the requirements.

The right to a national minimum wage is given to 'workers'. A 'worker' is defined in s 54 of the NMWA 1998 as an individual who has entered into or works under:

(a) a contract of employment; or

(b) any other contract, whether express or implied and (if it is express) whether oral or in writing, whereby the individual undertakes to do or perform personally any work or services for another party to the contract whose status is not by virtue of the contract that of a client or customer of any profession or business undertaking carried on by the individual; and any reference to a worker's contract shall be construed accordingly.

This wide definition is intended as an anti-avoidance measure. It seeks to exclude only the genuinely self-employed from its ambit and makes it extremely difficult for an employer to restructure its working relationships in order to avoid paying the national minimum wage and gaining an unfair competitive advantage in relation to market rivals. Agency and home workers are effectively also included by virtue of ss 34 and 35 of the NMWA 1998 respectively.

There are, however, specific exclusions, for example, share fishermen, voluntary workers, prisoners and people living and working within the family, such as nannies and au pairs; also, they do not apply to family members who work in the family business (National Minimum Wage Regulations 1999 (SI 1999/584) and the National Minimum Wage (Amendment) Regulations 2000). It has already been decided that pupil barristers are not 'workers' within the meaning of the Act (*Lawson and Others v Edmonds* (2000)).

Employers should express the minimum wage as an hourly rate. However the minimum wage need only be paid over the worker's 'pay reference period'. This is defined as a calendar month or, where the worker is paid by reference to a shorter period, that period (reg 10(1) of the National Minimum Wage Regulations 1999 (SI 1999/584)).

In determining whether the national minimum wage is being complied with, it is necessary to exclude certain items from gross pay and include others. The following are not included:

- loans or advances to workers;
- pension payments, lump sums on retirement and compensation for losing one's job;
- court or tribunal awards;
- redundancy payments;
- awards under suggestion schemes;
- payments during absences from work (for example, sick pay and maternity pay);

- benefits in kind, except living accommodation, for which there is a maximum permitted offset of £19.95 per week;
- the monetary value of vouchers, etc, which can be exchanged for money, goods or services;
- premium payments for overtime and shift work;
- unsociable hours payments and standby payments;
- service charges, tips and gratuities;
- payments made to reimburse the worker, for example, travel expenses;
- deductions made in respect of worker's expenditure, for example, cost of uniforms, tools, etc.

Where a worker has reasonable grounds for believing that he or she has been, or is being, paid less than the national minimum wage during the pay reference period, he or she may require his or her employer to produce any relevant records. The worker must supply the employer with a 'production notice'. The employer must then produce the records within 14 days following the date of receipt of the notice. A worker may complain to the tribunal where the employer either fails to produce the records or does not produce the relevant records.

Inland Revenue officials currently undertake the monitoring of the Act. They have the power to enter premises and inspect records, and can issue enforcement notices where they find that the minimum wage is not being paid. Enforcement officers recovered £500,000 worth of minimum wage underpayments and issued 66 enforcement notices between April and November 1999 (DTI press release P/2000/04). An employer has a right of appeal against an enforcement notice to an employment tribunal. Failure to comply with an enforcement notice may result in a 'penalty notice' being served. This will result in a financial penalty being imposed on the employer. Where a tribunal finds that the employer has failed to pay the national minimum wage, it may award additional remuneration to the worker. The NMWA 1998 also creates a criminal offence for failure on the part of the employer to pay the minimum wage, keep records, falsify records and obstruct officers. The First Annual Report on the national minimum wage showed that over £2 million had been won back by enforcement officers – *National Minimum Wage Annual Report, 1999–2000* (DTI).

The limitations on the effectiveness of the NMWA 1998 may either result from the level of minimum wage set – for example, the TUC would like it to be increased to £5 per hour, as a more realistic rate – or as a result of the exempted categories, either statutory or through case law. Although the case law may provide positive classification on defining terms such as 'working', in *British Nursing Association v Inland Revenue* (2001), the EAT held that employees who were employed on a night shift at home which involved taking telephone calls, notwithstanding that between calls they would undertake activities such as watching television, were engaged on 'time work' within the NMWA 1998 and were therefore entitled to be paid the minimum rate for all the hours they were on duty. The key factor was a continued obligation throughout the night.

For a detailed account of the national minimum wage, see the Second Report of the Low Pay Commission, *The National Minimum Wage: The Story so Far* (Cm 4571, 2000).

14.6.4 Implied terms

Implied terms may arise out of the custom and practice of a particular industry; for example, deductions from wages for bad workmanship were accepted as a term of contracts in the cotton industry. The courts may be the final arbiters as to whether an implied term is incorporated into the contract and, as can be seen in *Quinn v Calder Industrial Materials* (1996), such claims are not always successful.

In the case of *Henry v London General Transport Services Ltd* (2001), the EAT confirmed that there were four requirements in establishing implied terms by custom and practice:

- in relation to the incorporation into a contract of employment of a term by way of a custom and practice, the custom and practice so relied on must be reasonable, certain and notorious;

- that, where what is shown in relation to the custom and practice, the term thus supported is incorporated on the assumption that it represents the wishes of the parties;

- that strict proof is required of the custom and practice and that the burden of such proof is upon the party seeking to rely upon the consequential incorporation of the term into the contract;

- that there is some relevant distinction generally to be made between custom and practice, enabling changes to be made, and one enabling 'fundamental' changes to be made in a man's terms and conditions of employment.

Implied terms generally have to be read subject to any express terms, which may be to the contrary. The courts have moved towards a more objective test for determining incorporation based on 'necessity' or 'business efficacy', that is, is the term a 'necessary condition of the relationship?'. However, where the implied term is necessary to give efficacy to the contract, the implied term will take precedence over the express term. This is illustrated in *Johnstone v Bloomsbury HA* (1991) (see below, Chapter 17).

A hospital doctor was obliged to work a stipulated number of hours under his contract, plus additional hours if required. As a result, the doctor found himself working, on average, over 80 hours per week and, as a result, became ill. It was held that the express term regarding the additional hours had to be read subject to the implied term of care and safety. The implied term in this case was necessary to give efficacy to the contract.

A reasonableness test is also appropriate when determining whether implied terms are incorporated. This is particularly so where one of the parties is relying on custom and practice as the basis for incorporation (see Smith, I, 'The creation of the contract of employment', in *Employment Law Guide*, 2nd edn, 1996, p 15). An employee must know of the custom and practice if it is to be accepted as incorporated into the contract. In *Sagar v Ridehalgh and Sons Ltd* (1931), it was common practice in the defendant's mill to make deductions for bad work. This practice had operated for at least 30 years and all weavers had been treated the same. The plaintiff weaver challenged its validity. The court held that the matter of whether the plaintiff knew of its actual existence was immaterial in this case, as he had accepted employment on the same terms and conditions as the other workers at the mill. However, it is clear that a worker should have either express or constructive knowledge of such 'terms' if there are to be valid and enforceable (see *Meek v Port of London* (1913) and *Quinn v Calder Industrial Materials Ltd* (1996)).

A number of 'standard' implied terms have developed in respect of the employer/employee relationship. These take the form of duties imposed on the respective parties. A breach by the employee may result in disciplinary action or even dismissal; a breach by the employer may result in legal proceedings before a tribunal.

14.6.5 Duties imposed on the employer

The duties imposed on the employer are to provide work; to pay wages; to indemnify the employee; and to hold in mutual respect and provide for the care and safety of the employee.

To provide work

An employer will not be in breach of the implied duty to provide work, as long as he or she continues to pay his or her employees, even though there may be no work available. However, in certain situations, the employer may be liable for failing to provide work, for example, if a reduction in the employee's earnings occurs. This is most likely to affect those employees on piecework or commission. For example, in *Devonald v Rosser and Sons* (1906), Devonald's employers found that they could no longer run the works at a profit, so they gave Devonald, a piece-worker, one month's notice but closed the factory immediately. Devonald claimed damages for the wages he lost during this period, arguing that there was an implied term that he would be provided with work during the notice period. It was held that the necessary implication from the contract was that the master would find a reasonable amount of work up to the expiration of the notice. Furthermore, if the employee needs to work in order to maintain particular skills, then to deny him or her this right may also be a breach of this duty.

In *Collier v Sunday Referee Publishing Co Ltd* (1940), Collier was employed as a sub-editor with the defendant's newspaper. The defendant sold the newspaper and continued to pay the plaintiff, although he was not provided with any work. Collier claimed that the company was under a duty to supply work. It was held that there was a breach of the duty to provide work in this case, as the plaintiff had been appointed to a particular job, which had been destroyed on the sale of the newspaper, thereby denying him the right to maintain his skills as a sub-editor. However, Asquith J stated:

> It is true that a contract of employment does not necessarily, or perhaps normally, oblige the master to provide the servant with work. Provided I pay my cook her wages regularly, she cannot complain if I choose to eat all my meals out.

Interestingly, the courts took this duty one step further in *Langston v Amalgamated Union of Engineering Workers* (1974), in which Langston refused to join the trade union. As a result of union pressure, his employers were forced to suspend him from work on full pay. It was said (*obiter*) that, where a person employs a skilled employee who needs practice to maintain or develop those skills, there may be an obligation to provide a reasonable amount of work.

In *William Hill Organisation Ltd v Tucker* (1998), the Court of Appeal, in considering whether, where work is available and an employee is not only appointed to do that work but is ready and willing to do it, the employer must permit him to do it, concluded that the contract of employment gave rise to such an obligation.

As a result, unless there is an express provision on garden leave contained in the contract, the employer may be in breach of contract.

To pay wages

As a general rule, the employer must pay his or her employees their wages even if there is no work available. In relation to piece-workers, this means that they should be given the opportunity to earn their pay. However, it is possible for the employer to exclude or vary this implied term by providing that there will be no pay where there is no work available.

However, where an employee offers only partial performance of his or her contract, for example, where he or she is on a 'go-slow', the employer need not accept partial performance, in which case the employer need not pay for the employee's services, even on a *quantum meruit* basis (see *Miles v Wakefield MDC* (1987)). However, where the employer accepts this part performance, he or she will be required to pay the full wage. In determining whether the employer had accepted part performance, a restrictive interpretation was given in *Wiluszynski v Tower Hamlets LBC* (1989), in which employees were allowed into work, even though the employer had made it clear that it would not accept partial performance of their duties. Allowing the employees onto the premises was not found to be inconsistent with the employer's initial statement in respect of part performance and did not amount to the employer resiling from its original position. As a result, the employer in this case did not have to pay for the services received.

Whilst the employer is under a duty to pay wages, deductions from wages are regulated by Pt II of the ERA 1996, formerly the Wages Act 1986. First, the mode of payment is as agreed between the employer an employee (for example, directly into a bank account). Every employee is entitled to an itemised pay statement showing gross salary or wages, deductions, net salary or wages, variable deductions and fixed deductions and the purpose for which they are made (see below, Figure 4). Failure to provide this may result in a reference to an employment tribunal.

Furthermore, there is a general rule that no deductions can be made unless the deduction falls within one of the following:

- it is required or authorised by statute, such as PAYE;
- it is authorised by a provision in the employee's contract, for example, contributions to occupational pension schemes;
- the employee has agreed in advance in writing to the deduction being made.

There are exceptions which allow for deductions in respect of overpayment of wages, etc. There are also specific provisions relating to the retail industry, which provide that it is permissible to make deductions in respect of cash shortages and stock deficiencies. However, the right to deduct must be included in the contract of employment and any deductions should not exceed 10% of the gross wages payable on the day in question.

Any contravention allows the employee to complain to an employment tribunal within three months of the deduction being made.

Figure 4: Itemised pay statement

Employer:		Employee:
NI No:		Internal Code No:
Tax Code:		

Pay Date + Period:

Tax Period:

Pay + Allowances:	Deductions:	Balances:
Description:	Rate x Hours:	
Amount		
	DES:	Gross Tax:
	Tax:	DES:
	NI:	Tax:
	Others:	NI:
	Gross:	
	Deductions:	NET:

To indemnify the employee

Where the employee, in the course of his or her employment, necessarily incurs expenses on behalf of the employer, the employee is entitled to be reimbursed. This extends to such things as postage, parking fees, damage to property, etc.

To treat with mutual respect

The employer is under a duty to treat any employee with respect. The basis of the employment relationship is mutuality of respect, trust and confidence. In deciding whether there has been a breach of this term, the actions of the employer are of great importance.

In *Donovan v Invicta Airways Ltd* (1970), Donovan, an airline pilot, was subjected to abusive conduct by his employer. As a result, Donovan resigned. It was held that, in this particular case, the incidents were not substantial enough to justify treating the contract as having been broken. Where there has been a breach of the implied term of trust and confidence by the employer, the employee is not entitled to withhold performance of his contractual obligations – see *Macari v Celtic Football and Athletic Co Ltd* (1999). It is also clear that there is now a duty under which all of the parties to the contract of employment must treat each other with due consideration and courtesy. In *Isle of Wight Tourist Board v Coombes* (1976), a director was heard to describe his personal secretary as 'an intolerable bitch on a Monday morning'. This was held to be a breach of the duty of mutual respect and was conduct that entitled her to resign. In *Malik v BCCI SA (In Liq)* (1997), it was stated that the employer should not conduct itself in a manner likely to destroy or seriously damage the relationship of confidence and trust between employer and employee.

Failure to investigate grievances in certain specific instances has, in the past, been regarded as a breach of the obligation of trust and confidence on the part of the employer. This is illustrated in *Bracebridge Engineering v Darby* (1990), where a complaint of sexual harassment against a manager was not investigated. In *Reed v Stedman* (1999), it was held that an act of sexual harassment may also amount to a breach of the implied term of trust and confidence. More recently, the EAT has held in *WA Goold (Pearmak) Ltd v McConnell and Another* (1995) that there is a general implied term that employers will reasonably and promptly afford a reasonable opportunity to their employees to obtain redress of any grievance they may have.

There is generally no requirement that the employer provide a reference for an outgoing or former employee. However, in certain circumstances, failure to provide a reference may leave the employer open to a claim of victimisation under Art 6 of EC Directive 76/207 and the discrimination legislation – *Coote v Granada Hospitality Ltd* (1998) and *Chief Constable of West Yorkshire Police v Khan* (2001). (For further discussion of the decision in *Coote* and victimisation, see below, Chapter 15.) Also, if a reference is provided, the employer must ensure that the reference is a fair and accurate reflection of the employee's capabilities, etc. Following the decision in *Spring v Guardian Assurance plc* (1995), the employer may be liable in defamation, subject to the defence of qualified privilege and/or negligent misstatement, where he provides an inaccurate or misleading reference. The House of Lords in *Spring* held that an employer who supplies a reference is under a duty to take reasonable care in compiling it. Following the case of *TSB Bank plc v Harris* (2000), to provide a reference containing details of several complaints made about the employee, of which she was unaware, constitutes a breach of the implied term of trust and confidence by the employer. This case further supports the view that references should be balanced and fair.

In *Cox v Sun Alliance Life Ltd* (2001), the Court of Appeal found employers liable in negligence for failing to take reasonable care to be accurate and fair when they provided a reference which suggested that they had a reasonable basis for dismissing the claimant on the ground of dishonesty amounting to corruption. In fact, the charges of dishonesty had never been put to him, had not been made the subject of proper investigation and were shelved pending negotiation of an agreed resignation settlement.

According to Mummery LJ, discharge of the duty of care to provide an accurate and fair reference will usually involve making a reasonable inquiry into the factual basis of the statement in the reference. A similar approach to that set out in *British Home Stores Ltd v Burchell* (1978) in relation to dismissal on grounds of misconduct is appropriate. In order to take reasonable care to give a fair and accurate reference, an employer should confine unfavourable statements about the employee to those matters into which they had made reasonable investigation and had reasonable grounds for believing to be true. However, in order to discharge the duty of care, an employer is not obliged to carry on with an inquiry into an employee's conduct after the employee has resigned. If an investigation is discontinued, unfavourable comments should be confined to matters which had been investigated before the investigation.

In a helpful *obiter*, Mummery LJ advised that where the terms of an agreed resignation or the compromise of an unfair dismissal claim make provision for the supply of a reference, the parties should ensure, as far as possible, that the exact wording of a fair and accurate reference is fully discussed, clearly agreed and carefully recorded in writing on the COT3 at the same time as other severance terms.

To provide for the care and safety of the employee

This duty is based on the law of negligence and is dealt with in detail in Chapter 17, below. Suffice it to say here that the common law requires the employer to take reasonable care for the safety of his or her employees and this duty extends to the provision of competent fellow employees, a safe plant and equipment, a safe place of work and a safe system of work.

14.6.6 Duties imposed on the employee

There are a number of duties imposed on the employee, many of which are tied to the idea of trust and confidence, underpinned by the concept that the employee owes a degree of loyalty to the employer.

To obey lawful and reasonable orders

If an order given by the employer is reasonable and lawful, it must be obeyed. Indeed, failure to obey may give the employer the right to dismiss the employee. Whether an order is lawful and reasonable is a question of fact in each case, depending upon the nature of the job.

In *Pepper v Webb* (1969), an employer instructed his gardener to carry out certain planting work in the garden. The gardener swore at his employer and indicated that he was not prepared to obey the instructions. It was held that the employee was in breach of his implied duty, as the orders were not only lawful, but also reasonable in the circumstances. A change in working practices may also be a reasonable order. In *Cresswell v IRB* (1984), the introduction of a computerised system which tax officers were expected to operate was found to be a reasonable order, given their grading and their job descriptions.

Any dismissal for failing to follow an illegal order, that is, failing to commit a criminal offence, is unlawful and the employee will be able to pursue an action for either unfair or wrongful dismissal (see *Morrish v Henlys (Folkestone) Ltd* (1973), where a refusal to falsify the accounts did not amount to a breach of contract on the part of the employee). Further protection is provided by TURERA 1993 in respect of dismissals in connection with health and safety if an employee has refused to work where there is a serious and imminent danger; such dismissals are automatically unfair.

To act faithfully

This duty is fundamental to the relationship of employer and employee. The employee's first loyalty must be to the employer. The duty encompasses such things as confidentiality, not competing with the employer, etc.

In *Faccenda Chicken Ltd v Fowler* (1986), Faccenda employed Fowler as a sales manager. He resigned with a number of other employees and set up a chicken selling company in competition with his previous employer. Although there was no restraint of trade clause in the contract, the plaintiff alleged that the duty of confidentiality had been broken, as information such as lists of customers had been copied and used by the defendant. It was held that, as the scope of the duty to act faithfully varied according to the nature of the contract of employment, it was necessary to consider all the circumstances of the case, particularly the nature of the employment and the information obtained and used; that is, was the information of such a nature as to be a trade secret and, therefore, highly confidential? It was held that the employer's claim would be rejected, as the information was not so confidential that it could be covered by an implied prohibition on its use.

This case limits the protection afforded to the employer with respect to confidential information. The only information which will be protected is that which could be legitimately protected by a restraint of trade clause and does not appear to cover information 'recalled' by the employee, as opposed to information which is copied or memorised.

Working for another employer whilst still in the employ of the original employer may also be a breach of the duty to act faithfully. Generally, this will only amount to a breach where the second employer is in competition with the first employer, where the nature of the contract is one of exclusivity or where there is a conflict of interest. In all other circumstances, the courts will not seek to curb an employee's legitimate 'spare time' activities. If, for example, an employee was a car mechanic by day and worked in a public house at night, there would be no breach (see *Nova Plastics Ltd v Froggatt* (1982), in which it was held that, even where an employee worked for a competitor in his spare time, there had to be some evidence of potential harm).

In *Hivac Ltd v Park Royal Scientific Instruments Ltd* (1946), employees of the plaintiff company were found to be working in their spare time for a company which was in direct competition with their employer. The employees concerned were doing the same job at both establishments. It was held that the employees were under a duty not to work for a competitor of their employer where this work would conflict with their duty of fidelity and may inflict harm on their employer's business. The duty to act faithfully was found to have been breached in *Adamson v B and L Cleaning Services Ltd* (1995), where an employee put in a tender for the future business of his employer's customers.

The employer may prevent his or her employees either working for rival firms or setting up a business in competition with him or her after they have left their employment by including in the contract of employment an express term which restricts the employee's future employment in some way. Such clauses are known as *covenants in restraint of trade*. Many professional people, such as solicitors and accountants, will have this type of clause in their contracts. Restraint of trade clauses are only valid if they are reasonable in all the circumstances of the case; that is, the protection afforded the employer must not be excessive. Furthermore, the interests of the public must be considered – this is particularly relevant with respect to trade secrets, inventions, etc. Such clauses will also be subject to rules of construction and severance, which may result in part of a clause being struck out.

In *Home Counties Dairies Ltd v Skilton* (1970), Skilton was a milkman. His contract of employment contained a clause which provided that, for a period of one year after the termination of his contract with the plaintiff dairy, he would not sell milk or dairy produce to any person who had been a customer of the dairy for the last six months of his contract and whom he had served. Soon after leaving his employment, he set up his own milk round in the same area as the one in which he had worked for the dairy company. It was held that the former employer should be awarded an injunction to prevent Skilton from working this area. The clause in his contract was valid, as the time limit was reasonable in order to protect the interests of the dairy.

Restraint of trade clauses may not be found to be reasonable where the area of protection is unacceptably large. For example, in *Greer v Sketchley Ltd* (1979), a restraint of trade clause prevented Greer from working anywhere in the UK in a related business, even though his actual job covered only the Midlands. The Court of Appeal found that the restraint was invalid, as Sketchley did not currently operate over the whole of the UK and the likelihood of them expanding the business into other areas was too uncertain. Restraint of trade clauses may also be struck out if they are contrary to public policy, for example, depriving a community of a particular service – see *Bull v Pitney-Bowes* (1966).

Under the requirement of fidelity, the employee must not disclose confidential information which has been acquired in the course of his or her employment. The duty extends to trade secrets, financial state of the company, new designs, etc.

In *Cranleigh Precision Engineering Co Ltd v Bryant* (1965), Bryant was the managing director of a firm which designed swimming pools. He left the company and started his own business, using information which he had gained from his previous employment. It was held that Bryant was in breach of the implied term in his contract of employment, as he could only have gained this information from his previous employment. He had made improper use of information gained in confidence to the detriment of his former employer.

To use skill and care

The employee is under a duty to use reasonable skill and care in the performance of the job. If he or she does so and incurs loss or damage, the employer will indemnify him or her. However, should the employee be grossly incompetent, the employer may have grounds to dismiss him or her. The duty extends to taking proper care of the employer's property, as is illustrated by the decision in *Superlux v Plaisted* (1958), in which an employee was held liable for allowing his employer's goods to be stolen whilst in his care.

In *Lister v Romford Ice and Cold Storage Co Ltd* (1957), Lister, a lorry driver employed by the defendant company, negligently reversed his lorry, seriously injuring a fellow employee. The company claimed an indemnity from Lister, on the grounds that he had broken the implied term of skill and care in his contract of employment. It was held that the employer was entitled to an indemnity because the employee had failed to use reasonable skill and care, as required by the implied terms. Lister was, therefore, liable for the damages awarded to his fellow employee.

See, also, *Janata Bank v Ahmed* (1981), in which a bank manager who failed to check customers' creditworthiness adequately before giving them loans and arranging credit was held to be personally responsible for failing to use sufficient skill and care.

Not to take bribes or make a secret profit

While this duty is part and parcel of the general duty of fidelity, it extends to accounting for any monies or gifts received which may compromise an employee. A breach of this duty by an employee is an abuse of position and may result in a fair dismissal. This is illustrated in *Sinclair v Neighbour* (1967), in which a clerk in a betting shop took £15 from the till without the permission of his employer, whom he knew would refuse to let him do so. The clerk intended to replace it the next day. However, in the interim, the employer discovered what the clerk had done and dismissed him. It was held that the clerk had not acted honestly in attempting to deceive his employer and, therefore, the employer was entitled to dismiss him.

In *Reading v AG* (1951), Reading, who was a sergeant in the British Army based in Egypt, used his position to accompany lorries containing illicit spirits, so that they would not be stopped by the police. Over a period of time, Reading received £20,000 for his 'services'. When his role was finally discovered, he was arrested and the army authorities confiscated his money. When he was released from prison, he brought an action for the return of the money. It was held that Reading was in breach of the implied duty not to take bribes or make secret profits. He had misused his position of trust and had, therefore, to account for those 'profits' to his employer. He was not entitled to have any of the money returned to him.

In *British Syphon Co Ltd v Homewood* (1956), Homewood was employed as chief technician by the plaintiff company in the design and development department. During his employment, he designed a new type of soda syphon. He did not disclose his invention to his employers. He then left his employment and applied for letters patent in respect of his invention. It was held that the invention and the profits from it belonged to his employer. The invention was clearly related to his employer's business and they were, therefore, entitled to the benefits from it.

The common law position regarding employees' inventions has been qualified by ss 39–41 of the Patents Act 1977 and s 11 of the Copyright Designs and Patents Act 1988. In such cases, the invention or design will only belong to the employer if:

- it is made in the course of normal duties or duties specifically assigned and the invention could reasonably be expected to derive from that work;
- it is made in the normal course of duties and, at the time of the invention, there is a special obligation to further the employer's business interests.

SUMMARY OF CHAPTER 14

INDIVIDUAL EMPLOYMENT RIGHTS (1):
THE CONTRACT OF EMPLOYMENT

An employee is employed under a contract of employment (or contract of service), whereas an independent contractor is employed under a contract for services. The distinction is important because many employment rights only accrue in an employer/employee relationship:

- an express term in a document which defines status will override an implied term where there is conflict between them – *Stevedoring & Haulage Services Ltd v Fuller and Others* (2001).

The tests which have developed for establishing the employer/employee relationship are:

- the *control test*, which extends to not just what the employee does, but how it is done. As a single definitive test, the use of control is now rather limited;

- the *integration test*, which considers how far or to what extent the employee is integrated into the employer's business. This has not proved to be a popular test, but, as with the control test, may be used as part of the multiple test;

- the *multiple test* was developed in the case of *Ready Mixed Concrete (South East) Ltd v Minister of Pensions and National Insurance* (1968). The key factors are:

  ○ the provision of own work or labour in return for remuneration;

  ○ a degree of control; and

  ○ all other terms being consistent with the existence of a contract of service; *Lane v Shire Roofing Co (Oxford) Ltd* (1995).

- The *mutuality of obligations test* was developed to overcome the problems faced by the 'regular, casual' worker, who could not be deemed to be an employee using the other tests and, as a result, had to forego any employment rights:

  ○ *O'Kelly v Trusthouse Forte plc* (1983);

  ○ *McMeecham v Secretary of State for Employment* (1997);

  ○ *Carmichael v National Power plc* (2000);

  ○ *Montgomery v Johnson & Underwood Ltd* (2001);

  ○ *Motorola v Davidson and Melville Craig* (2001);

  ○ the Fixed-Term Workers Directive and the Fixed-Term Employees Regulations may assist in overcoming the problems faced by casual workers.

Continuity: most employment rights depend on continuity of employment on the part of the employee. This is governed by s 212 of the ERA 1996. See *Flack v Kodak Ltd* (1983).

National minimum wage

This is governed by the National Minimum Wage Act 1998. The current minimum wage is set at £4.10 per hour for persons aged 22 and over and £3.50 for those aged between 18 and 21. All workers aged 18 years and over are entitled to the minimum wage – this is defined in s 54 of the National Minimum Wage Act 1998. The rate is expected to increase in October 2002.

The Act is enforced by Inland Revenue officers. Employers are expected to keep up to date and accurate records.

Written statement of terms

Although there are no formalities involved in the formation of the contract of employment, every employee is entitled to a statement of written particulars within two months of the commencement of his or her employment (s 1 of the ERA 1996).

Express terms

Express terms are agreed between the employer and employee. Implied terms must be read subject to any express terms in the contract.

Implied terms

Implied terms arise out of custom and practice or through the courts, which will determine whether an implied term is part of the contract (*Johnstone v Bloomsbury HA* (1991)). The test for establishing implied terms can be found in *Henry v London General Transport Services Ltd* (2001).

The duties imposed on the employer are as follows:
- to provide work (*Collier v Sunday Referee Publishing Co Ltd* (1940));
- to provide wages;
- to indemnify his or her employees;
- to have mutual respect (*Donovan v Invicta Airways Ltd* (1970); *Macari v Celtic Football and Athletic Co Ltd* (1999); *TSB Bank plc v Harris* (2000); *Cox v Sun Alliance Life Ltd* (2001));
- to provide for the safety of his or her employees.

The duties imposed on the employee are:
- to obey lawful and reasonable orders (*Pepper v Webb* (1969));

- to act with loyalty (*Faccenda Chicken Ltd v Fowler* (1986); *Hivac Ltd v Park Royal Scientific Instruments Ltd* (1946); *Home Counties Dairies Ltd v Skilton* (1970); *Cranleigh Precision Engineering Co Ltd v Bryant* (1965));
- to act with skill and care (*Lister v Romford Ice and Cold Storage Co Ltd* (1957));
- not to take bribes or secret profits (*Reading v AG* (1951); *British Syphon Co Ltd v Homewood* (1956)).

CHAPTER 15

INDIVIDUAL EMPLOYMENT RIGHTS (2): EQUAL PAY AND DISCRIMINATION

15.1 INTRODUCTION

The legal requirement of ensuring equality between men and women's terms of employment can be found in the Equal Pay Act (EPA) 1970, Art 141 (formerly Art 119) of the EC Treaty and EC Directive 75/117 (the Equal Pay Directive). Although these legislative provisions protect men and women alike, the evidence suggests that a woman's average weekly earnings are only 78% of a man's earnings (New Earnings Survey 2000, Labour Market Trends). Therefore, in practical terms, most cases for equal pay are brought by women. This is further compounded by the segregation of women into jobs perceived as 'women's jobs', which are traditionally in the service sector and in the lower pay bracket. Job segregation is seen as a major obstacle to equality in employment. The National Minimum Wage Act 1998, discussed in Chapter 14, above, may have an impact in this area. However, there is an argument that the current national minimum wage has been set too low to be effective. (See Sachdev, S and Wilkinson, F, *Low Pay, the Working of the Labour Market and the Role of the Minimum Wage*, 1998.)

15.2 EUROPEAN COMMUNITY LAW

The continued impact of European Community (EC) law in the area of equality cannot be underestimated. Article 141 has direct effect and, therefore, domestic law must be applied and interpreted in the light of the Article. The decision in *Jenkins v Kingsgate (Clothing Productions) Ltd* (1981) upholds the principle that Art 141 is directly applicable in the national courts. Directive 75/117, whilst not in itself being enforceable against individual employers, requires Member States to amend their laws so as to comply with the Directive. Article 141 requires each Member State to ensure that the principle of equal pay, for both male and female workers, for equal work or work of equal value, is applied (Art 1). 'Pay' for this purpose means the ordinary basic or minimum wage or salary and any other consideration, whether in cash or kind, which the worker receives, directly or indirectly, in respect of his or her employment (for example, a company car).

Article 141 is enforceable by an individual (see *Kowalska v Freie und Hansestadt Hamburg* (1990)). It is supplemented by the Equal Pay Directive. Generally, such directives are not enforceable by an individual, as it is left to the Member State to comply with the directive, using whatever form or method they choose. However, the Equal Pay Directive is an exception to this, as, first, it gives meaning and clarity to Art 141 and, as a result, is applied through Art 141; secondly, it fulfils the test in *Van Duyn v Home Office* (1975), where it was held that a directive could be enforced by an individual if it was 'sufficiently clear, precise, admitted of no exceptions and, therefore, of its nature, needed no intervention by the national authorities'. The Directive states that:

> ... the principle of equal pay for men and women outlined in Article 141 ... means, for the same work or for work to which equal value has been attributed, the elimination of all discrimination on grounds of sex with regard to all aspects and conditions of remuneration.

Where a Member State fails to comply with the Article or Directive, the European Commission may make a challenge, in the form of legal action, against that Member State. An important and successful legal action was taken by the Commission against the UK for failing to implement the equal value provision in the EPA 1970. This led to an amendment to that Act, providing a new head of claim for equal value (see *Commission v UK* (1982)).

Many challenges have been brought by or on behalf of part time workers, and the majority of those workers in the labour market are women. For example, a challenge was made on the basis that the statutory qualifying periods denied part time employees access to employment rights and, as a result, discriminated against female employees. (See *R v Secretary of State for Employment ex p EOC* (1994) and *R v Secretary of State for Employment ex p Seymour-Smith and Perez (No 2)* (2000).)

Whilst it was held that a two year qualifying period for unfair dismissal complaints had a disparately adverse impact on women so as to amount to indirect discrimination contrary to Art 141 (formerly 119), the House of Lords concluded that the Secretary of State had objectively justified the requirement by providing evidence that to reduce the requirement might inhibit the recruitment of employees and had shown that it was unrelated to any discrimination based on sex. For a critique of *Seymour-Smith*, see Townshend-Smith, R, '*Seymour-Smith*: the closing stages' (2000) 29 ILJ 297.

Where two groups of employees, one predominantly female, the other male, perform for the most part identical work, different training and qualifications may result in the two groups using different knowledge and skills acquired through their different disciplines to carry out their job. As a result, they may not be employed to do the same work within Art 141 – *Angestelltenbetriebstrat der Wiener Gebietskrankenkasse v Wiener Gebietskrankenkasse* (1999).

A wide interpretation has been given to the meaning of 'pay' under Art 141 of the EC Treaty. It has been found to include occupational pension schemes (see *Barber v Guardian Royal Exchange Assurance Group* (1990)); piecework pay schemes (see *Specialarbejderforbundet i Danmark v Dansk Industri (acting for Royal Copenhagen A/S)* (1995)); sick pay (see *Rinner-Kuhn v FWW Spezial-Gebaudereinigung GmbH* (1989)); Christmas bonus (see *Lewen v Denda* (2000)).

The European Court of Justice (ECJ) in *Lommers v Minister Van Landbouw Natuurbeheer en Visserij* (2002) concluded that 'a scheme under which an employer makes nursery places available to employees is to be regarded as a "working condition" within Dir 76/207 rather than as "pay" within Art 141, notwithstanding that the cost of the nursery places is partly born by the employer'.

Although certain working conditions may have pecuniary consequences, such conditions may not fall within Art 141 unless there is a close connection existing between the nature of the work done and the amount of pay.

15.3 EQUALITY CLAUSE

The EPA 1970 incorporates an equality clause into all contracts of employment (s 1(1)). As a result of this clause, any term in the contract of employment which is less favourable to the woman (or man) as compared with a similar clause in a man's contract (or vice versa) will be deemed to be no less favourable. Similarly, if the woman's contract does not contain a beneficial term which is to be found in the man's contract, her contract will be deemed to contain such a clause.

The EPA 1970 is not restricted to claims for pay, but applies to any terms in the applicant's contract which are less favourable than the comparator's. Each term must be considered individually, rather than as part of the remuneration package, as decided in *Hayward v Cammell Laird Shipbuilders Ltd* (1988). Furthermore, a collective agreement may be only one aspect in adducing evidence of remuneration – *Brunhoffer v Bank der Österreichischen Postparkasse* (2001). In theory, the equality clause should operate automatically, without recourse to the employment tribunal system, although, in reality, many complainants have had to resort to the tribunals.

15.3.1 Claiming equality

In order to bring a claim under the EPA 1970, the applicant must show that he or she is employed under a contract of service or contract for services where there is a requirement for them personally to do the work (s 1(6)). This provides the opportunity for a greater number of people to be afforded some equality protection. In *Mirror Group Newspapers Ltd v Gunning* (1986) (a sex discrimination case), it was held that the question to be asked is, is the sole or dominant purpose of the contract the execution of work or labour by the contracting party? If the answer is no, then, clearly, the applicant is not employed. The flexibility of EC law can be seen in *Perceval-Price v Department of Economic Development* (2000), which permitted a person holding a 'statutory office' to claim equal pay under Art 141 as a 'worker'. This was not available under the EPA 1970.

The applicant must be in the same employment as her comparator, that is, she should be employed by the same employer at the same establishment, or by the same employer or an associated employer at an establishment where common terms and conditions are observed (s 1(6)). This sub-section recognises the need for as wide a choice as possible in selecting a comparator within the acceptable confines of the legislation; that is, it would be totally unreasonable to allow a comparison between unrelated employers or industries. The term 'common terms and conditions' was considered in *Leverton v Clwyd CC* (1989). Ms Leverton, the applicant, was a nursery nurse employed by Clwyd County Council. She selected, as her comparators in her equal value claim, male clerical staff who were employed by the county council but who worked at a different establishment. This comparison would only be valid, therefore, if she and her comparators were subject to 'common terms and conditions'. It was held that s 1(6) of the EPA 1970 required a comparison between the terms and conditions observed at the establishment at which the woman was employed and the establishment at which the men were employed, applicable either generally or to a particular class of employee to which both the woman and the men belonged. In this particular case, they were both employed under the same collective agreement, which was applied generally. It was irrelevant that there were some differences between the actual terms of their contracts. Section 1(6) was, therefore, satisfied.

Furthermore, in *British Coal Corp v Smith* (1996), the House of Lords concluded that 'common terms and conditions' meant terms and conditions which are comparable substantially on a broad basis. It is sufficient for the applicant to show that her comparators at both another establishment and her own establishment were, or would be, employed on broadly similar terms.

EC law provides further scope by allowing an applicant to avoid the restrictive nature of s 1(6), insofar as it confines 'associated employer' to private employers. Article 141 of the EC Treaty allows the applicant to select a comparator in the same establishment or service, so held the Employment Appeal Tribunal (EAT) in *Scullard v Knowles and South Regional Council for Education and Training* (1996). This, in turn, would allow public sector employees to compare themselves for the purpose of making equal pay claims. One possible limitation on this interpretation can be seen in *Lawrence v Regent Office Care Ltd* (1999), in which former employees of the county council who were now employed by private contractors were not permitted by the EAT to compare themselves with current employees of the county council.

Whilst the case of *Allonby v Accrington & Rossendale College* (2001) is primarily a sex discrimination case, the employment tribunal at the initial hearing was asked to consider whether s 1(6) of the EPA 1970 provided grounds for an equal pay claim. The tribunal held that as s 1(6) was not satisfied, there could be no equal pay case. However, the Court of Appeal has decided to refer the equal pay issue to the ECJ for it to consider whether Art 141 has direct effect so as to entitle the applicant to bring an equal pay claim against ELS, the agency which found her employment at the college. The argument being that in comparing herself with a lecturer employed by the college at a time when she was employed there, she was working in the same employment for the purposes of Art 141.

The decision in *Scullard* has been applied in *South Ayrshire Council v Morton* (2002) in which the Court of Session held that a claimant in an equal pay claim can now use a comparator who is not employed by the 'same employer' as defined in s 1(6). In the *Morton* case, a female headteacher employed by a local education authority in Scotland was permitted to compare herself with a male headteacher employed by a different Scottish education authority, using Art 141. This type of comparison is restricted to the public sector on the basis that 'any pay settlement conducted under statutory authority and under overall government control constitutes a national collective agreement of the kind contemplated in the *Defrenne* case'.

15.3.2 Comparator

The applicant must select a comparator of the opposite sex. The choice of comparator is a decision for the applicant, as can be seen in *Ainsworth v Glass Tubes Ltd* (1977), and she may apply for an order of discovery in order to select the most appropriate comparator (see *Leverton v Clwyd CC* (1989) (above)). However, and more importantly, the comparator must be, or have been, in existence. While, therefore, comparison with a predecessor of the opposite sex is allowed, as decided by the ECJ in *Macarthys v Smith* (1980), comparison with a hypothetical comparator is not permitted. This, in effect, prevents any claim from applicants in segregated industries where there is no one of the opposite sex falling within s 1(6) of the EPA 1970. However, comparison with a successor is now permitted by virtue of *Diocese of Hallam Trustees v Connaughton* (1996).

15.3.3 Grounds of claim

Equality can only be claimed on one of the following grounds:
- like work;
- work rated equivalent;
- work of equal value.

Like work (s 1(2)(a) of the EPA 1970)

'Like work' is defined by s 1(4) of the EPA 1970 as either the same work or work of a broadly similar nature, where the differences (if any) between the applicant's and comparator's jobs are not of practical importance in relation to the terms and conditions of employment. The application of s 1(4) can be seen in *Capper Pass Ltd v Lawton* (1977), where Mrs Lawton was a cook employed in a directors' dining room, where she provided lunches for up to 20 directors each day. She claimed equal pay on the basis of 'like work' with two male assistant chefs in the works canteen, who provided some 350 meals per day. It was held that a two stage test should be applied:

- is the work the same or, if not, is it of a broadly similar nature? The EAT suggested that a broad approach should be adopted to this question, without a minute examination of the differences between the jobs;

- if the work is broadly similar, are the differences of practical importance? In applying this test, it was concluded that Mrs Lawton was employed on 'like work', as both her work and that of her comparator fell within s 1(4).

Additionally, there may be other factors that have a bearing on whether s 1(4) of the EPA 1970 is satisfied. Additional responsibility may justify a difference in pay (see *Eaton Ltd v Nuttall* (1977)); whereas, in general, the time at which work is done should be ignored (*Dugdale v Kraft Foods Ltd* (1977)) unless it brings with it additional responsibilities, as in *Thomas v NCB* (1987). There, a male chef working permanent nights on his own was found not to be on 'like work' because of the extra responsibilities and the lack of supervision. This amounted to a 'difference of practical importance in relation to terms and conditions of employment', as illustrated in *Calder and Cizakowsky v Rowntree Macintosh Confectionery Ltd* (1993).

Finally, the tribunal is concerned with what the applicant and the comparator actually do in practice, not necessarily what their job descriptions are under their contracts. See *E Coomes (Holdings) Ltd v Shields* (1978), where a woman employed in a betting shop claimed equal pay with a male employee who appeared to be doing the same job as a counterhand. She was paid 62 p per hour, while he received £1.06. The employer claimed that the difference in pay resulted from the fact that the man was also required to deal with troublemakers. The reality was that he had never been called upon to cope with a disturbance and had never received any training in respect of this. The applicant was, therefore, found to be doing 'like work'.

Work rated equivalent (s 1(2)(b) of the EPA 1970)

An applicant may bring an equality claim if her job has been rated as equivalent with that of her male comparator by virtue of a job evaluation scheme. This can only be used where there is in existence a complete and valid scheme, the validity of which has been accepted by the parties who agreed to its being carried out. Indeed, in *Arnold v Beecham Group Ltd* (1982), it was held that there could be no implementation of a job evaluation scheme until the parties who agreed to it had accepted its validity. It would appear, therefore, that, even if it supports the position of the applicant, the employer is not compelled to implement it. Such schemes must comply with s 1(5) of the EPA 1970. The interpretation of this, resulting from the case of *Bromley v H and J Quick Ltd* (1988), is that all valid schemes, as well as being non-discriminatory, must be analytical and must not involve the subjective views of management as to the grading of an employee. Comparisons must, therefore, be made of the various demands upon the employees under the headings laid down in s 1(5), that is, effort, skill, decision, etc. As a result, some job evaluations will not satisfy the decision in *Bromley* or s 1(5) and can, therefore, be challenged.

Some guidance on analytical schemes is offered in *Eaton v Nuttall* (1977) and the Advisory Conciliation and Arbitration Service (ACAS) *Job Evaluation* booklet.

Equal value (s 1(2)(c) of the EPA 1970)

This head of claim originated from a case brought by the European Commission against the UK Government for failing to comply with Art 119 (now Art 141) of the EC Treaty and Directive 75/117, in that there was no provision in UK law for claims of equality where jobs were of equal value. This was highlighted by the fact that there was no right on the part of the employee to compel an employer to carry out a job evaluation scheme under s 1(2)(b) (see *Commission v UK* (1982)). As a result, the UK was forced to amend the EPA 1970 by inserting a provision on equal value. This had the effect of making the equality law available to a greater number of claimants.

From the wording of the EPA 1970, it was thought that this head of claim could only be used if there was no 'like work' or 'work rated equivalent' claim available. However, a potential loophole was spotted by at least one employer, which involved the use of the token man employed on 'like work' to prevent an equal value claim proceeding. In *Pickstone v Freemans plc* (1988), where the employer attempted to block an equal value claim in this way, the House of Lords concluded that the presence of a man doing like work to the applicant did not prevent the applicant bringing an equal value claim using another male comparator. In making this decision, consideration was had of EC law, with the conclusion that any other construction would:

> ... leave a gap in the equal work provision, enabling an employer to evade it by employing one token man on the same work as a group of potential women claimants who were deliberately paid less than a group of men employed on work of equal value with that of the woman. This would mean that the UK had failed yet again to fully implement its obligations under EC law.

15.3.4 Equal value procedure

The procedure in equal value claims is complex. The applicant makes an application to an employment tribunal. One of the provisions of the Employment Act 2002 gives complainants in equal pay claims the right to issue a questionnaire to potential respondents, which would then assist in the decision whether or not to institute proceedings. Initially, the claim is sent to ACAS with a view to settling the claim. If this does not occur, the claim is then the subject of a preliminary hearing, where it is decided whether there are reasonable grounds for determining that the work is of equal value. The purpose of this hearing is to weed out hopeless cases, for example, where the jobs have been deemed unequal under a valid job evaluation scheme (s 2A(1)(a) of the EPA 1970). Alternatively, the employment tribunal may refer the claim directly to an independent expert. Where a case is referred to an independent expert, he or she must provide the employment tribunal with an estimation of the length of time it will take him or her to prepare the report. The employer may introduce the genuine material factor defence (see below) at the preliminary stage, but, if he or she does so, he or she will not be allowed to plead it after the independent expert has reported back to the tribunal. If the tribunal is then satisfied that there are reasonable grounds on which the claim may proceed, the claim is then referred to an independent expert appointed from the ACAS panel. The expert carries out a thorough investigation of the jobs for comparison and reports in writing to the tribunal. Interestingly, the tribunal is not obliged to accept the report, as held in *Tennants Textile Colours Ltd v Todd* (1989). The onus is on the applicant to prove that her job is of equal value to that of the comparator.

What amounts to 'equal value'?

One of the problems for the tribunal has been what amounts to work of equal value. At employment tribunal level, there has been some inconsistency; for example, in *Wells v F Smales and Son (Fish Merchants)* (1985), the tribunal adopted a broad brush approach in concluding that female fish packers were engaged in work of equal value to that of a male labourer, even though some of the women's work was assessed at only 75% of the value of the men's work. The tribunal concluded that the differences were not material. In *Brown and Royal v Cearn and Brown Ltd* (1985), however, the independent expert concluded that the applicant's work was worth 95% of her comparator's work, yet the tribunal declined to conclude that this was work of equal value, as it was not 'precisely equal value'. In *Pickstone v Freemans* (1993), the industrial tribunal concluded that equal value does not have to be 100% value. Equal value also includes higher value, as can be seen in *Murphy v Bord Telecom Eireann* (1988), where the applicant was found to be on less pay yet on work of higher value than her comparator.

Genuine material factor defence (s 1(3) of the EPA 1970)

The EPA 1970 provides a defence in equal pay cases if the employer can show that the variation between the women's and the men's contract is genuinely due to a material difference or factor which is not a difference in sex. In the case of 'like work' or 'work rated equivalent' claims, that factor must be a material difference, whereas, in 'equal value' claims, it *may* be such a difference. The distinction has, in reality, been removed by the decision in *Rainey v Greater Glasgow Health Board* (1987), which went on to apply the criteria in *Bilka-Kaufhaus GmbH v Weber von Hartz* (1986) for establishing this defence. This requires the employer to show objectively justified grounds for the different treatment. There must be a real need on the part of the undertaking for the difference; it is not sufficient merely to show that the reason for the difference was not discriminatory. However, the need to justify any inequality in pay only arises where the disparity in pay is based on gender – see *Strathclyde Regional Council v Wallace* (1998). This has been supported in *Glasgow City Council v Marshall* (2000), although this interpretation has been challenged in *Brunhoffer v Bank der Österreichischen Postparkasse* (2001), in which it was held that there was a need for objective justification where a difference in pay between men and women is established.

The criteria in the *Bilka* case have been successfully used to uphold 'market forces' as a defence, as in *Rainey v Greater Glasgow Health Board* (1987), but can no longer be used to justify inequalities arising out of collective bargaining agreements, as was held in *Enderby v Frenchay HA* (1993). This case further confirms that the burden of proof moves to the employer to show that the pay differential is not discriminatory and is based on an objectively justified factor. (See, also, *Glasgow CC and Others v Marshall* (2000) for a restatement of this principle and a detailed explanation of what the employer must do to establish the defence.)

The following are examples of genuine material factors: the location at which the applicant and her comparator work may justify the difference in terms, for example, work in London as compared with the provinces (see *Navy, Army and Air Force Institutes v Varley* (1976)); 'red circling' – this occurs where the contractual terms of an employee or group of employees are legitimately preserved, for example, where the job may have been downgraded but existing staff have their terms protected. This is a legitimate defence, as long as the red circling is genuine and only applies to an existing person or pool of employees (*Snoxell v Vauxhall Motors Ltd* (1977)). The same is true of economic necessity (see *Benveniste v University of Southampton* (1989)), although, once the economic situation improves, the employer is bound to redress the disparity in terms. Following the decision in *Ratcliffe v North Yorkshire DC* (1995), competitive tendering may not amount to a genuine material difference/factor unless it can be shown to be gender neutral. (See Gill, D, 'Making equal pay defences transparent' (1990) 33 EOR 48.)

15.3.5 Remedies

The applicant must make her claim either whilst still in employment or within six months of leaving that employment. EC law does not impose a time limit for claims. However, the case law suggests that any claim based on EC law should be subject to the limits set for tribunal claims under domestic legislation (*Emmott v Minister for Social Welfare* (1991)). This has been reaffirmed in the case of *Etherson v Strathclyde Regional Council* (1992) and successfully challenged in *Preston v Wolverhampton Healthcare NHS Trust* (2000). The ruling by the ECJ in *Levez v TH Jennings (Harlow Pools) Ltd* (1999) also confirms that the limitation period is in breach of EC law – see also *Levez v TH Jennings (Harlow Pools) Ltd (No 2)* (1999).

If the applicant succeeds in her claim, she may recover arrears of pay for a period of up to two years prior to the date on which proceedings began.

In determining where a successful applicant should be placed on an incremental scale, any entitlement is to join the scale at the point where his or her comparator stood at the relevant date and to enjoy the same entitlement to incremental progression (*Evesham v North Hertfordshire HA* (2000)).

In conclusion, there is some debate about the continued efficacy of the discrimination legislation, including the EPA 1970 (*Equal Pay for Men and Women; Strengthening the Acts*, 1990). However, recent proposals are fairly radical, in that they recommend one single statute covering all aspects of equal treatment for men and women, including gender reassignment and sexual orientation. In respect of pay, it is proposed that employers be placed under a statutory duty to review their pay structures, in order to identify any areas of potential pay inequality and eliminate them. Employers would also be expected to publish the results of their review. Failure to carry out a review would lead to proceedings being taken by the Equal Opportunities Commission (EOC) for non-compliance. Extensive powers would also be given to employment tribunals to make changes to collective agreements or pay structures.

Whether any of these proposals become law is another matter, but, clearly, they highlight a number of serious deficiencies in the current legislation (see *Equality in the 21st Century: A New Approach*, 1998). An attempt to make the EPA 1970 more effective was made in 1997 with the publication of the *Code of Practice on Equal Pay*, published by the EOC. This also recommends that employers carry out a review of their pay systems and provides guidance on how to carry out such a review. However, like all Codes of Practice, it does not have the force of law, although it could be used in evidence. Its effectiveness is, therefore, questionable.

The Equal Pay Task Force has called for mandatory equal pay reviews to be carried out by employers; it also believes that the procedure in equal pay cases needs to be streamlined and that the absence of a comparator should not act as a bar to an equal pay claim. The study by the Equal Pay Task Force looks at the consequences of the gender pay gap. The Task Force state that 'the gender pay gap caused by discrimination in pay systems should be reduced by 50% within the next five years and eliminated entirely within eight years' (*Just Pay – Report of the Equal Pay Task Force*, 2001, EOC).

15.4 SEX AND RACE DISCRIMINATION

There is a steady flow of discrimination cases reaching the employment tribunals, clearly indicating that discrimination in the workplace continues to be a serious problem. There have been a number of studies of the causes of discrimination, but one major cause stands out – stereotyping, particularly in respect of recruitment and promotion (see Curran, M, *Stereotypes and Selection*, 1985).

The EOC has published guidelines on eradicating stereotyping from the selection process (*Fair and Efficient Selection*, 1993). However, it is clear that it still goes on, not solely in relation to race and gender, but also (and possibly more so) in respect of disability and age. Stereotyping may result in women, ethnic minorities and those with disabilities being directed into the less skilled and poorly paid jobs, where there is little chance of career development.

The law on sex and race discrimination is to be found in the Sex Discrimination Act (SDA) 1975 and the Race Relations Act (RRA) 1976 respectively. The RRA 1976 is modelled on the SDA 1975, although there are some differences, which will be highlighted below. However, for the most part, the statutes are the same and, to that extent, the applicability of the case law is interchangeable. The aim of the legislation is to eliminate discrimination and promote equality of opportunity. It is, however, arguable that legislation can be effective in doing this, unless it is supported by the political will to succeed, which, at the very least, means that effective penalties must be provided. It also raises the question of whether the Acts address the causes of discrimination, in particular, stereotyping resulting in job segregation, which is not unlawful under the SDA 1975; whilst it is unlawful under the RRA 1976, the legislative control is not particularly effective. Some protection is also afforded to women, racial and ethnic groups by EC law.

15.4.1 EC law

The Equal Treatment Directive (EC 76/207) provides that every Member State must introduce measures to enable individuals to pursue claims for equal treatment. An individual may pursue a claim against the State as an employer, for example, *Foster v British Gas plc* (1991) and *Doughty v Rolls Royce plc* (1992), which confirmed that an individual was allowed to rely on Art 5 of the Directive against a body which is:

... subject to the authority or control of the State or which has been made responsible, pursuant to a measure adopted by the State, for providing a public service under the control of the State and has for that purpose special powers beyond those which result from the normal rules applicable in relations between individuals.

The Directive enshrines the principle of equal treatment on grounds of sex and marital status. It applies to access to jobs, vocational guidance and training, collective agreements and working conditions, including dismissal. The Directive has been used by the European Commission to challenge the UK's failure to comply with it (*Commission v UK* (1984)); the subsequent legislation (SDA 1986) made sex discrimination in collective agreements unlawful.

The most significant change made by the 1986 Act arose from the decision in *Marshall v Southampton and South-West Hampshire AHA* (1986). The health authority had a policy which resulted in the dismissal of women because they had attained the State pension age, which is a different age for men and women. As a result Ms Marshall was forced to leave her employment; she then decided to challenge this policy. It is held by the ECJ that the term 'dismissal' in Art 5 of the Equal Treatment Directive must be given a wide meaning; that being so, the compulsory dismissal of workers pursuant to a policy concerning retirement related to conditions governing dismissal, which were then subject to Art 5. Where that policy then resulted in different retirement ages for men and women, there had been a contravention of the Article.

The importance of Directive 76/207 in continuing to provide support for individuals and bringing about change in the domestic provision cannot be underestimated. In *Coote v Granada Hospitality Ltd* (1998), the ECJ reaffirmed the importance of Art 6 of the Directive in providing all persons with a right to obtain an effective remedy in a competent court against measures which they consider to interfere with equal treatment for men and women. In this particular case the adequacy of the victimisation provisions under the SDA 1975 were successfully challenged.

The relationship between EC law and domestic law has been reaffirmed in *Blaik v Post Office* (1994), in which the EAT held that:

... if there is a sufficient remedy given by domestic law, it is unnecessary and impermissible to explore the same complaint under the equivalent provisions in a directive. It is only if there is a disparity between the two that it becomes necessary to consider whether the provisions in European Community law are directly enforceable by the complainant ...

A successful challenge was made to the two year qualifying period for protection against unfair dismissal on the basis that it amounted to indirect discrimination against women and was, therefore, contrary to Directive 76/207 (*R v Secretary of State for Employment ex p Seymour-Smith and Another* (1995)). However, in relation to the qualification periods for redundancy payments and possible discrimination against part time employees (who are predominantly female), the appeal was unsuccessful, as it was found to be justifiable (*R v Secretary of State for Employment ex p Seymour-Smith and Perez (No 2)* (2000)).

It should be stated that even EC law has its limitations. There are many areas of discrimination which have only recently been brought within the framework for protection from discrimination, for example, race, religion, disability and sexual orientation. However, Art 13 of the Treaty of Amsterdam (OJ 2000 L303/16) extends anti-discrimination to racial or ethnic origin, religion or belief, disability, age or sexual orientation. It also prohibits both direct and indirect discrimination, and specifically recognises hypothetical comparisons in respect of direct discrimination. Member States will be subject to a series of deadlines, by which each aspect must be legislated for.

The Framework Directive (2000/78) in implementing Art 13 pays particular attention to disability, age, religion and belief. What is interesting is that these grounds are not all treated equally by the Directive. Indeed, it has been suggested that the Directive introduces a hierarchy amongst the discrimination grounds – see Waddington, L, 'Article 13 EC: setting priorities in the proposal for a horizontal employment directive' (2000) 29(2) ILJ 176.

The Race Discrimination Directive (2000/43), which lays down the framework for combating discrimination on the grounds of racial or ethnic origin, has to be implemented by July 2003. It makes unlawful both direct and indirect discrimination on grounds of racial or ethnic origin. It also specifically recognises racial harassment as a distinct type of discrimination (Art 2(3)). Whilst it covers all aspects of employment, the Directive also permits genuine occupational requirements as long as they are founded on legitimate objectives and are proportional (Art 4). Positive action is also permissible (Art 5). (See Guild, E, 'EC Directive on Race Discrimination: surprises, possibilities and limitations' (2000) 30(4) ILJ 416.)

Also, the ECJ is not always prepared to interpret the Directive in a flexible way. For example, in *Kalanke v Freie Hansestadt Bremen* (1996), the ECJ ruled that preferential treatment for women who are equally qualified with men is contrary to Directive 76/207, even where women are underrepresented in the grade concerned. There has now been a proposed amendment to Art 2(4), which, if passed, would allow preferential treatment of a particular sex at the point of selection – in effect, positive action would be recognised. Currently, positive action is also contrary to the SDA 1975 (see *Jepson and Dyas-Elliot v The Labour Party* (1996)).

This has been qualified by the decision in *Badeck and Others* (2000), in which the ECJ held that the Equal Treatment Directive did not preclude a national rule which gives priority to female job applicants. This would apply where women are under-represented, and the male and female candidates have equal qualifications, provided that the rule guarantees that candidates are the subject of an objective assessment which takes account of the specific personal situations of all candidates.

15.4.2 Who is protected?

The legislation covers anyone who seeks employment under a contract of service or who is employed under a contract of service. It extends to those employed under a contract for services where these is a requirement for them personally to do the work (see *Mirror Group Newspapers Ltd v Gunning* (1986)). Protection from discrimination is also extended to discrimination by trade unions and employers associations, employment agencies and qualifying bodies such as the Association of Chartered Accountants, The Law Society and partnerships.

Specific protection is now afforded to part time employees by virtue of s 19 of the Employment Relations Act 1999, which provides that the Secretary of State for Employment shall make regulations for ensuring that part time employees are treated no less favourably than persons in full time employment. This has led to the Part-Time Workers (Prevention of Less Favourable Treatment) Regulations 2000. These Regulations also implement the EC Part-Time Workers Directive (97/81).

The Regulations make it unlawful to treat part time workers less favourably than full time workers, and cover pay, pensions, training and holidays. The right of employers to objectively justify the different treatment is enshrined in the Regulations. Rights are extended to workers who become part time having worked full time. The rise in sex discrimination claims is a direct result of these Regulations.

Although there are no immediate plans for a Code of Practice, employers are recommended to review posts to determine whether they could be performed by part time workers. For a critique of the impact of the Part-Time Workers (Prevention of Less Favourable Treatment) Regulations 2000, see McColgan, A, 'Missing the point? The Part-Time Workers (Prevention of Less Favourable Treatment) Regulations 2000 (SI 2000/1551)' (2000) 29 ILJ 260.

15.5 TYPES OF UNLAWFUL DISCRIMINATION

Discrimination is unlawful if it is based upon sex/gender or racial grounds or the marital status of the complainant. It is, therefore, unlawful to discriminate against a woman or man because of their gender or because they are married (see *Hayle and Clunie v Wiltshire Healthcare NHS Trust* (1998)). However, it is not unlawful to discriminate against someone because they are single (s 3(1) of the SDA 1975). It *is* unlawful to discriminate against someone on 'racial grounds'. This is defined as any of the following: colour, race, nationality, or ethnic or national origins (s 3(1) of the RRA 1976). 'Ethnic origins' have been given a wider interpretation than 'racial origins' and, as a result, have brought more groups within the scope of the RRA 1976, although there is still a problem for those groups who can be equated with a religion rather than a race – these people may not be protected by the legislation.

The test for establishing 'ethnic origin' can be found in *Mandla v Dowell Lee* (1983), in which it was decided that Sikhs constituted an ethnic group. It was stated by Lord Fraser that, in order for a group to constitute an 'ethnic group', it must be regarded as a distinct community by virtue of certain characteristics, some of which are essential:

> ... a long, shared history; a cultural tradition of its own; a common geographical area or descent from a number of common ancestors; a common language; a common literature; a common religion different from that of neighbouring groups or from the general community surrounding it; being a minority or being an oppressed or dominant group within a larger community ...

The test has been applied with some success to bring 'gypsies' within the RRA 1976 (see *CRE v Dutton* (1989)), but not Rastafarians (*Dawkins v Department of the Environment* (1993)), as the latter were deemed to be no more than a religious sect and, in any event, there was no 'long, shared history'. However, Jews may fall within the RRA 1976, although whether an action will succeed depends upon the reason for the discrimination; that is, if a Jew is discriminated against because of his or her religion, he or she will not be protected (see *Seide v Gillette Industries* (1980) and *Simon v Brimham Associates* (1987)). Each case must be considered on its merits.

'National origins' was defined in *Northern Joint Police Board v Power* (1997) as having identifiable elements, both historically and geographically, which, at least at some point in time, reveal the existence of a nation. The Court of Appeal went on to conclude that, as England and Scotland were once separate nations, the complainant could base his claim that he was discriminated against under the RRA 1976 because he was English.

It should be noted that both the SDA 1975 (s 5(3)) and the RRA 1976 (s 3(4)) require a 'like with like' comparison to be made, so that the 'relevant circumstances between the comparators are the same or not materially different' (*Bain v Bowles* (1991)).

Finally, the Human Rights Act (HRA) 1998 provides some protection from discrimination on the grounds of 'religion, politics, or other opinion, national or social origin, association with national minority, property, birth and other status'. Discrimination is prohibited under the HRA 1998 insofar as it relates to other Articles of the European Convention on Human Rights (ECHR), such as freedom of association, privacy, etc. All primary legislation must be read subject to the ECHR and such legislation must be interpreted in the light of legal decisions in respect of the Convention.

The HRA 1998 is likely to have an impact on areas of discrimination which are either not currently protected or are inadequately protected. For example, the right to have respect for one's private life (Art 8) is likely to encompass sexual orientation, sexual activity, dress codes and family life – such as working hours. Article 9 embodies the right to religious and political freedom. However, Art 14 does not provide a free-standing right not to be discriminated against. It prohibits discrimination solely in relation to the enjoyment of the substantive Convention rights.

Article 14 – Prohibition of Discrimination
The employment of the rights and freedoms set forth in this Convention shall be secured without discrimination on any ground such as sex, race, colour, language, religion, political or other opinion, national or social origin, association with a national minority, property, birth or other status.

An individual may challenge existing legislation on the basis of incompatibility; such a challenge will be heard by the High Court. The Secretary of State has the power to amend legislation deemed to be incompatible by an Order in Council. (See Ewing, KD, 'The Human Rights Act and labour law' (1998) 27 ILJ 275 for an analysis of the application of the HRA 1998 to employment law.)

15.5.1 Direct discrimination

Direct discrimination covers both overt and covert acts against the individual and is not confined to hostile or intentional acts of discrimination. Direct discrimination occurs where a person is treated less favourably on grounds of their sex, race or marital status. In order to establish this type of discrimination, comparison must be made with a person of the opposite sex or another race; however, a hypothetical person can be used for this comparison. Following the decision in *Badamoody v United Kingdom Central Council for Nursing, Midwifery & Health Visiting* (2002), where the applicant fails to establish an actual comparator, the employment tribunal must go on to construct a hypothetical comparator and test the case against that benchmark. Although this head of claim has been difficult to establish in the past, in recent years the following test has been formulated, which has helped the complainant and reinforces the fact that intention and motive, no matter how good, are not relevant. The test is as follows:

- has there been an act of discrimination? If yes,

- but for the sex or race of the complainant, would he or she have been treated differently, that is, more favourably? If the answer to this is in the affirmative, an act of direct discrimination has taken place (see *R v Birmingham CC ex p EOC* (1989), followed in *James v Eastleigh BC* (1990)). In the latter case, free swimming was provided for children under the age of three and persons who had attained the State retirement age. Mr and Mrs

James were both aged 61 and were both retired. When they went to the swimming baths owned by the defendant council, Mrs James was able to take advantage of free swimming, whilst her husband had to pay. Mr James alleged an act of direct discrimination, which breached s 29 of the SDA 1975, relating to discrimination in the provision of goods, facilities and services. Initially, the Court of Appeal held that there was no act of discrimination, as it was necessary to look at the reason for adopting the discriminatory policy, which, in this case, was to help the needy; therefore, the discrimination was not on grounds of gender. However, on appeal to the House of Lords, it was decided to apply the 'but for' test and ask the question, 'but for the complainant's sex, would he have received the same treatment?'; the answer was in the affirmative and, as a result, Eastleigh Borough Council had to alter their policy.

However, the 'but for' approach has been questioned, particularly in cases where discrimination is inferred. In *Zafar v Glasgow CC* (1998), it was held that the guidance provided in *King v The Great Britain China Centre* (1991) should be applied when inferring that discrimination had taken place. This places the burden of proof squarely on the applicant, but allows the tribunal to draw any inferences which it believes are just and equitable. The employer will then be required to give an explanation, which, if unsatisfactory or inadequate, will allow the tribunal to infer that an act of discrimination has taken place. The decision in *Zafar* goes on to support the dissenting judgment in *James*, which allows the tribunal to consider reason, intention and motive. Whether this decision will now make it harder for the applicant to establish direct discrimination remains to be seen. (See Watt, B, 'Goodbye "but-for", hello "but-why?"' (1998) 27 ILJ 121, which provides a detailed analysis of the possible impact of *Zafar*.) The Sex Discrimination (Indirect Discrimination and Burden of Proof) Regulations 2001 shift the burden of proof in direct discrimination cases to the extent that, once the complainant has established a *prima facie* case, that is, that there is sufficient evidence to infer discrimination, the burden will move to the respondent to offer a non-discriminatory reason for his actions. It is unclear at this stage whether it will have a significant impact on the guidance provided by the decision in *King*.

Further assistance in establishing direct discrimination can be found in the case of *Noone v North West Thames Regional HA* (1988), which concluded that, once the complainant has shown that there is a *prima facie* case of discrimination, even though actual evidence may be lacking, discrimination will be inferred unless the employer can show good reason for his or her actions which are not connected to the sex or race of the complainant.

The Court of Appeal in *Anya v University of Oxford* (2001) stresses the importance of looking for indicators from a time before or subsequently which may demonstrate that a decision to appoint, or not, was affected by racial bias. For example:

... evidence that one of the panel was not unbiased, or that equal opportunities procedures were not used when they should have been, may point to the possibility of conscious or unconscious racial bias having entered into the process.

The RRA 1976 is slightly wider in scope than the SDA 1975, as it extends to transferred discrimination. For example, if a white barmaid is instructed to refuse to serve black people and, on refusing to obey this order, is dismissed, she can claim direct discrimination under the RRA 1976: *Zarcynska v Levy* (1978). (See *Weathershield Ltd (Van and Truck Rentals) v Sargent* (1999), in which a receptionist was dismissed for refusing to obey an order not to take van hire requests from Blacks or Asians.)

15.5.2 Sexual and racial harassment

There is no separate provision relating to harassment at work in either the SDA 1975 or the RRA 1976. However, it is specifically covered by the Race Directive. Any complaint must be made under the heading of direct discrimination. The recognition of this as a serious head of claim is fairly recent. The definition of sexual harassment is wide and encompasses any conduct meted out in a particular way because of the complainant's gender or race; that is, it is not confined to conduct of a purely physical nature, even though many of the cases involve this type of conduct.

In *Strathclyde Regional DC v Porcelli* (1986), Mrs Porcelli was a laboratory assistant at a school under the control of the council. She was subjected to a variety of treatment from two male laboratory assistants, who were intent on driving her from her job. This conduct involved brushing against her and making suggestive remarks, as well as putting heavy equipment on the top shelves of the store. She made her claim and asked to be transferred. It was held that she had been discriminated against, as the type of treatment was related to her sex and a man in a similar position would not have been treated the same way. The employer was found to be vicariously liable for the actions of the male laboratory assistants by virtue of s 41 of the SDA 1975.

The courts have gone further, in holding that harassment need not be a course of conduct but can manifest itself in a single act of a serious nature. In *Bracebridge Engineering v Darby* (1990), it was held that employees committing such acts might be within the course of their employment, resulting in the employer being vicariously liable for such acts. Racial harassment is akin to sexual harassment and, to that extent, racial insults may also be a form of harassment. However, in establishing either type of discrimination, the complainant must show that the treatment is to their detriment, as that term is used in s 6 of the SDA 1975 and s 4 of the RRA 1976 (see *De Souza v Automobile Association* (1986)).

The EC has intervened on the question of sexual harassment by, first, adopting a resolution relating to sexual harassment at work (Resolution No 6015/90) and, second, agreeing to a recommendation and Code of Practice on the Protection and Dignity of Women and Men at Work. As a result, although the recommendation is not directly enforceable, the ECJ has ruled that the national courts must take such measures into account in applying national and Community law (*Grimaldi v Fonds des Maladies Professionelles* (1990)).

In *Wadman v Carpenter Farrer Partnership* (1993), it was held that the tribunal should look at the employer's code of practice in harassment cases to assess implementation. It should be noted that the Criminal Justice and Public Order Act 1994 introduced a criminal provision against harassment. The Protection from Harassment Act 1997 also creates a criminal offence of harassment, as well as providing civil remedies in the form of damages or an injunction. It is unclear how far this Act covers harassment in the workplace. The Act is limited, in that one act of harassment will not support an action and there is no vicarious liability provision.

As with all acts of discrimination, the employer may be found to be vicariously liable unless all reasonable precautions are taken to prevent the act of discrimination from taking place. Employers are expected to take preventative action even though such action may not have prevented the act complained of from taking place – *Canniffe v East Riding of Yorkshire Council* (2000). See Roberts, P, 'Employer's liability for sexual and racial harassment: developing the reasonably practicable steps defence' (2001) 30(4) ILJ 388. Although it was thought that the common law test for determining whether an employee was acting outside the course of the employment was also applicable to this statutory form of vicarious liability, it is clear from the current case law that the tribunals will not necessarily apply such a stringent test. In *Burton v De Vere Hotels Ltd* (1996), the employer was found to be vicariously liable where the harasser was a third party who subjected the employer's employees to racial insults as part of his nightclub act. In these circumstances, it was found that the employer would be vicariously liable, provided he could have prevented the harassment from taking place by applying the standards of good practice. In *Tower Boot Co Ltd v Jones* (1997), the Court of Appeal overruled the decision of the EAT by finding that the employer was vicariously liable for extreme acts of racial harassment perpetrated by his employees on a fellow employee, such as branding with a screwdriver and whipping, even though the EAT had felt that the employees were outside the scope of their employment. The Court of Appeal felt that a purposive construction should be given to s 32 of the RRA 1976 and s 41 of the SDA 1975, so as to deter acts of sexual and racial harassment in the workplace. (See, also, *Sidhu v Aerospace Composite Technology Ltd* (2000), in which an act of discrimination occurring on a works trip was found to be outside the course of employment, and Roberts and Vickers, 'Harassment at work as discrimination: the current debate in England and Wales' (1998) 3 IJDL 91.)

The common law approach (see Chapter 17) resulted in a restrictive interpretation, which would allow employers to avoid liability for more heinous acts of discrimination.

15.5.3 Discrimination and pregnancy

Discrimination related to pregnancy or maternity is part and parcel of direct discrimination. As a result, a pregnant woman can, at least in theory, challenge unfavourable treatment because of her pregnancy as an act of direct discrimination. At one time, it was thought that such treatment was not protected by the SDA 1975, on the basis that there could be no male comparator. This approach was supported in *Turley v Allders Department Stores Ltd* (1980)). However, some redress was provided by cases such as *Hayes v Malleable Working Men's Club* (1985) and *Webb v EMO Cargo Ltd* (1993), although both of these cases required comparison of the treatment of the pregnant woman with that of the sick man or, at the very least, a male employee who would be absent for an equivalent period. However the ECJ, in considering Webb's case, ruled that this comparison was no longer acceptable and that dismissal on account of pregnancy constituted direct discrimination (see, also, *Dekker v Stichting Vormingscentrum voor Jong Volvassen (VJW Centrum) Plus* (1991)).

Webb was referred back to the House of Lords (*Webb v EMO Air Cargo Ltd (No 2)* (1995)), where it was concluded that the ECJ ruling should be limited to permanent contracts rather than those existing or intending to exist for a fixed term only, for example, maternity cover. It is, therefore, arguable that, if this distinction is maintained, the UK provision does not comply with EC law. However, in *Caruana v Manchester Airport plc* (1996), the EAT decided that the ruling in *Webb* applied equally to fixed term contracts. This has been clarified by the decision in *Mahlburg*. In *Mahlburg v Land Mecklenburg-Vorpommern* (2000), the ECJ, in applying *Dekker* and *Habermann*, concluded that it was contrary to Art 2(1) of the Equal Treatment Directive for an employer to refuse to appoint a pregnant woman to a post of an unlimited duration on the ground that a statutory prohibition on employment arising on account of her pregnancy would prevent her from being employed in that post from the outset and for the duration of the pregnancy.

To replace an employee on maternity leave with a permanent employee, knowing that the pregnant employee wanted to return to her post, amounted to less favourable treatment within the SDA – *(NICA) Patefield v Belfast CC* (2000). She was therefore disadvantaged in the circumstances in which she had to work.

The ECJ has confirmed that protection of the pregnant woman under Art 5 of the Equal Treatment Directive and Art 10 of the Pregnant Workers Directive is not restricted to a woman employed for an indefinite period, but extends to one employed for a fixed term, even though, because of her pregnancy, she may be unable to work for a substantial part of the term of the contract. Dismissal of a worker on account of pregnancy constitutes direct discrimination on grounds of sex, whatever the nature and extent of the economic loss incurred by the employer as a result of her absence because of pregnancy. Whether the contract was concluded for a fixed or an indefinite period has no bearing on the discriminating character of the dismissal. In either case, the employee's inability to perform her contract of employment is due to pregnancy – *Tele Danmark A/S v Handels-Og Kontorfunktiunaererernes Forbund i Danmark acting on behalf of Brandt-Nielsen* (2001).

We can see the use of the purposive approach by the ECJ in considering whether the non-renewal of a fixed term contract on grounds related to pregnancy fell within Art 10 of the Pregnant Workers Directive or Arts 2(1) and 3(1) of the Equal Treatment Directive.

While the ECJ concluded that non-renewal of a fixed contract when it comes to the end of its stipulated term cannot be regarded as dismissal within Art 10, it can be viewed as a refusal of employment which, if it relates to a worker's pregnancy, constitutes direct discrimination contrary to Arts 2(1) and 3(1) of Directive 76/207 – *Jiménez Melgar v Ayuntamiento de los Barrios* (2001).

Whilst the 'sick man' comparator has no role in the treatment of the pregnant woman or woman on maternity leave, it still has a limited role to play (see *Brown v Rentokil Ltd* (1998)). For example, it has been held that a woman who was dismissed on grounds of absence due to an illness which arose from pregnancy was not necessarily discriminated against on grounds of sex. In this case, it was thought to be quite legitimate to compare the treatment of the woman with how a sick man would have been treated, although it was decided that protection for the pregnant woman extended to the end of the maternity leave period (*Handels og Kontorfunktionaernes Forbund i Danmark (acting for Hertz v Dansk Arbejdsgiverforening)* (1991)). Where, therefore, a woman is dismissed due to an illness originating from her pregnancy which occurs outside the maternity leave period, her treatment by her employer should be compared to that of the hypothetical sick man – see *Handels og Kontorfunktionaerenes Forbund i Danmark (acting on behalf of Larson) v Dansk Handel and Service (acting on behalf of Fotex Supermarket)* (1997).

Finally, even where national legislation allows an employer to send home a pregnant employee on the basis that they are unfit for work, he or she is still required to pay them full pay – see *Handels og Kontorfunktionaernes Forbund i Danmark (acting on behalf of Hoj Pedersen) v Faellesforeningen for Danmarks Brugsforeringer (acting on behalf of Kvickly Skive)* (1999).

Some of these issues may have less significance as a result of the Employment Rights Act 1996, which provides protection from dismissal for all pregnant employees and in connection with childbirth. Further rights relating to maternity and parental leave can be found in the Employment Relations Act 1999 and the Maternity and Parental Leave Regulations 1999.

15.5.4 Sexual orientation

The issues of discrimination on grounds of sexual orientation and the extent of the protection provided by the SDA 1975 and Directive 76/207 are contentious ones. Much publicity was given to the challenge made against the ban on the recruitment of homosexuals to the armed forces. The final outcome is that neither the SDA 1975 nor Directive 76/207 extend protection to discrimination on grounds of sexual orientation (see *R v Ministry of Defence ex p Smith* (1996) and *Grant v South West Trains Ltd* (1998)). The latter case involved the grant of travel concessions to partners of employees of South-West Trains; the exception being same sex partners. The ECJ concluded that an employer is not required by Community law to treat same sex relationships as those involving a partner of the opposite sex. It would require a change in the legislative provision for this situation to be recognised.

There may, however, be some redress as a result of the Human Rights Act 1998. Indeed, the European Court of Human Rights (ECtHR) has recently held that the Ministry of Defence was in breach of Art 8 (right to a private life) of the Convention in banning homosexuals from the armed forces (*Smith and Grady v UK* (1999)).

Considerable doubt has been cast on the applicability of Art 14 of the ECHR by the decision in *Secretary of State for Defence v MacDonald* (2001). The Court of Session in this case confirmed that 'sex' within the meaning of s 1(1) of the SDA 1975 does not include sexual orientation. Nor does the decision of the ECtHR in *Salgueiro da Silva Mouta v Portugal* (2001) result in Art 14 of the ECHR including sexual orientation. Once again, in the *MacDonald* case, the issue of comparison in s 5(3) was considered, and the conclusion reached was that the comparator was a person of the opposite sex attracted to the same sex, rather than a heterosexual. As Michael Rubenstein has pointed out on a number of occasions, this comparison does not equate to the same circumstances but is merely analogous – see 'Highlights' [2001] IRLR 413.

There may also be a possible action for sexual harassment under the SDA 1975 if the complainant can show that, for example, a lesbian employee would have been treated differently, that is, more favourably. It is unfortunate that the 'like with like' comparison required by s 5(3) results in such a restrictive comparison in such cases (*Smith v Gardner Merchant Ltd* (1998)).

The continued impact of the need for a like with like comparison to be made under the SDA 1975 is problematic in harassment cases, particularly where the applicant is subjected to verbal abuse. This was highlighted in *Pearce v Governing Body of Mayfield Secondary School* (2001), in which a teacher was forced to resign from her post due to a campaign of homophobic abuse from her students. The Court of Appeal restricted the comparator to a male homosexual who would have been treated to the same sort of sexual harassment. However, *Pearce* provided some hope regarding the application of the Human Rights Act 1998, in that Hale LJ (at p 675) concluded that the acts of homophobic abuse were capable of contravening Art 8 when read with the prohibition of discrimination under Art 14. She suggested, therefore, that 'a remedy might lie against a public authority under ss 6 and 7 of the Human Rights Act 1998 in respect of acts taking place on or after 2 October 2000'. The HRA 1998 would also allow the SDA 1975 to be read in such a way as to be compatible with those rights, so that sex was not confined to sexuality.

Whilst there is little protection for homosexuals, the courts have recognised that discrimination against transsexuals, that is, those undergoing or having undergone gender reassignment, is unlawful and falls within the remit of the SDA 1975 – see *P v S and Cornwall CC* (1996). To reaffirm this approach, the Sex Discrimination (Gender Reassignment) Regulations 1999 (SI 1999/1102) specifically bring this type of discrimination within the SDA 1975. (See, also, *Chessington World of Adventure Ltd v Reed* (1997).) The Framework Directive addresses the need for protection from discrimination on grounds of sexual orientation.

15.5.5 Indirect discrimination

Indirect discrimination is aimed at conduct which, on the face of it, does not treat people differently; that is, it is race and gender neutral. However, it is the impact of this treatment which amounts to discrimination. It can, therefore, be subtle in nature and may be difficult to prove. However, the SDA 1975 has been amended by the Sex Discrimination (Indirect Discrimination and Burden of Proof) Regulations 2001, which introduce a new definition of indirect discrimination in employment cases relating to sex discrimination (s 2(b)). Note that, for the moment, the 'old' definition applies to race cases. This will change when the Race Directive is implemented. The essentials are that:

- a requirement or condition is applied equally to both sexes and all racial groups; or (in employment cases) a provision, criterion or practice relating to sex discrimination;

- a considerably smaller proportion of the complainant's sex or race can comply with it, as compared to the opposite sex or persons who are not of that racial group; or which is to the detriment of a considerably larger proportion of women than men;

- the requirement or condition operates to the detriment of the complainant because he or she cannot comply with it;

- the requirement or condition can be justified irrespective of the gender or race of the complainant.

The burden of proof is initially on the complainant. Once a *prima facie* case has been made out, the burden moves to the employer to show that the requirement or condition is justified. Again, the intention of the employer is irrelevant in establishing indirect discrimination, although it becomes important to the tribunal in deciding whether compensation should be awarded, as both statutes provide that no compensation is payable for unintentional, indirect discrimination.

In isolating a requirement or condition, the complainant has in the past had to show that it operates as an absolute bar, in that it amounts to 'a must', without which an applicant could not proceed. This is highlighted by *Perera v Civil Service Commission* (1983). Perera was a barrister from Sri Lanka who applied for a post with the defendants. The selection criteria, which were applied to all candidates, included age, practical experience in the UK, spoken and written English, etc. Perera argued that these were requirements or conditions. It was held that they were not a 'must', without which an applicant could not succeed. The only relevant condition was that the applicant should be a barrister or solicitor and Perera fulfilled this condition.

This interpretation allowed an employer to apply a wide range of criteria in making selections for employment or promotion and, as long as they did not constitute a 'must', how he or she applied them was not called into question under the SDA 1975 or the RRA 1976. However, the decision in *Perera* has been challenged by the EAT in *Falkirk Council v Whyte* (1997). The EAT in this case confirmed that a 'desirable' qualification could amount to a requirement or condition where it was clear that the qualification operated as the decisive factor in the selection process. The EAT not only chose not to follow *Perera*, but also welcomed a more liberal approach to determining 'requirement or condition' and avoiding the need to establish an absolute bar. Past cases show that age limits may be discriminatory, as in *Price v Civil Service Commission* (1977), as may requirements to work full time (*Home Office v Holmes* (1984); *Briggs v North Eastern Education and Library Board* (1990)); a mobility clause which requires an employee to move to new locations may also amount to requirement or condition, as in *Meade-Hill and National Union of Civil and Public Servants v British Council* (1995). The new definition in employment cases is in line with this more liberal approach as seen in *Falkirk*.

In determining what amounts to a 'considerably smaller proportion', the complainant must show, usually by the use of statistical evidence, that there is an adverse impact on his or her particular race or sex (see *London Underground Ltd v Edwards (No 2)* (1998) for a flexible application of adverse impact). Many complainants fail by selecting the wrong pool for comparison.

In *Pearse v City of Bradford Metropolitan Council* (1988), Ms Pearse, a part time lecturer at Ilkley College, was unable to apply for a full time post at the college because the only persons eligible to apply were full time employees of the local authority. She alleged that this amounted to indirect discrimination and submitted statistics which showed that only 21.8% of the female academic staff employed at the college were employed on a full time basis, compared with the 46.6% of the male academic staff who could comply with the requirement/ condition regarding full time employment. It was held that Ms

Pearse should fail in her claim because she had selected the incorrect pool for comparison; the correct pool would have been those with the appropriate qualifications for the post, without reference to the requirement/condition in question, rather than those eligible.

Whether the complainant has selected the correct pool for comparison is a question of fact to be decided by the tribunal. However, as can be seen in *Kidd v DRG (UK) Ltd* (1985), statistical evidence is usually necessary to support claims and this must specifically relate to the pool for comparison. For example, if the requirement or condition affects part time workers and the applicant wants to show that the majority of part time workers are female, her statistical evidence must show this.

In deciding whether the complainant has selected the correct pool, the tribunal will not allow the complainant to limit the pool just because it suits her case. In *Jones v University of Manchester* (1993), the Court of Appeal held that the appropriate pool for comparison was all those with the required qualifications for the post, not including the requirement complained of. So, Mrs Jones' attempts to narrow the pool failed. The new wording is unlikely to require a comparison based on statistical evidence. A more theoretical comparison may suffice.

The term 'can comply' has also been open to interpretation by the tribunals. It has been determined that the words mean 'can in practice', rather than 'can as a theoretical possibility'. This is supported by the decisions in *Price v Civil Service Commission* (1977) and *Mandla v Dowell Lee* (1983).

Has the condition or requirement operated to the detriment of the complainant?

The complainant must show that he or she has suffered a detriment, that is, that the requirement or condition has disadvantaged him or her; in effect, the complainant must have *locus standi*. The following have been held to amount to a disadvantage: requiring a woman to work part time (*Home Office v Holmes* (1984)); transfer to a less interesting job (*Kirby v MSC* (1980)); and conduct amounting to sexual harassment (*Wileman v Minilec Engineering Ltd* (1988)).

Justification

Once the complainant has established the above requisites, the onus of proof moves to the employer to show that the requirement or condition is justified irrespective of the gender, race or marital status of the complainant. The criteria for establishing justification were clarified by the Court of Appeal in *Hampson v Department of Science* (1989), in which it was made clear that the test requires a balance to be struck between the discriminatory effect of the requirement or condition and the needs of the employer. The employer must show a real need on the part of the undertaking to operate such a practice (this must be objective; it will then be balanced against the discriminatory impact of the practice). If there is a less discriminatory alternative, the employer must take it.

The fact that a requirement or condition is not inherently discriminatory does not amount to justification within s 1(1)(b). As the operation of s 1(1)(b) is based on gender neutral requirements which have a disparate impact on a particular sex (or race), it is not acceptable justification of the practice to argue that it may operate in a non-discriminatory manner – *Whiffen v Milham Ford Girls' School* (2001).

15.5.6 Victimisation

Section 2 of the RRA 1976 and s 4 of the SDA 1975 both recognise victimisation as a separate form of discrimination. Victimisation occurs where the complainant is treated less favourably because he or she has: brought proceedings against the discriminator or another person under the RRA 1976, SDA 1975 or EPA 1970; given evidence or information in connection with proceedings brought by any person against the discriminator or another person under the RRA 1976, SDA 1975 or EPA 1970; alleged that the discriminator or any other person has committed an act which would amount to a contravention of the RRA 1976, SDA 1975 or EPA 1970; or done anything under or with reference to the SDA 1975, RRA 1976 or EPA 1970 in relation to the discriminator or another.

Until recently, the complainant had to show a clear connection between the action of the discriminator and his or her own conduct (presuming that it falls under one of the above); if there was no more than a casual connection, then the tribunal would be reluctant to find that victimisation had taken place. (See *Aziz v Trinity Street Taxis Ltd* (1988).) However, the decision in *Nagarajan v London Regional Transport* (1999) has overturned the decision in *Aziz*. As a result, the alleged victim no longer has to show that the discriminator had a motive which was consciously connected with the discrimination legislation. It would suffice to show that the discrimination provisions in s 4 of the SDA 1975 and s 2 of the RRA 1976 consciously or subconsciously influenced the discriminator.

The House of Lords in *Chief Constable of West Yorkshire Police v Khan* (2001) held that, whilst failure to provide a reference may amount to victimisation, the withholding of the reference must be linked to a protected act on the part of the applicant. In the present case, the reason why the reference was withheld was not because the applicant had brought discrimination proceedings, but rather because the employer temporarily needed to preserve his position in the outstanding proceedings. The evidence established that once the litigation was concluded, a reference would have been supplied. From this case, it is clear that the reason for the alleged act of victimisation is relevant and must be identified.

Segregation

Section 1(2) of the RRA 1976 makes unlawful the provision of separate facilities for members of different races, even where they are equal in quality. The purpose of this is to prevent any form of apartheid. However, the interpretation of this section by the tribunals shows that there is no onus to prevent voluntary segregation of racial groups (see *PEL Ltd v Modgill* (1980)). The SDA 1975 does not contain a similar provision.

15.6 SCOPE OF PROTECTION

Once the complainant has identified and established the grounds of discrimination, he or she must then show how they relate to s 6 of the SDA 1975 or s 4 of the RRA 1976, insofar as the discrimination is only unlawful if it occurs in the selection process, in respect of the terms on which persons are employed; within employment, in respect of opportunities for training, promotion or other benefits; and, finally, in respect of the dismissal of employees or subjecting them to any other detriment. For example, in *Saunders v Richmond-upon-Thames BC* (1978), it was held that it was not unlawful in itself to ask questions of a female applicant which would not be asked of a male applicant, although it may illustrate a discriminatory frame of mind.

15.6.1 Genuine occupational qualifications

Both s 7 of the SDA 1975 and the s 5 of the RRA 1976 permit discrimination by an employer if it falls within the specified genuine occupational qualifications, which include the following:

- the nature of the job demands a man or woman because of their physiology, excluding strength and stamina;
- authenticity;
- decency or privacy, for example, a female nurse in a girls' boarding school. However, in *Etam plc v Rowan* (1980), the genuine occupational qualification defence did not succeed, as the failure to employ a male sales assistant in a female clothes shop was held to be unlawful, as there were, in practice, female sales assistants who could assist in the changing rooms;
- a post which requires the employee to live in, where there are no separate sleeping and sanitary facilities and it is unreasonable to expect the employer to provide them;
- posts in a private home (which for the SDA 1975 exemption only involves social or physical contact with the person living in the home);
- the holder of the post supplies individuals or persons of a particular race with personal services promoting their welfare, education, etc. In *Lambeth*

LBC v CRE (1990) and *Tottenham Green Under-Fives Centre v Marshall (No 2)* (1991), it was held that the personal service must require direct contact between the provider of the service and the client if the genuine occupational qualification is to apply;

- a post which involves working abroad in a country whose laws and customs are such that the job can only be done by a man;
- the job is one of two, held by a married couple.

In addition, there are exemptions for acts done to safeguard national security and there is special protection for women during pregnancy and childbirth. However, the Employment Act 1989 allows an employer to treat a woman differently on grounds of health and safety where there was a statutory requirement in existence prior to the SDA 1975 which was for the protection of women in relation to pregnancy, maternity or other risks which are specially associated with women.

15.7 BRINGING A CLAIM

An applicant must bring a claim to the employment tribunal within three months of the date on which the act complained of was committed. A complaint brought after this limit will only be heard by the tribunal if it is just and equitable to do so. Where the act of discrimination is a continuing one, the time limit runs from the date on which it was last committed.

15.8 REMEDIES

A successful complainant may receive an award of compensation, which may include a sum for actual losses, such as expenses and wages, injury to feelings and future losses. However, no compensation will be awarded for indirect race discrimination unless it is intentional. An amount of not less than £500 should be awarded for injury to feelings, which should always form part of the award (*Sharifi v Strathclyde Regional Council* (1992)). The upper limit for compensation was £11,000. This was challenged in *Marshall v Southampton and South West Hampshire AHA (No 2)* (1993), where it was held by the ECJ that the limit on compensation contravened EC law and should, therefore, be removed; in addition, it was in order to award interest on compensation. Following *City of Bradford v Arora* (1991), an employment tribunal may award aggravated damages but, following *Deane v London Borough of Ealing* (1993), can no longer award exemplary damages. The Court of Appeal in *Sheriff v Klyne Tugs (Lowestoft) Ltd* (1999) has recognised a new head of damages for personal injury in discrimination cases. As a result, where an applicant can show that an act of discrimination resulted in personal injury, the employment tribunal must award compensation for it. Compensation may be awarded for injury to feelings and psychiatric injury resulting from an act of discrimination. Whilst they are distinct forms of injury, it is recognised that they are not always easily separable – *HM Prison Service v Salmon* (2001).

The employment tribunal also has the power to:

- make a declaration with respect to the rights of the complainant under the respective legislation – such a declaration is not enforceable and, at the most, can only be persuasive as far as the employer is concerned;

- make a recommendation for the employer to take specific action, for example, order the employer to cease discrimination with respect to an individual complainant. However, this does not extend to a general order to cease a discriminatory practice, nor, failing the decision in *Noone v North West Thames RHA (No 2)* (1988), does it extend to positive discrimination such as recommending that the applicant who has been the victim of discriminatory selection be awarded to the next available post.

15.9 THE EOC AND THE COMMISSION FOR RACIAL EQUALITY

The EOC and Commission for Racial Equality (CRE) have the following duties, which are broadly similar:

- to work towards the elimination of discrimination;

- to promote equality of opportunity between men and women and racial groups and to promote good race relations;

- to keep under review the working of the equal opportunities legislation and propose amendments as necessary.

The Commissions are also granted various powers:

- to assist applicants in bringing complaints of discrimination;

- to undertake or assist research and education activities;

- to issue Codes of Practice. There is now a Code of Practice on equal pay;

- to conduct formal investigations for any purpose connected with the carrying out of their duties. Following such investigations, the Commission may issue a non-discrimination notice.

15.10 DISABILITY DISCRIMINATION

The Disability Discrimination Act (DDA) 1995, which is modelled on the SDA 1975 and the RRA 1976, creates a right not to be discriminated against on grounds of disability in employment or in the provision of goods, facilities and services.

The DDA 1995 is restricted to employers who employ 15 or more employees. It is also confined to acts of direct discrimination, as opposed to indirect discrimination. The DDA 1995 protects the disabled employee at all stages of the employment process, that is, recruitment and selection, during the contracts existence and with respect to termination (s 4). In effect, the disabled employee has to show that he or she has been treated less favourably on grounds relating to his or her disability (s 5). There is, however, no need to make a 'like with like' comparison, as this is not required by the DDA 1975. In assessing whether the treatment is less favourable, comparison is with another person, not another disabled person – see *Clark v TDG Ltd t/a Novacold* (1999). However, unlike the SDA 1975 and the RRA 1976, the DDA 1995 provides a defence which allows the employer to *justify* the less favourable treatment (s 5). In establishing justification, the employer must show that:

> ... the reason for the act of discrimination was material to the circumstances of the case and substantial and that he has not, without justification, failed to comply with any duty under s 6 to make reasonable adjustments [*Baynton v Sauras General Engineers Ltd* (1999)].

In assessing whether there has been a breach of s 5, one contentious point had been whether there was a need for knowledge of the disability on the part of the employer. The tribunals have moved from the position in *O'Neill v Symm & Co* (1998), which required such knowledge as a result of the decision in *Clarke v TDG Ltd t/a Novacold* (1999) (knowledge being irrelevant in assessing less favourable treatment within s 5(1) and (9) and in respect of justification in s 5(3) – see *London Borough of Hammersmith and Fulham v Farnsworth* (2000)).

Such a lack of knowledge of the disability does not discharge the onus of justification under s 5(3) of the DDA 1995. 'A justification defence cannot be thought up after the event when it has never been considered during the period of employment,' that is, an employer cannot say that there is nothing they could have done because they did not know of the disability – *Quinn v Schwarzkopf Ltd* (2001). However, the decision in *Quinn* has been qualified by the decision in *Callagan v Glasgow CC* (2001). The EAT did not rule out the provision of the justification issue where the employer was unaware of the disability. In considering justification, the emphasis was placed on consideration of the treatment meted out by the employer and this did not depend upon the tribunal being satisfied that all possible protection had been given to the employee.

In determining whether there has been less favourable treatment within s 5(1) of the DDA 1995, the tribunal must consider whether the reason for the less favourable treatment is related to the disability – *London Clubs Management Ltd v Hood* (2001).

For example, in *Cosgrove v Caesar and Howie* (2001), where the applicant was dismissed after having been absent through illness for over a year, the employment tribunal compared her treatment with that of any employee who had been absent from work for over a year. Following the decision in *Clark v TDG Ltd t/a Novacold* (1999), this was not the correct approach – the question to be asked is: 'would the employer have dismissed some other to whom the material reason would not apply?'. In the present case, the material reason for the dismissal was the applicant's absence on medical grounds, which amounted to a disability, and there would have been no reason to dismiss someone else to whom the reason would not apply.

Section 5(3) requires tribunals to consider whether the reason given for less favourable treatment can properly be described as both material to the circumstances of the particular case and substantial. The employer should carry out an assessment based on appropriate medical evidence. The employment tribunal cannot challenge a risk assessment which is properly conducted and does not produce an irrational response – *Jones v Post Office* (2001).

There is a further duty on the employer by virtue of s 6 of the DDA 1995 to make adjustments to premises to ensure that the disabled person is not placed at a substantial disadvantage as compared with persons who are not disabled (s 6).

The duty to make reasonable adjustments is to be judged on whether he or she was aware of, or could reasonably be expected to know of, the person's disability (*Rideout v TC Group* (1998)). The duty under s 6 does not extend to the provision of a personal carer (*Kenny v Hampshire Constabulary* (1999)). The employer is provided with a justification defence. The test of whether the employer must make adjustments is one of reasonableness, which permits consideration of the cost and nature of the adjustments, as well as the practicability of making them. An employer is duty-bound under s 6 to consider the adjustments proposed by the applicant, whether they were reasonable and whether their implementation would have avoided the discriminatory act – *Fu v London Borough of Camden* (2001); *Johnson and Johnson Medical Ltd v Filmer* (2002).

It is, however, not the duty of the applicant or his medical advisors to suggest 'reasonable adjustments'. Section 6 places the duty on the employer – *Cosgrove v Caesar and Howie* (2001).

One contentious issue appears to be what is meant by 'disability' and 'disabled'. However, the DDA 1995 provides some assistance in s 1 by defining disability as 'a mental or physical impairment which has a substantial and long term adverse effect on a person's ability to carry out normal day to day activities'. (See, also, *Goodwin v The Patent Office* (1999) and *Greenwood v British Airways plc* (1999).) The Disability Discrimination (Meaning of Disability) Regulations 1996 provide further clarification. The Employment Appeal Tribunal has encouraged employment tribunals to adopt a purposive approach to the construction of the DDA 1995, with explicit reference being made to guidance issued by the Secretary of State and the Codes of Practice (see *Goodwin v The Patent Office* (1999)).

One issue centres on the interpretation of 'substantial and long term effect on his ability to carry out normal day to day activities'.

In assessing whether a person's ability to carry out such activities is affected, the employment tribunal may consider evidence relating to the performance of their duties at work, where these duties include 'normal day to day activities', for example, nursing (*Law Hospital NHS Trust v Rush* (2001)).

The focus for the employment tribunal should be on what the applicant cannot do, or can only do with difficulty, not what he can do (see *Leonard v Southern Derbyshire Chamber of Commerce* (2001)). Also, the impairment and its effect should be considered holistically; for example, an impairment to the hand should be considered in the light of an adverse effect on manual dexterity, ability to lift and carry everyday objects, instead of focusing on particular tasks or issues. Nor should tasks which are gender specific – for example, applying make up – be discounted as not being a normal day to day activity as it is carried out almost exclusively by women – see *Ekpe v Commissioner of Police of the Metropolis* (2001).

The onus is on the employment tribunal to make its own assessment from the evidence before it, and avoid being over-influenced by medical opinion rather than fact. Also, where the applicant is receiving medical treatment for the condition, so that the final outcome cannot be determined or the removal of the treatment would result in a relapse, the medical treatment must be disregarded in determining whether there is a substantial adverse effect – see *Abadeh v British Telecommunications plc* (2001).

Where the expert medical evidence demonstrates that the applicant has a disability which is controlled by medication, it still falls within the definition of disability – see s 1 of the DDA 1995 – *Kapadia v London Borough of Lambeth* (2000).

Finally, a difficult area for the employment tribunals is where the alleged disability is actually due to a functional or psychological 'overlay', that is, where a person claims to be suffering from a physical injury, which the doctor states is due to the individual's psychological state and is not related to any physical pathology. The problem for the tribunal is that the applicant is claiming a physical impairment (which does not in fact exist) whilst the tribunal must assess whether the mental impairment falls within s 1 of the DDA 1995 – that is, is a 'clinically well-recognised illness'. Interestingly, 'functional overlay' does not appear in the WHO's International Classification of Diseases or the American Psychiatric Association's *Diagnostic and Statistical Manual of Mental Disorders* – see *Rugamer v Sony Music Entertainment Ltd* (2001) and *McNicol v Balfour Beatty Rail Maintenance Ltd* (2001), in which the employment tribunals concluded that the applicants, both with 'functional overlay', did not have a mental impairment.

It could be suggested that this places a further responsibility on the tribunal to consider not whether the applicant has a disability, but why he has.

The problem in establishing mental impairment can be seen in *Morgan v Staffordshire University* (2002). By reference to Sched 1, para 1 of the DDA 1995, the EAT concluded that there were four routes to establishing 'mental impairment':

- proof of a mental illness as listed in the WHO classification of diseases;
- proof of a mental illness, specifically mentioned as such in a publication, which in effect verifies wide professional acceptance;
- proof of a medical illness recognised by a respected body of medical opinion;
- as a matter of medical opinion, which falls within the inclusive nature of Sched 1 to the DDA. However, this would require substantial and very specific medical evidence to support its existence.

It would appear that terms such as 'anxiety', 'stress' and 'depression' will not suffice to establish mental impairment unless the evidence clearly identifies a clinically well-recognised illness.

However, the issue of 'knowledge' on the part of the employer has been revisited in *HJ Heinz Co v Kenrick* (2000). In this case, Mr Kenrick was employed by Heinz from 1979 until his dismissal in 1997. He became ill in 1996, but his condition was never satisfactorily identified. He was warned by his employer that he risked being dismissed if he did not indicate a likely date of return to work. In April 1997, the company's medical adviser noted that he was still unfit for work and he was dismissed. After his dismissal, a diagnosis of chronic fatigue syndrome (CFS) was confirmed. In the subsequent legal action under the DDA 1995, Heinz argued that they could not be liable because they were not aware of his disability at the time of the dismissal. It was, however, accepted that CFS was a disability within the meaning of the DDA 1975. The EAT held that the employer had sufficient knowledge, through their medical adviser, of Kenrick's illness so as to be held to have treated him less favourably for a reason related to his disability. The tribunal further concluded that s 5 does not require the employer to have knowledge of the disability in order to have acted for a reason that relates to the disability. It is not anticipated that this case will open the floodgates. The intention of the tribunal is to '... require employers to pause to consider whether the reason for a dismissal might relate to disability'.

In addition, there is now a Code of Practice for the elimination of discrimination in the employment field against disabled persons or persons who have had a disability. The Government has recently formed the Disability Rights Commission, which will operate in a similar way to the EOC and CRE. As with all discrimination claims, a complaint may be made to an employment tribunal within three months of the alleged act of discrimination.

There have been numerous calls for amendments to the DDA 1975. As a result, in 1997, the Government set up the Disability Rights Task Force (DRTF), whose role is twofold: (a) to make recommendations on the role and functions of the Disability Rights Commission; and (b) to consider 'how best to secure comprehensive, enforceable civil rights for disabled people'. The Task Force's recommendations on proposed changes to the current legislation have now been published (*From Exclusion to Inclusion – a Report of the DRTF on Civil Rights for Disabled People*, 1998). The DRTF has called for changes to the meaning of 'disability' and 'disabled'; the removal of the justification defence for failure to make reasonable adjustments; and the lowering of the small employer threshold from 15 to two.

INDIVIDUAL EMPLOYMENT RIGHTS (2): EQUAL PAY AND DISCRIMINATION

European Community law

European Community (EC) law can be found in Art 141 (formerly Art 119) of the EC Treaty and Directive 75/117 (the Equal Pay Directive), which lay down the principle of equal pay for equal work, including work of equal value. Although EC law is confined to pay, this has been given a wide interpretation by the European Court of Justice (*Barber v Guardian Royal Exchange Assurance Group* (1990)).

The Equal Pay Act (EPA) 1970 incorporates an equality clause into every contract of employment, which has the effect of equalising unfavourable terms between men's and women's contracts and, should a claim for equal pay be pursued, the applicant must select a comparator of the opposite sex and show he or she is employed by:

- the same employer or associated employer;
- the same establishment or an establishment where common terms and conditions are observed (*Leverton v Clwyd CC* (1989); *British Coal Corp v Smith* (1996));
- *Allonby v Accrington and Rossendale College* (2001);
- *South Ayrshire Council v Morton* (2002).

There are three heads of claim:

- like work – defined in s 1(4) (*Capper Pass Ltd v Lawton* (1977); *Shields v Coomes (Holdings) Ltd* (1978));
- work rated equivalent – defined in s 1(5);
- work of equal value (*Pickstone v Freemans plc* (1988)).

Genuine material factor defence

The employer must objectively justify any differing terms between the contracts of male and female employees:

- *Rainey v Greater Glasgow Health Board* (1987);
- *Glasgow CC and Others v Marshall* (2000).

Sex, race and disability discrimination

Sex, race and disability discrimination are governed by the Sex Discrimination Act (SDA) 1975, the Race Relations Act (RRA) 1976 and the Disability

Discrimination Act (DDA) 1995. Further protection is provided by the Equal Treatment Directive (76/207), the Race Discrimination Directive (2000/43) and the Framework Directive which extends protection to homosexuals, the disabled, etc. The Part-Time Workers (Prevention of Less Favourable Treatment) Regulations 2000 extend protection from discrimination to part time workers. The legislation also needs to be interpreted in the light of the Human Rights Act 1998 which gives effect to the European Convention on Human Rights.

In order to bring a complaint under the RRA 1976, the complainant must establish 'racial grounds' or membership of a racial group (s 3(1); *Mandla v Dowell Lee* (1983)).

Direct discrimination

The test for establishing direct discrimination is the 'but for' test (*James v Eastleigh BC* (1990)):

- there may be an inference of discrimination (*Noone v North West Thames Regional HA* (1988); *Zafar v Glasgow CC* (1998));
- harassment is a form of direct discrimination. Sexual harassment is also covered by the Code of Practice on the Protection and Dignity of Men and Women at Work;
- protection from discrimination is afforded to a woman during pregnancy and the maternity leave period, and applies not only to those employed for an indefinite period but also those on fixed term contracts – *Teledanmark* case (2001); *Jiménez Melgar v Ayuntamiento de los Barrios* (2001).

Indirect discrimination

This occurs where, on the face of it, all employees or potential employees are treated the same, but in effect there is a disparate impact on one group because of their sex or racial group. The Sex Discrimination (Indirect Discrimination and Burden of Proof) Regulations 2001 have introduced new requirements for establishing indirect discrimination in employment cases relating to sex discrimination. The applicant must establish:

- a provision, criterion or practice;
- which is to the detriment of a considerably larger proportion of women than men;
- which cannot be justified irrespective of the gender of the complainant.

In race cases the complainant must establish:

- a requirement or condition has been applied equally to all racial groups;
- a considerably smaller proportion of their race can comply with it as

compared to persons not of that racial group;

- the requirement or condition operates to the detriment of the complainant because he or she cannot comply with it;
- finally, even where the complainant has been able to establish these three elements, the employer has the opportunity to justify the requirement or condition by showing that there is an objective necessity for the requirement or condition which is not based on the sex or race of the complainant.

Victimisation

Victimisation occurs where the complainant is treated less favourably because he or she has brought proceedings, etc, under the RRA 1976, SDA 1975 or EPA 1970:

- *Nagarajan v London Regional Transport* (1999);
- *Chief Constable of West Yorkshire Police v Khan* (2001).

Segregation

Segregation occurs where racial groups are intentionally segregated in some way (*PEL Ltd v Modgill* (1980)).

Genuine occupational qualifications

The employer has the opportunity to defend the act of discrimination on the basis that the sex or race of the employee is a genuine occupational qualification (SDA 1975 and RRA 1976).

Remedies

Remedies are in the form of compensation. Compensation may be provided for injury to feelings and psychiatric injury resulting from an act of discrimination (*HM Prison Service v Salmon* (2001)).

Disability discrimination

This is governed by the Disability Discrimination Act (DDA) 1995 and applies to employers who employ 15 or more employees:

- confined to direct discrimination;
- defence of justification;

and no 'like with like' comparison is required (*Clark v TDG t/a Novacold* (1999)):

- 'less favourable treatment' must be related to the disability (*London Clubs Management Ltd v Hood* (2001));
- complainant must show that they are disabled within the meaning of s 1 of the DDA 1995 – *Goodwin v The Patent Office* (1999); *Kapadia v London Borough of Lambeth* (2000);
- employer has a duty to make reasonable adjustments (*Rideout v TC Group* (1998); *Kenny v Hampshire Constabulary* (1999); *Fu v London Borough of Camden* (2000)).

The Disability Rights Commission oversees the operation of the DDA 1995 and the rights of disabled persons under the Act.

CHAPTER 16

INDIVIDUAL EMPLOYMENT RIGHTS (3): TERMINATION

16.1 INTRODUCTION

The contract of employment may be terminated at common law in various ways, some of which do not amount to a dismissal, for example, death, mutual agreement (see *Birch and Humber v University of Liverpool* (1985) and *Igbo v Johnson Matthey Chemical Ltd* (1986)), expiry of a fixed term contract (although this may amount to a statutory dismissal) and frustration. Frustration occurs where there is an unforeseen event which either makes it impossible for the contract to be performed at all, or at least renders its performance as something radically different from what the parties envisaged when they made the contract. The event must have occurred without the fault of either contracting party, for example, imprisonment or sickness. With respect to the former, in *Shepherd and Co Ltd v Jerrom* (1986), the applicant had entered into a four year apprenticeship when, after 21 months, he was sentenced to a minimum of six months in borstal. On his release, his employers refused to take him back and he complained of unfair dismissal. The tribunal rejected the employer's argument that the contract had been frustrated by reason of the custodial sentence, but the Court of Appeal allowed the employer's appeal.

The criteria for allowing frustration of a contract of employment were laid down in *Williams v Watsons Luxury Coaches Ltd* (1990). The factors to be taken into account are:

- length of previous service;
- how long it had been expected that the employment would continue;
- the nature of the job;
- the nature, length and effect of the illness or disabling event;
- the need of the employer for the work to be done and the need for a replacement to do it;
- the risk to the employer of acquiring obligations in respect of redundancy payments or compensation for unfair dismissal to the replacement employee;
- whether wages gave continued to be paid;
- the acts and the statements of the employer in relation to the employment, include the dismissal of, or failure to dismiss, the employee; and
- whether, in all the circumstances, a reasonable employer could be expected to wait any longer.

In addition, the Employment Appeal Tribunal (EAT) in this case recommended that any court should guard against too easy an application of the doctrine.

Frustration automatically terminates a contract without the need for affirmation or acceptance by the innocent party. If frustration is established, there will be no dismissal and, therefore, no right to claim unfair dismissal or redundancy payments. For this reason, the courts have shown a degree of reluctance in applying the doctrine of frustration fully to contracts of employment. Termination by dismissal occurs where there is dismissal by notice.

16.2 DISMISSAL FOR FUNDAMENTAL BREACH OR WRONGFUL DISMISSAL

16.2.1 Notice

If the employer wishes to terminate an employee's employment, the minimum period of notice (as stated in the contract of employment) must be given or, if there is nothing in the contract, the amount of notice required by s 86 of the Employment Rights Act (ERA) 1996. Section 86 states that, where an employee has been continuously employed for between one month and two years, he or she shall be given one week's notice; if employed for more than two years, he or she is entitled to one week's notice for each year of employment, subject to a maximum of 12 weeks.

Either party may waive their right to notice or terminate without notice in response to a serious breach of the contract by the other. The employer may give wages or salary in lieu of notice and s 49 does not prevent the employee from accepting such payment. In order to avoid legal action by the employee, the employer must have a legitimate reason in the eyes of the law for terminating the contract of employment. Where the employee wishes to terminate the contract of employment, the minimum period of notice, as stipulated in his or her contract, must be given. If this is not stated, a minimum of one week's notice must be given (s 86(2) of the ERA 1996).

16.2.2 Summary dismissal for fundamental breach

An employer may summarily dismiss an employee (that is, dismiss without notice) for conduct which is judged to be sufficiently serious. In these circumstances, the employee will lose the right to contractual and statutory notice. Conduct such as theft, violence, etc, will warrant such action on the part of the employer, and even misconduct may do so. However, in *Wilson v Racher* (1974), where the plaintiff was dismissed for using bad language in a row with his employer, his summary dismissal was found to be unfair, as the evidence was that, in general, he was a good employee and this had been a solitary incident. However, in *Denco Ltd v Joinson* (1991), the applicant was instantly dismissed for unauthorised access to computer information which the employer considered was done to assist the employee in his capacity as a union representative. The tribunal refused to accept that such conduct could justify dismissal without prior warning. The EAT allowed the employer's appeal, as there was a clear analogy with dishonesty. If the summary dismissal is not justified, the employee may bring an action at common law for wrongful dismissal.

There is an issue of whether the breach automatically ends the contract, or whether it is only so effective once the innocent party elects to accept the breach. The decision in *Boyo v London Borough of Lambeth* (1995) attempted to clarify the position by determining that an unaccepted dismissal did not bring the contract to an end, nor should acceptance be readily inferred. The Court of Appeal chose to follow the decision in *Gunton v London Borough of Richmond-upon-Thames* (1995).

16.3 WRONGFUL DISMISSAL

An action for wrongful dismissal at common law may be brought by an employee who does not qualify for the unfair dismissal protection provided by the ERA 1996; or it may be brought by an employee who has been dismissed unjustifiably without notice or who has not been given the required period of notice. Following the Industrial Tribunals Extension of Jurisdiction (England and Wales) Order 1994, an action for breach of the employment contract may be commenced in the employment tribunal, subject to an award limit of £25,000. Compensation in the form of wages and damages can, in general, only be awarded for the notice period and will be subject to the calculation of damages in contract. This has been confirmed by the decision in *Johnson v Unisys Ltd* (2001), where the applicant argued that his claim for dismissal should include compensation for breach of various implied terms which led to his mental breakdown. It was held that, if wrongful dismissal is the only cause of action, nothing can be recovered for mental distress or damage to reputation.

Whilst the case of *Johnson v Unisys* limits the implied terms of trust and confidence to the pre-dismissal employment relationship, the Court of Session in *King v University Court of the University of St Andrews* (2002) makes it clear that the duty is to be implied throughout all aspects of the ongoing relationship of employer and employee. As a result, it subsists 'during the stage at which the employers were investigating allegations against the employee and considering whether there were grounds for dismissal'.

The limitation imposed by *Johnson* is confined to a situation where the decision to dismiss has been taken. The decision in *Malik* is further supported by *Gogay v Hertfordshire CC* (2000), in which it was held by the Court of Appeal that where there has been a breach of the implied duty of trust and confidence, damages for a recognised psychiatric illness could be awarded. However, this limitation is not applicable where there is a breach of the duty of trust and confidence which makes it more difficult for an employee to obtain further employment (see *Malik v BCCI SA (In Liq)* (1997)). How far other contractual remedies such as specific performance and injunctions are available is open to debate. Injunctions restraining a dismissal have been issued where the rules of natural justice have not been followed in circumstances where the employee is in public employment.

In *Irani v South West Hampshire HA* (1985), the plaintiff was an ophthalmologist who was employed part time in an outpatient eye clinic. He was dismissed with six weeks' notice because of irreconcilable differences with the consultant in charge of the clinic. No criticism at all was made of his competence or conduct. In dismissing him, the employers were in breach of the disciplinary procedure established by the Whitley Council and incorporated into his contract of employment. He sought an injunction to prevent the employers from dismissing him without first following the appropriate disciplinary procedure. The employers argued that this would be contrary to the general rule that injunctions cannot be issued to keep a contract of employment alive. The plaintiff successfully obtained his injunction on the basis that, first, the case fell within the exception to the general rule, in that trust and confidence remained between the employer and the employee – the breakdown in confidence between the consultant and Irani did not affect the latter's relationship with the employer; and, secondly, damages were not an adequate remedy in this case, since Irani would become virtually unemployable throughout the National Health Service.

There have been further important decisions in this area, for example, *Ridge v Baldwin* (1964), in which a chief constable was dismissed without a proper opportunity to be heard in his own defence. He obtained a declaration that the decision to dismiss him was a nullity, as it was in breach of the rules of natural justice. See, also, *Powell v London Borough of Brent* (1987), in which an interlocutory injunction for specific performance was obtained. It had previously been thought that an order for specific performance could not be awarded in respect of a contract of employment because the requisite mutual trust and confidence has generally been destroyed. It is quite clear that the courts will be sympathetic to the issue of injunctions where the employee has not yet exhausted all of his or her rights under grievance and disciplinary procedures (see *Wadcock v London Borough of Brent* (1990) and *Robb v London Borough of Hammersmith and Fulham* (1991)).

16.4 UNFAIR DISMISSAL

Employees who qualify for protection under the ERA 1996 have the right not to be unfairly dismissed; that is, the employer must show that the reason for the dismissal was reasonable. The ERA 1996 provides greater protection and a wider range of remedies for the unfairly dismissed employee and, in this respect, is a much needed provision in the light of the inadequacies of the common law. However, as the law has developed, so has its complexity; statistics reveal the low success rate of complaints. For example, in the periods 1997–98 and 1998–99, only 12.9% of cases were successful following a hearing; the median award was £2,388. Of the 74,006 cases heard by the EAT in 1998–99, 44% were unfair dismissal cases. While it is still the largest single cause of complaint, the percentage of cases has fallen by 3% from 1997–98 (employment tribunal and EAT statistics, Labour Market Trends, September 1999).

The Employment Rights (Dispute Resolution) Act 1998 contains provisions to implement those aspects of the Green Paper, *Resolving Employment Rights Disputes: Options for Reform* (Cm 2707, 1994) which attracted wide support and required primary legislation. The most significant change under the Act is to grant ACAS powers to fund and provide an arbitration scheme for unfair dismissal claims. This is available as an alternative to an employment tribunal hearing and is voluntary on both sides. After some delay, the ACAS Arbitration Scheme came into force in England and Wales on 21 May 2001 and in Scotland by January 2002. The Scheme has got off to a sluggish start, with only one case heard in the first six months of the Scheme's operation (see *Anyone for Arbitration*, Employers' Law, November 2001, pp 22–23).

In *Fairness at Work*, the Government put forward a number of proposals aimed at strengthening the unfair dismissal remedy. These included:

- abolishing the maximum limit on the compensatory award;
- index-linking limits on the basic award, subject to a maximum rate;
- prohibiting the use of waivers for unfair dismissal claims but continuing to allow them for redundancy payments;
- creating a legal right for individuals to be accompanied by a fellow employee or trade union representative of their choice during grievance and disciplinary hearings; and
- reducing the qualifying period for claimants to one year.

The Employment Relations Act 1999 and a ministerial order have implemented these proposals with one exception. The ceiling on the compensation award has not been completely removed but the maximum limit has been raised from £12,000 to £50,000. This maximum is automatically indexed to retail prices and is £52,600.

Finally, the Employment Act 2002 amends the statutory unfair dismissal regime. A new statutory dispute resolution procedure has been introduced and every contract of employment will require employers and employees to comply with it. The statutory procedures set out in Sched 2 to the Act and deal with disciplinary and dismissal issues, and employee grievances.

16.4.1 Who qualifies under the ERA 1996?

Protection from unfair dismissal is only available to employees, that is, those employed under a contract of service. The basic rule is that an employee must have at least one year's continuous employment in order to qualify. This significant change to the qualifying period arose out of the Government's White Paper, *Fairness at Work* (Cm 3968, 1998), which resulted in the Unfair Dismissal and Statement of Reasons for Dismissal (Variation of Qualifying Period) Order 1999 (SI 1999/1436). This change from two years to one took effect on 1 June 1999. The two year qualifying period was held indirectly to discriminate against women in *R v Secretary of State for Employment ex p Seymour-Smith and Perez (No 2)* (2000). However, the House of Lords ruled that the Secretary of State was objectively justified under EC law in increasing the qualifying period from one to two years in 1985. This decision has largely been overtaken by the subsequent statutory amendment, although this does not have retrospective effect. There is a presumption that continuity exists. The onus is, therefore, on the employer to show that it does not.

The following people are specifically excluded from the unfair dismissal provisions of the ERA 1996:

- share fishermen;
- any employee who has reached the normal retirement age (this is recognised as 65 for both men and women under the Sex Discrimination Act 1986); or, if relevant, the contractual retirement age;
- persons ordinarily employed outside Great Britain;
- workers on fixed term contracts who have waived in writing their right to claim if the contract is not renewed;
- the police and armed forces;
- employees who are affected by a dismissal procedure agreement between the employer and an independent trade union which has been approved by the Secretary of State;
- employees who, at the time of their dismissal, are taking industrial action or are locked out, where there has been no selective dismissal or re-engagement of those taking part. Unofficial strikers may be selectively dismissed or re-engaged (ss 237 and 238 of the Trade Union Labour Relations (Consolidation) Act (TULR(C)A) 1992);

- where the settlement of a claim for dismissal has been agreed with the involvement of ACAS and the employee has agreed to withdraw his or her complaint.

16.5 CLAIMS

An applicant must bring a claim within three months of the effective date of termination (s 111 of the ERA 1996). The employment tribunal may extend this limit if it considers that it was not reasonably practicable for the applicant to present it in time (*Palmer v Southend-on-Sea BC* (1984)). However, the time limit tends to be rigorously applied. Such is the stringency of the approach that it has been held that an applicant may not use the excuse that his or her failure to claim was due to a mistake of 'a skilled adviser' such as a lawyer, trade union official or Citizen's Advice Bureau worker (see *Riley v Tesco Stores Ltd* (1980)). Thus, the date of termination, as well as the length of service, etc, is of importance in deciding whether a claim is made in time.

16.6 EFFECTIVE DATE OF TERMINATION

The same rules apply for unfair dismissal and redundancy, although with respect to redundancy it is known as 'the relevant date':

- Where the contract of employment is terminated by notice, whether by the employer or employee, the date of termination is the date on which the notice expires (s 97(1) of the ERA 1996). If an employee is dismissed with notice but is given a payment in lieu of notice, the effective date of termination is the date when the notice expires, as illustrated in *Adams v GKN Sankey* (1980).

- Where the contract of employment is terminated without notice, the date of termination is the date on which the termination takes effect, that is, the actual date of dismissal, not the date on which the notice would expire. In *Robert Cort and Sons Ltd v Charman* (1981), where an employee was summarily dismissed with wages in lieu of notice, the effective date of termination was the actual date on which he was told of his dismissal, not the date on which the notice would expire. The exception to this rule is provided by s 97(2) of the ERA 1996, by which the effective date is extended either where summary dismissal has occurred, despite the employee being entitled to the statutory minimum notice, or where the actual notice given was less than that required by statute. In both cases, the effective date is the expiration of the statutory notice period.

- Where the employer is employed under a contract for a fixed term, the date of termination is the date on which the term expires.

One important issue has been what the effective date of termination is where the employee invokes an internal appeals procedure. It appears that, if the appeal is subsequently rejected, the effective date is the date of the original dismissal (*J Sainsbury Ltd v Savage* (1981)), unless the contract provides for the contrary (*West Midlands Co-operative Society v Tipton* (1986)).

16.7 WHAT IS MEANT BY DISMISSAL?

The onus is on the employee to show that he or she has been dismissed within the meaning of the Act (s 95 of the ERA 1996). There are three ways in which dismissal can take place:

- Express termination of the contract of employment by the employer

  The employer may terminate the contract with or without notice. Such a dismissal may be made orally or in writing; however, if it is made orally, the words used should be unambiguous. For example, in *Futty v Brekkes Ltd* (1974), in a row with his foreman, the employee was told, 'If you do not like the job, fuck off'. This was interpreted by the employee as a dismissal and he left and found a job elsewhere. The employer argued that there had been no dismissal, as the words were to be interpreted in the context of the workman's trade. Furthermore, if a dismissal had been intended, the words used would have been formal. This argument was accepted by the industrial tribunal, which concluded that the employee had terminated his own employment.

  Where the words are ambiguous, the effect of the statement is determined by an objective test; that is, would the reasonable employer or employee have understood the words to be tantamount to a dismissal? One of the problems for the courts has been deciding whether there has been a dismissal within the meaning of the ERA 1996.

  A termination which is mutually agreed between the employer and employee is not a dismissal. However, the courts have, with some reluctance, upheld this practice, as it may work to the advantage of the employer in avoiding employment rights and thereby lead to an abuse of a dominant position. The courts will look closely to see whether there is genuine mutual agreement; this will be a question of fact in each case.

  In *Igbo v Johnson Matthey Chemicals Ltd* (1986), the applicant requested extended leave to visit her husband and children in Nigeria. This was granted by her employers on the condition that she signed a document which stated that she agreed to return to work on 28 September 1986 and, if she failed to do so, her contract of employment would automatically terminate on that date. She signed the document. She failed to return on the due date because she was ill and, as a result, her contract was terminated. The Court of Appeal held that the contract had been terminated, not by mutual agreement, but by dismissal. The document amounted to a means of avoiding employment rights and was, therefore, void by virtue of s 140(1) of the Employment Protection (Consolidation) Act 1978 (now s 203 of the ERA 1996).

It should be noted that, where the employee is under notice of termination and gives the employer a counter notice indicating an intention to leave before the expiry of the employer's notice, the employee is still deemed to have been dismissed for the purposes of the ERA 1996. Any counter notice must be in writing with respect to a claim for redundancy, but this is not a requirement in respect of unfair dismissal.

- Where the employee invites a termination of his contract either by his inaction or conduct

In *Martin v Yeoman Aggregates Ltd* (1983), Martin refused to get a spare part for the director's car. The director angrily told the employee to get out. Five minutes later, the director took back what he had said and instead suspended Martin without pay until he could act more rationally. Martin insisted that he had been dismissed. It was held that it was vital to industrial relations that both the employer and employee should have the opportunity to withdraw their words. It was up to a tribunal to decide whether the withdrawal had come too late to be effective.

Certainly, immediate retraction is effective. However, a subsequent retraction will only be effective with the consent of the other party.

Where the employer invites the employee to resign, this may amount to a dismissal. In *Robertson v Securicor Transport Ltd* (1972), Robertson had broken one of the works rules by signing for a load which had not actually been received. When his employers discovered what he had done, they gave him the option of resignation or dismissal. He chose resignation. It was held that resignation in these circumstances amounted to a dismissal by the employer because, in effect, there was no alternative action open to the employee. He would have been dismissed if he had not opted to resign on the invitation of his employer.

- Expiration of a fixed term contract

As we have seen, in certain situations, a fixed term contract may be excluded from the protection afforded by the ERA 1996; that is, where the employee agrees before the term expires to forgo any claim for unfair dismissal. However, if a fixed term contract is not renewed and it is not within the excluded category, the failure to renew amounts to a dismissal (whether it is a fair dismissal is another issue). The courts have found it necessary to distinguish between a fixed term contract and a contract which terminates on the completion of a particular job or task – the latter being outside the ERA 1996 provisions. Contracts terminable on the happening or non-happening of a particular event, even if it is a future event, have been found to be a 'task' contract. In *Brown v Knowsley BC* (1986), the distinction between a fixed term contract and a contract to perform a particular task was extended to cover contracts terminable on the happening or non-happening of a future event.

Section 2 of the ERA 1996 further requires that, if the agreement amounts to a fixed term contract, the duration of the contract must be certain, that is, there must be a date on which the contract expires. It follows, therefore, that a contract to do a specific job, which does not refer to a completion date, cannot be a fixed term contract, since the duration of the contract is uncertain.

Furthermore, at one time, it was thought that a fixed term contract must run for the whole of the term and must not be capable of termination before the term expired, for example, by a clause giving either party the right to terminate (see *BBC v Ioannou* (1975)). However, in *Dixon v BBC* (1979), it was held that a fixed term contract could exist even though either party could terminate it before it had run its full term.

16.7.1 Constructive dismissal

Constructive dismissal is an important concept, since the law recognises that an employee may be entitled to protection where he or she is put in a position in which he or she is forced to resign. Constructive dismissal arises where the employee is forced to terminate the contract with or without notice due to the conduct of the employer (s 95(1)(c) of the ERA 1996). One issue for the courts is whether the words or actions of the employee in resigning are unambiguous. In *Sovereign House Security Services Ltd v Savage* (1989), Savage, a security officer, was told that he was to be suspended pending police investigations into the theft of money from the employer's offices. Savage told his immediate superior to pass on the fact that he was 'jacking it in'. The Court of Appeal held that the employer was entitled to treat these words as amounting to a resignation.

The courts will, however, make some allowance for 'heat of the moment' utterances (see *Tanner v Kean* (1978)). The main focus for the courts is to decide whether the employer's conduct warrants the action taken by the employee. It is now firmly decided that, in order to permit the employee to constructively dismiss him or her, the employer's actions must amount to a breach of contract and must, therefore, be more than merely unreasonable conduct.

In *Western Excavating Ltd v Sharp* (1978), Sharp took time off from work without permission. When his employer discovered this, he was dismissed. He appealed to an internal disciplinary board, which substituted a penalty of five days' suspension without pay. He agreed to accept this decision but asked his employer for an advance on his holiday pay, as he was short of money; this was refused. He then asked for a loan of £40, which was also refused. As a result, he decided to resign, since this would at least mean that he would receive his holiday pay. At the same time, he claimed unfair dismissal on the basis that he was forced to resign because of his employer's unreasonable conduct. Initially, the tribunal found in Sharp's favour; that is, the employer's conduct was so unreasonable that Sharp could not be expected to continue working there. However, the case eventually went to the Court of Appeal, where it was decided that, before a valid constructive dismissal can take place, the employer's conduct must amount to a breach of contract such that it entitles the employee to resign. In this particular case, there was no breach by the employer and, therefore, there was no constructive dismissal.

It would appear that, if the breach by the employer is to allow the employee to resign, it must be a breach of some significance and must go to the root of the contract, for example, a unilateral change in the employee's terms (express or implied) and conditions of employment. For example, in *British Aircraft Corp v Austin* (1978), a failure to investigate a health and safety complaint was held to be conduct amounting to a breach of contract on the part of the employer which was sufficient to entitle the employee to treat the contract as terminated. If the employee does not resign in the event of a breach by the employer, the employee will be deemed to have accepted the breach and to have waived any rights. However, the law recognises that he or she need not resign immediately but may, for example, wait until he or she has found another job (see *Cox Toner (International) Ltd v Crook* (1981)).

It is also recognised that a series of minor incidents can have a cumulative effect, which results in a fundamental breach amounting to repudiation of the contract by the employer. In *Woods v WM Car Services (Peterborough)* (1982), it was held that the general implied contractual duty that employers will not, without reasonable or proper cause, conduct themselves in a manner calculated as being likely to destroy the relationship of trust and confidence between employer and employee, is an overriding obligation independent of and in addition to the literal terms of the contract.

In *Simmonds v Dowty Seals Ltd* (1978), Simmonds was employed to work on the night shift. His employer attempted to force him to work on the day shift by threatening to take industrial action if he refused to be transferred from the night shift. He resigned. It was held that he was entitled to resign and could regard himself as having been constructively dismissed because the employer's conduct amounted to an attempt to unilaterally change an express term of his contract, namely, that he was employed to work nights.

The employee may also be able to claim where he or she is forced to resign when the employer is in breach of an implied term in the contract of employment. However, it must be stressed that the employee must be able to show not only the existence of the implied term, but also what is required by the implied term, that is, its scope (see *Gardner Ltd v Beresford* (1978)). An implied term in a contract which provided for demotion in the event of incompetence defeated a claim of constructive unfair dismissal when applied to a helicopter pilot who was demoted following a dangerous incident (*Vaid v Brintel Helicopters Ltd* (1994)).

It is also possible for the conduct of an immediate superior to amount to a fundamental breach on the part of the employer, as long as the test for establishing vicarious liability is satisfied (*Hilton International Hotels (UK) Ltd v Protopapa* (1990)).

The case law illustrates that a wide range of conduct on the part of the employer may entitle the employee to resign. For example, in *Bracebridge Engineering Ltd v Darby* (1990), failing to properly investigate allegations of sexual harassment or failing to treat such a complaint with sufficient seriousness was held to be constructive dismissal. The employee is not expected to tolerate abusive language from his or her employer, particularly when he or she is being accused of something which he or she did not do (*Palmanor Ltd v Cedron* (1978)). Even where the employer orders his or her employee to relocate as a result of a mobility clause in the employee's contract, if the employee is given very short notice and no financial assistance, he or she may resign and claim constructive dismissal (*United Bank Ltd v Akhtar* (1989)). Finally, where an employee lodges a grievance which is not investigated because of a failure to implement a proper procedure, the employee's resignation may be justified (*WA Goold (Pearmak) Ltd v McConnell and Another* (1995)).

As a result of the decision in *Western Excavating Ltd v Sharp*, it is clear that unreasonable conduct alone which makes life difficult for the employee, so that he or she is put in a position where he or she forced to resign, will not automatically be deemed to be a constructive dismissal, unless it can be found to be a breach of the express or implied terms on the part of the employer. The employee may have to depend on the generosity of the courts in establishing a breach of an implied term.

In the case of *Pepper and Hope v Daish* (1980), in December 1978, Pepper, who was employed by the defendants, negotiated for himself an hourly wage rate. In January 1979, his employers increased the hourly rate of all workers by 5%, with the exception of Pepper. As a result, Pepper resigned and claimed constructive dismissal. It was held that Pepper would succeed in his claim. The tribunal was prepared to imply a term into his contract that he would be given any wage increases received by the hourly rate workers. Such a term had, therefore, been broken by his employer, forcing him to resign. Whether the courts will always be as generous in their interpretation is open to debate.

16.8 REASONS FOR THE DISMISSAL

An employee who is dismissed within the meaning of the ERA 1996 is entitled to a written statement of the reasons for his dismissal (s 92 of the ERA 1996). He or she must, however, have been continuously employed for one year (s 92(3) of the ERA 1996). However, this qualifying period is not applicable where a female employee is dismissed while she is pregnant or in connection with childbirth (s 92(4) of the ERA 1996). The employee must request the statement and it must be supplied within 14 days of this request. Failure to do so or providing particulars which are inadequate or untrue will allow the employee to make a complaint to an employment tribunal. If the tribunal finds in favour of the employee, it may declare the real reason for the dismissal and award the employee two weeks' pay. It has been held that a 'conscientiously formed belief that there was no dismissal was a reasonable ground for refusing to provide a written statement' (*Brown v Stuart Scott and Co* (1981)). The written statement is admissible in proceedings and any inconsistency between the contents of the statement and the reason actually put forward could seriously undermine the employer's case.

16.9 FAIR DISMISSALS

Once the employee has established dismissal, be it by the employer or constructively, the onus moves to the employer to show that he or she acted reasonably in dismissing the employee and, therefore, that the dismissal was fair (s 98 of the ERA 1996). Prior to 1980, the burden of proof in unfair dismissal claims at this stage was on the employer. The Employment Act 1980 amended the test, primarily by removing the requirement that the employer shall satisfy the employment tribunal as to the reasonableness of his or her action, and so rendered the burden of proof 'neutral'. A further amendment required tribunals to have regard to the size and administrative resources of the employer's undertaking in assessing the reasonableness of the dismissal. The specific reference to size and administrative resources is an encouragement to tribunals to be less exacting in their examination of the disciplinary standards and procedures of small employers.

The test of reasonableness requires consideration of what a reasonable employer would have done in the circumstances; that is, does it fall within 'the band of reasonable responses to the employee's conduct within which one employer might take one view, another quite reasonably another?' (*Iceland Frozen Foods v Jones* (1982), *per* Browne-Wilkinson J). Whether the test is satisfied is a question of fact in each case. More recently, in *Haddon v Van Den Bergh Foods Ltd* (1999), the EAT held that the 'range of reasonable responses' test was an unhelpful gloss on the statute and should no longer be applied by employment tribunals. The EAT qualified its decision in *Haddon* in the case of *HSBC v Madden* (2000). In this case, the EAT stated that, whilst only the Court of Appeal or a higher court can discard the range of reasonable responses test, a tribunal is free to substitute its own views for those of the employer as to the reasonableness of dismissal as a response to the reason shown for it. Instead, the test of fairness should be applied 'without embellishment and without using mantras so favoured by lawyers in this field'. The EAT recommended the approach adopted in *Gilham v Kent CC (No 2)* (1985), in which the Court of

Appeal emphasised that whether a dismissal was fair or unfair is a pure question of fact for the tribunal. However, the Court of Appeal in *Post Office v Foley; HSBC Bank v Madden* (2000) has now restored the 'band of reasonable responses' test. The proper function of the employment tribunal is to determine objectively whether the decision to dismiss the employee fell within the band of reasonable responses which a reasonable employer might have adopted. In practice, this may not be required in every case; nor is there a requirement to show that the employer's decision was so unreasonable as to be perverse.

However, employment tribunals continue to have regard to the substantive merits of a case, for example, length of service, previous disciplinary record and any other mitigating circumstances, with a view to maintaining consistency of treatment and procedural fairness. In other words, they will ask whether the employer has adhered to the ACAS Code of Practice on Disciplinary Practices and Procedures in Employment, which involves the provision of formal warnings, internal hearings, appeals procedures, etc. The Code may be used as evidence to show that the employer has not acted reasonably (s 207 of TULR(C)A 1992). (There is a new Draft Code of Practice on Disciplinary and Grievance Procedures, which also contains guidance on the new statutory right for workers to be accompanied at disciplinary and grievance hearings (2000).) Further rights in respect of disciplinary and grievance hearings can be found in ss 10–12 of the Employment Relations Act 1999, in particular, the right to be accompanied at a hearing; the right to complain to an employment tribunal if the employer fails to allow a worker to be accompanied; and the right not to be subjected to any detriment by his or her employer for pursuing his or her rights under ss 10 and 11.

Schedule 2 to the Employment Act 2002 introduces new statutory dispute resolution procedures and every contract of employment will require employers and employees to comply with them. A standard procedure for dismissal and disciplinary procedures is found in Chapter 1 of the provisions. It extends to the conduct of the meetings, as well as procedural fairness, and may have implications for the decision in *Polkey* (below).

The leading case on procedural fairness is *Polkey v AE Dayton Services Ltd* (1987). Polkey was employed as a van driver. In order to avoid more financial losses, his employer decided to make three van drivers redundant. There was no prior consultation; Polkey was merely handed a letter informing him that he was being made redundant. Polkey claimed that this amounted to unfair dismissal, as the failure to consult showed that the employer had not acted reasonably in treating redundancy as a sufficient reason for dismissing him. It was held that, in deciding whether the employer had acted reasonably, the tribunal should have regard to the facts at the time of the dismissal and should not base their judgment on facts brought to light after the dismissal, such as whether the failure to consult would have made any difference to the dismissal or whether the employee had in practice suffered an injustice.

The implementation of the disciplinary procedure is also of paramount importance. In *Westminster CC v Cabaj* (1996), the council's disciplinary code required three members of the council to be in attendance to hear appeals. The complainant's appeal was heard by the Chief Executive and two other members. The EAT held that this amounted to a significant error, as the appeals panel should have been constituted in a particular way. As a result, the dismissal was unfair.

The grounds on which a dismissal is capable of being fair are laid down in s 98 of the ERA 1996. In *Wilsorky v Post Office* (2000), the Court of Appeal held that it was a question of legal analysis to determine in which part of s 98 of the ERA 1996 a reason for dismissal falls. If it was incorrectly 'characterised', this was an error of law which would therefore be corrected on appeal.

16.9.1 Capability or qualifications

Section 98(3) states that capability is 'assessed by reference to skill, aptitude, health or any other physical or mental quality', whereas qualifications means 'any degree, diploma, or other academic, technical or professional qualification relevant to the position which the employee held'. In *Blackman v Post Office* (1974), Blackman was a telegraph officer. He was required to pass an aptitude test. He was allowed the maximum number of attempts (three), and he still failed. He was then dismissed. It was held that, as the taking of an aptitude test was a qualification requirement of that job, his dismissal was fair.

Before dismissing an employee for incompetence, the employer should have regard to the ACAS Code of Practice on Disciplinary Practices and Procedures in Employment, which offers some guidance on improving poor performance; certainly, no dismissal should take place without formal warnings providing the employee with an opportunity to redress his or her position, unless the potential consequences of the incompetence are so serious that warnings are inappropriate. In *Taylor v Alidair* (1978), a pilot was dismissed for a serious error of judgment when he landed a plane so badly that it caused extensive damage. The Court of Appeal held that the company had reasonable grounds for honestly believing that he was incompetent.

The employer must not only be able to show that, for example, the employee was incompetent or inadequately qualified, but also that, in the circumstances, it was reasonable to dismiss him or her – that is, what would the reasonable employer have done? The court will have regard to all the surrounding circumstances, such as training, supervision and what alternatives were available, for example, could the employee have been redeployed in another job, etc? The employer may also have to show that the employee was given a chance to improve his or her standing. If the employer is to be deemed to have acted reasonably, he or she must be able to show that dismissal was the last resort.

In *Davison v Kent Meters Ltd* (1975), Davison worked on an assembly line. She was dismissed as a result of assembling 500 components incorrectly. She alleged that she had merely followed the instructions of the chargehand. The chargehand maintained that he had not given her any instructions. It was held that the dismissal was unfair. Davison should have received supervision and training in the assembly of the components. It was clear from the evidence that she had not received any; therefore, her employer had not acted reasonably in dismissing her.

Persistent absenteeism may be treated as misconduct and should be dealt with under the disciplinary procedure. However, a long term absence, such as long term sickness, should be treated as incapability. Whether the employer's action to dismiss for long term sickness absence is reasonable will depend on the particular circumstances of each case, for example, the nature of the illness, the length of the absence, the need to replace the absent employee and the carrying out of an investigation of the illness (*London Fire and Civil Defence Authority v Betty* (1994)). The employer will be expected to make a reasonable effort to inform him or herself of the true medical position of the employee, although the consent of the employee is needed before access to medical records can be gained.

16.9.2 Conduct

In deciding whether a dismissal for misconduct is to be regarded as fair, attention must be paid to the nature of the offence and the disciplinary procedure. For example, gross or serious misconduct may justify instant dismissal, whereas a trivial act may only warrant a warning in line with the disciplinary procedure. In *Hamilton v Argyll and Clyde Health Board* (1993), it was found that the fact that the employer was prepared to offer the employee an alternative post did not mean that the misconduct could not be classified as 'gross'. The word 'misconduct' is not defined in the ERA 1996, but it is established that it covers assault, refusal to obey instructions, persistent lateness, moonlighting, drunkenness, dishonesty, failing to implement safety procedures, etc. Whether the commission of a criminal offence outside employment justifies a dismissal will depend upon its relevance to the actual job carried out by the employee.

Before any dismissal for misconduct takes place, the employer must have established a genuine and reasonable belief in the guilt of the employee. This may involve carrying out a reasonable investigation. A false accusation without reasonable foundation may result in the employee resigning and claiming constructive dismissal (*Robinson v Crompton Parkinson Ltd* (1978)). It should be remembered that reference must also be made to what the reasonable employer would have done; that is, the test is an objective one.

In *Taylor v Parsons Peebles Ltd* (1981), a works rule prohibited fighting. It was also the policy of the company to dismiss anyone caught fighting. The company had employed the applicant for 20 years without complaint. He was caught fighting and was dismissed. It was held that the dismissal was unfair. Regard must be had to the previous 20 years of employment without incident. The tribunal decided that the reasonable employer would not have applied the sanction of instant dismissal as rigidly because of the mitigating circumstances.

In *Whitbread and Co v Thomas* (1988), it was held that an employer who could not identify which member of a group was responsible for an act could fairly dismiss the whole group, even where it was probable that not all were guilty of the act, provided that three conditions were satisfied:

- the act of misconduct warranted dismissal;
- the industrial (now employment) tribunal is satisfied that the act was committed by at least one of the group being dismissed and all were capable of committing the act;
- the tribunal is satisfied that the employer had carried out a proper investigation to attempt to identify the persons responsible.

In *Parr v Whitbread plc* (1990), Parr was employed as a branch manager at an off-licence owned by the respondents. He and three other employees were dismissed after it was discovered that £4,000 had been stolen from the shop in circumstances which suggested that it was an inside job. Each of the four had an equal opportunity to commit the theft and the employers found it impossible to ascertain which of them was actually guilty. It was held, applying the test in the *Thomas* case, that the dismissals were fair.

16.9.3 Redundancy

Redundancy is *prima facie* a fair reason for dismissal. However, the employer must show that the reason for the dismissal was due to redundancy (s 98(2) of the ERA 1996). He or she must, therefore, be able to establish redundancy within the meaning of the ERA 1996. A dismissal for reason of redundancy will be unfair if the employer had not acted as the reasonable employer would have acted in the circumstances. The following matters, as laid down in *Williams v Compair Maxam Ltd* (1982), should be considered before the redundancies are put into effect:

- to give as much warning as possible;
- to consult with the trade union (see ss 188–92 of TULR(C)A 1992, as amended by the Collective Redundancies and Transfer of Undertakings (Protection of Employment) (Amendment) Regulations 1995 (SI 1995/2587));
- to adopt an objective rather than a subjective criteria for selection;
- to select in accordance with the criteria;
- to consider the possibility of redeployment rather than dismissal.

In *Allwood v William Hill Ltd* (1974), William Hill Ltd decided to close down 12 betting shops. Without any warning, they made all the managers redundant. They offered no alternative employment. The managers, as employees, complained that this amounted to unfair dismissal. It was held that, in the circumstances, this amounted to unfair dismissal. The employer should have considered possible alternatives, such as transfers to other betting shops. Furthermore, the way in which the redundancies had taken place was not the way in which a reasonable employer would have acted.

It is important to realise that, just because there is a redundancy situation within the meaning of the ERA 1996, it does not automatically follow that any dismissal due to redundancy will be fair. An important issue is whether the criteria used for selection of those employees who are to be made redundant are fair, for example, first in, first out (FIFO); last in, first out (LIFO); or part time staff first, which may also amount to discrimination. Contravention of customary practices may be evidence that the dismissal is unfair.

In *Hammond-Scott v Elizabeth Arden Ltd* (1976), the applicant was selected for redundancy because she was close to retirement age. The defendants had employed her for many years, but this was not taken into account when she was selected for redundancy. It was held that her selection for redundancy amounted to unfair dismissal because the employer had not acted reasonably in the circumstances. In view of her age, the length of service and the fact that she was close to retirement age, it would have had little financial effect on the company if they had continued to employ her until she retired.

Transferring the responsibility for deciding who will be made redundant from the employer to the employees involved in the redundancy may also amount to unfair dismissal. In *Boulton and Paul Ltd v Arnold* (1994), when an employee complained about her selection for redundancy, the employer offered to retain her, but on the terms that another employee would be made redundant in her place. She rejected this offer and claimed unfair dismissal. Her claim was upheld, as the EAT did not accept the employer's defence that she could have remained in employment. It also declared that it was unfair to move the onus to the employee in order to decide whether she or another employee would be selected for dismissal.

Where employees in similar positions are not made redundant and the reason why a particular employee was selected for redundancy was because he or she was a member or non-member of a trade union or participated in trade union activities, dismissal will be deemed to be automatically unfair (s 153 of TULR(C)A 1992). This is no longer subject to any qualifying period of service.

16.9.4 Statutory restrictions (s 98(2)(d) of the ERA 1996)

If the dismissal is because the continued employment of the employee would result in a contravention of a statute or subordinate legislation on the part of either the employer or the employee, the dismissal will be *prima facie* fair, for example, if the employee has been banned from driving, yet the job requires him or her to hold a current driving licence – if the employee continues to fulfil the job specification, he or she would be in breach of the Road Traffic Acts (*Fearn v Tayford Motor Company Ltd* (1975)); or if the employer, in continuing to employ someone, was found to be contravening the Food and Drugs Act 1955.

As with all cases of dismissal, the employer must act as the reasonable employer and must, therefore, consider any possible alternatives if the dismissal is to be regarded as fair (*Sandhu v Department of Education and Science and London Borough of Hillingdon* (1978)).

16.9.5 Some other substantial reason

Where the employer is unable to show that the reason for the dismissal was one of those referred to above, he or she may show 'some other substantial reason' (s 98(1)(b) of the ERA 1996). There is no exhaustive list of what is recognised in law as some other substantial reason. The employer must show not only that his or her actions were reasonable, but also that the reason was 'substantial'. The following have been held to be valid reasons for dismissal, although it should be appreciated that it is a question of fact in each case:

- a conflict of personalities which is primarily the fault of the employee. In *Tregonowan v Robert Knee and Co* (1975), the atmosphere in the employer's office was so bad, due to the complainant constantly talking about her private life, that her fellow employees could not work with her. Accordingly, she was dismissed and the tribunal upheld the dismissal. Dismissal should be a last resort after attempts to improve relations have taken place;

- failure to disclose material facts in obtaining employment, for example, mental illness (see *O'Brien v Prudential Assurance Co Ltd* (1979));

- commercial reasons, for example, pressure from important customers to dismiss the employee (*Grootcon (UK) Ltd v Keld* (1984));

- failure to accept changes in the terms of employment (see *Storey v Allied Brewery* (1977)). Any change must be justified by the employer as being necessary;

- non-renewal of a fixed term contract – the employer must show a genuine need for temporary contracts and that the employee knew of the temporary nature of the contract from the outset (*North Yorkshire CC v Fay* (1985));

- a dismissal which satisfies reg 8(2) of the Transfer of Undertakings (Protection of Employment) Regulations 1981 (SI 1981/1794) insofar as the dismissal is for an 'economic, technical or organisational reason entailing changes in the workforce and the employer is able to show that his actions were reasonable'. Where the employer can satisfy reg 8, the employee may be able to claim redundancy, as in *Gorictree Ltd v Jenkinson* (1984). Any other dismissal in connection with the transfer of the business is automatically unfair: see *Litster v Forth Dry Dock and Engineering Co Ltd* (1989), considered below.

16.10 SPECIAL SITUATIONS

The following are situations where dismissal is automatically unfair.

- Trade union membership or activity (s 152(1) of TULR(C)A 1992)

  Where the employee is dismissed because of an actual or proposed membership of an independent trade union, or because he or she is not a member of a trade union or refuses to become a member, the dismissal is automatically unfair. This is also the case where the employee has taken part or proposes to take part in any trade union activities. The employee need not have the required qualifying period of employment in order to bring an action for unfair dismissal under this section.

- Pregnancy or childbirth

  Section 99 of the ERA 1996 provides that an employee is automatically unfairly dismissed where the principal reason for the dismissal is pregnancy or a reason connected with pregnancy; or, following maternity leave period, dismissal for childbirth or a reason connected with childbirth.

  In *O'Neil v Governors of St Thomas Moore RCVA Upper School* (1996), a religious instruction teacher was dismissed whilst on maternity leave when it was discovered that the father of her child was the local Roman Catholic priest. The employer argued that the reason for the dismissal was the paternity of the child and her particular post at the school. The EAT declined to accept this and held that the main reason related to pregnancy and was, therefore, unlawful.

- Industrial action

  Dismissals during strike or lock-out are governed by s 238 of TULR(C)A 1992. Generally, dismissal of the participants during a strike, lock-out or other industrial action is not unfair, as long as all those participating are dismissed and none are re-engaged within three months of the dismissal. However, if only some of the participants are dismissed or have not been offered re-engagement within the three month period, an unfair dismissal claim may be brought. This exception is subject to the action being regarded as official by trade unions (s 20 of TULR(C)A 1992).

- Industrial pressure

  Where an employer dismisses an employee because of industrial pressure brought to bear by other employees, the dismissal may be unfair. Section

107 of the ERA 1996 provides that industrial pressure such as the threat of a strike if the applicant continues to be employed by the employer should be ignored by the tribunal, which must consider the dismissal on the basis of whether the employer had acted reasonably.

Where pressure is put on an employer to dismiss the applicant by a trade union, because the applicant was not a member of a trade union, the trade union may be joined by the employer or applicant as party to the proceedings. The tribunal may then make an award against the trade union if it finds that the dismissal was unfair.

- Section 100 of the ERA 1996 provides that an employee has the right not to be dismissed for:

  o carrying out, or proposing to carry out, any health and safety activities which he or she is designated to do by the employer;

  o bringing to his or her employer's attention, by reasonable means and in the absence of a safety representative or committee who could do so on his or her behalf, a reasonable health and safety concern (see *Harris v Select Timber Frame Ltd* (1994));

  o in the event of danger which he or she reasonably believes to be serious and imminent and which he or she could not reasonably be expected to avert, leaving or proposing to leave the workplace or any dangerous part of it, or (while the danger persisted) refusing to return;

  o in circumstances of danger which he or she reasonably believes to be serious and imminent, taking or proposing to take appropriate steps to protect him or herself or other persons from danger.

In *Lopez v Maison Bouquillon Ltd* (1996), an assistant in a cake shop complained to the police that a chef, who was married to the shop manageress, had assaulted her. She was then dismissed from her job. She claimed unfair dismissal, stating that it was reasonable for her to leave the workplace because of the assault. The tribunal found that the incident came within s 100 and, therefore, the dismissal was unfair.

The ERA 1996 also extends protection to the following: workers who refuse to comply with working hours which would contravene the Working Time Regulations 1998 (s 101A of the ERA 1996); workers who are dismissed on the grounds of asserting a statutory right, for example, bringing proceedings against an employer to enforce a statutory right (s 104 of the ERA 1996) – see *Mennell v Newell and Wright (Transport Contractors) Ltd* (1997); employees who are dismissed for making protected disclosures (s 103A of the ERA 1996) – protective disclosures are defined in ss 43A–J of the ERA 1996 and cover such matters as crime, protection of the environment, disclosure to a legal adviser, to the Crown or to a prescribed person. This protection arises from the Public Interest Disclosure Act 1998. Finally, s 25 of the National Minimum Wage Act 1998 amends the ERA 1996 by inserting new ss 104A and 105(7A), which provide that employees who are dismissed or selected for redundancy will be regarded as unfairly dismissed if the sole or main reason for the dismissal or selection was that, *inter alia*, they had asserted their right to the national minimum wage; or the employer was prosecuted for an offence under the National Minimum Wage Act 1998; or they qualify for the national minimum wage. Protection is also afforded for dismissals for taking proceedings, etc, against the employer under the Part-Time Workers (Prevention of Less Favourable Treatment) Regulations 2000.

16.11 REMEDIES

Where the dismissal is found to be unfair, the tribunal has the power to make an order for reinstatement, re-engagement or compensation (ss 112–24 of the ERA 1996).

16.11.1 Reinstatement

In the case of reinstatement, the tribunal must ask the applicant whether he or she wishes such an order to be made. The effect of an order for reinstatement is that the employer must treat the employee as if he or she had not been dismissed, that is, as if his or her employment is on the same or improved terms and conditions.

16.11.2 Re-engagement

If the applicant so wishes, the tribunal may make an order for re-engagement (s 115 of the ERA 1996). The effect of this is that the applicant should be re-engaged by the employer, or by an associated employer in employment which is comparable to the previous employment or amounts to other suitable employment. The tribunal will specify the terms on which the applicant should be re-engaged and this may make provision for arrears of pay. The making of orders for reinstatement and re-engagement is at the discretion of the tribunal, which will consider whether it is just and equitable to make such an order considering the conduct of the employee and whether it is practicable to do so.

Failure to comply fully with the terms of an order for reinstatement or re-engagement will result in an award of compensation being made by the employment tribunal, having regard to the loss sustained by the complainant, which is usually the basic award plus an additional award. The employer may raise 'impracticability' as a defence to such a claim.

16.11.3 Compensation

Certain employment protection awards are now automatically index-linked – see the Employment Relations Act 1999 (Commencement No 3 and Transitional Provision) Order 1999 (SI 1999/3374).

An award of compensation will be made where an order for reinstatement or re-engagement is not complied with or it is not practicable to make such an order. The various types of compensation are described below.

Basic award (s 118 of the ERA 1996)

The calculation of the basic award is dependent upon the number of years of continuous service which the applicant has attained:

Entitlement:	Age	Weeks' pay for each year of employment
	18–21	$^1/_2$
	22–40	1
	41–65	$1^1/_2$

The maximum number of years which can be counted is 20 and the maximum amount of weekly pay is currently £250. The maximum basic award is at present £7,500. The tribunal may reduce the basic award on the grounds of contributory conduct on the part of the applicant. Where there is also an award of a redundancy payment, the basic award will be reduced by the amount of that payment, as long as it is established that the dismissal was for reason of redundancy.

A 'week's pay' relates to gross pay; if the applicant is over 64, the award is reduced by one-twelfth for each month after the complainant's 64th birthday. The basic award will be two weeks' pay where the reason for the dismissal was redundancy and the employee unreasonably refuses to accept a renewal of the contract or suitable alternative employment.

Any statutory limits placed on awards are now to be index-linked and reviewed in September of each year (s 34 of the Employment Relations Act 1999).

Compensatory award (s 123 of the ERA 1996)

A compensatory award is in addition to the basic award and is awarded at the discretion of the tribunal. The amount of the award is decided upon by the tribunal by reference to what is 'just and equitable in all the circumstances, having regard to the loss sustained by the applicant in consequence of the dismissal'. At present, the maximum amount of this award is £52,600. The amount of the award may be reduced by failure on the part of the employee to mitigate his or her loss, contributory conduct and any *ex gratia* payment made by the employer.

In making the award, the tribunal will take into account loss of wages; expenses incurred in taking legal action against the employer; loss of future earnings; loss of pension rights and other benefits, for example, a company car; and the manner of the dismissal.

Additional award

An additional award can be made where the employer fails to comply with an order for reinstatement or re-engagement and fails to show that it was not practicable to comply with such an order. The amount of this additional award will be between 13 and 26 weeks' pay; if the dismissal is unfair because it is based on sex or race discrimination, the additional award will be between 26 and 52 weeks' pay.

Interim relief

There are now minimum awards of compensation for dismissal in 'special situations'. For example, the minimum amount for contravening s 100 is £3,400.

Where an employee alleges dismissal for union/non-union membership or trade union activities, he or she can apply to the employment tribunal for an order for interim relief (s 161 of TULR(C)A 1992).

Such an order will preserve the status quo until a full hearing of the case and has the effect, therefore, of reinstating or re-engaging the employee. In order to obtain an order for interim relief, an application must be made to the employment tribunal within seven days immediately following the effective date of termination. This must be supported by a certificate signed by an authorised trade union official where the allegation relates to dismissal for trade union membership or taking part in trade union activities. Finally, it must appear to the employment tribunal that the complaint is likely to succeed at a full hearing.

Even where these conditions are satisfied, the employment tribunal must then determine whether the employer is willing to reinstate or re-engage the employee. If the employer is not so willing, then the employment tribunal must make an order for the continuation of the employee's contract of employment until the full hearing, thus preserving continuity, pay and other employment rights.

Where the employer fails to comply with an interim relief order, the employment tribunal must:

- make an order for the continuation of the contract; and
- order the employer to pay such compensation as the tribunal believes is just and equitable, having regard to the loss suffered by the employee.

Where an employer fails to observe the terms of a continuation order, the employment tribunal shall:

- determine the amount of any money owed to the employee; and
- order the employer to pay the employee such compensation as is considered to be just and equitable.

There has been much academic debate about the success or otherwise of the unfair dismissal provisions. It has been said that the law has been unsuccessful in providing effective control over what is seen as managerial prerogative in relation to dismissals (see, for example, Collins, H, 'Capitalist discipline and corporatist law' (1982) 11 ILJ 78). One general weakness expounded by academics is the attitude of the appeal court judges to the legislation. They perceive that judges feel that they are being asked to intervene in areas which they believe individuals should resolve; as a result, judges end up endorsing the ordinary practices of employers, even though these may be flawed (see *Saunders v Scottish National Camps Association Ltd* (1980)). The right to protection from unfair dismissal can be seen as a fundamental human right, which therefore demands a complete overhaul of the current legislative provisions (see Hepple, R, 'The fall and rise of unfair dismissal', in McCarthy, W (ed), *Legal Intervention in Industrial Relations: Gains and Loses*, 1992, p 95).

16.12 REDUNDANCY

When an employee's services are no longer required by the business, either through the closing down of that business or perhaps because of the introduction of new technology, he or she will in general have been made redundant. Whether or not the employee is entitled to redundancy pay will depend upon whether the qualification rules and the key essentials are satisfied. The law in this area is weighted in favour of the employer, who, in order to avoid the higher compensation limits for unfair dismissal, may well try to disguise an unfair dismissal situation as redundancy. The law relating to redundancy can be found in the ERA 1996. The purpose of the ERA 1996 is to provide for the payment of compensation based on an employee's service and wages, in order to tide the employee over during the period in which he or she is without a job. However, any entitlement to redundancy payments only exists where it is established that the employee's dismissal was by reason of redundancy within the meaning of the ERA 1996.

16.12.1 Qualifications

In assessing whether an employee qualifies for redundancy payment, the rules are similar to the unfair dismissal provisions. The qualifying period for redundancy is two years. The final outcome of the decision in *R v Secretary of State for Employment ex p Seymour-Smith and Perez (No 2)* (2000) does not change this, even though a two year qualifying period was found by the

House of Lords to discriminate indirectly against women and was contrary to EC law. The onus is on the employer to show that continuity has been broken or that there are weeks which do not count towards continuity; once again, the same rules apply regarding continuity. Certain categories of employee are excluded from the provisions of the ERA 1996 (as referred to earlier), in some cases because existing arrangements between their employer and their trade union are better than the protection afforded by the ERA 1996.

16.12.2 Dismissal

The burden of proof in the initial stages of any claim for redundancy is on the employee to show dismissal. There is then a presumption that the dismissal was for reason of redundancy and the burden moves to the employer to show that redundancy was not the reason for the dismissal.

Where an employee meets the basic qualification requirements, it must be shown that he or she has been 'dismissed' within the meaning of s 136 of the ERA 1996. Again, the provisions which determine dismissal are the same as for unfair dismissal. According to s 139 of the ERA 1996, an employee shall be treated as dismissed by the employer if, but only if:

- the contract of employment is terminated by the employer with or without notice; or
- it is a fixed term contract which has expired without being renewed; or
- the employee terminates the contract with or without notice in circumstances such that he or she is entitled to terminate it without notice by reason of the employer's conduct; or
- the contract is terminated by the death of the employer or on the dissolution or liquidation of the firm.

It is clear, however, that the initiative to dismiss the employee must come from the employer. An employee who resigns is not entitled to redundancy payment unless the constructive dismissal provision is satisfied (*Walley v Morgan* (1969)).

Whether a dismissal is within s 136 or 139 is a question of fact in each case. For example, a variation in the terms of the employee's contract will amount to a dismissal if he or she does not agree to the new terms. If, however, the employee accepts the new terms, there can be no dismissal and continuity is preserved.

In *Marriot v Oxford and District Co-operative Society Ltd* (1970), the defendants employed Marriot as a foreman. He was informed that, from a certain date, he would be employed on a lower grade and his rate of pay would be reduced accordingly. It was held that the variation in the terms of the existing contract amounted to termination by the employer, which Marriot could treat as a dismissal.

Clearly, there may be a term in the contract which allows the employer to vary the terms. If the employee in this situation does not like the new terms and chooses to leave his or her employment, this will not amount to a dismissal for the purposes of the ERA 1996. One type of contentious term has proved to be the 'mobility clause' which many executive contracts contain. Where an employee refuses to comply with an express mobility clause requiring him or her to move, the refusal amounts to misconduct and, therefore, any dismissal cannot be treated as redundancy, but it could leave the employer open to a claim of unfair dismissal. Furthermore, if the employee attempts to anticipate the employer's actions and resigns, the resignation will not amount to a dismissal.

In *Morton Sundour Fabrics v Shaw* (1967), Morton employed Shaw as a foreman. He was informed that there might be some redundancies in the near future, but nothing specific was decided. In the light of what he had been told, he decided to leave the firm in order to take another job. It was held that he had not been dismissed and, therefore, was not entitled to redundancy payments. His precipitous action could not be shown to relate to the subsequent redundancies made by his employer.

Obviously, he would have succeeded had he waited until he received his notice of redundancy. However, when he resigned, there was no way of knowing exactly who would be made redundant (see *Doble v Firestone Tyre and Rubber Co Ltd* (1981), which followed the decision in *Morton*).

16.12.3 Dismissals for reasons of redundancy

In order for the employee to be entitled to redundancy payments, he or she must have been dismissed 'for reason of redundancy'. There is a presumption that, once the employee has shown dismissal, the reason for the dismissal was redundancy (s 163(2) of the ERA 1996). The onus is on the employer to show that the dismissal was for some reason other than redundancy.

Section 139(1) of the ERA 1996 provides a definition of 'redundancy':

[This is where] dismissal is attributable wholly or mainly to:

(a) the fact that his employer has ceased, or intends to cease, to carry on the business for the purposes of which the employee was employed by him, or has ceased, or intends to cease, to carry on that business in the place where the employee was so employed; or

(b) the fact that the requirements of that business for employees to carry out work of a particular kind, or for employees to carry out work of a particular kind in the place where they were so employed have ceased or diminished or are expected to cease or diminish.

In effect, there are three situations in which the dismissal can be said to be for redundancy. These are as follows:

Cessation of the employer's business

This covers both temporary and permanent closures of the employer's business in respect of the type of work carried on at the premises and is, on the whole, straightforward. In *Gemmell v Darngavil Brickworks Ltd* (1967), a brickworks closed for a period of 13 weeks in order for substantial repairs to be carried out. Some of the employees were dismissed. It was held that the dismissal was for reason of redundancy, even though part of the premises was still in use.

Closure or change in the place of work

Where the employer ceases to trade at a particular place, as opposed to the cessation of the type of work, the dismissal of any employees will usually be for reason of redundancy. This is subject to any term in the contract of employment which contains a 'clear and unambiguous mobility clause'. Such clauses will rarely be implied.

In *O'Brien v Associated Fire Alarms Ltd* (1969), O'Brien was employed by the defendants at their Liverpool branch. There was a shortage of work and he was asked to work in Barrow-in-Furness. He refused and was dismissed by his employer. He contended that the dismissal amounted to redundancy. It was held that, as there was no clause in O'Brien's contract of employment which would have allowed his employer to move him to a different location, the dismissal was for reason of redundancy.

Where the employer only moves his place of work a short distance and/or remains within the same town or conurbation, any offer of work to his existing employees at the new place of employment may prevent any dismissal from being for reason of redundancy. Obviously, this will depend on accessibility to the new premises, as well as the terms on which the offer is made – it should be remembered that the terms must not be worse than existing terms. It can, therefore, be within the employer's expectations that his or her employees will move to different premises without there being a redundancy situation if such an expectation is reasonable in all the circumstances of the case.

In *Managers (Holborn) Ltd v Hohne* (1977), the defendants occupied premises in Holborn, of which Hohne was a manageress. They decided to move their business to Regent Street, which was only a short distance away. Hohne refused to move there and claimed redundancy, on the basis that there was no term in her contract which required her to move. It was held that the new premises were just as accessible as the old ones and, therefore, it was reasonable for her employer to expect her to move without there being any issue of redundancy. There was no evidence of any additional inconvenience to Hohne if she agreed to move to the new premises. She did not, therefore, succeed in her action.

Finally, this provision has recently been interpreted in such a way that it will only be satisfied if the place where the employee actually works, rather than is expected to work, closes or changes. In *High Table Ltd v Horst* (1997), Mrs Horst was employed as a silver service waitress. Her letter of appointment specified that she was appointed as waitress to one particular client and she worked at their premises from July 1988 until she was dismissed. The staff handbook stated:

> Your place of work is as stated in your letter of appointment, which acts as part of your terms and conditions. However, given the nature of our business, it is sometimes necessary to transfer staff on a temporary or permanent basis to another location. Whenever possible, this will be within reasonable travelling distance of your existing place of work.

The client for whom Horst worked reduced its catering needs and, as a result, Horst was dismissed as redundant. She claimed unfair dismissal. The main issue for the Court of Appeal was, what is the test for determining redundancy? It held that the test was primarily a factual one and, on the facts, the place where she was employed no longer needed her. There was, therefore, a redundancy situation, which caused her to be dismissed. This decision casts doubt on the decision in *UK Automatic Energy Authority v Claydon* (1974). In that case, Claydon's contract of employment included a mobility clause. When he was asked to move from his employer's Suffolk plant to their Aldermaston premises, he refused and was dismissed. It was held that the mobility clause was valid and, although the work had ceased in Suffolk, it was reasonable for the employer to request a transfer to Aldermaston. The dismissal was, therefore, fair.

Whilst the decision in *Horst* appears to recognise the importance of an employee's redundancy rights and the desire to ensure that those rights are not negated by the unscrupulous use of mobility clauses, in real terms, the employer in this case wanted it to be a redundancy situation without any obligation to redeploy staff or increase the amount of compensation payable.

Diminishing requirements for employees

As a general rule, where the employer is forced to dismiss employees because of a reduction in the work available, such employees are surplus to the requirements of the business and any dismissal is for reason of redundancy. Furthermore, where there is a change in systems of work so that fewer employees are actually needed to do the job, this, too, can amount to redundancy. The courts are, from time to time, faced with the difficult task of deciding whether dismissal for failing to keep up with modern working practices is for reason of redundancy.

In *North Riding Garages v Butterwick* (1967), Butterwick had been employed at the same garage for 30 years and had risen to the position of workshop manager. The garage was taken over by the appellants and Butterwick was dismissed for inefficiency, on the ground that he was unable or unwilling to accept new methods of work, which would involve him in some administrative work. It was held that the dismissal was not for reason of redundancy because the employee was still expected to do the same type of work, subject to new working practices. As far as the court was concerned, employees who remain in the same employment for many years are expected to adapt to new techniques and methods of work and even higher standards of efficiency. It is only when the new practices affect the nature of the work so that, in effect, there is no requirement to do that particular kind of work that a redundancy situation may arise.

In *Hindle v Percival Boats Ltd* (1969), Hindle had been employed to repair of wooden boats for many years. This type of work was in decline because of the increasing use of glass-fibre. He was dismissed because he was 'too good and too slow' and it was uneconomical to keep him. He was not replaced; his work was merely absorbed by existing staff. It was held that Hindle's dismissal was not for reason of redundancy. The court felt that the employer was merely shedding surplus labour and that this was not within the ERA 1996.

Clearly, there are situations where shedding surplus labour will amount to redundancy; each case must be considered on its merits.

In *Haden Ltd v Cowen* (1982), Cowen was employed as a regional supervisor. He was based in Southampton and had to cover a large part of southern England as part of his job. He suffered a mild heart attack. His employer then promoted him to divisional contracts surveyor, as it was thought that this would make his life less stressful. One of the terms of his contract required him to undertake, at the discretion of the company, any duties which reasonably fell within the scope of his capabilities. The company was later forced to reduce the number of employees at staff level. Cowen was not prepared to accept demotion and was dismissed. He claimed both redundancy and unfair dismissal. It was held that Cowen was dismissed for reason of redundancy because there was no other work available within the terms of his contract, that is, as divisional contracts manager.

It is suggested that the true test of redundancy is to be found in this case and the issue to be considered is 'whether the business needs as much work of the kind which the employee could, by his contract, lawfully be required to do'. This is a question, not of the day to day function of the employee, but of what he or she could be expected to do under his or her contract of employment (see *Pink v White and Co Ltd* (1985)). Recent case law suggests that, even where a contract contains a 'flexibility clause', for example, 'and any work which may be required by the employer', there may still be a redundancy situation. In *Johnson v Peabody Trust* (1996), Johnson was employed as a roofer. A flexibility clause was introduced into his contract, which stated that he was expected to undertake general building work. By 1993, Johnson was doing more general work than roofing. He was then laid off. The EAT concluded that he was redundant. In looking at the basic task which he was expected to perform, it was determined that he was first and foremost a roofer and the need for such employees had diminished. However, a move from day shift to night shift work or vice versa may be 'work of a particular kind', as was held in *Macfisheries Ltd v Findlay* (1985).

In *Shawkat v Nottingham City Hospital NHS Trust (No 2)* (2001), the Court of Appeal held that the mere fact of a reorganisation of the business, as a result of which the employer requires one or more employees to do a different job from which he or she was previously doing, is not conclusive of redundancy. The tribunal must go on to decide whether that change had any, and if so what, effect on the employer's requirements for employees to carry out work of a particular kind. It does not necessarily follow from the fact that a new post is different in kind from the previous post or posts that the requirements of the employer's business for employees to carry out work of a particular kind must have diminished. Nor does the fact that an employee of one skill was replaced by an employee of a different skill compel the conclusion that the requirements for work of a particular kind have ceased or diminished. That is always a question of fact for the tribunal to decide.

In *Shawkat's* case, a tribunal was entitled to find that dismissal of a thoracic surgeon, following a reorganisation as a result of which he was asked to carry out cardiac surgery in additional to thoracic surgery, was not by reason of redundancy. The requirements for employees to carry out thoracic surgery had not diminished even though the reorganisation changed the work which the employees in the thoracic department, including the applicant, were required to carry out.

Finally, the definitive test, which upholds an earlier decision in *Safeway Stores plc v Burrell* (1997), can be found in *Murray and Another v Foyle Meats* (1999). The House of Lords in this case determined that a dismissal must now be regarded as being by reason of redundancy wherever it is attributable to redundancy; that is, did the diminishing requirement for employees cause the dismissal? This is a straightforward causative test.

16.12.4 Lay-off and short time (ss 147–49 of the ERA 1996)

Redundancy payment may be claimed where an employee has been laid off or kept on short time for either four or more consecutive weeks or for a series of six or more weeks (of which not more than three are consecutive) within a period of 13 weeks. The employee must give written notice to his or her employer, no later than four weeks from the end of the periods referred to, of his or her intention to claim redundancy payment, and should terminate the employment by giving either at least one week's notice or notice during the period stipulated in the contract of employment. Following this action by the employee, the employer may serve a counter-notice within seven days of the employee's notice, contesting the claim and stating that there is a reasonable chance that, within four weeks of the counter-notice the employee, will commence a period of 13 weeks' consecutive employment. This then becomes a matter for the tribunal.

If the employer withdraws the counter-notice or fails to employ the employee for 13 consecutive weeks, the employee is entitled to the redundancy payment.

16.12.5 Change in ownership and transfer of undertakings

Under the ERA 1996, continuity is preserved in the following situations, so that past service will count in the new employment:

- change of partners;
- where trustees or personal representatives take over the running of the company when the employer dies;
- transfer of employment to an associated employer;
- transfer of an undertaking, trade or business from one person to another.

Where there is a change in the ownership of a business and existing employees either have their contract renewed or are re-engaged by the new employer, this does not amount to redundancy and continuity is preserved (s 218(2) of the ERA 1996); an example of this is where the business is sold as a going concern, rather than a transfer of the assets. However, if the employee has reasonable grounds for refusing the offer of renewal, he or she may be treated as redundant (s 141(4)).

The Transfer of Undertakings (Protection of Employment) Regulations 1981 (SI 1981/1794) apply to the sale or other disposition of commercial and non-commercial undertakings (see s 33 of the Trade Union Reform and Employment Rights Act (TURERA) 1993, which brought the UK in line with EC Directive 77/187 – the Acquired Rights Directive). The transfer must be of the whole or part of a business, not merely a transfer of assets (*Melon v Hector Powe Ltd* (1980)); nor do the Regulations apply to a change in ownership resulting from a transfer of shares. Where there is the transfer of a business which falls within the Regulations, the contracts of employment of the employees are also transferred, as if they had been made by the transferee. This not only protects continuity, but also puts the new employer in the same position as the original employer. As a result, all existing rights, etc, attained by employees are preserved and become enforceable against the new business. Such transfers are subject to the consent of the employee. If the employee objects, the transfer will in effect terminate the contract of employment, but this termination will not amount to a dismissal (s 33(4) of TURERA 1993). If, following a transfer, there is a subsequent dismissal, the employee may claim unfair dismissal, or, if it is for 'an economic, technical or organisational reason', redundancy payment may be claimed.

The Court of Appeal in *RCO Support Services v Unison* (2002) held that there can be a TUPE transfer even where there is no transfer of significant assets and none of the relevant employees were taken on by the new employer. In the present case, there was a change in hospitals providing inpatient care within the same NHS trust area and new contractors took over the provision of cleaning and catering. In determining whether there had been a transfer of an undertaking, the tribunal had correctly applied the retention of identify test as well as considering the reasons why the employees were not taken on by the new employer.

The contentious issue concerning the position of employees who are dismissed prior to a transfer (thus potentially enabling the employers to evade the Regulations) has been resolved by *Litster and Others v Forth Dry Dock and Engineering Co Ltd* (1989), in which it was decided that, where employees are dismissed in these circumstances, they must be treated as if they were still employed at the time of transfer. As a result, the Regulations are to be applied to such employees. The transferee employer will be responsible for any unfair dismissals, unless they can be shown to be for an 'economic, technical or organisational' reason entailing a change in the workforce.

By virtue of reg 8(2), such dismissals are deemed to be for a substantial reason for the purposes of s 98(1) of the ERA 1996 and are fair, provided that they pass the statutory test of reasonableness. If the employer successfully establishes the 'economic technical or organisational' (ETO) defence, an employee can claim a redundancy payment if the transfer was the reason for the redundancy dismissal. The Court of Appeal considered the scope of the ETO defence in *Berriman v Delabole Slate Ltd* (1985). The court held that, in order to come within reg 8(2), the employer must show that a change in the workforce is part of the economic, technical or organisational reason for dismissal. It must be an *objective* of the employer's plan to achieve changes in the workforce, not just a possible consequence of the plan. So, where an employee resigned, following a transfer, because the transferee employer proposed to remove his guaranteed weekly wage so as to bring his pay into line with the transferee's existing workforce, the reason behind the plan was to produce uniform terms and conditions and was not in any way intended to reduce the numbers in the workforce.

A further contentious issue relating to the position of contracted out services has been resolved by the decision in *Dines and Others v Initial Health Care Services and Another* (1994). The Court of Appeal held that, where employees are employed by the new contracting company, the new company is obliged to take over the contract of employment on exactly the same terms (following the decision in *Kenny v South Manchester College* (1993)).

Following *Dines*, cases have extended the meaning of 'relevant transfer'. In *Betts v Brintel Helicopters and KLM* (1996), Brintel had, until 1995, exclusive rights to provide and service Shell's helicopter requirements for all of their North Sea oil rigs. In 1995, Shell decided to split the contract between Brintel and KLM, and 66 Brintel employees were left without jobs. Betts and six others claimed successfully that they were now employed by KLM. The High Court held that there had been a transfer of the 'activity' from Brintel to KLM, even though there was no transfer of employees or assets. (See, also, *ECM (Vehicle Delivery Service) Ltd v Cox and Others* (1999).)

An attempt to avoid the application of the Transfer of Undertakings (Protection of Employment) Regulations 1981 (SI 1981/1794) by 'hiving' down the transfer first to a subsidiary company and then to the ultimate transferee has been thwarted. In *Re Maxwell Fleet and Facilities Management Ltd (No 2)* (2000), the High Court held that liability for employees dismissed before the purported 'hive down' passed to the ultimate transferee by virtue of the application of the *Litster* principle. The employees in this situation were dismissed for a reason connected with the transfer and were, therefore, deemed to have been employed immediately before the transfer.

Finally, the Government is proposing to reform the Transfer of Undertakings (Protection of Employment) Regulations 1981 and has issued a Consultation Paper: *Government Proposals for Reform (Employment Relations Directorate)* DTI, September 2001.

The Collective Redundancies and Transfer of Undertakings (Protection of Employment) (Amendment) Regulations 1995 have amended the 1981 Regulations. In particular, reg 8(5) was introduced to reverse the decision in *Milligan v Securicor Cleaning Ltd* (1995) to the effect that an employee did not need to have two years' continuous employment in order to claim unfair dismissal on a transfer pursuant to reg 8. The effect of the decision was that someone who was dismissed after one week's employment because of a transfer could claim unfair dismissal, whereas an employee of 23 months' duration who was dismissed in a non-transfer situation could not! The decision has been overruled by the High Court in *R v Secretary of State for Trade and Industry ex p Unison* (1996).

Sections 99 and 105 of the ERA 1996 made it automatically unfair to select an employee for redundancy on grounds of pregnancy, childbirth or because he or she has made a health and safety complaint or has asserted a statutory right.

16.12.6 Offer of alternative employment

The offer of alternative employment is covered by s 141 of the ERA 1996. The general rule is that, where the employer makes an offer of suitable alternative employment, which is unreasonably refused by the employee, the employee will be unable to claim redundancy. This contract, which is either a renewal or a re-engagement, must take effect on the expiry of the old contract or within four weeks. Clearly, the main issue is what amounts to 'suitable'. Consideration must be had of the old terms and conditions as compared with the new ones, that is, the nature of the work; remuneration; hours; place;

skills; and experience, including qualifications, etc. Where the conditions of the new contract do not differ materially from the old contract regarding place, nature of the work, pay, etc, then the question of suitability does not arise. It is a question of fact in each case as to whether an offer can be deemed 'suitable', with the onus resting on the employer to establish suitability. However, the facts must be considered objectively.

In *Taylor v Kent CC* (1969), Taylor was made redundant from his post as headmaster of a school. He was offered a place in the pool of supply teachers from which temporary absences were filled in schools. There was no loss of salary or other rights, other than status. Taylor refused the offer. It was held that his refusal was reasonable. The offer was not suitable because of the loss of status, since he was being removed from a position as head of a school to an ordinary teacher.

A loss of fringe benefits has been held to be a reasonable refusal (*Sheppard v NCB* (1966)). However, the refusal of an offer of a job which may only last a short period could be deemed to be unreasonable (*Morganite Crucible v Street* (1972)). It was decided in *Spencer and Griffin v Gloucestershire CC* (1985) that the issue for the industrial (now employment) tribunal is twofold: first, whether the job offered is suitable; and, secondly, whether the employee has acted reasonably in refusing the offer.

In considering whether a refusal by the employee is reasonable, regard must be had for the personal circumstances of the employee, such as housing and domestic problems. It may be reasonable for an employee to refuse a job offer which involves a move to London when he or she lives in the Midlands, because of the housing problems associated with a move to the Home Counties. However, a refusal based upon a personal whim will be unreasonable. In *Fuller v Stephanie Bowman (Sales) Ltd* (1977), the applicant refused to move with her employers from a West End address to one in Soho, where the new business premises were above a sex shop. After a site visit to the premises, it was decided that the dislike of the sex shop was not enough to make the refusal of the offer reasonable, as it was not one of the worst streets in Soho and it was unlikely that the applicant would be mistaken for a prostitute. In *Rawe v Power Gas Corp* (1966), it was held to be reasonable to refuse a move from the south-east of England to Teeside because of marital difficulties.

Finally, even where the employment tribunal finds that the offer was suitable, it does not automatically follow that a refusal by the employee is unreasonable. For example, in *Cambridge and District Co-operative Society Ltd v Ruse* (1993), although the job was deemed to be suitable by the industrial tribunal, the employee had personal objections to the job offered, as he perceived a lack of status which supported his refusal of the offer.

It must be remembered that the onus is on the employer to show that the employee's rejection of the offer is unreasonable. Where the offer of alternative employment is accepted by the employee, there is deemed to be continuity of employment between the former contract and the new contract.

By virtue of s 132 of the ERA 1996, the employee is entitled to a trial period of four weeks (or longer, if agreed with the employer) if the contract is renewed on different terms and conditions. If the employee terminates his or her employment during the trial period for a reason connected with the new contract, he or she will be treated as having been dismissed on the date that the previous contract was terminated. Whether he or she will be entitled to redundancy will depend on whether it was a suitable offer of alternative employment and whether the refusal to accept it was reasonable (see *Meek v Allen Rubber Co Ltd and Secretary of State for Employment* (1980)). If the employer dismisses the employee during the trial period for any reason, the dismissal is to be treated as redundancy.

An employee is entitled to a reasonable amount of time off to seek work or retrain once notice of redundancy has been received (s 52 of the ERA 1996). This right is confined to those employees who meet the qualifying periods. Failure to provide time off may result in the employee making a complaint to an employment tribunal, which may award two-fifths of a week's pay.

16.12.7 Calculation of redundancy payment

The employee must inform the employer, in writing, of any intention to claim a redundancy payment. If the employer does not make the payment or there is a dispute over entitlement, the matter is referred to an employment tribunal. As a general rule, the claim must be made within six months of the date of termination of the contract of employment. This period can be extended at the discretion of the employment tribunal but cannot exceed 12 months.

Method of calculation

Although those under 20 years of age or who have reached retirement age do not qualify, the method of calculation is the same for unfair dismissal (considered above). The maximum award at present is, therefore, £7,500. An employee may lose entitlement to all or part of his or her redundancy payments in the following circumstances:

- if the claim is made out of time, that is, after a period of six months from the relevant date. However, as with unfair dismissal, an employment tribunal may allow an extension within the time limit if it is just and equitable to do so (s 164 of the ERA 1996);

- if employment is left prematurely, the employee having been warned of the possibility of redundancy in the future. An employee under notice of dismissal who leaves before the notice expires may also lose the right to payment. This will depend on whether the employer objects to the premature departure (s 142 of the ERA 1996);

- where the employee is guilty of misconduct, allowing the employer to terminate the contract for this reason (s 140(1) of the ERA 1996);
- strike action – if the employee is involved in a strike during his or her period of notice, he or she will still be entitled to redundancy payment. However, if his or her notice of dismissal is received whilst on strike, he or she will not be entitled to claim redundancy payment.

16.12.8 Procedure for handling redundancies

This is governed by s 188 of TULR(C)A 1992 (as amended by TURERA 1993) and the Collective Redundancies and Transfer of Undertakings (Protection of Employment) (Amendment) Regulations 1995 (SI 1995/2587). There is an obligation on the employer to consult a recognised trades union or elected employee representative 'in good time', as opposed to 'at the earliest opportunity'. Such consultation must take place even if only one employee is being made redundant. Where consultation cannot take place at the earliest opportunity, the fall back rules are as follows:

- at least 90 days before the first dismissal takes effect, where he or she proposes to make 100 or more employees redundant at one establishment within a period of 90 days or less;
- at least 30 days before the first redundancy takes effect, where he or she proposes to make 20 or more employees redundant at one establishment within a 30 day period.

Consultation must include consideration of the ways in which the redundancies can be avoided; a possible reduction in the numbers of employees being dismissed; anything which might mitigate the effects of the redundancy *ex gratia* payment, etc (ss 188–98 of TURERA 1993). The employer must also disclose the following during the consultations (s 188(4) of TULR(C)A 1992):

- the reasons for the proposed redundancies;
- the number and description of the employees whom it is proposed to make redundant;
- the total number of employees of that description employed at that establishment;
- the method of selection, for example, last in, LIFO, part timers first, etc;
- the method of carrying out the redundancies, having regard to any procedure agreed with the trade union.

During these consultations, the trade union may make any representations which it sees fit. The employer may not ignore these representations and must give the reasons if he or she chooses to reject them. However, in considering the fairness of the employer's conduct, in *British Aerospace plc v Green* (1995), the Court of Appeal adopted a broad brush approach in judging the overall fairness of the employer's conduct of the selection procedure and did not feel that it was necessary to examine individual applications of it too closely. Where there are special circumstances, such as insolvency, the employer need only do what is reasonably practicable to comply with the consultation requirements.

Effect of non-compliance with the procedure

Where the employer fails to comply with the consultation procedure in circumstances where it was reasonably practicable to expect him or her to do so, the trade union can complain to the employment tribunal. If the tribunal finds in favour of the trade union, it must make a declaration to this effect and may make a protective award to those employees who were affected. This award, which is discretionary, takes the form of remuneration for a protected period. The length of the protected period usually reflects the severity of the breach by the employer. However, the protected period:

- must not exceed 90 days, where it was proposed to make 100 or more employees redundant within 90 days;
- is 30 days, where it was proposed to make 20 or more redundant.

All employees covered by the protective award are entitled to up to 13 weeks' pay (Collective Redundancies and Transfer of Undertakings (Protection of Employment) (Amendment) Regulations 1995 (SI 1995/2587)).

16.12.9 Notification of redundancies to the Secretary of State

By virtue of s 193 of TULR(C)A 1992, an employer must notify the Secretary of State of his or her intentions where he or she proposes:

- to make 100 or more employees redundant at one establishment within a 90 day period – here, the notification must take place within 90 days;
- to make 20 or more employees redundant within a 30 day period – in which case the notification must take place within 30 days.

Failure to meet these requirements may result in prosecution. However, there is a 'special circumstances' defence where it is not reasonably practicable for the employer to comply with the law on notification.

INDIVIDUAL EMPLOYMENT RIGHTS (3): TERMINATION

The contract of employment may be terminated by agreement, death, frustration or performance. As a general rule, an employer must give notice if he or she wishes to terminate an employee's contract. The minimum periods of notice are laid down in s 86 of the ERA 1996. An employee wishing to terminate his or her contract must give at least one week's notice.

Summary dismissal

Summary dismissal is dismissal without notice for a serious breach of the contract.

Wrongful dismissal

Wrongful dismissal is summary dismissal without just cause (*Irani v South West Hampshire HA* (1985)). Compensation in the form of wages and damages will generally only be awarded for the notice period unless there has been a breach of the implied term of trust and confidence (*Malik v BCCI SA* (1997); *Gogay v Hertfordshire County Council* (2000)). However, no compensation can be awarded for mental distress or damage to reputation (*Johnson v Unisys Ltd* (2001)).

Unfair dismissal

Protection for unfair dismissal is provided by the ERA 1996. All employees must now satisfy the qualifying period of at least one year's continuous service and must not belong to the excluded groups.

Effective date of termination (s 97 of the ERA 1996)

Rules are the same for redundancy and unfair dismissal where:
- termination is with notice and the effective date/relevant date is the date on which the notice expires;
- termination is without notice and the effective date is the date on which termination takes effect.

Dismissal

The employee must show that he or she has been dismissed within the meaning of the ERA 1996. This may amount to:

- Express termination by the employer:
  - *Igbo v Johnson Matthey Chemicals Ltd* (1986);
  - *Martin v Yeoman Aggregates Ltd* (1983);
  - *Robertson v Securicor Transport Ltd* (1972).
- Expiration of a fixed term contract which is not renewed.
- Constructive dismissal where the employee is entitled to terminate his or her contract:
  - *Western Excavating Ltd v Sharp* (1978);
  - *Simmonds v Dowty Seals Ltd* (1978);
  - *Pepper and Hope v Daish* (1980).
- Written reasons for the dismissal:

  Where the employee makes a written request for a statement of the reasons for his or her dismissal, the employer must supply this information within 14 days (s 92 of the ERA 1996).

Fair dismissals

Once the employee has established dismissal, the onus moves to the employer to show that he or she acted reasonably and that, therefore, the dismissal was fair (s 98 of the ERA 1996).

The employer must show that:

- The actions were a reasonable response:
  - *Polkey v AE Dayton Services Ltd* (1987);
  - *Haddon v Van Den Bergh Foods Ltd* (1999);
  - *Post Office v Foley* (2000).

  ACAS Code of Practice on Disciplinary and Grievance Procedures. This will be replaced by a new procedure in the Employment Act 2002.
- The capability or qualifications of the employee were inadequate:
  - *Davison v Kent Meters Ltd* (1975).
- The conduct of the employee merited dismissal:
  - *Taylor v Parsons Peebles Ltd* (1981);
  - *Parr v Whitbread plc* (1990).
- There was a redundancy situation:
  - *Allwood v William Hill Ltd* (1974);
  - *Hammond-Scott v Elizabeth Arden Ltd* (1976).

- There were statutory restrictions.
- There was some other substantial reason.

Automatically unfair

The following dismissals are automatically unfair:
- trade union membership or activities;
- pregnancy and childbirth;
- industrial action;
- health and safety matters;
- protected disclosures.

Remedies

The remedies available for unfair dismissal are:
- reinstatement;
- re-engagement;
- basic award;
- compensatory award;
- additional award;
- interim relief order.

Redundancy

Redundancy occurs when an employee is dismissed because his or her services are no longer required or the business ceases. The employee may have a claim for redundancy payments. The employee must show:
- that he or she satisfies a qualification period of two years' continuous employment and does not fall within excluded classes (*R v Secretary of State for Employment ex p Seymour-Smith and Perez (No 2)* (2000));
- dismissal by his or her employer – *Marriot v Oxford and District Co-operative Society Ltd* (1970).

Once dismissal has been established, there is a presumption that the reason for the dismissal was redundancy. There are three situations which are deemed to be 'for reason of redundancy':
- cessation of the employer's business (*Gemmell v Darngavil Brickworks Ltd* (1967));
- closure or change in the place of work (*O'Brien v Associated Fire Alarms Ltd* (1969); *Managers (Holborn) Ltd v Hohne* (1977));

- diminishing requirements for employees (*North Riding Garages v Butterwick* (1967); *Hindle v Percival Boats Ltd* (1969); *Shawkat v Nottingham City Hospital NHS Trust (No 2)* (2001)).

Lay-off and short time

Redundancy payment may be made where an employee has been laid off or kept on short time.

Change in ownership and transfer of undertakings

Change in ownership occurs where there is a transfer of a whole or part of the business (*Melon v Hector Powe* (1980)).

The Transfer of Undertakings (Protection of Employment) Regulations 1981 (SI 1981/1794) apply to employees dismissed prior to the transfer (*Litster and Others v Forth Dry Dock and Engineering Co Ltd* (1989)). A transfer of an undertaking may occur even where there is no transfer of significant assets and none of the relevant employees are taken on by the new employer (*DCO Support Services v Unison* (2002)).

Offer of alternative employment

Taylor v Kent CC (1969) – an unsuitable offer may be refused.

Trial period

A trial period is four weeks.

Procedure for handling redundancies

The correct procedure for handling redundancies is to consult with representatives of a recognised independent trade union. Failure to consult may result in a protective award. Notification of redundancies should be given to the Secretary of State.

CHAPTER 17

EMPLOYERS' LIABILITY

17.1 INTRODUCTION

The tort of employers' liability arises out of the duty on an employer to take reasonable care for the safety of his or her employees whilst they are at work. (For a comprehensive study of employers' liability, see Munkman, J, *Employers' Liability*, 13th edn.) If, as a result of an accident at work, an employee is injured, he or she may be able to establish that the employer is in breach of the personal duty owed to him or her. However, should an action for employers' liability be unavailable, the injured employee may have the same rights as any other individual injured by another employee – namely, to pursue an action for vicarious liability (see below, 17.6).

It was not until the late 19th century that employees were able to proceed with such claims. The courts originally took the view that the doctrine of common employment precluded an action against the employer where the employee had been injured by the actions of a fellow employee (*Priestley v Fowler* (1837)); the rationale for this being that the employee had impliedly agreed to accept any risks incidental to his contract of employment. There was also concern expressed for the possible financial burden placed on employers having to pay compensation for industrial accidents if such actions were allowed to proceed. In addition, the defences of *volenti* and contributory negligence removed any chance of success in such claims, as *volenti* in particular was freely available to the employer. Gradually, the doctrine of common employment was removed and limitations placed on the use of *volenti* as a defence (*Smith v Baker and Sons* (1891)); as a result, the tort of employers' liability was allowed to develop.

Employers' liability is a negligence based tort, in that it is a specialised form of negligence arising out of a duty imposed by the employer/employee relationship. It is, therefore, necessary to refer to the basic elements of that tort. It gives the employee the right to sue the employer when injured at work for negligent acts by the employer arising out of the course of his or her employment. In order to ensure that the employer can pay any award of damages, the Employers' Liability (Compulsory Insurance) Act 1969 imposes a duty on the employer to take out the necessary insurance cover.

17.2 DUTY OF CARE

The employer's duty of care is owed to each individual employee and, as it is a personal duty, it cannot be delegated by the employer to anyone else. This was made quite clear in *Wilsons and Clyde Coal Co v English* (1938), where the day to day responsibility for a mine was delegated to a mine manager, as required by statute. However, the court concluded that the ultimate responsibility for health and safety remained with the employer (see, also, *McDermid v Nash Dredging and Reclamation Ltd* (1987) and *Morris v Breaveglen Ltd T/A Anzac Construction Co* (1993), which reaffirm this principle). The duty is only owed whilst the employee is acting within the course of his or her employment, that is, doing something reasonably incidental to the employee's main job.

In *Davidson v Handley-Page Ltd* (1945), the plaintiff was washing his teacup in the sink at his place of work when he slipped and hurt his leg whilst standing on a duckboard. The duckboard had become slippery because water was constantly splashed upon it. It was held that the employer was in breach of his duty, because the employee was carrying out a task which was reasonably incidental to his job; tea breaks were an accepted part of working life.

As a general rule, employees are not acting within the course of their employment whilst travelling to and from work. The exception to this was recognised in *Smith v Stages and Darlington Insulation Co Ltd* (1989), which offers some protection to peripatetic workers or any employee who may have to work away from his or her main base. Where employees are paid their normal wage for this travelling time, they will be within the course of their employment.

As the duty is of a personal nature, the standard of care will vary with the individual needs of each employee. It follows, therefore, that special regard must be had for the old, young, inexperienced and less able bodied. The general nature of the duty can be expressed as follows: the employer must take reasonable care in the way he conducts his operations so as not to subject his employees to unnecessary risks (*Smith v Baker and Son* (1891)).

17.2.1 Scope of the employer's duty

This was defined in *Wilsons and Clyde Coal Co v English* (1938). Following this case, the employer's duty has been determined as extending to the provision of:

- competent fellow employees;
- safe plant and appliances;
- safe place of work;
- safe system of work.

However, it has been recognised that there is an overlap between the duties owed at common law and the duties implied into the contract of employment, breach of which would allow the employee to pursue either cause of action. An example of this can be seen in *Johnstone v Bloomsbury HA* (1991), where it was concluded that requiring junior hospital doctors to work excessive hours may be a breach of the employer's implied duty, although the implied contractual duty, to take reasonable care for the safety of employees, would have to be read subject to the express terms in the contract of employment. The issue of working hours has been superseded to some extent by the Working Time Regulations 1998 (SI 1998/1833). It should be noted that junior doctors are expressly excluded from the Working Time Regulations 1998.

The remit of the employer's duty is open to expansion through the case law. It does not, however, extend to the provision of insurance cover against special risks – *Reid v Rush and Tomkins Group plc* (1989). In *McFarlane v EE Caledonia* (1994), a claim was made that an employer owed a duty to prevent psychiatric injury. The Court of Appeal concluded that, as the plaintiff was not directly involved in the accident and did not fall within the recognised categories of plaintiffs (now claimants) who can recover, as outlined in *Alcock v Chief Constable of South Yorkshire* (1991), the employer could not be liable.

It was originally held by the Court of Appeal in *Frost v Chief Constable of South Yorkshire* (1997) that an employer owed a duty of care to avoid exposing an employee to unnecessary risk of physical or psychiatric injury. However, on appeal (*White v Chief Constable of South Yorkshire* (1999)), the House of Lords reversed the Court of Appeal's decision. The House of Lords concluded that the police officers who attended the scene of the Hillsborough stadium disaster were secondary victims and, therefore, the criteria in *Alcock* must be met. However, the standard of care in discharging the duty will vary from case to case according to the nature of the job and the degree of fortitude to be expected of the employee. As a result, police officers who were at the ground in the course of duty, within the area of risk of physical and psychiatric injury, dealing with the dead and dying and who were thus exposed, by their employer's negligence, to the exceptionally horrific events which occurred, could recover damages.

However, the risks from passive smoking may well be within the remit of the employer's duty. As a result, a reasonable employer would be expected to produce and implement a no smoking policy (*Bland v Stockport CC* (1992)).

17.2.2 Competent fellow employees

The employer must ensure that all his or her staff are competent to do the job which they have been employed to do. The employer must, therefore, make sure that they have the necessary experience and qualifications, and, where necessary, must be prepared to train them accordingly. If an employee is injured as a result of the incompetence of a fellow employee, then the employer may be liable. The word 'incompetence' covers a range of ineptitudes; many of the cases arise out of practical jokes. In this situation, whether the employer is liable will depend on the depth of knowledge about the incompetent employee. If, for example, the employer has been put on warning or given notice that the employee is capable of committing an incompetent act, such as a practical joke, the employer will be liable.

In *O'Reilly v National Rail and Tramway Appliances Ltd* (1966), O'Reilly was employed with three others to break up scrap from railways. His colleagues persuaded him to hit, with his sledgehammer, a shell case embedded between the railway sleepers. When he did this, the shell exploded. It was held that the employer was not in breach of his duty because he had no previous knowledge that these workmen played practical jokes or were capable of encouraging such an act. He had not, therefore, failed to employ competent fellow employees.

The previous conduct of the incompetent employee is, therefore, extremely relevant. Where the employer has been given notice, he should take suitable action to ensure that such conduct does not result in something more serious; failure to take action will leave the employer open to a claim in the event of an accident arising out of the employee's incompetence. Depending on the nature of the previous conduct, dismissal of the incompetent employee may be justified.

In *Hudson v Ridge Manufacturing Co Ltd* (1957), Hudson was on his way to the sick room when a fellow employee tripped him up and broke his wrist. This employee was known as a practical joker and had been warned by his employer to stop fooling about. It was held that the employer was in breach of his duty because he was aware of his employee's tendency to fool around. He should have done more to curb this employee, even if this meant dismissal.

Interestingly, the employer will have primary liability in these circumstances for a deliberate and blatant act as well as the negligent act. However, an isolated incident will not incur liability, as can be seen in *Smith v Crossley Bros Ltd* (1951). A claim based on vicarious liability may be open to an injured employee where the employee is unable to show that the employer had breached this particular duty, for example, through lack of prior knowledge (see *Harrison v Michelin Tyre Co Ltd* (1985), below). However, the decision in *Waters v Commissioner of Police for the Metropolis* (2000) takes the issue one step further by placing a common law duty of care on the employer to protect his employees against victimisation and harassment by fellow employees, which may give rise to physical or psychiatric injury.

17.2.3 Safe plant and appliances

The employer must not only provide his employees with the necessary plant and equipment to do the job safely; he or she must also ensure that such plant and equipment is safe, that is, properly maintained. For example, guards must be provided on dangerous machinery to protect the employee from injury and these guards must be inspected regularly to ensure that they are securely in position and are not damaged in any way.

In *Bradford v Robinson Rentals Ltd* (1967), Bradford was employed as a driver. He was required to drive over 400 miles in extremely cold weather, in a van with a broken window and a heater that did not work. He suffered severe frostbite. It was held that the van was not safe and, therefore, the employer had failed in his duty to provide safe plant and equipment. Although the conditions were extreme, it was foreseeable that the employee would suffer some injury, if sent out on a long journey in a van in that condition. A further illustration of this duty can be seen in *Taylor v Rover Car Co Ltd* (1966). Taylor was using a hammer and chisel when a piece of metal flew off the chisel and blinded him in one eye. This batch of chisels was in a defective state when supplied by the manufacturers. It was held that Taylor's employer was liable because a similar incident had occurred four weeks previously (without anyone being injured). This meant that the employer should have known of the likelihood of such an accident occurring. To avoid this, the chisels should have been taken out of use and returned to the manufacturer.

If the previous incident in the *Taylor* case had not occurred, Taylor's only remedy at that time would have been against the manufacturer. However, the Employers' Liability (Defective Equipment) Act 1969 provides that, where an employee is injured at work as a consequence of defective equipment supplied by his employer and the defect is the fault of a third party, for example, the manufacturer, the employer will be deemed to be negligent and, therefore, responsible for the injury. This statute removes the need to establish foresight on the part of the employer in cases like *Taylor*.

In the earlier case of *Davie v New Merton Board Mills Ltd* (1959), the issue of whether an employer could be liable for a manufacturer's negligence where an employee was injured by a fragmented tool was considered. The conclusion was that the employer could not be responsible for a manufacturer's negligence. Obviously, the Employers' Liability (Defective Equipment) Act 1969 reverses this decision. This Act is potentially wide in scope: 'equipment' has been held to include a defective ship (*Coltman v Bibby Tankers Ltd* (1988)) and a flagstone (*Knowles v Liverpool CC* (1993)).

17.2.4 Safe place of work

The employer must ensure that his employees are not exposed to any dangers arising out of the place where the employee is expected to work. This covers any place under the control of the employer, including access and egress, and may extend to the premises of a third party, although, in the latter case, the employer may not reasonably be expected to go to the same lengths as he or she would on his own premises. However, as can be seen in *Wilson v Tyneside Window Cleaning Co* (1958), at the very least it may be necessary to warn the employee of the dangers when visiting/working on the premises of a third party.

In *Smith v Vange Scaffolding and Engineering Co Ltd* (1970), Vange employed Smith on a building site. There were other contractors on site. As Smith returned to the changing hut at the end of the working day, he tripped over the cable of a welding machine, which had been left there by a contractor. Vange were aware of the obstructions on site which made access to and from the place of work difficult and dangerous, but they had not complained to the other contractors. It was held that the employer had failed in his duty to his employee because, being aware of the situation, he should have made the necessary complaints to the main contractor. It was foreseeable that such an accident might occur and reasonable precautions should have been taken.

The remit of this duty extends to consideration of the nature of the place and the potential risks involved, the work to be carried out, the experience of the employee and the degree of control or supervision which the employer can reasonably exercise. There may be situations where providing a safe place of work overlaps with the employer's duty to provide a safe system of work. Finally, the duty may apply where the employer sends employees overseas to work. However, whether there has been a breach of duty will depend on whether the employer acted reasonably in the circumstances of that particular case.

In *Square D Ltd v Cook* (1992), an employee was sent to Saudi Arabia on a two month contract. His employer was satisfied that the site occupiers and the contractors were reliable companies and had a good health and safety record. In these circumstances, it was held that the employer could not be held to be responsible for the day to day running of the site, nor undertake safety inspections. However, the situation may be different where a number of employees were required to work there for long periods.

Providing a safe place of work extends to protecting staff from the risks of passive smoking. In *Waltons and Morse v Dorrington* (1997), it was stated that there is 'an implied term that the employer will provide and monitor for employees, so far as is reasonably practicable, a working environment which is reasonably suitable for the performance by them of their contractual duties. This extends to the right of an employee not to be required to sit in a smoke filled atmosphere'.

17.2.5 Safe system of work

The duty on the employer to provide a safe system of work extends to a consideration of the following by the employer: the physical layout of the job; safety notices; special procedures; protective clothing; training; and supervision.

In order to fulfil this duty, the employer must take into account all foreseeable eventualities, including the actions of any employees. Any system, to be safe, must reduce the risks to the employee to a minimum; it is accepted that not all risks can be eliminated. Furthermore, the employer must do more than introduce a safe system of work; he or she must ensure that it is observed by the employees. The case law highlights the breadth of this duty.

For example, it can extend to preventing staff being exposed to risk of violence if this is a foreseeable risk, as in *Charlton v Forrest Printing Ink Co Ltd* (1980). This aspect of the duty will also cover claims for compensation for work-related upper limb disorder, as in *Bettany v Royal Doulton (UK) Ltd* (1993). This was questioned as a result of the decision of the House of Lords in *Pickford v Imperial Chemical Industries plc* (1998). The House of Lords concluded that, in order to recover for work-related upper limb disorder, it must be organic in origin. In this particular case, whilst the plaintiff suffered from cramp of the hand, the question of whether it was due to repetitive movement and organic in origin was unresolved, due to inconclusive evidence. Furthermore, in *Alexander v Midland Bank plc* (1999), the Court of Appeal concluded that, where upper limb disorder is physical rather than psychogenic in origin and can be linked to an unsafe system of work, a personal injury claim will succeed.

Stress at work also falls within the remit of the employer's liability. In *Walker v Northumberland CC* (1994), Walker was employed as an area social services officer with responsibility for four teams of field workers. As the volume of work increased, Walker wrote reports and memoranda regarding the increased workload and the need for urgency in redistributing staff to assist. Nothing was done about this and, one year later, Walker suffered a nervous breakdown. Before returning to work, Walker's superior agreed to provide him with assistance. However, one month after he returned to work, assistance was withdrawn and, in September 1987, he suffered a second nervous breakdown. In 1988, he was dismissed on grounds of permanent ill health. It was held that the defendants were in breach of the duty of care owed to the plaintiff in respect of the second nervous breakdown which he suffered as a result of stress and anxiety occasioned by his job.

In *Lancaster v Birmingham CC* (1999), the county court awarded damages of £67,000 for mental injury as a result of work-related stress. Whilst this case did not break legal ground, it was the first time an employer had admitted liability. The employee in this case was able to establish each element of the negligence claim against her employer and show that she had a recognised illness, which was caused by work-related stress. As she had also persistently asked for training and administrative support, which had not been forthcoming, she was able to show that her injury was foreseeable. The case of *Sutherland v Hatton* (2002) introduces new guidelines for determining an employer's liability for psychiatric illness caused by stress at work. The key factors are whether such harm is reasonably foreseeable and 'whether the employer failed to take the steps which are reasonable in the circumstances bearing in mind the magnitude of the risk of harm occurring, the gravity of the harm which may occur, the costs and practicability of preventing it and the justification for running the risk'.

It was also stated that unless an employer knew of some particular problem or vulnerability, he is entitled to assume that the employee can withstand the normal pressures of the job.

The contentious issue surrounds instruction and supervision. Is it sufficient to order an employee to take safety precautions, or should they be supervised as well if the duty is to be satisfied? The answer depends on the degree of risk and the experience of the employee concerned, including how far the employee has been warned of the risks. It is, however, quite clear from the decision in *Pape v Cumbria CC* (1991) that merely providing protective clothing without warning of the risks may not be sufficient to discharge the duty.

In *Woods v Durable Suites Ltd* (1953), Woods worked in the veneer department at Durable Suites. He was an extremely experienced employee. As there was a risk of dermatitis from the synthetic glues, his employer posted up a notice, specifying the precautions to be taken. Woods had also been instructed personally by the manager in the protective measures but had not observed them fully. As a result, he contracted dermatitis. It was held that the employer was not liable for failing to provide a safe system of work because he had taken all reasonable care in posting up notices and providing barrier cream, etc. He was under no obligation, given the age and experience of Woods, to provide someone to watch over him to make sure he followed the precautions.

Constant supervision is, on the whole, not necessary where the employees have the necessary experience and have been trained or instructed accordingly. However, the degree of supervision is commensurate to the severity of the risk.

In *Bux v Slough Metals Ltd* (1974), Bux's job involved the removal of molten metal from a furnace and the pouring of this metal into a die-casting machine. Goggles were supplied and Bux was made aware of the risks. He refused to wear the safety goggles because they misted up and he complained to the supervisor, who informed him that no other goggles were available. He was injured when molten metal splashed into his eye. It was held that the employer was liable because, where the work was of a particularly hazardous nature, he must do more than merely provide safety equipment. He should constantly urge his employees to use or wear it.

Finally, in *King v Smith* (1995), King, a window cleaner employed by Smith, was seriously injured when he fell 35 ft from the exterior window sill on which he was standing to clean a window. The employers' rulebook contained an instruction that if a window could only be cleaned by standing on the sill, the employee must secure his safety belt to a structure, which would support his weight in the event of a fall. Unfortunately, in this particular case there were no anchorages for the safety belt. King claimed that his employer had failed to provide a safe system of work. The Court of Appeal concluded that there had been a breach of this duty, as, given the inherent danger involved, the employer should have prohibited the act rather than issue an instruction.

In considering this duty, the courts will need to determine whether the system is safe and whether it has been properly implemented. The employer needs to do both in order to avoid liability.

17.3 BREACH OF DUTY

Once duty is established, the remaining essentials are judged on the same basis as any action in negligence. The burden is on the employee to show that the employer is in breach of his or her duty. The employee must prove fault on the part of the employer, that is, has the employer failed to act as a reasonable employer? Alternatively, can *res ipsa loquitur* be established? If the employer has taken all reasonable precautions, considering all the circumstances of the case, then he or she will not be liable (see *Latimer v AEC Ltd* (1953)).

The standard of care will vary with respect to the individual needs of each employee. The employer must have special regard for the old, young, inexperienced and employees with special disabilities; that is, the standard of care will be increased.

In *Paris v Stepney DC* (1951), Paris worked for the council in one of their garages. One of his jobs, which he did frequently, was to chip out rust from under buses and other vehicles owned by the council. At that time, it was not customary to provide safety goggles for such work. Paris was already blind in one eye. One day, as he was chipping out rust, a fragment of rust entered his good eye and he was rendered totally blind. It was held that the employer had failed to exercise the necessary standard of care. It was foreseeable that there was an increased risk of greater injury to this particular employee because of the nature of his existing disability. He should, therefore, have been provided with safety goggles, which at the very least would have reduced the risk.

This case illustrates the basic rule that 'you must take your victim as you find him'. In applying this rule, whether there has been a breach will be a question of fact in each case, as illustrated in *James v Hepworth and Grandage Ltd* (1968), in which the employer erected large notices in their foundry, informing their employees that they should wear spats – a form of leg protection. Unbeknown to the employer, the plaintiff could not read; he was injured when molten metal hit his leg and ran into his shoe. He failed in his claim for damages, as it was held that he had observed the other workmen wearing spats and his failure to make enquiries indicated that, even if he had been informed about the notice, he would not have worn them.

The standard of care is increased in potentially high risk occupations where an employee may be illiterate or may not comprehend English. This can be seen in *Hawkins v Ian Ross (Castings) Ltd* (1970). The employer employed a large number of Asians as labourers. Hawkins was carrying a ladle of molten metal with the assistance of one such labourer. When he shouted to him to stop, the labourer did not understand and carried on walking. Hawkins overbalanced and was injured by the molten metal spilling over his leg. It was held that the employer had failed in his duty because, where he chooses to employ labourers or, indeed, any staff who may not have a good understanding of the English language, the standard of care is increased. Furthermore, this increase is not confined to the particular employee; it is extended to his or her workmates, as there is a foreseeable increase in the risk to them of having to work with people who do not understand instructions.

17.4 CAUSATION AND RESULTANT DAMAGE

Having established duty and breach, the employee must show that injury has been suffered as a result of the employer's breach of duty. Injury is not confined to physical injury; it includes damage to personal property, loss of earnings, etc. The test for establishing liability is the one used in negligence, that is, the 'but for' test. The question which has to be answered by the court is, therefore, but for the employer's breach of duty, would the employee have been injured? If the answer is no, causation is established.

In *McWilliams v Arrol Ltd* (1962), a steel erector employed by Arrol fell from the scaffolding that he was working on and was killed. The employer had provided safety harnesses in the past, but, since they had not been worn, they had been removed to another site. It was held that, although the employer was in breach of his duty, he was not liable because it could not be proved that McWilliams would have worn the harness, even if it had been available. The 'but for' test was not satisfied.

In *Fairchild v Glenhaven Funeral Services* (2002), the Court of Appeal held that victims of mesotheloima, a type of lung cancer, could not recover damages from their former employers where they did not remain in the same employment throughout the period of exposure, as they could not establish which employer caused the cancer. It was felt that it would be 'unjust to impose liability on one employer', as this causative element was not present. The House of Lords has recently overturned the decision of the Court of Appeal (2002). It would appear that in these circumstances, any employer who 'materially increases the risk to his employees' may be liable for the harm caused.

Even after causation has been established, the employer is not necessarily liable for all the damage to his or her employee. The employer will only be liable for foreseeable damage. This does not mean that the precise nature or extent of the injury has to be foreseen, only that some harm will result from the breach of duty. However, there is legal limit to the extent of liability imposed by *The Wagon Mound (No 1)* (1961) (see above, Chapter 10). Applying this rule, the employer will only be liable for the foreseeable consequences of his breach, that is, he will not be liable for the unexpected. In *Doughty v Turner Manufacturing* (1964), a lid made of asbestos and cement, covering a bath of sulphuric acid, was knocked accidentally into the acid. A chemical reaction took place between the cover and the acid. In the eruption which followed, Doughty was severely burned. It was held that the employer was not liable because the only harm which could be foreseen from the incident was splashing. A chemical reaction of this type resulting in an eruption was at the time unknown and, therefore, unforeseeable. This is regarded as a rather harsh decision, since it demands a degree of foresight as to the way in which the injury occurred. The decision is doubtful in the light of such cases as *Hughes v Lord Advocate* (1963) and *Smith v Leech Brain and Co* (1962). In the latter, Smith's lip was splashed with molten metal. At the time, unknown to anyone, his lip contained cancerous tissue, which became malignant as a result of the burn. He subsequently died of cancer. It was held that the employer was liable for his death from cancer because the risk of being splashed with molten metal was foreseeable. Smith's death was, therefore, merely an extension of the foreseeable injury, which was a burn. This latter case is a much more sympathetic interpretation of the rule in *The Wagon Mound (No 1)*.

17.5 REMEDIES AND DEFENCES

The principal remedy available for employers' liability is compensation for personal injury; the object being to put the claimant in the position he or she would have been in if the accident had never occurred. The limitation period for bringing such an action is three years from the date on which the cause of action arose or the date of knowledge, whichever is the later (Limitation Act 1980).

There are no defences unique to this particular tort. In general, the main ones pleaded are contributory negligence and *volenti*: the former may result in a reduction in the amount of damages payable; the latter is rarely accepted by the courts in actions founded in employers' liability.

17.6 VICARIOUS LIABILITY

As a general rule vicarious liability only arises out of the employer/employee relationship, although it can be found in the principal/agent relationship and as an exceptional case in the employer/independent contractor relationship. It is dependent upon this type of special relationship being established.

17.6.1 Meaning of vicarious liability

Vicarious liability is not a tort; it is a concept used to impose strict liability on a person who does not have primary liability, that is, not at fault (see Kidner, R, 'Vicarious liability: for whom should the employers be liable?' (1995) 15 LS 47). Literally, it means that one person is liable for the torts of another. The employer is, therefore, liable for the torts of his employee. This liability only arises while the employee is acting within the course of his or her employment. The concept has found favour with courts and claimants alike, because, realistically, the employer is likely to have the money to pay for any claim for damages, whereas the main tortfeasor, the employee, will not. This does not mean that the employee will escape liability. The employer can insist that he or she is joined in any action or, if the employer is found to be vicariously liable, may insist on an indemnity from his or her employee. The effect of this is that the employee will have to pay towards the damages imposed on the employer (see the Civil Liability (Contribution) Act 1978, which provides for this).

It must not be forgotten that this tort depends on the primary liability of the employee being established; that is, the employee must have committed a tort. Once this is done, the claimant has the option to sue the employer, the employee or both.

17.6.2 Employer/employee relationship

The claimant must establish that there is in existence an employer/employee relationship (or, in less common situations, a principal/agent relationship), that is, a contract of service as opposed to a contract for services. In the majority of cases, this may not be an issue, but just because the word 'employee' is used in the contract, it does not automatically follow that it is a contract of service (or employment). There are tests for establishing this relationship, which were considered in depth in Chapter 14, above.

17.6.3 Scope of vicarious liability

Once it is established that there is in existence a contract of service and that the employee has committed a tort, that is, that he or she has primary liability, the question of whether the employer should be vicariously liable can be considered. This stage is important because the employer will only be liable if the employee is 'acting within the course of his employment' when the tort is committed. It is, therefore, essential to consider what is meant legally by this term. If the employee is outside the scope of his or her employment, the injured person has no choice but to sue the employee, who may not be in a financial position to pay compensation.

17.6.4 Course of employment

The interpretation given by the courts is wide – in the past, they have favoured making the employer liable, if it is at all possible to do so. The onus is on the claimant to show that the employee is a servant and that the tortious act was committed whilst he or she was going about his or her employer's business. Once this is established, the onus moves to the employer, who must show that the tortious act was one for which he or she was not responsible. As a general rule, to be within the course of employment, one of the following must be established:

- the act must be incidental to the job that the employee was employed to do;
- the act should have been authorised by the employer, either expressly or impliedly;
- the authorised act has been carried out in a wrongful, negligent or unauthorised manner.

These can best be illustrated through the case law, which shows how far the courts are prepared to go in holding an employer vicariously liable. The following cases relate to situations where the employee was found to be 'within the course of his employment'.

In *Century Insurance Co Ltd v Northern Ireland Road Transport Board* (1942), Davison was employed as a tanker driver for the NIRTB. He was delivering petrol at a garage. Whilst the underground storage tank was being filled with petrol, Davison lit a cigarette and threw away the lighted match. The petrol vapour ignited, resulting in an explosion. The employer's insurance company claimed that the driver's actions regarding the cigarette were outside the course of his employment as being wholly unauthorised, thereby avoiding liability on the part of the employer and payment of compensation by the insurance company. It was held that the employer was vicariously liable for the negligent act of the employee. The lighting of the cigarette was an act of convenience on the part of the employee and, although it was not necessarily for the employer's benefit, it did not prevent him from being made liable. It was the time and place at which the employee struck the match that was negligent. The employee was seen to be carrying out the job he was employed to do in a negligent manner.

From this case it can been seen that such acts as taking a tea break, having a cigarette, going to the washroom, etc, are all acts which are incidental to the main job, although it is still necessary to consider all the facts of the case at the time of the tortious act; of course, the question as to whether, in the present climate of no smoking policies, the smoking of a cigarette would be seen as incidental to one's employment is debatable. The next case is regarded as the leading authority with respect to actions which are specifically prohibited by the employer.

In *Rose v Plenty* (1976), Plenty was employed as a milkman by the Co-Operative Dairy. A notice had been posted up in the depot which prohibited all milkmen from using young children to deliver milk and from giving lifts to them on the milk float. Plenty ignored this notice and engaged the assistance of Rose, a 13 year old boy. Rose was injured whilst riding on the milk float through the negligent driving of Plenty. It was held that, applying the decision in *Limpus v London General Omnibus Co* (1862), since the prohibited act was being done for the purpose of the employer's business and not for the employee's own benefit or purpose, Plenty was within the course of his employment and, therefore, the employer was vicariously liable.

Obviously, where the employee carries out a prohibited act, all the circumstances will have to be considered to see if the employee remains within the course of his or her employment. However, the key to establishing vicarious liability in such cases is to ask the question: 'Who is the intended beneficiary of the prohibited action?' In *Rose v Plenty*, Lord Denning applied his own earlier judgment in *Young v Edward Box and Co Ltd* (1951), in which he said:

> In every case where it is sought to make the master liable for the conduct of his servant, the first question is to see whether the servant was liable. If the answer is yes, the second question is to see whether the employer must shoulder the servant's liability.

This approach gives little weight to the issue of the 'course of employment' by adopting the view that, generally, it is the employer who will have the money to pay the compensation because of insurance cover and, therefore, if it is at all possible to do so, the employer should be made responsible for an employee's tortious acts. It should not be forgotten that the concept of vicarious liability may also enable an employee who has been injured by a fellow employee to recover compensation, even though a claim for employers' liability would fail. In *Harrison v Michelin Tyre Co Ltd* (1985), Harrison was injured when a fellow employee, Smith, deliberately tipped up the duckboard on which he was standing to work at his machine. The employer contended that Smith, who caused the injury, was on a 'frolic of his own' when he caused the injury. However, the court held that, although it was an unauthorised act, Smith was going about his job when he committed the act, which was so closely connected with his employment that he remained within the course of his employment, thereby resulting in the employer being vicariously liable. Some doubt about the decision in *Harrison* was expressed in *Aldred v Nacanco* (1987).

Vicarious liability extends to acts which may be crimes as well as torts, for example, assault and fraud. Where the employee uses force or violence, the courts will look closely at the circumstances surrounding its use and question whether it was necessary or excessive. Early case law illustrates that the use of force may result in the employer being vicariously liable. In *Poland v Parr and Sons* (1927), an employee saw some boys who he believed to be stealing from his employer's wagon. He struck one of them, who fell and was run over. The employer was held to be vicariously liable, as the servant was legitimately protecting his employer's property. However, as the social climate has changed, so has the attitude of the courts. This is illustrated in *Keppel Bus Co Ltd v Sa'ad bin Ahmad* (1974), in which the employer was found not to be vicariously liable for an assault carried out by a bus conductor on a passenger. Whether the employee has an implied authority to use force in a given situation, such as protecting his employer's property, and why and how that force is used are key issues.

The following cases consider the position where the employee is put in a position of trust and abuses that position so that a crime or tort is committed.

In *Morris v Martin and Sons Ltd* (1966), Morris's mink stole was sent by her furrier to Martins to be cleaned. Whilst there, an employee of Martin, who had been entrusted with the cleaning of the fur, stole it (committing the tort of conversion). It was held that the employer was liable for the act of conversion of their employee. Martins were bailees for reward of the fur and were, therefore, under a duty to take reasonable care of it. It was then entrusted to an employee to do an act which was within the course of his employment, that is, clean it. What the employee did in stealing the fur was merely an abuse of his job.

A critical element in this case was the fact that Martins had become bailees of the fur and would, therefore, probably have been liable for anything happening to it. There is a further limitation on the application of the rule in *Morris v Martin and Sons*; it can only serve to make the employer vicariously liable where the goods come into the employee's possession as part of his or her job. If, for example, an employee who was not involved in the cleaning of the fur had stolen it, the employer would not have been vicariously liable. The courts have reinforced the limit on the application of the decision in the *Morris* case by requiring a nexus between the criminal act and the circumstances of the employment. In *Heasmans v Clarity Cleaning Co Ltd* (1987), an employee of a firm contracted to clean offices, whose job involved the cleaning of telephones, dishonestly made use of the telephones to make private calls. It was held that the telephone calls were outside the purpose for which the man was employed.

For an employer to be liable for the criminal acts of his employees, there must be some nexus between the criminal act of the employee and the circumstances of his or her employment. In this case, the requirement to dust the telephones merely provided the employee with an opportunity to commit the crime – access to the premises was an insufficient nexus. How far the question of nexus is becoming an issue in all cases of vicarious liability can be seen in *Irving v Post Office* (1987) and *Aldred v Nacanco* (1987). Where an employee is involved in a fraud, the fact that the employer has placed the employee in a position to perpetrate the fraud may result in the employer being vicariously liable.

In *Lloyd v Grace, Smith and Co* (1912), Lloyd went to the defendant solicitors to discuss some properties that she had for investment purposes. She saw their managing clerk, who persuaded her to sell the properties and to sign some documents, which, unbeknown to her, transferred the properties to him. He then disposed of them for his own benefit. It was held that the solicitors were liable for the fraudulent act of their employee, even though they did not benefit from the fraud. They had placed him in a position of responsibility, which enabled him to carry out the fraud. Also, as far as the general public was concerned, he was in a position of trust and appeared to have the authority for his actions.

The facts of the *Lloyd* case are rather special and the decision is based on the special relationship between solicitor and client, which is one of trust. The court did not regard 'benefit to the employer' as an issue. In reality, there can be no set formula for deciding whether an employer should be vicariously liable. The fact that in many of the cases it appears that justice was seen to be done probably justifies Lord Denning's stance in *Young v Edward Box and Co Ltd* (1951).

It is pertinent to mention the case of *Lister v Hesley Hall Ltd* (2001), as it challenges the common law test for establishing vicarious liability. The case involved gross acts of sexual abuse by the warden of a boarding school against boarders aged between 12 and 15 years. The school was owned and managed by the respondents. The House of Lords held:

> In determining whether an employee's wrongful act has been committed in the course of his employment so as to make the employers vicariously liable, the correct approach is to concentrate on the relative closeness of the connection between the nature of the employment and the employee's wrongdoing. The question is whether the employee's tort was so closely connected with his employment that it would be fair and just to hold the employers vicariously liable. The conventional test formulated by *Salmond*, which deems as within the course of employment a wrongful and unauthorised mode of doing some act authorised by the employer, does not cope ideally with vicarious liability

for intentional wrongdoing. *Salmond* also observed, however, that an employer is liable even for acts which he has not authorised provided they are so connected with acts which he has authorised that they may rightly be regarded as modes, albeit improper modes, of doing them.

In the present case, the employee's position as warden and the close contact with the boys which that work involved created a sufficiently close connection between the acts of abuse which he committed and the work which he had been employed to do, so that it would be fair and just to hold the employers vicariously liable to the claimants for the injury and damage which they suffered at his hands. The sexual abuse was inextricably interwoven with the carrying out by the warden of his duties. The sexual assaults were committed in the employers' time and on their premises while the warden was also busy caring for the children. The fact that the warden performed his duties in a way which was an abuse of his position and an abnegation of his duty did not sever the connection with his employment.

The House of Lords went on to overrule the decision of the Court of Appeal in *Trotman v North Yorkshire CC* (1999). In effect, a purposive approach has been adopted in line with the interpretation of the statutory form of vicarious liability to be found in the SDA 1975, the RRA 1976 and the DDA 1995. Employers must realise that there will be situations where providing an opportunity to the employee to commit tortious acts will result in the employer being vicariously liable. In *Fennelly v Connex South Eastern Ltd* (2001), the Court of Appeal held that in determining 'course of employment' the job should be looked at in general terms, not by taking each task separately and then asking whether each step was authorised by the employer. See also *Balfron Trustees Ltd v Peterson* (2001).

17.6.5 Outside the course of employment

In considering those cases in which the employee has been held to be outside the course of employment, a significant issue has been the employee's deviation from the job that he or she was employed to do. Once again, there are no set criteria for judging this issue; it remains a question of fact in each case, based on the nature of the job and the actions of the employee. The standard is laid down in *Hilton v Thomas Burton (Rhodes) Ltd* (1961). Four workmen were allowed to use their employer's van, as they were working on a demolition site in the country. At lunchtime, they decided to go to a café some seven miles away. Before reaching the cafe, they changed their minds and set off to return to the site. On the return journey, one of them was killed through the negligent driving of the van driver. It was held that the employer was not vicariously liable. By travelling such a distance to take a break, they were no longer doing something incidental to their main employment; nor were they doing anything for the purpose of their employer's business. As far as the court was concerned, they were 'on a frolic of their own'.

Following this case, it is pertinent to ask how far the employee has deviated from his course of employment. This is a question of degree, which depends on the facts of each case. There are cases dealing with prohibited acts where it has been decided that the employee is outside the course of his or her employment. It should be noted that many of these decisions were made before *Rose v Plenty* (1976), which is seen as the watershed for such cases. It could, therefore, be argued that the decision in *Twine v Bean's Express Ltd* (1946), in which the employer was not liable for the injuries to a hitch-hiker who had been given a lift, contrary to the express instructions of the employer, would be different today, as the reasoning that no duty was owed because he was a trespasser is doubtful in the light of the decision in *Rose*. However, the problem of tortious acts which are also crimes has not been totally resolved, although it is possible to distinguish the case law on their facts.

In *Warren v Henly's Ltd* (1948), a petrol pump attendant employed by Henly's used verbal abuse when wrongly accusing Warren, a customer, of trying to drive away without paying for petrol. Warren called the police and told the attendant that he would be reported to his employer. This so enraged the attendant that he physically assaulted Warren. It was held that the employer was not liable. The act of violence was not connected in any way to the discharge of the pump attendant's duties. When he assaulted Warren, he was not doing what he was employed to do, but was acting in an unauthorised manner. The act was done in relation to a personal matter affecting his personal interests, not in respect of the protection of his employer's property, as was the case in *Poland v Parr* (1927).

Finally, both the Sex Discrimination Act (SDA) 1975 and the Race Relations Act (RRA) 1976 recognise a statutory form of vicarious liability which results in the employer being liable for acts of discrimination carried out by his or her employees. Whether the employer is so liable will depend on whether the employee is acting within the course of his or her employment when he or she commits the act. In *Irving v Post Office* (1987), a postman, whilst sorting mail, took the opportunity to write racist remarks on post addressed to his neighbour. It was held that the employer would not be liable for such actions, since the employee had gone beyond what he was employed to do, as the only authorised act in these circumstances would have been an amendment to the address.

The test was considered in *Tower Boot Co Ltd v Jones* (1997), where the complainant was subjected to deliberate branding with a screwdriver and whipping, as well as racial taunts by fellow employees. It was held by the Court of Appeal that the EAT had erred in applying the common law test in interpreting the statutory provision contained in s 32 of the RRA 1976. The words 'in the course of employment' for the purposes of s 32 of the RRA 1976 and s 41 of the SDA 1975 should be interpreted in the sense in which they are employed in everyday speech, and not restrictively by reference to the principles laid down by case law for establishing an employer's vicarious liability for the torts committed by an employee. If the common law approach were to be taken, this would result in an employer being able to avoid liability for particularly heinous acts of discrimination.

Both statutes recognise that an employer may escape being vicariously liable if it can be shown that all reasonably practicable steps were taken to prevent or stop the act of discrimination.

17.7 PRINCIPAL AND AGENT

The rules relating to the vicarious liability of a principal for the tortious acts of his or her agent operate in the same was as those for the employer/employee relationship. However, the key to the principal's liability will be based on whether the agent has exceeded the authority. As was seen in Chapter 11, above, an agent's authority can be extremely wide, in that it can be express, implied, ostensible or usual. There is, therefore, more scope for making the principal vicariously liable, even though, in *Lloyd v Grace, Smith and Co Ltd* (1912), the employee had only intended to benefit himself.

17.8 EMPLOYER AND INDEPENDENT CONTRACTOR

As a general rule, the employer is not liable for the torts of any independent contractor whom he or she chooses to employ. However, he or she may be made a joint tortfeasor with the independent contractor where he or she has:

- ratified or authorised the tortious act;
- contributed to the commission of the tort by the independent contractor, either by the way in which the work was directed or by interfering with the work;
- been negligent in the selection of his independent contractor. In *Balfour v Barty-King* (1957), Barty-King's water pipes were frozen. She asked two men at a nearby building site to help to defrost them. They did this by using a blowlamp, rather than a heated brick, on the lagged pipes in her loft. The lagging caught fire and the fire spread to the adjoining premises. It was held that Barty-King was jointly liable for the negligence of the contractor. She had chosen them, invited them onto her premises and then left them to do the job. She should have exercised more care, not only in her selection, but also in overseeing their work;
- a non-delegable duty, for example, under the Factory Act 1961 and related statutes (see *Wilsons and Clyde Coal v English* (1938));
- asked the independent contractor to carry out work which is particularly hazardous or is situated on the highway. In *Salsbury v Woodland* (1970), the

independent contractor was contracted to fell a tree in his client's garden, which was close to the highway. He was an experienced tree feller but was negligent in felling the tree. Telephone lines were brought down and the plaintiff, whilst attempting to move the wires from the highway, was struck by a car. It was held that the person employing the independent contractor was not liable. The work was not being carried out on the highway, and *near to* the highway is not the same thing as *on* the highway. Furthermore, this work would only be regarded as extra-hazardous if it had been carried out on the highway. The independent contractor had to bear sole responsibility.

The criteria for judging whether work is particularly hazardous involves looking at where the work is to be carried out, whether members of the public are at risk and what the dangers are (see *Honeywell and Stein Ltd v Larkin Bros Ltd* (1934)).

SUMMARY OF CHAPTER 17

EMPLOYERS' LIABILITY

Introduction

An employer is under a duty to take reasonable care in respect of the health and safety of his or her employees. This duty is personal, in that it is owed to each individual employee and cannot be delegated. The scope and nature of the duty was originally defined in *Wilsons and Clyde Coal Co v English* (1938). The duty is owed whilst the employee is acting within the course of his or her employment.

The course of employment extends to the carrying out of tasks reasonably incidental to one's job:

- *Davidson v Handley-Page Ltd* (1945);
- *Smith v Stages and Darlington Insulation Co Ltd* (1989).

The scope of the duty is fourfold:

- To provide competent fellow employees:
  - *O'Reilly v National Rail and Tramway Appliances Ltd* (1966);
  - *Hudson v Ridge Manufacturing Co Ltd* (1957).
- To provide safe plant and appliances:
  - *Bradford v Robinson Rentals* (1967);
  - Employers' Liability (Defective Equipment) Act 1969 – *Taylor v Rover Car Co Ltd* (1966); *Coltman v Bibby Tankers Ltd* (1988); *Knowles v Liverpool CC* (1993).
- To provide a safe place of work:
  - *Smith v Vange Scaffolding and Engineering Co Ltd* (1970).
- To provide a safe system of work:
  - *Charlton v Forrest Printing Co Ltd* (1980);
  - *Bettany v Royal Doulton (UK) Ltd* (1993);
  - *Pickford v Imperial Chemical Industries plc* (1998);
  - *Walker v Northumberland CC* (1994);
  - *Sutherland v Hatton* (2002).

Breach of duty

The claimant must establish a breach of duty on the part of the employer. The standard of care is that of the reasonable employer. The courts will generally consider the same factors as discussed in Chapter 10, above, in relation to negligence:

- *Fairchild v Glenhaven Funeral Services* (2002);
- *Latimer v AEC Ltd* (1953);
- *Paris v Stepney DC* (1951);
- *Hawkins v Ian Ross (Castings) Ltd* (1970);
- *James v Hepworth and Grandage Ltd* (1968).

Causation

The next stage is for the claimant to establish causation. The claimant must show that, 'but for' the defendant's breach of duty, the injury would not have occurred and that harm was foreseeable:

- *McWilliams v Arrol Ltd* (1962);
- *Doughty v Turner Manufacturing* (1964);
- *Smith v Leech Brain and Co* (1962).

Vicarious liability

An employer is, in general, liable for torts committed by his or her employees whilst they are acting within the course of their employment. For an employer to be liable:

- There must be in existence an employer/employee relationship (see Chapter 14).
- The employee must be acting within the course of his or her employment ie, must be doing something incidental to his or her job or carrying out an authorised act in a wrongful, negligent or unauthorised manner.
- 'Within the course of employment':
  - *Century Insurance Co Ltd v Northern Ireland Road Transport Board* (1942);
  - *Rose v Plenty* (1976);
  - *Harrison v Michelin Tyre Co Ltd* (1985);
  - *Poland v Parr and Sons* (1927);
  - *Morris v Martin and Sons Ltd* (1966);
  - *Lister v Hesley Hall Ltd* (2001).

- 'Outside the course of employment':
  - *Hilton v Thomas Burton (Rhodes) Ltd* (1961);
  - *Warren v Henly's Ltd* (1948);
  - *Aldred v Nacanco* (1987);
  - *Heasmans v Clarity Cleaning Co Ltd* (1987);
  - *Irving v Post Office* (1987).

The concept of vicarious liability arises where there is in existence a 'special relationship'. It can, therefore, also arise between principal and agent and, in limited circumstances, between employer and independent contractor:

- *Balfour v Barty-King* (1957);
- *Salsbury v Woodland* (1970);
- *Honeywell and Stein Ltd v Larkin Bros Ltd* (1934).

CHAPTER 18

CONSUMER CREDIT

18.1 INTRODUCTION

In our 'live now, pay later' society, credit is a fact of everyday life for most people. Credit is obtained by a wide range of methods, for example, loans, credit cards and mail order catalogues; and for many years, the media has related stories of 'loan sharks' and unscrupulous money lenders taking advantage of consumers. The Consumer Credit Act (CCA) 1974 was passed following the Crowther Committee Report (*Report of the Committee on Consumer Credit* (Cmnd 4569, 1971)) and its purpose was to provide greater protection to those buying on credit – for example, the CCA 1974 repealed and replaced most of the Hire Purchase Act 1964 – and to rectify the imbalance in the bargaining positions of the respective parties.

European Community directives have been issued (for example 87/02/EEC, to harmonise the laws relating to consumer credit in Member States), but the directives largely follow the pattern of the CCA 1974 and so, major legislative changes have not been necessary in the UK.

It is extremely important that any business providing credit is aware of and complies with the regulatory framework of control of the CCA 1974, as it creates criminal offences for non-compliance, controls on advertising and a licensing system for credit providers, outside which businesses cannot operate.

18.1.1 Examples of credit agreements

- Hire purchase

  Under such an agreement, the customer is given use and possession of goods in return for payment by instalments. The ownership in the goods is not transferred unless and until all payments are made and the option to purchase is exercised (usually by payment of an additional nominal sum). Accordingly, the customer may never acquire ownership in the goods, even though that could have been his or her objective from the outset, and the goods may be repossessed for non-payment.

- Credit sale

  In this type of agreement, the customer agrees to buy the goods but pays the purchase price by instalments. Ownership passes immediately and the goods cannot be repossessed for non-payment. If a buyer fails to pay, he or she can only be sued for the arrears.

- Conditional sale

  At first sight, this agreement appears to be similar to both credit sale and hire purchase, but in legal terms it is a distinct type of agreement. Here, the buyer agrees to purchase ownership and pay by instalments but ownership does not actually pass to him or her until he or she has made a specified number of payments. The distinction between conditional sale and credit sale lies in the time at which ownership is transferred.

- Personal loans

  Fixed term loans are available from banks and other financial institutions and are repaid by instalments, which include interest payments. Such loans are commonly obtained to purchase goods and holidays; it should be realised that, if the loan was used, for example, to pay for a car, there would be two separate contracts – a contract for the sale of goods and a loan agreement.

- Overdraft

  Under an overdraft agreement, the holder of a current account at a bank is able to draw against his or her account up to an agreed amount when the account is in debit. Therefore, the customer is borrowing money and usually has to pay interest on the borrowing.

18.1.2 The terminology of the CCA 1974

The specific terminology of the CCA 1974 must be explained before the provisions of the Act can be understood:

Creditor   The person/body who supplies the credit/finance.

Credit broker A person/body who carries on a business, which includes introducing individuals requiring credit to persons/bodies carrying on a consumer credit business or to other credit brokers. So, a garage which arranges for a customer to obtain hire purchase finance for a car from a finance company is a credit broker.

Debtor   The customer/borrower/person who is obliged to repay the finance.

Credit   Not only cash loans, but also any other form of financial accommodation (s 9(1) of the CCA 1974), such as hire purchase.

18.1.3 Agreements within the scope of the CCA 1974

The CCA 1974 applies to regulated agreements. There are three main types:

- consumer credit agreements;

- consumer hire agreements;
- linked transactions.

Consumer credit agreements

Section 8(2) of the CCA 1974 states:

> A consumer credit agreement is a personal credit agreement by which the creditor provides the debtor with credit not exceeding [£25,000].

Section 8(3) indicates such agreements are 'regulated'. It should be noted that the credit limit for application of the Act was increased from £15,000 to £25,000 by the Consumer Credit (Increase of Monetary Limits) Order 1998 (SI 1998/996).

In such agreements, the amount of the credit extended determines the application of the CCA 1974. The Act does not apply where the credit extended exceeds £25,000 and 'credit extended' refers to the principal sum advanced. Accordingly, charges such as interest payments should not be included in the calculation of whether the credit extended is within the current statutory limit. This is aimed at preventing the creditor from including all sums payable under the credit agreement (such as administration fees and insurance premiums) so that the agreement appears to fall outside the ambit of the CCA 1974. Thus, the 'credit' extended has to be distinguished from the 'total payable'; it must also be distinguished from the 'total charge for credit', which means the cash price deducted from the 'total payable' (see *Huntpast Ltd v Leadbetter* (1993)). For details of matters to be or not be included in the 'total charge for credit', the Consumer Credit (Total Charge for Credit Agreements and Advertisements) (Amendment) Regulations 1999 (SI 1999/3177), which came into force on 14 April 2000, should be referred to.

It should further be appreciated that the Act only applies where the credit is extended to an 'individual', but s 189 indicates that this 'includes a partnership or other unincorporated body of persons not consisting entirely of bodies corporate'. Arguably, Parliament felt that businesses such as sole traders needed the same protection from the unscrupulous as did private individuals.

Consumer hire agreements

Under s 15 of the CCA 1974, this is an agreement:

> ... made by an individual (the 'hirer') for the bailment of goods to the hirer, being an agreement which:
>
> (a) is not a hire purchase agreement; and
>
> (b) is capable of subsisting for more than three months; and
>
> (c) does not require the hirer to make payments exceeding £25,000.

The nature of regulated consumer credit and consumer hire agreements was examined by the House of Lords in *Dimond v Lovell* (2000). L damaged D's car and, whilst it was being repaired, D hired a car from A. Under the hire agreement, payment was not required until the claim against L's insurers was settled, so credit was extended. L's insurers refused to pay the hire charge on the basis that the hire agreement was a regulated consumer credit agreement which was unenforceable because it did not contain all the terms required by regulations made under the CCA 1974 (see 18.4); as the agreement was not enforceable, D did not have to pay the hire charge and therefore L's insurers were not liable for it. L's insurers also argued that D had not 'mitigated' her loss (see 8.7.2) because she could have hired a car much more cheaply at 'spot rate' (the prevailing price in the market generally). On this latter argument, the House of Lords indicated that, if the hire agreement was enforceable, she could only have obtained, as damages, the 'spot rate' hire charge (see also *Burdis v Livsey* (2002)). In relation to the nature of the hire agreement, the House of Lords decided that it was a regulated consumer credit agreement rather than a regulated consumer hire agreement because, technically, it did not indicate that it was capable of lasting more than three months. It was agreed that this regulated consumer credit agreement was unenforceable for non-compliance with regulations; as D did not have to pay, the hire charge was not a loss suffered within her claim against L and L's insurers were not liable.

'Linked transactions' (s 19 of the CCA 1974)

These are agreements which are entered into by the debtor with the creditor or a third party in relation to the regulated agreement but which are not part of the regulated agreement. Linked transactions take one of three forms:

- Compulsory

  One which has to be entered into by the terms of the principal agreement, for example, a maintenance agreement on a washing machine.

- Financial

  Where the transaction is a debtor-creditor-supplier agreement (see below, 18.1.4) and is financed by the principal agreement, for example, if A pays for goods by credit card, the contract under which he obtains the credit card is the principal agreement which finances A's purchase of the goods, because the credit card company pays the supplier of the goods and A repays the card company later with interest. A credit card agreement is a regulated agreement under s 14 of the CCA 1974, but it should be noted that cheque guarantee cards are outside the definition of s 14 (see *Metropolitan Police Comr v Charles* (1977)). However, some cards have multi-functions, one or more of which may bring them within s 14, for example, a cheque guarantee card which is also a credit card.

- Suggested

  This may occur where a person is induced to enter another transaction by the suggestion of the creditor, owner or credit broker, in order to persuade the creditor to enter the principal agreement. For example, a credit broker might suggest that he can arrange a loan with a creditor if A is willing to insure repayment of the loan under an insurance policy which he will also arrange. Here, the loan agreement would be the principal agreement and the insurance policy, the linked transaction.

The significance of a linked transaction is that it will be affected by any action taken in respect of the principal agreement. So, if the principal agreement is cancelled under s 69, the related insurance policy would be discharged. The right of cancellation is discussed below, 18.5.3.

18.1.4 Types of regulated consumer credit agreements

Depending on the nature of the particular situation, a regulated agreement may be one of various types. The distinction can be important in determining which provisions of the CCA 1974 will apply. (Some agreements will fall into more than one category and are known as *multiple agreements* (s 18(1)) and each divisible part is regulated by the CCA 1974 accordingly.)

Debtor-creditor agreement

An agreement where finance only is supplied by the creditor to the debtor, as in the case of a bank loan. Such an agreement could be a *restricted* or *unrestricted use* credit agreement (see s 11 of the CCA 1974).

Unrestricted use credit agreements

This is an agreement where the creditor has no control over how the credit extended to the debtor is used. Thus, if the debtor gets a bank loan for home improvements by a credit to his current account, the bank cannot physically prevent him from using that loan to pay for a holiday. Of course, he may be in breach of his loan agreement in such circumstances.

Restricted use credit agreements

In such agreements, the creditor can control the use to which the credit extended to the debtor is put. If a debtor obtained a loan from a bank to buy a car, it could be part of the agreement that the bank pays the money borrowed directly to the seller of the car. This clearly prevents the debtor from misleading the bank as to the purpose of any loan applied for. Possibly, such agreements protect consumers from themselves! In *Dimond v Lovell* (see 18.1.3), the Court of Appeal said that the hire agreement was (*inter alia*) a restricted use credit agreement.

Debtor-creditor-supplier agreements

These are agreements where there is a link between the creditor and the supplier of the goods/services given to the debtor. Common examples would be:

- Purchase by credit card

  The debtor is the purchaser, who must repay the credit card company; the supplier is the retailer; and the creditor is the credit card company, because, under a pre-existing arrangement with retailers (which is the *link* between creditor and supplier), the card company pays the retailer for the debtor's purchase. Incidentally, this type of transaction would be an unrestricted use agreement, as the card company does not dictate what the card is used for.

- Purchase of goods on credit from a retailer who himself finances the credit

  This can be done by allowing the debtor to pay by instalments; this would be usual for purchases by store card.

- Hire purchase agreements

  A retailer of expensive goods such as cars will not be able to sell them unless customers can buy on credit, but he or she may not be in a financial position to wait two or three years for his or her money. Therefore, the retailer will have to enter into a contract with a finance company, under which any car a customer wants is sold ('on paper') to the finance company by the retailer and the finance company lets the customer have the car on hire purchase terms. In this situation, the customer's contract is with the finance company, *not* the retailer, though the agreement forms are usually filled out at the retailer's premises. Hire purchase is a restricted use consumer credit agreement and fulfils the CCA 1974 definition of a debtor-creditor-supplier agreement. (The finance company is the creditor, the person acquiring the car on hire purchase is the debtor and the retailer (though merely a credit broker in this case) is treated as the supplier.)

In relation to debtor-creditor-supplier agreements, the consumer gets special protection under s 75 of the CCA 1974, which allows the debtor to bring an action *against the creditor* for any misrepresentation or breach of contract *by the supplier*. (But whether misrepresentation or breach by the supplier would give the debtor the right to rescind or treat the credit contract as repudiated is not clear, despite the decision in *United Dominions Trust v Taylor* (1980).) To put s 75 into context, the following situations can be considered:

- The consumer pays a travel company for his holiday by credit card. Before the date that he is due to go on holiday, the travel company goes into liquidation, so that the consumer gets no holiday and the travel company will not have the funds to repay him.

  Here, the consumer could claim his refund from the credit card company.

- A furniture retailer induces a consumer to purchase a three-piece suite by a negligent misrepresentation that the covers are machine washable.

  Here, the consumer may bring an action for misrepresentation against the credit card company which issued the card.

Whilst, in theory, s 75 of the CCA 1974 appears to place a heavy burden on the creditor, if the debtor pursues a claim against the creditor, the creditor can claim an indemnity from the supplier – presuming that he or she is still in existence. There are limitations on the use of s 75, in that it does not apply to a non-commercial agreement (defined in s 189 of the CCA 1974 as a consumer credit agreement where the creditor/owner does not act in the course of business); nor does it apply to a claim in respect of any item where the cash price does not exceed £100 or is more than £30,000. However, in these circumstances, the debtor could still take action against the supplier.

The application of s 75 has not proved to be straightforward, particularly where credit card holders have used the section to pursue claims against banks. First, it does not apply to credit card agreements made before 1 July 1977; secondly, where there is a main card holder and a second authorised user, only the main card holder has the right to use s 75, which means that, if defective goods are purchased by the second user, s 75 may not operate; and, thirdly, where the card has been used abroad, banks are keen to avoid liability on the basis that the law of the country in which the purchase is made should apply (see *Jarrett v Barclays Bank plc* (1996)).

Fixed sum credit

Fixed sum credit is where the actual amount of the loan is fixed from the start of the agreement, subject to the statutory limit for regulated agreements. The relevant figure is the actual amount of the sum being loaned, excluding the amount payable as interest or deposit. It is irrelevant that it may be repaid or received by instalments. A hire purchase agreement is one of fixed sum credit. The actual amount of fixed sum credit determines whether the agreement is covered by or is outside the financial limits of the CCA 1974. In *Dimond v Lovell* (see 18.1.3), the hire agreement was said to be a fixed sum credit in the Court of Appeal.

Running account credit

Running account credit is where credit is fixed up to an agreed limit, for example, credit card agreements and bank overdrafts. Again, such agreements will be regulated agreements within the CCA 1974, as long as the credit limit does not exceed the current specified figure (£25,000).

18.1.5 Exempt and partially exempt agreements

Though apparently falling within the definition of the CCA 1974, some agreements are exempt from the provisions of that Act. 'Extortionate credit bargains' (see below, 18.5.1) are not exempt; others are only partially regulated by the CCA 1974.

Small agreements (s 17 of the CCA 1974)

A small agreement is either a regulated consumer credit agreement or a regulated consumer hire agreement where the amount of credit or hire/rental charges do not exceed £50. (Note that the Department of Trade and Industry consultative document, Deregulation of UK Consumer Credit Legislation (1995), proposes raising the sum to £150.) The rules for determining whether the credit exceeds the limit are by reference to fixed sum and running account credit (explained above).

Small agreements are *exempt* from some, but not all, of the provisions of the CCA 1974; for example, the rules relating to formation of credit agreements (see below, 18.4.2) do not apply. However, the main provisions contained in Pt IV, relating to seeking business, the requirement on the creditor to supply information on request and the provisions restricting remedies on default, will apply (see below, 18.3, 18.5.2 and 18.5.6).

Exempt agreements

Certain agreements are exempt from the provisions of the CCA 1974 by virtue of s 16 of that Act and the Consumer Credit (Exempt Agreements) Order 1989 (SI 1989/869) (as amended by SI 1999/1956).

The exemptions cover situations where it is probably unnecessary to provide protection for debtors and, accordingly, though the 1989 Order exempts debtor-creditor-supplier agreements where there are no more than four payments in a 12 month period, this exemption does not apply to any hire purchase or conditional sale agreement. (One of the purposes of the CCA 1974 was to protect consumers in relation to hire purchase agreements.) Everyday examples of exempt agreements are milk and newspaper bills, which are usually paid in arrears, so credit is given. In *Dimond v Lovell* (see 18.1.3) in the House of Lords, Lord Hoffman indicated that the hire car company could have made the agreement 'exempt', and therefore enforceable, by stating in the agreement that the hire charge had to be paid within 12 months.

Other examples of exempt agreements are:

- mortgages;
- debtor-creditor-supplier agreements for running account credit where the whole of the credit given has to be paid off in a lump sum. Certain charge

cards will require the whole of the outstanding balance to be repaid at the end of each month;

- credit sale agreements where no interest is charged when the purchase price is repaid over an agreed period. This type of arrangement is what is commonly offered by furniture retailers in their television advertising.

Non-commercial agreements

Such agreements are made by a creditor who is not acting in the course of any business carried on by him (s 189 of the CCA 1974), for example, a private individual giving a loan to a friend. In *Hare v Schurek* (1993), a business only giving credit very occasionally was not required to be licensed under the CCA 1974 (see below, 18.2, for CCA 1974 licensing provisions). Thus, in relation to the definition of a non-commercial agreement, such a business should not be regarded as acting in the course of a business it carries on when giving credit.

Non-commercial agreements are exempt from the CCA 1974 provisions relating to, for example, form and contents (see 18.4.2); the right to cancel (see 18.5.3); cooling off periods (see 18.5.3); and licensing (see 18.2).

18.2 LICENSING

The licensing system was introduced to regulate creditors and thereby protect consumers, but it is clear that there are still unlicensed money lenders who charge exorbitant rates of interest and enforce payment by threats. The people who are most likely to be caught in this trap are the poor, because banks and other financial institutions which are licensed under the CCA 1974 are loathe to extend credit to them because of their low income; perhaps those who need the protection of the law most are not receiving it.

Businesses which provide facilities for regulated agreements must be licensed by the Office of Fair Trading; a licence is required whether the business's main activity is the provision of credit or whether such provision is ancillary to its main activities (for example, debt collection, debt counselling and credit references).

The licences which can be granted are *standard* licences (given on an individual basis) and *group* licences (for example, covering a group of professionals such as solicitors or accountants). Standard licences are granted for five years; group licences for 15 years. Licences under the CCA 1974 are not required by local authorities or businesses granting credit over £25,000 or granting credit only to companies. A licence may be granted to cover only stated aspects of the credit business; if a licence was granted to cover debt collection and debt counselling only, the holder could not legally extend credit within the provisions of the CCA 1974.

Applicants for licences have to satisfy the Director General of Fair Trading as to their fitness to be granted the licence. In considering such fitness, the Director General will take account of such matters as convictions for fraud, theft and breaches of the Trade Descriptions Act 1968 (s 25 of the CCA 1974). In *North Wales Motor Auctions Ltd v Secretary of State* (1981), the refusal of a licence because the applicant was not a fit person, on account of convictions for fraud on the Inland Revenue, was upheld. The Director General will also ensure that the applicant is not applying to trade under a name which is misleading. In *Hunter-Jaap v Hampshire Credit Consultants Ltd* (1986), it was held that a trader may be prevented from using a name (even his own name) which, with intent to deceive, might mislead the public into thinking that it is someone else's business.

The Director General also has the power to vary, withdraw or suspend current licences (ss 30–32 of the CCA 1974). Licensees or applicants for licences may appeal against the Director General's decision to the Secretary of State (as occurred in *North Wales Motor Auctions Ltd v Secretary of State* (above)). Where an unlicensed trader makes an agreement which comes within the provisions of the CCA 1974, that agreement is not enforceable unless the Director General makes an order allowing enforcement (s 40 of the CCA 1974). Failure to get such an order would mean that the unlicensed trader would not be able to sue the debtor for non-payment under the agreement; however, this provision would not protect the consumer against an unlicensed money lender who used unlawful means, such as coercion, to obtain payment.

Unlicensed trading is a criminal offence, as is trading under a name other than that on the licence (s 39 of the CCA 1974). Conviction may result in a fine of up to £5,000 and/or up to two years' imprisonment (s 167 of the CCA 1974).

18.3 PROMOTION OF CREDIT AGREEMENTS

18.3.1 Introduction

People are often caught in the 'credit trap' because they do not appreciate the practical consequences of using credit; equally, many consumers do not realise how much credit costs them and find it difficult to assess what is the best credit deal for them. So, a person wishing to buy a freezer might not be sure whether to buy by credit card, by bank loan or on hire purchase.

The law seeks to protect the consumer in these situations by measures such as controls on advertising and specifying the information that a prospective debtor must be given.

18.3.2 Canvassing offences

The CCA 1974 creates the following criminal offences:

- sending documents to a minor, inviting him or her to enter a credit agreement or to apply for information about credit (s 50 of the CCA 1974); a defence is available if there was no reasonable cause to believe that the addressee was a minor;

- giving a person an unsolicited credit token (s 51 of the CCA 1974), for example, a credit card, though the provisions of s 51 do not render renewals unlawful; and

- canvassing off trade premises for debtor-creditor agreements (ss 48 and 49 of the CCA 1974).

It is a criminal offence to make an unsolicited call at a person's home and to make oral statements to him or her about credit terms available in relation to debtor-creditor agreements. Commission of the offence can be avoided where the 'canvasser' has a written request to call at premises. Most people are familiar with salesmen calling round and saying that they are 'not trying to sell anything, but if you would like to know more about our product or service you can fill out our card for one of our salesman to call'. By responding positively, the consumer makes a written request, soliciting the salesman to call, and no offence is committed. Of course, the subsequent sales talk will then include reference to credit terms available.

18.3.3 Advertising of credit

In the context of control of the advertising of credit, the word 'advertisement' is a wide concept, encompassing television and radio advertising, labels, distribution of samples, films, circulars and catalogues, to mention just a few (see the full definition in s 189 of the CCA 1974).

The CCA 1974 creates two main criminal offences relating to advertising credit, which apply even to the advertising of 'exempt' agreements:

- Conveying information which, in a material respect, is false or misleading (s 46(1) of the CCA 1974).

  In *Metsoja v Pitt and Co Ltd* (1989), a car dealer was able to advertise a '0% finance' deal by giving smaller part-exchange allowances. This was held to be misleading and the dealer was convicted of an offence under s 46(1) of the CCA 1974.

- Advertising the supply of goods under a restricted use credit agreement where the advertiser is not also prepared to sell those goods for cash. If there is no comparable cash price, the consumer is unable to assess the advisability of acquiring the goods on credit.

There are further criminal offences relating to non-compliance with regulations made under s 44 of the CCA 1974 as to the form and content of advertisements of credit (s 47(1) of the CCA 1974). The Consumer Credit (Advertisements) Regulations 1989 (SI 1989/1125, as amended in respect of the calculation of the Annual Percentage Rate (APR) by SI 1999/3177 – see below) refer to three types of advertisement – 'simple', 'intermediate' and 'full' – and specify the information that such advertisements must contain. A 'full' advertisement must, amongst other things, state deposit details, give a warning that there is a risk of losing any property that the credit is secured against if repayments are not made, and state the APR. The APR has also been called the 'true rate of interest' and is the rate which should be used to compare one method of obtaining credit against another, rather than a simple comparison of flat rates of interest. The method of calculating the APR is now provided for in the Consumer Credit (Total Charge for Credit, Agreements and Advertisements) (Amendment) Regulations 1999 (SI 1999/3177), in line with EC Directive 98/7.

Under the Consumer Credit (Quotations) Regulations 1989 (SI 1989/1126) (made under s 52(1) of the CCA 1974), any quotation relating to credit terms had to contain broadly the same information as the 'full' credit advertisement, but these have now been revoked by the Consumer Credit (Quotations) (Revocation) Regulations 1997. The Consumer Credit (Content of Quotations) and the Consumer Credit (Advertisements) (Amendment) Regulations 1999 regulate the information to be included in the quotation.

18.3.4 Adequacy of protection

Whilst the laws relating to promotion of credit go a long way to protecting the consumer, the problem still remains that many consumers either do not read or do not understand the information made available. Despite the attempts to protect young people from being persuaded into obtaining credit, application forms for 'plastic' cards are common magazine inserts and television advertising of credit is on the increase. Finally, it is worth noting that an offence against the advertising provisions does not in itself affect the validity and enforceability of a credit agreement (s 170 of the CCA 1974).

18.4 PRE-CONTRACT PROTECTION OF THE CONSUMER

18.4.1 Introduction

The desire to protect the consumer from entering into a credit agreement without a full realisation of what he is undertaking extends to the making of the contract and, accordingly, the CCA 1974 makes the following provisions:

- Section 55(1) enables regulations to be made requiring disclosure of specific information to the debtor before the contract is made. Section 55(2) indicates that failure to comply with regulations renders the agreement unenforceable, unless a court orders that it can be enforced (s 65(1) of the CCA 1974), for example, *Eastern Distributors Ltd v Goldring* (1957) (decided under previous legislation). In such circumstances, the creditor could not recover possession of goods from a debtor who defaulted on payment, nor could he recover any arrears.

- Section 60(1) requires the Secretary of State to make regulations concerning the form and content of the consumer credit agreement, so that the debtor can be aware of his or her rights and obligations under the agreement. (Section 61 of the CCA 1974 requires that such regulations are complied with for the agreement to be properly executed and s 65 renders an improperly executed agreement unenforceable in the absence of a court order that action may be taken to enforce it.)

- To reflect the growth in the number of *credit reference agencies* and to provide protection and redress for those persons who are incorrectly rated as to their creditworthiness, ss 157–59 allow someone who has been refused credit to request the name and address of the credit reference agency from the creditor/owner. The customer is then entitled to make a written request to the agency for a copy of his or her file (subject to a fee of £2). The customer can then take steps to have the file amended, if necessary.

18.4.2 The Consumer Credit (Agreements) Regulations 1983

The Consumer Credit (Agreements) Regulations 1983 (SI 1983/155, as amended by SI 1999/3177) relate to the provisions of ss 55 and 60. Accordingly, the contractual document must:

- be printed or typed (though 'blanks' can be filled in in handwriting) and signed by *both* parties. The debtor must sign *personally*, but the creditor (often a company) can sign through an agent;

- indicate APR, amount of any deposit, amount and timing of instalments, number of instalments, amount of credit given, difference between cash and credit price, total charge for credit and total amount payable;

- give details of the debtor's right to terminate and (where applicable) the restriction on the creditor's right to repossess 'protected goods' (see below, 18.5.6);

- give details of any security provided by the debtor;

- include details of the right of cancellation (if applicable) (see below, 18.5.3) and the details must be stated in a box; this draws the debtor's attention to his or her right;

- include the names and postal addresses of the parties and, if goods are involved (as in, for example, hire purchase and credit sale), details of the goods.

All copies of the agreement must contain the same information, subject to some exceptions in relation to signatures (see below, 18.4.3).

These provisions should mean that the debtor has all the information that he or she needs before signing the agreement, but the question must arise as to how many consumers actually avail themselves of the opportunity to read all of the information before signing.

18.4.3 Copies of regulated agreements (ss 62 and 63 of the CCA 1974)

When the debtor signs the agreement, he or she must receive a copy of what he or she signs (the *first* statutory copy); if the creditor does not sign at the same time, the debtor must also receive the *second* statutory copy, which is a copy of the concluded contract with both signatures, within seven days of the creditor signing. Where only the first statutory copy is required, the creditor must send, by post to the debtor, within seven days of conclusion of the contract, a *notice of his or her right to cancel* (if applicable).

In order to determine how many copies of the agreement are required, consider the following examples of debtor-creditor-supplier agreements on hire purchase terms:

Situation 1:

1   sales assistant completes details of hire purchase agreement on the proposal form;
2   debtor signs the form = his or her *offer* to contract;
3   debtor is given first statutory copy (of what he or she has just signed);
4   shop sends form to finance company for signature;
5   creditor signs = *acceptance* = *contract made* (up to this point, the debtor could withdraw his or her offer, in which case no contract would be made). Under s 57 of the CCA 1974, notice of withdrawal of offer can be given to people other than the prospective creditor, for example, the credit broker or supplier who conducted the antecedent negotiations;
6   within 7 days of signing, creditor sends second statutory copy (with both signatures) to debtor = copy of contract.

Situation 2:

1   sales assistant completes details on hire purchase proposal form;
2   debtor signs = *offer* to contract;
3   creditor's representative (for example, shop manager) signs immediately after debtor = *acceptance* = contract;
4   shop gives debtor a copy of the contract (with both signatures).

Failure to comply with these regulations renders the contract unenforceable without a court order under s 65(1) of the CCA 1974.

It is clear from this section that failure to comply with the legal rules relating to formalities renders the contract unenforceable unless the court grants an enforcement order. Section 127 of the CCA 1974 restricts or denies the power of a court to grant such orders; in *Wilson v First County Trust* (2001), the Court of Appeal held that preventing the court from making such an order (s 127(3)) was incompatible with the rights of the lender under Art 6 of the European Convention on Human Rights.

18.5 PROTECTING THE DEBTOR AFTER THE CONTRACT IS MADE

A wide range of provisions continue to protect debtors even after the contract is made. A specific instance that is known to many consumers is that there are legal restrictions on the right of a finance company to repossess hire purchase goods for non-payment.

18.5.1 Extortionate credit bargains (ss 137–40 of the CCA 1974)

The CCA 1974 gives the court power to reopen a credit agreement and take action if it finds that a credit agreement is extortionate. A 'bargain' is defined as extortionate when payments imposed on the debtor are grossly exorbitant or grossly contravene the ordinary principles of fair dealing. The court will take into account the prevailing interest, age, capacity and experience of the hirer/debtor. In considering whether the agreement is extortionate, the court must also consider the degree of risk accepted by the creditor and the nature and value of the security. The court can rewrite the agreement or set aside the contract. They do, however, seem to be reluctant to intervene on some occasions.

In *Ketley v Scott* (1981), Mr Scott had negotiated a loan for which he was paying interest at the rate of 48% per annum. He had an overdraft at the bank and the loan was negotiated in a hurry, without full enquiries being made. He defaulted on the loan and the plaintiffs sued him. Mr Scott claimed that the interest rate was extortionate. It was held that there was a high degree of risk involved in the loaning of money and, therefore, the interest charged was not disproportionately high. (See, also, *Davies v Direct Loans Ltd* (1986).)

Application may be made to the court under these provisions in respect of *any* consumer credit agreement – the £25,000 limit does not apply here.

It should be noted, however, that the creditors who impose extortionate demands are likely to be unlicensed ones who deal with the most vulnerable members of society, who either do not know their rights or may be 'persuaded' not to exercise them. Furthermore, lawyers have speculated that courts will be reluctant to intervene under the provisions of the CCA 1974 – perhaps the *caveat emptor* principle has left its mark on the judiciary.

18.5.2 Disclosure of information

It is important that consumers are regularly made aware of the current state of their obligations under a credit agreement; most consumers will receive monthly statements of their current bank accounts so as to enable them to check their financial position. The CCA 1974 places obligations on the creditor to ensure that consumers are aware of their financial situation:

- If the debtor under a fixed term credit agreement makes a written request for a statement of his or her current position under the agreement, the creditor must respond in writing within 12 days (s 77(1) of the CCA 1974) and the creditor's statement is binding (s 172(1) of the CCA 1974). Thus, if a creditor stated that the sum owed was less than it actually was, he or she would be unable to enforce payment of the true sum owed unless, by virtue of s 172(3)(b), the court thinks that the enforcement is just. In relation to running account credit agreements, the information provided by the creditor must include a statement of what is currently owed, amounts which will become payable and the dates on which such amounts will be payable (s 78(1) of the CCA 1974).

- Regardless of any request by the debtor, statements of running account credit agreements must be sent to the debtor at least once every 12 months (s 78(4) of the CCA 1974).

18.5.3 The debtor's right to cancel the agreement

The right is given by s 67 of the CCA 1974 and the Consumer Protection (Cancellation of Contracts Concluded away from Business Premises) Regulations 1987 (SI 1987/2117).

It has already been seen (see above, 18.4.3) that the prospective debtor can withdraw his or her offer to contract before the creditor accepts; the right to cancel allows a debtor to cancel a validly concluded contract without being in breach. The right may apply to regulated agreements, subject to certain exceptions such as small agreements and overdrafts (see s 74 of the CCA 1974).

In order for the right to cancel to be available, the following conditions must be fulfilled:

- oral representations (such as 'sales talk') were made in the hirer's (under a consumer hire agreement) or debtor's presence about the agreement before it was made. In *Moorgate Services Ltd v Kabir* (1995), it was indicated that the representation must be material/capable of inducing the agreement, though proof that it was so intended or in fact induced the agreement, was not necessary;

- such representations were made by the creditor, a party to a 'linked' transaction or the person conducting antecedent negotiations;

- the hirer or debtor signed the agreement off trade premises. The general idea here was to protect people who signed agreements in their own homes, perhaps to 'get rid of' a door-to-door salesman. However, an agreement signed in the pub could also be cancellable because the definition of 'trade premises' means the premises of the creditor, owner, a party to a 'linked transaction' or the person who conducted the antecedent negotiations (s 67(b)). It should also be noted that, under SI 1987/2117 (see above), where an agreement is made during an unsolicited visit by a trader, for example, at the consumer's home or place of work, it is unenforceable against the consumer unless he or she is sent a notice of his or her right to cancel within seven days, and he or she has a seven day 'cooling off' period. In the past, some businesses tried to avoid the cancellation provisions by driving the consumer to their premises to sign the agreement!

In order to cancel the agreement, the hirer/debtor must give written notice to the creditor (or to any other person specified in s 69 of the CCA 1974) that he or she is cancelling. The usual 'cooling off' period or time allowed for cancellation is five days from receipt of the second statutory copy of the agreement, or the notice of cancellation where the hirer/debtor receives only one copy of the agreement (see above, 18.4.3).

The effect of cancellation (ss 70–73 of the CCA 1974) is as follows:

- the agreement is erased and there is no liability under it;

- all sums cease to be payable and all sums paid out are recoverable (for example, a deposit);

- the hirer or debtor is not obliged to return the goods but must hand them over if the owner calls at a reasonable time;

- the hirer or debtor has a duty to take care of the goods for 21 days after notice of cancellation. During that period, he or she is liable if he or she accidentally damages the goods; on expiry of the 21 days, he or she is only liable if he or she deliberately damages the goods;

- the hirer has a lien on the goods for the repayment of sums paid under the agreement;

- any part-exchange goods can be recovered within 10 days or a part-exchange allowance must be given to the hirer;

- any linked transaction is also terminated;

- if a debtor has received credit under a loan agreement, no interest is payable if he or she repays it within one month of cancellation or before the first repayment is due. If he or she fails to repay within that period, he or she must pay the interest agreed on the loan.

18.5.4 The debtor's right to terminate the agreement

The CCA 1974 gives debtors the right to terminate certain credit agreements during the currency of the agreement; the right can be exercised in relation to regulated hire purchase and conditional sale agreements. Termination must be distinguished from cancellation, which wipes out the contract and means that no liability accrues under it. Termination brings the contract to an end at the date of termination, but any obligations already accrued are enforceable. At first sight, the fact a debtor can bring the contract to an end and does not have to pay future instalments appears to be a protection for the debtor in financial difficulties. In practice, however, termination may not prove to be a financially sound decision.

The right to termination is exercised by notice to the creditor (s 99(1) of the CCA 1974) or any other person entitled to receive the payment under the agreement (for example, the dealer or supplier of the goods). Although termination might appear to be a problem in conditional sales where the ownership has already passed, the CCA 1974 provides that, on termination, ownership reverts to the previous owner (s 99(5) – but subject to s 99(4)).

Termination has the following consequences (s 100 of the CCA 1974):

- arrears due at the date of termination are payable;
- the debtor is liable to pay damages if he or she has failed to take reasonable care of the goods (fair wear and tear excepted);
- the debtor must return the goods when the creditor calls to collect them;
- the debtor must pay to the creditor such sum (if any) as brings the total paid by the debtor up to half the total price agreed. However, this provision does not apply where the agreement makes no such provision or provides that a smaller sum is payable or a court orders that a smaller sum is payable. It is this provision which the debtor should consider carefully before terminating, as termination could prove very costly. As an alternative to termination, he or she might be able to re-negotiate the contract and pay smaller amounts over a longer period. The debtor might also consider the possibility of re-financing the debt, so that the creditor can be paid off in full.

It should also be noted that s 101 of the CCA 1974 provides for termination of consumer hire agreements. The hirer must give written notice, which is subject to a minimum period. The agreement must have run for at least 18 months before the right to terminate can operate.

18.5.5 Creditor's right of termination

Most hire purchase and conditional sale agreements give the creditor the right to terminate the agreement and repossess the goods for breach of contract. The commonest form of breach is default in payment.

Of course, the creditor could merely sue for arrears owing, but this is rather an onerous undertaking where the debtor continually defaults. The creditor would clearly prefer to terminate the agreement and recover the goods, which he or she could then sell. Some consumer credit agreements may contain accelerated payment clauses, allowing the creditor to claim the whole of the outstanding balance where the debtor is in default; this, again, is preferable to suing for arrears for each default in payment. Accelerated payment clauses are valid, provided that they are not interpreted as penalty clauses (see above, Chapter 8); this can be avoided by providing for an appropriate rebate on interest for early repayment.

Despite the fact that the law may allow the creditor to terminate the contract and make claims for the balance outstanding or repossession of the goods, the debtor still receives protection because the provisions of the CCA 1974 control the exercise of such rights. Where the debtor is in breach and the creditor wishes to terminate the contract, he or she must serve a default notice on the debtor (s 87 of the CCA 1974). The default notice must state the nature of the breach and what is to be done to remedy it; at least seven days must be given to remedy the breach (s 88 of the CCA 1974). The form of the notice is prescribed by the Consumer Credit (Enforcement, Default and Termination) Regulations 1983 (SI 1983/1561). If the debtor complies, the contract continues as if there had been no breach (s 89 of the CCA 1974). In the case of a default in payment, the default notice should specify the amount owed (see *Woodchester Lease Management Services Ltd v Swain & Co* (1998)), the date by which it must be paid and the consequences of non-compliance; if the debtor fails to comply with the notice, the contract can be treated as terminated. The debtor's liability on such termination would be to:

- pay arrears owing up to date of termination;
- return goods to the creditor when he or she calls for them, after having given the debtor a written request for re-delivery;
- pay damages if he or she has failed to take reasonable care of goods;
- possibly pay such sum as brings the total paid up to half the total price (see above, 18.5.4).

However, these consequences will not automatically follow. The debtor or hirer, having been served with a default notice or in the event of any other action being taken to enforce a regulated agreement, may apply to the court for a time order, allowing him or her extra time to make payments or rectify the breach. Such orders can be varied, extended or revoked by the court (s 129 of the CCA 1974). The terms of a time order will depend on the debtor's circumstances. The court will also consider what is 'just', bearing in mind the creditor's position and the debtor's future prospects. During the period of the time order, the creditor cannot take any action to terminate the agreement, recover possession of any land or goods or remove or vary any rights of the debtor (s 130 of the CCA 1974). Following the decision in *Southern District Finance v Barnes* (1995), where a default notice has been served, the court will have the power under s 129 to rewrite the agreement, resulting in the rescheduling of the whole of the outstanding balance under the loan and, if necessary, where it is 'just', vary the rate of interest.

The CCA 1974 does not actually state the consequences of failing to send a default notice or of sending one which does not comply with the prescribed form, but it has been suggested that a repossession of the goods in such circumstances would give the debtor the right to sue for damages for conversion or trespass to goods or for breach of an implied warranty of quiet possession.

However, there is one limitation on the liability of the debtor who fails to comply with a default notice provided by the rules relating to 'protected goods' (see 18.5.6).

18.5.6 Protected goods

Where the debtor under a hire purchase or conditional sale agreement has paid one-third or more of the total price but the ownership is still with the creditor who terminates the agreement for the debtor's default, the goods cannot be repossessed, unless the debtor consents, without a court order (s 90 of the CCA 1974). A creditor who repossesses goods in contravention of this provision does so at his or her peril. Although the creditor may keep the repossessed goods which he or she owns, the agreement is at an end and the debtor is released from all liability and is entitled to recover all sums already paid (s 91 of the CCA 1974). In such a case, the debtor will have had free use and possession of goods for a period. Furthermore, any guarantor of the credit agreement would be released from liability and could recover any security given. A guarantor is someone who guarantees that the creditor will receive payment due to him or her from the hirer/debtor. It is a secondary responsibility based solely on the responsibility of the hirer to pay.

In *Capital Finance Co Ltd v Bray* (1964), Bray acquired a car under a hire purchase agreement. He fell behind with the repayments and an agent of the finance company repossessed the car without obtaining Bray's consent or a court order. The finance company realised that it had made a mistake and the car was duly returned to Bray. Unfortunately, Bray continued to default on the repayments and the company sued for repossession. It was held, on granting a repossession order, that Bray was entitled to recover all the money he had previously paid to the finance company.

In *Bentinck Ltd v Cromwell Engineering* (1971), a car was the subject of a hire purchase agreement. The car was involved in an accident. The hirer took the car to a garage for repair; he then failed to pay any more hire purchase instalments and did not collect the car. The finance company traced the car and repossessed it. They sold the car and sought to recover depreciation costs from the hirer. He claimed that they had repossessed the car without consent. It was held that, when a hirer has abandoned goods and shows that he or she no longer has any interest in them, the owner can repossess even 'protected goods' without a court order.

18.5.7 Action to recover possession of protected goods

The CCA 1974 gives the county court jurisdiction over actions relating to protected goods. All those concerned, including any guarantor or indemnifier, must be made parties to the court action. The court can make the following orders in relation to the goods (s 133 of the CCA 1974).

Return order

The hirer is asked to return the goods to the owner/creditor. If the hirer fails to return the goods, the only fallback position is to send in the bailiffs.

Suspended return order

This is awarded when the hirer has a reasonable excuse for default, for example, redundancy or ill health. The court can vary the terms of the original agreement in order to enable the hirer to meet his or her obligations. It can reduce the amount of each instalment and extend the period of time to pay, if this is deemed to be necessary. These are known as time orders. The effect of a suspended order can therefore be summarised as follows:

- the agreement continues but with a variation in terms;
- the owner cannot claim extra interest for the longer period of time;
- if the hirer breaks any terms specified in the varied agreement, it is possible for the court to make an order that the creditor can repossess without going back to court, that is, implement the suspended order;
- the court can vary the time order upon application from the hirer or the owner, if the hirer's financial circumstances get better or worse;
- the hirer may avoid the suspended order by paying off the unpaid balance and becoming the owner of the goods.

Transfer order

This order gives part of the goods back to the owner and allows the hirer to retain part of the goods and become owner of them. The hire purchase agreement is then at an end.

18.5.8 Early settlement of debts

The CCA 1974 allows a debtor to pay off his or her debt earlier than agreed (s 94 of the CCA 1974). In order to do so, he or she must give written notice to the creditor of his or her intention and settle the outstanding debt in full. As the creditor gets paid earlier than he or she expected, it would be unfair for him or her to claim interest payments in full; a rebate on the interest must be allowed, which is calculated in accordance with the Consumer Credit (Rebate on Early Settlement) Regulations 1983 (SI 1983/1562).

18.6 DEFECTIVE GOODS ACQUIRED ON CREDIT TERMS

Under credit sale, conditional sale, consumer hire and hire purchase agreements, the debtor/hirer will receive goods. If such goods prove to be defective, the law provides protection by way of statutory implied terms as follows:

Credit sale and conditional sale agreements

The implied terms of ss 12–15 of the Sale of Goods Act 1979 apply to such agreements (see above, 9.2.4).

Consumer hire

The implied terms of ss 6–10 of the Supply of Goods and Services Act 1982 apply to consumer hire agreements (see above, 9.3.1).

Hire purchase agreements

The implied terms of ss 8–11 of the Supply of Goods (Implied Terms) Act 1973 apply to hire purchase agreements. The implied terms are similar to those relating to sale of goods contracts, namely: title; description; satisfactory quality; fitness for purpose; and correspondence with sample. The draft Sale and Supply of Goods to Consumers Regulations 2002 will make amendments to these implied terms in the same way as for the implied terms of a sale of goods or a hire contract (discussed in Chapter 9).

18.7 THE DEALER/SUPPLIER AS AGENT OF THE CREDITOR – A SUMMARY

We have seen that the dealer or supplier is often regarded as the agent of the creditor under the CCA 1974; for example, the garage supplying a vehicle to a debtor is usually the agent of the finance company which lets the debtor have the car on hire purchase terms.

To summarise, he or she is agent in the following circumstances:

• to receive notice of cancellation;

• to receive the goods;

• to receive notice of withdrawal of offers;

• to receive notice of the rescission of the contract;

• to receive notice of termination.

Also, by virtue of s 56(2) of the CCA 1974, the dealer is to be treated as the agent of the creditor in antecedent negotiations.

SUMMARY OF CHAPTER 18

CONSUMER CREDIT

- Consumer credit is regulated for the most part by the Consumer Credit Act (CCA) 1974. This applies to 'regulated agreements' (for example, consumer credit and consumer hire agreements) and primarily controls the provision of credit to individuals as opposed to companies.
- In order for the provisions of the CCA 1974 to apply, the credit extended must not exceed £25,000. *Small* agreements are exempted from some of the provisions of the CCA 1974. *Exempt* agreements are not regulated by the provisions of the CCA 1974 (subject to a few exceptions).

Licensing

- Businesses providing finance for regulated agreements must be licensed by the Office of Fair Trading.
- Issue of a licence is subject to the applicant being a fit person to hold a licence. Licences can be refused, revoked or varied and may limit the credit facilities that the licence holder can offer. Unlicensed trading is a criminal offence.

Promotion of credit agreements

- The CCA 1974 creates criminal offences, such as soliciting a minor to take credit. There are specific criminal offences in relation to non-compliance with provisions in relation to the form and content of advertisements of credit.

Pre-contract protection of the consumer

- The Act enables a person who is refused credit to see any information held by a credit reference agency and to amend it if necessary.
- The Consumer Credit (Agreements) Regulations 1983 (as amended) specify the form and content of credit agreements and copies thereof; non-compliance renders the agreement unenforceable without a court order.

Protection of the debtor after the contract is made

- Extortionate credit bargains can be re-opened by the courts.
- The debtor is entitled to statements of the current state of the credit agreement.

- Credit agreements signed off trade premises after oral representations are made can be cancelled within five days of receipt of the second statutory copy of the agreement, by written notice to the creditor/credit broker.
- The debtor can terminate hire purchase, conditional sale and consumer hire agreements by written notice to the creditor/credit broker.

The creditor's right to terminate the agreement

- The contract usually allows the creditor to terminate for the debtor's default in payment. The creditor must serve a default notice on the debtor before termination, allowing the debtor seven days to pay arrears.
- The debtor can apply to the courts for a time order, allowing him or her more time to pay.
- If the debtor has paid one-third or more of the price, the goods are 'protected' and cannot be repossessed for default, unless the debtor consents, without a court order. If the creditor wrongfully repossesses 'protected' goods, the contract is at an end. Although the creditor may keep the goods, the debtor is released from all liability and is entitled to recover money already paid under the agreement.

Early settlement of debts

- Where the debtor pays his or her debts early, he or she is entitled to a rebate on the interest payable under the agreement.

Defective goods acquired on credit terms

- In all such agreements, there are implied terms relating to title, description, satisfactory quality, fitness for purpose and correspondence with sample.

FURTHER READING

Chapter 1   Law and Legal Sources

Barnett, H, *Constitutional and Administrative Law*, 3rd edn, 2000, London: Cavendish Publishing

Bell, J and Engle, G (Sir), *Cross: Statutory Interpretation*, 3rd edn, 1995, London: Butterworths

Bennion, F, 'Statute law: obscurity and drafting parameters' (1978) 5 Br JLS 235

Cross, R, *Cross, Harris and Hart: Precedent in English Law*, 4th edn, 1991, Oxford: Clarendon

Feldman, D, 'The Human Rights Act and constitutional principles' (1999) 19(2) JLS 1

Goodhart, A, 'The *ratio decidendi* of a case' (1959) 22 MLR 117

Holdsworth, W, 'Case law' (1934) 50 LQR 180

Jenkins, C, 'Helping the reader of Bills and Acts' (1999) 149 NLJ 798

Kennedy, T, *Learning European Law*, 1998, London: Sweet & Maxwell

Laws, J (Sir), 'Law and democracy' [1995] PL 72

Mansell, W and Meteyard, B, *A Critical Introduction to Law*, 2nd edn, 1999, London: Cavendish Publishing

Sedley, S (Sir), 'Human rights: a 21st century agenda' [1995] PL 386

Slapper, G and Kelly, D, *The English Legal System*, 5th edn, 2001, London: Cavendish Publishing

Young, J, 'The politics of the Human Rights Act' (1999) 26(1) JLS 27

Chapter 2   The Criminal and Civil Courts

Carlen, P, *Magistrates' Justice*, 1976, Oxford: Martin Robertson

Harrison, R, 'Why have two types of civil court?' (1999) 149 NLJ 65

Malleson, K, 'The Criminal Cases Review Commission: how will it work?' [1995] Crim LR 928

Pedley, FH, 'The small claims process' (1994) 144 NLJ 1217

Richardson, PJ (ed), *Archbold on Criminal Pleading, Evidence and Practice*, 1997, London: Sweet & Maxwell

Slapper, G and Kelly, D, *The English Legal System*, 2001, London: Cavendish Publishing

Woolf (Lord), *Access to Justice – Final Report to the Lord Chancellor on the Civil Justice System in England and Wales*, 1996, London: HMSO

Chapter 3 Alternative Dispute Resolution

Abel, R, 'The comparative study of dispute institutions in society' (1973) 8 Law and Society Rev 217

Baldwin, J, *The Small Claims Procedure and the Consumer*, 1995, London: Office of Fair Trading

Beale, H and Dugdale, T, 'Contracts between businessmen: planning and the use of contractual remedies' (1975) 2 Br JLS 45

Committee on Administrative Tribunals and Inquiries, *Franks Report*, Cmnd 218, 1957, London: HMSO

Genn, H and Genn, Y, *The Effectiveness of Representation at Tribunals*, 1989, London: LCD

Mackay (Lord), *The Administration of Justice*, 1994, London: Sweet & Maxwell

Payne, R, 'To counsel, not confront: the law on ADR' (1999) *Counsel*, February, p 30

Pedley, FH, 'The small claims process' (1994) 144 NLJ 1217

Annual Reports of the Council on Tribunals, London: HMSO

Chapters 4–8 Contract Law

Furmston, MP, *Cheshire, Fifoot & Furmston's Law of Contract*, 14th edn, 2001, London: Butterworths

Koffman, L and McDonald, E, *The Law of Contract*, 4th edn, 2001, Croydon: Tolley

Oughton, D and Davis, M, *Sourcebook on Contract Law*, 2nd edn, 2000, London: Cavendish Publishing

Poole, J, *Contract Law*, 6th edn, 2001, London: Blackstone (OUP)

Smith, JC, *The Law of Contract*, 4th edn, 2002, London: Sweet & Maxwell

Stone, R, *The Modern Law of Contract*, 5th edn, 2002, London: Cavendish Publishing

Treitel, G, *The Law of Contract*, 10th edn, 1999, London: Sweet & Maxwell

Chapter 9   Sale and Supply of Goods

Atiyah, PS, *Sale of Goods*, 10th edn, 2001, London: Pitman

Macleod, J, *Consumer Sales Law*, 2002, London: Cavendish Publishing

Oughton, D and Lowry, J, *Consumer Law*, 2nd edn, 2000, London: Blackstone (OUP)

Sealy, LS and Hooley, RJA, *Text, Cases and Materials in Commercial Law*, 2nd edn, 1999, London: Butterworths

Chapter 10   Negligence

Conaghan, J and Mansell, W, *The Wrongs of Tort*, 2nd edn, 1997, London: Pluto

Harpwood, V, *Principles of Tort Law*, 4th edn, 2000, London: Cavendish Publishing

Hedley, S, *Butterworths Core Text: Tort*, 2000, London: Butterworths

Jones, M, *Textbook on Torts*, 8th edn, 2002, London: Blackstone (OUP)

Lunney, M and Oliphant, K, *Tort Law: Text and Materials*, 2000, Oxford: OUP

Rogers, WVH, *Winfield and Jolowicz on Tort*, 15th edn, 1999, London: Sweet & Maxwell

Stephenson G, *Sourcebook on Tort*, 2nd edn, 2000, London: Cavendish Publishing

Chapter 11   Agency

Fridman, G, *The Law of Agency*, 6th edn, 1990, London: Butterworths

Hardy, IE, *Casebook on Agency*, 1986, London: LLP

Markesinis, B and Munday, R, *An Outline of the Law of Agency*, 4th edn, 1998, London: Butterworths

Stone, R, *Law of Agency*, 1996, London: Cavendish Publishing

Chapter 12   Partnership Law

Banks, R and Anson, C (eds), *Lindley on Partnership*, 1995, London: Sweet & Maxwell

Morse, G, *Partnership Law*, 4th edn, 1998, London: Blackstone (OUP)

Prine, T and Scanlan, G, *The Law of Partnership*, 1995, London: Butterworths

Chapter 13   Company Law

Bourne, N, *Principles of Company Law*, 3rd edn, 1998, London: Cavendish Publishing

Gower, LCB, *Modern Company Law*, 1997, London: Stevens

Chapter 14   The Contract of Employment

Anderman, SD, *Labour Law: Management Decisions and Works Rights*, 4th edn, 2000, London: Butterworths

Barnard, C, *EC Employment Law*, 2nd edn, 2000, Oxford: OUP

Bowers, J, *Employment Law*, 5th edn, 1999, London: Blackstone (OUP)

Bowers, J and Honeyball, S, *Textbook on Labour Law*, 4th edn, 1996, London: Blackstone (OUP)

Jefferson, M, *Principles of Employment Law*, 4th edn, 2000, London: Cavendish Publishing

Painter, RW and Holmes, AEM, *Cases and Materials on Employment Law*, 4th edn, 2002, Oxford: OUP

Sargeant, M, *Employment Law*, 2001, London: Pearson

Chapter 15   Employment Rights: Discrimination

Bowers, J, *Employment Law*, 5th edn, 1999, London: Blackstone (OUP)

Bowers, J and Honeyball, S, *Textbook on Labour Law*, 4th edn, 1996, London: Blackstone (OUP)

Honeyball, S, 'Pregnancy and sex discrimination' (2000) 29(1) ILJ 43

Jefferson, M, *Principles of Employment Law*, 4th edn, 2000, London: Cavendish Publishing

Kingsmill, D, 'A review of women's employment and pay' (www.kingsmillreview.gov.uk)

Painter, RW and Holmes, A, *Cases and Materials on Employment Law*, 3rd edn, 1999, London: Blackstone (OUP)

Twomey, B, 'Disability and the labour market: results from the summer 2000 Labour Force Survey' (2001) Labour Market Trends p 241

Chapter 16 Employment Rights: Termination

Anderman, S, *The Law of Unfair Dismissal*, 3rd edn, 2000, London: Butterworths

Barrett, B, and Howells, R, *Occupational Health & Safety Law*, 1997, London: Financial Times

Bowers, J, *Employment Law*, 5th edn, 2000, London: Blackstone (OUP)

Carty, H, 'Dismissed employees: the search for a more effective range of remedies' (1989) 52 MLR 449

Collins, H, 'The meaning of job security' (1991) 20 ILJ 227

Dickins, L et al, *Dismissed*, 1985, London: Blackwell

Elias, P, 'Fairness in unfair dismissal' (1981) 10 ILJ 201

Ewing, K, 'Remedies for breach of the contract of employment' [1993] CLJ 405

Freer, A, 'The range of reasonable responses test – from guidelines to statute' (1998) 27 ILJ 335

Grunfeld, C, *The Law of Redundancy*, 3rd edn, 1989, London: Sweet & Maxwell

Jefferson, M, *Principles of Employment Law*, 4th edn, 2000, London: Cavendish Publishing

Korn, A, *Compensation for Dismissal*, 2nd edn, 1997, London: Blackstone (OUP)

Larkin, D, 'Compensation for repetitive strain injury' (2000) 29(1) ILJ 88

Lewis, R and Clark, J, *Employment Rights, Industrial Tribunals and Arbitration: The Case for Alternative Dispute Resolution*, 1993, London: Institute of Employment Rights

Painter, RW, Puttick, K and Holmes, AEM, *Employment Rights*, 2nd edn, 1998, London: Pluto

Chapter 17 Employers' Liability

Harpwood, V, *Principles of Tort Law*, 4th edn, 2000, London: Cavendish Publishing

Munkman, J, *Employers' Liability*, 13th edn, 1996, London: Butterworths

Stephenson, G, *Sourcebook on Tort*, 2nd edn, 2000, London: Cavendish Publishing

Chapter 18 Consumer Credit

Dobson, P, *Sale of Goods and Consumer Credit*, 5th edn, 1996, London: Sweet & Maxwell

Lowe, R and Woodroffe, G, *Consumer Law and Practice*, 4th edn, 1995, London: Sweet & Maxwell

Oughton, D and Lowry, J, *Consumer Law*, 1997, London: Blackstone (OUP)

Rosenthal, D, *Guide to Consumer Credit Law and Practice*, 1994, London: Butterworths

INDEX